Advanced Financial Accounting

seventh
edition

Advanced Financial Accounting

Richard Lewis MSc, FCA

Co-Director of the Centre for Higher Education Research and Information,
Open University

David Pendrill BSc(Econ), MSc, FCA, CTA, LTCL

Esmée Fairbairn Professor of Accounting and Financial Management,
University of Buckingham

 Prentice Hall
FINANCIAL TIMES

An imprint of **Pearson Education**
Harlow, England • London • New York • Boston • San Francisco • Toronto • Sydney • Singapore • Hong Kong
Tokyo • Seoul • Taipei • New Delhi • Cape Town • Madrid • Mexico City • Amsterdam • Munich • Paris • Milan

Pearson Education Limited

Edinburgh Gate
Harlow
Essex CM20 2JE
England

and Associated Companies around the world

Visit us on the World Wide Web at:
www.pearsoned.co.uk

_____

First published under the Pitman imprint 1981
Second edition published 1985
Third edition published 1991
Fourth edition published 1994
Fifth edition published under the Financial Times Pitman Publishing imprint 1996
Sixth edition published under the Financial Times Prentice Hall imprint 2000
Seventh edition published 2004

© Richard Lewis, David Pendrill and David S. Simon 1981, 1985
© Richard Lewis and David Pendrill 1991, 1994, 1996, 2000, 2004

ISBN 0 273 65849 2

British Library Cataloguing-in-Publication Data
A catalogue record for this book can be obtained from the British Library.

10 9 8 7 6 5 4 3 2 1
08 07 06 05 04

Typeset in 10/12pt Minion by 30.
Printed and bound in Great Britain by Bell and Bain Ltd, Glasgow.

The publisher's policy is to use paper manufactured from sustainable forests.

Brief contents

Contents

Part 3 · Accounting and price changes   617

Historical cost

Preface

This is undoubtedly a demanding time for practitioners and students of financial reporting. Accountants and business people in European Union countries need to master not only their national regulations but also the rules of the International Accounting Standards Board. Both sets of rules are voluminous, ever growing and presently undergoing a process of rapid change as a consequence of the convergence programme designed to bring national and international standards into line with one another.

The ASB, in the UK, has developed its *Statement of Principles for Financial Reporting*, a conceptual framework designed to underpin the development of accounting standards which adopts a rather different view from that of the accruals-based approach of traditional financial accounting. However, some of the principles are inconsistent with present company law and several of the Financial Reporting Standards in issue are inconsistent with the *Statement of Principles*. Company law is presently under review, with the publication of a White Paper which proposes major changes to the mechanism for setting and enforcing accounting rules in the UK. Once the law is changed, then it will be necessary to change numerous Financial Reporting Standards. It can perhaps be seen that the failure in the past to develop a generally-agreed theory underpinning financial accounting is not without its practical costs.

A 2002 EU Regulation requires all quoted companies in Europe to prepare their consolidated financial statements in accordance with international standards, rather than national standards, by the year 2005. Accounting rule setters in the various member states are attempting, with varying degrees of enthusiasm, to achieve convergence between their own standards and those of the IASB, but this process is difficult to achieve because of considerable, often major, differences between the respective standards and because the IASB is itself revising a large number of standards as part of its improvements project. National standard setters are therefore in the uncomfortable position of shooting at a moving target.

The EU Regulation applies only to the consolidated financial statements of quoted companies, although member states may permit, or require, the use of international standards in the single-entity financial statements of those companies as well as in both the single entity and consolidated financial statements of unquoted companies. At the time of writing it is unclear whether the various member states will require universal application of international standards or whether two sets of standards, national and international, will co-exist for application to different financial statements in the same country. In the view of the authors, even the consolidated financial statements of quoted companies in different EU countries are unlikely to be comparable until long after 2005, let alone the financial statements of unquoted companies.

While the world's standard setters still have their disagreements, most of them seem to suffer from the same condition – asking for more and more about what is in relative terms less and less. The phrase 'knowledge economy' might have become a stale cliché but it still has a relevance in that the major assets of an increasing number of businesses are knowledge and expertise rather than physical assets. Yet standard setters have poured far more of their energies into the production of longer and ever more detailed standards relating to tangible assets than they have to the critical questions of how an entity should report on the extent to which it has invested in enhancing its store of knowledge and what it has done to protect that store, for example through its staffing policies.

Another disappointing feature of the shared practices of standard setters is their reluctance to move away from the view that there is one and only one way of valuing an asset or a liability that should be reported. The standard setters argue that it would be confusing to report both the replacement cost and historical cost of an asset or the market value and original value of a liability. One of their strongest arguments is that the users of financial statements would not understand the different bases but, at the same time, they issue standards of such detail and complexity that the layperson attempting to interpret financial statements can now no longer even see the trees; the wood disappeared some while ago.

The practice of providing very detailed information about what is such a limited range of assets and liabilities does suggest that financial accounting practice is an area where, increasingly, spurious accuracy reigns.

We are grateful for the permission of the Accounting Standards Board to reproduce extracts from their large list of publications. As in previous editions, we have included a selection of questions from the professional examination papers of the Association of Chartered Certified Accountants, the Chartered Institute of Management Accountants and the Institute of Chartered Accountants in England and Wales. We gratefully acknowledge the permission of these three bodies to reproduce their questions, although we are disappointed that the ACCA will not permit us to include questions set in the two years preceding publication of the book, even though those questions are available on their website. We have chosen to include questions based on UK standards but would emphasise that both the ACCA and CIMA set alternative examination papers based on international accounting standards, should readers wish to make use of these.

A downloadable *Solutions Manual*, prepared by John Wyett, to whom both the authors and readers of this text owe a considerable debt, is available to Lecturers on the password-protected website to the book, **www.booksites.net/lewispendrill**, where we intend also to publish annual *Updates*.

As always, we wish to thank our long-suffering wives, Pamela and Louise, for all their help in reading and commenting on draft chapters and checking proofs, and for reminding us in such positive tones that there is a life beyond *Advanced Financial Accounting*.

RWL
DP

The framework of financial reporting

The search for principles

overview

In this chapter we first introduce the subject matter of the book and explore the role of accounting theory before turning to some of the attempts which have been made to construct a conceptual framework for financial reporting. We examine the ongoing US Conceptual Framework Project and the International Accounting Standards Board (IASB) *Framework for the Preparation and Presentation of Financial Statements* before concentrating on the work of the UK Accounting Standards Board (ASB) that led to the publication of its *Statement of Principles for Financial Reporting* in December 1999.

Introduction

One of the most difficult tasks facing authors is deciding how to start their books. An elegant epigram or an eye-catching sentence might well fix the attention of prospective readers or, more importantly, potential purchasers of the book, but such devices do not seem appropriate in this case. We feel that it would be best to start the book in a fashion which reflects its approach, i.e. we shall adopt a practical stance and start by discussing what we mean by the three words which constitute the title of the book – *Advanced Financial Accounting*. It will be convenient to start at the end of the title and then work back.

A number of definitions of accounting are available in the literature, and of these we will select the oft-quoted description provided by the Committee of the American Accounting Association (AAA), which was formed in order to prepare a statement of basic accounting theory. In its report, which was published in 1966, the Committee defined accounting as:

> the process of identifying, measuring, and communicating economic information to permit informed judgements and decisions by users of the information.[1]

We feel that the definition is a useful one in that it focuses not on the accounting process itself but on the reasons why information is required. It is all too easy for accountants to become obsessed with the techniques of their craft and to forget that the application of these techniques is not an end in itself but merely a means to an end. In this book we shall constantly reiterate such questions as 'Why is this information required?' or 'How will this data be used?' We believe that a proper study of accounting must start with an examination of the needs of decision makers.

The distinction between financial and management accounting is a convenient one to make, but it must not be regarded as one which divides the two areas of study into watertight compartments. It would be better if the phrases 'financial' and 'management' accounting

---

[1] *A statement of basic accounting theory*, AAA, New York, 1966, p. 1.

were replaced by 'external' and 'internal' accounting, as management accounting has financial implications while managers have more than a passing interest in financial accounting. But, however one describes the differences, it is generally agreed that financial, or external, accounting is primarily concerned with the communication of information about an entity to those who do not share in its management, while management, or internal, accounting refers to the communication of information to the managers of the particular entity. Thus the American Financial Accounting Standards Board (FASB) has defined financial reporting as activities which are intended to serve 'the informational needs of external users who lack the authority to prescribe the financial information they want from an enterprise, and therefore must use the information that management communicates to them'.[2] This is a helpful definition which indicates that in this book we will be concerned with financial information that is given to users rather than information which is required by an individual or group of individuals who are in a position to enforce their request.

A more recent description of the objective served by financial statements has been provided by the UK Accounting Standards Board (ASB), whose publications loom large in this book. In its *Statement of Principles for Financial Reporting*,[3] the Board states that:

> The objective of financial statements is to provide information about the reporting entity's financial performance and financial position that is useful to a wide range of users for assessing the stewardship of the entity's management and for making economic decisions.

The reference to the making of economic decisions links back to the AAA's description of accounting and reminds us of the essentially utilitarian nature of the activity. The concept of stewardship reminds us of accounting's historical roots which were based on the desire of owners of assets to receive reports from their stewards on the way in which the assets entrusted to their charge had been used.

A more modern interpretation of the concept of stewardship suggests that it has two aspects. The obligation to render accounts, or provide financial statements, might be expected to motivate stewards (managers) to act in ways which best serve the interests of owners, while the receipt of such information might help owners make economic decisions (e.g. sell shares or sack the managers), thus indicating that the two purposes of the provision of financial information identified by the ASB are closely interrelated.

Another way in which our attitude to stewardship has changed is that there is now the question of whether stewardship is owed to parties other than the economic owners of the assets. Do managers have an obligation to report to other groups such as employees? Although many would contend that economic ownership is all, and that reporting to other groups is simply a means to the end desired by the owners, there are others who would argue that in a modern business enterprise shareholders are not the only stakeholders entitled to receive reports. We shall return to this theme later in the book.

In this book we shall concentrate on the question of accounting for limited companies. We do, of course, recognise that there are many other forms of entity which are of importance, including charities, universities, central and local government and their associated agencies. Our reason for deciding to concentrate on the topic of limited companies is not because we think that the other forms of entity do not merit the concern of financial accountants, but because we recognise that, at least at present, most accounting courses are concerned with the private profit-seeking sector of the economy. Our readers will appreciate

---

[2] Statement of Financial Accounting Concepts (SFAC) 1, *Objectives of Financial Reporting by Business Enterprises*, FASB, Stamford, Conn., 1978, Para. 28.

[3] *Statement of Principles for Financial Reporting*, ASB, London, December 1999.

that many of the topics that will be discussed in the context of limited companies are of direct relevance to other forms of economic entity.

We should also provide some indication of the interpretation that should be placed on the adjective 'advanced' in the title of this book. It does not mean that the text will concentrate on detailed and complex manipulations of debits and credits, although we shall of course have to deal with such matters from time to time. In the context of this book, 'advanced' means that we shall concentrate on the identification, measurement and communication of economic information in the light of our acceptance of the view of the ASB that such information is required to help in decision making. Thus we shall concentrate on such questions as what information is relevant to decision makers, how the information is relevant to decision makers, how the information should be measured, and the manner in which it should be communicated. In so doing we shall describe and evaluate alternative approaches to the solution of accounting problems.

The definitions of accounting which we quoted above stop at the 'communication' of information. However, it must be emphasised that the interpretation of information is a vital part of an accountant's work, and it is clear that this aspect must be regarded as being an integral part of the process of communication. It should be noted that the definition of accounting does not extend to decision making. Of course, many accountants do become involved in decision making, but when they do so they are performing a managerial rather than an accounting role. We would not for one moment wish to argue that accountants should not become involved in management, but it is essential to distinguish between accounting and decision making. It is important that information provided by accountants should be as free as possible from personal bias but, if accountants do not keep the distinction between accounting and decision making clear in their own minds, there is a great danger that they might, possibly quite unconsciously, bias the information provided towards the decision which they would wish to see made.

The above discussion might suggest that we see the work of an accountant as being of a purely technical nature in which he or she is allowed little latitude for professional judgement. This is not the case, because we believe that the accountant must strive to find out and attempt to satisfy the information needs of decision makers and, as we shall show, this is no easy task.

Accounting theory

Academic accountants tend to bemoan the lack of generally accepted accounting theory. This is understandable because theory is the stock in trade of academics. Some 'practical' accountants are probably rather pleased that there is no generally agreed theory of accounting because such practical people are suspicious of theory and theorising as they believe that it gets in the way of 'real work'. However, those who take this view are probably ignorant of the role that theory can play in practical matters and do not realise that an absence of theory does give rise to many real and practical difficulties.

The description of accounting theory provided by Hendriksen shows clearly the practical uses of theory. Hendriksen defines accounting theory as 'logical reasoning in the form of a set of broad principles that (i) provide a general frame of reference by which accounting practice can be evaluated and (ii) guide the development of new practices and procedures'.[4]

---

[4] E.S. Hendriksen and M.F. Van Breda, *Accounting Theory*, 5th edn, R.D. Irwin, Homewood, Ill., 1992.

Expressed in this way, it is obvious that the function of theory is to assist in the resolution of practical problems. The existence of a theory would mean that we could say and explain why, given a number of assumptions, method X (perhaps current cost accounting) is to be preferred to method Y (say historical cost accounting).

There have been numerous attempts to construct a theory of accounting.[5] In the early stages of development an *inductive* approach was employed. Thus the practices of accountants were analysed in order to see whether patterns of consistent behaviour could be derived from the observations. If a general principle could be observed, then procedures which deviated from it could be castigated as being unsound. These first attempts were mainly directed towards the establishment of explanatory theories, i.e. theories which explained why certain rules were followed.

This approach failed for two main reasons. One is the difficulty of distinguishing consistent patterns of behaviour from a mass of procedures which had developed with the growth of accountancy and the problem of establishing any general set of explanatory statements. The second, and possibly more important, reason was that the approach did not help to improve accounting practice in any significant way. The approach only allowed the theorist to say 'what is' and not 'what ought to be'.

In response to these problems a different method of theory construction emerged in the 1950s. This method was normative in nature, i.e. it was directed towards the improvement of accounting practice. The method also included elements of the deductive approach, which essentially consists of the derivation of rules on the basis of logical reasoning from a basic set of objectives. The theories generally consisted of a mixture of deductive and inductive approaches, the latter being used to identify the basic objectives. These approaches to theory construction were extremely valuable in that they generated a number of books and papers which have had a profound effect on the development of accounting thought, in particular in the area of current value accounting.[6]

Since that time, we have seen the development of numerous bodies throughout the world concerned with setting accounting standards. Perhaps not surprisingly, these standard setters have found it difficult to resolve particular accounting issues, so they have sought to construct a conceptual framework or set of principles which could be used to underpin accounting standards and to provide guidance to practitioners in areas where no accounting standard exists. Although the British Accounting Standards Steering Committee, a predecessor of the ASB, issued a discussion document *The Corporate Report*[7] as early as 1975, the most ambitious attempt to create such a framework has undoubtedly been that of the Financial Accounting Standards Board (FASB) in the USA. As we shall see, enormous expenditure on this project in the 1970s and early 1980s was not sufficient to prevent it running into difficulties with the consequence that there has been very little output since the mid-1980s.

In spite of these difficulties, the approach of the FASB has had considerable influence on subsequent developments in other countries, including the following attempts to develop conceptual frameworks:[8]

---

[5] Hendriksen and Van Breda, *op. cit.*, provides a detailed and authoritative description of these attempts.

[6] Some of the more important developments are summarised in Chapter 19.

[7] Accounting Standards Steering Committee, *The Corporate Report*, London, 1975. This important and wide-ranging document did not receive the attention which it deserved because it was followed closely by the publication of the Report of the Inflation Accounting Committee (the Sandilands Report), which was considered to have much greater immediate relevance. We discuss the Sandilands Report in Chapters 19 and 20 of this book.

[8] This is not intended as an exhaustive list. Many bodies in other countries have attempted to prepare conceptual frameworks and have drawn upon the work of the FASB. Examples include Australia, Canada and New Zealand.

- *Making Corporate Reports Valuable*, Discussion Document by the Research Committee of the Institute of Chartered Accountants of Scotland (ICAS), edited by Peter N. McMonnies, Kogan Page, London, 1988.
- *Framework for the Preparation and Presentation of Financial Statements*, International Accounting Standards Committee (IASC), London, 1989 and, subsequently, adopted by the International Accounting Standards Board (IASB) in April 2001.
- *Guidelines for Financial Reporting Standards*, Report to the Research Board of the Institute of Chartered Accountants in England and Wales by Professor David Solomons, Institute of Chartered Accountants in England and Wales (ICAEW), London, 1989.
- *The Future Shape of Financial Reports*, Discussion paper by the ICAEW Research Committee and the ICAS Research Board, 1991.
- *Statement of Principles for Financial Reporting*, ASB, London, December 1999.

With the exception of the ICAS Discussion Document, *Making Corporate Reports Valuable*,[9] which takes a much less blinkered approach, all of these documents work within the confines of a typical set of financial statements comprising position statement/balance sheet, performance statement or statements, cash or funds flow statement and supplementary notes. Their basic approach is summarised in Figure 1.1.

As we shall see, problems arise at every stage of the process but, in particular, at the stages of recognition and measurement.

We shall look first at the US Conceptual Framework Project and then briefly at the IASB *Framework for the Preparation and Presentation of Financial Statements* before taking a more detailed look at the development of the ASB's *Statement of Principles*.

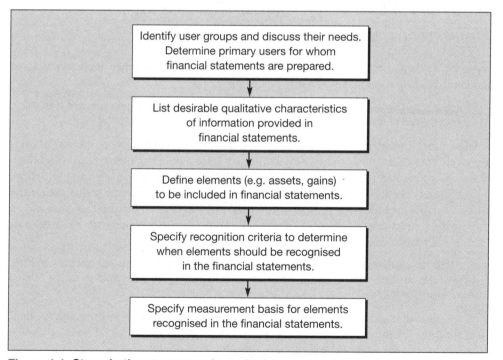

Figure 1.1 Steps in the structure of a typical conceptual framework

---

[9] We shall examine some of the ideas of this report later in the book, particularly in Chapters 13 and 21.

The FASB conceptual framework project

Since the mid-1970s, the US FASB has been engaged in a major project to develop a 'conceptual framework' for accounting which it defined as:

> a constitution, a coherent system of interrelated objectives and fundamentals that can lead to consistent standards and that prescribes the nature, function and limits of financial accounting and financial statements. [10]

As the project developed, the FASB issued a number of documents entitled *Statements of Financial Accounting Concepts* (SFACs). For reasons which will be explained below, many observers thought that the project had come to an end with the publication of SFACs Nos 5 and 6 in 1984 and 1985 but, in the late 1990s, the FASB began to develop a further SFAC, which was published as No. 7 in February 2000. The following Statements are relevant in the context of this book:[11]

1 *Objectives of Financial Reporting by Business Enterprises* (November 1978).
2 *Qualitative Characteristics of Accounting Information* (May 1980).
5 *Recognition and Measurement in Financial Statements of Business Enterprises* (December 1984).
6 *Elements of Financial Statements* (December 1985).
7 *Using Cash Flow Information and Present Value in Accounting Measurements* (February 2000).

We shall briefly consider each of these in turn.

SFAC No. 1 *Objectives of Financial Reporting by Business Enterprises*

As we have seen earlier in the chapter, the FASB is firmly of the view that financial reporting is intended to help users make decisions:

> Financial reporting is not an end in itself but is intended to provide information that is useful in making business and economic decisions . . . (Para. 9)

It follows that it is necessary to determine who the users are and to explore the sort of decision which they have to take. The FASB identifies a large number of user groups with both a direct and an indirect interest. The former include such groups as owners, lenders, suppliers, potential investors and creditors, customers, management, directors and taxing authorities while the latter include such groups as financial analysts and labour unions, who advise those with a direct interest. In spite of recognition of these user groups and discussion of their needs, the Statement comes to the conclusion that:

> . . . Thus, financial reporting should provide information to help investors, creditors and others assess the amounts, timing and uncertainty of prospective net cash inflows to the related enterprise. (Para. 37)

While some find it difficult to accept that this focus on investors and creditors follows logically from the identification of so many user groups and the discussion of their needs, the next step in the logic seems to be even more suspect:

---

[10] *Scope and Implications of the Conceptual Framework Project*, FASB, Stamford, Conn., 1976, p. 2.
[11] SFAC No. 3 was superseded by SFAC No. 6 and SFAC No. 4 was concerned with Objectives of Financial Reporting by Nonbusiness Organizations, which is outside the scope of this book.

Financial reporting should provide information about the economic resources of an enterprise, the claims to those resources (obligations of the enterprise to transfer resources to other entities and owners' equity) and the effects of transactions, events and circumstances that change resources and claims to those resources. (Para. 40)

A cynical observer might comment that it is extremely convenient that the outcome of the user-oriented approach is the conclusion that users need the sort of reports that they have traditionally received in the past, namely a position statement or balance sheet together with an income statement!

SFAC No. 2 *Qualitative Characteristics of Accounting Information*

In SFAC No. 2, the FASB specifies a hierarchy of desirable characteristics for accounting information. Decision usefulness is paramount and to be useful information must be both relevant and reliable. While the statement provides numerous other desirable qualities in a hierarchy, it clearly recognises that there will often be a conflict between two or more of these characteristics. Thus at the highest level, relevant information may not be reliable while reliable information may not be relevant. We will examine a similar attempt to specify desirable characteristics later in the chapter within the context of the UK ASB's *Statement of Principles for Financial Reporting*.

SFAC No. 6 *Elements of Financial Statements* (superseded SFAC No. 3)

This SFAC provides definitions of the ten elements of financial statements, namely:

- Assets
- Liabilities
- Equity
- Investments by owners
- Distributions to owners
- Comprehensive income[12]
- Revenue
- Expenses
- Gains
- Losses

It follows that nothing should be included in the financial statements unless it satisfies one of the definitions provided. Even then, it should not be included in the financial statements unless it satisfies the recognition criteria laid down in SFAC No. 5.

---

[12] While other terms in this list will be familiar to readers, it may be helpful to reproduce the FASB definition of Comprehensive income: 'Comprehensive income is the change in equity of a business enterprise during a period from transactions and other events and circumstances from nonowner sources. It includes all changes in equity during a period except those resulting from investments by owners and distributions to owners' (SFAC No. 6, Para. 70).

SFAC No. 5 *Recognition and Measurement in Financial Statements of Business Enterprises*

Having set down the desirable characteristics of accounting information and the definitions of the elements of financial statements, the crucial step in the US Conceptual Framework Project came with SFAC No. 5. This is the document which was intended to specify both when an element should be recognised (that is, included in the financial statements) and, once included, how it should be measured.

The Statement lays down four fundamental recognition criteria but accepts that trade-offs between them will have to be made in practice. It then discusses various different possible bases of measurement which could be used in a set of financial statements, including historical cost, current cost, current market value, net realisable value and present value of future cash flows. However, it does not come down clearly in favour of any one basis of measurement but, rather, leaves the choice of accounting measurement to standard setters and accountants.

For many observers, this was the end of the Conceptual Framework Project for, instead of providing guidance of what should be included in financial statements and what basis of measurement should be used, it failed to do so. Three short quotations from the Statement will help readers appreciate why the late Professor David Solomons described SFAC No. 5 as a 'cop-out':[13]

> Items currently reported in financial statements are measured by different attributes, depending on the nature of the item and the relevance or reliability of the attribute measured. The Board expects the use of different attributes to continue. (Para. 66)

> The concept of earnings described in this statement is similar to net income in present practice . . . (Para. 33)

> The Board expects the concept of earnings to be subject to the process of gradual change or evolution which has characterised the development of net income . . . (Para. 35)

Here was a framework designed to help standard setters improve financial reporting providing little guidance but rather expecting things to continue much as they had done before! Such an outcome had been predicted by the British Professor Richard Macve in 1981 in a report commissioned by the Accounting Standards Committee, the predecessor of the ASB.[14] Professor Macve concluded that, while the quest for a conceptual framework or general theory is important in identifying questions that need to be answered, it would be idle to hope that such a framework could be developed that would give explicit guidance on practical problems.

SFAC No. 7 *Using Cash Flow Information and Present Value in Accounting Measurements*

To the surprise of many, the FASB published two exposure drafts of a proposed Statement of Financial Accounting Concepts in the late 1990s and these were followed, in due course, by the publication of SFAC No. 7 in February 2000.[15] This Statement attempts to provide a

---

[13] David Solomons, 'The FASB's Conceptual Framework: an evaluation', *Journal of Accountancy*, June 1986, pp. 114–24.

[14] Richard Macve, *A conceptual framework for financial reporting: the possibilities of an agreed structure*, ICAEW, London, 1981.

[15] The exposure drafts were *Using Cash Flow Information in Accounting Measurements* (June 1997) and *Using Cash Flow Information and Present Value in Accounting Measurements* (March 1999).

framework for the use of present values of future cash flows as a basis for accounting measurement. In the view of SFAC No. 7, where present values are used, the objective should be to arrive at the price of an asset or liability in a hypothetical market. While recognising that present values will often be calculated by discounting the most likely outcome by a risk-adjusted discount rate, the FASB would prefer to see present values reflecting any uncertainty inherent in the future cash flows by using expected cash flows, that is possible cash flows weighted by their probability of occurrence, discounted at a risk-free rate of interest. The Statement is quite clear in proposing that the calculation of the present value of liabilities should reflect the credit standing of the particular entity for which the valuation is being calculated.

SFAC No. 7 is a difficult and rather rambling read and, as with the earlier Statements, it is difficult to envisage it providing much help in the solution of problems of financial reporting in the foreseeable future.

In spite of Professor Macve's conclusion and the difficulties which have been faced by the FASB in applying their Conceptual Framework in practice, other bodies have continued their search for this Holy Grail and we turn next to the attempt of the IASC.

The IASC/IASB framework

Given that national standard setters, like the FASB and ASB, were facing difficulties in resolving many accounting issues, it is perhaps not surprising that the IASC, with members drawn from some 100 countries, faced even greater difficulties.[16] It too attempted to construct a conceptual framework although on a much less grand scale than that which was originally envisaged by the FASB.

The IASC published its extremely short *Framework for the Preparation and Presentation of Financial Statements* in July 1989 and we may immediately obtain a feel for its contents by listing the major headings of the document:

- Introduction
- The Objective of Financial Statements
- Underlying Assumptions
- Qualitative Characteristics of Financial Statements
- The Elements of Financial Statements
- Recognition of the Elements of Financial Statements
- Measurement of the Elements of Financial Statements
- Concepts of Capital and Capital Maintenance

Most of these may be clearly related to the relevant Statements of Financial Concepts of the FASB, which we have outlined above. The additions are sections on 'Underlying Assumptions' and 'Concepts of Capital and Capital Maintenance'. The first of these describes the accruals basis and going concern concept while the second outlines the major capital maintenance concepts which can be used in the measurement of profit, namely financial capital maintenance (nominal or real) and physical capital maintenance, respectively, without choosing between them.[17]

---

[16] We discuss the increasing role of the IASC and its successor, the International Accounting Standards Board (IASB) in international standard setting in Chapter 3, Sources of authority: the rise of international standards.

[17] We will discuss these concepts in considerable depth later in the book, initially in Chapter 4 and subsequently in Part 3.

Yet again, standard setters looking to this framework for help in resolving most accounting issues will be disappointed. Its failings are most evident at the measurement stage. Thus the section on measurement discusses four different measurement bases which are employed to different degrees and in varying combinations in financial statements, namely historical cost, current cost, realisable value and present value. However, no guidance is given on which should be selected for any given element recognised. When this is coupled with the lack of guidance on the capital maintenance concept to be employed in measuring profit for a period, the document seems unlikely to resolve many accounting issues. A quotation from the final paragraph (Para. 110) gives support to this conclusion:

> The selection of the measurement bases and concept of capital maintenance will determine the accounting model used in the preparation of financial statements. Different accounting models exhibit different degrees of relevance and reliability and, as in other areas, management must seek a balance between relevance and reliability. This Framework is applicable to a range of accounting models and provides guidance on preparing and presenting the financial statements constructed under the chosen model. At the present time, it is not the intention of the Board of IASC to prescribe a particular model other than in exceptional circumstances, such as for those enterprises reporting in the currency of a hyperinflationary economy. This intention will, however, be reviewed in the light of world developments.

Well over a decade has now passed but this framework has not been tightened. It was adopted by the IASB in April 2001 but we may rest assured that that body will not be able to resist attempts to improve the framework in due course.

With this background, let us now turn to the attempts of the ASB to develop its *Statement of Principles for Financial Reporting*.

The ASB's *Statement of Principles*

The ASB has been committed to the development of a *Statement of Principles for Financial Reporting* since its formation in 1990. This was made clear in paragraph 4 of the ASB's *Foreword to accounting standards*, issued in June 1993:

> FRSs (Financial Reporting Standards) are based upon the Statement of Principles for Financial Reporting currently in issue, which addresses the concepts underlying the information presented in financial statements. The objective of this Statement of Principles is to provide a framework for the consistent and logical formulation of individual accounting standards. The framework also provides a basis on which others can exercise judgement in resolving accounting issues.

Despite this brave statement, the Board managed to issue many FRSs before it published its own *Statement of Principles* in December 1999.

The first attempt

Individual draft chapters of a *Statement of Principles* were issued by the ASB and, following amendment in response to comments, these were collected together in an exposure draft published in November 1995. The headings of the seven chapters in this exposure draft were as follows:

1　The objective of financial statements
2　The qualitative characteristics of financial information
3　The elements of financial statements
4　Recognition in financial statements
5　Measurement in financial statements
6　Presentation in financial statements
7　The reporting entity

The first five of these chapters covered material familiar from the FASB *Statements of Financial Accounting Concepts* and the IASC *Framework for the Preparation and Presentation of Financial Statements* which we have discussed above. Chapter 6 specified the contents of a set of financial statements and how information should be presented in those statements. Chapter 7 concerned itself with the treatment of different levels of investment, including subsidiaries, associates and joint ventures.

In the preparation of this draft, the ASB sensibly tried to start with a clean sheet by ignoring the constraints imposed by company law. Appendix 2 to the draft specifically drew attention to a number of important conflicts between the draft *Statement* and the law. However, where such conflicts exist, the principles could only be followed if use were to be made of the true and fair override or if the law were to be changed. The ASB undoubtedly hopes and anticipates that changes in the law will follow general acceptance of its *Statement of Principles*.

The draft *Statement of Principles* adopted a balance sheet focus. Thus, like its predecessors, it provided definitions of assets and liabilities and proposed that only items which satisfy those definitions may be recognised in the balance sheet and then only when certain recognition criteria are satisfied.

Given the greater relevance of current values to decision taking, it proposed a greater use of current values using a concept known as 'value to the business', to which we shall return many times in this book.

Ownership interest is defined as assets less liabilities and the total gains or losses for a period are to be calculated by deducting the opening ownership interest from the closing ownership interest and adjusting for any contributions from or distributions to owners. Such gains or losses were to appear in one of the two performance statements, either in the Profit and Loss Account or, as another gain or loss, in the Statement of Total Recognised Gains and Losses. The draft specified certain rules to guide this selection, in particular that gains and losses on fixed assets, whether realised or unrealised, should appear in the Statement of Total Recognised Gains and Losses rather than in the Profit and Loss Account.

Perhaps not surprisingly, the ASB received more comments on this document than any other document it has published. While many recognised the need for a Statement of Principles, criticism of this particular draft Statement was vociferous, with the firm of Ernst & Young playing a particularly important role.[18] This criticism was such that the ASB withdrew the draft *Statement of Principles* in July 1996 and issued a progress paper entitled 'Statement of Principles for Financial Reporting – the way ahead'. In that document, the ASB stated its intention to issue a revised exposure draft and this was published, rather later than expected, in March 1999.

Although the ASB accused its critics of misunderstanding its proposals, much of the criticism seemed to have been well founded. The balance sheet focus adopted in the draft has a

---

[18] *See*, for example: *The ASB's Framework: Time to Decide*, Ernst & Young, London, February 1996; and *The ASB's Statement of Principles – Blueprint or Blind Alley?*, Ron Paterson (Ernst & Young), University of Wales (Aberystwyth), February 1998.

number of strengths but does not seem in accord with either current practice or the principles on which the Board has based some of its published standards. The draft certainly failed to provide sufficient justification for such a fundamental departure from a position with which many accountants feel comfortable.

Although they may be accused of overlooking the fact that a large proportion of listed companies have revalued at least some of their fixed assets on a piecemeal basis, critics also attacked the proposals to move towards a greater use of current values. They argued that such values are less reliable and that, even if all assets and liabilities recognised in a balance sheet were to be shown at current values, the total ownership interest would not represent the wealth or value of the business as discussed in economists' models. Given this, any measure of gains and losses based upon comparing two such balance sheet totals is unlikely to provide a sensible measure of the increase in the wealth of owners.

The way in which gains and losses were to be recognised in either the Profit and Loss Account or the Statement of Total Recognised Gains and Losses also came in for criticism. While the authors would applaud the attempts of the ASB to discard the confusing and rather unhelpful distinction between realised and unrealised profit, it is not surprising that practitioners, who have worked with such concepts for the whole of their working lives, were not willing to give them up without a fight.

With this brief look at the major criticisms made of the first draft Statement of Principles, let us now turn to the revised exposure draft issued in March 1999.

The revised exposure draft

The revised exposure draft was issued in March 1999, this time accompanied by an introductory booklet and a technical supplement. The introductory booklet contained both a question and answer section and an overview of the draft statement. The technical supplement sets out the reasons for some of the Board's conclusions and why it had rejected possible alternatives. Having been taken by surprise by the negative reaction to the first exposure draft, the ASB was clearly concerned to defuse criticism of this second attempt at developing a Statement of Principles and took great pains to explain and sell its revised draft. Skilful presentation, coupled with a clear exposition of the limited role of the Statement and the considerable flexibility which it still allows, appeared to defuse criticism of the revised draft and permitted the issue of the actual *Statement of Principles for Financial Reporting* later that same year, in December 1999.

The *Statement of Principles*

The *Statement of Principles for Financial Reporting* contains the same eight chapters as the revised exposure draft with only minor changes to the words and layout. These chapters are:

1 The objective of financial statements
2 The reporting entity
3 The qualitative characteristics of financial information
4 The elements of financial statements
5 Recognition in financial statements
6 Measurement in financial statements
7 Presentation of financial information
8 Accounting for interests in other entities

We shall provide a brief synopsis of each of these chapters before assessing the extent to which the *Statement* is likely to contribute to an improvement in the quality of future accounting standards.

Chapter 1 The objective of financial statements

Perhaps not surprisingly the *Statement of Principles* provides us with the following objective:

> The objective of financial statements is to provide information about the reporting entity's financial performance and financial position that is useful to a wide range of users for assessing the stewardship of the entity's management and for making economic decisions. (p. 16)

It identifies a number of users of general-purpose financial reports and discusses their needs for information. The user groups include investors, lenders, suppliers and other trade creditors, employees, customers, governments and their agencies and the public. Like the US Conceptual Framework Project, discussed above, the *Statement of Principles* comes to the conclusion that it is possible to meet the objective by focusing exclusively on the needs of investors, which it describes as the defining class of user.

It concludes that investors and others need information about the reporting entity's financial performance and financial position to help them to evaluate the entity's ability to generate cash (including the timing and certainty of its generation) and to assess its financial adaptability.

Chapter 2 The reporting entity

This chapter specifies the boundary of the reporting entity by reference to the scope of control. Thus an entity with direct control of its activities, assets and liabilities should prepare single entity financial statements while an entity which also has indirect control of the activities, assets and liabilities of a subsidiary should also prepare consolidated financial statements.

Control has two aspects: first, the ability to deploy the economic resources involved and, second, the ability to benefit (or to suffer) from this deployment. The Statement makes it clear that it is the relationship existing between entities in practice, rather than the theoretical level of influence, that is to be considered in determining whether or not control exists.

Chapter 3 The qualitative characteristics of financial information

The *Statement* sets out the desirable characteristics of financial information in a hierarchy which we have reproduced as Figure 1.2. To be useful financial information must be (i) relevant to users, (ii) reliable, (iii) comparable and (iv) understandable.

Financial information is relevant if it would influence economic decisions and it would be able to do this if it has predictive value or confirmatory value. Information with predictive value would help users to assess what is likely to happen in future while information with confirmatory value would help them to confirm or correct previous predictions which they have made. In many, if not most, cases information will have both confirmatory and predictive value.

To be reliable, information must be free from material error and possess certain subsidiary characteristics:

- *Faithful representation.* It must faithfully represent what it purports to represent so that, for example, the substance of a transaction must be portrayed when this differs from its legal form.

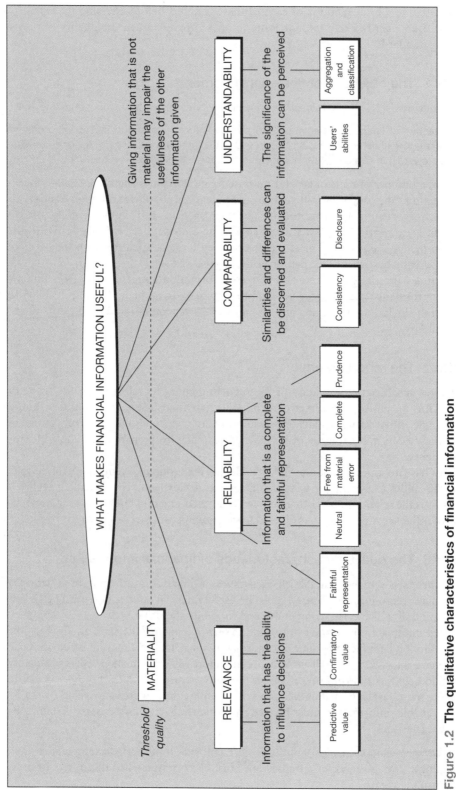

Figure 1.2 The qualitative characteristics of financial information

Source: Statement of Principles for Financial Reporting, Accounting Standards Board, December 1999, p. 34. © ASB Publications Limited 2000. Reproduced with permission.

- *Neutral.* The information should be neutral, in other words, it should not be subject to deliberate or systematic bias. We shall have more to say about this when we discuss prudence below.
- *Free from material error.* Information which includes a material error is unlikely to be reliable.
- *Complete.* It should be complete to the extent possible.
- *Prudent.* In the Statement, prudence is defined as follows:

> . . . Prudence is the inclusion of a degree of caution in the exercise of the judgements needed in making the estimates required under conditions of uncertainty, such that gains and assets are not overstated and losses and liabilities are not understated. In particular, under such conditions it requires more confirmatory evidence about the existence of, and a greater reliability of measurement for, assets and gains than is required for liabilities and losses. (Para. 3.19)

This definition of prudence still contains an element of bias insofar as it specifically warns against the overstatement of gains and assets but is silent on the understatements of gains and assets and warns against the understatement, but not the overstatement, of losses and liabilities. Even so, the new definition does involve some significant implications in that it requires that the concept must be applied within the bounds of reasonable estimates and hence renders the making of excessive provisions or the creation of hidden reserves unacceptable. The definition is not, however, one that is amenable to objective interpretation so disputes between directors and auditors about what is or is not prudent are unlikely to disappear. A message of some of the causes célèbres of 2001 and 2002 might suggest that, perhaps contrary to expectations, the auditors may not always be the more prudent party!

Information should be comparable both for a reporting entity over time and across different reporting entities. This is a tall order but, in particular, requires disclosure of accounting policies as well as of details of changes and the effects of changes in accounting policies.

In order to specify understandability as a desirable characteristic, it is necessary to make some assumption about the ability of users. The ASB assumes that the targeted users 'have a reasonable knowledge of business and economic activities and accounting and a willingness to study with reasonable diligence the information provided' (Para. 3.27(c)). However, this is qualified a little later when it is stated that 'information that is relevant and reliable should not be excluded from the financial statements simply because it is too difficult for some users to understand' (Para. 3.37).

The *Statement* clearly recognises that there will be conflicts between desirable characteristics such that trade-offs will be necessary. One example of such a conflict is between relevance and reliability: timely information may be highly relevant but not very reliable in an uncertain world but, if we wait for reliable information, it may no longer be timely and therefore no longer relevant. Another example is the conflict between neutrality and prudence, both subsidiary characteristics of reliability, to which we have drawn attention above.

Chapter 4 The elements of financial statements

This chapter defines seven elements of financial statements:

- assets
- liabilities
- ownership interest
- gains
- losses
- contributions from owners
- distributions to owners

Ownership interest is defined as assets less liabilities while gains and losses, contributions from owners and distributions to owners are defined by reference to various changes in ownership interest. The crucial definitions are therefore those for assets and liabilities, which clearly demonstrates the determination of the ASB to retain a balance sheet focus in spite of the heavy criticism of that approach following publication of the first exposure draft:

> **Assets are rights or other access to future economic benefits controlled by an entity as a result of past transactions or events. (Para. 4.6)**
>
> **Liabilities are obligations of an entity to transfer economic benefits as a result of past transactions or events. (Para. 4.23)**

We shall consider these terms in considerable detail later in the book, particularly in Chapters 5 and 7.

Chapter 5 Recognition in financial statements

There are two prongs to the recognition of transactions or events in a set of financial statements: first, there must be sufficient evidence that an asset or liability has been created or that there has been an addition to an asset or liability. Second, the new asset or liability, or addition thereto, must be capable of measurement at a monetary amount with sufficient accuracy.

So, to be included in a set of financial statements, the item must satisfy the definition of an element in Chapter 4 of the *Statement of Principles* and must be measured reliably. This would mean that certain expenditure previously treated as a deferred asset, such as deferred advertising expenditure, may not be recognised in future. In this way, the ASB hopes to limit the carrying forward of expenditure to match against perhaps dubious benefits in the future:

> The Statement imposes a degree of discipline on this process because only items that meet the definitions of, and relevant recognition criteria for, assets, liabilities or ownership interest are recognised in the balance sheet. (Para. 5.29)

Chapter 6 Measurement in financial statements

Having rejected, perhaps too easily, the notion that individual assets and liabilities should be reported on two or more bases of measurement, the ASB then has to choose whether assets and liabilities should be measured at historical cost or on a basis of measurement that reflects current value. The first exposure draft was explicit that the ASB favoured the use of current value, as can be seen from the following quotation:

> The Board therefore believes that practice should develop by evolving in the direction of greater use of current values to the extent that this is consistent with the constraints of reliability and cost. (First exposure draft, Para. 5.38)

This was criticised as an attempt on the part of the ASB to move away from historical cost accounting towards a system of current cost accounting. This the ASB denied and, certainly in the Statement, it is very careful not to expose this hostage to fortune.

The ASB now favours the use of the mixed measurement system, sometimes described as modified historical cost accounting. As envisaged by the *Statement*, some assets will be valued on a historical cost basis while others will be valued at current value. The practice whereby some entities have remeasured their tangible fixed assets at a current value on one

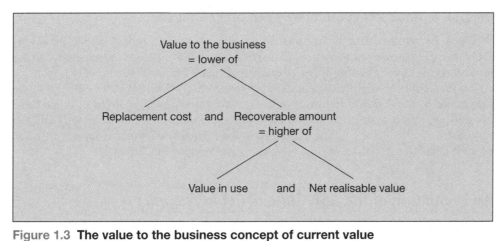

Figure 1.3 The value to the business concept of current value

Source: Statement of Principles for Financial Reporting, Accounting Standards Board, December 1999, para. 6.8. © ASB Publications Limited 2000. Reproduced with permission.

particular date but then left that revised value in the financial statements for many years to come is no longer permissible.[19]

The concept of current value which the ASB favoured at the date of publication of the *Statement* was value to the business, otherwise known as current cost or deprival value, which it defines as shown in Figure 1.3. However, as part of, or one might suggest as part of the cost of, the programme of convergence between UK and international Financial Reporting Standards, the ASB may have to switch its allegiance from value to the business to the use of fair value which, in its international variant, is firmly based upon market values. We shall return to the concept of current value many times in this book, particularly in Chapters 4, 5, 20 and 21.

If some companies choose to measure assets and liabilities on a historical cost basis while others choose to use current value, it is difficult to see how their respective financial statements will satisfy the desirable quality of comparability.

Chapter 7 Presentation of financial information

According to this chapter, the primary financial statements should comprise three documents:

- Statement of financial performance[20]
- Position statement or balance sheet
- Cash flow statement

The chapter lays down general principles for presentation of the highly structured and aggregated information necessary in financial statements, the notes to these statements and in the accompanying information. The latter includes such documents as the Chairman's Report, the operating and financial review and five-year historical summaries.

---

[19] See FRS 15 *Tangible Fixed Assets*, ASB, February 1999.

[20] Present standard accounting practice in the UK requires the inclusion of two performance statements: a Profit and Loss Account and a Statement of Total Recognised Gains and Losses. The reference to 'Statement of performance' in the singular anticipated the ASB proposal to combine these statements in the Discussion Paper *Reporting Financial Performance: Proposals for Change*, published in June 1999, and subsequently in FRED 22 *Revision of FRS 3 Reporting Financial Performance*, published in December 2000. We will discuss these proposals in Chapter 11.

Chapter 8 Accounting for interests in other entities

This final chapter deals with the treatment of investments in other entities both in the single-entity financial statements and in consolidated financial statements and is closely related to the material on the reporting entity discussed earlier in Chapter 2 of the *Statement of Principles*.

The *Statement* specifies that the accounting treatment in financial statements should be determined by the degree of influence which the investor has over the investee. When there is significant influence or joint control, the investee is an associate or joint venture and the appropriate method of accounting to be used in the consolidated financial statements is the equity method of accounting. We shall discuss this thoroughly in Chapter 15.

An evaluation of the ASB *Statement of Principles*

As we have seen, one of the major criticisms of the first exposure draft of the *Statement of Principles* was that it adopted a balance sheet focus as opposed to the transactions focused and matching approach of what was then current practice. The *Statement* reiterates this balance sheet focus and considers that it is necessary in order to prevent the attempts by some entities to delay the recognition of items of expenditure by carrying them forward as assets to match against, perhaps dubious, future benefits.

A second major criticism of the first exposure draft was that the ASB was attempting to move away from a system of historical cost accounting to a system of current cost accounting. The ASB has always claimed that this was not its intention although it, quite sensibly, favours the greater use of current values where appropriate. In the *Statement*, it has undoubtedly stepped further back and envisages the use of a mixed measurement system using both historical costs and current values for a long time to come. It has to be recognised that, if entities are permitted to choose whether to use historical cost based values or current values, the desirable quality of comparability across entities is lost completely.

A third criticism of the first exposure draft concerned the way in which gains and losses were divided between the Profit and Loss Account and the Statement of Total Recognised Gains and Losses. There is undoubtedly greater understanding and acceptance of the Statement of Total Recognised Gains and Losses now than when the first exposure draft was published.[21] Indeed, the Discussion Paper *Reporting Financial Performance: Proposals for change* (June 1999) and subsequent Financial Reporting Exposure Draft (FRED) 22 *Revision of FRS 3 'Reporting Financial Performance'* (December 2000) advocates the combination of both documents into a single Statement of Performance. The major debate has therefore focused on the more detailed proposals in these later documents.

In order to defuse potential criticism, the ASB plays down the importance of the *Statement of Principles* by drawing attention to the many other factors which will have to be considered in setting accounting standards, namely:

(a) legal requirements,
(b) cost–benefit considerations,
(c) industry-specific issues,
(d) the desirability of evolutionary change, and
(e) implementation issues.[22]

---

[21] The first exposure draft was published in November 1995 just some three years after the issue of FRS 3 *Reporting Financial Performance* in October 1992. It was FRS 3 which introduced the requirement for entities to produce the new primary statement, a Statement of Total Recognised Gains and Losses, for accounting periods ending on or after 22 June 1993.

[22] *Statement of Principles for Financial Reporting*, Introduction, Para. 14.

In particular, Appendix 1 draws attention to the major conflicts between the *Statement* and existing company law. It recognises very clearly that, as in the past, the law will continue to constrain the activities of the ASB for some considerable time in the future.

All of this leaves the ASB considerable flexibility in future but does raise a fundamental question about the role of any *Statement of Principles for Financial Reporting* if the principles which it lays down can be overridden on so many other grounds!

Summary

In this chapter we have first provided an introduction to this book. We have then stressed the need for 'theory' to guide and underpin practice and have examined some attempts to build theories of accounting. After a brief examination of early attempts to develop theory, we have outlined the attempts of the US Financial Accounting Standards Board and International Accounting Standards Committee to develop conceptual frameworks for financial reporting. We have then focused, in more detail, on the work of the ASB in developing its, more modestly titled, Statement of Principles.

The *Statement of Principles for Financial Reporting*, published in December 1999, goes to great pains to explain why the ASB has adopted its particular approach and, by so doing, attempted to head off the enormous criticism generated by its first exposure draft on this subject. In this, it appears to have been extremely successful.

Part of the reason for the lack of vociferous criticism is undoubtedly the fact that the *Statement of Principles* leaves the ASB with a considerable amount of flexibility. Inevitably choices will have to be made with trade-offs between different desirable characteristics and judgements on the necessary level of reliability for recognition of elements in the financial statements and the basis of their measurement. As we shall see in various places in the book, there are a number of cases where the ASB has issued accounting standards which are inconsistent with its own *Statement of Principles*. We would do well to remember that the setting of accounting standards is very much a political process which those with vested interests will wish to influence.

We have also seen that, although the *Statement of Principles* is written without taking into account the constraints imposed by the law, these constraints cannot possibly be ignored by those charged with the task of preparing accounting standards. The question of who does and who should set the rules by which the accounting game is played are important and complex issues and these form the subject matter of the next two chapters.

Recommended reading

ASC, *The Corporate Report,* London, 1975.

T.G. Evans, *Accounting Theory,* Thomson/South-Western College Publishing, Mason, O., 2002.

E.S. Hendriksen and M.F. Van Breda, *Accounting Theory,* 5th edn, Irwin, Homewood, Ill., 1992.

ICAS, *Making Corporate Reports Valuable,* Kogan Page, London, 1988.

R. Macve, *A Conceptual Framework for Financial Reporting: The Possibilities of an Agreed Structure,* ICAEW, London, 1981.

R. Macve, *A Conceptual Framework for Financial Accounting and Reporting – Vision, Tool or Threat?,* Garland, New York and London, 1997.

K.V. Peasnell, 'The function of a conceptual framework for corporate financial reporting', *Accounting and Business Research*, Autumn 1982.

M.K. Power, 'On the idea of a conceptual framework for financial reporting', in *Philosophical perspectives on accounting: Essays in honour of Edward Stamp*, M.J. Mumford and K.V. Peasnell (eds), Routledge, London and New York, 1993.

D. Tweedie, 'The conceptual framework and the Accounting Standards Board', in *Essays in accounting thought: A tribute to W.T. Baxter*, I. Lapsley (ed.), ICAS, Edinburgh, 1996.

Questions

1.1 The ASB's Statement of Principles sets out the concepts which underpin its development of financial reporting standards.

Required
Discuss why the ASB has adopted this conceptual approach and whether any difficulties may be encountered.

ICAEW, Financial Reporting, November 1994   **(10 marks)**

1.2 The Statement of Principles identifies the elements of financial statements. The measurement basis which is applied to these elements can significantly affect the reported financial performance and financial position of a company.

Requirements
(a) Identify the two main measurement bases used in financial reporting and explain how each should be applied in practice.   (8 marks)
(b) Explain the impact that subsequent remeasurement of elements of financial statements can have on reported financial performance and financial position.   (7 marks)

ICAEW, Financial Reporting, September 2001   **(15 marks)**

1.3 The Statement of Principles deals with the presentation of financial statements i.e. disclosure in primary statements and supporting notes.

Requirements
(a) Discuss the purposes and usefulness of the information on financial position and performance disclosed in published financial statements.   (10 marks)
(b) Provide a brief explanation of two inherent limitations of financial statements.

(5 marks)

ICAEW, Financial Reporting, December 2001   **(15 marks)**

Sources of authority: the United Kingdom

There is a large and increasing body of rules with which accountants need to be familiar when preparing or interpreting a set of financial statements. In some countries most of the rules are laid down in the law while, in other countries, the law contains principles only with the major rules being laid down in accounting standards.

Companies must comply with both the relevant law and applicable accounting standards, although the sanctions that will be applied for non-compliance with each may differ. Companies that have their shares publicly traded on a Stock Exchange must also comply with the rules of that Stock Exchange.

In this chapter, we explore all three sources of rules – the law, accounting standards and the Stock Exchange – within the present UK context. Here and throughout the book, we concentrate on 'big GAAP', the rules which apply to large companies and groups, rather than the special rules which apply to small and medium-sized companies.

In 1998, the Government embarked on an extensive review of British company law. After considering the Final Report of the Company Law Steering Group, it published a White Paper in July 2002 which proposes major changes to rule making in the United Kingdom. We examine the proposals to delegate the making of rules on the form and content of company financial statements and reports to a Standards Board, based on the present ASB but with a wider remit, and to extend the role of a Reporting Review Panel, based on the present Financial Reporting Review Panel (FRRP).

Increasingly, national standard setting is being superseded by regional and international standard setting and we examine this extremely important development in the following chapter.

Introduction

In Chapter 1 we explained that there is no general theory of accounting in existence to guide us in the preparation of financial statements. We explored the attempts of several bodies to build conceptual frameworks of accounting and concentrated on the work of the ASB in developing its *Statement of Principles for Financial Reporting*. In spite of the lack of theory, there are many rules which govern the preparation of financial statements and in this chapter we turn to the framework for the setting and enforcement of such rules in the United Kingdom.

Rule setters affecting the United Kingdom come in three main forms, each of which has different powers and sanctions available to it:

1 *Government at both the United Kingdom and European Union levels.* These operate through legislation.
2 *Securities markets.* In the United Kingdom the Stock Exchange imposes rules which must be complied with by companies that have their shares and other securities traded on the Exchange.

3 *Standard setting bodies in the private sector.* In the United Kingdom, standard setting takes place nationally through the work of the ASB. The European Union Regulation which requires all European companies that have their shares publicly traded on securities markets in Member States to prepare their consolidated financial statements in accordance with International Accounting Standards by the year 2005[1] raises the status of those international standards as well as raising a number of questions about future relationships between national standard setters and the IASB, which we shall discuss in some depth in the following chapter.

We shall first examine each of the three sources of authority within the UK context before turning to the proposals in the Government White Paper, *Modernising Company Law*, published in July 2002.[2]

Legislation

Background

The advent of the limited liability company by registration under a general Act of Parliament in the mid-nineteenth century made possible the separation of management from ownership, which is such a dominant feature of business organisation today. With this separation came the need for directors to render accounts (financial statements, in modern terminology) to shareholders to show the performance and financial position of the company. It followed that it was necessary to determine what should be included in such accounts and how they should be prepared.

It would have been possible for the law to have left the specification of the form and content of such accounts to be determined by contract between the shareholders and directors, or even to have left the directors to decide what information should be made available in the particular circumstances. However, the law initially flirted with the regulation of accounting disclosure in the period 1844–56 and then became permanently involved with regulating the contents of company accounts early in the twentieth century. The Companies Act 1929 increased the information which companies had to disclose while extensive disclosure has been required since the Companies Act 1948.[3]

Before the Companies Act 1981, the accounting requirements of company law allowed companies considerable latitude. The directors were required to prepare accounts which showed a true and fair view and which contained the minimum information specified by the various Companies Acts. These accounts, together with the accompanying auditors' and directors' reports, had to be laid before the shareholders and filed with the Registrar of Companies within certain time limits. While the basic position is unchanged, substantial alterations were made by the Companies Act 1981.

---

[1] Regulation PE-CONS 3626/02, European Union, June 2002. See Chapter 3, Sources of authority: the rise of international standards

[2] *Modernising Company Law*, Cm. 5553–I and 5553–II, HMSO, July 2002. See also **www.europa.eu.int/ comm.internal_market/en/company/account/news/index.htm**

[3] Readers who wish to study this historical development of accounting further are referred to H.C. Edey, 'Company accounting in the nineteenth and twentieth centuries', in *The Evolution of Corporate Financial Reporting*, T.A. Lee and R.H. Parker (eds), Nelson, London, 1979, and J.R. Edwards, *A History of Financial Accounting*, Routledge, London, 1989: Chapters 9, 10 and 11 of the latter are particularly relevant.

The Companies Act 1981 was mainly concerned with the implementation of the EC Fourth Directive, a directive heavily influenced by the more prescriptive approach to accounting found in France and Germany. As a consequence, the Act was much more prescriptive than previous legislation in the UK. Although it still contained the overriding principle that accounts should give a true and fair view, it increased substantially the amount of information to be disclosed and reduced considerably the flexibility which companies previously enjoyed. Thus, whereas directors were previously able to choose the particular formats and valuation rules which seemed most appropriate in the circumstances, the Companies Act 1981 specified much more tightly the formats and valuation rules to be used.

The provisions of the Companies Act 1981 are now contained in the Companies Act 1985, which was a consolidating Act, but this in turn has been amended by the subsequent Companies Act 1989 and numerous Statutory Instruments.

The Companies Act 1989 implemented the EC Seventh Directive on consolidated accounts and the EC Eighth Directive on auditors, as well as dealing with many other matters.

Small and medium-sized companies have long enjoyed the opportunity of filing abbreviated accounts with the Registrar of Companies. However, as a consequence of the attempts of successive governments to reduce the burden of regulation on small companies, new rules were introduced in 1997 to reduce the volume of disclosure required of small companies and groups. The Companies Act 1985 (Accounts of Small and Medium-Sized Companies and Minor Accounting Amendments) Regulations 1997 (SI 1997/220) established a revised Schedule 8 to the 1985 Companies Act, which now contains all the provisions of the law relating to the accounts which small companies must send to their members. This law, together with the accounting standard *Financial Reporting Standard for Smaller Entities* (FRSSE) now provides a less burdensome regulatory framework for small companies and groups.[4]

In this book we shall concentrate on what is sometimes called 'Big GAAP', that is Generally Accepted Accounting Practice for large companies and groups. While we will from time to time draw attention to some of the exemptions available to small and, to a lesser extent, medium-sized companies and groups, we will not deal with these systematically or in any detail.

Concentrating now on large companies, the law requires that full accounts, including group accounts where appropriate, are sent to all shareholders and debenture holders of the company, although permission is given for a listed public company to send a summary financial statement to its shareholders.[5] The latter provision was intended to reduce the cost of sending full accounts to large numbers of relatively unsophisticated shareholders, particularly following the large privatisation issues of the 1980s. Full accounts have to be laid before the company in general meeting except that a private company may elect not to do so.[6] Such provisions are designed to ensure that shareholders and debenture holders receive financial information about companies, while recognising that it may not be necessary formally to present the accounts of a private company at a general meeting.

In addition to the above, companies are required to make their accounts available to the public by filing them with the Registrar of Companies within certain time limits, namely ten months after the end of the accounting year for a private company and seven months after the end of an accounting year for a public company.

---

[4] The first FRSSE was issued in November 1997 and updated versions have been issued in December 1998, December 1999 and December 2001. It is intended that the Standard be updated periodically to incorporate relevant parts of new FRSs and Abstracts of the Urgent Issues Task Force (UITF).

[5] Companies Act 1985, s. 251 (as inserted by the Companies Act 1989, s. 15). This section was implemented by the Companies (Summary Financial Statement) Regulations 1990, SI 1990/515. See Chapter 17, pp. 555–7

[6] Companies Act 1985, s. 252 (as inserted by the Companies Act 1989, s. 16).

The current position

The Companies Act 1985, as amended by the Companies Act 1989, requires that the accounts of a large company give the information specified in Schedule 4 using one of the profit and loss account and balance sheet formats provided. However, compliance with this requirement is not sufficient to ensure compliance with the law for there is an overriding requirement that every balance sheet shall give a true and fair view of the state of affairs of the company and that every profit and loss account shall give a true and fair view of the profit or loss of the company for the financial year.[7]

Hence, having prepared the accounts containing the required disclosure, the accountant must then step back and decide whether or not the overall impression created is true and fair. If the accounts do not give such an impression, additional information must be provided. If the provision of additional information still does not result in a true and fair view, then the accounts must be changed, even if this means that they do not comply with the other statutory rules. Particulars of any departure, the reasons for it and its effect must be disclosed in the notes to the accounts.

The statutory requirements outlined above pose a number of problems for the accountant. Familiarity with the disclosure requirements of the Companies Acts is required, as is knowledge of the measurement or valuation rules to apply in arriving at the figures to be disclosed. Also the accountant must be aware of what is meant by the words 'true and fair'. We will look at each of these three aspects in turn.

The first problem involves detailed knowledge of the Companies Acts and the various guides thereto and considerable practice in applying those rules in various circumstances. We assume that readers have some knowledge of the requirements of the Companies Acts although, where relevant, we will reproduce the statutory rules in later chapters.

The second problem involves the selection of measurement or valuation rules to apply in arriving at the various figures which appear in the set of accounts. This requires a considerable knowledge of accounting, which this book will help to provide.

Until the Companies Act 1981 accountants would have looked to accounting principles, conventions, recommendations and standards to help them with this task. Although, as we shall see, such sources are extremely important, certain basic accounting principles have now been incorporated into the law. Thus, the law requires that accounts should be prepared in accordance with five accounting principles:

1 Going concern
2 Consistency
3 Prudence
4 Accruals
5 Separate determination of each asset and liability

Statute law now requires that these principles must be applied unless there are special reasons for departing from them. Where such special reasons exist, a note to the accounts must state the details of the departure, the reason for it and its effect.[8] We shall discuss the first four of these principles later in this chapter and the fifth principle in Chapter 9.

The Act provides that companies may prepare their accounts using either historical cost accounting rules or alternative accounting rules.[9]

---

[7] Companies Act 1985, s. 226.

[8] Companies Act 1985, Schedule 4, Part II, s. A, Paras 9–15.

[9] The historical cost accounting rules are contained in the Companies Act 1985, Schedule 4, s. B while the alternative accounting rules are contained in Schedule 4, s. C.

The alternative accounting rules are so framed to permit companies to use piecemeal revaluations in their historical cost accounts or to prepare current cost accounts as their main accounts, although in either case it is necessary to provide certain information to enable partial reconstruction of the historical cost accounts.

Some UK accountants are strongly opposed to the inclusion of such accounting principles and valuation rules in the law. They argue that it provides a straitjacket which may impede accounting development and two examples will illustrate their arguments.

First, company law includes a provision that 'only profits realised at the balance sheet date shall be included in the profit and loss account'. For reasons which we explain in Chapter 4, the ASB has taken the wise decision that a poorly defined concept of realisation is an inappropriate criterion for determining whether or not gains or losses should be recognised in the financial statements. However, while it has been possible for the ASB to ignore this legal constraint in drafting its *Statement of Principles for Financial Reporting*, it is not possible to ignore it when drafting accounting standards. As a consequence, the ASB is hampered in its attempts to reform accounting practice by a poorly thought out and somewhat dated legal provision.

Second, the alternative accounting rules permit the preparation of current cost accounts as a company's main accounts. As we explain in Part 3 of the book, Current Cost Accounting was very much in vogue in the 1970s and early 1980s, when the Companies Act 1981 was enacted. However, it is now very much out of favour and, to the best of our knowledge, no UK company now prepares its financial statements using current cost accounting. The statutory reference to current cost accounts now looks rather dated and out of line with the current approach of the ASB.

When accounts have been prepared, the accountant must decide whether they show a true and fair view and, if not, in what respects they need to be altered. These words 'true and fair' were first introduced together in the Companies Act 1948, following the recommendations of the Cohen Committee.[10] They have never been defined by statute but, rather, their meaning has become established by usage. A good definition has been provided by G.A. Lee:

> Today, 'the true and fair view' has become a term of art. It is generally understood to mean a presentation of accounts, drawn up according to accepted accounting principles, using accurate figures as far as possible, and reasonable estimates otherwise; and arranging them so as to show, within the limits of current accounting practice, as objective a picture as possible, free from wilful bias, distortion, manipulation or concealment of material facts.[11]

So, in order to decide whether or not a set of accounts presents a true and fair view, it is necessary for the accountant to have recourse to a constantly changing body of accounting principles and standards.[12]

Stock Exchange rules

Where companies have shares listed on the Stock Exchange or quoted on the Alternative Investment Market, they must comply with the additional disclosure requirements laid down by the Stock Exchange. These rules require the provision of both some more information and some more frequent information than that required by law.

---

[10] *Report of the Committee on Company Law Amendment*, Cmnd. 6659, HMSO, London, 1945.
[11] G.A. Lee, *Modern Financial Accounting*, 3rd edn, Nelson, London, 1981, p. 270.
[12] For a fuller discussion of the term 'true and fair' readers are referred to David Flint, *A True and Fair View in Company Accounts*, Gee and Co., London, 1982.

Examples of greater disclosure are the requirements for more detailed analysis of certain creditors, namely bank loans, overdrafts and other borrowings, in the annual financial statements, as well as the requirement for directors to disclose whether or not they have complied with the provisions of the *Combined Code on Corporate Governance*.[13]

The best example of the requirement for more frequent information is the requirement for quoted companies to prepare and publish an interim report, containing certain minimum information. This provides investors and other users with more timely information on which to base their decisions.

Accounting concepts

We have seen how statute law requires companies to disclose a considerable amount of information and lays down broad principles which must usually be applied in arriving at the figures disclosed. We have also seen how this information is extended for companies subject to the rules of the Stock Exchange.

In order to prepare accounts complying with the law and, where appropriate, the Stock Exchange rules, an accountant must turn to what are referred to as generally accepted accounting principles, conventions or concepts. These were first developed during the latter part of the nineteenth century but have been the subject of continuous development as new situations have arisen and new ideas have emerged.

Many such principles could be listed, but a useful starting point would seem to be the fundamental accounting concepts of SSAP 2 *Disclosure of Accounting Policies*. SSAP 2 was originally issued in November 1971 but, as we shall see below, has now been replaced by FRS 18 *Accounting Policies*, issued in December 2000.

The fundamental accounting concepts of SSAP 2 were defined as 'the broad basic assumptions which underlie the periodic financial accounts of business enterprises'.[14]

Four concepts were listed and these are the same as the first four principles listed in the Companies Act 1985 as shown above. Users of the accounts were entitled to assume that the concepts have been applied in the preparation of a set of accounts unless warning is given to the contrary.

The four concepts were as follows:

1 *Going concern*: Following the application of this concept, the accounts are drawn up on the basis that the enterprise will continue in operational existence for the foreseeable future. Thus, the accountant does not normally prepare the accounts to show what the various assets would realise on liquidation or on the assumption of a fundamental change in the nature of the business. It is assumed that the business will continue to do in the future the same sort of things that it has done in the past. If, of course, such continuation is not expected, then the going concern concept must not be applied. So if, for example, liquidation seems likely then the valuation of assets on the basis of sale values would be appropriate. The accountant must then give warning to the users that the usual going concern concept has not been applied.

2 *Accruals*: While this is an easy concept to describe and, indeed, to apply in situations that are commonly encountered, its implementation sometimes gives rise to problems.

[13] *Combined Code on Corporate Governance*, The London Stock Exchange Limited, London, 1998. This Code has been developed from the earlier Cadbury and Greenbury Reports.

[14] SSAP 2 *Disclosure of Accounting Policies*, Para. 14.

Revenues and costs are not calculated on the basis of cash received or paid. Revenues are recognised when they are earned, usually at the date of a transaction with a third party. Against such revenues are charged, not the expenditures of a particular period, but the costs of earning the revenue which has been recognised.

3 *Consistency.* The consistency concept requires like items to be treated in the same manner both within one set of accounts and from one period to another.

Such a concept could easily prevent progress if applied too rigidly for, if a better accounting treatment than the existing method was discovered, it could never be applied because it would be inconsistent with the past! Obviously, it will be necessary to depart from this concept on occasions but then it is necessary to give warning that such departure has occurred and to show clearly what the effect has been.

4 *Prudence.* This concept has specified that accountants do not take credit for revenue until it has been realised but that they do provide for all known liabilities. This asymmetrical approach was designed to introduce a bias that tended to understate profit and undervalue assets. Although such a concept might at first sight be thought to benefit users, it may instead damage their interests. Thus a shareholder may sell his or her shares at a low price because the financial statements show low profits and low asset values. As we have seen in Chapter 1, the ASB is attempting to refine the definition of the prudence concept along the following lines:[15]

> Prudence is the inclusion of a degree of caution in the exercise of the judgements needed in making the estimates required under conditions of uncertainty, such that gains and assets are not overstated and losses and liabilities are not understated. In particular, under such conditions it requires more confirmatory evidence about the existence of, and a greater reliability of measurement for, assets and gains than is required for liabilities and losses.

FRS 18 *Accounting Policies* was issued in December 2000 to update SSAP 2 to bring it into line with the thinking contained in the *Statement of Principles*. The key provision of the standard is that:

> An entity should adopt accounting policies that enable its financial statements to give a true and fair view. Those accounting policies should be consistent within the requirements of accounting standards, Urgent Issues Task Force (UITF) Abstracts and companies legislation.[16]

Under the terms of FRS 18, users may still assume that the going concern and accruals concepts have been applied, unless they are given clear warning to the contrary, but the roles of consistency and prudence have changed.

These last two concepts have disappeared. Instead, in line with the thinking of the *Statement of Principles*, the appropriateness of accounting policies should be judged against the following objectives:

- Relevance
- Reliability
- Comparability
- Understandability

[15] *Statement of Principles for Financial Reporting*, ASB, London, December 1999, Para. 3.19.
[16] FRS 18 *Accounting Policies*, Para. 14.

When judging the appropriateness of accounting policies, the entity needs to consider two constraints:

- The need to balance the above objectives.
- The need to balance the cost of providing information with the likely benefit to users of the financial statements.

The ASB did not find the distinction drawn by SSAP 2 between accounting bases and accounting policies to be of any value and does not use the former term. The new term now in use is *Estimation techniques*, which is defined as:

> the methods used by an entity to arrive at estimated monetary amounts, corresponding to the measurement basis selected for assets, liabilities, gains, losses and changes to share-holders' funds.[17]

Estimation techniques thus include methods of depreciation and the bases for estimating the provision for doubtful debts. The standard includes an Appendix devoted to the distinction between changes in accounting policies and changes in estimation techniques which is important because, only changes in accounting policies give rise to a prior period adjustment under the provisions of FRS 3 *Reporting Financial Performance*.

Even where an accountant complies with FRS 18, he or she still has considerable flexibility in the way in which assets are valued and profit determined. There are, for example, many methods of depreciating fixed assets or of valuing stocks and work-in-progress; there are many ways of accounting for deferred taxation and for translating the accounts of overseas subsidiaries. From the numerous accounting methods available, an accountant must choose the appropriate policy to apply in the circumstances of the particular company.

As we have seen in Chapter 1, there are many different users of financial statements and their needs for information may conflict: in addition, as we have seen in this chapter, we have no precise idea of what is meant by the words 'true and fair'. Add to this the fact that the valuation of any asset or liability by its very nature, even under the historical cost system, involves taking a view of the future, and it is not surprising that different accountants will arrive at different views of the same business reality and hence report different figures.

Recommendations and freedom of choice

In order to help their members to choose the appropriate accounting policies, the various professional bodies have issued recommendations on accounting principles. For example, the Institute of Chartered Accountants in England and Wales (ICAEW) issued 29 such recommendations between 1942 and 1969, and these provided guidance on all manner of accounting matters. These recommendations were persuasive rather than mandatory and often permitted a choice from various methods of accounting for a particular set of transactions.

Most accountants appreciated the freedom which these recommendations provided and perhaps welcomed, as a bonus, the fact that the existence of flexibility made it difficult for anyone to prove that mistakes had been made. However, many thoughtful accountants took a more principled position and argued that the complexities of business were such that it was not desirable, nor even possible, to specify in advance a set of accounting rules to be applied rigidly in all circumstances. They argued that there would always be occasions when any preordained rules would be inappropriate and that the benefits resulting from the

---

[17] FRS 18, Para. 4.

existence of flexibility, in terms of meaningful reporting on such occasions, more than out-weighed the disadvantage that equally competent accountants might produce different results in the same circumstances.

A number of incidents in the late 1960s brought the existence of such flexibility to the attention of the general public and in 1968 Sir Frank Kearton, Chairman of Courtaulds and the Industrial Reorganisation Corporation, wrote to the President of the ICAEW to complain about 'the plethora of generally accepted accounting principles'. The problem was brought to a head in 1968 in connection with the GEC/AEI and Pergamon/Leasco affairs.[18]

In 1969 the late Professor Edward Stamp wrote a letter to *The Times* in which he was very critical of some aspects of the accountancy profession, in particular its lack of independence and its lack of a theoretical foundation for the preparation of accounts. His letter provoked an angry reaction from the accountancy profession in the person of Ronald Leach, President of the ICAEW. Suffice it to say that the criticism and ensuing debate led to the issue of a 'Statement of intent on accounting standards in the 1970s' by the ICAEW in 1969 and to the subsequent formation of the Accounting Standards Steering Committee.

Standardisation

From 1970 to 1990

The 'Statement of intent on accounting standards in the 1970s' issued by the Council of the ICAEW in 1969 set out a plan to advance accounting standards along the following lines:

(a) narrowing the areas of differences and variety in accounting practice;
(b) disclosure of accounting bases;
(c) disclosure of departures from established definitive accounting standards;
(d) wider exposure for major new proposals on accounting standards;
(e) a continuing programme for encouraging improved standards in legal and regulatory matters.

To this end, an Accounting Standards Steering Committee was set up by the ICAEW, the ICAS and the Institute of Chartered Accountants in Ireland. The Committee was later joined by representatives of the Association of Certified Accountants (now the Association of Chartered Certified Accountants – ACCA) and the Institute of Cost and Management Accountants (now the Chartered Institute of Management Accountants – CIMA) in 1971 and by representatives of the Chartered Institute of Public Finance and Accountancy (CIPFA) in 1976. From 1 February 1976 its name was changed to the Accounting Standards Committee (ASC) and it was reconstituted as a joint committee of the six member bodies acting through the Consultative Committee of Accountancy Bodies (CCAB).

Until 1982, the ASC consisted of more than 20 members, all of whom were qualified accountants. Membership of the committee was part-time and unpaid. The ASC had no power to issue standards in its own right but, once a standard had been set by the committee and approved and issued by the councils of the six CCAB members, individual members of the various professional accountancy bodies were required to comply with the standard. Thus, we had a body of professional accountants imposing rules above those required by the law of the land and attempting to enforce them through the constituent member bodies. Such a process was criticised on two counts.

---

[18] These are dealt with in E. Stamp and C. Marley, *Accounting Principles and the City Code: the Case for Reform*, Butterworths, London, 1970.

First, the people who can be expected to benefit from standards are the users of accounts. If such is the case, then it may be argued that these users should have a larger say in the formulation of standards. Indeed, accounting standards may have considerable impact on economic behaviour which some would argue should, in a democratic state, be taken into consideration by duly elected Members of Parliament.[19] To give an example, FRS 17 *Retirement Benefits*, issued in November 2000, proposed that any deficit in a company pension scheme should be recognised as an expense in the company's profit and loss account. Even before this standard was fully implemented, it contributed to the decisions of many large companies to close their defined benefit pension schemes to new members and this will have severe consequences for the welfare of large sections of the population. We will return to this topic in Chapter 10.

Second, for standards to be effective, it is essential that they are enforced. However, the law places the onus for preparing accounts clearly on the shoulders of directors, and professional accountancy bodies have no authority over such directors unless the directors happen to be professional accountants.[20] Even where professional accountants are involved, the ultimate penalty for non-compliance was disciplinary action against those members, and the professional bodies appear to have been loath to take such action.

The ASC was aware of these and other criticisms and a number of changes were made as a result of two papers: *Setting accounting standards: a consultative document*, known colloquially as the Watts Report after the then chairman of the ASC, Mr Tom Watts, published in 1978, and *Review of the standard setting process*, known as the McKinnon Report after its chairman, published in 1983.

As a consequence of these reports, membership of the ASC was opened up to include non-accountants representing user groups, and some new types of pronouncement were introduced. However, the Watts Report's recommendation that a panel be established to review non-compliance with accounting standards by listed companies was not acted upon at that time.

The 1983 Review introduced the publication of two new types of statement, the Statement of Intent (SOI) and the Statement of Recommended Accounting Practice (SORP). While the SOI, a short public statement explaining how the ASC proposed to deal with a particular accounting matter, was used very rarely, the SORP was a completely different type of statement issued on topics considered not to be of sufficient importance to warrant the issue of an accounting standard. These non-mandatory SORPs hark back to the earlier recommendations of the professional accountancy bodies. It was intended that such statements would be issued for matters which are of widespread application but not of fundamental importance, or for matters which are of limited application, in specific industries or particular areas of the public sector. In the case of statements of limited application, SORPs were prepared by the specific industry or areas of the public sector and then 'franked', that is approved, by the ASC.[21]

In spite of the changes which were made, the ASC came under increasing criticism in the 1980s. Its lack of powers of enforcement became blatantly obvious in the context of SSAP 16 *Current Cost Accounting*, when at one time only some 25 per cent of the companies to which it applied were actually complying with its provisions. In addition, the ASC faced enormous

---

[19] For an account of the effect of standard setting on economic behaviour *see* S.A. Zeff, 'The rise of "economic consequences"', *Journal of Accountancy*, December 1978.

[20] The so-called accounting scandals that emerged in the USA in 2001 and 2002 have provided an impetus for governments, not just in the USA, to produce tougher legislation to punish directors who connive in the production of misleading financial statements.

[21] An example of the first type of SORP is *Accounting for Charities*, issued in May 1988. Some examples of franked SORPs are those issued by the Oil Industry Accounting Committee and the Committee of Vice-Chancellors and Principals of the Universities of the United Kingdom.

difficulties in developing standard practice for controversial areas such as accounting for business combinations and intangible assets.

A decline in the credibility of the ASC led to the establishment of the Dearing Committee, named after its chairman, now Lord Dearing, which produced its report, *The Making of Accounting Standards* (the Dearing Report), in September 1988. This, in turn, has led to fundamental changes in the process of setting and enforcing accounting standards in the United Kingdom.

The current regime – structure

The Dearing Report took the view that standards should no longer be set by an inadequately financed ASC made up of part-time unpaid members, with only a small technical staff, and with no powers of ensuring compliance with its standards. It therefore recommended major changes.

In the view of the Dearing Report, effective standard setting required considerably more resources than had been available in the past. Given that a large constituency of users benefit from the existence of accounting standards, it was thought to be unreasonable for the process of standard setting to be financed wholly by the accountancy profession. Dearing therefore recommended a large increase in the finance available and a sharing out of the cost of standard setting.[22]

As a consequence of the Dearing Report, a Financial Reporting Council, drawn from a wide constituency of interests, was set up to guide the standard setting process and to ensure that it is properly financed. Standards are now set by the Accounting Standards Board (ASB), which has the power to issue standards in its own right. In addition, a Financial Reporting Review Panel (FRRP)was established to examine contentious departures from accounting standards by large companies.

An Urgent Issues Task Force (UITF) has also been set up as a committee of the ASB to provide timely and authoritative interpretations on the application of standards. In addition, there are three more specialised committees which support the work of the ASB. These are the Financial Sector and Other Special Industries Committee, the Public Sector and Not-for-Profit Committee and the Committee on Accounting for Smaller Entities (CASE). As a consequence, the present structure is as shown in Figure 2.1 on p. 34.

The ASB is a much smaller body than its predecessor. It consists of not more than nine members with a full-time Chairman and Technical Director, supported by a much larger technical and administrative staff to permit a higher level of research. As recommended by the Dearing Report, it has the power to issue standards in its own right and, for this, a two-thirds majority is required.

The introduction of the FRRP was more revolutionary, although the establishment of such a body had been proposed in the Watts Report in 1978. It is a panel of some twenty members chaired by a QC. The function of the Review Panel is to examine the accounts of large companies to ensure that they give a true and fair view and comply with the Companies Act 1985 and applicable accounting standards.

Although the government chose not to give statutory backing to accounting standards, it introduced provisions which facilitate the operations of the Review Panel. The first of these is a requirement for directors of all large (but not small or medium-sized) companies to state in the notes to the accounts whether or not those accounts have been prepared in accordance

---

[22] The operating cost of the present regime, which amounted to some £2 769 000 in the year to 31 March 2002, comes from three main sources: the accountancy profession, government and city institutions, which include the Financial Services Authority. A substantial sum is also raised by the sale of ASB publications and from interest receivable.

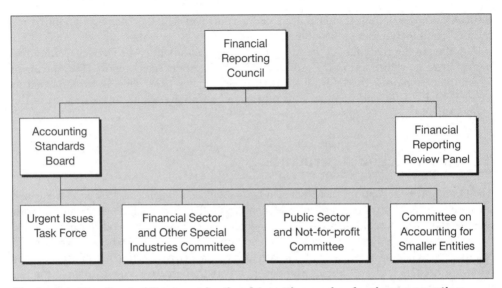

Figure 2.1 Structure of the organisation for setting and enforcing accounting standards

with applicable accounting standards, drawing attention to material departures and explaining the reasons for them.[23] The second is the introduction of procedures for the revision of accounts which are considered to be defective. These include a procedure whereby accounts can be revised voluntarily by the directors and a procedure whereby the Secretary of State for Trade and Industry or other authorised persons are able to apply to the court for an order requiring the revision of a company's accounts.[24] The FRRP is an 'authorised person' under these provisions and concentrates on the accounts of public and large private companies.

The current regime – progress

One of the many problems which confronted the ASB, and indeed the ASC before it, was the lack of a conceptual framework for accounting. As we have discussed in Chapter 1, the ASB immediately set to work to build such a framework and eventually published an exposure draft of its *Statement of Principles for Financial Reporting* in November 1995. Following a hostile reaction to that draft, it was withdrawn and a revised exposure draft was issued in March 1999. The *Statement of Principles* was published shortly afterwards in December 1999.

While some people might argue that no standards should have been set until the *Statement of Principles* had been finalised, it would have been quite impossible for the ASB to adopt such an approach. Indeed, it is becoming more widely recognised that the search for one conceptual framework is a search for the Holy Grail. Given the multiple users of accounts, there are probably many different conceptual frameworks, with a consequent implication for the adoption of multicolumn reporting.[25] If such is the case then we should not be under any illusion that the *Statement of Principles* will solve all the problems of accounting although, of course, it may enable us to remove some of the many inconsistencies which exist at present.

---

[23] Companies Act 1985, Schedule 4, Part III, Para. 36A.
[24] These provisions are contained in the Companies Act 1985, s. 245.
[25] See Chapter 21.

While work proceeded on the development of the *Statement of Principles*, the ASB continued its work on standard setting. In its first 13 years of operation, it has produced an enormous volume of regulation in the form of Financial Reporting Standards (FRSs), which we have listed in Table 2.1.[26]

Table 2.1 Financial Reporting Standards issued by ASB, 1990–2002

1	Cash Flow Statements	1991, revised 1996
2	Accounting for Subsidiary Undertakings	1992
3	Reporting Financial Performance	1992, amended 1993
4	Capital Instruments	1993
5	Reporting the Substance of Transactions	1994, amended 1994
6	Acquisitions and Mergers	1994
7	Fair Values in Acquisition Accounting	1994
8	Related Party Disclosures	1995
9	Associates and Joint Ventures	1997
10	Goodwill and Intangible Assets	1997
11	Impairment of Fixed Assets and Goodwill	1998
12	Provisions, Contingent Liabilities and Contingent Assets	1998
13	Derivatives and other Financial Instruments: Disclosures	1998
14	Earnings per Share	1998
15	Tangible Fixed Assets	1999
16	Current Tax	1999
17	Retirement Benefits	2000
18	Accounting Policies	2000
19	Deferred Tax	2000

These standards have changed the face of financial reporting considerably. FRS 3 *Reporting Financial Performance*, in particular, changed the presentation of the profit and loss account and introduced the new primary statement, the Statement of Total Recognised Gains and Losses. As we shall see in Chapter 11, the pace of change is now so fast that this standard is itself already under review.[27] Other standards, such as FRS 4, FRS 5 and FRS 12 have addressed areas in which major abuses had occurred in the past. Yet other standards have tackled fundamental and difficult areas of accounting such as what to do with the large amounts paid for goodwill and intangible assets in an age when such assets may be far more important than tangible assets. One of the more difficult and controversial topics still on the agenda of the ASB is the measurement of derivatives and other financial instruments. We will, of course, deal with all of these topics later in this book.

---

[26] On its formation, the ASB adopted a large number of Statements of Standard Accounting Practice (SSAPs) published by its predecessor and many of these are still in force. Examples are SSAP 9 *Stocks and Long-term Contracts* and SSAP 20 *Foreign Currency Translation* although both of these are under review in 2002/2003 as part of the convergence project to bring national and international standards into line with one another.

[27] See Discussion Paper, *Reporting Financial Performance: Proposals for Change*, ASB, London, June 1999, and FRED 22 *Revision of FRS 3 'Reporting Financial Performance'*, ASB, December 2000.

While the ASB has been working on the above and many other issues, the UITF has been providing timely guidance on contemporary accounting problems. Its guidance is provided in the form of Abstracts and, by the end of 2002, it had issued 35 such Abstracts.[28]

The FRRP does not systematically examine the accounts of all the companies within its ambit. Rather it acts only when something which appears to be wrong is drawn to its attention. Its references come from three broad sources: qualified audit reports or recorded non-compliance, cases referred by individuals or corporate bodies, and press comment.

Some of these references are not pursued beyond an initial examination but most have been pursued with the directors concerned. The Review Panel has not as yet considered it necessary to apply for a court order for rectification of accounts, although a fund of £2m is available to finance such action. In cases where companies have been found to be at fault, the Panel has been able to reach voluntary agreement with the directors concerned, usually requiring them to rectify errors in the next set of accounts or interim statement.

During 2001, the accounts of 53 companies were brought to the attention of the Panel.[29] This is an increase over the previous year but represents a significant decrease compared with references in earlier years of the Panel's existence. During the year, 27 cases were concluded and seven press notices were issued.

There appears to be widespread approval of the work and operations of the FRRP and it is now seen as a possible role model by other countries.

Advantages and disadvantages of standardisation

Before we consider the proposals of the Government White Paper, *Modernising Company Law*, it is perhaps helpful if we review both the advantages and the disadvantages of standardising accounting practice, for the process of standardisation is not without its critics.

Accounting may be described as the language of business. As with any communication, it is important that the preparers of a document and the users adopt the same language. Standards may be regarded as the generally accepted language.

As recent accounting scandals have made very clear, when directors prepare accounts for their companies, they are unlikely to be indifferent to the position shown by those accounts. If there are many generally accepted accounting bases in existence, the choice of a particular policy may not be free from bias. The establishment of accounting standards, with the consequent need to justify departures from them, limits the possibility of exercising such bias and strengthens the hands of the auditor.

It is also clear that the process of setting standards, that is the issue of discussion papers, exposure drafts and standards, provokes considerable thought and discussion among members of the accounting profession. Although this has done much to make accounting an exciting area of study, most thoughtful accountants would probably now agree that one can have too much of a good thing!

---

[28] Some examples of the topics covered are:
   UITF Abstract 6 'Accounting for post-retirement benefits other than pensions', November 1992,
   UITF Abstract 9 'Accounting for operations in hyper-inflationary economies', June 1993,
   UITF Abstract 29 'Website development costs', February 2001 and
   UITF Abstract 33 'Obligations in capital instruments', February 2002.

[29] *2001 Annual Review*, Financial Reporting Council: Report by Chairman of the Financial Reporting Review Panel, p. 56, Para. 4.

One of the most pertinent criticisms of the process of standardisation was made by Professor W.T. Baxter writing about recommendations on accounting principles in 1953,[30] long before the Accounting Standards Steering Committee was formed. He argued that authoritative backing for one particular accounting treatment may have adverse effects. Although it may help practical men [and women] in their day-to-day work, in the longer run it may hinder experimentation and progress. An accountant or auditor may become loath to depart from a particular recommendation or standard and the educational process may become one of learning rules rather than searching for theories or truth. Indeed he argued that, if truth subsequently shows a recommendation or standard to have been wrong, then it may be hard for authoritative bodies to admit that they were wrong.

Both the ASC and the ASB have been well aware of these criticisms. Thus the *Foreword to accounting standards*, issued by the ASB in June 1993, makes it quite clear that the requirement to give a true and fair view may in exceptional circumstances require a departure from accounting standards and permits such a departure, although particulars of the departure, the reasons for it and its financial effects must then be disclosed in the financial statements (Paras 18 and 19). It also recognises that the standards are not absolute but will require amendment as the business environment and accounting thought evolves (Para. 33). As we shall see later in the book, there have been many cases where standards have been revised and these have often involved substantial changes in required standard accounting practice.[31] The standard setters certainly do not hesitate to recognise that previous standards may have been, or have become, deficient.

The Government's proposals

British company law has developed since the mid-nineteenth century and has been added to in a piecemeal fashion, by both statute and case law, for well over a century. It is now bulky and complex and widely recognised to be in need of reform. To this end, the Government launched a Company Law Review in 1998 and, after much consultation, the Company Law Review Steering Group issued its final report, 'Modern Company Law For a Competitive Economy', in June 2001.[32] The Government considered this final report and, in July 2002, it issued a White Paper, *Modernising Company Law* setting out its proposals.[33]

The White Paper makes many proposals concerned with simplifying the formation and operation of companies, particularly small companies, in order to encourage enterprise. Here, we will concentrate on its proposals for reporting by limited companies and for the setting of rules for reporting by companies in future.

---

[30] W.T. Baxter, 'Recommendations on accounting theory', in *Studies in Accounting Theory*, 2nd edn, W.T. Baxter and S. Davidson (eds), Sweet & Maxwell, London, 1962, pp. 414–27. See also D.R. Myddelton, *Accountants Without Standards? – Compulsion or Evolution in Company Accounting*, IEA Hobart Paper 128, IEA, London, 1995.

[31] One example of such a change is the replacement of SSAP 22 *Accounting for Goodwill* by FRS 10 *Goodwill and Intangible Assets*. As we shall see in Chapter 13, the latter takes a fundamentally different approach to that of SSAP 22.

[32] Company Law Review Steering Group, 'Modern Company Law For a Competitive Economy', Final Report, Vols I and II, June 2001. This report, together with earlier publications of the Steering Group are available on **www.dti.gov.uk/cld/reviews/condocs.htm**.

[33] *Modernising Company Law*, Cm. 5553–I and 5553-II, HMSO, July 2002. Volume II contains some Draft Clauses of a proposed Companies Bill. Both volumes are available on **www.dti.gov.uk/companiesbill**.

The White Paper envisages that the present requirement for companies to prepare a directors' report will be abolished and that companies will be required to publish the following documents each year:

- Financial Statements. The exact nature of these is not specified but they are expected to include a balance sheet, a single performance statement and a cash flow statement as well as consolidated financial statements where appropriate.
- Supplementary Statement. This would replace the directors' report for most companies.
- For the most economically significant companies only, an Operating and Financial Review. The White Paper envisages that this requirement will apply to about a thousand companies or groups and specifies possible criteria for identifying these.[34]
- For quoted companies only, a Directors' Remuneration Report.
- An optional Summary Statement. It is envisaged that all companies, not just listed companies as at present, will be able to publish a Summary Statement, although shareholders will be given the right to receive the full reports if they so wish.

It is proposed that small and medium-sized companies should no longer be able to file abbreviated financial statements with Companies House and that the deadlines for filing annual reporting documents with the Registrar of Companies will be reduced for both public and private companies to six and seven months respectively after the year end. It is also proposed that quoted companies will have to publish their annual reporting documents on the internet within four months of their year ends.

Much detail still needs to be filled in as the Companies Bill develops but the way in which the Government intends to implement the detailed rules makes the proposals of the White Paper quite revolutionary. The Government recognises that it is difficult for the law to respond quickly to a rapidly changing business world or to changes in accounting thought. It is clearly concerned at the rather uncomfortable current mix of regulation by company law and accounting standards, with its resulting inconsistencies and overlaps. It therefore follows the recommendations of the Steering Group by proposing that, while a future Companies Act will specify the documents required of each type of company, it will delegate the setting of rules on the form and content of company financial statements to a Standards Board, the precise name of which would have to be decided but which would be based upon the present ASB. It envisages that this new Standards Board will have a wider remit than the present ASB and that, in particular, it will have responsibility for specifying the detailed content of both the Operating and Financial Review and the Summary Statement and possibly some responsibility for keeping the Combined Code under review. This would give much greater power and responsibility to the Standards Board.

The White Paper envisages that the law and standards would be enforced as at present by a Reporting Review Panel, for larger companies, and the Secretary of State, for smaller companies. Although the Reporting Review Panel would be based on the present FRRP, the Government suggests a change of name to reflect a widening responsibility for all the annual reporting documents of a company, not just its financial statements.

The proposed approach would seem likely to be much more responsive to changes in the world of business and accounting thought. However it gives considerable power to private-sector bodies, the members of which have not been elected and who are therefore not democratically accountable. As we shall see in the next chapter, the authority for rule making, for quoted companies at least, is moving away from the national standards setters to the IASB. In this context, the proposed approach of the government White Paper appears to be rather insular. It is to international and regional standardisation that we turn in the next chapter.

---

[34] Interested readers are referred to *Modernising Company Law*, Volume I, Part 4, paras 4.35 to 4.39.

Summary

In this chapter, we have examined the regulatory framework of accounting in the UK. Thus we have examined company law, the Stock Exchange rules and accounting standards. We have seen how accounting standards grew out of the earlier recommendations of professional accountancy bodies and have examined how the Accounting Standards Committee operated from 1970 to 1990. We have explained why the ASC was replaced by the Accounting Standards Board in 1990 and examined how the ASB operates, supported by a number of sub-committees, including the Urgent Issues Task Force, and the Financial Reporting Review Panel. We have also examined the fundamental accounting concepts laid down in SSAP 2 and later in company law and shown how these have been modified by the provisions of FRS 18.

The Government launched a major company law review in 1998 and published a White Paper in July 2002. We have examined the main relevant proposals of this White Paper, in particular the proposed change to the way in which accounting rules are set. The White Paper envisages that the next Companies Act will delegate the power to set the rules on the form and content of company financial statements and other reports to a new Standards Board, based on the present ASB but with a wider remit. It also proposes the establishment of a Reporting Review Panel based on the present FRRP but again with a wider remit. It remains to be seen whether these proposals will be enacted and, if so, how they will interact with developments in the international arena to which we turn in the next chapter.

Recommended reading

W.T. Baxter, 'Accounting standards – boon or curse?', *Accounting and Business Research*, ICAEW, Winter 1981.

M. Bromwich, *The Economics of Accounting Standard Setting*, Prentice Hall, London, 1985.

R. Leach and E. Stamp (eds), *British Accounting Standards: The First Ten Years*, Woodhead-Faulkner, Cambridge, 1981.

The Making of Accounting Standards (The Dearing Report), ICAEW, London, 1988.

D.R. Myddelton, '*Accountants Without Standards? – Compulsion or Evolution in Company Accounting*', IEA Hobart Paper 128, IEA, London, 1995.

G. Whittington, 'Accounting standards: A mixed blessing?', in *Essays in accounting thought: A tribute to W.T. Baxter*, I. Lapsley (ed.), ICAS, Edinburgh, 1996.

Some useful websites

www.asb.org.uk
www.dti.gov.uk/companiesbill
www.dti.gov.uk/cld/reviews/condocs.htm

Questions

2.1   Your managing director has approached you saying that he is 'confused at all the different accounting bodies that have replaced the old Accounting Standards Committee'.

You are required to draft a memorandum to your managing director explaining the purpose, a description of the type of work and, where applicable, examples of the work to date of the following:

(a)	Financial Reporting Council	(3 marks)
(b)	Accounting Standards Board	(4 marks)
(c)	Financial Reporting Review Panel	(5 marks)
(d)	Urgent Issues Task Force	(3 marks)

CIMA, Advanced Financial Accounting, May 1993   **(15 marks)**

2.2   Before the introduction of accounting standards, accounting practices varied from enterprise to enterprise – there was inconsistency and occasionally practices were inappropriate. Intercompany and inter-period comparisons were difficult as enterprises changed accounting policies and resorted to, for example, 'window-dressing' and 'reserve accounting'.

Discuss the extent to which the publication of more than 20 accounting standards has overcome these problems. Illustrate your discussion by reference to specific accounting standards.

ICAEW, Financial Accounting 2, July 1993   **(12 marks)**

2.3   'At their simplest, accounts comprise a summary of cash receipts and payments. Concepts such as accruals and substance over form lead to increased complexity and may make it difficult for a user to interpret the results and financial position of a company. The key focus of future accounting standards and legislation should be simplification, not increased disclosure and more complex rules.'

Using examples, illustrate the complexities which may make it difficult for the various users to understand published accounts. Comment on any recent action taken by the Accounting Standards Board or the Government which has affected the complexity of accounts and discuss, reaching a conclusion, whether simplification of company accounts should be a key objective for the Accounting Standards Board and the Department of Trade and Industry.

ICAEW, Auditing and Financial Reporting, final exam, July 1996   **(12 marks)**

2.4   The following is an extract from a press note published by the Financial Reporting Review Panel (FRRP):

> FINDINGS OF THE FINANCIAL REPORTING REVIEW PANEL IN RESPECT OF THE ACCOUNTS OF S PLC FOR THE YEAR ENDED 31 MARCH 2001
>
> The Financial Reporting Review Panel has had under consideration the Report and Accounts of S plc for the year ended 31 March 2001 and has discussed them with the company's directors.
>
> The matters raised by the Panel related to aspects of the company's implementation of Financial Reporting Standard (FRS) 15 – *Tangible Fixed Assets*, regarded as standard in respect of financial statements relating to accounting periods ending on or after 23 March 2000.

The company's stated accounting policy in respect of properties was not to provide any depreciation on any given property until approximately ten years before the end of its useful life, from which point the depreciable amount was written off over the remainder of the useful life. In respect of plant and equipment, it was the company's policy not to commence depreciation until the accounting year following that in which the assets were acquired. In the Panel's view, neither of these policies complied with the requirements of FRS 15.

As reported in their Report and Accounts for the year ended 31 March 2002, the directors have accepted the Panel's findings. The directors have amended the 2001 comparative figures by way of prior year adjustment.

Required:
(a) **Explain the role of the Financial Reporting Review Panel (FRRP).**   (8 marks)
(b) **Explain why the FRRP disagreed with S plc's depreciation policies and explain why it made this disagreement public.**   (6 marks)
(c) **Explain whether the FRRP's role could be left to the external auditor.**   (6 marks)

CIMA, Financial Accounting – UK Accounting Standards, May 2002   (**20 marks**)

chapter 3

Sources of authority: the rise of international standards

overview

Given the globalisation of capital markets and the intention of the European Union (EU) to create an integrated capital market, international developments in accounting have assumed a much greater importance than they did in the past. In this chapter, we examine the contribution of the International Accounting Standards Committee (IASC) and its successor from April 2001, the International Accounting Standards Board (IASB), as well as that of the EU.

We look at the way in which international standards have been set as well as some of the difficulties the IASC faced in both introducing and enforcing them. We outline the agreement between the IASC and the International Organisation of Securities Commissions (IOSCO) under which the IASC worked extremely hard to prepare a set of core standards but which IOSCO failed to endorse wholly for cross-border listing purposes.

We then examine the EU Accounting Directives, that is the Fourth Directive on company accounts and the Seventh Directive on consolidated accounts, and explain why they have achieved much less harmonisation than had initially been hoped. We then go on to explain the change in policy of the EU under which it has rejected the use of new Directives and supported International Accounting Standards, which will, in future, be issued as International Financial Reporting Standards.

We explain the EU Regulation of June 2002, which requires all publicly traded companies incorporated in the EU to prepare their consolidated financial statements using International Accounting Standards/International Financial Reporting Standards by the year 2005. This gives an enormous boost to those standards but the timescale is extremely tight and, as we explain, there are many problems to be faced.

International standardisation

Introduction

It seems reasonable to suggest that, if standards have merit within the boundaries of one country, there would be merit if they were applied more generally.

In a period in which investors based in one country choose between investments in many countries, a lack of comparability between financial statements drawn up in different countries may well lead to incorrect decision taking and thereby to an inefficient allocation of scarce resources. As individual countries have pursued a policy of standardisation, so too a number of bodies have become concerned with international standardisation. Both the United Nations (UN) and the Organisation for Economic Co-operation and Development (OECD) have been concerned with the regulation of accounting and, as might be expected, these bodies have been primarily concerned with the regulation of disclosure by multinational companies. In the more recent past, we have seen the formation and subsequent disbandment of the 'G4+1' which was an international group of standard setters that consisted of the standard setters from Australia, Canada, New Zealand, the UK and the USA, together with representatives of the IASC. This group attempted to formulate a common, Anglo-Saxon approach to financial reporting issues and published Position Papers intended to influence the work of the standard setters in their respective countries.[1] The group disbanded in January 2001 in anticipation of the formation of the new IASB in April 2001.

For the remainder of this chapter, we shall concern ourselves with the two most important attempts at international standardisation relevant in the UK. We shall look first at the approach of the IASC and its successor, the IASB, and then at the approach of the EU. In the final section, we will examine the enormous boost given to International Accounting Standards by the EU Regulation, issued in 2002, which requires all publicly traded companies in Member States to prepare their consolidated financial statements in accordance with International Accounting Standards by the year 2005. We also examine some of the potential problems to which this Regulation gives rise.

The International Accounting Standards Committee

Although the possibility of international standards had been debated during the first half of the twentieth century, the most successful programme began with the formation of the IASC in 1973. The founder members were drawn from professional accountancy bodies in the following countries: Australia, Canada, France, Germany, Japan, Mexico, the Netherlands, the UK, the Republic of Ireland and the USA. By the time it was replaced by the IASB in 2001, the membership of the IASC consisted of 153 professional accountancy bodies from 112 countries.

The objectives of the IASC as stated in the original 1973 agreement were:[2]

> to formulate and publish in the public interest basic standards to be observed in the presentation of audited accounts and financial statements and to promote their worldwide acceptance and observance.

Under a revised agreement in November 1982, the reference to basic standards was removed and the revised objectives became:[3]

> (a) to formulate and publish in the public interest accounting standards to be observed in the presentation of financial statements and to promote their worldwide acceptance and observance, and
>
> (b) to work generally for the improvement and harmonisation of regulations, accounting standards and procedures relating to the presentation of financial statements.

In order to achieve these objectives, members joining the IASC entered into the following undertaking:

> to support the work of IASC by publishing in their respective countries every International Accounting Standard approved for issue by the Board of IASC and by using their best endeavours:

---

[1] See, for example, the G4+1 Position Papers, 'Recommendations for achieving convergence on the methods of accounting for business combinations', subsequently published by the ASB as a Discussion Paper in December 1998, 'Reporting Financial Performance: proposals for change', subsequently published by the ASB as a Discussion Paper in June 1999, and 'Share-based payment', subsequently published by the ASB as a Discussion Paper in July 2000

[2] IASC Constitution, London, 1973.

[3] See *Preface to Statements of International Accounting Standards*, IASC, London, January 1983, para. 2.

(i) to ensure that published financial statements comply with International Accounting Standards in all material respects and disclose the fact of such compliance;

(ii) to persuade governments and standard-setting bodies that published financial statements should comply with International Accounting Standards in all material respects;

(iii) to persuade authorities controlling securities markets and the industrial and business community that published financial statements should comply with International Accounting Standards in all material respects and disclose the fact of such compliance;

(iv) to ensure that the auditors satisfy themselves that the financial statements comply with International Accounting Standards in all material respects;

(v) to foster acceptance and observance of International Accounting Standards internationally.[4]

The undertaking emphasises the fact that the IASC had no direct power to implement or enforce its standards. Rather it had to rely on its members to persuade the relevant institutions in their particular countries to adopt and enforce the standards. This was no easy task given the very different ways in which countries regulate accounting; in some countries it involves persuading the relevant standard-setting bodies to comply while, in other countries, it involves the much more difficult task of persuading the government that changes to the law are necessary.

Even before the IASC had been established, Irving Fantl identified three major barriers to international standardisation:[5]

(a) differences in background and traditions of countries;
(b) differences in the needs of various economic environments;
(c) the challenge to the sovereignty of states in making and enforcing standards.

These were enormous problems for the IASC, although it took considerable steps to try to overcome the barriers. Thus, it worked closely with the major national standard-setting bodies to ensure that it was involved before a country's position became entrenched. In addition, like the ASB, it consulted widely and formed a consultative committee drawn from a number of international bodies including the International Association of Financial Executives Institutes, the International Confederation of Free Trade Unions and the World Bank.

What then did the IASC achieve in the 28 years of its existence?

By 1990 the IASC had issued 31 International Accounting Standards and these provided a set of inexpensive ready-made standards that could be adopted by those countries which had not developed their own mechanism for standard setting. While many of the International Accounting Standards covered topics on which a UK standard had already been set, this was not always the case. For example, IAS 14 *Reporting Financial Information by Segments* (1981) was published many years before the issue of SSAP 25 *Segmental Reporting* (1990); and IAS 18 *Revenue Recognition* (1982) dealt with a subject on which neither the ASC nor the ASB has yet issued a standard.[6]

As might have been expected, the activities of the IASC attracted considerable criticism and, during the 1980s, it was accused of Anglo-Saxon domination and of issuing standards which were too flexible. It took action on both counts.

The Committee appointed a number of non-Anglo-Saxon Chairmen, including Georges Barthès from France (1987–9), Eiichi Shiratori from Japan (1993–5) and Stig Enevoldsen from Denmark (1998–2000).

By the close of the 1980s, the IASC recognised that it had reached a new phase in its work and its emphasis changed from the production of new standards to the tightening of its

---

[4] *Ibid.*, para. 4.
[5] I.L. Fantl, 'The case against international uniformity', *Management Accounting*, May 1971.
[6] The ASB subsequently issued a Discussion Paper *Revenue Recognition* in July 2001.

existing standards. Even now, however, many international standards specify not just one *benchmark* treatment but also an, often very different, *allowed alternative* treatment.

The work of the IASC assumed a much higher profile from 1995, when it entered into an agreement with the IOSCO to develop a set of 'core standards for cross-border capital raising and listing purposes'.[7] The intention was that once International Accounting Standards had been endorsed by IOSCO and accepted by the national securities regulators, this would permit quoted companies to produce their financial statements using International Accounting Standards rather than having to prepare a set of financial statements drawn up in accordance with the GAAP of the country in which the stock exchange is situated or to provide a reconciliation with the local rules of that country.

After a period of frenetic effort, the IASC concluded the development of this set of core standards with its approval of IAS 39 *Financial Instruments: Recognition and Measurement* in December 1998. In spite of this effort by the IASC, it took some considerable time for IOSCO to endorse these core standards. The main reason for the delay was opposition from the powerful US Securities and Exchange Commission (SEC) for, if the IASC set of core standards were to be accepted, this would mean that foreign companies quoted in the USA would be able to prepare their financial statements in accordance with international standards rather than in accordance with what the SEC sees as being the much more rigorous and voluminous rules of the SEC and the (American) Financial Accounting Standards Board (FASB). Such an approach would be unlikely to find favour with US corporations still subject to US GAAP and might have serious implications for the subsequent development of that US GAAP itself. It is pertinent to suggest that the US perceptions have probably been changed somewhat by the Enron and other crises of 2001 and 2002, which have cast serious doubt on the alleged superiority of the US accounting standards!

When the IOSCO endorsement did come in May 2000,[8] it came in the form of a recommendation to members of IOSCO to accept financial statements prepared in accordance with thirty core International Accounting Standards. However, the sting in the tail was that it also permitted members, if they so wished, to require reconciliation to the local GAAP or to require supplementary disclosure. This permitted countries like the USA and Canada to continue requiring a reconciliation, which imposes enormous costs on the companies concerned. Not surprisingly, such a limited endorsement came as a disappointment to the members of the IASC and to others who had worked so hard to achieve international harmonisation.

The International Accounting Standards Board

The completion of the core international accounting standards provided a suitable opportunity to address the rather anachronistic structure of the IASC and, in 2001, a new IASC Foundation was formed as a not-for-profit corporation. This is the parent company of the new IASB, which assumed responsibility for setting International Accounting Standards from 1 April 2001.

The IASB consists of 14 members, 12 full-time and 2 part-time, and its first Chairman is Sir David Tweedie, the distinguished first Chairman of the UK Accounting Standard Board for its first ten years of operation.

---

[7] Joint press release, IASC Board and IOSCO Technical Committee, Paris, 9 July 1995.
[8] 'IASC Standards – Assessment Report', Report of the Technical Committee of the International Organisation of Securities Commissions, IOSCO, Montreal, May 2000. See the IOSCO website at **www.iosco.org**.

The constitution of the new IASB provides the following objectives:

- To develop, in the public interest, a single set of high quality, understandable and enforceable global accounting standards that require high quality, transparent and comparable information in financial statements and other financial reporting to help participants in the world's capital markets make economic decisions.
- To promote the use and rigorous application of those standards.
- To bring about convergence of national accounting standards and International Accounting Standards to high quality solutions.

The focus of the IASB is now clearly on the global players and it is quite clear that, in order to achieve its objectives, the IASB must work very closely with national standard setters. To this end, seven of the IASB members have been appointed as liaison members with their respective national standards setters.[9]

At its first meeting in April 2001, the IASB adopted all the existing International Accounting Standards but decided that future standards that it issues will be described as International Financial Reporting Standards (IFRS). A list of International Accounting Standards extant at 1 January 2003 is provided in Table 3.1.

The IASB is supported by a large Standards Advisory Council, available for consultation and advice, as well as an International Financial Reporting Interpretations Committee,[10] concerned with the publication of interpretations of International Accounting Standards and International Financial Reporting Standards.

Harmonisation in the European Union

The use of Directives

When the European Economic Community (EEC) was established by the Treaty of Rome on 25 March 1957 one of the objectives to be achieved by member states was 'the approximation of their respective national laws to the extent required for the common market to function in an orderly manner'.[11] To achieve this objective a number of programmes of law harmonisation have been undertaken. One of these is the company law harmonisation programme under the provisions of Article 54(3)(g) which calls for 'the co-ordination of the safeguards required from companies in the Member States, to protect the interests both of members and of third parties'.

When the EU Commission has obtained agreement on a set of proposals on a particular topic, it places a Draft Directive before the Council of Ministers. If the Directive is adopted, governments of member states then have a specified period to enact legislation and incorporate the provisions of the Directive into their national law.

In practice, many countries were unable to keep to the timetables imposed by the early Directives and, for the Seventh Directive, the time limits set were much longer than for previous Directives. This was, however, to a large extent necessary to accommodate fundamental changes that have been required in some member states.

---

[9] Countries which have this liaison arrangement are (1) Australia and New Zealand, (2) Canada, (3) France, (4) Germany, (5) Japan, (6) the USA and (7) the UK.

[10] This IFRIC replaces the Standing Interpretations Committee formed in 1997 under the previous structure.

[11] Treaty of Rome, Article 3(h).

Table 3.1 **International Accounting Standards at 1 January 2003**

		Most recent version
IAS 1	Presentation of Financial Statements	1997*
IAS 2	Inventories	1993*
IAS 7	Cash Flow Statements	1992
IAS 8	Net Profit or Loss for Period, Fundamental Errors and Changes in Accounting Policies	1993*
IAS 10	Contingencies and Events Occurring After the Balance Sheet Date	1999*
IAS 11	Construction Contracts	1993
IAS 12	Income Taxes	2000
IAS 14	Segment Reporting	1997
IAS 15	Information Reflecting the Effects of Changing Prices	1994
IAS 16	Property, Plant and Equipment	1998*
IAS 17	Leases	1997*
IAS 18	Revenue	1993
IAS 19	Employee Benefits	2000
IAS 20	Accounting for Government Grants and Disclosure of Government Assistance	1994
IAS 21	The Effects of Changes in Foreign Exchange Rates	1993*
IAS 22	Business Combinations	1998*
IAS 23	Borrowing Costs	1993
IAS 24	Related Party Disclosures	1994*
IAS 26	Accounting and Reporting by Retirement Benefit Plans	1994
IAS 27	Consolidated Financial Statements and Accounting for Investments in Subsidiaries	2000*
IAS 28	Accounting for Investments in Associates	2000*
IAS 29	Financial Reporting in Hyperinflationary Economies	1994
IAS 30	Disclosures in the Financial Statements of Banks and Similar Financial Institutions	1994
IAS 31	Financial Reporting of Interests in Joint Ventures	2000
IAS 32	Financial Instruments: Disclosure and Presentation	1998*
IAS 33	Earnings per Share	1997*
IAS 34	Interim Financial Reporting	1998
IAS 35	Discontinuing Operations	1998
IAS 36	Impairment of Assets	1998
IAS 37	Provisions, Contingent Liabilities and Contingent Assets	1998
IAS 38	Intangible Assets	1998
IAS 39	Financial Instruments: Recognition and Measurement	2000*
IAS 40	Investment property	2000*
IAS 41	Agriculture	2001

Notes: (1) IASs 3, 4, 5, 6, 9, 13 and 25 have been superseded.

(2) As we shall see later, Standards marked with an asterisk are being revised in 2002–2003.

While a number of Directives have been adopted, the two of most concern to accountants are the Fourth Directive on company accounts and the Seventh Directive on consolidated accounts.[12] The former was adopted on 25 July 1978 and implemented in the UK by the Companies Act 1981. The latter was adopted on 13 June 1983 and implemented by the Companies Act 1989. In this section of the chapter we look briefly at these two Directives.

The Fourth Directive

The original draft of the Fourth Directive was published in November 1971, some time before the UK became a member of the EEC. Not surprisingly, the draft was heavily influenced by the current law and practice in France and Germany. When the UK joined the EEC in March 1973, it pressed for certain changes to the draft and, as a result, an amended draft was issued in February 1974. Although not all of the changes suggested by the UK were accepted, the requirement to give a 'true and fair view' was admitted as an overriding objective of accounts and the Directive was eventually adopted by the Council of Ministers on 27 July 1978.

As we have explained in the previous chapter, the major changes prescribed by the Fourth Directive were as follows:

(a) limited companies have to adopt compulsory formats for both the balance sheet and the profit and loss account;
(b) defined methods of valuing assets, the so-called 'valuation rules', must be followed.

In addition, the Directive provided definitions of small and medium-sized companies and permitted member states to offer such companies exemptions from complying with certain requirements of the Directive.[13]

We have already seen how the provisions of the Fourth Directive have been implemented in the UK, but it is worth spending a little time looking at the impact of the Fourth Directive in the EU as a whole.

Given the very different accounting systems which exist in member countries, it is perhaps not surprising that it took some ten years for the Fourth Directive to be adopted. Although this Directive undoubtedly moved the accounting requirements of the various countries closer together, there are two major factors which have limited its effectiveness in achieving harmonisation.

First, as we have seen, the Directive contains an overriding requirement that accounts must give a 'true and fair view'. As we have explained in Chapter 2, although it is difficult to define such a term, accountants in the UK have long experience of working with it and are familiar with what it means. In many EU countries the term was unknown and, although it has been translated and included in their respective national legislation, it is certainly not interpreted or applied in the same way in all of those countries as it is in the UK.

Second, in order to be able to obtain agreement, it was necessary to include a large number of options in the Fourth Directive and there are over 60 points on which countries were able to exercise a choice.[14] Member states had to decide whether or not to incorporate

---

[12] These directives may be found in the *Official Journal of the European Communities*. The text of the Fourth Directive is in Volume 21, L222, 14 August 1978, while the text of the Seventh Directive is in Volume L193/1, 18 July 1983. They may also be found on the Europa-Internal Market-Accounting website at **www.europa.eu.int/comm/internal_market/en/company/account/news/index.htm**

[13] Fourth Directive, Articles 11, 27 and 47.

[14] T.R. Watts (ed.), *Handbook on the EEC Fourth Directive*, ICAEW, London, 1979, p. 1.

the particular options in their national legislation and could, in fact, even permit individual companies a choice from alternative treatments under the national legislation.

One example is the possible exemptions for small and medium-sized companies. Some countries, such as the UK, gave most of these, while other countries did not. As a result, the information provided by small companies in different countries is not comparable.

A second example is that countries could adopt historical cost valuation rules or either permit or require the application of alternative accounting rules. The UK, through the provisions of the Companies Acts, permits the use of such alternative accounting rules, while other countries do not. Given the requirement for the provision of information that would enable the reconstruction of historical cost accounts when alternative accounting rules are used, this means that many international comparisons are possible only on the basis of the historical cost figures.

A third example is provided by the possible choice of formats. The Directive provided two balance-sheet formats and four profit-and-loss-account formats. Although part of the choice was merely between a horizontal and a vertical format, there are differences between the information disclosed in the two pairs of profit-and-loss-account formats. Member states could either impose one balance-sheet format and one profit-and-loss-account format on all companies or they could specify all formats and permit companies to choose between them. The UK Companies Acts have given the widest possible choice with the result that, even in the UK, different companies disclose somewhat different information. Other countries have been more rigid and, hence, there is a lack of comparability.

Even if all countries were to adopt the same formats, the inability to define terms with precision means that there is a superficial comparability only. For example, the profit-and-loss-account format of Article 25 requires the disclosure of, *inter alia*, cost of sales, distribution costs and administrative expenses. Even if we ignore the flexibility of the underlying valuation rules, it is highly likely that different companies will analyse similar expenses between these three categories in different ways and, hence, although the same descriptions are used, the figures may not be comparable.

The above examples are not given to belittle the efforts that have been made to try and achieve harmonisation in the EU but rather to ensure that readers do not overestimate their impact.

The Seventh Directive

Although a proposed Seventh Directive was first issued in May 1976 and an amended proposal was issued in December 1978, it was not until June 1983 that the Seventh Directive was actually adopted.[15] As with the Fourth Directive it was a long and difficult task to reach agreement on when consolidated accounts should be prepared and what they should contain. This should not surprise us when it is realised that some EU countries had no legal requirement for consolidated accounts at all.[16] One of the major difficulties was defining the circumstances in which consolidated accounts should be required and a large part of the Directive was devoted to this problem.[17]

In the UK the basic legal position was that group accounts were required when one company owned more than half of the equity share capital in another company or had the legal power of control over that other company, irrespective of whether the investing company

---

[15] *Official Journal of the European Communities*, Volume L193/1, 18 July 1983.
[16] Examples were Greece and Luxembourg.
[17] Seventh Directive, s. 1, 'Conditions for the preparation of consolidated accounts' (Articles 1–15).

actually exercised that power. The proposed Directive was initially concerned to ensure that information was provided about concentrations of economic power and, as a consequence, consolidated accounts were required when companies were managed in practice by a 'central and unified management'. Ownership was only important to the extent that it led to a presumption that such central management might exist.

A criterion based on the existence of an economic unit is much more difficult to apply than one based on the legal power of control, and accountants in the UK were relieved to find that the Directive came down in favour of a definition based on the existence of this legal power of control.[18]

Some other problems which had to be resolved in this connection were whether or not consolidated accounts should be required when an individual or partnership controls companies; whether consolidated accounts should be required for subgroup holding companies where the ultimate parent company is in another EU country or non-EU country; and whether horizontal consolidations should be required for companies in the EU where, for example, two French companies are both under the control of a US company. We will examine accounting for groups of companies in Chapter 14.

The second part of the Directive is concerned with the preparation of consolidated accounts. As is the case for the accounts of individual companies, there is an overriding requirement that consolidated accounts give a 'true and fair view' as well as the requirement that they give the information specified by the Directive using the valuation rules and formats specified in the Fourth Directive as far as appropriate.

There is no doubt that the Seventh Directive has had a much greater impact on accounting in other EU countries than it has had in the UK, where many of its provisions were already established by existing law and accounting standards. However, this is not to say that it has had no impact at all in the UK. As in the case of the Fourth Directive, rules previously set by accounting standards are now a part of the law and the introduction of new definitions has widened the coverage of consolidated accounts to include certain off-balance-sheet finance schemes as well as certain partnerships and joint ventures. We deal with these topics in Chapters 9 and 15.

As in the case of the Fourth Directive, member states were given a large number of options in the Seventh Directive. The different ways in which they have exercised these options has inevitably limited the degree of harmonisation achieved.

The EU Regulation of 2002 and the problems that it poses

The EU Regulation of 2002

It is now recognised that, in spite of all the efforts which led to their development, the Accounting Directives have achieved much less harmonisation in the EU than was originally anticipated. Perhaps not surprisingly, they have been found to be an inflexible source of rules, difficult to change in a business world which is constantly changing.

The European Commission has explored the way forward on accounting harmonisation in the EU.[19] It has rejected both the use of new Directives and the establishment of a

---

[18] Seventh Directive, s. 1. As we shall see in Chapter 14 it is still possible for member states to require consolidated accounts where there is unified management but no legal power of control (Article 1, Para. 2).

[19] See, for example, *Accounting Harmonisation: A new strategy vis-à-vis international harmonisation*, Communication from the Commission, COM 95 (508), November, 1995, EU *Financial Reporting Strategy: the way forward*, Com. (2000) 359, June 2000 and *Proposal for a regulation of the Parliament and of the Council on the application of International Accounting Standards*, COM (2001) 80, February 2001.

European standard-setting body. Instead it has opted to support the work of the IASB, accepting that there will be a consequent need to amend the existing Accounting Directives where necessary to enable companies to comply with International Accounting Standards (IASs) and International Financial Reporting Standards (IFRSs).

The way that it has done this is by the issue of a Regulation in June 2002.[20] Unlike a Directive, which requires legislation by member states, a Regulation takes effect throughout the EU without the need for member states to incorporate its provisions in their own national law.

This rather short Regulation will have enormous impact upon accounting in the EU. It requires that, with minor exceptions, all publicly traded companies governed by the law of a member state of the EU must prepare consolidated financial statements in accordance with IASs and IFRSs and related Interpretations for all accounting periods starting on or after 1 January 2005. Although the Regulation only requires that **consolidated** financial statements comply with international standards, it also gives member states the option of permitting or requiring the use of international standards in the single entity financial statements of the publicly traded parent company. It also gives member states the option of permitting or requiring the use of international standards in the single entity financial statements and/or the consolidated financial statements of European companies that are not publicly traded. It remains to be seen how member states will use these options although, as we discuss below, the way in which they do so may give rise to considerable difficulties in practice.

In order to permit consolidated financial statements to comply with both international standards and the Directives, it has already been necessary to amend the valuation rules included in the Fourth and Seventh Directives. This was done by means of a Directive in May 2001[21] and this opens the way for companies in EU countries to use fair values for certain financial instruments in accordance with the requirements of IAS 39, *Financial Instruments: Recognition and Measurement* (revised 2000 and under revision again in 2002). Unlike the use of a Regulation, the use of a Directive does, of course, require legislation by the individual member states and the deadline imposed for implementation of this Directive is 1 January 2004. It is clear that further amendments to the Directives will be necessary to permit international standards to be applied.

The Regulation is very clear that international standards are to be imposed on publicly traded companies by 2005. It is estimated that some seven thousand companies in the EU fall within this category and, of these, less than three hundred have used international standards in the past. A large number of companies will therefore be applying international accounting standards for the first time and to help them, as well as companies elsewhere in the world, the IASB issued an exposure draft (ED 1) of an IFRS entitled *First Time Application of International Financial Reporting Standards* in July 2002. The UK ASB issued a Consultation Paper, which reproduced the IASB ED 1, at the same time.[22]

ED 1 would require that, when companies first adopt international standards by making an explicit and unreserved statement of compliance, those statements should comply with the international standards and interpretations effective at the reporting date. However it does provide some exemptions, in particular where the cost of obtaining the relevant information would be out of proportion to its benefits.[23]

---

[20] Regulation PE-CONS 3626/02, EU, June 2002.

[21] EU Directive PE-CONS 3624/01. See the Europa website given in n.12 above.

[22] Consultation Paper, *IASB proposals for first-time application of International Financial Reporting Standards*, ASB, July 2002.

[23] For details of these exemptions, interested readers are referred to the Exposure Draft or, in due course, to the IFRS based on ED 1.

The timescale allowed for so many companies to make this major change is extremely short and the requirement to use international standards gives rise to a considerable number of potential problems with which we will deal under five headings in the following section.

The EU Regulation – some problems

Lack of understanding

While there is a considerable similarity of approach between UK standards and international standards, there is a much greater difference between the rules of some other member states and those international standards. It will be necessary for directors and accountants in all EU countries to understand these international standards and how to apply them well before 2005 because of the need to provide comparative figures. These directors and accountants will usually have been raised on a very different set of rules and may therefore find it difficult to understand and assimilate international accounting standards.

There is a considerable amount of evidence that, although companies state that their financial statements comply with international accounting standards and have been given a clean audit report, the financial statements do not, in fact, do so. One example of such evidence is a piece of research published in July 2001 by the UK Association of Chartered Certified Accountants[24] which concludes that compliance is more problematic for companies domiciled in some Western European countries, notably France and Germany. It appears that even the members of large international accountancy firms in some countries do not really understand how international standards should be applied. If this is the case, then clearly a large education programme is needed before 2005 to familiarise accountants throughout the EU with the requirements of IASs and IFRSs.

Considerable differences and the need for convergence

There are considerable differences between the national accounting rules of individual countries in Europe and the international standards and this must be bridged if there is to be European standardisation. The new term used is 'convergence' and, as a first step towards this end, several countries have conducted studies of the differences between their own rules and the international standards. For example, the UK ICAEW published a study in 2000 entitled *The Convergence Handbook* prepared by David Cairns and Christopher Nobes.[25] Even though the UK standards are relatively close to the international accounting standards, Cairns and Nobes identify an enormous number of differences between them and make suggestions for resolving those differences. However, sometimes they favour the UK approach and, at other times, they favour the international approach. Other countries that are studying the difference between their national rules and the international standards are not necessarily coming to the same conclusions on the appropriate way forward.

The IASB is working hard with national standard setters to resolve differences and has embarked on an improvements project to revise international standards to bring them into

---

[24] Donna Street and Sidney Gray, *Observance of International Accounting Standards: Factors explaining non-compliance*, ACCA Research Report No. 74, July 2001.

[25] David Cairns and Christopher Nobes, *The Convergence Handbook: A comparison between International Accounting Standards and UK financial reporting requirements*, ICAEW, 2000. An update to this has subsequently been published: David Cairns, *The Implications of IAS for UK Companies: An Update to the Convergence Handbook*, ICAEW, 2002.

line with current best practice and to remove options. To this end, it issued an exposure draft of proposed 'Improvements to International Accounting Standards' in May 2002, which proposed changes to the twelve IASs listed in Table 3.2.

Table 3.2 **IASs to be revised in 2003 under the IASB Improvements project**

IAS 1   Presentation of Financial Statements*

IAS 2   Inventories+

IAS 8   Net Profit or Loss for the Period, Fundamental Errors and Changes in Accounting Policies*

IAS 10   Events after the Balance Sheet Date+

IAS 16   Property, Plant and Equipment+

IAS 17   Leases*

IAS 21   The Effects of Changes in Foreign Exchange Rates+

IAS 24   Related Party Disclosures+

IAS 27   Consolidated Financial Statements and Accounting for Investments in Subsidiaries*

IAS 28   Accounting for Investments in Associates*

IAS 33   Earnings Per Share+

IAS 40   Investment Property*

+ Separate FREDs on these topics were issued by the UK ASB in May 2002. See FREDs 24 to 29.

* A Consultation Paper on these six topics, entitled 'IASB Proposals to Amend Certain International Accounting Standards' was also issued by the UK ASB in May 2002.

These twelve IASs are not the only ones scheduled for improvement for there are major revisions in train for IAS 22 *Business combinations*, IAS 32 *Financial instruments: Disclosure and presentation* and IAS 39 *Financial instruments: Recognition and measurement*.

At the same time that the IASB issued its proposed improvements in May 2002, the UK ASB issued seven Financial Reporting Exposure Drafts (FREDs) designed to move us towards convergence on the six topics marked + in Table 3.2, the seventh draft being concerned with 'Financial Instruments: Hedge Accounting'. At the same time it published a Consultation Paper, 'IASB proposals to amend certain international accounting standards', outlining its plan to implement changes in respect of the other six topics in Table 3.2, each marked with an asterisk, in 2005 but not before. Even after these changes, there will remain major differences between UK standards and international standards, which we will discuss in the context of the relevant chapters.

There is no doubt that the period until 2005 is likely to be extremely confusing for accountants, both in the EU and elsewhere, as they try to understand IASs which are constantly changing. Even keeping up with national standards will be difficult as individual countries attempt to change their own rules to bring them into line with the constantly changing international accounting standards. At the present time, attempts to achieve convergence involve shooting at a moving target!

Differential enforcement

If international standards are to be effective throughout the EU then it is essential that there is some enforcement mechanism to ensure that they are properly applied. Clearly the IASB does not have this mechanism at the present time but must rely on auditors of publicly traded groups throughout the EU. As we have explained in the previous chapter, the standards structure in the UK does have the Financial Reporting Review Panel to enforce UK standards and this panel could no doubt turn its efforts to the enforcement of international, rather than UK, standards. However, other EU countries do not have such a mechanism and hence we may arrive at a situation where international standards are enforced much more rigorously in some countries that in other EU countries. This can only diminish the effectiveness of a European capital market.

The endorsement mechanism

In order to ensure political acceptance of IASs in the EU, the Regulation requires that they be endorsed by an Accounting Regulatory Committee. This committee, composed of representatives of member states, is supported by a technical committee, the European Financial Reporting Advisory Group (EFRAG). EFRAG reviewed all IASs (1–41) and Standing Interpretations (1–33), that were extant in 2002, and recommended endorsement en bloc. However, even if this recommendation is accepted by the Accounting Regulatory Committee on this occasion, there are many who have concerns about this endorsement mechanism. The question they would pose is what happens if the Accounting Regulatory Committee fails to endorse an IAS or proposes changes to such a standard for use in the EU? If this were to happen then it could lead to one set of IASs for the EU and a slightly different set for the rest of the world, hardly ideal for a global capital market!

One or two sets of standards in each member state

As we have seen above, publicly traded companies are required to use IASs in their consolidated financial statements but, until relevant rules are introduced in member states, we do not know whether such companies will have to use national standards or international standards in their single entity financial statements. Nor do we know what the position will be with regard to companies that are not publicly traded. Whatever the outcome, there will be problems to be addressed.

If member states were to require non-publicly traded companies to use national standards, then countries would be faced with the cost and confusion of having two sets of standards applying to their companies. There is even the possibility, in the short term, that the non-publicly traded company would have to comply with certain national standards which are more stringent than the corresponding international standard. This would seem to be quite bizarre.

If member states were to require all companies to use IASs, then national standards will become redundant and, so too, may national standards setters. Why would it be necessary to finance a body of national standard setters if standards are being set by the IASB?

Conclusion

While the requirement of the EU 2002 Regulation is extremely clear, that Regulation gives rise to enormous problems. Implementation is likely to be difficult, painful and costly, especially within the very tight timetable that has been laid down and, in the view of the authors, it will be many years after 2005 before there is real standardisation within the EU.

Summary

Given the globalisation of capital markets and the desire of the EU to establish an integrated capital market, international and regional standardisation is now of fundamental importance to the development of accounting, both worldwide and in the EU. We have therefore examined the structure and work of the IASC and, in particular, its agreement with IOSCO to prepare a set of core international standards and the disappointing IOSCO recommendations to its members. Next we considered the structure and objectives of the IASB, which opened its doors to business in April 2001.

We then considered the attempts of the EU to harmonise accounting practice in Europe by the use of the Fourth and Seventh Directives and explained why such Directives have not been as successful as was once hoped and why the EU has gradually changed its approach to standardisation in Europe.

In 2002, the EU adopted a Regulation requiring all publicly traded companies in the EU to prepare their consolidated financial statements using International Accounting Standards (IASs) and International Financial Reporting Standards (IFRSs) for accounting periods beginning on or after 1 January 2005. This very clear focus on publicly traded companies seems eminently sensible but the Regulation gives rise to a number of difficult problems, which we have discussed at some length. Given the magnitude of the task, 2005 is uncomfortably close, and much remains to be done, especially in the field of education and training. In addition, member states must decide whether or not single entity financial statements and the consolidated financial statements of non-publicly traded companies should comply with international standards as well. If they decide against this approach, we face the prospect of having two sets of standards operating side by side in various countries of the EU. If, however, member states decide in favour of the universal application of the international standards, then the future for national standard setters seems rather bleak.

Recommended reading

D. Alexander and S. Archer, *Miller European Accounting Guide*, 4th edn, Aspen Law and Business, New York, 2001.

J. Blake and M. Hossein (eds), *Readings in International Accounting*, International Thomson Business Press, London, 1996.

D. Cairns, *International accounting standards survey 2000 – an assessment of the use of IASs in the financial statements of listed companies*, International Financial Reporting, Henley-on-Thames, 2001. See also Updates to this survey.

D. Cairns and C. Nobes, *The Convergence Handbook: A comparison between International Accounting Standards and UK financial reporting requirements*, ICAEW, 2000. Also *The Implications of IAS for UK Companies: An Update to the Convergence Handbook*, David Cairns, ICAEW, 2002.

B. Carsberg, *The role and future plans of the International Accounting Standards Committee*, in *Essays in accounting thought: A tribute to W.T. Baxter*, Irvine Lapsley (ed.), ICAS, Edinburgh, 1996.

F.D.S. Choi, C.A. Frost and G.K. Meek, *International Accounting*, 4th edn, Financial Times Prentice Hall, Harlow, 2002.

J. Flower with G. Ebbers, *Global Financial Reporting*, Palgrave, Basingstoke, 2002.

J. Flower and C. Lefebvre (eds), *Comparative Studies in Accounting Regulation in Europe*, Acco, Leuven, 1997.

A. Haller, 'Financial accounting developments in the European Union: Past events and future prospects', *The European Accounting Review 2002*, 11:1, 153–90.

S. McLeay (ed.), *Accounting regulation in Europe*, Macmillan, Basingstoke, 1999.

C. Nobes and R. Parker, *Comparative International Accounting*, 7th edn, Financial Times Prentice Hall, Harlow, 2002.

L.H. Radebaugh and S.J. Gray, *International accounting and multinational enterprises*, 5th edn, Wiley, New York and Chichester, 2002.

C. Roberts, P. Weetman and P. Gordon, *International Financial Accounting: A comparative approach*, Financial Times Prentice Hall, Harlow, 2000.

P. Walton, A. Haller and B. Raffournier (eds), *International Accounting*, International Thomson Business Press, London, 1998.

Some useful websites

www.europa.eu.int/comm/internal_market/en/company/account/news/index.htm
www.iasb.org.uk
www.iosco.org

Questions

3.1 It is a requirement of the Companies Acts that the accounts of limited companies must show a true and fair view of the state of affairs at the end of a period and the profit or loss for the period.

Requirement
(i)   Explain the role that the Companies Acts have in the preparation and presentation of published accounts;
(ii) explain the relationship between accounting standards, the Companies Acts and European Union Directives; and
(iii) provide two examples of how accounting standards extend the requirements of the Companies Acts and one example of an accounting standard that differs from the Companies Acts.

ICAEW, Financial Reporting, September 2002   (15 marks)

3.2 'In recent years, there has been growing interest in, and efforts directed towards, the harmonisation of international accounting.' (*Advanced Financial Accounting* by Taylor and Underdown (CIMA/Butterworth Heinemann)).

You are required to explain this statement.

CIMA, Advanced Financial Accounting, November 1993   (15 marks)

3.3 You are the chief accountant of Britain plc. Britain plc has a number of subsidiaries located in various parts of the world. One of these subsidiaries is Faraway Ltd. Faraway Ltd prepares its financial statements in accordance with local Accounting Standards. The accountant of Faraway Ltd has prepared the financial statements for the year ended 30 September 2001 – also the accounting reference date of Britain plc. The profit and loss account for the year ended 30 September 2001 (together with comparatives) drawn up in local currency (LC) was as shown below.

	Year ended 30 September	
	2001	*2000*
	LC000	*LC000*
Turnover	56 000	53 000
Cost of sales	(34 000)	(32 000)
Gross profit	22 000	21 000
Other operating expenses	(10 000)	(9 800)
Operating profit	12 000	11 200
Interest payable	(4 000)	(3 800)
Profit before tax	8 000	7 400
Tax	(3 000)	(2 800)
Profit after tax	5 000	4 600
Dividends paid	(2 500)	(2 400)
Retained profit	2 500	2 200
Retained profit 1 October 2000 (1 October 1999)	10 000	7 800
Retained profit 30 September 2001 (30 September 2000)	12 500	10 000

The local Accounting Standards that are used in preparing the financial statements of Faraway Ltd are the same as UK Accounting Standards with the exception of the following:

1. Faraway Ltd values its stocks using the LIFO basis. This valuation is acceptable for local tax purposes. Relevant stock values are as follows:

Date	*Stock value under LIFO*	*Stock value under FIFO*
	LC000	*LC000*
30 September 2001	9 500	10 000
30 September 2000	7 700	8 000
30 September 1999	8 600	9 000

The stock levels of Faraway Ltd often vary from year to year and prices do not rise evenly. The rate of local corporate taxation is 36%.

2. On 1 October 1993, Faraway Ltd acquired an unincorporated business for 50 million units of local currency. The fair value of the net assets of this business on 1 October 1993 was 30 million units of local currency. The resulting goodwill was written off to the profit and loss reserve as permitted by local Accounting Standards. At the date of acquisition, the directors of Faraway Ltd ascertained that the useful economic life of this goodwill was 10 years.

The accountant of Faraway Ltd has sent the financial statements to you with a suggestion that consolidation would be much easier if all group companies used International Accounting Standards to prepare their individual financial statements.

Required
(a) **Restate the profit and loss account of Faraway Ltd in local currency (both the current year and the comparative) so as to comply with UK Accounting Standards.** (14 marks)
(b) **Evaluate the practicality of the suggestion that all group companies should use International Accounting Standards.** (6 marks)

CIMA, Financial Reporting – UK Accounting Standards, November 2001   (**20 marks**)

3.4 'Now that the EU has decided to harmonise financial reporting by Regulation rather than by the issue of new Directives, the financial statements of all companies in Europe will be comparable by the year 2005.'

Discuss.

University of Buckingham, Advanced Financial Accounting, December 2002   (**25 marks**)

What is profit?

We start this chapter with a discussion of the economic concept of profit and consider a number of different ways in which profit may be defined and measured. This requires us to consider, first, the measurement of wealth at the beginning and end of a period and, second, the comparison of these opening and closing amounts when the value of the measuring rod, the pound, may be changing. We demonstrate that the traditional approach of historical cost accounting is just one of several approaches which could be adopted and that it has serious limitations for many of the purposes for which it is used. This section of the chapter also serves as an introduction to Part 3 of the book, where we discuss, in some depth, major alternatives to the traditional historical cost accounting approach.

The chapter also has a more immediate practical purpose in that the later sections explore the legal definition of distributable profit, which is relevant when determining the maximum dividend that can be paid by a limited company, and the closely related question of when a profit is deemed to have been realised.

Introduction

The layperson has no doubt about the way in which the question 'What is profit?' should be answered. Profit is the difference between the cost of providing goods or services and the revenue derived from their sale. If a greengrocer can sell for 10p an apple which cost him 6p, his profit must be 4p. Accountants also used to inhabit this seemingly comfortable world of simplicity, but they are now aware that such a world is not only uncomfortable but possibly dangerous. We can perhaps agree that profit is the difference between cost and revenue, but there is more than one way of measuring cost. Historical cost – the cost of acquisition – is only one alternative, which may indeed be one of the least helpful for many purposes. Furthermore, it is not even obvious that we should measure the difference between costs and revenue in monetary terms – actual pounds – for another unit of measurement has been suggested: the purchasing power of pounds.

In order to answer the question 'what is profit?' it is perhaps best to start by considering the most useful of hypothetical examples in accounting theory – the barrow boy who trades for cash and rents his barrow.

Consider such a barrow boy whose only asset at the start of a day's trading is cash of £2000. Let us suppose that he rents a barrow and a pitch for the day which together cost him £20. Let us further assume that he spends £150 in the wholesale market for a barrow-load of vegetables, all of which are sold for £240. The trader therefore ends the day with cash of £2070 and we can all agree that the profit for that day's trading is £70.[1] In other words we have taken the barrow boy's profit to be the increase in monetary wealth resulting from his trading activities.

---

[1] Actually this is not strictly true, for one might wish to impute a charge for the labour supplied by the barrow boy and would say that his profit is the excess of £70 over the imputed labour charge.

Let us extend the illustration by supposing that the barrow boy has changed the style of his operation. He now owns his barrow and trades in household sundries of which he can maintain a stock. If we wish to continue to apply the same principle as before in calculating his profit, we would need to measure his assets at the beginning and the end of each day. Thus we would need to place a value on his stock and his barrow at these two points of time as well as counting his cash.

All this may appear to be very simple, but it is by no means trivial, for the above argument contains one important implication, that profit represents an increase in wealth or 'well-offness', and one vital consequence, that in order to measure the increase in wealth it is necessary to attach values to the assets owned by the trader at the beginning and end of the period.

Let us now consider the implied definition of profit in a little more detail. The argument is that a trader makes a profit for a period if either he is better off at the end of the period than he was at the beginning (in that he owns assets with a greater monetary value) or would have been better off had he not consumed the profits. This essentially simple view was elegantly expressed by the eminent economist Sir John Hicks, who wrote that income – the term which economists use to describe the equivalent, in personal terms, of the profit of a business enterprise – could be defined as:

> the maximum value which [a man] can consume during a week and still expect to be as well off at the end of the week as he was at the beginning.[2]

This definition cannot be applied exactly to a business enterprise since such an entity does not consume. The definition can, however, be modified to meet this point, as was done by the Sandilands Committee,[3] which defined a company's profit for a year by the following adaptation of Hicks's dictum:

> A company's profit for the year is the maximum value which the company can distribute during the year and still expect to be as well off at the end of the year as it was at the beginning.[4]

The key questions that have to be answered in arriving at such a profit are, 'How do we measure "well-offness" at the beginning and end of a period?' and 'How do we measure the change in "well-offness" from one date to another?'

This is not the end of the matter for we may wish to make a distinction between that part of the increase in 'well-offness' which was available for consumption and that which should not be so regarded. In traditional accounting practice a distinction has been made between realised and unrealised profits such that only the former is normally available for distribution. Subsequently company legislation[5] introduced into statute law the concept of distributable profits and the legal aspects of the assessment of this element of profit will be discussed in the final section of this chapter.

Turning to our two questions, we will first examine the question of how we may measure 'well-offness' or 'wealth' of a business at a point in time. There are two approaches. First, the wealth of a business can be measured by reference to the expectation of future benefits; in other words, the value of a business at a point of time is the present value of the expected future net cash flow to the firm. The second approach is to measure the wealth of a business by reference to the values of the individual assets and liabilities of the business. Actually these two approaches can be linked by the recognition of an intangible asset, often called goodwill, which can be defined as the difference between the value of the business as a whole and the sum of the values of the individual assets less liabilities.

---

[2] J.R. Hicks, *Value and Capital*, 2nd edn, Oxford University Press, Oxford, 1948, p. 172.
[3] *Report of the Inflation Accounting Committee*, Cmnd 6225, HMSO, London, 1975.
[4] *Ibid.*, p. 29.
[5] Companies Act, 1980 and 1981.

Present value of the business

We will assume that readers are familiar with the principles and mechanics of discounted cash flow techniques.

The present-value approach is based on the assumption that the owner of a business is only interested in the pecuniary benefits that will accrue from its ownership ('I am only in it for the money'). Well-offness at any balance sheet date is then measured by the present value of the expected future net cash flows at that date and profit for the period is the difference between the present values at the beginning and end of the period after adjustment for injections and withdrawals.

This requires some formidable problems of estimation of both cash flows and appropriate discount rates, but such estimates are made either explicitly or implicitly (usually the latter) when businesses or individual assets are bought and sold. The present-value approach is an important and useful one when applied to the valuation of businesses or shares in a business in order to determine whether their sale or purchase would be worthwhile at a given price. It may well be thought, however, that the problems of estimation are such as to render the approach unsuitable for the measurement of an entity's periodic profit on a regular basis, specifically given the qualitative characteristics of financial information discussed in Chapter 1. But there is a more fundamental objection to the use of this method for financial accounting in that it is agreed that the regular reporting of profits should not be based solely on future expectations. The present-value approach is, of course, based entirely on expectations of the future and depends on decisions involving the way in which assets will be employed. It is argued that one of the objectives of accounting is to aid decision making and it is hardly appropriate if the fundamental measure of profit is based on the assumption that all decisions have already been made. This point was made by Edwards and Bell, who wrote:

> A concept of profit which measures truly and realistically the extent to which past decisions have been right or wrong and thus aids in the formulation of new ones is required. And since rightness or wrongness must, eventually, be checked in the market place, it is changes in market values of one kind or another which should dominate accounting objectives.[6]

This quotation provides a neat introduction to the asset-by-asset approach.

Measurement of wealth by reference to the valuation of individual assets

In this section we shall discuss some of the different methods that may be used to value assets. We shall at this stage concentrate on the problems associated with the determination of an asset's value using the different bases and shall defer the question of the suitability of the different bases of asset valuation for profit measurement until later.

---

[6] E.O. Edwards and P.W. Bell, *The Theory and Measurement of Business Income*, University of California Press, Stanford, CA, 1961, p. 25.

Historical cost

The historical cost of an asset can usually be determined with exactitude so long as the records showing the amount paid for the asset are still available. The matter, however, is not always that simple. The historical cost of a fixed asset purchased when new may well be known, but it will usually be impossible to say what proportion of the original total cost should be regarded as being applicable to that portion of the asset which remains unused at a point in time. For example, imagine that we are dealing with a two-year-old car which cost £20 000 and which we expect to have a total life of five years – do we say that the historical cost of the unused portion of the car is three-fifths of £20 000, i.e. £12 000? This is, of course, the class of question which is answered by the use of some more or less arbitrary method of depreciation. As we will show later, much the same sort of expedient is used in various forms of current-value accounting.

Readers will be aware of the difficulties involved in the determination of the historical cost of trading stock – whether stock should be valued on the basis of 'average', FIFO, etc. The problem is even more acute when trading stock involves work-in-progress and finished goods, as the question of the extent to which overheads should be included in the stock figure must be considered. Similar problems arise when determining the cost of fixed assets which are constructed by a firm for its own use.

There is another class of assets for which it may be difficult to find the historical costs. These are assets which have been acquired through barter or exchange, a special case of which are assets which are purchased in exchange for shares in the purchasing company. In such instances it will usually be necessary to estimate the historical cost of the assets acquired. This is usually done by reference to the amount that would have been realised had the assets, which had been given in exchange, been sold for cash. In some cases it might prove to be extremely difficult to make the necessary estimates as there may not be a market in the assets concerned.

Yet further problems occur where a number of assets are purchased together; for example, where a company purchases the net assets of another company or unincorporated firm. For accounting purposes it is necessary to determine the cost of the individual assets and liabilities which have been acquired and this involves an allocation of the global price to the individual assets and liabilities which are separately identified in the accounting system; any balancing figure represents the amount paid for all assets and liabilities not separately identified in the accounting system and is described as goodwill.[7] Such an allocation has traditionally been made using 'fair values', which usually results in the individual assets being valued at their replacement costs and liabilities being valued at their face values.

The contents of this section may seem fairly obvious, but it is important to remember that the determination of an asset's historical cost is not always an easy task.

'Adjusted' historical cost

By 'adjusted' historical cost we mean the method whereby the historical cost of an asset is taken to be its original acquisition cost adjusted to account for changes in the value or purchasing power of money between the date of acquisition and the valuation date. This method of valuation forms the basis of the accounting system known as current purchasing power accounting (see Chapter 19).

---

[7] Such an approach is also necessary when preparing consolidated financial statements and this is discussed in Chapter 14.

The practical difficulties of this approach include all those which were discussed in the preceding section on historical cost but to these must be added the problems involved in reflecting the changes in the value of money. This is done by using a price index, which is an attempt to measure the average change in prices over a period.

Great care must be taken when interpreting the figures produced by the adjusted historical cost approach. It must be remembered that this method does not attempt to revalue (i.e. state at current value) the assets; it is money and not the asset which is revalued. The adjusted historical cost method can be contrasted with those approaches under which assets are stated at their current values. It is these approaches which are the subjects of the following sections.

Replacement cost

Replacement cost (RC) is often referred to as an entry value because it is the cost to the business of acquiring an asset. In crude terms it may be defined as the estimated amount that would have to be paid in order to replace the asset at the date of valuation.

This is a useful working definition, but it is crude as it begs a large number of questions, some of which will be discussed below.

The definition includes the word 'estimated' because the exercise is a hypothetical one in that the method is based on the question, 'How much would it cost to replace this asset today?' Since the asset is not being replaced, the answer has to be found from an examination of the circumstances prevailing in the market for the asset under review. If the asset is identical with those being traded in the market, the estimate may be reasonably objective. Thus, if the asset is a component which is still being manufactured and used by a business, its replacement cost may be found by reference to manufacturers' or suppliers' price lists. However, even in this apparently straightforward case, there may still be difficulties in that the replacement cost may depend on the size of the order. Typically a customer placing a large order will pay a lower price per unit than someone buying in small lots. In some types of business the difference between the two sets of prices may be significant, as is evidenced by the different prices paid for food by large supermarkets and small grocery shops. This observation leads to the conclusion that in certain instances it will be necessary to add to the above definition of replacement cost that the estimate should assume that the owner of the asset would replace it in 'the normal course of business', in other words that the replacement would be made as part of the normal purchasing pattern of the business.

The difficulties inherent in the estimation of replacement cost loom very much larger when we turn our attention to assets which are not identical to those that are currently being traded in the market, including those which have been made obsolete by technological progress. A special, and very important, class of non-identical assets is used assets because all used assets will differ in some respect or other from other used assets of a similar type.

A more detailed discussion of the ways in which the replacement cost of assets is found will be provided later in the book, but it will be helpful if we indicate some of the possible approaches at this stage:

1 *Gross/net replacement cost:* The most common approach, particularly if the asset has been the subject of little technological change, is to take the cost of a new asset (the gross replacement cost) and then deduct an estimate of depreciation; for example, if the asset is two years old and is expected to last for another three years then, using straight-line depreciation, the net replacement cost is three-fifths of the gross replacement cost.

2 *Market comparison*: In the case of some used assets, such as motor vehicles, the asset might be valued by reference to the value of similar used assets. It may prove necessary to adjust the value found by direct comparison to account for any special features pertaining to the particular asset. Thus, the approach includes a subjective judgement element which is combined with the reasonably objective comparison with the market.

3 *Replacement cost of inputs*: In certain cases – particularly fixed assets manufactured by owners for their own use and work-in-progress and finished goods – it might be possible to determine an asset's replacement cost by reference to the current replacement cost of the various inputs used in the construction of the asset. Thus the necessary labour input could be costed at the wage rates prevailing at the valuation date with similar procedures being applied to the other inputs – raw materials, bought-in components and overheads.

Whilst in practice the focus of valuation is often the physical asset itself, we need to recognise that this is a proxy for that which is actually being valued – the services provided by the asset.

Take, as an example, a machine which is expected to operate for another 2000 hours. A new machine might have a life of 4000 hours and have operating costs which are less than those of the machine whose replacement cost we are seeking to estimate. In this case, the replacement cost of the old machine would be half the cost of the new machine less the present value of the savings in the operating costs. If there is a 'good market' in second-hand machines the replacement cost of used machines will approximate this value, but if this is not the case the replacement cost will be based on the cost of a new machine after adjusting for differences in capacity and operating costs.

Net realisable value

The net realisable value of an asset may be defined as the estimated amount that would be received from the sale of the asset less the anticipated costs that would be incurred in its disposal. It is sometimes called an exit value as it is the amount realisable when assets leave the firm.

One obvious problem with this definition is that the amount which would be realised on the disposal of an asset depends on the circumstances in which it is sold. It is likely that there would be a considerable difference between the proceeds that might be expected if the asset were disposed of in the normal way and the proceeds from a forced and hurried sale of the assets. Of course, it all depends on what is meant by the 'normal course of business' and, while the phrase may be useful enough for many practical purposes, it must be remembered that it is often not possible to think in terms of the two extreme cases of 'normal' and 'hurried' disposals. There may be all sorts of intermediate positions between these extremes. It can thus be seen that there may be a whole family of possible values based on selling prices which depend on the assumptions made about the conditions under which assets are sold and that, particularly in the case of stock, great care must be taken when interpreting the statement that the net realisable value of an asset is £x.

As is true for the replacement cost basis of valuation, the difficulties associated with the determination of an asset's net realisable value are less when the asset in question is identical, or very similar to, assets which are being traded in the market. In such circumstances the asset's net realisable value can be found by reference to the prevailing market price viewed from the point of view of a seller in the market. The replacement cost is, of course, related to the purchaser's viewpoint. If there is an active market, the difference between an asset's replacement cost and its net realisable value may not be very great and will depend on the expenses and profit margins of traders in the particular type of asset.

The relationship of the business to the market will determine whether, in the case of that business, an asset's replacement cost exceeds its net realisable value or vice versa. It is likely that the barrow boy to whom reference was made earlier would find that the replacement cost of his barrow could be greater than its net realisable value, while the reverse is likely to hold for his vegetables. It is generally, but not universally, true that a business will find that the replacement costs of its fixed assets will exceed their net realisable values, while in the case of trading stock the net realisable value will be the greater.

Generally the estimation of the net realisable value of a unique asset is even more difficult than the determination of such an asset's replacement cost. It may be possible to use a 'units of service' approach in that one could examine what the market is prepared to pay for the productive capacity of the asset being valued, but the process is likely to be more subjective. In the replacement cost case, the owner is the potential purchaser and will base his valuation on his own estimate of the productive capacity of the asset but, in the net realisable value case, the hypothetical purchaser will have to be convinced of the asset's productive capacity.

A further difficulty involved in the estimation of net realisable value is the last phrase in the definition – 'less the anticipated costs that would be incurred in its disposal'. This sting in the definition's tail can be extremely significant, especially in the case of work-in-progress, in relation to which the estimation of anticipated additional costs may be difficult and subjective.

Present value

It might be possible to apply the present-value approach to the valuation of individual assets. To do so would require the valuer to attach an estimated series of future cash flows to the individual asset and select an appropriate discount rate. This may be possible in the case of assets which are not used in combination with others, such as an office block which is rented out, but most assets are used in combination to generate revenue. Thus, a firm purchases raw materials which are processed by many machines in their building to produce the finished goods which are sold to earn revenue. In such circumstances as these it would seem impossible to say what proportion of the total net cash flow should be assigned to the building or to a particular machine. Hence it would not be possible to calculate a present value for the individual building or for a particular machine but only for groups of assets which can be identified as a separate income-generating unit.

Capital maintenance

Let us for a while ignore the practical problems associated with the valuation of assets at an instant in time and assume that one can generate a series of figures (depending on the basis of valuation selected) reflecting the value of the bundle of assets which constitutes a business and hence, after making appropriate deduction for creditors,[8] arrive at a series of figures showing the owners' equity in or net assets of the enterprise at different instants in time.

If this can be done, is the profit for a period found by simply deducting the value of the net assets at the start of the period from the corresponding value at the end of the period? In

---

[8] The valuation of liabilities is a much less developed subject than the valuation of assets, but things are changing and more attention is now being paid to this topic. In order to focus on the principles underlying the concept of capital maintenance and its relationship to the measurement of profit we will defer the subject of the valuation of liabilities to Chapter 7.

other words if, using the selected basis of valuation, the value of the assets at the time t_0 was £1000 and the value at the time t_1 £1500, is the profit for the period £500? The answer is, probably not.

We must remember that we have defined profit in terms of the amount that can be withdrawn or distributed while leaving the business as well off at the end as it was at the beginning of the period. Now assume that in this simple example the valuation basis used is replacement cost and, for the sake of even more simplicity, that no capital has been introduced or withdrawn during the period and that the firm only holds one type of asset, the replacement cost of which has increased by 50 per cent. (Thus the company holds the same number of assets at the end as it did at the beginning of the period.) Let us also assume that prices in general have not increased over the period.

The question which has to be answered is, how much could be distributed by way of a dividend at the end of the period without reducing its 'well-offness' below that which prevailed at the start of the period? It could be argued that £500 could be paid, as that would leave the value of the assets constant. It could also be argued that nothing should be paid because in order to pay a dividend the company would have to reduce its holding of assets. If the latter view is accepted, it means that the whole of the increase in the value of the assets should be retained in the business in order to maintain its 'well-offness'. It will be seen that each of the approaches described in this simple example will be found in different accounting models, but at this stage we simply want to show that it is not sufficient to find the difference between values at two points in time. The profit figure will also depend on the amount which it is deemed necessary to retain in the business to maintain its 'well-offness', that is on the concept of *capital maintenance* which is selected. We shall describe the various approaches to capital maintenance in a little more detail below.

There are thus two choices to be made: the basis of asset valuation and the aspect of capital which is to be maintained. In theory each of the possible bases of valuation can be combined with any of the different concepts of capital maintenance with each combination yielding a different profit figure. In practice the two choices are not made independently of each other in that, as we will show, there are some combinations of asset value/capital maintenance which are mutually consistent and yield potentially helpful information, while others appear not to provide useful information, usually because the two choices are made on the basis of an inconsistent approach to the question of the objectives served by the preparation of financial accounts.

We can summarise the argument thus far by stating that the profit figure depends on (a) the basis of valuation selected, and (b) the concept of capital maintenance used, and is found in the following way:

1 Find the difference between the value of the assets less liabilities at the beginning and end of the period after adjusting for capital introduced or withdrawn.
2 Decide how much of the difference (if any) needs to be retained in the business to maintain capital.
3 The residual is then the profit for the period.

We will now turn to more detailed examination of the possible ways of viewing the capital of the company (or of its owners) which is to be maintained. It will be helpful to categorise the various approaches to capital maintenance in the following way:

- Financial capital maintenance
  - Not adjusted for inflation (Money financial capital maintenance)
  - Adjusted for inflation (Real financial capital maintenance)

- Operating capital maintenance[9]
  - From the standpoint of the entity
  - From the standpoint of the equity shareholders' interest.

We shall deal with the above in turn. In order to avoid repetition, readers should assume that there have been no capital injections or withdrawals.

Money financial capital maintenance

With money financial capital maintenance the benchmark used to decide whether a profit has been earned is the book value of the shareholders' interest at the start of the period.

If money capital is to be maintained then the profit for the period is the difference between the values of assets less liabilities at the start and end of the period with no further adjustment. Money financial capital maintenance is used in traditional historical cost accounting which is not to say that, as we will show in Example 4.1, it cannot be combined with other bases of asset valuation.

Real financial capital maintenance

With real financial capital maintenance (which is often referred to simply as real capital maintenance) the benchmark used to determine whether a profit has been made is the *purchasing power* of the equity shareholders' interest in the company at the start of the period. Thus, if the equity shareholders' interest in the company is £1000 at the start and the general price level increases by 5 per cent in the period under review, a profit will only arise if, on the selected basis, the value of the assets less liabilities, and hence the equity shareholders' interest[10] at the time, amounts to at least £1050.

Both the money financial capital and real financial capital maintenance approaches concentrate on the equity shareholders' interest in the company and are hence sometimes referred to as measures of profit based on *proprietary capital maintenance*.

Operating capital maintenance

The operating capital maintenance concept is less clear-cut than the financial capital maintenance approach. Broadly, it is concerned with the physical assets of the enterprise and suggests that capital is maintained if at the end of the period the company has the same level of assets as it had at the start. A very simple example of the operating capital approach is provided by the following example.

Suppose a business starts the period with £100 in cash, 20 widgets and 30 flanges and ends the period with £130 in cash, 25 widgets and 32 flanges. Then the profit for the period, using the operating capital maintenance approach, could be regarded as being:

$$\text{Profit} = £30 \text{ in cash} + 5 \text{ widgets} + 2 \text{ flanges.}$$

---

[9] There is no consensus on the names of the various bases of capital maintenance. For example, the term 'nominal money' might be used instead of 'money capital', or 'physical capital' rather than 'operating capital'. We believe the terms used in this book both provide better descriptions and are more widely used in the literature than the alternatives.

[10] Preference shares being treated as liabilities for this purpose.

For certain purposes one could stop here, for the list of assets given above shows the increase in wealth achieved by that business over the period. To state profit in this way does provide a very clear picture of what has happened and shows in an extremely objective fashion the extent to which the business has grown in physical terms. Accountancy, however, is concerned with providing information stated in monetary terms.

In order to take this additional step it is necessary to select a basis of valuation, for this would then enable the accountant to place a single monetary value on the profit.

Let us assume that it is decided that replacement cost is the selected valuation basis and that the replacement costs at the end of the year are widgets £100 each and flanges £150 each. The profit for the period would then be stated as follows:

	£
Increase in cash	30
Increase in widgets, 5 × £100	500
Increase in flanges, 2 × £150	300
Profit	830

The above example is obviously simplistic in so far as companies hold a large number of different sorts of assets and, only in the most static of situations, will the assets held at the end of the year match those which are owned at the start of the period. However, the example does illustrate the sort of thinking which will be developed in later chapters.

The example was based on the variant of the operating capital maintenance measure which states that a company only makes a profit if it has replaced, or is in a position to replace, the assets which were held at the start of the period and which have been used up in the course of the period. A more sophisticated alternative would be to consider the output which is capable of being generated by the initial holding of assets and design an accounting model which would only disclose a figure for profit if the company is able to maintain the same level of output.

Most variants of the operating capital maintenance approach relate the determination of profit to the assets held by the business, i.e. look at the problem from the standpoint of the business. The operating capital approach is thus often referred to as an *entity measure of profit*. It is, however, possible to combine the operating capital maintenance concept with the proprietary approach. Thus, a profit based on an entity concept can be derived which can be adjusted to show the position from the point of view of the equity holders. If, for example, part of the assets are financed by long-term creditors, it might be assumed that part of the additional funds required, in a period of rising prices, to maintain the business's operating capital will also be contributed by the long-term creditors. Hence, the profit attributable to equity holders would be higher than the profit derived from the strict application of the entity concept. Assume that a company has the following opening balance sheet:

	£		£
Equity shareholders	60	Assets	
		10 items of stock at £10 each	100
Debentures	40		
	100		100

Stock is valued at its replacement cost and the proportion of debt finance in the capital structure (i.e. the gearing) is 40 per cent. For simplicity we will assume the debentures are interest free.

Assume that the company holds the stock for a period and then sells all 10 items for cash at £18 each so that the closing balance sheet includes just one asset, cash of £180. In the period the replacement cost of stock has risen from £10 to £15 per unit.

If the operating capital maintenance concept is followed, then, in order to maintain the operating capital of the entity, an amount of £150, that is 10 items at the new replacement cost of £15, would be needed. Thus, the entity profit would be:

	£
Closing capital in cash	180
less Amount necessary to replace 10 items at £15	150
Entity profit	30

However, in order to maintain the operating capital of the equity shareholders' interest in the entity, an amount of £90 rather than £150 would be needed. Shareholders were financing 60 per cent of the stock and 60 per cent of £150 is £90. Thus, the proprietary profit would be:

Net assets at end of period:	£
Cash	180
less Debentures	40
Equity interest	140
Amount necessary to maintain the equity interest in entity	90
Profit attributable to equity shareholders	50

The additional £20 of profit may be described as a gearing gain and represents the profit which accrued to the shareholders because the company borrowed money and invested it in stock which rose in value. It is therefore 40 per cent of the increase in the replacement cost of stock: $40\% \times (150 - 100)$.

If the gearing gain were distributed, the operating capital of the entity would fall, unless the debentures were increased to maintain the original gearing ratio of 40 per cent.

An extended illustration is provided in Example 4.1, in which the combinations of three different bases of valuation and three different concepts of capital maintenance are shown.

Example 4.1 Different profit concepts

In this example the three valuation bases used are historical cost (HC), replacement cost (RC) and net realisable value (NRV), and the three measures of capital maintenance are money financial capital, real financial capital and operating capital.

Suppose that a trader has an inventory consisting of 100 units at the start of the year (all of which were sold during the year) and 120 units at the end of the year, but has no other assets or liabilities.

Assume that the trader has neither withdrawn nor introduced capital during the period.

Suppose that the following prices prevailed:

Opening position (100 units)

Basis of valuation	Unit price £	Total capital £
Historical cost	10.00	1000
Replacement cost	11.00	1100
Net realisable value	11.50	1150

Closing position (120 units)

Basis of valuation	Unit price £	Total capital £
Historical cost	15.00	1800
Replacement cost	17.00	2040
Net realisable value	18.00	2160

In order to use the real financial capital approach it is necessary to know how a suitable general price index moved over the year. For illustrative purposes, we shall assume a high rate of inflation. We will assume that an index moved as follows:

	Index
Beginning of the year and date on which the opening inventory was purchased	100
Date on which the closing inventory was purchased	118
End of year	120

(a) Money financial capital

The opening money financial capital depends on the selected basis of asset valuation and profit is the difference between the value of the assets at the end of the period and the corresponding figure for opening money capital.

Basis of valuation	Closing value of assets £	Opening money capital £	Profit £
Historical cost	1800	1000	800
Replacement cost	2040	1100	940
Net realisable value	2160	1150	1010

(b) Real financial capital

(i) *Historical cost.* The closing inventory of £1800 (as measured by its historical cost) was acquired when the general price index was 118. The index has risen to 120 by the year end and thus the historical cost of inventory expressed in terms of pounds of year-end purchasing power is £1800 × 120/118 = £1831.

Opening money capital based on historical cost was £1000. The index stood at 100 at the beginning of the year and rose to 120 by the year end. Thus the real financial capital which has to be maintained is £1000 × 120/100 = £1200.

The profit derived from the combination of historical cost valuation and real financial capital is hence £1831 – £1200 = £631 (expressed in 'year-end pounds').

(ii) *Replacement cost*. As the replacement cost is a current value it is automatically expressed in year-end pounds and hence the closing value of inventory is £2040.

Opening money capital using replacement cost was £1100 which, expressed in year-end pounds, is equivalent to £1320 (£1100 × 120/100). The profit for this particular combination is thus £2040 – £1320 = £720.

(iii) *Net realisable value*. The argument is similar to that which was used above and the profit derived from a net realisable value/real financial capital concept combination is calculated as follows:

	£
Closing inventory at net realisable value (automatically expressed in pounds of year-end purchasing power)	2160
Opening money capital (based on net realisable value) restated in year-end pounds, £1150 × 120/100	1380
Profit	780

(c) Operating capital

In this simple example it can be seen that the wealth of the business has increased by 20 units and the only question is how the 20 units should be valued:

Basis of valuation		Profit £
Historical cost (using first in, first out)	20 × £15.00	300
Replacement cost	20 × £17.00	340
Net realisable value	20 × £18.00	360

The various profit figures are summarised in the following table:

	Capital maintenance concept		
Basis of valuation	Money financial £	Real financial £	Operating capital £
Historical cost	800	631	300
Replacement cost	940	720	340
Net realisable value	1010	780	360

The usefulness of different profit measures

In Example 4.1 nine different profit figures emerged. It is impossible to say that one of these is the 'correct' figure. They are all 'correct' in their own terms, although it may be argued that some of them are generally more useful than others. The different measures reflect reality in different ways. We will meet some of these measures later in this book in the context of the various proposals that have been made for accounting reform.

It might be useful if at this stage we examined a number (but by no means all) of the different objectives which are served by the preparation of financial statements and consider which of the different profit measures would appear to be the more useful in each case.

We will first discuss the question of whether a business should be allowed to continue in existence. For simplicity we will assume that the business is a sole proprietorship. Consider the profit figure of £780 derived from the combination of the net realisable value asset valuation method and real financial capital maintenance. This figure shows the potential increase in purchasing power which accrued to the owner of the business by virtue of his decision not to liquidate the business at the beginning of the year. Had he taken that option, the owner would have received £1150, which expressed in terms of year-end pounds amounts to £1380, i.e. he could at the beginning of the year purchase an 'average' combination of goods and services amounting to £1150 but it would cost £1380 to purchase the same quantity of goods and services at the end of the year. By allowing the business to continue, the owner has increased his wealth by £780 in that, should he liquidate the business at the end of the year, he would release purchasing power amounting to £2160. Now this analysis does not enable the owner to tell whether he was right to allow the business to continue in operation, but the figures do allow him to compare his increase in wealth with that which he would have achieved had he liquidated the business at the beginning of the year and invested his funds elsewhere. In the words of Edwards and Bell (see p. 645) the owner has been able to check in the market place his decision not to wind up the business.

But, of course, the past is dead and it is current decisions which are important, the decision to be taken in this case being whether or not the business should be liquidated at the end of the year. It would be naive to assume that the figure of past profit can be expected to continue in the future. However, the decision maker has to start somewhere and most people find it easier to think in incremental terms. With this approach the decision maker might say: 'In the conditions which prevailed last year I made a profit of £x. I accept that next year there will be a number of changes in the circumstances facing the business and I estimate that the effect of these changes will be to change my profit by £y.' It is clear that if this approach is adopted a profit figure related to the decision maker's objectives (in this case assumed to be the maximisation of the potential consumption) is a valuable input to the decision-making process.

Let us now consider the subject of taxation. A government might well take the view that a company should be able to maintain its productive capacity and that taxation should only be levied on any increase in the company's wealth as measured against that particular yardstick. In that case, one of the set of profit figures derived from the application of physical capital maintenance might be thought to be most suitable on the grounds that, to use the figures given in our example, if the company started the year with 100 units, then in order to maintain the productive capacity it should hold 100 units at the end of the year. The government would, if it took this view, wish to base its taxation levy on the physical increase of wealth of 20 units. Arguments for and against the use of one of the three members of the physical capital maintenance set could be deployed, but these will not be pursued at this stage. There are obviously severe practical difficulties in the use of the physical units approach where the company owns more than one type of asset and, as will be discussed later, other more practical methods have been used which allowed governments to apply a taxation policy which approximated to that postulated above.

Later in this chapter we will point out the limitations of the historical cost approach and, in fairness, we should now consider whether the profit derived from the traditional accounting system (historical cost asset values and money capital maintenance) could be said to be particularly apposite for any purpose. It is sometimes suggested that the traditional profit figure is of use in questions concerned with distribution policy, for, to quote Professor W.T. Baxter:

The ordinary accounting concept has obvious merits; it is familiar and (inflation apart) cautious, and most of its figures are based on objective data; its widespread use has therefore been sensible where the decisions are about cash payments (e.g. tax and dividends), since it reduces the scope for bickering and the danger of paying out cash before the revenue has been realized.[11]

How do we choose?

We have identified nine different methods of measuring profit and one possible way forward would be to include in a company's annual financial statements a list of these different profit figures. However, if this is not considered practical, the question becomes which basis or bases is/are the most suitable for inclusion in published accounts. The reference to the plural 'bases' holds upon the possibility that it might be found desirable to include more than one profit concept in the financial statements.

A sensible approach to this question would be a consideration of the purposes for which a knowledge of a company's profits are used, which is in effect the consideration of the aims and objectives of published financial accounts. A very long list of such purposes can be provided, but it might be helpful if these were analysed under four different headings, i.e. control, consumption, taxation and valuation. It must, however, be recognised that the divisions between these headings are not watertight and that they share numerous common features.

The limitations of historical cost accounting

Later chapters of this book deal with the subject of current purchasing power and current value accounting and will, by implication, highlight some of the deficiencies of the traditional form of accounting, i.e. the historical cost basis of valuation and money financial capital maintenance.[12] It might, however, be helpful if by way of introduction we tested the traditional system against the objectives enumerated above.

Control

It is a widely held view that the prime objective of the preparation and publication of regular financial reporting is – so far as public limited companies are concerned – to provide a vehicle whereby the directors can account to the owners of the company on their *stewardship* of the resources entrusted to their charge. This involves providing shareholders with information about the progress of the company as well as details of the amounts paid to directors by way of remuneration. In theory shareholders can, when supplied with this information,

---

[11] W.T. Baxter, *Accounting Values and Inflation*, McGraw-Hill, London, 1975, p. 23. It may be strange to quote the words of one of the foremost advocates of current value accounting in support of historical cost accounting. However, Professor Baxter, on whose work this section of the book is largely based, was seeking to show that different profit concepts may be useful for different purposes.

[12] The weaknesses of the traditional accounting model are lucidly and concisely set out by the Accounting Standards Committee in *Accounting for the Effects of Changing Prices; a Handbook*, published in 1986, and by the Accounting Standards Board in its Discussion Paper, 'The Role of Valuation in Financial Reporting', published in 1993. See Chapters 19–21.

take certain steps to remedy the position if the information suggests that all is not well. One mechanism that is available to shareholders is to effect a change in directors, but in practice it is rare for shareholders directly to oust directors because of the publication of unfavourable results. This end might be achieved by the indirect process of a takeover, in that shareholders might accept an offer for their shares on the grounds that they believe that the new management will be more effective than existing management. An individual shareholder can, of course, achieve similar ends by selling his shares but in so doing he must compare what he considers to be the value of the shares with the existing management with the current market price (see the section on valuation later in this chapter).

The above discussion is based on the view that the directors need only account for their stewardship to their shareholders, but it has been suggested that the concept of stewardship should be extended – at least so far as large companies are concerned – to cover the need to report to the community at large. This view, propounded for example in *The Corporate Report*,[13] is based on the view that large companies control the use of significant proportions of a country's scarce resources and that, consequently, large companies should report to the community at large on the way in which the resources have been used. It will be realised that such a view does not attract the support of all business people and accountants, who might well be concerned with the nature of the control devices which might follow if this view were adopted. The pressure of public opinion might be an acceptable control device, but many would be concerned that this might not be regarded as being sufficiently strong and that recourse might be made to government intervention or 'interference' or, ultimately, nationalisation.

If stewardship is narrowly defined to cover simply the reporting by directors to shareholders of how they have used shareholders' funds, then it is possible to argue that historical cost accounting is reasonably adequate. A historical cost balance sheet lists the assets of the company and the claims by outsiders (liabilities) on the company; however it will not identify *all* the assets, as it will usually omit many intangible assets such as the skill and knowledge of the employees, degree of monopoly power, etc. The main point, however, is whether stewardship should be narrowly defined in the manner suggested above. If shareholders, and others, are to apply effective control they should be helped to form judgements about how well the directors have used the resources entrusted to them.

As we indicated earlier in the chapter there are a number of different possible approaches to the question of how one can measure how successful a company – and by implication its managers – has been over a period. At this stage it is perhaps sufficient to point out that historical cost accounting will not – except in the simplest of cases where a high proportion of a company's assets is made up of cash – be of much assistance. Historical cost accounts, in general, simply show the acquisition cost or the depreciated historical cost of a company's assets and not their current values, let alone the value of the company as a whole.

It is sometimes argued that, even if historical cost accounts do not provide an absolute measure of success, they can at least allow comparisons to be made between the quality of performance achieved by different companies. This statement is sometimes justified by arguments such as, 'Inflation affects all companies to more or less the same extent and therefore a comparison of profitability measured on a historical cost basis, e.g. rate of return on capital employed, enables a rough comparison to be made of relative success'.

Two points need to be made. The first concerns inflation. As will be shown, the problem is not just inflation – a general increase in prices or a fall in the value of money – but includes the treatment of changes in relative prices. For, even in an inflation-free economy, there will be

---

[13] Scope and Aims Committee of the Accounting Standards Steering Committee, *The Corporate Report*, Accounting Standards Steering Committee, London, 1975.

changes in individual prices. The limitations of historical cost accounting in the context of changes in relative prices can be seen by considering the following simple example.

Suppose that two companies start operations as commodity dealers, in an inflation-free environment, with £1000 each. Company A spent its £1000 on commodity A while Company B invested its £1000 in commodity B. Assume that neither company bought or sold any units during the period and that over the period the market value[14] of commodity A increased by 2 per cent and commodity B increased by 20 per cent. Historical cost accounts will not show that Company B performed better in the sense that it chose to invest in a commodity which experienced a greater increase in value.

The second point which should be made about the argument advanced above is that it is not true that inflation affects all companies to more or less the same extent. This point will be developed later when we will show that price changes (both general and relative) affect different companies in very different ways and that it is in fact the case that historical cost accounts are most unhelpful when it comes to the comparison of performance.

Consumption

Probably one of the most important uses of the profit figure is in determining the amount of any increment of wealth which is available for distribution and how it should be shared between the various groups entitled to share in such a distribution, i.e. the different classes of shareholders, the directors and employees (either directly through profit-sharing schemes or indirectly through wage claims) and the community through taxation. There are what might be called 'legal' and 'economic' aspects to this question. Company law requires that dividends may only be paid out of profits, and tax law specifies the amount of taxation which has to be paid; however, subject to these constraints, plus any other legal limitations arising from such things as profit-sharing agreements, it is for the directors to make economic judgements about the level of dividends and, again subject to numerous institutional and possible legal constraints, the level of wages. Empirical evidence suggests that companies' dividends are related to the level of reported profit. It is also safe to suggest that sole traders and partners act in a similar fashion in that, when deciding on the level of their drawings, they will be influenced by the profits of their businesses.

The concept of capital maintenance based on historical cost accounting principles has, in periods of anything but modest price changes, proved to be a dangerous benchmark when used to assess the amount which a company can pay out by way of dividend or through taxation. For example, the maintenance of money financial capital is not, except in the simplest of cases, the same as the maintenance of the company's productive capacity. The point is an obvious one, for we could visualise a company which started business with £10 000 which it invested in 1000 units of stock. If the price of the stock increases and if the whole of the company's historical cost profit is taxed or consumed away, its money financial capital will be maintained, but it is clear that the company will have to reduce the physical quantity of stock.

It should be recognised that there is a great deal of difference between using the capital maintenance approach as a benchmark to measure profit and requiring companies to maintain their capital. Presumably distribution decisions should be made on the basis of consumption needs and perceived future investment opportunities inside and outside the company, and in many cases it would be sensible not to restrict distributions to profits. It is

---

[14] For simplicity we will ignore transaction costs and assume, in the case of both commodities, that there is no difference between the commodities' replacement costs and net realisable values.

necessary that company law should attempt to provide a measure of protection to creditors, but this should not be done in an inflexible way.[15]

It will be argued in later chapters that there is a need to devise a measure of profit that will provide a signal that if more than the amount of profit is consumed or taxed away then the substance of the business – however that may be defined – will be eroded. However, this is not to say that the substance of the business should never be reduced by way of dividend: in other words, a partial liquidation of the business might in certain circumstances be beneficial to shareholders without being detrimental to the interests of creditors and employees.

Taxation

In the UK, as in many other countries, a company's tax charge is based on its accounting profit, although some adjustments will usually have to be made to that profit in order to compute the profit subject to taxation. The general rule is, however, clear: the higher the accounting profit, the higher, all other things being equal, the amount that will be paid in tax.

For reasons similar to those discussed in the above section on consumption, the traditional accounting system does not constitute a suitable basis for the computation of the taxation obligations of businesses. This view depends on the not unreasonable assumption that governments would wish companies to be at least able to maintain the substance of their businesses. As we have shown, it is possible for historical cost accounting to generate a profit figure even when there has been a decline in the productive capacity of the business or, in less extreme cases, the reported profit might far exceed the growth in the company's productive capacity. Thus the use of historical cost accounting as the basis for taxation means that in periods of rising prices the proportion of the increase in a company's wealth which is taken by taxation may be very much larger than that which is implied by the nominal rate of taxation. In extreme cases taxation might be payable even where there has been a decline in the productive capacity of the business.

The rapid and extreme inflation of the mid-1970s made governments and others very much aware of the inadequacy of historical cost accounting for the purposes of taxation. Special measures were enacted which allowed businesses some relief against taxation for the impact of increasing prices, namely stock appreciation relief[16] and accelerated capital allowances. In contrast, financial accounting practice remained and remains essentially rooted in the traditional model of historical cost valuation combined with money financial capital maintenance, although, as described later in this book, the debate on possible reforms continues.

Valuation

The information contained in a company's financial statements is a significant, but not the sole, input to decisions concerning the valuation of a business or of a share in a business. At this stage it is perhaps sufficient to point out that the value of any asset, including a business or a share, depends on the economic benefits which are expected to flow to the asset's owner. It requires neither much space nor forceful argument to suggest that a knowledge of the historical cost of a company's assets will not be of much help in assessing the value of a

---

[15] Current legal practice regarding distributable profit is outlined in the next section of this chapter.

[16] Stock appreciation relief was a means of mitigating the extent to which companies had to pay tax on illusory profits arising from the increase in the replacement cost of stock during the periods in which they were held.

company or of its shares. Indeed, it was never the view of accountants that historical cost accounts should be used in this way. However, this view has never fully been accepted by the users of accounts, who have, understandably from their point of view, believed that the information provided by a company's accounts should help them form judgements concerning valuation. In fact the case for accounting reform does not rest simply on the existence of inflation, which still appears to be a permanent feature of our economy, but on the recognition that the wish of users to be supplied with information which will help them assess the value of companies and shares therein is a legitimate demand and one which will be better served by accounts based on current value principles than by historical cost accounts.

Interim summary

So far in this chapter, we have considered the meaning of profit and have shown that there are very many ways of measuring this elusive concept. These depend essentially on the choice made regarding the basis of asset valuation and the aspect of capital which is to be maintained. We have also discussed the limitations of historical cost accounting when tested against the more important purposes which a 'reasonable person' might expect financial accounts to serve. In Part 3 of the book, we will consider in some detail a number of the more important accounting models which have been developed and used in practice. But before doing so, we will turn our attention briefly to the subject of distributable profits.

Distributable profits

Because the liability of its shareholders is limited to the amount which they have paid or agreed to pay in respect of their shares, creditors of a failed limited company will normally only have recourse to the assets of the company itself. The assets representing the share capital, and any other reserves which are treated as being similar to share capital, may be seen as a buffer or cushion which provides some protection to creditors in the event of a failure. If a company were permitted to use its assets to repay this 'permanent' capital, the buffer would be reduced or disappear entirely with the result that the creditors' position would be more risky.

Although the law cannot prevent companies from reducing their 'permanent' capital by making losses, it does attempt to restrict the reduction of capital in other circumstances and, where a reduction of capital is permitted, it is strictly regulated. One way in which the law achieves its aim is by restricting payments of dividends to the distributable profits of the company. Another way is by the regulation of any transactions involving the purchase or redemption of a company's own shares and of any capital reduction or reorganisation schemes. We look at the former here and the latter in Chapter 18.

It has long been the case that dividends can only be paid out of profits but, surprisingly, until the passage of the Companies Act 1980, statute law offered no guidance on what constituted profits available for distribution. There were a number of leading cases, some of which were distinguished by their age rather than their economic rationale, which combined to produce some rather odd and confusing results.[17]

---

[17] Interested readers are referred to E.A. French, 'Evolution of the Dividend Law of England', in *Studies in Accounting*, W.T. Baxter and S. Davidson (eds), ICAEW, London, 1977.

The implementation of the Second and Fourth EU Directives necessitated the inclusion of provisions relating to distributable profits in UK statute law and, as a result, the Companies Act 1985 contains the following definition:

> . . . a company's profits available for distribution are its accumulated, realised profits, so far as not previously utilised by distribution or capitalisation, less its accumulated, realised losses, so far as not previously written off in a reduction or reorganisation of capital duly made.[18]

The above represents the only legal requirement placed on private companies, but additional rules apply to public companies and investment companies.

A public company may not pay a dividend which would reduce the amount of its net assets below the aggregate of its called-up share capital plus its undistributable reserves.[19] For this purpose the Act defines undistributable reserves as:

(a) the share premium account;
(b) the capital redemption reserve;
(c) excess of accumulated unrealised profits over accumulated unrealised losses (to the extent that these have not been previously capitalised or written off);
(d) any other reserve which the company may not distribute.

Before turning to the special case of investment companies we will discuss the implications of the above for public and private companies. Note that no distinction is made between revenue and capital profits, both are distributable; the key element is whether the profits have been *realised*, a term which will be discussed in further detail below.

A private company may, legally, pay a dividend equal to the accumulated balance of realised profits less realised losses, irrespective of the existence of unrealised losses. In contrast, the effect of the 'net asset rule' or 'capital maintenance rule' imposed on public companies is to require such a company to cover any net unrealised losses.

Thus, suppose a company's balance sheet is as given below:

	£	£
Share capital		50
Share premium		25
Unrealised profits	20	
Unrealised losses	(35)	(15)
Realised profits less realised losses		40
Net assets		100

If the concern were a private company it could pay a dividend of £40, but if it were a public company the maximum possible dividend would, because of the net asset rule, be restricted as follows:

	£	£
Net assets		100
less Share capital and undistributable reserves		
Share capital	50	
Share premium	25	
Excess of unrealised profits over unrealised losses[20]	0	75
Maximum dividend payable by public company		25

[18] Companies Act 1985, s. 263(3).
[19] Companies Act 1985, s. 264(1).
[20] Note that the excess of unrealised profits over unrealised losses is zero rather than the 'mathematical' excess of minus 15.

The effect of the net asset rule is to reduce the possible dividend by the net unrealised losses:

	£
Realised profits less realised losses	40
less Excess of unrealised losses over unrealised profits	15
Maximum dividend	25

Given the general bias in accounting to treat losses and provisions as being realised, it should be appreciated that unrealised losses are likely to be rare in practice. As we shall see later in the chapter, one of the few examples is a loss recognised on the reversal of a previously recognised unrealised gain.

An investment company is a listed public company whose business consists of investing its funds in securities with the intention of spreading the risk and giving its shareholders the benefits of the results of its management of funds. Such a company can, if it satisfies a number of conditions,[21] including a prohibition on the distribution of capital profits, give notice to the Registrar of Companies of its intention to be regarded as an investment company.

Except for the fact that it may not distribute capital profits, an investment company may calculate its maximum dividend on the same basis as any other public company. However, it is afforded greater flexibility by s. 265 of the Companies Act 1985 which provides an alternative method of calculating the maximum dividend payable. An investment company can, subject to a number of conditions, pay a dividend equal to the amount of its accumulated realised revenue profits less its accumulated revenue losses (both realised and unrealised). Thus, it may ignore any capital losses subject to the restriction that, after the payment of the dividend, the company's assets must be equal to or greater than one-and-a-half times its liabilities. Thus, if an investment company wishes to take advantage of the provision in s. 265 of not restricting its dividend by virtue of the existence of capital losses, it must apply this 'asset ratio test'.

It should be noted that the asset ratio test will be affected by the way in which it is proposed to fund the dividend, in that the result will depend on whether the dividend will reduce assets (if paid out of a positive cash balance) or increase liabilities (if paid from an overdraft). Suppose, for example, that an investment company has assets of £1200 and liabilities of £600. Then the maximum dividend on each basis will be:

(a) Dividend paid out of cash (i.e. liabilities held constant)

	Initial position £	After dividend £	Maximum dividend £
Assets	1200	900(3)	300
Liabilities	600	600(2)	

(b) Dividends paid out of an overdraft (assets held constant)

	Initial position £	After dividend £	Maximum dividend £
Assets	1200	1200(3)	
Liabilities	600	800(2)	200

[21] For a detailed list of conditions readers should refer to the Companies Act 1985, s. 266.

The various provisions outlined above are summarised in Table 4.1 and illustrated in Example 4.2.

Table 4.1 **Tests for maximum dividend**

Type of company	*Test*
Private	The dividend must not exceed accumulated realised profits less accumulated realised losses.
Public (other than investment companies)	The dividend must not exceed accumulated realised profits less accumulated realised losses, less accumulated net unrealised losses.
Investment companies	The maximum dividend is the higher of: (a) the amount derived from the above rule applicable to all public companies with the modification that realised capital profits must be excluded; and (b) the amount of accumulated realised revenue profits less accumulated revenue losses, both realised and unrealised, provided that, after payment of the dividend, assets are equal to at least one and a half times the liabilities.

Example 4.2

The balance sheet of Company A is summarised below:

	£	£
Total assets		4000
less Total liabilities		1000
		3000
Share capital		200
Share premium account		800
Unrealised profits		
Revenue	100	
Capital	200	300
Unrealised losses		
Revenue	(200)	
Capital	(800)	(1000)
Realised profits less realised losses		
Revenue	2300	
Capital	400	2700
		3000

We will now work out the maximum dividend on the assumption that Company A is (a) a private limited company, (b) a public limited company and (c) an investment company.

(a) Private company

For such a company, the maximum dividend is the accumulated net realised profits, that is £2700.

(b) Public company

The public company is subject to the capital maintenance rule that, after distribution, the net assets must equal the share capital plus undistributable reserves. In this case the undistributable reserves comprise only the share premium account, for the excess of unrealised profits over unrealised losses is zero. Hence, the maximum dividend is given by:

	£	£
Net assets		3000
less Share capital	200	
Share premium	800	1000
Maximum dividend		2000

In the case of the public company, the maximum dividend of the private company (£2700) has been reduced by the net unrealised losses of £700. (Unrealised losses £1000 less unrealised profits £300.)

(c) Investment company

By definition, an investment company must not distribute its capital profits. Hence our starting point must be realised revenue profits of £2300 subject, however, to the capital maintenance rule. Under this rule, the maximum dividend would be £2000 as for the public company in (b) above.

Using the alternative method allowed by s. 265, the maximum dividend is the excess of the realised revenue profits over net unrealised revenue losses, i.e. £2300 – (200 – 100) = £2200, subject to the application of the asset ratio test.

(i) If a dividend of £2200 were paid in cash, total assets would fall from £4000 to £1800, which is more than 1.5 times the liabilities of £1000.

(ii) If the dividend of £2200 was paid by overdraft, liabilities would increase to £3200, which would require asset cover of 1.5 × £3200 = £4800, i.e. more than the existing assets of £4000.

Hence the maximum dividend is £2200, but only if such a payment did not increase the liabilities. The lower limit of the maximum dividend is £2000 (as this can be justified on the alternative capital maintenance rule) while a dividend of between £2000 and £2200 would be possible if only a proportion of the dividend was paid out of an overdraft.

Realised profits

It is clear from the above discussion that the most important task in determining a company's distributable profits is deciding what constitutes its realised profits less losses.[22] Given the importance of the term, we might expect the Companies Acts to provide us with a comprehensive definition, but we would be extremely disappointed.

The Companies Acts provide both specific and general guidance; although the specific guidance is helpful, the general guidance is much less helpful. Let us look at the more detailed guidance first.

---

[22] This section on realised profits draws heavily on the ICAEW research paper, B.V. Carsberg and C.W. Noke, *The Reporting of Profits and the Concept of Realisation*, ICAEW, 1989. Interested readers are also referred to the Draft Technical Release (TECH 25/00), *The determination of realised profits and distributable profits in the context of the Companies Act 1985*, ICAEW and ICAS, 2000, although, for reasons explained later in this section, this draft is unlikely to be developed any further.

Section 275 of the Companies Act 1985 states that provisions are realised losses except for a provision made in respect of a fall in value of a fixed asset appearing on a revaluation of all the fixed assets of the company, whether including or excluding goodwill. This rather strange statement appears to mean that a fall in the value of one fixed asset may be treated as unrealised provided the aggregate value of fixed assets exceeds their aggregate net book value, thus taking a portfolio approach to fixed assets not often found in accounting. For this purpose, directors merely have to consider the values of all fixed assets and do not have to recognise those values in the financial statements although disclosure of what has been done is required. In the absence of such a general revaluation of fixed assets, a reduction in a previously unrealised profit would be treated as an unrealised loss unless the reduction is such that the revised value falls below the depreciated historical cost of the asset; in the latter case, the difference between the revised value and the depreciated historical cost is regarded as being a realised loss.

The Act also provides that where a fixed asset is revalued and depreciation is subsequently based on the revalued amount, the excess of depreciation based on the revalued amount over depreciation based on historical cost is to be treated as a realised profit. Thus the unrealised profit on revaluation is gradually converted into realised profit over the remaining useful life of the asset. Put another way, whatever is done in the profit and loss account, it is necessary only to charge depreciation based on historical cost in arriving at the realised profits of a company.

To give an example of such depreciation, let us suppose that a company purchased a fixed asset for £50 000 when its expected useful life was ten years and its expected residual value was zero. Using the straight line method of depreciation, the annual charge would be £5000 and, after four years, the net book value would be £30 000. If, after these four years, the asset were revalued to £42 000, there would be an unrealised revaluation surplus of £12 000, that is £42 000 less £30 000. The future annual depreciation charge in accordance with FRS 15 *Tangible Fixed Assets*, would normally be £42 000 ÷ 6 = £7000.

The excess of the revised depreciation charge of £7000 over historical cost depreciation of £5000 will then be treated as realised profits of the company year by year for the purpose of determining its distributable profits. Thus, by the end of the ensuing six years, the original unrealised revaluation surplus of £12 000 will have been regarded as realised and hence distributable.

Quite clearly the realised profits of a company may be a different figure from the balance on its profit and loss account!

Let us turn next to the more general guidance provided by the law. As a consequence of Companies Act 1989, the Companies Act 1985, s. 275 now contains the following definition:

> References . . . to 'realised profits' and 'realised losses', in relation to a company's accounts, are to such profits or losses of the company as fall to be treated as realised in accordance with principles generally accepted, at the time when the accounts are prepared, with respect to the determination for accounting purposes of realised profits or losses.

This hardly provides an adequate definition of realised profits. Rather it leaves the definition of realised profits to accountants, subject, of course, to the need for judicial interpretation in the courts if the accountants' methods are challenged. For reasons which we discuss below, accounting standard setters have found it extremely difficult to provide a satisfactory definition of realised profits.

A basic problem is that the definition includes reference, not to generally accepted accounting principles, but to 'principles generally accepted with respect to the determination for accounting purposes of realised profits'. There is some considerable doubt over whether such principles actually exist. Accounting principles have been primarily concerned with a different objective, namely providing a true and fair view of a company's position and results. In attempting to achieve such an objective, accountants have been more concerned with the recognition of profit than with whether it is realised or distributable.

Paragraph 12 of Schedule 4 to Companies Act 1985 further complicates matters by stating that:

The amount of any item shall be determined on a prudent basis, and in particular:

(a) only profits realised at the balance sheet date shall be included in the profit and loss account.

Many accountants see this as providing an undesirable constraint on the development of more informative accounting.[23] Indeed the ASC invoked the true and fair override to avoid the requirement to comply with the above principle in cases where it was thought to be inappropriate. One example is the treatment of exchange gains on foreign currency loans outstanding on a balance sheet date, which we discuss in Chapter 16.

Given the above position, it is perhaps not surprising to find little guidance on how to determine realised profits. One source of guidance was the ICAEW Technical Release 481, issued in 1982, which came to the conclusion that:

A profit which is required by SSAPs to be recognised in the profit and loss account should normally be treated as a realised profit, unless the SSAP specifically indicates that it should be treated as unrealised.

Although this might have seemed an attractive way forward, it does seem to be a rather suspect interpretation of the law. Indeed, it appears to be somewhat close to a tautology: a profit and loss account must only include realised profits but, by definition, whatever an accountant puts in the profit and loss account is realised!

Given the above difficulties, the ASC requested the Research Board of the ICAEW to commission a study, and the resulting paper 'The Reporting of Profits and the Concept of Realisation', by B.V. Carsberg and C.W. Noke, was published in 1989. If the ASC was expecting guidance on what was and what was not a realised profit, it must have been extremely disappointed. Carsberg and Noke identified six different meanings of realisation which have been used.

We shall focus on just two of these possible concepts of realisation. The narrower of the two is that which was embodied in the definition of prudence contained in the now withdrawn SSAP 2:[24]

revenue and profits are not anticipated, but are recognised by inclusion in the profit and loss account only when realised in the form either of cash or of other assets the ultimate cash realisation of which can be assessed with reasonable certainty; provision is made for all known liabilities (expenses and losses) whether the amount of these is known with certainty or is a best estimate in the light of the information available. (Para. 14)

This concept concentrates on the reasonable certainty of the ultimate receipt of cash. Clearly realisation has occurred if cash has been received but realisation is also deemed to occur if certain types of assets, such as debtors, are held which are reasonably certain to be turned into cash.

The wider concept regards profit as realised if it can be assessed with reasonable certainty. Thus, it considers the main purpose of the concept as being to ensure reliability of measurement.

---

[23] See, for example, 'The ASC in chains: whither self-regulation now?', Professor David P. Tweedie, *Accountancy*, March 1983, pp. 112–20. This article was written many years before David Tweedie became Chairman of the Accounting Standards Board in 1990.

[24] As explained in Chapter 2, SSAP 2 *Disclosure of Accounting Policies* (November 1971) has now been replaced by FRS 18 *Accounting Policies* (December 2000).

Readers may find the distinction between these two concepts difficult to grasp so it is perhaps helpful to look at some examples.

Where a company makes a cash sale, there is no doubt that the profit is realised under either concept. Similarly, where a sale is made on credit, the profit is treated as realised subject to the possible need for a provision for doubtful debts. The creation of the debt payable in the short term provides evidence of the ultimate cash proceeds and also provides a reliable measure of the profits.

Let us think next of an investment in a listed security which increases in price during a period. Under the narrower concept of realisation, profit would not be considered realised because the ultimate cash proceeds at some unspecified time in the future cannot be assessed with reasonable certainty. However, under the wider concept, profit would be treated as realised because the listed price of the share on the balance sheet date provides reliable evidence that a profit has been made. Conventionally accountants would adopt the narrower concept and would treat the holding gain as unrealised.

When we turn to foreign exchange gains on unsettled short-term debtors and creditors, we find that SSAP 20 requires that such gains be taken to the profit and loss account as realised profits. Under the narrower concept of realisation, these would not be treated as realised profits in view of the fact that the exchange rate may reverse between the balance sheet date and the date of receipt or payment. However, under the wider concept, there is reliable evidence, in the form of a published exchange rate, for the fact that a profit has been made. It is true that this may be reversed in the subsequent period but that will be a matter for the subsequent period. Here the ASC appears to have adopted the wider concept of realisation, although, interestingly, the adoption of this wider concept is not applied to the treatment of exchange gains on unsettled long-term monetary items, for here the gains are specifically described as unrealised.[25]

We hope that these examples provide an indication of the lack of consistency in defining realised profits in practice. In order to provide some consistency, Carsberg and Noke recommended that the standard setters should prepare a statement defining realisation and, in their view, the definition should be framed in terms of the reliability of measurement. Instead of attempting to define or redefine realisation, the ASB has taken a rather different approach in the development of its *Statement of Principles*. As we have seen in Chapter 1, it has developed recognition criteria which do not depend upon realisation; we shall return to this below.

Do the provisions make sense?

It is possible to question the philosophy on which the law of distributable profits is based and to press for changes to that law. Why, after all, should dividends be restricted to distributable profits defined in terms of realisation?[26]

Let us approach the question in two stages. First, why should dividends be restricted to profits and, second, if such a restriction is to apply, why should it relate to realised profits?

If a company's directors are acting in the interests of its shareholders then the decision on whether or not a distribution is made should depend on the rates of return available to

[25] See Chapter 16, pp. 480–3.

[26] The ideas which follow may be explored in E.A. French, 'Evolution of the dividend law of England', in *Studies in Accounting*, W.T. Baxter and S. Davidson (eds), ICAEW, London, 1977, and D.A. Egginton, 'Distributable profit and the pursuit of prudence', *Accounting and Business Research*, No. 41, Winter 1980.

shareholders outside the company, compared with the rates of return available within the company. If the company has inferior investment opportunities to those of the shareholders, then the restriction of a dividend to the distributable profits of the company would lead to an inefficient allocation of economic resources. The position of creditors needs to be considered and there is a case for protecting the 'buffer' available to creditors. In practice it is likely that the buffer will only be of relevance if the company goes into liquidation or substantially reduces its scale of operations. In such circumstances the real protection for creditors is the amount which will be realised from the sale of assets. In the case of some assets, especially current assets, realisable values may be well in excess of book values, but in the case of many fixed assets, particularly of a failed company, book value might exceed net realisable value. Hence, it might be argued that the test that should be applied is to specify that after distribution the realisable value of the company's assets exceed, possibly by a safety margin, the amounts due to creditors.

Even if we accept that dividends should be restricted to profits, why should the distribution be limited to realised profits?

It is sometimes argued that if a gain is realised, then the money is available to pay the dividend without the need to consider asset valuation. However, as Professor Egginton has pointed out, the argument has two weaknesses, one damaging and the other fatal! The damaging weakness is that conventional accounting often treats profits as realised well before cash is received. The fatal weakness is that even when profits have been received in cash, this cash will usually have been converted into other assets long before any dividends are paid. Hence, whether profits have been received or not, there is no guarantee that cash is available.

This is an area of the law which includes a number of poorly thought-out rules based on dubious reasoning, and accountants are forced to operate within an extremely unhelpful framework. It is of some consolation that in the vast majority of cases the limiting factor in determining a dividend is not the availability of distributable profits but the availability of cash and the alternative uses to which it may be put!

The ASB approach

According to the present law, only profits realised at a balance sheet date may be included in a profit and loss account. However, given the difficulties which we have discussed above, it is not surprising that the ASB has found the concept of realisation a poor test of whether or not a gain or loss should be recognised in financial statements. As we have explained in Chapter 1, the ASB *Statement of Principles*[27] is drawn up ignoring the realisation constraint as well as other constraints imposed by the law.

The *Statement of Principles* contains recognition criteria which are based upon the reasonable certainty that an asset or liability exists and whether it can be measured with sufficient reliability. This would achieve the purpose intended by the recommendation in the report by Carsberg and Noke, discussed above, but in a rather different way. In the view of the authors, this attempt to separate recognition from realisation makes good sense.

The ASB anticipates that its approach will lead to changes in company law and this now seems likely following the publication of the White Paper *Modernising Company Law* in July 2002.[28] This White Paper makes an enormous number of proposals for change of which two are pertinent here.

---

[27] *Statement of Principles for Financial Reporting*, ASB, London, December 1999.
[28] *Modernising Company Law*, Cm. 5553-I and Cm 5553–II, Draft clauses of Companies Bill, July 2002. The White Paper is available from the Modernising Company Law pages of the Department of Trade and Industry website at **www.dti.gov.uk/companiesbill**.

First, as we have seen in Chapter 2, the White Paper proposes that the next Companies Act will not contain detailed rules on the form and contents of annual financial statements and reports. Rather power to make these detailed rules will be delegated to a Standards Board, modelled on the present ASB but with a wider remit. This delegation will permit the new Standards Board to make the rules for what is or is not to be recognised in a company's performance statement and its rules will undoubtedly make no reference to realisation as a criteria for recognition.

Second, the White Paper proposes:

> the revision of the distribution rules to clarify what is a 'distribution', replacing the common law rules in the area with a complete codification, and enabling the delegation of some of the more technical accounting provisions to the proposed Standards Board.[29]

Although many draft clauses of a Companies Bill were published in July 2002,[30] unfortunately no definition of distribution or draft clauses on this topic are provided to help us to see how the new law is likely to develop.

Changes in company law inevitably involve a long gestation period and it has to be recognised that the approach taken by the ASB is likely to lead to all manner of difficulties and possible confusion until a new Companies Act is enacted. While it was possible to ignore the constraints imposed by law in drawing up the *Statement of Principles* it is not possible to do so in drafting accounting standards and the ASB is only too well aware that some parts of its accounting standards are in conflict with its own *Statement of Principles*.

Summary

In this chapter, we have first looked at the economic concept of profit and explored different ways of measuring it. These involve first measuring the wealth or well-offness of a company at the beginning and end of an accounting period and then comparing these two amounts with the aid of a capital maintenance concept. Although wealth could be measured in respect of the business as a whole, it is more likely to be determined as the sum of the values of the individually identified assets and liabilities. Using this approach, possible measurement bases for assets include historical cost, replacement cost, net realisable value and present value. When prices are changing, comparison of the opening and closing wealth requires the selection of a capital maintenance concept, the three main candidates for which are money financial capital maintenance, real financial capital maintenance and operating capital maintenance. We have examined briefly the usefulness of the different profit measures which result, and, in particular, the limitations of the traditional historical cost/money capital maintenance approach to the measurement of profit.

We have also examined the legal definition of distributable profits, the amounts which may be paid out to the shareholders of a limited company, and the related, but rather unhelpful, legal definition of realised profits, which have developed over the past century, largely as part of the common law. Under present company law, only realised profits may be included in a profit and loss account and, as we have seen in Chapter 1, this legal restriction has been hampering the ASB in its attempts to reform financial reporting. Fortunately, the Government White Paper *Modernising Company Law*, issued in July 2002, proposes that the

---

[29] *Ibid.*, Cm. 5553-I, Part II, Chapter 6, para. 6.5.
[30] *Ibid.*, Cm. 5553-II, Companies Bill – Draft clauses.

next Companies Act will delegate the making of detailed rules on the form and content of company accounts to a new Standards Board, a successor to the ASB but with a somewhat wider remit. It also proposes that the new Act will include changes to the distribution rules, which will replace the common law rules with a complete codification.

Recommended reading

B.V. Carsberg and C.W. Noke, *The Reporting of Profits and the Concept of Realisation*, ICAEW, London, 1989.

R.H. Parker, G.C. Harcourt and G. Whittington (eds), *Readings in the Concept and Measurement of Income*, 2nd edn, Philip Allan, Oxford, 1986.

A useful website

www.dti.gov.uk/companiesbill

Questions

4.1 Some commentators on financial reporting practices argue that financial statements produced under the historic cost convention do not provide relevant information to users of those statements in times of rising prices.

Requirements
(a) Identify the main limitations of historic cost accounting, explaining the nature of those limitations.   (5 marks)
(b) Discuss how the use of other capital maintenance concepts to that applied under historic cost accounting might provide more useful information to users of financial statements.   (5 marks)

ICAEW, Financial Reporting, May 1995   **(10 marks)**

4.2 (a) Give a brief summary of the current value replacement cost accounting system (entry values).   (6 marks)
(b) Give a brief summary of the current value net realisable value accounting system (exit values).   (6 marks)
(c) To what extent do you consider it would be useful to prepare financial statements which used entry values for the profit and loss account and exit values for the balance sheet and why?   (8 marks)

ACCA Level 2, The Regulatory Framework of Accounting, December 1989   **(20 marks)**

4.3 Three unrelated companies, Tower plc (a public company), Book Ltd (a private company) and Holdings plc (a quoted investment company) have summarised balance sheets, as on 30 June 1985, as set out below with relevant additional information.

(a) **Tower plc**

	£m		£m
Share capital	2.0	Fixed assets	3.3
Share premium account	0.5		
Revaluation reserves	1.0	Net current assets	2.7
Profit and loss account	2.5		
	6.0		6.0

(1) A partial revaluation of fixed assets took place during the year with the following result:

	£m
Surplus on land	0.65
Surplus on buildings	0.35
Surplus on plant and machinery	0.10
Deficit on fixtures and fittings	(0.10)
	1.00

The directors consider that the value of the remaining fixed assets not revalued is equal to their net book amounts.

(2) Depreciation is provided at 2% on buildings, 15% on plant and machinery, and 20% on fixtures and fittings. All fixed assets are depreciated for the full year on the cost or revalued amounts.

(3) Fixed assets comprise:

	£m
Land	1.2
Buildings	0.8
Plant and machinery	0.8
Fixtures and fittings	0.3
Development costs	0.2
	3.3

(b) **Book Ltd – Current Cost Balance Sheet**

	£000		£000	£000
Share capital	45	Fixed assets		50
Current cost reserve	40	Investment in Worm Ltd		40
Retained profit	55	Current assets		
		Stock	10	
		Long-term work-in-progress	30	
			40	
		Cash	10	50
	140			140

(1) No provision has yet been made for the losses of the subsidiary, Worm Ltd. It is estimated that the net assets of Worm Ltd in which Book Ltd has an interest of 60% are £50 000.

(2) The current cost reserve comprises:

	£000
CCA adjustments passed through profit and loss account	13
Uplift of fixed assets to CCA values	27
	40

(3) Long-term work-in-progress includes a profit element of £6000 calculated in accordance with SSAP 9.

(c) **Holdings plc**

	£000		£000	£000
Share capital	650	Fixed assets		
Share premium	325	Tangible		20
Reserves	4 380	Investments		5 647
		Current assets		
		Debtors	98	
		Investments	2 436	
		Cash	147	
			2 681	
		Creditors falling due		
		within 1 year	1 793	888
				6 555
		Creditors falling due in		
		more than 1 year		(936)
		Provisions		(264)
	5 355			5 355

Reserves consist of:

	£000
Unrealised capital losses	(48)
Unrealised revenue profits	140
Unrealised revenue losses	(17)
Realised capital profits	2 890
Realised capital losses	(1 241)
Realised revenue profits	2 666
Realised revenue losses	(10)
	4 380

Requirements

(a) State concisely, for each of the three types of company mentioned, the principles for calculating distributable profits under the Companies Act 1980 (now part of the Companies Act 1985). (5 marks)

(b) Calculate for each of the three companies the maximum legally distributable profits. (7 marks)

(c) Discuss the reasons why it is not normally commercially or practically desirable to make the maximum distribution. (7 marks)

ICAEW, Financial Accounting II, December 1985   **(19 marks)**

4.4 The balance sheet of Omega as at 30 September 1992 contained the following balances and notes:

		£000
Share capital		10 000
Reserves:		
Share premium	*Note 1*	1 000
Revaluation reserve	*Note 2*	1 780
Other Reserves:		
Merger reserve	*Note 3*	550
Profit and loss account – 1992	*Note 4*	1 940
Profit and loss account b/f		(200)
Capital and reserves		15 070
Liabilities		15 070
Total assets		30 140

Note 1 The share premium arose on the issue of shares on 1 October 1989.

Note 2 The revaluation reserve arose as a result of a revaluation of certain of the fixed assets on 1 October 1991. It comprises a gain of £2 000 000 on the revaluation of plant and machinery, which is the balance remaining after the transfer to the profit and loss account of £200 000 representing the depreciation on the revaluation surplus; and a loss of £220 000 arising from the revaluation of office premises. The directors propose to revalue the remaining fixed assets which currently appear at historic cost in a subsequent financial year.

Note 3 The merger reserve represented the premium of £1 450 000 on shares issued on the acquisition on 1 October 1991 of a subsidiary, Alpha plc, in accordance with the merger provisions of the Companies Act 1985 less goodwill of £900 000 arising on a separate transaction. The goodwill has an estimated useful economic life of 15 years.

Note 4 The profit and loss account balance is the balance after:

(i)   Writing off the total acquisition goodwill of £400 000 arising on the acquisition on 1 October 1991 of an unincorporated business carried on by Beta Associates. The estimated useful economic life of the goodwill is 10 years.

(ii) Creating a provision of £1 200 000 representing a permanent diminution in the value of a subsidiary, Gamma plc.

(iii) The transfer of the £200 000 mentioned in Note 2 from the revaluation reserve to the profit and loss account representing the amount by which the total depreciation charge for the year exceeded the amount that would have been provided if the plant had not been revalued.

(iv) Crediting an exchange gain of £38 000 that arose on the translation of a long-term loan taken out in French francs on 1 October 1991. The loan was taken out to use in the United Kingdom because the interest rate was favourable at the date the loan was raised.

Required

(a) **Calculate the amount of distributable profit for Omega on the basis that it is:**

(i)   **A public company.**

(ii) **An investment company.**   (10 marks)

(b) **Explain briefly:**

(i)   **The disclosure requirements relating to distributable profits in a single company and group context.**

(ii) The effect on the distributable profits of the holding company if the group has sufficient distributable profits in aggregate to make a distribution to the holding company's shareholders but the holding company itself has insufficient distributable profits.

(iii) The effect on the distributable profits of the holding company if the holding company has sold one subsidiary company to another subsidiary for a consideration that exceeds the carrying value of the investment in the holding company's accounts.

(iv) The effect on the distributable profits of the holding company if a subsidiary company which has a coterminous accounting period declares a dividend after the end of the holding company's year end. (10 marks)

ACCA, Advanced Financial Accounting, December 1992 (**20 marks**)

Financial reporting in practice

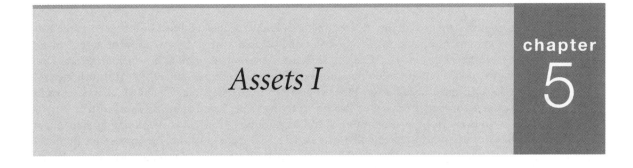

Assets I

overview

A key practical and theoretical issue in accounting is when should an asset be recognised and how should it be measured? In what circumstances does expenditure result in an asset and when in an expense? If an asset is to be recognised should it be recorded at cost, and how should that cost be measured, or at a current value that may be more or less than the asset's historical cost? Most assets do not last forever and so we must decide how we should measure the consumption of the asset.

In this chapter we concentrate on fixed assets, including investment properties, and will discuss the issues involved both in the way in which they are initially recognised in the financial statements and in the way in which changes in their carrying value are effected. Thus we will cover both depreciation and impairment reviews and the use of current values. We will in the following chapter cover other topics related to assets: inventory, research and development and accounting for grants, while we will deal with contingent assets in Chapter 7, along with contingent liabilities.

The various statements and standards covered in the chapter are:

- FRS 15 *Tangible Fixed Assets* (1999)
- FRED 29 *Property, Plant and Equipment and Borrowing Costs* (2002)
- IAS 16 *Property, Plant and Equipment* (revised 1998)
- IAS 23 *Borrowing Costs* (revised 1993)
- SSAP 19 *Accounting for Investment Properties* (amended 1994)
- FRS 10 *Goodwill and Intangible Assets* (1997)
- FRS 11 *Impairment of Fixed Assets and Goodwill* (1998)
- IAS 36 *Impairment of Assets* (1998)
- *Exposure draft of an amendment to FRS 15 and FRS 10* (2000)

The proposals of FRED 29, which was issued as part of the convergence programme between UK and international standards, are intended to lead to the replacement of FRS 15 by two standards. One would be based on the existing International Standard, IAS 23 *Borrowing Costs*, and the other on a planned revised version of IAS 16 *Property, Plant and Equipment*.

Introduction

In Chapter 4 we introduced the various approaches to the valuation of assets in a balance sheet. These included historical cost, historical cost adjusted for inflation, replacement cost, net realisable value and present value. We shall, in Part 3 of the book, explore systems of accounting which attempt to adjust for the effects of changing prices in various ways but in this and the following chapter we will discuss a number of problems of accounting measurement and disclosure of assets in the context of current financial accounting practice. The current system used in the UK has long been known as the 'modified historical cost account-ing system' although, in its *Statement of Principles*, the ASB now uses the term 'mixed measurement system' (see Chapter 1). It is a system of accounting in which most assets are shown at an amount based upon historical cost while other assets are shown at their current values. In the UK and a few other countries,[1] fixed assets may be shown at their current values even when this is higher than the carrying values based upon historical cost.

While efforts to replace historical cost accounting by current cost accounting as the main basis of accounting have failed, the debate has had a considerable impact on financial accounting practice. During the 1970s and 1980s, those inflationary decades, both the accountancy profession and the UK Government made moves towards the greater use of current values in financial statements and the main elements of that particular saga are described in Chapter 19. In a period of low inflation much of the heat has gone out of the debate, but there are some important legacies of the controversy including the 'alternative accounting rules' of the Companies Act 1985 and the fact that the subject of revaluation is now an important aspect of any financial reporting standard dealing with assets. As we explained in Chapter 1, it is quite clear that the ASB favours the greater use of current values in financial statements and this enthusiasm is undoubtedly shared by the present IASB.

The nature of assets

The ASB deals with the general nature of assets in its *Statement of Principles* issued in December 1999, in which assets are defined thus:

> Assets are rights or other access to future economic benefits controlled by an entity as a result of past transactions or events. (Para. 4.6)

Note that the key elements are *control* (not ownership), *future economic benefits* and the need to identify *past transactions or events* that gave rise to the asset. We shall show how these ele-ments affect the treatment of assets in the course of the chapter.

Tangible and intangible assets

Company legislation and accounting standards make much of the distinction between tangible and intangible assets. The balance sheet formats of the Companies Act require the separation of the two types of assets while they are dealt with different financial reporting standards. In the past when manufacturing was king and 'real' assets were things that you could touch it might have been appropriate to treat the two classes of assets as being fundamentally different but in the modern economy where knowledge, brands and rights may be far more significant sources of wealth than plant and equipment the distinction seems far less sensible.

The distinction may actually be very unhelpful because it deflects us from understanding the basic principle that an asset is only an asset if it is a source of future economic benefits. Its tangibility or intangibility has nothing to do with that. A piece of plant and equipment is a potential heap of rust; the right to the 'Mars' brand is a very 'real' source of wealth.

---

[1] The ASB is part of a group of national standard setters from jurisdictions in which the revaluation of fixed assets is permitted together with the IASB. This is referred to as the 'Revaluation Group' and comprises representatives from standard-setting bodies of Australia, New Zealand, South Africa and the UK. Upward revaluations of fixed assets are not permitted in most countries including major players such as Canada, Germany, Japan and the USA.

An interesting example of the somewhat odd outcome that emerges from the debates about an asset's tangibility relates to websites. A well-designed and skilfully targeted website will generate considerable economic benefits and hence must be regarded as constituting an asset, but is it tangible or intangible? This question, and here one is rather reminded of angels dancing on pins, was addressed by the Urgent Issues Task Force (UITF) which published an abstract on the subject in February 2001.[2]

It was concluded that a website does indeed constitute an asset if there existed reasonable grounds for supposing that future economic benefits would exceed the costs to be capitalised. If the case could be made, the amount to be capitalised would be the expenditure related to infrastructure costs (including the cost of registering the domain name and software) and the costs of designing the site and in preparing and posting the content of the site.

It might be thought that the asset has more of a virtual than a physical substance but even so the UITF experienced some difficulty in determining whether it should be treated as a tangible or an intangible asset. They did, however, identify a precedent in paragraph 2 of FRS 10 *Goodwill and Intangible Assets* where it is stated that software development costs that are directly attributable to bringing a computer system into working condition should be treated as part of the cost of the related hardware rather than as a separate intangible asset. On the basis of this somewhat imperfect analogy, the UITF decided that website development costs should be treated as a tangible asset.

It is not altogether clear how this view can be squared with the FRS 15 definition of a tangible asset that includes the requirement that it has a 'physical substance' (see p. 100). A more important question, however, is does it matter whether website expenditure is tangible or intangible? We shall return to this question on p. 122 after dealing with the standards relating to these tangible and intangible assets respectively.

A multiplicity of standards

In its recent work the ASB has more closely linked the issues surrounding the special case of the intangible asset of goodwill arising from a business combination with intangible assets in general. One consequence is that there are now three key interlinking standards, FRS 10 *Goodwill and Intangible Assets*, FRS 11 *Impairment of Fixed Assets and Goodwill* and FRS 15 *Tangible Fixed Assets*, which are based on consistent principles, as well as three surviving SSAPs, 19, 9 and 13, which deal with investment properties, stocks and work-in-progress, and research and development. We will, in this chapter, focus on FRS 15, FRS 10 and SSAP 19, but will also discuss some elements of FRS 11. We will return to a more extensive discussion of goodwill and impairment in Chapter 13 where we deal with the subject of business combinations.

The nature of the issues

Before proceeding to the detailed discussion it might be helpful to identify the main issues relating to accounting for assets that need to be considered:

1 What is the actual nature of the asset that is to be recorded? It may be necessary to distinguish between the economic benefits that accrue from the ownership of the asset, the right to acquire the asset (an option), or the right to receive some or all of the returns that will be generated by the asset.

---

[2] UITF Abstract 29, 'Website development cost'.

2 Who controls the right to benefit from the use of the asset? This might not be the same entity as its legal owner.

3 What was the cost of acquiring an asset?

4 Does the asset have a finite useful economic life? If so, how should it be depreciated?

5 What is the current value of the asset and on what basis should the current value be determined? These questions need to be answered even for historical cost accounts to help decide whether the carrying value of the asset needs to be written down.

6 To what extent, and how, should current values be recognised in historical cost accounts?

7 What is the appropriate treatment of gains and losses from the revaluation and disposal of assets?

While we deal with most of these issues in this chapter some, like the second, control of the right to benefit from the use of the asset, are best dealt with in later chapters of the book.

The basis of valuation

We will start not with the first issue but with the fifth, because the answer to the question 'What is the asset's current value?' has an important impact on many of the issues. We will in Part 3 of the book deal with some of the theoretical aspects of current value but, at this stage, we will confine our discussion to the two concepts that have impacted on UK and International Standards, namely *fair value* and *value to the business*.

While, in its early standards, the ASB used the fair value approach to obtaining current values, it subsequently adopted the more sophisticated and logically consistent value to the business model that, as it points out in its *Statement of Principles*, provides the most relevant basis for arriving at the current value of an asset.[3] Unfortunately the IASB remains committed to the fair value approach that, as we shall see, reappears in the UK in FRED 29. It appears that the ASB is prepared to accept the less satisfactory fair value approach to current value as part of the cost of convergence.

Value to the business

We will start by considering *value to the business*, also known as *deprival value*, which we briefly introduced in Chapter 1 and to which we will return, in more detail, in Chapter 20. The key question in determining an asset's value to the business (the loss the entity would suffer if deprived of the asset) is whether an entity would, if deprived of the asset, replace it. If it would, the loss, and hence the value to the business, is the asset's replacement cost.[4] But in some instances the entity would not choose to replace the asset because the economic benefit that comes from ownership is less than the cost of replacement. In such a case the value to the business, which would be less than the replacement cost, would depend on what a 'rational entity' is intending to do with the asset; the critical question is whether the asset is being held for sale or not. If the best thing the entity could do is sell the asset (but not replace it) then the value to the business is the asset's net realisable value: sales proceeds less the future costs of sale.

---

[3] Para. 6.7.

[4] Strictly, the loss includes any consequent costs due, for example, to delays in production. In practice these consequential losses are, unless they are substantial, ignored.

However, there may be some assets which are not worth replacing but which it would not be sensible to sell, because they are worth more to keep than would be realised through their sale. A good example of such an asset is an old specialised machine which would not be replaced but which is still producing cash flows with a present value far in excess of its net realisable value. In such a case, the asset would be retained and used rather than sold.

Assets that fall into this intermediate category are valued by reference to their value in use, which is defined as:

> The present value of the future cash flows obtainable as a result of the asset's continued use, including those resulting from its ultimate disposal.[5]

The higher of the net realisable and value in use is the assets *recoverable amount*; we will discuss this subject in more detail later in the chapter when we introduce FRS 11.

So when a company exercises its option to show assets at current value, rather than on the basis of historical cost, the value to the business will usually be its replacement cost, or to be more precise in the case of a fixed asset, the replacement cost of that portion of the assets that has not been consumed. If the asset is not worth replacing, its value to the business is its recoverable amount.

The above can be summarised as follows:

> Value to the business = lower of: Replacement cost
> Recoverable amount
>
> Recoverable amount = higher of: Value in use
> Net realisable value

Fair value

Let us now turn to fair value, which is defined in FRED 29 as:

> the amount for which an asset could be exchanged between knowledgeable, willing parties in an arm's length transaction.[6]

In other words fair value is the market value of an asset in a good market, that is one where there are willing buyers and sellers, where the parties are knowledgeable and where there are no forced sales.

The problem with this approach is that it ignores the different hypothetical positions of the willing partners. The market value is always dependent on the asset holder's relation to the market. Take for example a motor vehicle retailer who lives on the difference between the price he pays a knowledgeable and willing seller, such as BMW, and receives from a willing and knowledgeable purchaser, who may be one of our readers. The difference between these two prices is often quite considerable – how else might one account for the plush car showrooms?

The FRED 29 definition is quite deficient in that it provides no guidance as to which of the two possible figures represent the fair value of the retailer's inventory of BMWs. The definition has to be interpreted in the light of other factors. To value inventory at its realisable value would be to take credit for a profit yet to be realised and would thus be rejected in favour of replacement cost. The value to the business rule would produce the same answer

---

[5] FRS 11, Para. 2.
[6] Para. 6

but would do so in a more satisfactory and logical fashion. If the retailer would replace the cars then their current value is given by their replacement cost; if they are not worth replacing the value is given by their recoverable amount, in this case their net realisable value.

Another major weakness in the definition of fair value as set out in FRED 29 is that it does not deal explicitly with those cases where there is not a market for the asset, as might often be the case for highly specialised items of plant and equipment. In such cases, FRED 29 would require the asset to be valued on the basis of its depreciated replacement cost.[7] But, as we pointed out earlier this approach might not be valid if the asset's value in use is less than the depreciated replacement cost. The exposure draft does not deal with this point.

Tangible fixed assets

For convenience we will consider the various issues surrounding the accounting treatment of tangible fixed assets in the same order as is found in FRS 15 *Tangible Fixed Assets*,[8] which was issued in 1999. The main issues and related provisions of FRS 15 are summarised in Table 5.1.

Table 5.1 **Summary of main issues and related provisions of FRS 15 *Tangible fixed assets***

Issues	Provisions
Initial measurement of TFAs	At cost
Capitalisation of finance costs	Optional
Write-down of TFAs to their recoverable amounts	Required
Treatment of subsequent expenditure on TFAs	Write-off to P&L, with three exceptions
Revaluation of TFAs	Optional
Depreciation of TFAs	Required, other than for land and investment properties, but may be immaterial
Treatment of gains and losses on disposal and revaluation of TFAs	Show in P&L if due to consumption of economic benefits, otherwise in STRGL but with exceptions
Disclosure requirements	Various

Tangible fixed assets (TFAs) are defined in FRS 15 as:

Assets that have physical substance and are held for use in the production or supply of goods or services, for rental to others, or for administrative purposes on a continuing basis in the reporting entity's activities. (Para. 2)

This definition seems clear enough[9] but it does beg at least one important question. To what extent should an item be regarded as a single asset or a collection of assets? A factory is

---

[7] FRED 29, Para. 31.

[8] It appears that the convergence process will lead to a change in terminology in that, following IASB practice, FRED 29 includes in its title the phrase 'Property, plant and equipment' which, in the minds of the ASB members, has a similar meaning to 'Tangible fixed assets' (FRED 29, Para. 4).

[9] But see p. 97 where it is explained that the UITF believes that a website has a physical substance.

clearly a collection of assets while a motor car would almost always be treated as a single asset. But the question is not always capable of a simple answer. Take, as an example, trailers that are towed by articulated trucks. The tyres of the trailers constitute a substantial portion of the total cost of the trailer but have a much shorter life than that of the bodies of the trailers. The owner of a large trailer fleet might well find it sensible to treat the tyres separately from the bodies and, for example, to apply a different depreciation pattern to the tyres as compared to the bodies.

This is an important topic that FRS 15 touches upon but does not completely resolve. It is recognised that when an asset is made up of two or more major components with substantially different useful economic lives, then each component should be accounted for separately for depreciation purposes (FRS 15, Para. 83). But this, perhaps, does little more than shift the debate to what is the nature of a component.

One way of approaching the question is to consider the acquisition of the asset and argue that an identifiable asset is one that was acquired as a result of a single event but, as described earlier, the ASB's definition allows an asset to be acquired as a consequence of more than one event. Thus, in Appendix IV to FRS 15, which deals with the development of the standard, the Board is reduced to relying on such phrases as that the decision will '*depend upon the individual circumstances*' and expressing the expectation that entities will use '*a common sense approach*' (FRS 15, p. 77, emphasis added). The use of such phrases by standard setters is usually a pretty fair indication that there are issues still to be resolved.

The initial cost of a tangible fixed asset

Whether a TFA is acquired or self-constructed, its initial cost is made up of its purchase price and '*any costs directly attributable to bringing it into working condition for its intended use*' (Para. 8, emphasis added). Thus general overheads should not be included, but the cost does include, as well as any directly attributable labour costs, '*the incremental costs to the entity that would have been avoided only if the tangible fixed asset had not been constructed or acquired*' (Para. 9(b), emphasis added).

While it is clear that the Standard calls for the identification of truly marginal costs, it is likely that, in practice, the usual overhead recovery rates will be used as proxy to arrive at the incremental costs.

Of particular interest are the costs that the ASB say should not be included: Para. 11 states:

> Abnormal costs (such as those relating to design errors, industrial disputes, idle capacity, wasted materials, labour or other resources and production delays) and costs such as operating losses that occur because a revenue earning activity has been suspended during the construction of a tangible fixed asset are not directly attributable to bringing the asset into working condition for its intended use.

This paragraph seems both impractical and inconsistent. Its impracticability stems from the assumption that such things as design errors are 'abnormal'. Anyone who has experience of any large-scale construction knows that designers and engineers do not get everything right the first time and that a reasonable amount of rectification and redesign is part of the normal cost of construction.

The inconsistency is to be found in the different treatments of acquired and self-constructed tangible fixed assets. In the case of an acquisition the cost is the cost, which may or may not be the 'best price' at which it might have been purchased in the market and, in the case of complex assets, is likely to include an element for cost recovery of the 'inefficiencies' listed in Para. 11 of

FRS 15. Hence, it is possible to capitalise the entity's purchasing inefficiency and the supplier's production inefficiency and excess profit, but not the entity's production inefficiency.

A more consistent and realistic approach would be to measure and record the cost actually incurred in constructing the asset, warts (inefficiencies) and all, and then apply the usual tests of impairment to determine whether the carrying value should be written down to its recoverable value (see p. 104).

Another major problem that can arise in determining the initial cost of an asset occurs when the asset is not acquired in isolation but as part of a package that might, in the extreme, involve the purchase of an entire business. As we will show in Chapter 13 it is necessary, in such circumstances, to attempt to arrive at the fair values, or to be more precise, values to the business, of the assets involved using the bases we described earlier.

FRED 29 includes a proposal that has not previously been found in UK standards which relates to assets that have been acquired in exchange. The exchange of assets appears to be much more common in Eastern European countries and the exposure draft proposes that, where such exchanges occur, the cost of the assets should be measured by reference to the fair value of the assets given up or, if more clearly evident, the fair value of the assets acquired. This would preclude the use of the carrying amount of the asset that has been given up in the exchange, unless it was impossible to determine reliably either of the two fair values.

The capitalisation of borrowing costs

Considerable uncertainty surrounds the question of whether borrowing (finance)[10] costs should be capitalised when a fixed asset, say a building, is paid for in advance, often by a series of progress payments, or when such an asset takes a considerable time to bring into service. The debate about whether or not borrowing costs should be capitalised is often conducted with a fervour reminiscent of the more extreme medieval religious conflicts, but the basic point is, however, extremely simple.

The only point at issue is when the cost of borrowing should be charged to the profit and loss account. If the cost is not capitalised it will be charged over the life of the loan, whereas if it is capitalised the cost will be charged to the profit and loss account over the life of the asset as part of the depreciation expense. The rationale for the view that borrowing costs should be capitalised can best be demonstrated by the use of a simple example.

Assume that the client, A Limited, is offered the following choice by the builder, B Limited: 'The building will take two years to construct, you can either pay £10 million now or £12 million in two years' time.' If A Limited decides to select the first option, it may well have to borrow the money on which it will have to pay interest. If A Limited selects the second option, it will still have to pay interest, but in this case the interest will be included in the price paid to B Limited.

The above example is extreme, but it does highlight the principles involved. If we assume that both companies have to pay the same interest rate, then A Limited will be in exactly the same position at the end of two years whatever option is selected, and it does not seem sensible to suggest that the cost of the building is different because in one case the interest is paid directly by the client while in the second case the interest is paid via the builder.

The basic stance adopted in FRS 15 is that an entity can choose to capitalise or not to capitalise borrowing costs but, having chosen, it must be consistent.

---

[10] FRS 15 refers to finance costs but, following international practice, FRED 29 uses the term borrowing costs.

The ASB acknowledges that it would have been better if it climbed off the fence and either prohibited the capitalisation of borrowing costs or made it mandatory. It agrees that there are conceptual arguments for the capitalisation on the grounds of comparability as demonstrated in the above example. However, the ASB was influenced by the argument that, if capitalisation were made mandatory, then companies would demand that notional interest charges should also be capitalised. This would be relevant in cases where entities did not need to resort to borrowing to acquire the fixed asset but instead relied on their internal resources that have, not a direct cost, but an opportunity cost related to the benefit that the entity would have obtained had the resources not been used for this particular project. This is, the Board states, 'a contentious issue' and, until an internationally acceptable approach is agreed, the Board will continue with the optional approach that it says is consistent with that taken by IAS 23, *Borrowing Costs*, as revised in 1993.

The provisions of FRS 15 relating to the capitalisation of borrowing costs may be summarised as follows:

1 When an entity adopts a policy of capitalisation of finance costs that are directly attributable to the construction of tangible fixed assets, the finance cost should be included in the cost of the asset and the policy should be consistently applied (Paras 19 and 20).
2 When the entity borrows funds specifically to be used for the project the amount to be capitalised should be restricted to the actual costs incurred and should be capitalised on a gross basis, i.e. before the deduction of any tax relief (Paras 21 and 22).
3 If the funds used are part of the entity's general borrowings the amount to be capitalised should be based on the average cost of capital but, in calculating the cost, funds raised for specific purposes should be excluded (Paras 23 and 24).
4 Capitalisation should begin when:
   (a) finance costs are being incurred and
   (b) expenditure for the asset are being incurred and
   (c) activities to get the asset ready for use are in progress (Para. 25).
5 Capitalisation should stop when all the activities are substantially complete (Para. 29).
6 Where a policy of capitalisation is adopted that fact should be disclosed, together with:
   (a) the aggregate amount of finance costs included in the cost of tangible fixed assets;
   (b) the amount of finance costs capitalised during the period;
   (c) the amount of finance costs recognised in the profit and loss account during the period;
   (d) the capitalisation rate used to determine the amount of finance costs capitalised during the period (Para. 31).

FRED 29

There are no significant differences between the provisions of FRS 15 and FRED 29 so far as borrowing costs are concerned. The exposure draft does, however, indicate that debate on this issue has not yet come to an end in that it is reported that the IASB, when considering the revision of IAS 23, became inclined to the view that all borrowing costs be reporting as an expense in the period in which they are incurred (Para. 20) but it recognised that to do so would conflict with the views of national standard setters. Hence, more thought will be given to the matter as part of an IASB project dealing with measurement of the initial recognition of assets.

The writing down of new tangible fixed assets to their recoverable amounts

It is, as we shall see, a main theme of FRS 11 *The Impairment of Fixed Assets and Goodwill*, that fixed assets are not carried at more than their recoverable amounts and we deal with this later in the chapter. At this stage it is necessary just to point to Paras 32 and 33 that state that, when a new TFA is acquired, through either purchase or construction, it should not be carried at an amount that exceeds its *recoverable amount*.

Subsequent expenditure

'Subsequent expenditure' is a relatively new, useful term that covers all expenditure on the TFA after it has come into use.

One of the more slippery areas of accounting is the distinction between repairs and enhancement with the temptations often pulling in opposite directions. The enterprise wishing to minimise its tax bill would tend to write off as much as possible to repairs, while an enterprise more concerned with showing a good profit would opt for capitalisation.

FRS 15 is clear that expenditure to ensure that a fixed asset maintains its previously assessed standard of performance should be written off to the profit and loss account as it is incurred (Para. 34). The circumstances under which subsequent expenditure can be capitalised are set out in Para. 36, which we will reproduce in full.

Subsequent expenditure should be capitalised in three circumstances:

(a) where the subsequent expenditure provides an enhancement of the economic benefits of the tangible fixed asset in excess of the previously assessed standard of performance.

(b) where a component of the tangible fixed asset that has been treated separately for depreciation purposes and depreciated over its individual useful economic life is replaced or restored.

(c) where the subsequent expenditure relates to a major inspection or overhaul of a tangible fixed asset that restores the economic benefits of the asset that have been consumed by the entity and have already been reflected in depreciation.

The drafting of the paragraph is not entirely clear but the concepts are pretty simple. Paragraph 36(a) states that capitalisation is appropriate when the asset has been improved in some way, such as extending its life or improving its efficiency. Paragraph 36(b) takes us back to the question of when an asset is an individual asset or a bundle of assets. As mentioned earlier, an asset with two or more major components may have different depreciation patterns for each of the components and this clause is simply a consequence of this. Paragraph 36(c) refers to situations, such as those found in the airline industry, where there is a mandatory inspection and overhaul of the asset every, say, three years. Then the cost of the inspection and the overhaul can be capitalised and written off over the period until the next inspection is due.

The revaluation of tangible fixed assets

The various attempts to introduce a system of financial reporting based primarily on current values are described elsewhere in this book. In this section we will be concerned with what the ASB refers to as the 'mixed measurement system'. Under this system some assets are carried in the balance sheet at their current values and some are not. While historical costs accounting has always required the writing down of assets, by, for example, depreciation, revaluation in an upward direction is not permitted in most countries of the world.[11] However the revaluing of certain TFAs, particularly property, has long been common in the UK, a practice which has been given additional legislative force by the inclusion of the alternative accounting rules in the Companies Act 1985.

In previous pronouncements the ASB and its predecessor, the Accounting Standards Committee, set out the arguments for and against the greater use of current values, sometimes tending to favour such a practice[12] and sometimes not.[13] In FRS 15 the ASB's position seems to be one of studied neutrality as evidenced by the awe-inspiring declaration in a paragraph printed in bold and hence part of the standard itself, that:

Tangible fixed assets should be revalued where the entity adopts a policy of revaluation. (Para. 42)

So it should only be done when you want to do it!

Given that the entity has adopted a policy of revaluation the standard sets out the parameters within which the policy should be applied. These are summarised below.

1 The policy should be applied consistently to all assets within an individual class of tangible fixed assets but need not be applied to all classes of such assets (Para. 42).
2 Assets subject to the policy of revaluation should be included in the balance sheet at their current values (Para. 43).

The ASB has tried to ensure some consistency of practice within a given class of assets and outlawed the previous practice whereby companies would revalue one or more assets in a class at one point in time but then not update that value. It has thus outlawed the use of obsolete revaluations!

Classification of tangible fixed assets

In the UK the formats for financial reporting contain three groups for TFAs:

- Land and buildings
- Plant and machinery
- Fixtures, fittings, tools and equipment

However, in applying the provisions of this standard entities may adopt narrower classes, e.g. freehold properties. Little guidance is given as to what would be an appropriate class other than the not very forceful phrase that 'entities may, within reason, adopt . . . narrower classes' (Para. 62).

There is one exception to the rule that requires all assets within the same class to be revalued. These are assets that are held outside the UK or the Republic of Ireland for which it is impossible to obtain a reliable valuation. Such assets can continue to be carried at historical cost but the fact that this override has been used must be stated.

---

[11] One of the authors used a machine with an American spell check which gave an error message every time he typed 'revalued'. See n. 1 above, on the 'Revaluation Group'.

[12] See *Accounting for the Effects of Changing Prices*, published in 1986.

[13] See ED 51 *Accounting for Fixed Assets and Revaluations*, issued in 1990.

Frequency

Most quoted entities made use of the alternative accounting rules but generally did so on a spasmodic basis.[14] Large numbers of companies, particularly quoted companies, have incorporated revaluations into their financial statements, often cherry-picking assets for this treatment. These revaluations have usually related to properties but the revalued amounts have rarely been updated on an annual basis. Thus, in addition to showing their TFAs at 'historical costs' and 'current values', companies have frequently included assets at 'obsolete current values'. This third category is obviously unhelpful in that it tells the user nothing of value and has now wisely been outlawed by the ASB. It appears that many companies which have used obsolete revaluations have now reverted to the use of historical cost-based valuations rather than incur the cost of systematically revaluing all assets in a particular class at current value on an annual basis. Thus we are probably now closer to a historical cost system of accounting than we have been for many years!

The standard requires that, if an entity opts for a policy of revaluation in respect of a particular class of tangible fixed assets, the balance sheet should reflect the current values of those assets. This does not mean, however, that revaluation need be an annual process (Para. 44). In general, the requirements of the standard would be satisfied if there were a full revaluation every five years with an interim valuation in year 3. In addition an interim valuation should be carried out in any year where it is 'likely that there has been a material change in value' (Para. 45).

Special considerations apply to entities that hold a portfolio of non-specialised properties.[15] In such cases it is suggested that a full valuation could be achieved on a rolling programme designed to cover all the properties over a five-year cycle, together with interim valuations where it is likely that there has been a material change in value.

We have in the preceding paragraphs been free with the phrases '*full valuation*', '*interim valuation*' and '*likely to be a material change in value*'. What do these phrases actually mean?

The differences between full and interim valuations are described in the case of properties but not for other types of TFAs. For properties a full valuation would include a detailed inspection of the property, enquiries of local planning authorities, solicitors, etc. and research into market transactions involving similar properties and the identification of market trends (Para. 47). The less detailed interim valuation would involve the last of these together with the confirmation that there have been no significant changes to the physical fabric of the property and an inspection (but not a detailed inspection) if there are indications that such would be necessary (Para. 48).

No effective guidance is provided as to what is meant by a material change. In attempting this the standard does little more than restate its position by explaining that 'A material change in value is a change in value that would reasonably influence the decision of a user of the accounts' (Para. 52).

Who should make the valuations?

With the single exception referred to below revaluations should be made by qualified valuers. These may be internal, employed by the entity, but if they are, then the valuation process should be reviewed by a qualified external valuer.

---

[14] FRS 15, p. 73.

[15] FRS 15 follows the definitions used by the Royal Institute of Chartered Surveyors (RICS) that are reproduced in Appendix 1 to the standard. In summary, non-specialised buildings are those which can be used for a range of purposes.

The exception relates to those assets for which there exists an active second-hand market, as is the case for used cars, or where suitable indices exist that enable the entity's directors to establish the asset's value with reasonable certainty. In such instances the valuations can be made by the directors but if this option is selected the valuations should be done on an annual basis.

Bases of valuation

Assets other than properties

The basic principle for the revaluation of all tangible assets, other than property, is set out in Para. 59:

> **Tangible fixed assets other than properties should be valued using market value, where possible. Where market value is not obtainable, assets should be valued on the basis of depreciated replacement cost.**

For the reasons we explained earlier, while the use of the imprecise phrase 'market value' is far from helpful, it was clear that the ASB believed, at the time it issued FRS 15, that the 'practical interpretation' of this paragraph leads to the use of the value-to-the-business model. This view, following FRED 29, seems to have changed in the interest of convergence.

Properties

A distinction must be made between *specialised properties and non-specialised properties.* Drawing on the work of the RICS, the ASB states that specialised properties are 'those which, due to their specialised nature, are rarely, if ever, sold on the open market for single occupation for continuation of their existing use, except as part of a sale of the business in occupation' (FRED 29, p. 57). Examples of specialised properties listed include oil refineries, power stations, hospitals, universities and museums. In addition a property may be regarded as specialised if, although otherwise normal, it is of such a substantial size given its location that there is no market for such properties.

Valuation of specialised properties

Because of the lack of a market for such assets they should be valued by reference to their depreciated replacement cost (Para. 53(c)).

Valuation of non-specialised properties

In assessing current value, an important difference between properties and most other tangible assets is that the value of properties depends heavily on the use to which the property is put. Consider as an example a warehouse in the middle of an area which had once been industrial but which is now increasingly residential. The value of the property as a warehouse might be much less than its value as a shell for conversion into flats, but, even so, the entity needs a warehouse and would, if deprived of the asset, replace it. Thus, following the principles underlying value to the business, the asset should be valued on the basis of its replacement cost. But we must be clear as to what is being replaced: in this case it is a warehouse not a potential housing site. Hence, FRS 15 specifies that, if they are being revalued, non-specialised assets:

> should be valued on the basis of existing use value (EUV), with the addition of notional directly attributable acquisition costs where material. Where the open market value (OMV) is materially different from EUV, the OMV and the reasons for the difference should be disclosed in the notes to the accounts. (Para. 53(a))

If the asset is surplus to the entity's requirements the above argument does not hold and hence these should be valued on the basis of the OMV less any expected material directly attributable selling costs (Para. 53(c)).

Detailed definitions of EUV and OMV are provided in the standard. Both models are based on an opinion of the best price at which the sale of an interest in the property would have been completed unconditionally for cash consideration at the date of valuation, on the assumption that there is a good market for the property and specifically that there is no possibility of a bid by a prospective purchaser with a special interest. The last of these factors means that the value would not be enhanced by the possibility that a specific potential purchaser, perhaps the owner of the adjacent property, might be prepared to pay more for the property than anyone else.

The essential difference between the two bases, EUV and OMV, is that the estimate of existing use value is based on the additional assumption 'that the property can be used for the foreseeable future only for the existing use' (p. 60).

The adoption of the proposals set out in FRED 29 would change this approach to the valuation of non-specialist buildings. Since FRED 29 is based on the fair value concept non-specialist buildings would be valued on the basis of their open market values rather than on the basis of their existing use value.

Reporting losses and gains on revaluation

There can be no question that losses on revaluation reduce owners' equity and gains on revaluation enhance it. The only issue that presently detains us is how the loss or gain should be reported; should it be through the profit and loss account or through the statement of total recognised gains and losses (STRGL)?

In FRS 15 a distinction is made between those losses that are caused by 'clear consumption of economic benefits' and other losses. A loss of the first type, which is regarded as being akin to depreciation, is usually due to a factor which is intrinsic to the asset, such as physical deterioration, while the second type of loss may be characterised by a general fall of value in the type of asset concerned.

The starting position is that 'All revaluation losses that are caused by a clear consumption of economic benefits should be recognised in the profit and loss account' (Para. 65).

Otherwise losses should be recognised in the STRGL.

Now for the complications. If the carrying amount falls below the depreciated historical cost then, in general, any further revaluation losses, whatever their cause, should be recognised in the profit and loss account. But there is an exception to this where it can be shown that the recoverable amount exceeds the revalued amount, in which case the loss should be recorded in the STRGL to the extent that the recoverable amount exceeds the revalued amount (Para. 65).

In order to help understand this it might be helpful to be reminded that a non-specialised property is valued by reference to its OMV. It may well be that the value of the property has fallen, because of a general fall in the market, but the directors of the entity can demonstrate that the recoverable amount (the present value of the cash flows that flow from the owner-ship of the asset) is greater than the OMV. The asset is still written down to its OMV, and owners' equity reduced, but as the loss is not regarded as resulting from a consumption of economic benefit it can be recorded in the STRGL.

Revaluation gains should in general be recognised in the STRGL other than to the extent that gain reverses revaluation losses on the same asset that were recognised in the profit and loss account (Para. 63).

Because the basis of valuation underpinning FRED 29 does not incorporate the notion of recoverable amount, the exposure draft's proposals on the treatment of revaluation losses is that:

- All revaluation losses that exceed existing revaluation surpluses should be charged to the profit and loss account

- Losses that are reversals of previously recognised gains should be shown in the STRGL. (Para. 38)

This would undoubtedly be a much more straightforward, if less theoretically sound, approach to apply in practice.

Reporting losses and gains on disposal

The profit or loss on the disposal of a tangible fixed asset should be accounted for in the profit and loss account of the period in which the disposal occurs as the difference between the dis-posal proceeds and the carrying amount, whether carried at historical cost (less any provisions made) or at a valuation. (Para. 72)

This formulation, which follows the relevant provision of FRS 3, Para. 21, gives rise to a seri-ous inconsistency. If the entity had, at some stage in the past, revalued the asset the revaluation gain would not have passed through the profit and loss account but would instead have been recorded in the STRGL. But if the asset had not been revalued the whole of the gain goes through the profit and loss account. The ASB recognises that this is inconsis-tent and in FRED 17, the exposure draft for FRS 15, it proposed that the whole of the gain should appear in the STRGL.

For a number of reasons the responses to FRED 17 made it clear that this proposal was not acceptable. It seems that the main reasons for this reaction were the view that it would be premature to make the change in advance of a more far reaching review of the STRGL and that the proposed treatment was inconsistent with the treatment of gains and losses on the disposal of businesses, subsidiaries and investments. Thus it appears, as we discuss in Chapter 11, that further changes are on their way.

Disclosures relating to revaluation

Paragraph 74 specifies what has to be disclosed, and includes details of the timing of valu-ations, the names and status of those who carried them out as well as the total amount of material notional directly attributable acquisition costs or expected selling costs that are included in the valuation.

Depreciation

Prior to the issue of FRS 15 depreciation merited its own standard. It was the subject of SSAP 12, which was issued in 1977, amended in 1981 and revised in 1987. The 1977 version was firmly rooted in the historical cost tradition while the 1987 revision was relevant to both historical cost and current value accounting.

To those well versed in the ethos of historical cost accounting and the mechanics of double entry bookkeeping depreciation is a pretty straightforward matter. The asset that the entity owns will be a source of economic benefit for a number of time periods and hence the recognition of the cost of the asset should be spread over the same period. To such folk, depreciation is all about spreading the cost or, to use a clumsier expression, expensing the asset.

To many other people, including many who run successful businesses, the idea is not so simple because they have difficulty in grasping the concept that the accountant wants to recognise the using up of an asset. The layman has difficulty in distinguishing this from a fall in the value of the asset and becomes completely confused when told that depreciation is necessary in a period in which the value of the asset is actually increasing.

Well brought-up accountants, on the other hand, know that they must distinguish between two events: the consumption of a portion of the asset and the increase in value of that part of the asset that remains:

> The fundamental objective of depreciation is to reflect in operating profit the cost of the use of the tangible fixed assets (i.e. amount of economic benefits consumed) in the period. This requires a charge to operating profit even if the asset has risen in value or been revalued. (FRS 15, Para. 78)

One major element of the continuing saga of accounting standards for depreciation is the desire of standard setters to ensure that all assets other than land, the one asset which most people would agree might not be consumed, are depreciated. There is, however, pressure from the business community to identify other exceptions. Investment properties provide an interesting example of an asset about which there has been a continuing debate. The requirement that investment properties be depreciated was included in the original 1977 version of SSAP 12 but was dropped, after pressure from property companies, from the 1981 version. In that year the ASC issued SSAP 19 *Accounting for Investment Properties* which, although threatened with review, is still in issue. We discuss SSAP 19 later in this chapter.

As we shall see, the ASB accepts that there are some assets either whose life is so long or whose likely residual value is so high that an annual depreciation charge would not be material. They do not, it must be noted, retreat from the position that all tangible assets (except land) depreciate, but they are prepared to concede that some do not depreciate very much. FRS 15 is therefore more flexible than its predecessors in accepting that depreciation need not be recognised in certain limited circumstances, but it extracts a price, the *Impairment Review*. If depreciation is not to be recognised on the grounds of immateriality the entity must undertake an impairment review. We will discuss this topic later in the chapter and at this point simply explain that an impairment review is a systematic process that tests whether an asset's carrying value exceeds its recoverable amount.

Depreciation is more easily applied to a single identifiable asset whose cost and condition can be relatively easily measured and whose economic contribution to the entity easily assessed, the latter point being relevant to decisions as to whether the carrying value of the asset should be reduced to its recoverable value. But life is not always as conveniently simple as this and assets are often used in combination. A particularly noteworthy feature of FRS 15 is the way in which it deals with the topic of combined and interrelated assets (see p. 113).

FRS 15 and depreciation

The topics covered in the depreciation section of FRS 15 can be summarised as follows:

- General principles
- Changes in the methods used to account for depreciation
- Changes in estimates of remaining useful life and residual value
- Combined assets
- Renewals accounting
- Disclosure

General principles

Depreciation is defined as:

> The measure of the cost or revalued amount of the economic benefits of the tangible fixed asset that have been consumed during the period.
>
> Consumption includes the wearing out, using up or other reductions in the useful economic life of a tangible fixed asset whether arising from use, effluxion of time or obsolescence through other changes in technology or demand for the goods and services produced by the asset. (Para. 2)

The underlying principle is:

> The depreciable amount of a tangible fixed asset should be allocated on a systematic basis over its useful economic life. The depreciation method used should reflect as fairly as possible the pattern in which the asset's economic benefits are consumed by the entity. The depreciation charge for each period should be recognised as an expense in the profit and loss account unless it is permitted to be included in the carrying amount of another asset. (Para. 77)

Depreciable amount is defined as:

> The cost of a tangible fixed asset (or, where an asset is revalued, the revalued amount) less its residual value. (p. 10)

The final sentence in Para. 77 is logically necessary if depreciation is to be included in the costs of stocks and work-in-process or the cost of a self-constructed fixed asset.

There are, of course, a number of methods of charging depreciation and two, straight line and reducing balance, are described in the text of the standard. In general, the method of depreciation employed should be consistent with the pattern of consumption of the benefit. If approximately constant annual benefits are expected throughout the asset's useful economic life, the straight line method would be appropriate. If, however, greater benefits were derived in the earlier years of the asset's life, then the reducing balance is likely to be the more appropriate method. If the pattern of consumption is uncertain, the Board notes that the straight line method is usually employed (Para. 81).

Interest methods of depreciation

There are other, arguably more sophisticated, methods of depreciation that take into account the time value of money. These are known as 'interest methods of depreciation' and, of these, the best known method is the annuity method. The basic idea is that the total cost of an asset is not simply the purchase price but it also includes the 'borrowing cost'. Suppose an asset costs £1 million and that it is to be entirely financed by borrowing over the total estimated life of the asset; the 'total' cost of the asset is then £1 million plus the cost of finance, say, £700,000. The interest charge would be at its maximum in year 1 and then reduce as the loan is paid off. Thus, if the benefits from the use of the asset are more or less constant each year and it is desired to match these benefits with a constant annual expense, a 'real straight line approach', then the depreciation element of the total expense would need to increase each year to offset the falling interest costs.

FRS 15 does not refer, either positively or negatively, to interest depreciation methods, but in June 2000, the ASB issued an exposure draft of an amendment to FRS 15 and FRS 10, which would outlaw the general use of such interest methods of depreciation:

> The annuity method, and other interest methods of depreciation that are designed to take into account the time value of money, should not be used to allocate the depreciable amount of a tangible fixed asset over its useful economic life. (Para. 1)

This proposed prohibition is not based upon any fundamental criticism of the interest methods of depreciation. Indeed, the exposure draft states quite clearly 'in principle, interest methods more fairly reflect the economic cost of the benefits consumed in each accounting period' (Para. 2). Rather, the proposed prohibition was based upon grounds of comparability. If most companies are not using interest-based depreciation methods, then no companies should be permitted to use interest-based depreciation methods!

A second reason for the prohibition can also be recognised. Use of the annuity method of depreciation results in a low–high pattern of depreciation charges over the life of the fixed asset; the depreciation expense is 'back-end loaded'. This is therefore less conservative than the more usual straight line method of depreciation. The ASB did not wish to prohibit the use of back-end loaded depreciation methods in general, for the exposure draft accepted that a low–high pattern of depreciation will be appropriate where this reflects the expected pattern of consumption of economic benefits without regard to the time value of money.

No such provision is found in FRED 29 which, like FRS 15, manages to avoid specific reference to interest-based methods of depreciation. At the time of writing (January 2003) the proposed amendment to FRS 15 and FRS 10 had never been implemented nor withdrawn. The ASB's web page[16] states that the issue of interest methods of depreciation will be considered in the context of its leasing project (see Chapter 9) but also points out that FRS 15 is to be superseded by FRED 29. The relevance of the latter comment is not obvious, however, since there are no differences between FRS 15 and FRED 29 on this issue.

Depreciation and materiality

As we noted earlier, one of the more interesting features of FRS 15 is its acceptance that the depreciation charge may not always be material. The drafting of the relevant part of the standard is a little strange in that it does not say that depreciation need not be recognised but instead says what must happen when it is not recognised.

> Tangible fixed assets, other than non-depreciable land, should be reviewed for impairment, in accordance with FRS 11, at the end of each reporting period when either:
>
> (a) no depreciation charge is made on the grounds that it would be immaterial (either because of the length of the estimated remaining useful life or because the estimated residual value of the tangible fixed asset is not materially different from the carrying value of the asset); or
>
> (b) the estimated remaining economic life of the tangible fixed asset exceeds 50 years.
>
> (Para. 89)

[16] **www.asb.org.uk** (current projects).

Of the two grounds for immateriality, high residual value is generally more problematic than long life, as assets with very long lives, such as paintings and sculptures, can usually be readily identified. This is much less true of the high residual value group and hence the standard sets out a number of factors which could be used to justify the case for immateriality, including whether the assets are regularly maintained and whether, in the past, similar assets have been sold for amounts close to their carrying values.

Changes in the method of depreciation

A change is only permitted on the grounds that the new method will give a fairer presentation of the results and financial position (Para. 82). The change is not to be regarded as a change in accounting policy and hence the carrying amount of the asset at the date of change is simply depreciated, using the new method, over its remaining useful life.

Changes in estimated useful remaining life and residual value

The useful remaining economic life of a TFA should be reviewed at the end of each accounting period if 'expectations are significantly different from previous estimates' (Para. 93) while, 'Where the residual value is material it should be reviewed at the end of each reporting period' (Para. 95).

The standard, in respect of remaining useful life, seems rather unhelpful and tautological in that it is not possible to know whether expectations have changed without carrying out a review, albeit a superficial one.

The residual value should be measured on the basis of the same prices as apply to the carrying value of the asset, either the prices at acquisition or a subsequent valuation.

Note that one review, that for assets with long lives, only has to be carried out if there are significantly different expectations while the other, for assets with high residual values, has to be done annually. But this does depend on what is regarded as material in the case of the residual value. Of course if it is very material, depreciation may not be recognised, in which case an annual impairment review would be required.

The accounting consequences in changes of estimates of both types are the same: in each case no change is made to past results and the current carrying value is written off over the revised period or on the basis of the new assumption of residual value.

Combined assets

When an asset is made up of two or more of what the standard describes as 'major components' that have substantially different economic lives then each component should be treated separately for the purposes of depreciation (Para. 83). This is, of course, an approach that has been adopted for many years in the case of land and buildings but there are many other circumstances where it might sensibly be applied.

Renewals accounting

Renewals accounting is a technique that has been developed to deal with what might be termed an *infrastructure system* or *network*. An example of such might be a subway or light railway system. The trains, stations and other major identifiable assets can be treated as separate items but the system also includes, and depends on, a myriad of wires, computer chips and other small components. Such a situation poses some interesting questions. Should the cost of the small components be written off in the year of acquisition or should they be treated as other TFAs (for TFAs they surely are) and written off over their useful economic lives?

Neither approach is satisfactory. The first is unsatisfactory because it might produce a very unrealistic charge to profit and loss that would not adequately reflect the economic benefit consumed. It also would allow for manipulation of the reported profit, that is, cut back essential expenditure if there was a desire to increase profit, spend heavily in advance if there was a desire to reduce profit. The alternative approach is unrealistic in a practical sense, in that it would cost far too much to account individually for the millions of small components.

Renewals accounting can – in appropriate circumstances – be used to overcome the dilemma. The use of renewals accounting depends on knowing the level of expenditure required to maintain the operating capacity of the system. As an example it might be agreed that it requires £20 million per annum to be spent on the replacement of the smaller components in order to maintain the operating capacity of the system, which might be defined as the ability to operate the same number of trains travelling at the same average speed at the same level of reliability. Then, under renewals accounting, £20 million is the annual depreciation charge to be made to the profit and loss account and added to accumulated depreciation. The actual expenditure per year is capitalised and added to the cost of the asset. Hence, if the entity actually spends £20 million in a year, the carrying value would be maintained, if less, the carrying value is reduced and, if more, it would be increased. Note the primacy that is given to the charge to the profit and loss account. Assuming that £20 million is indeed a good estimate of the average cost then £20 million is the annual expense irrespective of the pattern of spending.

The treatment is not without its theoretical problems, for it could be argued that any excess expenditure over the £20 million is in effect a prepayment because less will have to be incurred in future years, while the effect of spending less is to create something very akin to an accrued expense. In other words, would it be better to reflect the differences between actual and planned expenditure in the working capital part of the balance sheet rather than in the cost of fixed assets?

In practice it is unlikely that the differences between planned and actual expenditure would be very large, in that one of the conditions that has to be satisfied, if renewals accounting is to be used, is that the system is mature, or in a steady state, and that the annual cost of maintenance is relatively constant (Para. 99). The other significant condition is that the required level of annual expenditure is derived from an asset management plan that has been certified by a suitably qualified and independent person (Para. 97).

Disclosure requirements relating to depreciation

The disclosure requirements are to be found in Para. 100. In summary they require that, for each class of TFA, the following be shown:

- the depreciation method used;
- the useful economic lives or the rates of depreciation used;
- the financial effects of any changes in estimates of either the remaining useful life or residual value, but only if material;
- the cost, or revalued amount, accumulated depreciation and net carrying amount at the beginning of the financial period and at the balance sheet date;
- a reconciliation of the movements.

In addition, Para. 102 requires that if there has been a change in the method of depreciation, the effect, if material, and the reason for the change should be disclosed.

FRED 29 and depreciation

Part of the cost of convergence is the adoption of less satisfactory standards and the treatment of depreciation provides a good example of this. In both instances of difference between FRS 15 and FRED 29, the latter adopts the inferior approach. The two areas are Renewals accounting and Charges in the estimates of residual values.

Renewals accounting

FRED 29 makes no reference to renewals accounting, which means that it provides no help in dealing with the dilemma we described on p. 113. This is a serious omission and the ASB has asked respondents to the exposure draft whether the absence of guidance from the standard would prevent entities from using renewals accounting and whether they believe that UK entities should be permitted to continue to use the method.

Changes in the estimates of residual values

When expected residual values change, FRS 15 requires that they be based on prices that are consistent with those used in determining the carrying value of the asset, either the prices at acquisition or, if the asset is not being carried at historical cost, the prices that prevailed at the most recent revaluation. In contrast FRED 29, in accordance with IAS 16, proposes that the prices used should be those at the date of the restatement of the residual value. FRED 29 states:

> An estimate of an asset's residual value is based on the amount recoverable from disposal, at the date of the estimate of similar assets that have reached the ends of their useful lives and have operated under conditions similar to those in which the asset will be used. (Para. 46)

While in many cases the differences between the two approaches will in practice be immaterial the FRED 29 proposal does mix up different bases of measurement, historical cost and current valuation. Consider the following example.

Suppose a company, which records assets on the basis of historical cost, buys an asset for £800 000 which has a life of five years and an estimated residual value of £300 000 and further suppose that all prices increase by 50 per cent at the start of year 3.

FRS 15

Annual depreciation charge £100 000 but excess provision for depreciation of £150 000 written back in year 5, as the residual value is £450 000 not £300 000.

FRED 29

Depreciation in years 1 and 2: £100 000. But since, due to the doubling of the prices, assets that are five years old are being sold for £450 000, the company would at the end of year 3 have to write off £150 000 (£600 000 − £450 000) over three years, so the depreciation charges for years 3–5 would be £50 000 per year, but, if prices stayed constant, there would be no excess depreciation to write back.

Compliance with International Accounting Standards

The implementation of FRED 29 would to a very large extent bring convergence between UK and International Standards. Table 5.2 summarises the changes that would be made if the proposals of FRED 29 were implemented also serves as a distillation of the existing differences between FRS 15 and the international standards and exposure drafts. The table shows that the only fundamental difference is in the basis for arriving at current value.

Table 5.2 Summary of the differences between FRED 29 and FRS 15

Topic	FRED 29 treatment	FRS 15 treatment
Basis of current value	Fair value (market value)	Current value (value to the business)
Terminology	(a) Property, plant and equipment (b) Borrowing costs	(a) Tangible fixed assets (b) Finance costs
Assets acquired in exchange	Should where possible be measured in terms of the fair value of assets given up	No coverage
Treatment of revaluation losses	Does not distinguish between losses caused by the consumption of economic benefit and other losses, nor does it take account of an asset's recoverable value	Distinguishes between such losses and takes account of recoverable value
Renewals accounting	Not covered	Included
Price level to be used in the revision of residual values	At the date of the revision	Either those relating to the date of acquisition or those prevailing at the most recent revaluation of the asset, whichever is appropriate

Investment properties

One important group of TFA, investment properties, needs to be considered separately because of the different accounting treatment that applies in their case. Investment properties have been a major feature of two interrelated debates: to depreciate or not depreciate and to revalue or not to revalue.

The original, 1977, version of the first standard on depreciation, SSAP 12, did not exclude investment properties from its scope and required all buildings, including those held for investment, to be depreciated. This was fiercely contested by property companies whose profits would, of course, be substantially reduced if they had to provide for depreciation on their buildings. It was argued that the profits of property companies would be distorted if depreciation were charged to the profit and loss account while the surpluses on revaluation had, under the provisions which were then in force of SSAP 6 (*Extraordinary Items and Prior Year Adjustments*), to be credited to reserves.

The ASC's response (which may, according to taste, be described as reflecting the committee's weakness or its flexibility) was to allow companies owning investment properties exemption from this provision, and this exemption was confirmed with the issue, in 1981, of SSAP 19 *Accounting for Investment Properties*, which specified the conditions under which depreciation need not be charged on properties held as investments.

It was argued in SSAP 19 that, for the proper appreciation of the position of the enterprise, it is of prime importance for users of the accounts to be aware of the current value of the investment properties and the changes in their values. For this purpose investment properties are defined as an interest in land and/or buildings:

(a) in respect of which construction work and development have been completed; and

(b) that is held for its investment potential, any rental income being negotiated at arm's length.

The following are specifically excluded from the definition:

(a) A property that is owned and occupied by a company for its own purposes is not an investment property.

(b) A property let to and occupied by another group company is not an investment property for the purposes of its own accounts or the group accounts.

The standard was revised in July 1994, to take account of the introduction of the new performance statement, the statement of total recognised gains and losses, but otherwise the revised version is virtually identical to the original version and reflects more the attitudes of 1981 than those of 1994.

In outline, SSAP 19 specifies:

● 'Investment properties should not be subject to a depreciation charge as otherwise required by SSAP 12 (now FRS 15), except for properties held on a lease which should be depreciated on the basis set out in SSAP 12 at least over the period when the unexpired term is 20 years or less' (SSAP 19, Para. 10). In other words, leaseholds with more than 20 years to run can be depreciated while other leases must be depreciated.

● Investment properties should be included in the balance sheet at their 'open market value', which might be defined as the best price at which the asset might reasonably be expected to be sold. The bases of valuation should be disclosed in a note to the accounts.

● The names of the persons making the valuation, or particulars of their qualification, should be disclosed together with the bases of valuation used by them. If the person making the valuation is an employee or officer of the company or group that owns the property, this should be disclosed.

● The carrying value of the investment properties and the investment revaluation reserve should be displayed prominently.

● With one exception (see below), changes in the market value of investment properties should not be taken to the profit and loss account but should be treated as a movement on an investment revaluation reserve and, consequently, be included in the STRGL. The exception is when there is a deficit on an individual property that is expected to be permanent; in this case the deficit should be charged to the profit and loss account.[17]

The ASB notes that the application of the standard will usually represent a departure from the legal requirement to provide depreciation on any fixed asset which has a limited economic life, but justifies this on the grounds that this treatment will more closely adhere to the overriding requirement to provide a true and fair view. In such circumstances the financial statements must include a statement giving particulars of the departures from the specific requirements of the Act with the reasons for and effect of the departure.[18]

Not everyone would agree with the stance, originally taken by the ASC in 1981 and confirmed by the ASB in 1994, in that it does appear that a fuller, truer and fairer picture would

[17] There is an exception to the exception in the case of investment companies and unit trusts, where deficits on individual investment properties may only be shown in the STRGL (SSAP 19, p. 13, as amended in 1994).

[18] Companies Act 1985, s. 222(5) as amended by Companies Act 1989, s. 4.

be revealed if both the increase in value and the proportion of the total value that has been consumed by the passage of time were shown in the financial statements.

It does appear that the life of SSAP 19 is limited in that in FRS 15 the ASB makes the point that it was considering the treatment of investment properties, in tandem with the international project on this subject. The ASB believes that it is appropriate to maintain the status quo until this work is completed[19] and hence investment properties were excluded from the scope of FRS 15, as they are from FRED 29.

Intangible assets

Some intangible assets are very identifiable and separable; patents and the right to use a famous brand name, are examples. Intangible assets like these can be easily bought and sold. But this is not true for other types of intangible asset.

In this 'Information Age', the skill and loyalty of its staff may be an entity's only significant asset. While this is an economically significant asset it is not, since the abolition of slavery, readily saleable. In practice the only way that the owner of such an entity can sell this asset is to dispose of the company that employs the skilled staff, in which case the sales proceeds will be very much greater than the sum of the carrying values of the assets and liabilities that have been recognised in the company's balance sheet.

In many cases it is very difficult to disentangle intangible assets from other residual elements that make up goodwill. This is why the ASB has chosen to deal with both goodwill and intangible assets in the same standard, FRS 10, *Goodwill and Intangible Assets.*

In the Discussion Paper[20] that preceded FRS 10 the Board expressed the view that certain intangible assets such as brands and the titles of published works could not be disposed of separately from the business and that there was, in any event, no generally agreed way of valuing such assets. Hence, the Board intimated that it was of a mind to specify that intangible assets that were part of a business acquisition should be subsumed within the value attributable to goodwill. This suggestion was met with strong opposition as corporate respondents said that such assets were critical to their business and that it was important to account for them separately (App. III, Para. 22).

The Board accepted that point and hence accepted that intangible assets can sometimes be separated from goodwill and shown as such, as long as they satisfy the legal and conceptual requirements for identifiability and can, at the time they are initially recognised, be measured with sufficient reliability. However, given what will in many cases be a pretty hazy distinction, the second principle underlying FRS 10 is that in order to avoid the results of the entity being shown in a more, or less, favourable light, merely by classifying expenditure as an intangible asset rather than goodwill, the accounting treatment of intangible assets and goodwill should be aligned (App. III, Para. 23).

We will return to FRS 10 in Chapter 13 when dealing with goodwill, and in this chapter we shall concentrate on the standard's treatment of intangible assets.

[19] FRS 15, p. 94.
[20] *Goodwill and Intangible Assets*, ASB, 1993.

FRS 10 and its treatment of intangible assets

In this section of the chapter we will discuss the following topics:

- The nature of intangible assets and the conditions necessary for recognition as a separate asset
- The determination of their carrying value at initial recognition
- The depreciation of intangible assets
- The revaluation of intangible assets
- Disclosure requirements

The nature of intangible assets

Intangible assets are defined as:

> **Non-financial fixed assets that do not have a physical substance but are identifiable and are controlled by the entity through custody or legal rights. (Para. 2)**

Identifiable assets are defined in FRS 10, in line with company legislation, as assets that are capable of being disposed of without disposing of a business of the entity.[21] So the test is, in simple terms, can the asset be sold without forcing the entity to get out of one or more of its businesses?

It is recognised that control can be exercised other than through the possession of legal rights; it can also be exercised through *custody*. An example of control through custody is technical or intellectual knowledge that is maintained secretly.

Initial carrying value

In determining the value at initial recognition we need to consider three cases – *intangible assets purchased separately from a business*, *internally developed intangible assets* and *intangible assets that are purchased as part of the acquisition of a business*.

The first is straightforward: an intangible asset purchased separately **should** be capitalised at its cost (Para. 9).

An internally developed intangible fixed asset **may** be capitalised only if it has a readily ascertainable market value (Para. 14). Note that in this case the entity has the choice whether to capitalise the asset or not. This means that it is very difficult to compare the results of companies in industries where, by the nature of the business, internally generated intangible assets are of significance.

The test of whether the internally generated asset can be recognised is whether it has a readily ascertainable market value which is a value that is established by reference to a market where:

(a) the asset belongs to a homogenous population of assets that are equivalent in all material respects; and

(b) an active market, evidenced by frequent transactions, exists for that population of assets (Para. 2).

---

[21] This seems to be a case where the use of the word does not accord with its basic meaning, as there are many 'identifiable' assets, such as the human resource of a business, that are readily identifiable but do not satisfy the accounting definition.

This is a stringent condition for recognition and would preclude assets such as brands and publishing titles that are one-offs that are not equivalent 'in all material respects' to a group of other assets.[22]

The third type of asset, an intangible fixed asset acquired as part of a purchase of a business:

> should be capitalised separately from goodwill if its value can be measured reliably on initial recognition. It should initially be recorded at its fair value, subject to the constraint that, unless the asset has a readily ascertainable market value, the fair value should be limited to an amount that does not create negative goodwill arising on acquisition. (Para. 10)

So there are two tests for recognition. Is the asset separable and, if so, can it be measured reliably?

The measurement test depends on whether it is possible to determine the asset's fair value. We discussed the problematic definition of fair value earlier in the chapter, and would repeat our conclusion here, that the use of fair values based solely on market values can be problematic. In the case of intangible fixed assets, FRS 10 recognises that many intangible assets are unique and are not traded in the market and the ASB accepts that acceptable techniques for their valuation have been developed including multiples of turnover and, where these exist, they can be used to provide a fair value for intangible assets.

In order to avoid the creation of negative goodwill a restriction is placed on the fair value that can be assigned to intangible assets. The fair value is reduced until the negative value of goodwill disappears, unless, that is, the carrying value of the intangible asset satisfies the more stringent test of being based on a readily ascertainable market value.

Depreciation of intangible fixed assets

We have already, in the context of FRS 15, discussed the arguments as to whether all fixed assets, other than land, should be depreciated. Intangible assets provide, of course, a very fruitful field for this debate.

FRS 10 takes a more relaxed line on the need to depreciate than FRS 15 where the view was that 'all tangible fixed assets, other than land, depreciate but the amount may not be material'. It is recognised in FRS 10 that certain intangible assets, not possessing a physical form that must wither with time, can have an indefinite life. Thus:

> Where goodwill and intangible assets are regarded as having indefinite useful economic lives, they should not be amortised. (Para. 17; note the word 'should')

The estimation of the useful life of a fixed asset is usually fairly subjective but this is particularly true in the case of intangible assets. The standard does specifically warn against using the uncertainty of the estimate as grounds for selecting an unrealistically short life (Para. 22). In addition to the impairment reviews, the useful lives of intangible assets should be reviewed at the end of each reporting period and revised if necessary (Para. 33).

The standard draws a distinction between those assets whose estimated lives are less than 20 years and those which have either an estimated life of 20 or more years or an indefinite life. The choice of 20 years as the cut-off is 'based largely on judgement' (App. III, Para. 33).

---

[22] As we will explain later in the following chapter FRS 10 does not cover the potential intangible assets that might result from development expenditure.

Assets with a life not exceeding 20 years

Because of the greater subjectivity, and because of the problems of separability when they are acquired as part of a purchase of a business, intangible assets are subject to more rigorous requirements than tangible assets. Intangible assets must be the subject of an impairment review:

(a) at the end of the first full financial year following the acquisition (the 'first year' review): and
(b) in other periods if events or changes in circumstances indicate that the carrying values may not be recoverable (Para. 34).

Assets with a life of 20 years or more, including those with an indefinite life

There is a rebuttable presumption that the useful life of purchased goodwill and intangible assets is limited to periods of 20 years or less. This presumption can be rebutted only if:

(a) the durability of the acquired business or intangible asset can be demonstrated and justifies estimating a life to exceed 20 years; and
(b) the goodwill or intangible asset is capable of continued measurement (so that annual impairment reviews will be feasible) (Para. 19).

Thus a case has to be made to justify a life of 20 years or more and an annual impairment review is required.

Revaluation of intangible assets

Only an intangible asset that has a readily ascertainable market value (see p. 119) may be revalued to its market value. If such a policy is selected then, in line with the provisions of FRS 15 for tangible assets, if one asset is revalued all intangible assets of the same class must be revalued and the operation must be repeated sufficiently often to ensure that the carrying value does not differ materially from the market value (Para. 43).

The effect of Para. 43 is that those intangible assets that were recognised as part of the purchase of the business on the grounds *inter alia* that they could be reliably measured, but for which a readily ascertainable market value does not exist, cannot be revalued. One of the members of the ASB argued, in a note of dissent, that it was inconsistent to accept that the reliability of measurement that was sufficient for initial recognition could not be the basis of subsequent valuation (App. IV, Para. 8).

Impairment losses can be reversed only in respect of those assets that have a readily ascertainable market value or, in what are regarded as rare circumstances, where both the original impairment loss and its subsequent reversal are attributable to external events (Para. 44). It is argued that to allow reversal in other circumstances would, in effect, be allowing the capitalisation of internally generated intangible assets.

Disclosure requirements

In general the disclosure requirements, to be found in Paras 52 to 59, are similar to those set out in FRS 15 in respect of tangible fixed assets. The additional requirements include the need to state, if appropriate, the grounds for rebutting the 20-year life presumption, which should be a reasoned explanation based on the specific factors contributing to the durability of the asset.

Compliance with international accounting standards

The corresponding international standard IAS 38, issued in 1998, does not differ from FRS 10 in substance but there are some differences in detail, including:

- IAS 38 does not accept that intangible assets can have an indefinite life and hence requires amortisation of such assets in all circumstances.
- Internally developed intangibles can, under the international standard, be capitalised as long as costs can be measured reliably. Thus a readily ascertainable market value is not required. But since IAS 38 specifically states that the costs of generating brands, mastheads and similar assets cannot be measured reliably, there are unlikely to be significant differences in practice between the two approaches.

Differences in the treatment of tangible and intangible fixed assets

We referred earlier to the difficulties that standard setters experienced in distinguishing between tangible and intangible assets. We are now in a position to consider the consequences of the decision. They may be summarised as follows:

- More stringent rules are applied to the recognition of intangible assets; e.g. an internally generated intangible asset can only be recognised if it has a readily ascertainable market value.
- An entity might choose not to recognise an internally generated intangible asset but would have to recognise a self-constructed tangible asset.
- It is more likely that depreciation would not be charged against intangible assets.
- Intangible assets are more likely to be subject to impairment reviews.

The more stringent rules applied to the recognition of intangible assets has a profound effect on the extent to which conventional financial statements can adequately report on the major assets that comprise an enterprise. The tangible assets of a successful management consultancy company will be minimal in comparison to the value of the business, as the real assets of such a company are to be found in such things as the skills and competence of its staff, its reputation and access to clients. It is very unlikely that such assets will have readily ascertainable market values and hence cannot be recognised if they have been internally generated. But if they have been acquired as part of the purchase the assets will find their way to a balance sheet, albeit as part of goodwill. So much for comparability!

Impairment reviews

It is a long-established principle that a fixed asset should be written down if its carrying value exceeds its economic worth to the entity but, prior to the publication of FRS 11, *Impairment of Fixed Assets and Goodwill*, there was little guidance on how to measure the economic worth of the asset and how any losses should be treated. For reasons, that we will describe below, the concept of recoverable amount, that will be rejected in the case of individual assets if the proposals of FRED 29 are implemented, would survive in the context of impairment reviews. The reason for this is that an impairment review is normally conducted on the basis of the cash flows associated with a bundle of assets, or *income-generating units*, and not the fair values of the assets. However, the provisions of FRS 11 fit more logically with FRS 15 than they would with a standard based on FRED 29.

FRS 11 *Impairment of Fixed Assets and Goodwill*

This standard is the last of the trinity dealing with fixed assets. Its main purpose is to set the principles and methodology for accounting for the impairment of fixed assets and goodwill which necessitates the reduction of their carrying values to their recoverable amounts. We have already introduced the term *recoverable amount*, which we defined as the higher of an asset's net realisable value and value in use.

The standard does not deal with investments covered by the Board's projects on derivatives and other financial instruments.

An impairment review is an exercise involving the valuation of an individual asset, where it is possible to assign the generation of cash flows to an individual asset, or, otherwise, the smallest bundle of assets to which a series of cash flows can be related.

In discussing FRS 11 we will cover the following topics:

- When to perform an impairment review
- The calculation of recoverable amount
- The bundle of assets to be valued or the 'income-generating unit'
- The estimation of cash flow
- The choice of discount rates
- The allocation of impairment losses
- Subsequent monitoring of cash flows
- Disclosure

When to perform an impairment review

We have already touched upon the special requirements for goodwill and intangible assets (see p. 121). For the generality of assets a review need only be carried out if 'events and changes in circumstances indicate that the carrying amount of the fixed asset or goodwill may not be recoverable' (Para. 8).

The events or circumstances can relate specifically to the asset, such as the emergence of a new, more efficient version, or to the business in which the asset is used, perhaps the making of large losses over an extended period. It is, of course, not possible to define precisely what constitutes a significant event that should trigger a review. This must be a matter of judgement at the margin, although there will be events of such magnitude that there will be no doubt as to the need for a review.

The calculation of recoverable amount

> Recoverable amount is the higher of an asset's net realisable value and its value in use and . . . , in making the comparison between value in use and net realisable value, regard must be paid to deferred tax balances that would arise in each case. (Para. 19).

Otherwise the calculations are made on the basis of pre-tax flows.

It is then necessary to compare the carrying value of the asset with the recoverable amount. Only where the recoverable amount is lower than the carrying value is it necessary to write down the asset.

While the standard sets out, in some considerable detail, how the calculations of value in use should be made, it also points out that in many cases a simple estimate will be enough to demonstrate that the value in use is either above the carrying value or below net realisable value, thus obviating the need for a more detailed calculation.

Income-generating units

Ideally, the value in use of assets should be estimated on an individual basis but this is often not possible, because of what the economists call the allocation problem, that is the impossibility of dividing the cash flows generated by the whole business between the individual assets. Thus, it is necessary to identify *income-generating units* that are found by dividing the total income stream of the entity into as many largely independent income streams as is reasonably possible. With the exception of any central assets which cannot meaningfully be apportioned across the units, all the identifiable assets and liabilities, excluding deferred tax balances, interest-bearing debt, dividends payable and other items relating wholly to finance, should be attributed to, or apportioned between, the various income-generating units.

Thus the main business is divided into two or more 'mini-businesses', as independent as possible. In practice, the businesses may not be very 'mini' for, given the highly integrated nature of many enterprises, it may not be possible to break down some very large entities into more than two or three income-generating units. An illustration of this is one of the examples provided in the standard. This is of a transport company that operates a number of trunk routes each fed by a number of supporting routes. In this case the units are each of the trunk routes together with their supporting routes.

In some cases it is possible to apportion central assets, such as the head office, to the different units using some rule of thumb such as proportion of turnover. This is more likely to be possible when the units are fairly homogeneous in nature. When they are very different, involving, say, a large-volume manufacturing plant and a small highly specialised research laboratory, this might not be possible. In such cases it may be necessary first to undertake a review at the level of the individual units, ignoring the asset value and the income flows relating to the central asset, and then to combine the units with the central assets and to again compare carrying value with recoverable amount. It might be that no impairment is identified at the individual unit level but is found at the aggregate level.

As we will explain in Chapter 13 a similar approach is used for goodwill.

The estimation of the cash flows

The standard is quite prescriptive in the way it requires the cash flows necessary to allow an asset's (or more likely an income-generating unit's) value in use to be estimated. The estimates must be based on two elements, first the most up-to-date budgets and plans that have been approved by management which, other than in exceptional circumstances, should be for a period not exceeding five years. Thereafter the cash flows should be based on the assumption of steady or declining (but not increasing) growth rates and that, again with a let-out in exceptional circumstances, the growth rate used should not exceed the long-term average of the country or countries in which the entity operates (Para. 36). Note that the rules are framed in terms of the growth rate not the rate itself, hence if the average rate of growth in the period covered by the budgets was, say, 3 per cent it would be permissible to extrapolate this rate of growth into the future so long as it was consistent with estimates of the growth rate in the appropriate country or countries.

In general the cash flow estimates should be based on the current condition of the assets and should include neither future expected cash savings from future reorganisations for which provision has not yet been made nor future capital expenditure that will enhance the asset in excess of its originally assessed standard of performance (Para. 38). There is one exception to this provision that applies in the case of a newly acquired income-generating unit such as a subsidiary. In instances such as these the purchase price might well reflect the synergies that will result from the acquisition but which will depend on additional expenditure. In these cases the cash flow estimates can, up till the end of the first full year following the acquisition, take the costs and benefits resulting from that expenditure into account (Para. 39).

Discount rate

> The present value of the income-generating unit under review should be calculated by discounting the expected cash flows of the unit. The discount rate used should be an estimate of the rate the market would expect on an equally risky investment. It should exclude the effects of any risk for which the cash flow has been adjusted and should be calculated on a pre-tax basis. (Para. 41)

The standard goes on to suggest ways by which the rate can be estimated, placing great emphasis on the need to ensure that the rates used for comparison are derived from cash flows from operations with the same risk profile or are adjusted for risk. The ASB is a trifle sanguine about the ease with which adjustments can be made for risk. As an example, it states (Para. 45) that it is likely that the use of a discount rate equal to the rate of return that the market would expect on an equally risky investment is likely to be the easiest way of dealing with risk, which begs the question of how one finds an equally risky investment. It goes on the state that an equally acceptable alternative is to adjust the cash flows for risk and then to discount using a risk-free rate, e.g. government bond rate, which begs the question of how to adjust the cash flows for risk (Para. 45)!

The standard warns against the danger of double-counting inflation: if cash flows are expressed in current prices they should be discounted using a real discount rate, if expressed in future prices a nominal discount rate should be employed (Para. 46).

The allocation of impairment losses

When the impairment review is conducted at the level of the income-generating unit it might not be possible to identify the asset whose carrying value should be reduced. If it is not obvious then the procedure specified in FRS 11 is to allocate the impairment loss first to those assets whose value is the most subjective. Hence the order is:

1 Goodwill
2 Any capitalised intangible asset
3 The tangible assets, on a pro rata or more appropriate bases (Para. 48)

Subsequent monitoring of cash flows

In those cases where the recoverable amount is based on the, generally, more subjective of the possible two measures, the asset's *value in use*, the standard requires that, for the period of five years following the review, the cash flows actually achieved should be compared with those used in the review (Para. 54). Such a comparison can have only three outcomes: the actual cash flows may be broadly in line with those that had been estimated, in which case no further action is required, or the position may turn out to be better or worse than had been originally anticipated.

If the cash flows turn out to be better than had been forecast then it might be possible to recognise a complete or partial reversal of the impairment loss.

If the actual cash flows are worse than had been expected, then the additional loss that would have been shown, had the actual cash flows been used, must be recognised.

Disclosure requirements

These appear at Paras 67–73 and may be summarised as follows:

- Impairment losses shown in the profit and loss account should, if appropriate, be shown as an exceptional item; those appearing in the STRGL should be disclosed separately.
- For assets shown at depreciated historical costs the impairment losses should be included within cumulative depreciation.
- If the loss is measured by reference to value in use, the discount rate used should be disclosed and, if a risk-free rate is used, an indication of the risk adjustments made to the cash flow should be provided.
- If an impairment loss is reversed, information relating to the circumstances and assumptions used in the calculation of the recoverable amount must be provided.
- If, in the measurement of value in use, the period before the assumption of steady or declining growth extends to more than five years, the note should state both the length of the period and its justification; if the long-term growth rate exceeds the average, the rate used and its justification should also be provided.

It can be seen that superficially a great deal of information has to be provided, especially in relation to value-in-use calculations but, in practice, there must be some doubt as to the extent that the disclosures will be useful to users of the financial statements, who may have difficulty in determining the reasonableness of the assumptions underpinning the calculations.

Compliance with international accounting standards

The equivalent international standard is IAS 36 *Impairment of Assets*, which was issued in 1998. The basic approach of the two standards is the same and, while the detailed requirements are very similar, among the more interesting differences are:

- The FRS treats intangible assets in much the same way as goodwill while the IAS aligns their treatment to that of tangible assets. As a consequence, for the allocation of impairment losses, the FRS sets them off first against intangible assets, while the IAS sets them off against all assets pro rata; for the recognition of the reversal of impairment losses, the IAS does not restrict the reversal of losses in respect of intangible assets.
- The FRS requires estimates of value in use to be monitored for five years, the IAS does not.
- The IAS has additional disclosure requirements.

Summary

In this chapter, we have examined the accounting treatment of both tangible and intangible fixed assets. We have examined the initial recognition and measurement of such assets, the need for depreciation and how to handle changes that occur over time, including impairment. We have seen that, whereas most countries in the world require the use of historical cost accounting, the UK is one of the few countries to permit upward revaluations of fixed assets under its 'mixed measurement approach'.

We have seen that the financial reporting standards relating to fixed assets are very flexible at a fundamental level while they are more rigid at the operational level. Thus companies may choose whether or not to capitalise borrowing costs and, perhaps much more seriously, may choose whether to show their various classes of fixed assets on the basis of historical cost or at current values. The choices which they make may lead to enormous differences between financial statements in practice and hence raise serious questions about the comparability of financial statements.

There has been considerable vacillation on the key issue of how to determine current values. It appeared that the ASB had finally settled on the value-to-the-business approach, the basis that is now enshrined in its *Statement of Principles*, but this now seems to be in flux as it appears that the Board is prepared to accept the alternative fair value approach in order to achieve convergence between UK and international standards.

One very major issue remains sorely neglected. For an increasing number of businesses the major assets are intangible, including staff competence, knowledge and reputation. Such assets do not usually appear among the assets of a business unless they have been acquired as part of the purchase of another business when they may appear as part of the figure for goodwill. We are still some way from developing financial reporting standards that require the recognition of such major assets in financial statements in a systematic fashion.

Recommended reading

'Avoiding depreciation', *Company Reporting*, No. 134, August 2001.

C.R. Baker, *Impairment tests for goodwill instead of amortisation: the potential impact on British companies*, Colchester, University of Essex Department of Accounting, Finance and Management, 2001.

W.T. Baxter, 'Depreciation and interest', *Accountancy*, October 2000.

B. Lev, 'Rethinking accounting – Intangibles at a cross road: what's next?', *Financial Executive* March/April 2002.

Excellent up-to-date and detailed reading on the subject matter of this chapter and on much of the contents of this book is provided by the most recent edition of:

UK and International GAAP, A. Wilson, M. Davies, M. Curtis and G. Wilkinson-Riddle, (eds), Ernst & Young, Butterworths Tolley, London. At the time of writing, the latest edition is the 7th, published in 2001.

Questions

5.1 The valuation and depreciation of fixed assets are covered by both mandatory accounting standards and the Companies Acts as sources of authority.

Requirement
Identify the main accounting issues involved in the valuation and depreciation of fixed assets and discuss to what extent these are addressed in the above sources of authority.

ICAEW, Financial Reporting, November 1995   (**10 marks**)

5.2 The managing director of your company has always been unhappy at depreciating the company's properties because he argues that these properties are in fact appreciating in value.

Recently he heard of another company which has investment properties and does not depreciate those properties.

You are required to write a report to your managing director explaining:
(a) **the consequence of not depreciating the company's existing properties;**   (2 marks)
(b) **the meaning of investment properties;**   (5 marks)
(c) **the accounting treatment of investment properties in published financial statements.**

(8 marks)

CIMA, Advanced Financial Accounting, May 1991   (**15 marks**)

5.3 X Ltd is a retail supermarket chain which regularly constructs its own superstores. During the year ending 31 December 1995, X Ltd began work on a new site.

On 1 January 1995, a leasehold interest in the site (of 50 years) was purchased for £20 million.

It was considered that a further £10 million would be required to build and fit the superstore. £6 million of the additional £10 million would be spent on the construction of the building and £4 million on fixtures and fittings. Past experience has led the management of X Ltd to believe that the fixtures and fittings would have an average useful economic life of ten years from first use before requiring replacement.

On 1 January 1995, X Ltd borrowed £30 million to finance the project. The £30 million carries no interest but is repayable on 31 December 1997 at a premium of £9.93 million (i.e. £39.93 million is to be repaid in total).

The superstore is to be brought into use on 1 January 1996.

Requirements
(a) **Set out the arguments for and against the capitalisation of borrowing costs on constructed fixed assets.**   (9 marks)
(b) **Assuming that borrowing costs ARE capitalised where appropriate, calculate:**
    (i) **the total amount to be included in fixed assets in respect of the development at 31 December 1995, and**
    (ii) **the total amount to be charged to the profit and loss account in respect of the development for the year ending 31 December 1996.**   (11 marks)

Present value factors are shown below.

Years t			
		Present value of £1 to be received after t years	
	5%	*10%*	*15%*
1	0.952	0.909	0.870
2	0.907	0.826	0.756
3	0.864	0.751	0.658
4	0.823	0.683	0.572
5	0.784	0.621	0.497

CIMA, Financial Reporting, November 1995   (**20 marks**)

5.4 C & R plc is a large company which operates a number of retail stores throughout the United Kingdom. The company makes up financial statements to 30 September each year.

On 1 October 1996 the company purchased two plots of land at two different locations, and commenced the construction of two retail stores. The construction was completed on 1 October 1997.

Details of the costs incurred to construct the stores are as follows:

	Location A £000	Location B £000
Cost of land	500	700
Cost of building materials	500	550
Direct labour	100	150
Site overheads	100	100
Fixtures and fittings	200	200

The construction of the stores was financed out of the proceeds of issue of a £10 million zero coupon bond on 1 October 1996. The bond is redeemable at a price of £25 937 000 on 30 September 2006. This represents the one and only payment to the holders of the bond.

Both stores were brought into use on 1 October 1997. The store at Location A was used by C & R plc but, due to a change of plan, the store at Location B was let to another retailer at a commercial rent.

It is the policy of C & R plc to depreciate freehold properties over their anticipated useful life of 50 years, and to depreciate fixtures and fittings over 10 years. The cost of such properties (including fixtures and fittings) should include finance costs, where this is permitted by the regulatory framework in the United Kingdom.

Requirements
(a) **Compute the amounts which will be included in fixed assets in respect of the stores at Locations A and B on 30 September 1997.**
    Give full explanations for the amounts you have included.   (11 marks)
(b) **Compute the charge to the profit and loss account for depreciation on the fixed assets at the two locations for the year to 30 September 1998, stating clearly the reasons for your answers.**   (9 marks)

CIMA, Financial Reporting, November 1997   (**20 marks**)

5.5 L plc has never revalued its land and buildings. The directors are unsure whether they should adopt a policy of doing so. They are concerned that FRS 15 – *Tangible Fixed Assets* has an "all or nothing" approach which would impose a duty on them to maintain up-to-date valuations in the balance sheet for all land and buildings into the indefinite future. They are also concerned that the introduction of current values will make the accounting ratios based on their balance sheet appear less attractive to shareholders and other users of the financial statements.

Required

Authors' note: Students should ignore part (c) of this question as the relevant data has not been provided.

(a) Explain why FRS 15 requires those companies who revalue fixed assets to revalue all of the assets in the relevant classes and why these valuations must be kept up to date.

(7 marks)

(b) Explain whether it is logical for FRS 15 to offer companies a choice between showing all assets in a class at either cost less depreciation or at valuation.   (4 marks)

(c) Calculate the figures that would appear in L plc's financial statements in respect of land and buildings if the company opts to show the factories at their valuation. You should indicate where these figures would appear, but do NOT prepare any detailed notes in a form suitable for disclosure.   (6 marks)

(d) Explain how the revaluation of fixed assets is likely to affect key accounting ratios and explain whether these changes are likely to make the company appear stronger or weaker. Do NOT calculate any ratios in respect of L plc.   (8 marks)

CIMA, Financial Accounting – UK Accounting Standards, November 2001   (**25 marks**)

5.6 You are the management accountant of Historic Ltd. Historic Ltd makes up its financial statements to 30 September each year. The financial statements for the year ended 30 September 2000 are currently being prepared. The Directors have always included fixed assets under the historical cost convention. However, for the current year, they are considering revaluing some of the fixed assets. They obtained professional valuations as at 1 October 1999 for the two properties owned by the company. Details of the valuations were as follows:

	Historical cost NBV *£000*	*Current use value* *£000*	*Market value* *£000*
Property One	15 000	16 800	17 500
Property Two	14 000	12 000	12 500

No acquisitions or disposals of properties have taken place since 1 October 1999 and none are expected in the near future. The buildings element of the two properties comprises 50% of both historical cost and the revalued amounts. Each property is reckoned to have a useful economic life to the company of 40 years from 1 October 1999.

Given the results of the valuations, the Directors propose to include Property One at its market value in the financial statements for the year to 30 September 2000. They wish to leave Property Two at its historical cost. They have no plans to revalue the other fixed assets of the company, which are plant and fixtures.

Requirements

(a) State briefly the key arguments for and against including fixed assets at revalued amounts.   (6 marks)

(b) Evaluate the Directors' proposal to revalue Property One as at 1 October 1999 but to leave all other fixed assets at historical cost. Your answer should include reference to appropriate Accounting Standards.   (4 marks)

(c) The Directors have decided to revalue the fixed assets of the company in accordance with their original wishes, amended where necessary to comply with appropriate Accounting Standards. Compute the net book value of each property as at 30 September 2000. You should clearly explain where any differences on revaluation will be shown in the financial statements.   (5 marks)

CIMA, Financial Reporting, November 2000   **(15 marks)**

5.7 K is a CIMA member who has recently established a limited company which specialises in biotechnology applications. The company has just reached the end of its first year of trading. K is working through the accounting records prior to drafting the company's first annual report. The fixed assets section of the balance sheet is causing him some difficulty. The company has invested heavily in sophisticated equipment and K is checking whether the associated costs have been accounted for in accordance with the requirements of FRS 15 – *Tangible Fixed Assets.*

K is reviewing the file relating to a sophisticated oven that is used to heat cell cultures to a precisely controlled temperature:

	£
(i) List price paid to supplier	50 000
(ii) Wages and materials costs associated with testing and calibrating oven, up to start of operations	800
(iii) Ongoing wages and materials costs associated with calibrating oven since start of operations	2 000
(iv) Expected costs of disposing of oven at the end of its useful life	16 000

The oven is used to heat cell cultures to a temperature range that must be closely controlled. The oven's controls will have to be regularly checked and calibrated throughout its working life.

The oven will have to be dismantled and sterilised by an expert contractor at the end of its life and then disposed of at a special facility. K has already provided £16 000 against these costs, in accordance with the requirements of FRS 12 – *Provisions, Contingent Liabilities and Contingent Assets.*

The machine's expected useful life is five years. K is planning to adopt the straight-line basis of depreciation. The market value/value in use of the machine at the year end is £28 000. This decrease in value from new is partly because the oven has been used to culture dangerous organisms and so it is much less valuable. K is unsure whether to value equipment at cost less depreciation or at valuation. This decision will be based on an analysis of the resulting figures in terms of two of the 'pervasive concepts' (those of relevance and reliability) contained in FRS 18 – *Accounting Policies.*

Required
(a) Calculate the cost of the oven, applying the requirements of FRS 15. Explain your treatment of items (ii), (iii) and (iv).   (10 marks)
(b) (i) Calculate the figures that will appear in respect of the oven in the profit and loss account for the company's first year and the balance sheet at the year end under both the historical cost and valuation bases.   (4 marks)
    (ii) Discuss the relevance and reliability of both sets of figures you have calculated in answer to requirement (b) (i) above.   (6 marks)

CIMA, Financial Accounting – UK Accounting Standards, November 2002   **(20 marks)**

5.8 (a) Accounting practices for fixed assets and depreciation can be said to have developed in a piecemeal manner. The introduction of FRS 11 'Impairment of Fixed Assets' has meant that a standard on the measurement of fixed assets was required to provide further guidance in this area. FRS 15 'Tangible Fixed Assets' deals with the measurement and valuation issue.

Required

Describe why it was important for a new accounting standard to be issued on the measurement of fixed assets. (6 marks)

(b)   Aztech, a public limited company manufactures and operates a fleet of small aircraft. It draws up its financial statements to 31 March each year,

Aztech also owns a small chain of hotels (carrying value of £16 million), which are used in the sale of holidays to the public. It is the policy of the company not to provide depreciation on the hotels as they are maintained to a high standard and the economic lives of the hotels are long (20 years remaining life). The hotels are periodically revalued and on 31 March 2000, their existing use value was determined to be £20 million, the replacement cost of the hotels was £16 million and the open market value was £19 million. One of the hotels included above is surplus to the company's requirements as at 31 March 2000. This hotel had an existing use value of £3 million, a replacement cost of £2 million and an open market value of £2.5 million, before expected estate agents and solicitors fees of £200 000. Aztech wishes to revalue the hotels as at 31 March 2000. There is no indication of any impairment in value of the hotels.

The company has recently finished manufacturing a fleet of five aircraft to a new design. These aircraft are intended for use in its own fleet for domestic carriage purposes. The company commenced construction of the assets on 1 April 1998 and wishes to recognise them as fixed assets as at 31 March 2000 when they were first utilised. The aircraft were completed on 1 January 2000 but their exterior painting was delayed until 31 March 2000.

The costs (excluding finance costs) of manufacturing the aircraft were £28 million and the company has adopted a policy of capitalising the finance costs of manufacturing the aircraft. Aztech had taken out a three year loan of £20 million to finance the aircraft on 1 April 1998. Interest is payable at 10% per annum but is to be rolled over and paid at the end of the three year period together with the capital outstanding. Corporation tax is 30%.

During the construction of the aircraft, certain computerised components used in the manufacture fell dramatically in price. The company estimated that at 31 March 2000 the net realisable value of the aircraft was £30 million and their value in use was £29 million.

The engines used in the aircraft have a three year life and the body parts have an eight year life; Aztech has decided to depreciate the engines and the body parts over their different useful lives on the straight line basis from 1 April 2000. The cost of replacing the engines on 31 March 2003 is estimated to be £15 million. The engine costs represent thirty per cent of the total cost of manufacture.

The company has decided to revalue the aircraft annually on the basis of their market value. On 31 March 2001, the aircraft have a value in use of £28 million, a market value of £27 million and a net realisable value of £26 million. On 31 March 2002, the aircraft have a value in use of £17 million, a market value of £18 million and a net realisable value of £18.5 million. There is no consumption of economic benefits in 2002 other than the depreciation charge. Revaluation surpluses or deficits are apportioned between the engines and the body parts on the basis of their year end carrying values before the revaluation.

Required:

(i)   **Describe how the hotels should be valued in the financial statements of Aztech on 31 March 2000 and explain whether the current depreciation policy relating to the hotels is acceptable under FRS 15 'Tangible Fixed Assets'.** (6 marks)

(ii) **Show the accounting treatment of the aircraft fleet in the financial statements on the basis of the above scenario for the financial years ending on:**

    (a) **31 March 2000.** (4 marks)

    (b) **31 March 2001, 2002.** (6 marks)

    (c) **31 March 2003 before revaluation.** (3 marks)

Candidates should use FRS 15 'Tangible Fixed Assets' in answering all parts of the above question.

ACCA, Financial Reporting Environment (UK Stream), June 2000   **(25 marks)**

Assets II

The main issues surrounding the treatment of assets have been introduced in the preceding chapter. In this chapter, we will focus on accounting for inventories and long-term contracts. While these are both covered in SSAP 9, FRED 28 proposes that this should be replaced by two standards. We will also cover accounting for research and development activities and accounting for government grants, both revenue and capital. Thus we will in this chapter discuss:

- SSAP 9 *Stocks and Long-term Contracts* (revised 1988)
- IAS 2 *Inventories* (revised 1993)
- IAS 11 *Construction Contracts* (revised 1993)
- FRED 28 *Inventories and Construction and Service Contracts* (2002)
- IAS 18 *Revenue* (revised 1993)
- SSAP 13 *Accounting for Research and Development* (revised 1989)
- SSAP 4 *Accounting for Government Grants* (revised 1990)

The treatment of long-term contracts requires us to address the question of when revenue should be recognised and, to this end, we will also refer to the appropriate part of the following:

- Discussion Paper, *Revenue recognition* (July 2001)

Introduction

It used to be said in jest that in drawing up the annual accounts of an enterprise the first figure to be set down was that of profit, then all the ascertainable figures, until finally the value of stock emerged as a balancing item. This sentiment is certainly echoed in the introductory remarks to the original version of SSAP 9 *Stocks and Work in Progress*, issued in May 1975:

> No area of accounting has produced wider differences in practice than the computation of the amount at which stocks and work in progress are stated in financial accounts. This statement of standard accounting practice seeks to define the practices, to narrow the differences and variation in those practices and to ensure adequate disclosure in the accounts.

SSAP 9, albeit revised in 1988, has survived for over a quarter of century but will soon be replaced as part of the convergence programme. This replacement is heralded by the issue of FRED 28 which, if implemented, would result in two Financial Reporting Standards, one *Inventories* which is based on the proposed revised text of the international standard with the same title, IAS 2; the other, *Construction and Service Contracts*, is based on IAS 11, *Construction Contracts* which, it is understood, the IASB is not likely to revise in the foreseeable future.

The fact that there are very few differences between the provisions of SSAP 9 and FRED 28 may be testimony to the absence of controversy surrounding the area of stock and work-in-progress, although some would argue that it provides evidence of the lack of theoretical work in the area. One interesting development is the recognition that long-term contracts are not confined to the construction industry. While SSAP 9 was drafted in terms of long-term contracts that related to the construction of tangible asssets its principles have been applied to other types of contracts, notably those for services. This topic is the subject of IAS 18 *Revenue* but, as the ASB and other standard setters are working on the subject of revenue recognition at present, the ASB does not feel it appropriate to propose that the UK adopt the full text of IAS 18. Instead, to ensure that accounting for long-term service contracts continues to be addressed in UK standards, the relevant paragraphs of IAS 18 have been incorporated into the draft standard. We will discuss these paragraphs later in the chapter.

SSAP 13 *Accounting for Research and Development* and SSAP 4 *Accounting for Government Grants*, which we shall introduce in the second part of the chapter, have also been around for some time but are not presently slated for replacement. They contain few issues of principle but SSAP 13 brings us back to the often faced question of when does expenditure result in the creation of an asset?

Stocks and long-term contracts

SSAP 9

SSAP 9 differs from most other statements in that a large proportion of the document is devoted to appendices that deal with practical problems. The ASC was of the view that the problems that arise in this area are of a practical rather than of a theoretical nature. Appendix 1 deals with the relevant practical considerations but, as was always the case with appendices, it did not form part of the SSAP. There are two other appendices: Appendix 2, which consists of a glossary of terms, and Appendix 3, which is concerned with the presentation of information relating to long-term contracts.

We will assume that readers are familiar with the basic principles of stock valuation and the different methods employed in the historical cost system and, hence, we will concentrate on the few, but important, principles underlying SSAP 9.

Stocks other than long-term contracts

> The amount at which stocks are stated in periodic financial statements should be the total of the lower of cost and net realisable value of the separate item of stock or of groups of similar items. (SSAP 9, Para. 26)

A simple enough statement. Stock should normally be shown at cost but might sometimes be written down. But to state that stock should normally be stated at cost does not take us very far, for, as readers will be aware, the determination of the cost of stock and work-in-progress is by no means a simple task and much of the statement, including the appendices, is devoted to that subject. The basic principle is that the cost of stock and work-in-progress should comprise:

> that expenditure which has been incurred in the normal course of business in bringing the product or service to its present location and condition. Such costs **will** [our emphasis] include all related production overheads, even though these may accrue on a time basis. (SSAP 9, Paras 17–19)

Overheads

The cost of stock and work-in-progress is to include costs of production and conversion (as defined in the statement). The specification of the treatment of overheads reflects one way in which the standard fulfils its objective of narrowing variations in practice. There has been much debate on the extent to which production overheads should be included in the valuation of stock. At one extreme – the variable costing approach – is the view that overhead allocation is by its very nature arbitrary and that stock should be valued by reference to the costs (usually just direct material and labour) that can be directly related to the stock in question. A view that lies between this extreme and the ASC's position is that production overheads that relate to activity rather than time (e.g. cost of power) should be included in the cost of stock. These approaches are rejected by SSAP 9, which requires the inclusion of all production overheads, including those that accrue on a time basis. It appears that this alternative was adopted because the ASC felt that all production overheads, whether or not they arise on a time basis, are required to bring the stock to its 'present location and condition'.

Costs which include time-related production overheads will, all other things being equal, vary with the level of output; the lower the output the greater the cost of, say, rent per unit. Thus, the statement refers to the need to base the allocation of overheads on the company's normal level of activity,[1] so ensuring that the cost of unused capacity is written off in the current year. Appendix 1 of SSAP 9 provides some guidance on the question of how the normal level of activity should be determined, but it is clear that judgement will have to play a part in the resolution of this matter.

The ASC specifically rejected the argument that the omission of production overheads can be defended on the grounds of prudence. This emerges in Appendix 1, Para. 10, which states:

> The adoption of a conservative approach to the valuation of stocks and long-term contracts has sometimes been used as one of the reasons for omitting selected production overheads. In so far as the circumstances of the business require an element of prudence in determining the amount at which stocks and long-term contracts are stated, this needs to be taken into account in the determination of net realisable value and not by the exclusion from cost of selected overheads.

Stock valuation methods

The conventional methods of stock valuation (FIFO, LIFO, etc.) are described in the Statement's Appendix 2, the glossary of terms. The standard does not give any guidance about the methods that should be used; but the ASC's view of the principle that should be followed is given in Appendix 1, where it is stated that 'management must exercise judgment to ensure that the methods chosen provide the fairest practicable approximation to cost'.[2] It can be seen that the ASC placed emphasis on the need to show as accurately as possible the cost of stock and rejected those methods such as LIFO which are used, especially in the United States, to produce a profit figure which approximates to a current cost operating profit (see Chapter 20). It now appears that the IASB, when revising IAS 2 *Inventories*, will, at last, also outlaw the use of LIFO. When this is done, it will greatly help to ensure that accounting standards will converge in a sensible direction.

[1] SSAP 9, Appendix 1, Para. 8.
[2] SSAP 9, Appendix 1, Para. 12.

The writing down of stock

We will now turn to the methods that must be adopted when stock is to be written down. We will not, however, at this stage refer to the problems of establishing the net realisable value, which has been dealt with in Chapter 4.

SSAP 9 requires that stock should be written down to its net realisable value. Prior to the publication of the standard, some companies stated stock at replacement cost where this was lower than net realisable value and cost. The use of replacement cost is rejected in SSAP 9 on the grounds that it may result in the recognition of 'a loss that is greater than that which is expected to be incurred' (SSAP 9, Para. 6).

Our final comment on the provisions of SSAP 9, Para. 26, quoted at the beginning of this section, relates to the requirement that the comparison of cost and net realisable value should be on an item-by-item basis or by reference to groups of similar items. The reason for this is that this provision is given in Para. 2, where it is stated that 'to compare the total realisable value of stocks with the total cost could result in an unacceptable setting off of foreseeable losses against unrealised profits'. In other words, the practice contravenes the concept of prudence.

The alternative accounting rules

The standard recognises that companies taking advantage of the alternative accounting rules set out in the Companies Act 1985 may show stock at the lower of current replacement cost and net realisable value (Para. 6). As we will see there is no equivalent statement in FRED 28.

Long-term contracts

Long-term contracts merit separate consideration. Because of the time taken to complete such contracts, to defer recording turnover and the recognition of profit until completion might, in the words of the standard, 'result in the profit and loss account reflecting not so much a fair view of the activity of the company during the year but rather the results relating to contracts which have been completed by the year end' (SSAP 9, Para. 7).

Thus, SSAP 9 states that it is appropriate to (and by appropriate the ASC meant that companies should) take credit for ascertainable turnover and profit while contracts are in progress, subject to various conditions specified in the standard.

This may well be an eminently practical and sensible view, but it did seem to be in conflict with the attitude adopted in SSAP 2 *Disclosure of Accounting Policies*, which was only withdrawn with the issue of FRS 18 in December 2000, where it was stated that 'where the accruals concept is inconsistent with the prudence concept . . ., the latter prevails'.[3] The provision of SSAP 9 relating to long-term contracts does appear to suggest that the accruals concept should prevail over prudence. In that the ASB has now adopted a radically different stance whereby prudence is no longer seen to be, of itself, a desirable characteristic, it can be seen that SSAP 9 was the forerunner of what was to follow. The difference between the two standards reflects the lack of consistency that was a feature of the pioneering period of standard setting.

The provision that attributable profit should (not *might*) be recognised in the financial statements was perhaps the most controversial aspect of the original SSAP 9. A number of large companies had consistently eschewed the recognition of profit on uncompleted contracts and some continued this practice after the implementation of SSAP 9, accepting the consequential qualifications in their audit reports.

[3] SSAP 2, Para. 14(b).

In addition, there would appear to be a conflict between this requirement of SSAP 9 and the legal requirement that only realised profits may be credited to the profit and loss account (see Chapter 4). Even if attributable profit on long-term contract work-in-progress is not realised, it may, nonetheless, be included in the profit and loss account if this is necessary to give a true and fair view. The use of this true and fair view override on a number of occasions in the UK aroused considerable criticism from other members of the EU, who did not envisage that it would be used so often. This is an issue that will be addressed in the Companies Act which results from the publication of the recent White Paper, *Modernising Company Law.*[4] At present, it looks as if company law will delegate all matters relating to the form and content of company financial statements to a Standards Board and, as a consequence of this, the emphasis placed upon the distinction between realised and unrealised profits will disappear.

Definition of long-term contracts

A long-term contract can relate to the design or construction of a single substantial asset or the provision of a service (or a combination of assets or services which constitute a single project) where the activity falls into different accounting periods. If a contract is to fall within the definition, it will normally have to last for more than a year, but shorter contracts may also be included if they are sufficiently material so that the failure to record turnover and attributable profit would distort the financial statements.

Turnover, related costs and attributable profit

Long-term contracts should be assessed on a contract by contract basis and reflected in the profit and loss account by recording turnover and related costs as contract activity progresses. (SSAP 9, Para. 28)

Also:

Where it is considered that the outcome of a long-term contract can be assessed with reasonable certainty before its conclusion, the prudently calculated attributable profit should be recognised in the profit and loss account as the difference between the reported turnover and related costs for that contract. (SSAP 9, Para. 29)

So the accounting seems pretty straightforward and obvious:

> Reported turnover – Related costs = Attributable profit

But how are the various elements determined? The standard does not help very much, although some guidance is given:

Turnover is ascertained in a manner appropriate to the stage of completion of the contract, the business and the industry in which it operates. (SSAP 9, Para. 28)

Some assistance is also provided in Appendix 1 (Para. 23) where it is stated that turnover may be ascertained by reference to valuation of the work carried out to date. Alternatively there may be specific points where separately ascertainable sales values and costs can be identified because, for example, delivery or customer acceptance has taken place. The

[4] Cm. 5553-I and Cm. 5553-II

paragraph goes on to state that the standard does not provide a definition of turnover because of the number of different possible approaches. It does, however, point out that the Standard does require disclosure of the means by which turnover is ascertained.

Neither the standard nor any of the appendices refer to the calculation of related cost, so we will now turn to this and the estimation of attributable profit. We will start with two conceptually simple cases.

If the outcome of a long-term contract cannot be ascertained with reasonable certainty, no profit should be reflected in the profit and loss account. However, if, despite the uncertainty, the contract is not expected to make a loss, 'it may be appropriate to show as turnover a proportion of the total contract value using a zero estimate of profit' (SSAP 9, Para. 10). In the latter situation in order to satisfy the relationship between turnover, cost and profit, the related costs would be made equal to the reported turnover. If, on this basis, related costs appeared to be greater than the actual costs incurred to date, the turnover would be reduced and made equal to the actual costs.

The second 'simple' case is where the contract is expected to make a loss. In that situation, in accordance with the prudence concept, the whole of the loss should be recorded as soon as it is foreseen. Turnover would be determined in the normal way and the related cost would be equal to the actual cost to date plus the provision for foreseeable future losses.

Now let us consider a case where it would be necessary to recognise some profit. Attributable profit is defined as:

> that part of the total profit currently estimated to arise over the duration of the contract, after allowing for estimated remedial and maintenance costs and increases in costs so far as not recoverable under the terms of the contract, that fairly reflect the profit attributable to that part of the work performed at the accounting date. (SSAP 9, Para. 23)

Thus, it is first necessary to estimate the total profit and then decide how it should be allocated. The principles involved are illustrated in Example 6.1.

Example 6.1

Suppose that Engineer Limited started a three-year contract at the beginning of year 1 with a total contract value of £180 000 and costs of £120 000 that it is anticipated will be incurred as follows:

Year 1	Year 2	Year 3	Total
£30 000	£60 000	£30 000	£120 000

The expected profit is thus £60 000.

Case 1

We will assume that both turnover and profit are to be recognised in proportion to the costs incurred. Hence, assuming all goes to plan, the contract would be reported in the profit and loss accounts as follows:

	Year 1 (25%) £	Year 2 (50%) £	Year 3 (25%) £
Reported turnover	45 000	90 000	45 500
Related costs	30 000	60 000	30 000
Attributable profit	£15 000	£30 000	£15 000

Case 2

Depending on the nature of the contract it might be deemed appropriate to record turnover on a different basis, perhaps on the values placed on the work completed to date by an independent consultant.

Assume that the value of the work certified is as follows:

	Value of work certified	Value of work completed in year	Fraction
	£	£	£
End of year 1	30 000	30 000	$\frac{1}{6}$
End of year 2	90 000	60 000	$\frac{1}{3}$
End of year 3	180 000	90 000	$\frac{1}{2}$

Profit might be based on cost (Case 2a) or turnover (Case 2b) that would result in the reporting of the following figures.

Case 2a

Profit related to cost

	Year 1		Year 2		Year 3	
	£		£		£	
Reported turnover	30 000		60 000		90 000	
Related cost	15 000		30 000		75 000	
Attributable profit	£15 000	(25%)	£30 000	(50%)	£15 000	(25%)

Case 2b

Profit related to turnover

	Year 1		Year 2		Year 3	
	£		£		£	
Reported turnover	30 000		60 000		90 000	
Related cost	20 000		40 000		60 000	
Attributable profit	£10 000	$(\frac{1}{6})$	£20 000	$(\frac{1}{3})$	£30 000	$(\frac{1}{2})$

Thus, we can see that under the provisions of SSAP 9, even in this simple case, three different patterns of turnover, cost and profit might be reported, and in practice more variations are possible.

Now let us assume that all does not go to plan and the actual cost in year 2 was £80 000 rather than the expected £60 000, but that no further difficulties are expected and that the original estimate for the cost of year 3 of £30 000 still holds.

Consider the position as at the end of year 2; there are two possibilities which will be illustrated by reference to Case 2a above. Either the additional unexpected expenditure can be written off in year 2 reducing the profit for the year by £20 000 to £10 000, leaving the profit for year 3 at £15 000, or the revised profit less that already recognised in year 1 could be spread over years 2 and 3 on the basis of cost, i.e. in the ratio 8:3.

The revised profit is £40 000 and the profit recognised in year 1 was £15 000, hence the profits for the remaining two years would be:

Year 1	£18 182	(8/11)
Year 3	£6 818	(3/11)
	£25 000	

Thus, we have the paradox that the profit for year 3 is reduced because of difficulties experienced in year 2. This does not appear to be sensible, but the approach would be permissible under the terms of SSAP 9.

Example 6.1 illustrates the point that the related cost is normally a balancing figure derived from the relationship between reported turnover and attributable profit. The statement does not deal with the situation where related costs exceed actual costs. Suppose that we have the following for the first year of a contract:

		£
Turnover		200 000
Related cost		160 000
Attributable profit		£40 000
Actual cost to date		£130 000

In practice it is likely that the turnover figure would be reduced to £170 000 to make the equation balance.

Long-term contracts and the balance sheet

Before moving to a discussion of the way in which long-term contract balances are shown in the balance sheet, we need to introduce another factor, payments on account, which is defined as 'all amounts received and receivable at the accounting date in respect of contracts in progress' (SSAP 9, Para. 25).

The relevant section of the standard reproduced below is perhaps unnecessarily complex.

Long-term contracts should be disclosed in the balance sheet as follows:

(a) the amount by which recorded turnover is in excess of payments on account should be classified as 'amounts recoverable on contracts' and separately disclosed within debtors;

(b) the balance of payments on account (in excess of amounts (i) matched with turnover; and (ii) offset against long-term contract balances) should be classified as payments on account and separately disclosed within creditors;

(c) the amount of long-term contracts, at costs incurred, net of amounts transferred to cost of sales, after deducting foreseeable losses and payments on account not matched with turnover, should be classified as 'long-term contract balances' and separately disclosed within the balance sheet heading 'Stocks'. The balance sheet note should disclose separately the balances of:
   (i) net cost less foreseeable losses; and
   (ii) applicable payments on account;

(d) the amount by which the provision or accrual for foreseeable losses exceeds the costs incurred (after transfers to cost of sales) should be included within either provisions for liabilities and charges or creditors as appropriate. (SSAP 9, Para. 30)

To unravel the above it is best to start by concentrating on the situation where there are no losses, either incurred or contemplated.

Let us start by looking at the costs.

If the actual costs incurred to date exceed the cumulative related costs (the total charged to cost of sales), there is an asset, long-term contract balances, which is separately disclosed within stocks.

As stated earlier the standard does not consider a situation where related costs exceed actual costs; in practice this will not arise because, in all probability, turnover would be adjusted.

Let us now consider the receipt of cash from the customer.

If the cumulative reported turnover exceeds cumulative payments on account there is an asset, amounts recoverable on contracts, which is separately disclosed within debtors.

If the reverse holds (more cash received on account than reported as turnover), the credit balance is set off against long-term contract balances. If the credit (payments less turnover) is greater than the debit (long-term contract balances), the resulting credit is described as payments on account, which is separately disclosed within creditors.

Thus in respect of each contract, which has to be considered separately, the possible combinations of assets and liabilities are:

(a) two assets: long-term contract balances and amounts recoverable on contract; or
(b) a liability: payments on account.

The above points are illustrated in Example 6.2.

Example 6.2 **No losses**

Assume that the position on three contracts at a year end is as follows:

	(1)	*(2)*	*(3)*
	£	£	£
Cumulative turnover	520	520	520
Cumulative actual cost	510	510	510
Cumulative related cost	450	450	450
Cumulative payments on account	440	555	630

The cumulative attributable profit for each of the contracts is £70, i.e. £520 – £450.

The relevant balance sheet items are shown below. Note that each contract will be considered on an individual basis, balances arising on one contract are not set off against balances on other contracts and hence the figures that will appear in the balance sheet are shown in the total column.

	Contract			*Total*
	(1)	(2)	(3)	
	£	£	£	£
Stock – long-term contract balances	60 (a)	25 (b)	NIL	85
Debtors – amount recoverable on contracts	80 (a)	NIL	NIL	80
Creditors – payments on account	NIL	NIL	50 (c)	50

Notes
(a) Actual costs less related costs; £510 – £450 = £60.
    Cumulative turnover less cumulative payments on account; £520 – £440 = £80.
(b) Long-term contract balance as (a), £60
    less Excess of payments on account
    over turnover, £555 – £520 £35
    £25
(c) Long-term contract balance, as (a) £60
    less Excess of payments on account
    over turnover, £630 – £520 £110
    (£50)

Foreseeable losses

All losses, as soon as they are foreseen, should be recognised in the financial statements. The estimate of future loss should be charged to the profit and loss as part of the related cost. The credit is first offset against the long-term contract balance (before any set-off for the excess of cumulative payments on account over cumulative reported turnover). If the long-term contract balance is insufficient to cover the expected loss, the balance is included within either provisions for liabilities and charges or creditors, as appropriate, i.e. depending on the degree of certainty with which the estimate is made.

Example 6.3

Consider the following two contracts:

	(1) £	(2) £
Cumulative turnover	200	110
Cumulative actual costs	250	200
Cumulative related costs	250	110
Cumulative payments on account	180	160
Losses to date (£250 – £200)	50	–
Expected future losses	40	70

If we assume that this is the first year of each contract, the profit and loss account will include the following:

	(1) £	(2) £	Total £
Turnover	200	110	310
Related costs (cost of sales)	290	180	470
Gross loss	90	70	160

If the projects were in other than their first year, the amounts included would depend on what had been charged or credited in the previous years.

The various balance sheet figures are:

	(1) £	(2) £	Total £
Stock – long-term contract balances	NIL	NIL	NIL
Debtors – amounts recoverable on contracts	20(a)	NIL	20
Creditors – payments on account	NIL	30(b)	30
Provision/accrual for foreseeable losses	40	NIL	40

Notes

(a) Cumulative turnover less cumulative payments on account, £200 – £180 = £20.

(b) For contract 2, actual costs exceed related costs so we start with a long-term contract balance of £90, i.e. £200 – £110.

Expected future losses of £70 are set off against that balance, reducing it to £20.

But, there are excess payments on account, £50 since payments on account, £160, exceed turnover, £110. This credit balance, £50, is set off against the debit, £20, representing the long-term contract balance.

The net credit of £30 will appear in the balance sheet as a provision or accrual as appropriate.

FRED 28

The most obvious difference between SSAP 9 and FRED 28 is of size: the former is a thick document while the exposure draft is a slim volume of only 49 pages. This is due to the absence of the technical appendices that were such a feature of the SSAP.

There are, with one possible exception, no major differences in principle between the standard and the exposure draft although the ASB[5] points out that the references to prudence included in the standard did not survive into the exposure draft where, in line with the ASB's *Statement of Principles* and FRS 18 *Accounting Policies*, reliability is emphasised at the expense of prudence. There are some relatively minor differences, one relating to the way in which the figures are derived, the other to the way in which they are presented.

The possible exception is the fact that the exposure draft, unlike the standard, makes no reference to the possibility of an entity showing reporting stock and work-in-progress at the lower of current replacement cost and net realisable value which is permitted under the alternative accounting rules.

FRED 28 allows for the principles to be applied not only to single contracts but also to separately identifiable components of a single contract and to groups of contracts so long as the group is made up of inter-related contracts that had been negotiated as a single package, whereas SSAP 9 has no such provision.

As we explained earlier (p. 140) SSAP 9 has quite complex disclosure requirements relating to the balance sheet presentation of long-term contracts. The disclosure requirements of the exposure draft are much simpler; all that is required is the presentation of:

- gross amount due from customers
- gross amount due to customers

The only complexity is that the gross amounts are actually net, the gross amount being the net amount of the costs incurred plus recognised profits less the sum of recognised losses and progress billings. If the resulting value is positive the amount is due from customers, if negative the amount is due to customers. Thus, other than the debtors figure arising from unpaid progress billings, there would be only one item, which could be a current asset or liability and which would incorporate stock and work-in-progress, on the balance sheet in relation to uncompleted long-term contracts.

Revenue recognition

In 2001 the ASB published a major discussion paper, *Revenue Recognition*. There is, as yet, no accounting standard in the UK relating to the recognition and measurement of revenue with the result that different entities and industries sometimes adopt inconsistent practices. The purpose of this discussion paper was to stimulate debate that would assist in formulating an appropriate standard. A number of important issues are covered by the paper including the possible accounting treatments of sales that allow the purchaser the right of return, barter transactions and the effect of agency agreements.

At this stage we only need to draw on the view expressed in the document that full performance of a contract is only sometimes necessary for revenue to arise and that the general principle should be that revenue 'should be recognised to the extent that the seller has performed and the performance has resulted in benefit accruing to the customer'.[6] It is in this context that the provisions of FRED 28 need to be considered.

---

[5] FRED 28, Para. 6.
[6] ASB *Revenue Recognition* (July 2001) p. 3.

The preface to the exposure draft points out that while, in the main, the provisions of SSAP 9 were applied to long-term construction contracts they had also been applied to other types of contracts, in particular contracts for services. Accounting for such services is covered by IAS 18 *Revenue*. As the ASB and others are currently working on the subject of revenue recognition, the Board would not wish to propose that the UK adopted the whole of IAS 18. But in order to ensure that the topic is addressed in the UK, the ASB included the relevant parts of IAS 18 in the draft standard on construction and service contracts. These are included at Paras 45A to 45J of FRED 28. The key provision[7] is that, when the outcome of a transaction involving the rendering of services can be estimated reliably, the associated revenue should be recognised by reference to the stage of completion of the transaction at the balance sheet date. Reliability of estimation depends on *all* of the following conditions applying:

- the amount of the revenue can be measured reliably;
- it is probable that the economic benefits will flow to the enterprise;
- the stage of completion of the transaction at the balance sheet date can be measured reliably;
- the costs incurred to date and those required to complete the transaction can be measured reliably.

If the outcome of the transaction cannot be estimated reliably revenue should be recognised only to the extent that the expenses incurred to date are recoverable.[8] In such circumstances no profit should be recognised.

Research and development

Many enterprises spend large sums of money on research and development in the hope that, by incurring such expenditure, future profits will be higher than they otherwise would be. In other words, they incur expenditure on research and development in the expectation of creating an intangible asset that will yield benefits in the future. By the very nature of the process, some research and development activities will be unsuccessful and hence no asset will be created. Any expenditure on such projects must certainly be written off against profits of the year in which it is incurred. Other research projects will be successful and will result in the creation of an asset. Under historical cost accounting, it would be reasonable to suggest that expenditure on unsuccessful projects should be written off against the profits of the year in which they were incurred, while expenditure on successful projects should be capitalised at an appropriate figure and written off against profits of the periods in which benefits are expected to arise.

The accounting treatment proposed above seems quite clear, but two major problems arise as soon as an attempt is made to apply it. First, even where a project appears to have been successful, the size and timing of future benefits are often very uncertain; if such is the case, the lack of a reliable evidence[9] would appear to require the expenditure to be written off. Second, the people who must make the decision on whether or not the research and development has been successful are not independent of the entity but are the directors who are interested in the outcome of the research and development. Because of their involvement, such directors may be susceptible to bias, either innocent or fraudulent, and, in view of the uncertainties involved, it may be extremely difficult for an auditor to challenge the views of the directors.

---

[7] FRED 28, Para. 45B.

[8] FRED 28, Para. 45H.

[9] In earlier editions we referred to the need to follow the prudence convention. However, although the prudence convention has been dethroned its influence continues.

SSAP 13 *Accounting for Research and Development*

Accounting for research and development was the subject matter and title of SSAP 13, originally issued in 1977. A later version SSAP 13 (revised), which was issued in 1989, follows the same principles, although it increased the amount of disclosure required. We shall refer to SSAP 13 (revised) *Accounting for Research and Development* (January 1989). This version, like its predecessor, follows the definitions of research and development expenditure adopted by the Organisation for Economic Co-operation and Development (OECD), which divides such expenditure into three categories:

1 Pure (or basic) research: experimental or theoretical work undertaken primarily to acquire new scientific or technical knowledge for its own sake rather than directed towards any specific aim or application.
2 Applied research: original or critical investigation undertaken in order to gain new scientific or technical knowledge and directed towards a specific practical aim or objective.
3 Development: use of scientific or technical knowledge in order to produce new or substantially improved materials, devices, products or services, to install new processes or systems prior to the commencement of commercial production or commercial applications, or to improve substantially those already produced or installed.

Given the uncertainties surrounding the benefits from research and development expenditure and the requirement of SSAP 2, then still extant, that, in case of conflict, prudence should prevail over the accruals concept, one approach would have been to write off all such expenditure to the profit and loss account as incurred.[10]

Although this approach may be simply applied and removes the need for judgement on the part of directors and auditors, many people would argue that it makes little economic sense. To take an example, we may think of two similar companies that have spent an identical amount on research and development. The efforts of one company have been successful while the efforts of the other company have not. If both companies are required to write off all research and development expenditure as it is incurred, then this essential difference between the two companies is not apparent from an examination of their financial statements. An important element of business reality does not feature in those statements.

Capitalisation of development expenditure

SSAP 13 takes a less conservative approach. Although it requires companies to write off all expenditure on pure and applied research as it is incurred, it permits, but does not require, the capitalisation of certain development expenditure which must then be matched against the revenues to which it relates.

The adoption of this permissive approach introduces the possibility of bias on the part of directors, who must decide whether or not an asset exists on a balance sheet date. In order to reduce this bias to a minimum, the standard lists the following conditions that must be satisfied before development expenditure may be carried forward:[11]

(a) there is a clearly defined project; and
(b) the related expenditure is separately identifiable; and

---

[10] This was, in fact, the approach proposed in the original exposure draft on the subject, ED 14 *Accounting for Research and Development*, issued in 1975.
[11] SSAP 13 (revised), Para. 25.

(c) the outcome of such a project has been assessed with reasonable certainty as to:
  (i) its technical feasibility; and
  (ii) its ultimate commercial viability considered in the light of factors such as likely market conditions (including competing products), public opinion, consumer and environmental legislation; and
(d) the aggregate of the deferred development costs, any further development costs, and related production, selling and administration costs is reasonably expected to be exceeded by related future sales or other revenues; and
(e) adequate resources exist, or are reasonably expected to be available, to enable the project to be completed and to provide any consequential increases in working capital.

It will be seen that, unlike the position with most internally generated intangible fixed assets, development expenditure can be recognised in the absence of readily ascertainable market value but, instead, expenditure can only be capitalised if the above, reasonably stringent, conditions, are met.[12]

Disclosure requirements

In order to facilitate interpretation, the standard requires that the notes to the accounts contain a clear explanation of the accounting policy followed, although this was, in any case, required under the provisions of SSAP 2, as it now is with FRS 18. It requires disclosure of the total amount of research and development expenditure charged in the profit and loss account, analysed between the current year's expenditure and the amortisation of deferred development expenditure. Finally, it requires disclosure of movements on the deferred development expenditure account each year. The Companies Act 1985 specifically requires that the directors explain why expenditure has been capitalised and state the period over which the costs are being written off.[13]

Compliance with international standards

Research and development expenditure is covered by IAS 38, *Intangible Assets* which, as we described in Chapter 5, does not require an intangible asset to have a readily ascertainable market value for it to be recognised. While SSAP 13 is consistent with the general approach of IAS 38 there is one significant difference. While both standards set down similar criteria which must be satisfied before development expenditure may be capitalised the consequences differ. When the criteria are satisfied, IAS 38 requires capitalisation (IAS 38, Para. 45) while SSAP 13 permits capitalisation (SSAP 13, Para. 25).

Government grants

It is appropriate to deal with the accounting treatment of government grants as a postscript to a chapter on assets because the topic is often closely related to the subject of fixed assets and depreciation. The topic is the subject matter of SSAP 4, *The Accounting Treatment of*

---

[12] The Companies Act 1985 requires that costs of research are charged to the profit and loss account (Schedule 4, Para. 3(2)(c)) but permits the carrying forward of development costs 'in special circumstances' (Schedule 4, Para. 20(1)). Satisfaction of the criteria for the carrying forward of development expenditure in SSAP 13 is generally accepted as providing the 'special circumstances' referred to in the Act.

[13] Companies Act 1985, Schedule 4, Para. 20(2).

Government Grants, which was originally issued in 1974. The standard proved to be inadequate, not only because it was itself poorly conceived but also because of other developments. Grants themselves became more complex than was envisaged when SSAP 4 was published, while the provisions of the standard proved to be inconsistent with those of the Companies Act 1985 and of IAS 20, *Accounting for Government Grants and Disclosure of Government Assistance* which was issued in 1982. Hence a revised standard, SSAP 4 (revised), *Accounting for Government Grants*, was issued in July 1990.

SSAP 4 *The Accounting Treatment of Government Grants*

The two accounting concepts on which SSAP 4 (revised) is based are accruals and prudence. The first implies that grants should be credited to the profit and loss account so as to match the expenditure towards which they are expected to contribute; the second that grants should not be recognised in the profit and loss account until the conditions for their receipt have been satisfied and that there is a reasonable assurance that the grants will be received.

Readers may feel that the reference in the standard to the accruals and prudence conventions would at the time have been unnecessary because they are two of the four fundamental accounting concepts specified in SSAP 2. However, by presenting the accruals concept in the way stated above, the ASC avoided a discussion of a fundamentally different alternative approach that all government grants should be regarded as a source of finance provided by government and hence retained in the balance sheet as a non-distributable reserve; including it as a reserve would imply that it is an element of owners' equity, but a part which has been provided by the government.

There are certain advantages of such an approach including clarity – it would describe clearly what has actually happened – and comparability in that it would assist comparisons between, for example, the two companies, one operating in an area where grants are available and the other not.

Revenue-related grants

Revenue-related grants, according to the original SSAP 4, did not produce any accounting problems 'as they clearly should be credited to revenue in the same period in which the revenue expenditure to which they relate is charged' (SSAP 4, Para. 2).

This may have been a reasonable description of the situation in 1974, but subsequently grants took many different forms and were derived from different sources than was the case in 1974. In the latter context it is noteworthy that, in the original SSAP 4, the ASC did not see a need to define government; by implication government was the UK Central Government. In contrast, the revised SSAP 4 defines government as including 'government and intergovernmental agencies and similar bodies whether local, national or international' (SSAP 4, Para. 21); it thus includes the European Union.

The matching of grants received to expenditure is straightforward when the grant is made towards specified items of expenditure. However, certain grants might not be related to specific items of expenditure; they might, for example, be paid to encourage job creation. In such circumstances the recognition of the grant in the profit and loss account should be matched with the identifiable net costs of achieving the objective. As is pointed out in the explanatory note to the revised standard, this may not be straightforward, as account needs to be taken of the associated income generated by the activity in arriving at the net cost. If, for example, the grant is given on condition that jobs are created and sustained for a period of, say, three years, the grant should be matched to the net cost of providing the jobs. Thus, if the revenue generated by the activity is higher in the third year, a higher proportion of the grant should be recognised in the earlier years.

In some cases the grant may be paid to support one activity – training, for instance – but will only become payable when the company incurs expenditure in another, usually related, area – perhaps the purchase of capital equipment. In other words, the grant will not be paid unless the company purchases the equipment, but the size of the grant depends on the company's training expenditure. SSAP 4 provides that where such a link is established the grant should be matched to the expenditure which it is intended to support, in this case training, but, as is the general rule under SSAP 4, nothing should be credited to the profit and loss account until the necessary conditions have been fulfilled – in this case until the equipment has been purchased.

The part of any revenue-related grant received but not yet recognised in the profit and loss account because the necessary conditions have not yet been satisfied should be included in the balance sheet as deferred income.[14]

Capital-related grants

Two methods of dealing with capital-related grants are identified in SSAP 4 (revised):

(a) Show the grant as deferred income that is credited to the profit and loss account over the life of the asset on a basis consistent with the depreciation policy adopted for the asset.
(b) Reduce the cost of the asset and hence reduce the annual depreciation charges.

The other possible option of not crediting the grant at any stage to the profit and loss account but retaining it in the balance sheet as a source of funds is not considered for the reasons given earlier.

In choosing between the two alternatives, the ASC came to the surprising, if not astonishing, conclusion that 'both treatments are acceptable and capable of giving a true and fair view' (SSAP 4 (revised), Para. 15). It is difficult to see how showing in the balance sheet the cost of an asset at 100 per cent of its purchase price or, say, depending on the size of the grant, 80 per cent of the price, can both show a 'true and fair' view. It does seem the ASC had, on this occasion, distorted that splendidly elastic phrase too far.

The ASC's position appears even stranger in that it records that it had received Counsel's opinion that the second alternative, the reduction in cost, is illegal in the light of Paras 17 and 26 of Schedule 4 to the Companies Act 1985. However, the ASC stuck to its guns. Both alternatives are available to enterprises under the provisions of SSAP 4 (revised), but only the first can be used by enterprises whose financial statements are governed by the Companies Acts.

Disclosure requirements

The disclosure requirements of SSAP 4 (revised) require the following information to be revealed:

(a) The accounting policy adopted in respect of government grants (this in any case is required by FRS 18 *Accounting Policies*, and its predecessor SSAP 2 *Disclosure of Accounting Policies*).
(b) The effects of government grants on the results of the period and the financial position of the enterprise.

---

[14] SSAP 4, Para. 15.

(c) Information regarding any material effect on the results of the period from government assistance other than grants (for example, free consultancy or subsidised loans) including, if possible, quantitative estimates of the effect of the assistance.

(d) Any potential liability to repay grants should, if necessary, be disclosed in accordance with SSAP 18 *Accounting for Contingencies*, which has now been replaced by FRS 12 *Provisions, Contingent Assets and Liabilities*.

Compliance with international standards

The equivalent international standard is IAS 20 *Accounting for Government Grants and Disclosure of Government assistance*, the main provisions which are consistent with those of SSAP 4. In particular IAS 20 also allows asset-related grants either to be treated as deferred income or to be deducted immediately from the cost of the asset, but the difference is that the IASB does not, of course, have to concern itself with the provisions of the Companies Act, 1985.

Summary

In this chapter we have discussed three veteran standards that have been around for over twenty years. One of them, SSAP 9, is likely to be replaced by two standards but these, although they will look very different and be less concerned with technical issues, will be based on virtually the same principles as SSAP 9. A seemingly important development over the life of the three standards has been the removal of the prudence convention from its previous dominant position. While its demotion is likely to discourage the making of excessive provisions, the absence of significant changes between SSAP 9 and FRED 28 suggests that, in other respects, the removal of prudence will not make very much difference.

SSAP 4 and 13 are not on the ASB's current programme so are likely to be with us for some time. This perhaps is reasonable in the case of SSAP 13 but it is unfortunate that the highly unsatisfactory SSAP 4 is not high on the list for review,

Recommended reading

Excellent up-to-date and detailed reading on the subject matter of this chapter and on much of the contents of this book is provided by the most recent edition of:

UK and International GAAP, A. Wilson, M. Davies, M. Curtis and G. Wilkinson-Riddle (eds), Ernst & Young, Butterworths Tolley, London. At the time of writing the most recent edition is the 7th, published 2001.

Questions

6.1 N Ltd is an independent company which manufactures clothing. For many years, N Ltd has worked exclusively for Store plc, a national group of department stores, manufacturing gloves. Store plc supplies the patterns for the gloves and specifies the fabric and colours that N Ltd must use. Store plc actively discourages its suppliers from manufacturing for other retailers and expressly forbids them from using its patterns or fabric colours for anything sold to another customer.

N Ltd manufactures gloves steadily throughout the year, building up stocks in advance of the major order that Store plc places every year in order to meet demand in the autumn and winter months.

Store plc used to order 500 000 pairs of gloves from N Ltd every year.

Store plc has suffered declining sales and has closed several of its stores. In April 2001, it warned N Ltd that it will reduce its annual purchases to 400 000 pairs of gloves. N Ltd took immediate steps to reduce its production capacity in response to this reduced order.

N Ltd has a year end of 30 September 2001. At that date, the company had 40 000 pairs of gloves in stock. It also had work-in-progress of 5000 pairs of gloves that were 100% complete in terms of fabric and were 50% complete in terms of labour and overhead. Raw materials stocks comprised £10 000 of fabric in Store plc's colours. N Ltd actually completed a total of 430 000 pairs of gloves during the year ended 30 September 2001.

The fabric content of a pair of gloves costs N Ltd £1.00 per pair.

N Ltd has summarised expenses incurred during the year as follows:

	Fixed overheads	Variable overheads	Labour
	£	£	£
Manufacturing	20 000	40 000	400 000
Administrative	15 000	10 000	50 000
Distribution	8 000	6 000	12 000
	43 000	56 000	462 000

Required

(a) SSAP 9 – *Stocks and long-term contracts* requires that stocks be valued at the lower of cost and net realisable value.

Describe the problems associated with determining net realisable value for closing stocks. You should describe the particular problems associated with determining the net realisable value of N Ltd's closing stocks. (6 marks)

(b) SSAP 9 defines the cost of stock as 'the expenditure which has been incurred in the normal course of business in bringing the product to its present location and condition'.

(i) Calculate the cost of N Ltd's closing stocks. (5 marks)

(ii) Identify the accounting issues associated with calculating the cost of closing stocks for N Ltd and explain how you have dealt with them. (5 marks)

(c) Explain why the valuation of closing stock is particularly important in the preparation of financial statements. (4 marks)

CIMA, Financial Accounting – UK Accounting Standards, November 2001   **(20 marks)**

6.2 Wick plc has produced the following trial balance as at 31 August 2002 as a basis for the preparation of its published accounts:

	Debit £'000	*Credit* £'000
Freehold property – at valuation	3500	
Freehold property – accumulated depreciation		100
Plant and machinery – at cost	1000	
Plant and machinery – accumulated depreciation		400
Plant held for rental income	400	
Fixtures and fittings – at cost	500	
Fixtures and fittings – accumulated depreciation		300
Stock as at 1 September 2001	200	
Debtors	650	
Provision for doubtful debts		50
Cash at bank	130	
Trade creditors		700
Bank loan		800
Deferred taxation		310
VAT payable		120
Ordinary share capital – shares of £1 each		2000
Share premium		500
Revaluation reserve		150
Profit and loss account as at 1 September 2001		300
Sales		3250
Purchases and direct labour costs	1600	
Distribution costs	400	
Administration costs	500	
Interim dividend paid	100	
Total	**8980**	**8980**

Additional information

(1) As a new venture, the company started work on a long-term contract in October 2001 and the above trial balance includes transactions relating to this contract which was in progress as at 31 August 2002. The agreed total contract price is £600 000 and there was work certified of £250 000, included in Sales, as at 31 August 2002. Costs to 31 August 2002 amounted to £400 000, included in Purchases, with estimated costs to completion of £300 000. Progress payments received by 31 August 2002 amounted to £340 000; these have been debited to Cash at bank and credited to Debtors.

(2) Stock at 31 August 2002 was valued at £300 000 and comprised finished goods of £50 000 and goods awaiting completion of £250 000. These amounts exclude the long-term contract.

(3) Depreciation has yet to be provided for as follows:

● Freehold property – 2.5% p.a. on valuation. The land element is £1.5 million.
● Plant and machinery – 10% p.a. on cost.
● Plant held for rental is for short-term hire and was acquired in the year ended 31 August 2002 – 20% p.a. on cost.
● Fixtures and fittings – 20% p.a. on cost.

It is company policy to provide a full year's depreciation charge in the year of acquisition.

(4) The bank loan was taken out on 1 September 2000 and is repayable in five equal annual instalments starting from 1 September 2001. Interest is charged at 7% p.a. on the balance owing on 1 September each year and has not yet been paid for the current year.

(5) The company is proposing a final dividend of 10p per share.

(6) Corporation tax of 30% of pre-tax profit is to be provided for, including an increase in the deferred taxation provision of £100 000.

Requirements

(a) **Prepare the profit and loss account for the year ended 31 August 2002 and a balance sheet as at that date for Wick plc in a form suitable for publication, providing the disclosure note for Stock.** (20 marks)

   NOTE: You are not required to prepare any other disclosure notes.

(b) **Identify and explain two areas in accounting for long-term contracts where judgement has to be exercised.** (5 marks)

ICAEW, Financial Reporting, September 2002 **(25 marks)**

6.3 G Ltd is a company specialising in the construction of sophisticated items of plant and machinery for clients in the engineering industry. Details of two contracts outstanding at 30 September 1995 (the balance sheet date) are as follows:

Contract with H Ltd

This contract was started on 1 January 1995 and is expected to be complete by 31 March 1996. The total contract price was fixed at £20 million and the total costs to be incurred originally estimated at £15 million, occurring evenly over the contract. The contract has been certified by experts as being 60% complete by 30 September 1995. Due to inefficiencies caused by industrial relations difficulties in the summer of 1995, the actual costs incurred on the contract in the period 1 January 1995 to 30 September 1995 were £10 million. However, the management is confident that these problems will not recur and that the remaining costs will be in line with the original estimate. In accordance with the payment terms laid down in the contract, G Ltd invoiced H Ltd for an interim payment of £10 million on 31 August 1995. The interim payment was received from H Ltd on 31 October 1995.

Contract with I Ltd

This contract was started on 1 April 1995 and was expected to be complete by 31 December 1995. The total contract price was fixed at £10 million and the total contract costs were originally estimated at £8 million. However, information received on 15 October 1995 suggested that the total contract costs would in fact be £11 million. The contract was certified by experts as being two-thirds complete by the year end and the costs actually incurred by G Ltd in respect of this contract in the period to 30 September 1995 were £7.5 million. No progress payments are yet due under the payment terms specified in the contract with I Ltd.

Requirements

(a) **Explain the principles which are used to establish the timing of recognition of profits/losses on long-term contracts.**
   You should assume that recognition of profits/losses takes place in accordance with the provisions of SSAP 9 *Stocks and long-term contracts*, and should refer to fundamental accounting concepts, where relevant. (10 marks)

(b) **Compute, separately for each of the contracts with H Ltd and I Ltd:**
   (i) **The amount of turnover and cost of sales that will be recognised in the profit and loss account of G Ltd for the year ended 30 September 1995.**

(ii) The contract balances (including nil balances, if appropriate) that will be shown at 30 September 1995 on the following accounts:
- long-term contract work-in-progress
- amounts recoverable on contracts
- provision for losses
- trade debtors.   (10 marks)

CIMA, Financial Reporting, November 1995   **(20 marks)**

6.4 Lewis plc specialises in bridge construction and had two contracts in progress at its year end, 30 April 1999.

Stornoway Bridge
Construction on this contract started in May 1997. Contract details extracted from the company's costing records as at 30 April 1999 were:

	£m
Total contract selling price	350
Work certified to date	210
Costs to date	175
Estimated costs to completion	75
Progress payments received	250

Work certified to date as at 30 April 1998 was £140 million and the appropriate amount of profit was recognised for the year ended 30 April 1998. No changes to the above total estimated contract costs have occurred since 30 April 1998.

On 11 May 1999 the customer's surveyor notified Lewis plc of a fault in one of the bridge supports constructed during a severe frost in February 1999. This will require remedial work in June 1999 at an estimated cost of £20 million.

Harris Link Bridge
Construction on this contract started in July 1998. Contract details extracted from the company's costing records as at 30 April 1999 were:

	£m
Total contract selling price	400
Work certified to date	45
Costs to date	40
Estimated costs to completion	395
Progress payments received	25

The company calculates attributable profit on the basis of work certified for all contracts.

Requirements
(a) Calculate the amounts to be included in the financial statements of Lewis plc for the year ended 30 April 1999, preparing all relevant extracts of the financial statements excluding accounting policies notes and any disclosures relating to cash flows.
                                                                         (15 marks)
(b) Explain how the requirements of SSAP 9, Stocks and long-term contracts, apply the prudence and accruals concepts to accounting for long-term contracts.   (5 marks)

ICAEW, Financial Reporting, June 1999   **(20 marks)**

6.5 S plc is a shipbuilder which is currently working on two contracts:

	Deep sea fishing boat £000	Small passenger ferry £000
Contract price (fixed)	3000	5000
Date work commenced	1 October 2000	1 October 2001
Proportion of work completed during year ended 30 September 2001	30%	Nil
	£000	£000
Invoiced to customer during year ended 30 September 2001	900	Nil
Cash received from customer during year ended 30 September 2001	800	Nil
Costs incurred during year ended 30 September 2001	650	Nil
Estimated cost to complete at 30 September 2001	1300	
Proportion of work completed during year ended 30 September 2002	25%	45%
	£000	£000
Invoiced to customer during year ended 30 September 2002	750	2250
Cash received from customer during year ended 30 September 2002	700	2250
Costs incurred during year ended 30 September 2002	580	1900
Estimated cost to complete at 30 September 2002	790	3400

S plc recognises turnover and profit on long-term contracts in relation to the proportion of work completed.

Required

(a) **Calculate the figures that will appear in S plc's profit and loss account for the year ended 30 September 2002 and its balance sheet at that date in respect of each of these contracts.** (14 marks)

The Accounting Standards Board's *Statement of Principles for Financial Reporting* (SoP) effectively defines losses on individual transactions in such a way that they are associated with increases in liabilities or decreases in assets. Liabilities are defined as 'obligations of an entity to transfer economic benefits as a result of past transactions or events'.

Required

(b) **Explain how the definition of losses contained in the SoP could be used to justify the requirement of SSAP 9 – *Stocks and Long-term Contracts* to recognise losses in full on long-term contracts as soon as they can be foreseen.** (6 marks)

CIMA, Financial Accounting – UK Accounting Standards, November 2002   (**20 marks**)

6.6 H plc is a major electronics company. It spends a substantial amount of money on research and development. The company has a policy of capitalising development expenditure, but writes off pure and applied research expenditure immediately in accordance with the requirements of SSAP 13 – *Research and Development*.

The company's latest annual report included a page of voluntary disclosures about the effectiveness of the company's research programme. This indicated that the company's prosperity depended on the development of new products and that this could be a very long process. In order to maintain its technical lead, the company often funded academic research studies into theoretical areas, some of which led to breakthroughs which H plc was able to patent and develop into new product ideas. The company claimed that the money spent in this way was a good investment because for every twenty unsuccessful projects there was usually at least one valuable discovery which generated enough profit to cover the whole cost of the research activities. Unfortunately, it was impossible to tell in advance which projects would succeed in this way.

A shareholder expressed dismay at H plc's policy of writing off research costs in this manner. He felt that this was unduly pessimistic given that the company earned a good return from its research activities. He felt that the company should invoke the Accounting Standards Board's true and fair override and capitalise all research costs.

Required
(a) **Explain why it might be justifiable for H plc to capitalise its research costs.**   (5 marks)
(b) **Explain why SSAP 13 imposes a rigid set of rules which prevent the capitalisation of all research expenditure and make it difficult to capitalise development expenditure.**
     (5 marks)
(c) **Explain whether the requirements of SSAP 13 are likely to discourage companies such as H plc from investing in research activities.**   (5 marks)
(d) **Describe the advantages and disadvantages of offering companies the option of a true and fair override in preparing financial statements.**   (5 marks)

CIMA, Financial Accounting – UK Accounting Standards, November 2001   (**20 marks**)

6.7 MWT plc is a company involved in the design and manufacture of aircraft. During the year ended 31 March 1995, the company had commenced the following projects.

A. **Project Alpha** involves research into the development of a lightweight material for use in the construction of aircraft. To date, costs of £175 000 have been incurred, but so far the material developed has proved too weak.

B. **Project Beta** involves the construction of three aircraft for a major airline at a total contract price of £75 million. Costs incurred to 31 March 1995 amounted to £21 million, and payments on account received, relating to £20 million of those costs, amounted to £24 million. It is estimated that the contract will cost another £40 million to complete.

C. **Project Gamma** involves the development of a new engine for an overseas customer for a total contract price of £7 million. The total cost of the project is estimated to be £5 million. Only £1.4 million had been incurred to 31 March 1995. Payments on account, relating to those costs, of £2.4 million have been received.

D. **Project Delta** involves the refurbishment of a fleet of ten aircraft for another major airline. The total contract price is £30 million. To 31 March 1995, costs of £24 million have been incurred, and, because of materials shortage, it is estimated that it will cost another £12 million to complete. Although £20 million had been invoiced to 31 March 1995, relating to cost incurred to that date, only £19 million had been received at that date.

E. **Project Epsilon** commenced in February 1995 involving the production of light aircraft for a flying school for a total contract price of £18.2 million. Costs incurred to 31 March 1995 amounted to £1 million of a total estimated contract cost of £17 million. Invoices raised to 31 March 1995 amounted to £3 million of which £2.6 million had been received by that date.

Requirement

(a) Explain, with appropriate figures, how each of the above projects should be treated in
    the financial statements of MWT plc.   (15 marks)

(b) Show the relevant extracts from MWT plc's profit and loss account and balance sheet
    for the year ended 31 March 1995.   (5 marks)

CIMA Financial Reporting, May 1995   **(20 marks)**

6.8 Forfar plc is an innovative engineering company with a substantial research and development budget. It is company policy to capitalise all expenditure relevant to development
work wherever possible and the following projects were in progress at the year end,
30 November 1998:

Project A100

The company incurred costs of £200 000 in the year ended 30 November 1998 to exploit
research into the production of engineering equipment with reduced energy requirements.
The company has produced a prototype model but commercial production is not expected
for several years.

  No other feasibility studies have been carried out. The company also incurred expenditure of £100 000 on computer equipment to assist in testing and analysis and this is expected
to have a useful economic life of five years.

Project A401

The company incurred technical research costs of £50 000 in November 1998 on behalf of a
customer who commissioned Forfar plc to investigate the feasibility of high-energy battery
cells. Forfar plc expects to recover the costs incurred plus a mark-up of 20% from their customer for this work. Market research costs of £20 000 have also been incurred by Forfar plc
in November 1998 but these will be reimbursed at cost by the customer and an invoice was
raised for this in December 1998. None of the technical research work has yet been invoiced
though the project is successful and the work will be completed by January 1999.

Project C900

The company had capitalised development expenditure of £500 000 by 30 November 1997
on this project and incurred a further £70 000 during the year ended 30 November 1998.
Commercial production of the new product started on 1 June 1998 and the company anticipates sales as follows:

Year ended	£
30 November 1998	250 000 actual
30 November 1999	300 000 budget
30 November 2000	500 000 budget
each year thereafter	600 000 budget

The company expects competitors will move into this market by 30 November 2002 and the
product will no longer be profitable after that date.

  In addition to the above costs, the company spent £150 000 on plant in December 1995
to assist with this project and has been depreciating this over five years to date. The plant has
no further use once the product is developed.

Project G150

The company's technical director considers that there is the possibility of producing new
generation computer-controlled engineering equipment. £400 000 was spent in the year
ended 30 November 1998 to investigate the likelihood of a viable research project. In addition, technical staff costs on this project amounted to £55 000 in the year.

Project B105

This project was started in December 1994 to develop a new generation solar power panel. Costs capitalised to 30 November 1997 amounted to £550 000. Market research carried out in July 1998 at a cost of £25 000 indicated demand would reach 5000 panels per annum; the company's finance director has calculated 7500 panels per annum would need to be sold in order to break even.

Requirements

(a) **Briefly identify and explain the appropriate accounting treatment required for the year ended 30 November 1998 for each of the above projects.**   (6 marks)

(b) **Calculate and disclose the appropriate amounts for the financial statements of Forfar plc for the year ended 30 November 1998.**   (14 marks)

Note: You are not required to produce any information for the directors' report, accounting policies or cash flow statement.

ICAEW, Financial Reporting, December 1998   **(20 marks)**

6.9 Amesbury plc produces and distributes computer-controlled machinery. As accountant for the company, you have been provided with the following information regarding the company's activities in researching and developing products in the year ended 31 October 1993:

(1) Expenditure on developing a new computerised tool for a long-established customer has amounted to £150 000. The work is now well advanced and the customer is likely to authorise the start of commercial production within the next 12 months. The customer is reimbursing Amesbury plc's costs plus a 10% mark-up. To date the company has received £70 000 having invoiced £100 000 for agreed work done.

(2) A review of the company's quality control procedures has been carried out at a cost of £100 000. It is considered that the new procedures will save a considerable amount of money in the testing and analysis of existing and new products.

(3) The development of Product M479 has reached an advanced stage. Costs in the year ended 31 October 1993 amounted to £400 000. In addition there has been expenditure on fixed assets required for the development of this product amounting to £120 000 of which £60 000 was incurred in the year ended 31 October 1992. The fixed assets have a five-year life with no residual value and are depreciated on the straight-line basis with a full year's depreciation in the year of acquisition.

Market research, costing £20 000, has been carried out and this indicates the product will be commercially viable although commercial production is unlikely to start until April 1994. The company expects that Product M479 will make a significant contribution to profit.

(4) Commercial production started on 1 June 1993 for Product A174. The costs of developing this product had been capitalised as follows:

	£
Development expenditure capitalised as on 31 October 1992	200 000
Expenditure incurred in the year ended 31 October 1993	50 000
	250 000

The company has taken out a patent which will last for ten years. The associated legal and administrative expenses amounted to £10 000.

Actual and estimated sales for Product A174:

Year ended 31 October	£
1993	250 000
1994	750 000
1995	1 000 000
1996	500 000
1997	250 000

After 31 October 1996 the company's market share and profitability from the product are expected to diminish significantly due to the introduction of rival products by competitors.

(5) It is company policy to capitalise development expenditure wherever possible.

Requirement
Prepare all relevant extracts of the published financial statements for the year ended 31 October 1993 in accordance with current accounting standards and legislation, explaining your treatment of items (1) to (4).

Note: You are not required to prepare extracts of the cash flow statement or the directors' report.

ICAEW, Financial Reporting, November 1993   **(15 marks)**

6.10 Global plc, which prepares accounts to 31 January each year, operates in several different countries and has recently obtained government financial assistance both in the UK and abroad:

(1) A foreign government has granted £4m to cover the establishment of a new factory. The factory and associated plant installation were completed in November 1992 at a cost of £10m for the land and buildings (land element – £2m) and £5m for the plant. Asset lives were estimated at 50 years for the premises and 10 years for the plant; a full year's depreciation is charged in the year of acquisition.

The grant was dependent on an inspection by government officials and the company retaining ownership of the factory for the next five years. The grant was released by the foreign government on 27 March 1993 following their inspection in January 1993.

The country in which the factory is situated has had a turbulent history with frequent changes of government but has enjoyed a period of relative stability over the past three years. No previous governments have granted assistance to foreign companies.

(2) A local authority in the UK has provided a grant of £130 000 which covers the total initial establishment costs of a new training programme for company staff. The grant is dependent on the company expanding its existing training unit and increasing the number of trainees in direct production areas within the local factory by 20 per cent. The increased number of trainees would have to be sustained for at least three years.

The grant was received in January 1993. Expected costs of the complete programme are £300 000 of which £100 000, relating to initial establishment costs, has been incurred to date.

Actual and projected trainee numbers provided by the production director are:

| | *Years ending 31 January* | | | |
	1993	*1994*	*1995*	*1996*
Welding shop	9	10	9	10
Lathe area	7	9	11	11
Computer-controlled machinery	11	14	13	14
Trainee general managers	3	2	2	2
	30	35	35	37

Requirement
Calculate the amounts which should be included in the financial statements for the year ended 31 January 1993, preparing all relevant notes in accordance with SSAP 4, Government grants.

ICAEW, Financial Reporting II, May 1993　　　　　　　　　　　　　**(8 marks)**

Liabilities

overview

This is the first of four chapters dealing with liabilities. In it we will discuss the nature of liabilities and how they should be recognised and valued. We will also look at the special type of liabilities known as provisions as well as contingent liabilities and, for convenience, contingent assets. We will deal with accounting for financial instruments, including derivatives, and the special cases of leases and pensions in the following three chapters.

The standards covered in this chapter are

- FRS 12 *Provisions, Contingent Liabilities and Assets* (1998)
- IAS 37 *Provisions, Contingent Liabilities and Contingent Assets* (1998)

Introduction

Liabilities used to be the poor relation in the standard-setting family. When we published the first edition of this book in 1981 the subject did not rate a chapter. Assets were all the rage; liabilities were simply the amounts that the entity owed to be deducted from assets to give the 'net assets'. But the world has changed and now the issue of accounting for liabilities has become one of the more fascinating and complex aspects of accounting theory and practice. Why has this all happened?

The first point to make is that we, and here 'we' encompasses the generality of accountants not just the authors, were wrong. Liabilities were a more important topic than accountants had recognised but far more thinking had been done about the valuation of assets, because it was easier to identify possible different bases of measurement: replacement cost, net realisable value, etc., than was the case with liabilities. But there are other reasons: the last twenty years has seen the introduction or, possibly a more apposite description, the invention of a whole range of far more complex financial instruments, which are often combined with assets and liabilities to create sophisticated financial packages that are capable of bringing to their owners great financial joy or total financial devastation. The language of accounting has changed; words and phrases like *derivatives* and *hedge accounting*, both of which we will discuss in the next chapter, have moved from the periphery to the centre of the profession's lexicon.

The forced liquidation of companies because of their inability to pay their debts is not a new phenomenon. Indeed, much of the early history of the accountancy profession was concerned with liquidations. However, while not discounting some of the spectacular failures of the Victorian era, we are all aware that modern disasters are getting bigger and worse and hence there is the need for users of financial statements to be supplied with appropriate information that will help them form a view as to the financial viability of entities. But the decisions as to the nature of information that should be supplied are still largely based on opinion, for there is even less coherence in the attempts to devise a theory of accounting for liabilities than has been achieved in the corresponding debate about assets. The liabilities debate is, however, starting to take off and we shall refer to some its strands in the course of this and the following chapters.

The debate associated with the treatment of various aspects of liabilities has intensified in recent years, both internationally and locally, for the countries that are members of the European Union. The convergence programme, which we discussed in Chapter 3, is increasing its pace and is now involving areas, like liabilities, where there has been a relative lack of conceptual thinking. As far as EU members are concerned, the game is becoming even more heated since the promulgation of the EU Regulation which requires that from 1 January 2005 all listed companies in the EU will have to prepare their consolidated financial statements in accordance with international standards.[1]

The three sources of funding

A company acquires capital funding through three sources:

- from owners – through either direct contribution of share capital or the retention of profits
- by borrowing
- through gifts.

The last named might seem an unusual source but in fact governments and other agencies do make significant contributions to some companies. Let us start with these.

Grants and gifts

We discussed the subject of accounting for government grants in Chapter 6 where we pointed out that a logical case could be made for retaining on the balance sheet a section, separate from owners' equity and liabilities, representing the volume of funds that have been provided by government and similar agencies. However, as we pointed out, SSAP 4 *Accounting for government grants*, does not take this line. Instead the standard requires that the government grant should be credited to the profit and loss account either immediately or over time. Hence, a transfer is made between the 'gift' source of finance and shareholders' funds; the grant is thus treated as a gift to the owners rather than to the business itself. A more unusual form of gift is sometimes found in small family-owned businesses where a very long-term loan is granted, possibly interest free, where, under foreseeable circumstances, there is no intention that the loan should be repaid. In such, admittedly rare, cases the source of finance would be treated as a liability.

Debt and equity

The two other sources of funding are referred to as debt (or liabilities) and equity. Debt, or liabilities, are the resources provided by outsiders and equity comprises the resources provided by the owners of a company. The use of the word equity to describe the source of funds provided by owners can sometimes lead to confusion, because it is narrower than the term shareholders. In the context of companies with share capital, there may be both equity shares and non-equity shares, such as preference shares, in issue. As we shall see, the latter

---

[1] See Chapter 3.

shares are usually more appropriately described as liabilities than equity, the latter term being restricted to the owners who hold the residual interest in the income and capital of the company.

In the sections that follow it will be necessary to consider the nature of the accounting problems that have to be faced when considering liabilities. These are recognition, measurement, presentation and disclosure.

Recognition

The fundamental questions are when has the entity made a commitment that falls to be recognised in the financial statements and when has it discharged that commitment so that the liability can be removed from the balance sheet?

Measurement

Once a liability is to be recognised, at what amount should it be recognised in the balance sheet? A related question is the measurement of the expense relating to the liability and deciding on the period in which it should be charged in the financial statements.

Presentation

Presentation covers such things as where, in the financial statements, a liability should appear as well as where changes in the value of the liabilities should be disclosed, whether in the profit and loss account or the statement of total recognised gains and losses. In some ways, presentation is not a good description of the issues dealt with under this heading because they include matters such as the distinction between long-term creditors, short-term creditors and provisions as well as that between debt and equity. Perhaps a better description would be presentation and classification.

Disclosure

This is concerned with what information should be disclosed and how it should be disclosed.

Liabilities

The nature of liabilities

We should start by considering what the basic nature of liability is, and where better to start than with the *Statement of Principles for Financial Reporting* that provided the following definition:

> **Liabilities are obligations of an entity to transfer economic benefits as a result of past transactions or events. (Para. 4.23)**

The concepts involved are straightforward. Perhaps the key word in the definition is 'obligations'. A liability only exists when the entity cannot avoid the future transfer of economic benefit – which might take the form of cash or the provision of goods or services. The word obligation is not, in this context, always capable of objective interpretation. There can be no doubt about the nature of a legal or contractual obligation but there may be other circumstances where the entity has no realistic alternative other than to transfer economic benefit. An example could be a business that may, for commercial considerations, have no realistic alternative to refunding the price of goods that fail to meet the expectations of customers, even though it has no legal obligation to do so. Such obligations, which are not legally binding, are often termed *constructive obligations*.

> *Ownership interest* or *equity* is the residual amount found by deducting all the entity's liabilities from all of the entity's assets. (Para. 4.37)

The *Statement of Principles* goes on to make a point that is obvious but which is worth restating, that owners, unlike creditors, do not have the ability to insist that a transfer is made to them regardless of the circumstances.

The recognition of liabilities

UK financial reporting standards are remarkably silent on the topic of the recognition and derecognition of liabilities; the topic is not addressed in FRS 4, *Capital instruments* (see Chapter 8), which tacitly assumes that there will be no difficulty in deciding whether something should be recognised and is more concerned with whether the item represents debt or equity. The only standard that directly addresses the recognition or derecognition of liabilities is FRS 5 *Reporting the Substance of Transactions*. This states at Para. 20:

> Where a transaction results in an item that meets the definition of an asset or liability, that item should be recognised in the balance sheet if –
>
> (a) there is sufficient evidence of the existence of the item (including, where appropriate, evidence that a future inflow or outflow of benefit will occur), and
>
> (b) the item can be measured at a monetary amount with sufficient reliability.

This is in line with the criteria for recognition specified in the ASB *Statement of Principles*, which were discussed in Chapter 1.[2]

The FRS 5 definition of a liability is that one exists if there are circumstance in which the entity is unable to avoid, legally or commercially, an outflow of benefits. This seems a very straightforward and sensible approach but, as we will see later it is proving to be one of the more difficult areas to resolve in the convergence programme.

The measurement of liabilities

We will discuss the measurement of financial liabilities and liabilities that have a market value in the following chapters and so at this stage we will focus on the measurement of liabilities arising from the obligation to provide goods and services where, typically, the customer has paid in advance. We will also use this part of the chapter to provide an introduction to a theoretical model of measuring the value of a liability, that is referred as the relief value approach. We will in this section draw heavily on an ASB 'exploratory essay', the first and so far the only one publications of this type to be published by the Board, written by Andrew Lennard and entitled, *Liabilities and how to account for them.*[3]

---

[2] FRS 5 *Reporting the Substance of Transactions*, Para. 18. The subject of the recognition of liabilities is also of course covered in the *Statement of Principles for Financial Reporting* but the discussion is mostly about the nature of evidence; it does not change the basic notion that a liability exists when benefits flow out of the entity.

[3] *Liabilities and how to account for them*, ASB Oct. 2002. The publication carries the disclaimer that it represents the views of the author and not the Board and that there are no plans to develop proposals for an accounting standard directly from the paper.

The simple example on which much of the argument of the paper is based is that of a business that receives in advance a non-refundable fee of £100 to perform a service that it believes that will cost £60 to discharge. Until the obligation is discharged, the business has a liability, but at what value should it appear in the balance sheet? Some have argued[4] that there might be circumstances (strong confidence that the work can be completed for £60 would be an important condition) in which the liability would be shown at £60 with profit of £40 being recognised immediately. This would be consistent with the view that in very special circumstances, the making of the sale is the 'critical event' in the transaction.

It may, at this stage, be helpful to consider how, in the absence of accounting rules, the liability might be measured if we removed the assumption of certainty. In such a case the liability could be measured on the basis of the best estimate of what it would cost to discharge the order. Such an approach is not purely theoretical because, if another business were to offer to discharge the service on behalf of the original supplier, that estimate would provide the benchmark against which the offer might be judged; if the proposed price is less than the estimated cost of providing the service then, all other things being equal, the offer is worth accepting.[5] An approach on these lines would measure the liability on the basis of its settlement value, where settlement value is analogous to exit values as applied to assets. Lennard argues strongly against the use of settlement values as the basis of the measurement of liabilities. He believes that the purchase consideration, in this case £100, represents the minimum figure at which the liability should be stated because this 'ensures that future ("unearned") returns are not anticipated, but are reflected only when they arise, on settlement of the liability'.[6]

Such an approach places emphasis on the timing of the recognition of revenue rather than on an economic assessment of the value of the liability. This is clear later in the paper where Lennard goes on to argue that, while the financial statements should be useful in predicting future cash flows, they should not consist of representations of future cash flows.[7]

Let us accept Lennard's argument for a moment and consider the situations where the liability would be stated in excess of the floor value of £100. This will occur if it becomes apparent that the contract has become onerous, in that it is now expected to cost more than £100 to fulfil. In such a case the business has a choice: it could seek to be released from the contract or grit its teeth and suffer the loss. Then, again ignoring legal issues and possible long-term consequences, it will select the least costly of these two options. Hence, Lennard argues that the liability should generally be measured by reference to the consideration but in some circumstances, such as onerous contracts, it should be measured at the lower of the cost of performance and the cost of release.

In other words the relief value of the liability to the business is found from the formulation in Figure 7.1.

This formulation is the counterpart of the definition of the 'value to the business' of the asset, see Figure 1.3, where consideration is the equivalent of replacement cost, settlement amount being akin to recoverable amount and cost of performance and cost of release replacing value in use and net realisable value.[8]

There is, however, one major difference between the two definitions. The 'value to the business' measure, or to give its alternative name 'deprival value', shows the amount the

[4] Richard A. Samualson, 'Accounting for Liabilities to Perform Services', *Accounting Horizons*, Vol. 7, No. 3, 1993.

[5] We have here ignored any legal complications that may arise from the possible switch of supplier as we have any possible damage to the reputation of the original supplier.

[6] A. Lennard, *Liabilities and how to account for them*, London, ASB, 2002, para. 24.

[7] *Op. cit.* para. 87.

[8] A very much earlier formulation of relief value was provided by W.T. Baxter, *Accounting Values and Inflation*, Maidenhead, McGraw-Hill, 1975.

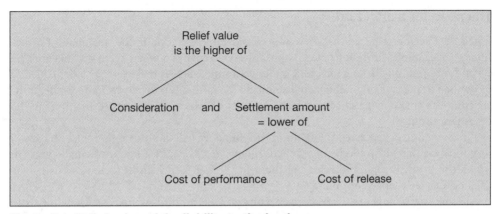

Figure 7.1 **Relief value of the liability to the business**

entity would need to receive, should it be deprived of the asset, to make it as well off as it was before the loss. Can the same be said about relief value? It seems not. To return to our simple example, if a fairy godmother waved a magic wand and made the liability disappear how much better off would the business be, or in other words how much should they be prepared to pay the fairy to cast her spell? The answer is the amount that the business would not then be required to pay, which is the expected cost of providing the goods or service, and not the original consideration of £100.

The question of how to measure liabilities for services and the associated question of when to recognise revenue is likely to continue for some time.

Provisions and contingencies

Provisions and contingent items are bound up with doubt and uncertainty. There may be no doubt that a provision is a liability – something is owed or an obligation has to be discharged – but there may be doubt as to how much is owed or when it has to be paid. In the case of a contingent asset or liability there may be doubt as to whether the thing exists at all. Doubt and uncertainty very easily give rise to uneven accounting treatment and, as we shall show, prior to the intervention of the ASB, this was particularly true in the case of provisions and, to a lesser extent (because the ASC had published SSAP 18 *Accounting for Contingencies*) in the case of contingent assets and liabilities. The ASB issued a Discussion Paper in November 1995 and an Exposure Draft, FRED 14, in June 1997 which was followed by FRS 12 *Provisions, Contingent Liabilities and Assets* in September 1998.

FRS 12 Provisions, Contingent Liabilities and Assets

We deal first with provisions and then go on to consider contingent liabilities and assets, the last named being included in a standard which is largely devoted to liabilities because the treatment of contingent assets and contingent liabilities share many common features.

The need for a standard

It had long been recognised that there was considerable variation in the treatment of provisions. For example, provisions were almost always recognised when there was likely to be expenditure resulting from goods sold under warranty, whereas they were far less frequently recognised in the case of potential environmental liabilities. But there was more to the problem than inconsistent practice: the lack of clarity allowed accountants to manipulate the figures for profit.

If provisions can be related to intention ('we think we will do this') rather than obligation ('we must do this') it would be possible to smooth profits by creating provisions in years in which the profit is high and releasing them in years in which profits are low (using the defence that 'we changed our mind').

Another way of apparently creating a healthy growth in profits was to engage in 'big bath' accounting. This often occurred following an acquisition of a new subsidiary or in a reorganisation of some kind, possibly following a change in management after disappointing financial results. The profit and loss account was charged not only with committed expenditure but also with planned expenditure for several years. The failure of users of financial statements to understand the significance of excess provisions and its beneficial effect on the reported profits of the years following the acquisition or reorganisation helped to boost the careers of a number of so-called 'company doctors'.

FRS 12 is a standard that is concerned with measurement and hence addresses three main issues: When should a provision be recognised? How should it be measured? How should it be disclosed?

We will deal with these in turn.

Provisions

Recognition of provisions

The summary of FRS 12 (Para. d) provides a succinct statement of the main issues:

> A provision should be recognised when an entity has a present obligation (legal or constructive) as a result of a past event, it is probable that a transfer of economic benefits will be required to settle the obligation, and a reliable estimate can be made of the amount of the obligation. Unless these conditions are met, no provision should be recognised.

A provision should only be made if a liability cannot be avoided, and this particular condition will usually be easily dealt with if there is a legal contract involved, but the standard also refers to non-legal or constructive obligations. These are obligations that arise because the reporting entity has created a valid expectation on the part of other parties that it will discharge its responsibilities towards them either because of its past actions or because it has clearly stated that it will do so (Para. 2).

If a provision is to satisfy the definition of a liability, it must have arisen from a *past event* or *obligating event*, in other words it must result from some past action of the entity such that it has 'no realistic alternative to settling the obligation created by the event' (Para. 17). The ASB strongly makes the point that financial statements deal with the entity's financial position at the end of its reporting period, and not its possible position in the future, and that no provision should be made for the costs of operating in the future or for providing against occurrences which the entity can avoid by changing its style of operations. An example of this is provided in the standard (Para. 19), namely that of an entity which might, because of commercial pressures or legal requirements, have good evidence that it will need to incur certain expenditures if it is to operate in a particular way in the future. The example quoted is the possible need to fit a smoke filter in a certain type of factory. It is argued that this should not give rise to a provision because the entity can avoid the expenditure by changing its operating methods and, hence, there is no present liability. Intuitively, there is something a bit odd about this, for it implies that the financial statement should ignore what might potentially be a catastrophic event if, say, the likely costs of complying with new environmental requirements mean that the existing business ceases to be economically viable. The answer is that, if the potential event is high in probability and large in magnitude, its impact on the business might be reflected through the write-down of certain assets (see impairment of assets in Chapter 5) or by the removal of the assumption that the business is a going concern. These two actions are related to the future while a provision has to be firmly rooted in the past.

The decision as to whether a constructive liability exists may not be straightforward, especially if we need to identify the past or obligating event. That event might simply be the announcement of a decision. Consider the situation of a company, which, possibly because it wants to construct a plant with an 'uncertain' environmental impact, needs to build up the goodwill of the local community and so decides to underwrite the costs of a local arts festival. Suppose that following the announcement of the possibility of the grant the local organisers take some action resulting from that announcement which increases their financial exposure. Should the company recognise a provision even if it had not yet signed a formal agreement and could legally change its mind? If, as seems likely given the facts stated, the company believes that it must stand by the announcement, then a provision should be recognised.

The measurement of provisions

The basic rule is that:

> **The amount recognised as a provision should be the best estimate of the expenditure required to settle the present obligation at the balance sheet date. (Para. 36)**

Of course, but how in a world of uncertainty do we measure it? In some cases use can be made of elementary statistical techniques such as *expected values*. For example, a store might at its year end have 100 000 items still under warranty and, on the basis of experience, estimate that 5 per cent will need to be repaired, and that the average cost of repair is £300.

Then the expected value of the cost of servicing the warranty that should be recognised as a provision is:

$$(0.95 \times 0 + 0.05 \times £300) \times £100\,000 = £1\,500\,000$$

In the case of a single event a distinction needs to be drawn between the *best estimate* and the *most likely outcome*. Consider the example provided in the standard. It is of an obligation to rectify a serious fault in a plant where the 'most likely' outcome is that the repairs can be completely rectified at the first attempt at a cost of £1m. But this is not certain, so the provision should be for a greater amount, or 'best estimate', to allow for the possibility of additional expenditure. This is a variant of the expected value approach in that the additional amount would depend on both the magnitude of the cost of the additional work but also the probability that it will be necessary.

The need for prudence as conventionally defined – the asymmetric statement that profits and assets should not be overstated and expenses and liabilities not understated – is introduced in Para. 43 but the ASB goes on quickly to warn against going too far. To quote directly, 'if the projected costs of a particularly adverse outcome are estimated on a prudent basis, that outcome is not then deliberately treated as more probable than is realistically the case' (Para. 43). This phrase, which must of one of the least elegant examples of ASB drafting, seems to exhort us to be prudent but not to overdo it.

Present values

> Where the effect of the time value of money is material, the amount of the provision should be the present value of the expenditures expected to be required to settle the obligation. (Para. 45)

In the case of provisions it is recommended that the easiest way of dealing with risk is to use a discount rate that reflects the risks specific to the liability, but if this option is selected the cash flows to be discounted should not themselves be adjusted for risk; rather, the 'best estimates' should be used. An acceptable alternative is to adjust the cash flows for risk and use a risk-free rate of discount.

Changes in provisions

> Provisions should be reviewed at each balance sheet date and adjusted to reflect the current best estimate. (Para. 62)

Provisions and the recognition of assets

> The recognition of a provision might also give rise to the recognition of an asset, but this can only be done when it is clear that the future economic benefits will flow to the entity. (Para. 66)

Disclosure requirements

The disclosure requirements are set out in Paras 89 and 90; the first paragraph deals primarily with numbers, the second mainly with words. The numerical statement should reflect the changes in provisions that have occurred during the accounting period: provisions created, used and reversed as well as increases in present values due to the passage of time and the consequences of changes in the discount rate. The words that should be supplied include, for each class of provision, the nature of the liability, some indication about the associated risk and a note of the extent of any expected reimbursements.

Contingent assets and liabilities

Company law has for a long time required the disclosure, by way of a note to the financial statements, of information concerning contingent liabilities, but there is no such requirement concerning contingent assets.

Accounting for contingencies was the subject and title of SSAP 18, issued in 1980, and this called for both the recognition, within financial statements, of certain contingent liabilities, but only in extreme cases, and the provision of note information about contingent assets but only where there was a high probability that they would unwind in the entity's favour. FRS 12, which replaced SSAP 18, also forbids the recognition of contingent assets under any circumstances but adopts a different, less useful, definition of contingent liabilities.

Contingent assets

It will be helpful to start the discussion with the definition of a contingent asset.

> **A possible asset that arises from past events and whose existence will be confirmed only by the occurrence of one or more uncertain events not wholly within the entity's control. (Para. 2)**

A bet on a horse race would seem to satisfy the definition pretty well, so too, to take a more commercial example, would be a drug which is the subject of clinical trials. However, prudence will usually dictate that such possible assets are not accorded the status of contingent assets – which will continue to be very rare beasts.

Contingent assets: disclosure requirements

'An entity should not recognise a contingent asset' (Para. 31), but what should be disclosed? This is covered in Para. 94, which states that where 'an inflow of economic benefits is probable', the nature of the contingent assets should be disclosed with, if practicable, an estimate of their financial effect measured on the same principles as FRS 12 applies to provisions.

Contingent liabilities

The definition of a contingent liability has two elements; the first is the counterpart of the contingent asset while the second breaks new ground. A *contingent liability* is defined as:

(a) **A possible obligation that arises from past events and whose existence will be confirmed only by the occurrence of one or more uncertain future events not wholly within the entity's control; or**

(b) **a present obligation that arises from past events but is not recognised because:**

    (i) **it is not probable that a transfer of economic benefits will be required to settle the obligation; or**

    (ii) **the amount of the obligation cannot be measured with sufficient reliability (Para. 2).**

The second part of the definition (which was not included in the SSAP 18 definition) provides a convenient vehicle for picking up items which are actually provisions, insofar that they represent *present obligations*, but which do not fully satisfy the tests for recognition set out in Para. 14, either because it is 'not probable' that the liability will have to be discharged, or because it is not possible to make a 'reliable estimate' of the liability. Thus FRS 12 requires that such pseudo-provisions should be treated in the same way as 'real' contingent liabilities. This may be convenient but it seems unfortunate that, as a result, the concept of contingency is muddied.

Figure 7.2, which is taken from FRS 12, shows a decision tree for distinguishing between provisions and contingent liabilities. The figure shows that, if it is unlikely that there is a present obligation, and that there is only a remote possibility that the liability, if it did exist, would have to be discharged, then the item can be ignored. But, if there is a reasonable chance that there is an obligation, but with very little chance that it will have to be discharged, then it should be disclosed by way of a note to the financial statements as part of contingent liabilities.

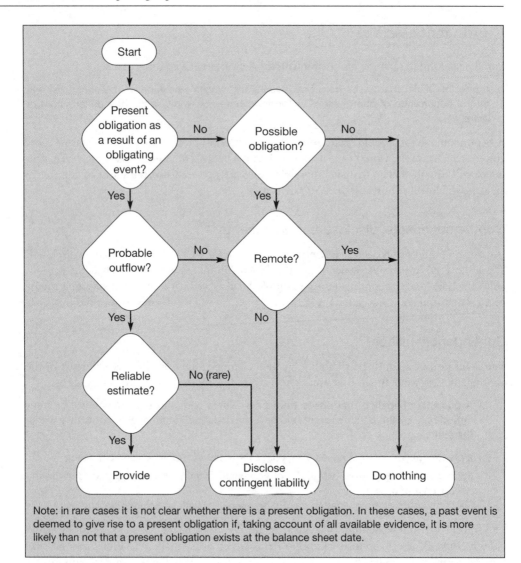

Figure 7.2 Decision tree

Source: ASB FRS 12, *Provisions, Contingent Liabilities and Assets* (1998). © ASB Publications Limited 2000. Reproduced with permission.

Contingent liabilities: disclosure requirements

As is the case with contingent assets, contingent liabilities should not be recognised but, as might be expected, the test for whether the item should be shown in the notes to the financial statements is not the same for the two items. In the case of contingent assets note disclosure is required when the inflow of benefits *is probable* while in the case of contingent liabilities disclosure can only be avoided if *the possibility of payment is remote* (Para. 91). For each class of contingent liability that passes the test information should be provided on their estimated financial effect, the uncertainties relating to the amount or timing of any outflow and an indication of the possibility of any reimbursement.

Compliance with international standards

FRS 12 was developed jointly with the international standard on the same topic, IAS 37 *Provisions, Contingent Liabilities and Contingent Assets*. Hence, all the requirements of the IAS are included in the FRS and there are no differences of substance between their common requirements. The FRS also deals with the circumstances under which an asset should be recognised when a provision is recognised and gives more guidance than the IAS on the discount rate to be used in the present value calculation.

Summary

In this chapter, we have introduced the subject of accounting for liabilities and have noted that this is an area where the theoretical debate is only just beginning.

We have examined the definition of a liability and explored the recognition and measurement of liabilities. We have then explored the treatment of provisions and have explained the approach of the ASB, designed particularly to stop abuses that involved the making of excessive provisions. Finally, we have discussed the nature and treatment of contingent liabilities and assets.

FRS 12 and IAS 37 were both issued in 1998 and were drafted in accordance with the same principles. Hence this is one of the relatively few areas where there is already convergence between the UK and international standards.

Recommended reading

W.T. Baxter *Accounting values and inflation*, McGraw-Hill, Maidenhead, 1975.

IATA (in association with KPMG), *Frequent flyer programme accounting*, IATA, Montreal, 1995.

'Revenue recognition' *Company Reporting* No. 142, April 2000.

P. Weetman, *Assets and liabilities: Their definition and recognition*, Certified Accountants Publications Limited, London, 1988.

Excellent up-to-date and detailed reading on the subject matter of this chapter and on much of the contents of this book is provided by the most recent edition of:

UK and International GAAP, A. Wilson, M. Davies, M. Curtis and G. Wilkinson-Riddle (eds), Ernst & Young, Butterworths Tolley, London. At the time of writing the most recent edition is the 7th, published 2001.

Questions

7.1 Provisions are particular kinds of liabilities. It therefore follows that provisions should be recognised when the definition of a liability has been met. The key requirement of a liability is a present obligation and thus this requirement is critical also in the context of the recognition of a provision. However, although accounting for provisions is an important topic for standard setters, it is only recently that guidance has been issued on provisioning in financial statements. In the UK, the Accounting Standards Board has recently issued FRS 12 Provisions, Contingent Liabilities and Contingent Assets.

Required:

(a) (i) Explain why there was a need for more detailed guidance on accounting for provisions in the UK. (7 marks)

(ii) Explain the circumstances under which a provision should be recognised in the financial statements according to FRS 12: Provisions, Contingent Liabilities and Contingent Assets. (6 marks)

(b) Discuss whether the following provisions have been accounted for correctly under FRS 12: 'Provisions, Contingent Liabilities and Contingent Assets'.

World Wide Nuclear Fuels plc disclosed the following information in its financial statements for the year ending 30 November 1999:

Provisions and long-term commitments

(i) Provision for decommissioning the Group's radioactive facilities is made over their useful life and covers complete demolition of the facility within fifty years of it being taken out of service together with any associated waste disposal. The provision is based on future prices and is discounted using a current market rate of interest.

Provision for decommissioning costs	£m
Balance at 1.12.98	675
Adjustment arising from change in price levels charged to reserves	33
Charged in the year to profit and loss account	125
Adjustment due to change in knowledge (charged to reserves)	27
Balance at 30.11.99	860

There are still decommissioning costs of £1231m (undiscounted) to be provided for in respect of the group's radioactive facilities as the company's policy is to build up the required provision over the life of the facility

Assume that adjustments to the provision due to change in knowledge about the accuracy of the provision do not give rise to future economic benefits. (7 marks)

(ii) The company purchased an oil company during the year. As part of the sale agreement, oil has to be supplied for a five year period to the company's former holding company at an uneconomic rate. As a result a provision for future operating losses has been set up of £135m which relates solely to the uneconomic supply of oil. Additionally the oil company is exposed to environmental liabilities arising out of its past obligations, principally in respect of remedial work to soil and ground water systems, although currently there is no legal obligation to carry out the work. Liabilities for environmental costs are provided for when the Group determines a formal plan of action on the closure of an inactive site and when expenditure on remedial work is probable and the cost can be measured with reasonable certainty. However in this case, it has been decided to provide for £120m in respect of the environmental liability on the acquisition of the oil company. World Wide Nuclear Fuels has a reputation for ensuring that the environment is preserved and protected from the effects of its business activities. (5 marks)

ACCA, Financial Reporting Environment (UK Stream), December 1999   **(25 marks)**

7.2   FRS 12 – *Provisions, contingent liabilities and contingent assets* was issued in September 1998. Prior to its publication, there was no UK Accounting Standard that dealt with the general subject of accounting for provisions.

Extract plc prepares its financial statements to 31 December each year. During the years ended 31 December 2000 and 31 December 2001, the following event occurred:

> Extract plc is involved in extracting minerals in a number of different countries. The process typically involves some contamination of the site from which the minerals are extracted. Extract plc makes good this contamination only where legally required to do so by legislation passed in the relevant country.
>
> The company has been extracting minerals in Copperland since January 1998 and expects its site to produce output until 31 December 2005. On 23 December 2000, it came to the attention of the directors of Extract plc that the government of Copperland was virtually certain to pass legislation requiring the making good of mineral extraction sites. The legislation was duly passed on 15 March 2001. The directors of Extract plc estimate that the cost of making good the site in Copperland will be £2 million. This estimate is of the actual cash expenditure that will be incurred on 31 December 2005.

Required

(a) **Explain why there was a need for an Accounting Standard dealing with provisions, and summarise the criteria that need to be satisfied before a provision is recognised.**

(10 marks)

(b) **Compute the effect of the estimated cost of making good the site on the financial statements of Extract plc for BOTH of the years ended 31 December 2000 and 2001. Give full explanations of the figures you compute.**

The annual discount rate to be used in any relevant calculations is 10%.   (10 marks)

CIMA, Financial Reporting – UK Accounting Standards, May 2001   (**20 marks**)

7.3   FRS 12 – *Provisions, Contingent Liabilities and Contingent Assets* requires contingencies to be classified as remote, possible, probable and virtually certain. Each of these categories should then be treated differently, depending on whether it is an asset or a liability.

Required

(a) **Explain why FRS 12 classifies contingencies in this manner.**   (5 marks)

The Chief Accountant of Z plc, a construction company, is finalising the work on the financial statements for the year ended 31 October 2002. She has prepared a list of all of the matters that might require some adjustment or disclosure under the requirements of FRS 12.

(i) A customer has lodged a claim against Z plc for repairs to an office block built by the company. The roof leaks and it appears that this is due to negligence in construction. Z plc is negotiating with the customer and will probably have to pay for repairs that will cost approximately £100 000.

(ii) The roof in (i) above was installed by a subcontractor employed by Z plc. Z plc's lawyers are confident that the company would have a strong claim to recover the whole of any costs from the subcontractor. The Chief Accountant has obtained the subcontractor's latest financial statements. The subcontractor appears to be almost insolvent with few assets.

(iii) Whenever Z plc finishes a project, it gives customers a period of three months to notify any construction defects. These are repaired immediately. The balance sheet at 31 October 2001 carried a provision of £80 000 for future repairs. The estimated cost of repairs to completed contracts as at 31 October 2002 is £120 000.

(iv) During the year ended 31 October 2002, Z plc lodged a claim against a large firm of electrical engineers which had delayed the completion of a contract. The engineering company's Directors have agreed in principle to pay Z plc £30 000 compensation. Z plc's Chief Accountant is confident that this amount will be received before the end of December 2002.

(v) An architect has lodged a claim against Z plc for the loss of a laptop computer during a site visit. He alleges that the company did not take sufficient care to secure the site office and that this led to the computer being stolen while he inspected the project. He is claiming for consequential losses of £90 000 for the value of the vital files that were on the computer. Z plc's lawyers have indicated that the company might have to pay a trivial sum in compensation for the computer hardware. There is almost no likelihood that the courts would award damages for the lost files because the architect should have copied them.

Required

(b) **Explain how each of the contingencies (i) to (v) above should be accounted for. Assume that all amounts stated are material.** (3 marks for each of (i) to (v) = 15 marks)

CIMA, Financial Accounting – UK Accounting Standards, November 2002   **(20 marks)**

7.4 L plc sells gaming cards to retailers, who then resell them to the general public. Customers who buy these cards scratch off a panel to reveal whether they have won a cash prize. There are several different ranges of cards, each of which offers a different range of prizes.

Prize-winners send their winning cards to L plc and are paid by cheque. If the prize is major, then the prize-winner is required to telephone L plc to register the claim and then send the winning card to a special address for separate handling.

All cards are printed and packaged under conditions of high security. Special printing techniques make it easy for L plc to identify forged claims and it is unusual for customers to make false claims. Large claims are, however, checked using a special chemical process that takes several days to take effect.

The directors are currently finalising their financial statements for the year ended 31 March 2002. They are unsure about how to deal with the following items:

(i) A packaging error on a batch of 'Chance' cards meant that there were too many major prize cards in several boxes. L plc recalled the batch from retailers, but was too late to prevent many of the defective cards being sold. The company is being flooded with claims. L plc's lawyers have advised that the claims are valid and must be paid. It has proved impossible to determine the likely level of claims that will be made in respect of this error because it will take several weeks to establish the success of the recall and the number of defective cards.

(ii) A prize-winner has registered a claim for a £200 000 prize from a 'Lotto' card. The financial statements will be finalised before the card can be processed and checked.

(iii) A claim has been received for £100 000 from a 'Winner' card. The maximum prize offered for this game is £90 000 and so the most likely explanation is that the card has been forged. The police are investigating the claim, but this will not be resolved before the financial statements are finalised. Once the police investigation has concluded, L plc will make a final check to ensure that the card is not the result of a printing error.

(iv) The company received claims totalling £300 000 during the year from a batch of bogus 'Happy' cards that had been forged by a retailer in Newtown. The police have prosecuted the retailer and he has recently been sent to prison. The directors of L plc have decided to pay customers who bought these cards 50% of the amount claimed as a goodwill gesture. They have not, however, informed the lucky prize-winners of this yet.

Required

(a) Identify the appropriate accounting treatment of each of the claims against L plc in respect of (i) to (iv) above. Your answer should have due regard to the requirements of FRS 12, *Provisions, contingent liabilities and contingent assets.*

(3 marks for each of items (i) to (iv) = 12 marks)

(b) It has been suggested that readers of financial statements do not always pay sufficient attention to contingent liabilities even though they may have serious implications for the future of the company.

    (i) Explain why insufficient attention might be paid to contingent liabilities. (4 marks)

    (ii) Explain how FRS 12 prevents companies from treating as contingent liabilities those liabilities that should be recognised in the balance sheet. (4 marks)

CIMA, Financial Accounting – UK Accounting Standards, May 2002 **(20 marks)**

Financial instruments

overview

In this chapter we deal with capital instruments and the broader category of financial instruments, including derivatives, as well as hedge accounting. This is currently an area of much flux and uncertainty. Standard setters are only now coming to grips with the vexed subjects of derivatives and hedge accounting but perhaps the major cause of uncertainty is the impact of the convergence programme. The relevant International Standards, IAS 32 and 39, are still evolving while the UK standards are also being reviewed. The relevant UK Exposure Draft, FRED 30, is itself tentative in some places in referring to the need to await the completion of developments in the international standard-setting arena while some of its proposed changes depend on changes being made to UK company law.

The UK statements covered in this chapter are:

- FRS 4 *Capital Instruments* (1993)
- FRED 23 *Financial Instruments: Hedge Accounting* (2002)
- FRS 13 *Derivatives and other Financial Instruments: Disclosure* (1998)
- FRED 30 *Financial Instruments: Disclosure and Presentation and Financial Instruments: Recognition and Measurement* (2002)

The international standards to which we refer are:

- IAS 32 *Financial Instruments: Disclosure and Presentation* (revised 1998)
- IAS 39 *Financial Instruments: Recognition and Measurement* (revised 2000)

Both were in the process of revision as at January 2003.

Introduction

A financial instrument can involve very simple things like cash, or something far more complicated, such as a derivative. At this stage it might be useful to introduce the definition of a financial instrument as set out in FRED 30 *Financial Instruments: Disclosure and Presentation*,[1] which is itself derived from IAS 32.

A *financial instrument* is any contract that gives rise to both a financial asset of one entity and a financial liability or equity instrument of another entity.

A *financial asset* is any asset that is:

a) Cash;

b) A contractual right to receive cash or another financial asset from another entity;

---

[1] FRED 30, Para. 5, p. 32.

c) A contractual right to exchange financial instruments with another entity under conditions that are potentially favourable; or

d) An equity instrument of another entity.

A *financial liability* is any liability that is a contractual obligation:

a) To deliver cash or another financial asset to another entity; or

b) To exchange financial instruments with another entity under conditions that are potentially unfavourable.

An *equity instrument* is any contract that evidences a residual interest in the assets of an entity after deducting all of its liabilities.

This is not an easy definition to understand and one always knows that there are problems when, as is the case with financial assets, the definition of a term includes the term itself. It is perhaps helpful to realise that the definition excludes physical assets and the obligations to provide services in the future. We will in this chapter concentrate on financial liabilities but will also need to touch on financial assets, especially in relation to derivatives and hedging transactions.

The present position with respect to accounting for financial instruments can best be described as 'messy'. The situation as this book went to press was that the ASB had issued FRED 30 as the forerunner of two possible standards, *Financial Instruments: Disclosure and Presentation and Financial Instruments: Measurement.* The messiness of the present position is that the proposed standards are based on proposed amended versions of two International Standards, IAS 32 *Financial Instruments: Disclosure and Presentation,* and IAS 39 *Financial Instruments: Recognition and Measurement.* Also, the implementation of some of the changes proposed in FRED 30 would require changes in UK company law. The proposed issue of the two new UK standards would lead to the withdrawal of two existing standards, FRS 4 *Capital Instruments* and FRS 13 *Derivatives and other Financial Instruments: Disclosures.*

In the circumstances we feel it would best help readers if we divided the chapter into two parts. In the first, we will concentrate on the basic principles underlying the issue and discuss the current but soon to be discarded standards. We will in so doing take account of their likely demise, but we need to remember the incremental nature of the developments in accounting standards. It is increasingly difficult fully to understand an accounting standard if one does not have some knowledge of its predecessor or predecessors. In the second part of the chapter, we will outline the contents of FRED 30 and comment on the likely progress of the convergence programme.

FRS 4 *Capital Instruments*

FRS 4 was the first ASB standard to deal with the issue of accounting for liabilities[2] and, while it is has been announced that it will be withdrawn as part of the convergence programme it still provides a useful introduction to the issues surrounding accounting for financial liabilities, and some appreciation of its contents will greatly assist in understanding the numerous developments that are currently taking place. The convergence programme is bringing about changes in classification and terminology in a number of areas and, in this case, the phrase capital instruments is being replaced by the broader term

[2] Although SSAP 18 dealt with contingent liabilities.

financial instruments, that includes both financial liabilities and financial assets. We will, for convenience, continue to use the term capital instruments in our discussion of FRS 4.

It is instructive to start by considering the objective of FRS 4, which is:

> to ensure that financial statements provide a clear, coherent and consistent treatment of capital instruments, in particular as regards the classification of instruments as debt, non-equity shares or equity shares; that costs associated with capital instruments are dealt with in a manner consistent with their classification, and, for redeemable instruments, allocated to accounting periods on a fair basis over the period the instrument is in issue; and that financial statements provide relevant information concerning the nature and amount of the entity's sources of finance and the associated costs, commitments and potential commitments. (Para. 1)

The paragraph makes specific reference to classification, appropriate measurement and disclosure but makes no mention of recognition. There is a brief discussion of recognition in FRS 5 *Reporting the Substance of Transactions* and the subject is covered in a little more depth in Chapter 5 of the *Statement of Principles.*

We should start by defining the term *capital instruments.*

> All instruments that are issued by reporting entities which are a means of raising finance, including shares, debentures, loans and debt instruments, options and warrants that give the holder the right to subscribe for or obtain capital instruments. In the case of consolidated financial statements the term includes capital instruments issued by subsidiaries except those that are held by another member of the group included in the consolidation. (Para. 2)

Another important definition is that of *finance costs.* These are:

> The difference between the net proceeds of an instrument and the total amount of the payments (or other transfers of economic benefits) that the issuer may be required to make in respect of the instrument. (Para. 8)

With these two definitions in mind the main points of FRS 4 can be summarised.

Balance sheet presentation

Capital instruments must be categorised into four groups for single companies and or six groups for consolidated financial statements as shown in Table 8.1.

Table 8.1 **Categorisation of capital instruments**

	Analysed between	
Shareholders' funds	Equity interests	Non-equity interests
Liabilities	Convertible liabilities	Non-convertible liabilities
Minority interests in subsidiaries	Equity interests in subsidiaries	Non-equity interests in subsidiaries

The period prior to the issue of FRS 4 had seen the issue of various hybrid forms of capital instruments that seemed to combine elements of debt and equity. Examples of the hybrid securities are convertible bonds where holders are given the right to convert into equity shares at a favourable price at some future time. Often the terms are such that the conversion is virtually certain to occur and existing shareholders benefit from obtaining capital at a relatively low rate of interest until conversion, when their ownership interest in the company is diluted.[3]

Because of their complexity, and the lack of a clear accounting standard, there was inconsistency in treatment and opportunities, which were from time to time taken, to paint the balance sheet in a more favourable light than reality might otherwise have allowed. All other things being equal, the higher the level of debt relative to shareholders' funds the higher the degree of risk, because failure to pay interest could lead to the insolvency of the company, whereas the failure to pay dividends would not have such a devastating effect. Similarly, from the point of view of equity shareholders, a high level of non-equity shares means that equity holders are subject to greater uncertainty in terms of their returns because of the prior claims of the non-equity holders. Hence the opportunity of painting the balance sheet in a rosy hue if there are possibilities that instruments which are essentially debt can be presented as part of shareholders' funds, or if non-equity interests can be classified as part of equity shares. As will be seen, the provisions of FRS 4 are such as to ensure that if an instrument contains any element of debt it should be treated as debt or, if the instrument is properly part of shareholders' funds, then, if the instrument contains any trace of non-equity, it should be recorded as non-equity.

Allocation of finance costs

Finance costs associated with liabilities and shares, other than equity shares, should be allocated to accounting periods at a constant rate on the carrying amount. This is the actuarial method that is illustrated in the examples that follow. Initially capital instruments should be recorded at the net amount of the issue proceeds and only the direct costs incurred in connection with the issue of the instruments should be deducted from the proceeds in arriving at this net amount. The finance cost for the period is added to the carrying amount and payments deducted from it. Thus, as will be seen, the carrying figure in the balance sheet may not be the same as the nominal value of the liability, but in the case of redeemable instruments this would result in the carrying amount at the time of redemption being equal to the amount payable at that time. Gains and losses will only occur on purchase or early redemption and the standard specifies clearly how these should be treated.

> Gains and losses arising on the repurchase or early settlement of debt should be recognised in the profit and loss account in the period during which the repurchase or early settlement is made. (FRS 4, Para. 32)

Accrued finance costs, to the extent that they will be paid in the next period, may be included with accruals, but even if this option is exercised, the accrual must be included in the carrying value for the purpose of calculating the finance costs and any gains or losses on repurchase or early settlement (FRS 4, Para. 30).

In some cases the amount payable on the debt may be contingent on uncertain future events such as changes in a price index. Such events should not be anticipated and the finance costs and carrying amount should only be adjusted when the event occurs (FRS 4, Para. 31).

---

[3] For an introduction to these hybrid forms of financial instruments, readers are referred to D.J. Tonkin and L.C.L. Skerratt (eds), *Financial Reporting 1988–1989*, ICAEW, 1989: chapter entitled 'Complex Capital Issues', by B.L. Worth and R.A. Derwent; and L.C.L. Skerratt and D.J. Tonkin (eds), *Financial Reporting 1989–1990*, ICAEW, 1989: chapter entitled 'Complex Capital Issues'.

We shall illustrate both the actuarial method specified in FRS 4 and the conflict between the provisions of the standard and the more economically illiterate aspects of company legislation by considering the example of the issue of three hypothetical debentures under terms that look more different than they actually are.

Example 8.1

Let us consider three issues of debentures, each with a nominal value of £100 and each for a five-year period.

(a) Debenture A carries a coupon rate of 20 per cent per annum: it is to be issued and redeemed at par.
(b) Debenture B carries a coupon rate of 16 per cent per annum: it is to be issued at a discount of £12, at a price of £88, and is to be redeemed at par.
(c) Debenture C carries a coupon rate of 18 per cent per annum: it is to be issued at par but redeemed at a premium of £15 at £115.

We shall assume that the interest on each debenture is payable annually at the end of each year and shall ignore taxation and transaction costs.

The effective interest rate on Debenture A is 20 per cent and the terms of Debentures B and C have been chosen to produce identical effective interest rates of 20 per cent. In other words, if we discount the cash flows from and to the debenture holders, all these debentures produce a net present value (NPV) of zero at a 20 per cent discount rate (Table 8.2).

Table 8.2 **Net present values of debentures**

Debenture	NPV at 20%
A	$+100 - 20a_{\overline{5}|} - 100v^5$
	$= +100 - 20(2.9906) - 100(0.4019)$
	$= +100 - 59.8 - 40.2$
	$= 0$
B	$+88 - 16a_{\overline{5}|} - 100v^5$
	$= +88 - 16(2.9906) - 100(0.4019)$
	$= +88 - 47.8 - 40.2$
	$= 0$
C	$+100 - 18a_{\overline{5}|} - 115v^5$
	$= +100 - 18(2.9906) - 115(0.4019)$
	$= +100 - 53.8 - 46.2$
	$= 0$

In all cases the effective rate of interest, that is the cost of the finance, is 20 per cent, but whereas for Debenture A this is all paid in interest, for Debentures B and C the cost is partly paid as a difference between the redemption price and the issue price.

Accounting for Debenture A poses no problems. The annual interest expense of £20 (20 per cent of £100) will be charged in the profit and loss account each year, while the liability will appear at the nominal value of the debentures, that is £100. Accounting for Debentures B and C does pose some problems and we will deal with each in turn.

Discount on debentures

Debenture B is issued at a discount. While the interest of £16 (16 per cent of £100) will undoubtedly be charged to the profit and loss account each year, it is also necessary to decide how to account for the discount on issue, the amount of £12.

The liability would be recorded at the nominal value of £100 and company law permits us to treat the discount on debentures as an asset.[4] Once we have recorded the discount as an asset, the next question is how this should be dealt with. As the discount is effectively part of the cost of the finance, we might expect this cost to be reflected in the profit and loss account. However, company law specifically permits the writing off of discounts on debentures to a share premium account.[5]

Thus, where a company has a share premium account, we may either write off the discount to the share premium account or we may write off the discount to the profit and loss account. In the latter case it is possible to write off the discount immediately or to write it off over the five-year period. Let us look at each possibility in turn.

Use of share premium account

Although company law clearly permits the writing off of this discount to the share premium account, this results in part of the cost of borrowing bypassing the profit and loss account and hence in an overstatement of profits. This odd quirk of company law has been around for some time, as have its critics.

As long ago as 1962, the Jenkins Committee, which was set up to advise the government on changes in company legislation, reported that it thought that the law should be amended:

> . . . to prohibit the application of the (share premium) account in writing off the expenses and commission paid and discounts allowed on any issue of debentures or in providing for any premiums payable on redemption of debentures, since these are part of the ordinary expenses of borrowing.[6]

Despite the numerous Companies Acts that have been enacted since 1962, this oddity remains and it is difficult to see how it can be justified. The charging of a discount to the share premium account means that the profit and loss account does not bear the full cost of the borrowing, but it also seems to be inconsistent with the rationale for creating a share premium account in the first place. The purpose of a share premium account is to ensure that, with certain exceptions, subscribed capital cannot be repaid to shareholders. If the profit and loss account is relieved of part of the cost of the business, then, effectively, part of the subscribed capital is available for distribution.

Charge to profit and loss account

If it is to be charged to the profit and loss account the 1985 Act merely states that 'it shall be written off by reasonable amounts each year and must be completely written off before repayment of the debt'.[7]

However FRS 4 requires that the 'finance cost of debt should be allocated to periods over the term of the debt at a constant rate on the carrying amount'.[8]

Using the actuarial method[9] the liability is recorded at the present value of the cash flows discounted at the market rate of interest, which we have assumed to be 20 per cent. The interest expense each year would be found by multiplying the present value of the cash flows at the start of the year by the effective interest rate. As can be seen from Table 8.3 this results in an increasing liability and an increasing interest expense throughout the term of the loan.

---

[4] Companies Act 1985, Schedule 4, Para. 24(1).
[5] Companies Act 1985, s. 130(2).
[6] Report of the Company Law Committee, Cmnd. 1749, HMSO, London, 1962, Para. 163.
[7] Companies Act 1985, Schedule 4, Para. 24(2)(a).
[8] FRS 4, Para. 28.
[9] Which is also called the effective rate method, the 'compound yield method' (Inland Revenue) or the 'interest method' (FASB).

Table 8.3 **Actuarial method for Debenture B**

(i) Year	(ii) Opening balance	(iii) Interest 20% of (ii)	(iv) Total (ii) + (iii)	(v) Payment at year end	(vi) Closing balance (iv) – (v)
	£	£	£	£	£
1	88.0	17.6	105.6	16.0	89.6
2	89.6	17.9	107.5	16.0	91.5
3	91.5	18.3	109.8	16.0	93.8
4	93.8	18.8	112.6	16.0	96.6
5	96.6	19.4*	116.0	116.0†	–

* Includes rounding adjustment.   † Interest 16.0 + Redemption price 100.0.

In addition to satisfying the requirements of FRS 4 this is the approach that is required in the USA[10] and by SSAP 21 *Accounting for Leases and Hire Purchase Contracts* when accounting for the obligation under a finance lease (see Chapter 9).

Premium on redemption

Debenture C, which carries a coupon rate of interest of 18 per cent is issued at par but redeemed at a premium of £15. Under the existing legal framework it is not clear whether the liability should be recorded initially at the nominal value of £100 or at the amount payable, the redemption price of £115. If it is recorded initially at £100, then a premium must be provided by the end of the five-year period. If it is recorded initially at £115, then an asset 'premium on debentures' must also be established and we have a situation analogous to the issue of a debenture at a discount that has been discussed above. In either case it is necessary to decide how to deal with the premium.

Not surprisingly we find that the law permits the write-off of this premium to share premium account but, for the reasons explained above, the authors are of the view that it should be charged to the profit and loss account over the life of the debentures. Using the actuarial method the liabilities at the balance sheet dates and the annual expense figures can be calculated as shown in Table 8.4.

Table 8.4 **Actuarial method for Debenture C**

(i) Year	(ii) Opening balance	(iii) Interest 20% of (ii)	(iv) Total (ii) + (iii)	(v) Payment at year end	(vi) Closing balance (iv) – (v)
	£	£	£	£	£
1	100.0	20.0	120.0	18.0	102.0
2	102.0	20.4	122.4	18.0	104.4
3	104.4	20.9	125.3	18.0	107.3
4	107.3	21.5	128.8	18.0	110.8
5	110.8	22.2	133.0	133.0*	–

* Interest 18.0 + Redemption price 115.0.

[10] Readers are referred to Richard Macve, 'Accounting for long-term loans', in *External Financial Reporting*, Bryan Carsberg and Susan Dev (eds), Prentice-Hall, Englewood Cliffs, NJ, 1984. This essay in honour of Professor Harold Edey discusses the treatment of long-term loans in both the UK and the USA.

Finance costs for non-equity shares

The treatment of finance costs relating to non-equity shares is based on the same principles as debt (FRS 4, Para. 42), with two additional specific rules. These are:

> Where the entitlement to dividends in respect of non-equity shares is calculated by reference to time, the dividends should be accounted for on an accruals basis except in those circumstances (for example where profits are insufficient to justify a dividend and dividend rights are non-cumulative) where ultimate payment is remote. All dividends should be reported as appropriations of profit. (Para. 43)

> Where the finance costs for non-equity shares are not equal to the dividends, the difference should be accounted for in the profit and loss account as an appropriation of profits. (Para. 44)

An example of a situation where there may be a difference between the finance costs and the dividends are shares that may be redeemed at a premium.

We have already introduced the actuarial method and shown that the method is logical and allocates the cost of borrowing fairly over the period of the loan, as well as ensuring that the whole of the finance costs are charged to the profit and loss account. The use of the method would also achieve consistency across a wide range of different capital instruments in issue, including non-equity shares, although, in this case, the provisions of company law, on which FRS 4 is based, would require us to show the cost as an appropriation of profit rather than an expense.

Issue costs

The calculation of the constant rate of interest and the initial carrying value in the balance sheet depends upon the 'net proceeds' of the issue of the capital instruments. The net proceeds are defined as:

> The fair value of the consideration received on the issue of a capital instrument after deduction of issue costs. (Para. 11)

Issue costs are defined as:

> The costs that are incurred directly in connection with the issue of a capital instrument, that is, those costs that would not have been incurred had the specific instrument in question not been issued. (Para. 10)

The use of the phrase 'fair value' reminds us that the carrying value of the capital instrument will not always be found without some degree of estimation. An example of such a case would be the joint issue of a debt and warrant when the amount received for the issue of the joint instrument will need to be allocated to provide the fair value of the debt and warrant respectively. The most likely source of evidence would be the market values of similar securities.

The standard is restrictive as to what should be included in issue costs (Para. 96). Such costs should not include any which would have been incurred had the instrument not been issued, such as management remuneration or indeed the costs of researching and negotiating alternative sources of finance. Those costs that do not qualify as issue costs should be written off to the profit and loss account as incurred. The standard requires that issue costs be accounted for by reducing the proceeds of the issue of the instrument and should not be regarded as assets because they do not provide access to any future economic benefits. The consequence of setting the issue costs against the proceeds is to increase the interest charge in the profit and loss account; in other words, it ensures that the issue costs are written off over the life of the capital instrument.

Use of the share premium account

It might be thought that the provisions of FRS 4 would include the stipulation that entities subject to the Companies Act should no longer take advantage of the provision whereby they can charge issue costs and discounts against the share premium account. They only go some way towards this desirable end. Issue costs, which would include discounts, have to be charged to the profit and loss account but the standard specifically draws attention to the fact that the issue costs may subsequently be charged to the share premium account by means of a transfer between reserves (Para. 97).

The distinction between shareholders' funds and liabilities

A capital instrument is a liability if it contains an obligation to transfer economic benefit, including contingent obligations, otherwise it is part of shareholders' funds. It is usually clear whether an instrument requires the company to make some sort of transfer to the owner of an instrument or whether any such transfer is made at the discretion of the company, but there are two exceptions to the general rule. The first relates to an obligation that would only arise on the insolvency of the issuer. If there is no expectation of that event, and the entity can be accounted for on a going concern basis, that contingent liability can be ignored. Similarly, an obligation that would only crystallise if a covenant attached to a capital instrument were breached can also be disregarded unless, of course, there is evidence that such a breach will occur.

Some preference shares effectively impose an obligation on the issuing entity to transfer economic benefit, that is pay a dividend, because to do otherwise would be even more costly. Until now, these economic facts have been disregarded and, if capital instruments were called preference shares, they automatically appeared in the owners' equity section of the balance sheet. FRED 30 proposes that in cases where the payment of a dividend is, in practice, unavoidable, the instrument be treated as a liability. Thus, as in many areas of accounting, substance would have to take precedence over form.

Warrants

Share warrants are instruments that state that the holder or bearer is entitled to be issued with a specified number of shares, possibly upon the payment of an additional fixed price. In the view of the ASB, the original amount paid for the warrant must be regarded as part of the subscription price of the shares which may, or may not, be issued at some time in the future, and it is for this reason that FRS 4 specifies that warrants be reported within shareholders' funds (Para. 37).

The Board does, however, recognise that the topic of warrants raises a number of issues that are outside the scope of FRS 4. It refers[11] in particular to the view that, if the price paid on the exercise of the warrant is less than the fair value of the shares issued, this should be reflected in the financial statements by, presumably, increasing shareholders' funds and recognising as an expense the 'cost' incurred in issuing shares in this way. Another controversial issue is what should be done if the warrant lapses without being exercised. Should the amount initially subscribed to the warrant continue to be treated as part of share capital or be regarded as a gain by the company? The issue depends essentially on whether the warrant holders are regarded as sharing in the ownership of the company. If they are so regarded then the benefit from the lapse in the warrant is not a gain to the company but a transfer between owners, and hence the initial subscription should be treated as part of share capital. If, on the other hand, the warrant holders are not regarded as owners (the view taken by the ASB), the amount released by the lapse of the warrants should be reported as a gain within the statement of recognised gains and losses.

In summary, the provisions of FRS 4 relating to the taking up and lapsing of warrants are:

1 When a warrant is exercised, the amount previously recognised in respect of the warrant should be included in the net proceeds of the shares issued (Para. 46).

2 When a warrant elapses unexercised, the amount previously recognised in respect of the warrant should be reported in the statement of total recognised gains and losses (Para. 47).

The distinction between equity and non-equity

FRS 4 reinforces the requirements of company law by requiring that the balance sheet should show the total amount of shareholders' funds with an analysis between the amount attributable to equity interests and the amount attributable to non-equity interests (Para. 40).

The need therefore is to distinguish between equity and non-equity interests. Company law provides a succinct definition of equity share capital, which means in relation to a company, its issued share capital excluding any part of that capital which, neither as respects dividends nor as respects capital, carries any right to participate beyond a specified amount in a distribution.[12]

The ASB believes that this definition does not give sufficient guidance in the more complex cases and hence it provides a far more detailed statement of the distinction that starts with a definition of non-equity shares. These are shares possessing any of the following characteristics:

(a) Any of the rights of the shares to receive payments (whether in respect of dividends, in respect of redemption or otherwise) are for a limited amount that is not calculated by reference to the company's assets or profits or the dividends on any class of equity share.

(b) Any of their rights to participate in a surplus in a winding-up are limited to a specific amount that is not calculated by reference to the company's assets or profits, and such limitation has a commercial effect in practice at the time the shares were issued or, if later, at the time the limitation was introduced.

(c) The shares are redeemable according to their terms, or the holder, or any party other than the issuer, can require their redemption. (Para. 12)

Following all the above, equity shares are defined simply as 'shares other than non-equity shares' (Para. 7).

The ASB thinking is quite clear. Its definition attempts to ensure that only 'true' equity is treated as such. In so far as the existence of non-equity capital represents a risk that may be taken into account by equity shareholders when making investment decisions, this approach can be seen as being protective of the interest of existing and potential equity shareholders.

As stated earlier, the provisions of FRED 30 would sensibly lead to the reclassification of some non-equity shareholders' funds as liabilities.

---

[11] See the section on the development of the standard, Paras 11–13.

[12] Companies Act 1985, s. 744.

The distinction between convertible and non-convertible liabilities

A convertible debt is one that allows the holder of the security to exchange the debt for shares in the issuing company on the terms specified in the debt instrument.

Prior to the issue of FRS 4, existing practice was to report convertible debt as a liability, a practice that FRS 4 noted is uncontroversial where conversion is uncertain or unlikely. But there are those who would argue that, if conversion were probable, convertible debt should be reported outside liabilities in order to give a fairer representation of the economic position of the company. In drafting FRS 4, the ASB, arguing that a balance sheet is a record of the financial position of a company at a point of time, not a forecast of future events, specified that all convertible debt should be included with liabilities. As we shall see, in the section of this chapter dealing with the disclosure requirements of the standard, adequate information must be provided regarding the terms and conditions relating to the various capital instruments in issue.

There is a more sophisticated line of argument that suggests that merely reporting convertible debt as part of liabilities ignores the equity rights which are inherent in the issue of convertible debt. As we shall see, the IASC, in IAS 32 *Financial Instruments: Disclosure and Presentation*, required split accounting for convertible debt. Under this approach the proceeds of issue of convertible debt are allocated between the two components, the equity rights and the liabilities. The consequence of this is that the finance charge relating to the debt is increased over that which would be recorded if the whole of the proceeds of the issue were treated as a liability. The reason for this is that the total amount payable to the convertible debt holders, assuming no conversion, consists of a string of interest payments and the redemption price remains the same irrespective of the method of accounting used. If the initial recorded value of the debt were smaller, as it would be if the proceeds of the issue were split, then the finance cost would be increased to cover the amount of the proceeds that were allocated to the equity interest.

Happily for lovers of simplicity, the ASB rejected this more complex presentation, although it will emerge if the proposals of FRED 30 are accepted. In the meantime the standard practice for the presentation of convertible debt is straightforward:

> Conversion of debt should not be anticipated. Convertible debt should be reported within liabilities and the finance cost should be calculated on the assumption that the debt will never be converted. The amount attributable to convertible debt should be stated separately from that of other liabilities. (Para. 25)

> When convertible debt is converted, the amount recognised in shareholders' funds in respect of the shares issued should be the amount at which the liability for the debt is stated as at the date of conversion. No gain or loss should be recognised on conversion. (Para. 26)

Debt maturity

As recognised in company legislation, users of accounts need to be given adequate information about the scheduling of the repayment of debt in order to help them assess the companies' short-term solvency and long-term liquidity position.

The requirements of FRS 4 are a little more extensive than those of the Companies Act in that they include an additional cut-off date of two years. The requirement is that:

An analysis of the maturity of debt should be presented showing amounts falling due:

(a) in one year or less, or on demand;
(b) in more than one but not more than two years;
(c) in more than two years but not more than five years; and in more than five years. (Para. 33)[13]

The maturity of the debt should be determined by reference to the earliest date on which the lender can require repayment. (Para. 34)

Life is, of course, not without its complications and the ASB had to consider the case of a borrower who had already made arrangements to refinance the existing loan. The question here is whether the maturity of the loan should be measured by reference only to the capital instrument currently in issue, or whether account should be taken of the re-financing arrangements that have been established. It would clearly be misleading to ignore the significant fact that facilities have been established in order to extend the period of the loan. Therefore the ASB states:

Where committed facilities are in existence at the balance sheet date that permit the refinancing of debt for a period beyond its maturity, the earliest date at which the lender can require repayment should be taken to be the maturity date of the longest refinancing permitted by a facility in respect of which all the following conditions are met:

(a) The debt and the facility are under a single agreement or course of dealing with the same lender or group of lenders.
(b) The finance costs for the new debt are on a basis that is not significantly higher than that of the existing debt.
(c) The obligations of the lender (or group of lenders) are firm: the lender is not able legally to refrain from providing funds except in circumstances the possibility of which can be demonstrated to be remote.
(d) The lender (or group of lenders) is expected to be able to fulfil its obligations under the facility. (Para. 35)

This is clearly a stringent set of conditions.

In order that the users of the accounts are made aware of the use of the above provision it is also required that:

Where the maturity of debt is assessed by reference to that of refinancing permitted by facilities in accordance with paragraph 35, the amounts of the debt so treated, analysed by the earliest date on which the lender could demand repayment in the absence of the facilities, should be disclosed. (Para. 36)

FRS 4 and consolidated financial statements

There are a number of special issues relating to consolidated financial statements.

There may be circumstances when shares issued by a subsidiary and held outside the group should be included in liabilities rather than minority interest (Para. 49). This treatment is required when the group, taken as a whole, has an obligation to transfer economic benefit; for example, if another member of the group has guaranteed payments relating to the shares.

---

[13] This is a correction of the original version that was effected in FRS 13. The original, incorrect, version referred to periods of less than 2 or 5 years and more than 2 or 5 years, thus leaving in doubt the treatment of liabilities that had exactly two or five years to run.

In addition:

(a) The amount of minority interests shown in the balance sheet should be analysed between the aggregate amount attributable to equity interests and amounts attributable to non-equity interests (Para. 50).

(b) The amounts attributed to non-equity minority interests and their associated finance costs should be calculated in the same manner as those for other non-equity shares. The finance costs associated with such interests should be included in minority interests in the profit and loss account (Para. 51).

Some further explanation is required regarding the circumstances under which shares issued by subsidiaries would not be shown in minority interest. As already noted, one of the FRS 4 principles is that if any element of obligation to transfer economic resources attaches to a capital instrument, then it should be treated as a liability. Thus, if guarantees have been given in respect of dividends payable on the shares or on their redemption, there is a liability, albeit contingent, to transfer economic resources. In such circumstances the shares should be included under liabilities.

Disclosure requirements

FRS 4 is very much concerned with the provision of adequate, some might argue more than adequate, disclosure, and, in the previous pages, we have referred to a number of the proposals that bear on this matter. The remaining disclosure requirements may be summarised as follows:

(a) Disclosure relating to shares (Paras 55–59)
  (i) An analysis should be given of the total amount of non-equity interests in shareholders' funds relating to each class of non-equity shares and series of warrants for non-equity shares.
  (ii) A brief summary of the rights of each class of shares should be given, other than for equity shares with standard characteristics. Details should also be provided of classes of shares which are not currently in issue but which may be issued as a result of the conversion of debt or the exercise of warrants.
  (iii) Details of dividends for each class of shares and any other appropriation of profit in respect of non-equity shares should be disclosed.
(b) Disclosure relating to minority interests (Paras 60–61)
  (i) The minority interests charge in the profit and loss account should be analysed between equity and non-equity interests.
  (ii) If there are non-equity minority interests the rights of the holders against other group companies should be described.
(c) Disclosure relating to debt (Paras 62–64)
  (i) Details of convertible debt should be provided.
  (ii) Brief descriptions should be provided where the legal nature of the instrument differs from that associated with debt; for example, when the obligation to repay is conditional.
  (iii) Gains and losses on the repurchase or early settlement of debt should be disclosed in the profit and loss account as separate items within or adjacent to 'interest payable and similar charges'.

(d) General disclosure requirements
  (i) When the disclosure requirements relating to the amounts of convertible debt, non-equity interests in shareholders' funds and non-equity interests in minority interests are given in the notes, the relevant balance sheet caption should refer to the existence of the relevant capital instruments (Para. 54).
  (ii) Where the brief summaries required in respect of a(ii), b(i), c(i) and c(iii) above cannot adequately provide the information necessary to understand the commercial effect of the relevant instruments, that fact should be stated together with particulars of where the relevant information may be obtained. In any event the principal features of the instruments should be stated (Para. 65).

Application notes

FRS 4 includes a section on Application Notes that describes how the principles of the reporting standard should be applied to capital instruments with certain features. The instruments covered in this section are:

- Auction market preferred shares (AMPS)
- Capital contributions
- Convertible capital bonds
- Convertible debt with a premium put option
- Convertible debt with enhanced interest
- Debt issued with warrants
- Deep discount bonds
- Income bonds
- Index-linked loans
- Limited recourse debt
- Participating preference shares
- Perpetual debt
- Repackaged perpetual debt
- Stepped interest bonds
- Subordinated debt

Space does not allow coverage of these notes and the interested reader should refer to the standard itself.

Hedge accounting

Amongst the reasons why the subject of accounting for liabilities has become far more interesting are the developments in the area of hedging.

A hedging transaction, or a hedge, is a way of reducing risk associated with an investment that the entity has made or contract that it has made; this is known as *the hedged item*. The hedge involves the entity entering into another contract, *the hedging instrument*, whose cash flow will vary inversely with those of the hedged item. A simple example would be an entity that wants to make a substantial investment, say in a building, in country A but is very concerned about the loss it would make if there was a substantial fall in the value of the currency of that country. It may have powerful strategic reasons to make such an investment but might be in a position that could not cope with a substantial loss. It could reduce the extent of any potential loss by investing in a contract whereby it would gain if the value of the currency falls. If the market did not share the entity's pessimism about the long-term value of the currency, it could enter the foreign currency market and agree to sell *x* million units of the currency of country A in six months' time. If the currency were to fall it would cost the entity less to acquire the agreed amount of the currency and the greater the fall the greater would be the gain. More complex packages could involve more than one hedge instrument.

Hedge accounting comes into play when the application of the normal accounting rules would mean that the gain or loss on the hedged item would be recognised in a different period to the offsetting gain or loss on the hedge instrument or instruments. There is obviously strong pressure to show the net impact of a hedging operation in one accounting period but to do so might involve breaking the normal rules, hence the need to consider whether, and if so to what extent, the normal rules should be 'adjusted' to reflect the fact that the transactions are part of a hedging operation.

FRED 23 *Financial Instruments: Hedge Accounting*

The objective of any standard based on FRED 23, issued in May 2002, would be to establish principles for the use of hedge accounting when accounting for financial instruments.

FRED 23 proposes that, in order for a financial instrument to qualify for hedge accounting, two criteria have to be met: a hedging relationship and hedge effectiveness.

1 *Hedging relationship*: A hedge cannot be created in arrears: there must be formal documentation of the hedging relationship available at the date of its inception. The effectiveness of the hedge must be capable of reliable measurement and, if a forecast transaction is being hedged, it must be highly probable and must present an exposure to variations in cash flows that could ultimately affect reported net profit or loss.

2 *Hedge effectiveness*: The effectiveness of a hedge is related to the achievement of the hedging instrument or instruments in generating changes in fair values or cash flows that offset those relating to the hedged item. In order to satisfy the requirements of FRED 23, the hedge must both be expected to be effective at the outset and prove to be effective during its life. The draft states that a hedge is effective if the extent of the offset lies between 80 per cent and 125 per cent.

The introduction to the exposure draft points out that hedge accounting takes many forms and the purpose of a standard based on it would not require or prohibit the adoption of any particular form of hedge accounting.[14] It would, however, cover three areas:

Hedges for net investment on foreign operations

The part of any gain or loss on the hedging instrument that is determined to be an effective hedge should be recognised in the statement of total recognised gains and losses and be treated in the same way as the gains and losses on the hedged item while the part of the gain or loss which is not an effective hedge should be reported in the profit and loss account (Para. 16).

An ineffective hedge

An ineffective portion of any hedge would have to be recognised immediately in the profit and loss account (Para. 16).

---

[14] FRED 23, p. 10.

Terminated hedges

If hedge accounting is terminated because the transaction that was hedged is no longer expected to occur the loss or gain on the hedge should be recognised immediately in the profit and loss account. If it is terminated for another reason, the loss or gain should be recognised immediately in the profit and loss account, or the statement of total recognised gains and losses, so as to offset the gains and losses on the hedged item (Para. 17).

Derivatives

This is an area where reasonably simple concepts are made complex by the use of technical terminology; some might call it jargon. So let us start with the basic definition:

> **A derivative instrument is one whose performance is based (or derived) on the behaviour of the price of an underlying asset (often simply known as the 'underlying'). The underlying asset itself does not need to be bought or sold. A premium may be due.**[15]

Let us start by considering one of the simplest forms of derivative, an *option*. Under a *call* option, the purchaser pays a sum of money in order to have the right to purchase shares at an agreed price at some point in the future. Under a *put* option, the purchaser has the right to sell shares at the agreed price at some time in the future.

Let us look at an example of a call option. Suppose that, in May, the price of the shares of Gambling plc are £3 each and an investor, who believes that the share price will increase considerably, pays 40 pence a share for the right to buy 1000 shares in October at £4.50 each, the *strike price*. If, in October, the price of the shares exceeds £4.50 by a sufficient margin to cover the price paid for the option and other transaction costs, the purchaser of the option will gain because he or she could buy the shares at £4.50 and then sell them at the then current market price. If the price falls between £4.50 and £4.90, it would still be worth buying the shares, although the investor would not cover the price paid for the option.

The 40 pence will be the price of the option as determined by the market. While most markets now employ electronic trading, derivatives trading is still carried out in bull pits by people wearing different coloured jackets communicating through hand signals. Most books on derivatives paint this rather charming scene before moving on to some pretty heavy mathematics.

The value of the option will constantly vary and will depend largely on two factors:

- the difference between the strike price and the current price of the share, *the underlying price*;
- the volatility of the underlying price, which is usually derived from a formula that is related to the history of the share's price movements.

It would be rare for anyone to hold a single option, unless it is part of a hedging operation, for options will normally be held as part of a portfolio of similar derivatives which will, according to the degree of risk averseness exhibited by the owner, be a balanced one that seeks to attempt to minimise the possibilities of making considerable losses but which also means that there is a lesser chance of making vast profits. But, of course, the great thing about options is that, so long as there is an active market, buyers can change their minds and sell the option or buy more options.

---

[15] Francesca Taylor, *Mastering Derivatives Markets*, FT/Pitman Publishing, London 1996, p. 2.

Another factor affecting value is the terms on which the option can be exercised and, in particular, whether it can only be exercised on the expiry date of the agreement, a *European* option, or at any time up to and including the expiry date, an *American* option.

There are basically two types of operators in the derivatives market, *hedgers* and *traders*. A hedger is someone who has a position to cover. For example, a company that has made a major investment in a project denominated in an overseas currency and is concerned that the currency may fall in terms of its own currency, might purchase a put option to sell a quantity of the overseas currency, that it does not own, at the current price. If the currency falls, the loss the company would make in converting its overseas remittances from the project would be offset by the gain from the put option. A trader is one who is interested in making money from trading in derivatives, and lest traders are thought to be in some way less worthy than hedgers it must be remembered that without the traders there would be at best a very illiquid market for derivatives.

This is not the place to provide a lengthy introduction to the market for derivatives although we should point out that is, in numerical terms, huge. Even in 1996 it was estimated that the derivatives market was at $30 trillion (that means 13 noughts), which would have made it three times as large as the then global equity market.[16] But it might be helpful to outline some of the main types of derivatives and explain some of the more important terms that are found in this jargon-laden industry.

The four primary derivative markets are:

- Equities
- Foreign exchange
- Commodities (such as energy, metals and agricultural goods)
- Interest rates

Some derivatives, especially those for interest rates, take the form of swaps, a term that would readily be understood by most school children. Take as example two companies both of which have a good reputation in their home country and hence can borrow at more advantageous terms than can others, especially overseas companies. Suppose that the two companies also operate in the home country of the other and both want to borrow money in the overseas country. The swap occurs when each company borrows at the advantageous terms from which it benefits in its home country and they exchange the benefits between them.

A futures contract is one that involves an agreement to deliver a stated quantity of a given commodity in return for a pre-arranged price at some future date. A farmer, for example, concerned that the price of his crop might fall because of a glut, might agree to sell his crop in advance of production for a price that will reflect the overall market view of the trend of market prices. In other words, the hedger has brought certainty while the trader has assumed the risk. The trader will probably not continue to carry the risk for the whole of the time it takes to grow the crop, as the futures contract is likely to be traded frequently as different views are formed as to the likely price.

Options differ from futures and swaps in that they involve the payment by one of the parties of a premium. The importance of a premium is that it allows the holder not to go ahead with the transaction if he believes that to do so would not be in his best interest. The purchaser of a call option where a premium is paid does not have to buy the shares. In contrast the parties to futures contracts have no choice; both must deliver their sides of the bargain.

---

[16]   Francesca Taylor, *Mastering Derivatives Markets*, FT/Pitman Publishing, London, 1996, p. xii.

The valuation of financial instruments

It would be something of an understatement to observe that there is a lack of consensus on the appropriate accounting treatment of financial instruments.

On the whole, but there are exceptions, standard setters seem to be moving towards the market value approach, especially in respect of derivatives. Thus, in a paper prepared by the Financial Instruments Joint Working Group (JWG)[17] and published in 2000,[18] the view was expressed that virtually all financial instruments should be measured at fair value and that virtually all gains and losses arising from changes in fair value should be recognised in the profit and loss account. The US Financial Accounting Standards Board require derivatives to be shown at market value[19] while the present draft of IAS 39, *Financial Instruments: Recognition and Measurement* would require all derivatives and other financial instruments held for trading, together with any financial assets that are available for sale, to be measured at fair value. As we will see later in this chapter, the ASB is not yet prepared to charge quite as fast down the fair value track.

Those who advocate the use of fair values believe that using them would better represent the effect that a company's use of derivatives and other financial instruments have had on its operations, in the sense that users might see the extent to which a market-related value of a subset of the company's assets and liabilities have moved. Those who would prefer to see a cost-based valuation approach applied to financial instruments feel that the adoption of a fair value basis would lead to greater volatility in reported earnings that might well distort the underlying pattern of trading results. These people who tend to be bankers and corporate treasurers, do not want to see their reported results distorted, for example by wide swings in stock market prices; they would prefer to wait until the actual results of hedging or financial operation are known before disclosing the results.

The fair value approach does seem more appropriate for the financial trading company whose rationale is to live, or die, through its financial activities than it is for other companies whose financial activities are to support their main business. Thus there are those who favour a dual regime using different bases for different types of company and this is, in effect, the position taken by the ASB in FRED 30.

But perhaps there is a simple way out of the argument? The authors have long been amongst those who argue that entities should be required to provide the values of their assets on more than one basis of valuation, for example replacement cost and net realisable value. The usual reason for the rejection of this idea is the, rather patronising, assertion that this would confuse the users of accounts. It is difficult to see how this argument can be used against the proposal that financial instruments be shown on the basis of cost and their fair value. Any user who understands and can appreciate the messages contained in financial statements about derivatives and other financial instruments should not be confused by the presentation of two bases of valuation. They both have messages to tell and users should be able to interpret both and appreciate that their interpretation of those messages should in part depend on the nature of the business of the company whose financial statements they are reviewing.

---

[17] The JWG was comprised of representatives or members of accounting standard setters or professional bodies drawn from Australia, Canada, France, Germany, Japan, New Zealand, the five Nordic countries, the UK, the USA and the International Accounting Standards Committee.

[18] Draft standard *Financial instruments and similar items*, Joint Working Group.

[19] SFAS 133 *Accounting for Derivative Instruments and Hedging Activities*.

This view accords with the position taken by the majority in a survey of members of the Association of Corporate Treasurers, who believed:

- a mixed model of cost and fair value accounting for derivatives will always be overcomplicated;
- an accounting standard on derivatives that people are trying to apply to both financial and non-financial institutions will never meet the requirements of both;
- the accounting of derivatives should remain at cost; the disclosure should include sufficient information on a company's risk management policies and fair value information to allow investors accurately to understand a company's treasury performance.

Only a small number of respondents were in favour of the JWG approach that all derivatives should be shown at fair value.[20]

The view that a much more useful picture can be provided by narrative disclosure has much to commend it, especially in areas where the selection of a single figure for inclusion in the financial statements must perforce present an incomplete story.

Mention of the narrative approach brings us neatly to FRS 13 *Derivatives and other Financial Instruments: Disclosure*. It would have been impossible at the time FRS 13 was published, September 1998, for the ASB to have produced a standard that dealt with the method of valuing derivatives and similar financial instruments, so a standard was produced that laid down the information that should be provided that would help users to understand what was happening, and in particular the risks to which the company is subject, rather than specifying the basis on which amounts should appear in the financial statements. At the time of issue, it was thought that FRS 13 was an interim standard that would be replaced as accounting standard-setting technology advanced, allowing the framing of regulations that specified the basis on which figures should appear in the financial statements. While this view is partly true, the use of narrative reporting that was, in a way, pioneered by FRS 13 is also likely to be developed and improved.

FRS 13 *Derivatives and other Financial Instruments*

Disclosures

This standard is unusual in a number of ways. Not only is it the most complicated standard issued to date, containing many terms and concepts which do not impinge on the professional life of the vast majority of accountants, but also it is an admission that the then (1998) state of the art of financial accounting was not capable of dealing adequately with the reporting of the more complex forms of derivatives and other types of financial instruments. The ASB's concerns were expressed in a discussion paper, *Derivatives and other Financial Instruments*, issued in July 1996, which focused on three main issues: the measurement of financial instruments, the use of hedge accounting and the disclosures relating to financial instruments. Among what FRS 13 describes (p. 137) as the tentative conclusions of the discussion paper was the view that it was not appropriate to measure financial instruments on a historical cost basis, but that they should be measured at fair value. However, the Board was not yet able to advance on the measurement front, nor deal with the issue of hedge accounting, but felt it was necessary to promulgate a standard on disclosure.

---

[20] Association of Corporate Treasurers, January 2002 Newsletter, **www.treasurers.org**.

Scope and objective

FRS 13 is concerned only with those entities that have one more of their financial instruments listed or publicly traded on a stock exchange or market as well as all banks and similar institutions. Its provisions do not apply, however, to insurance companies.

A financial instrument is defined in exactly the same terms as it is in the later FRED 30, which we quoted earlier in the chapter, namely:

> **any contract that gives rise to both a financial asset of one entity and a financial liability or equity instrument of another entity. (FRS 13, Para. 2)**

Financial instruments include both primary financial instruments – such as bonds, debtors, creditors and shares – as well *derivative financial instruments*, which are themselves defined in the same section as FRS 13 as:

> **a financial instrument that derives its value from the price or rate of some underlying item.**

The underlying items can take a variety of forms including equities, commodities, interest rates, exchange rates and stock market and other indices.

However, complicated though the nest of interrelations contained within the instrument may be, there must be a chain of events that leads to the transfer of either cash or an equity instrument from one party to another. Thus, just to give a few examples, debtors, shares, forward contracts and options are financial instruments while physical assets, prepayments and obligations, like many warranties that will be satisfied by the provision of services, are not. Lest it be thought that any entity that has debtors will be covered by the standard, remember that to qualify the financial instruments must be publicly traded.

The objective of the standard is to ensure that entities within its scope disclose information to help users assess its objectives, policies and strategy for holding or issuing financial instruments. In particular, the information should help users assess:

(a) the risk profile of the entity for each of the main financial risks that arise in connection with financial instruments and commodity contracts with similar characteristics; and

(b) the significance of such instruments and contracts to the reported financial position, performance and cash flows, regardless of whether the instruments or contracts are on the balance sheet (recognised) or off the balance sheet (unrecognised). (Para. 1)

Risks associated with financial instruments

The standard identifies the following four types of risk associated with financial instruments, of which only the first two have, and even then to a limited extent, been reported upon in financial statements.

- *Credit risk* – the possibility that a party to the contract may fail to perform according to the terms of the contract.
- *Liquidity risk* – the chance that an entity will fail to raise the funds that would enable it to meet its commitments under the contract.
- *Cash flow risk* – the possibility that future cash flows will fluctuate in amount.
- *Market price risk* – the possibility that future changes in market prices will change the value, or burden, of a financial instrument. The main components of market price risk are:
  - *Interest rate risk*
  - *Currency risk*
  - *Other market risk*; this includes the risks associated from changes in commodity and share prices.

The structure of FRS 13

The standard requires both narrative and numerical disclosures; the same narrative disclosures are required of all entities while the requirement for numerical disclosure differs between:

- entities that are not financial institutions
- banks and similar institutions
- other types of financial institutions.

We are in this section dealing only with the first of the above.

One of the more helpful features of the standard is the three examples it provides in Appendix III, of hypothetical disclosures that might be provided by different entities. One relates to a bank, the others to non-financial entities; of these, one, that is said to be representative of the vast majority of entities, is fairly simple, the other is more complex. Interested readers should refer to this appendix.

Mode of presentation

It is envisaged, but it is not required, that the disclosures specified by the standard should be placed in the context of a discussion of the entity's activities, structure and funding. This discussion should typically also consider the financial risk profile as a whole. This means that it will be helpful to provide the narrative requirements of the standard in a statement such as an operating and financial review. The way in which the information is presented is left to the entity, but it is required to ensure that the narrative information is cross-referenced to the Notes to the Financial Statements. The required numerical information should be included in the notes.

The standard covers a lot of ground, and large entities with numerous complex schemes, involving many types of financial instrument, could nullify the objective of the standard by providing data in excessive detail. The Board is aware of this point and enjoins entities to be prepared to use a high degree of aggregation in fulfilling their obligations under the standard, which could mean that it might be impossible to relate the explanations directly to the balance sheet captions (another unusual feature of FRS 13), and entities are encouraged to provide additional information to allow the figures to be traced back to the balance sheet unless that would unduly complicate the position (Para. 25).

Main elements to be disclosed

The length of the standard makes it impossible for us to do anything more than provide a highly simplified and selective summary of the main points that have to be disclosed. In making our selection we have been influenced by those areas, such as the use of current values, that we have emphasised elsewhere in this book. The following are the main aspects for which disclosure is required:

- *Objectives, policies and strategies.*
- *Interest rate disclosures* indicating liabilities at fixed interest rates, variable interest rates and on which no interest is paid.
- *Currency rates disclosure* providing an analysis of the net amount of financial (or monetary) assets and liabilities in terms of the principal currencies involved.
- *Liquidity disclosure*, including a breakdown of the dates at which financial liabilities fall due for payment.
- *Fair value disclosure*, providing information about both the carrying values and fair values of financial assets and liabilities.

- Disclosures about *financial assets and financial liabilities used for trading.*
- Disclosures about *hedging.*
- Disclosures about *commodity contracts.*

FRED 30 and the convergence programme

As we stated earlier in this chapter the convergence project will have a significant impact on accounting for liabilities, but there remain considerable uncertainties. The two international standards on which UK practice will converge are currently under review while UK company law will need to be changed if the likely changes are to be implemented in the UK.

The situation as at the beginning of 2003 is summarised in Table 8.5.

Table 8.5 Financial instruments: the current position

FRED 30 proposes two UK standards:

- *Financial Instruments: Disclosure and Presentation*
- *Financial Instruments: Measurement*

Based on published IASB proposals for revisions to:

- IAS 32 *Financial Instruments: Disclosure and Presentation*
- IAS 39 *Financial Instruments: Recognition and Measurement*

This will lead to the withdrawal of:

- FRS 4 *Capital instruments*
- FRS 13 *Derivatives and other Financial Instruments: Disclosures*

Proposed timetable:

- The revised IAS 32 will be implemented in the UK for all listed companies and all other banks from 1 January 2004.
- The presentation requirements of the revised IAS 32, but not the disclosure requirements, will be implemented in the UK for all unlisted entities, other than those included above from I January 2004.
- The recognition and derecognition requirements of the revised IAS 39 will not be implemented in the UK, but all its other provisions will have to be followed from 1 January 2004 by entities that choose to adopt fair value accounting.

Changes in company legislation will be required; if these are not made in time this timetable will have to change.

Even if the uncertainties are resolved, convergence would not be finally achieved because the ASB is not prepared to accept all the provisions of IAS 32 and 39, as can quickly be demonstrated by a perusal of the two draft statements set out in FRED 30. The starting points for both drafts are the clean versions of IAS 32 and 39, that is, the versions including the proposed changes; these drafts are then 'tracked' to show the additions and deletions that are proposed by the ASB.

In the sections that follow we will use the four-way classification introduced in the previous chapter, that is recognition, measurement, classification (presentation) and disclosure, to outline both the changes that would be made to UK practice if the proposals of FRED 30 were to be implemented and the differences that would still remain between the UK and international standards.

Changes to UK practice and remaining differences between UK and international standards

Recognition

Changes to current UK practice

The ASB has concerns about the recognition, and presentation, aspects of IAS 32 and 39 and hopes that the IASB will reconsider these before 2005. Hence the Board is not, at this stage, proposing any changes to the UK standards.

Remaining differences between UK and international standards

The different views on recognition are demonstrated by the fact that the while proposed revision of IAS 39 is entitled *Financial Instruments: Recognition and Measurement*, the proposed FRS omits the word 'recognition', which is not unreasonable given that the proposed UK standard does not contain the relevant paragraphs 27 to 65 of the proposed international standard.

In Appendix III of FRED 30, pp. 297–300, it is pointed out that the ASB's approach to the recognition and derecognition of financial instruments is based on the 'risks and rewards' approach whereby for an asset to be recognised the entity would need to be in a position where it had access to the benefits underlying the asset and was exposed to the risks associated with those benefits; the corresponding features for recognition would be a requirement to pay out benefits, and the associated risk. The IASB approach, as reflected in its proposals for the revision of IAS 39, is different; its view is that the question that needs to be answered is whether the transfer can reverse. If that possibility exists then the asset or liability cannot be derecognised.

The ASB believes that it would be inappropriate to issue a UK standard until the position of the IASB becomes clearer. In the meantime, it is pointed out that, while the underlying principles of the UK and likely international approaches are very different, their application will lead to the same conclusions for many straight-forward transactions.[21]

Measurement, including hedge accounting

Changes to current UK practice

The changes will impact on measurement and hedge accounting for it is proposed that, with effect from 1 January 2004, if an entity chooses to use *fair value accounting* in preparing its financial statements then it will be required to use, subject to certain modifications, IAS 39's fair value measurement and accounting system.

Let us start by introducing fair value accounting. ASB's understanding, expressed in FRED 30, is that the government would propose to amend legislation to add to the historic cost and the alternative accounting rules a third regime, based on fair value accounting.

The new rules would extend the opportunities for entities to measure certain financial assets and liabilities at fair value and to pass the changes in fair value through the profit and loss account rather than through the statement of total recognised gains and losses.

The exposure draft proposes that entities that adopt the fair value accounting rules, and only those entities, should be required to adopt almost all the measurement and hedge accounting requirements of IAS 39. These entities are likely to be relatively few and specialised, being those, that are not banks or insurance companies, that mark-to-market their trading books and recognise any resulting gains in the profit and loss accounts.

---

[21] FRED 30, p. 299.

Remaining differences between UK and international standards

At this point we need to return to FRED 23 *Financial instruments: hedge accounting.* FRED 23 and IAS 39 are both based on the same foundations, that is, to qualify for hedge accounting, the hedge needs to be pre-designated and effective. However, IAS 39 goes further than FRED 23 in that it contains additional restrictions on the use of hedge accounting and contains provisions on the type of hedge accounting to be used. As pointed out above, the only UK entities that FRED 30 would require to adopt the more stringent conditions of IAS 39 are the relatively few entities that adopt the fair accounting rules.

Moving to the more general issue of the measurement of financial instruments IAS 39 proposes that all derivatives, all financial instruments held for trading and any financial assets that are available for sale should be measured at fair value. All other financial instruments (i.e. financial assets held to maturity, loans and receivables originated by the reporting entity and all financial liabilities that are neither derivatives nor held for trading) should be measured at amortised cost.[22]

Under the present proposals only those UK entities who choose to make use of the fair value accounting rules would be required to use the IAS 39 measurement rules; other entities would continue on the present basis whereby liabilities are, 'generally speaking, ... measured at cost-based amounts rather than at some sort of updated value'.[23]

One other difference would remain between the proposed UK and international standards, and this relates to the important subject of *recycling* that the IASB would allow but which the ASB abhors. Recycling occurs when gains or losses relating to ongoing activities are first recognised in the statement of total recognised gains and losses, or to use the international jargon 'in equity', but which reappear, when, say, a hedge matures, in the profit and loss account. It does seem odd to recognise the same gain or loss more than once and so we hope that the UK position prevails.

Presentation (disclosure)

Changes to current UK practice

Changes are proposed to balance sheet terminology in that the division between 'shareholders' funds' and 'liabilities' should be replaced by a split between equity and non-equity interests. This has more than a terminological impact because some instruments that are presently treated as being part of shareholders' funds would be treated as a non-equity interest. One example is preference shares. These are in substance liabilities because they were issued on terms that effectively mean that the entity must transfer economic resource to their holders. FRED 30 proposes, in terms of the distinction between debt and equity, that substance should take priority over form and that certain financial instruments that are now included in equity should in the future be treated as a non-equity item.

The effect of the above would be seen not only in the balance sheet, of course, since the amounts paid in respect of preference shares that are in substance liabilities, and treated as such, would be reported as an interest expense rather than dividends. But other changes are being proposed, in that dividends paid and proposed, would no longer appear in the profit and loss account but would instead be disclosed in the reconciliation of movements in shareholders' funds.

It would, of course, only be possible to make the above changes if amendments are made to company legislation.

---

[22] FRED 30, p. 301.
[23] FRED 30, p. 6.

It is also proposed to make changes to the treatment of convertible debt and to adopt split accounting (see p. 186). The actual split is calculated by reference to market values; thus, in order to estimate the non-equity element of a convertible debt, an estimate would have to be made of the fair value of a similar liability without a related equity element.

While the ASB seems unhappy at the more permissive provisions of IAS 32, as compared to FRS 5 (see p. 211), on the matter of offsetting debits and credits, it has incorporated them into FRED 30. IAS 32 merely requires that the entity does have an enforceable right to set off and the intention to do so. In particular it does not require the right of offset to be capable of surviving the insolvency of the other party.

Remaining differences between UK and international standards

There are no significant differences between the provisions of FRED 30 and the proposed international standards on this matter.

Disclosure

Changes to current UK practice

At present in the UK companies have to publish a range of narrative and numerical risk disclosures relating to their financial instruments, which the ASB describes as 'extensive and relatively detailed'.[24] FRED 30 proposes that these be replaced by those set out in IAS 32 which, although they mirror the UK approach, are less detailed.

Remaining differences between UK and international standards

There would be no difference in what is to be disclosed but there would be some differences as to who has to disclose. The international standards would apply to all entities. The present UK position is that they should apply only to listed entities and banks and even then, in the case of groups, only to the consolidated financial statements.

Conclusion

It is to be hoped that the various endeavours to which we referred in this chapter will be achieved by the scheduled dates in order to remove the unnecessary complications from an area which is by its very nature pretty complex. This is not to say, however, that we are confident that matters are moving in the right direction.

We believe that the minds of standard setters, both domestically and internationally, are too firmly fixed on the notion that there is only one solution to every problem, in this case that it is their job is to identify the 'best' accounting treatment for any particular class of transactions. A rather different view is that there is more than one way of portraying reality and that in a number of areas, for example the valuation of financial instruments, a strong case can be made for requiring the valuations to be provided on more than one basis. This would put a greater onus on the users of financial statements, but we believe that it would be better to explain to users why more than one approach to reporting is being adopted rather than present a partial view.

---

[24] FRED 30, p. 13.

Summary

We started the chapter by introducing the subject of capital instruments and discussed the contents of FRS 4 *Capital Instruments*. This standard is exclusively concerned with liabilities but we described how attention is now being paid to the broader theme of financial instruments, which covers financial assets as well as liabilities.

The relationship between assets and liabilities is at the heart of hedge accounting, the next topic included in the chapter. Hedge accounting comes into play when transactions are linked and the normal rules controlling the recognition of gains and loses are relaxed so that gains and losses of linked transactions may be recognised in the same period. In this context we summarised the proposals of FRED 23 *Financial Instruments: Hedge Accounting*.

Derivatives are instruments whose performance is based on the price movements of an underlying asset. We described the most widely used forms of derivatives and outlined the arguments that are being advanced in the debate between those who believe that derivatives should be recognised in the financial statements at fair value and those who advocate a cost-based approach. As at January 2003 the only UK standard on derivatives, FRS 13 *Derivatives and other Financial Instruments: Disclosures*, is concerned solely with disclosure issues and says nothing about measurement. We summarised the content of the standard.

The issue of financial instruments, including derivatives, is looming large in the accounting standards convergence programme and we ended the chapter by describing the stance taken by the ASB as reflected in FRED 30, which is an exposure draft for two proposed standards, *Financial Instruments: Disclosure and Presentation* and *Financial Instruments: Measurement*. We outlined the changes that the implementation of the FRED 30 proposals would bring to UK practice as well as the differences that would remain between UK and international standards. The differences are now being addressed as part of the convergence programme – with the added spur for EU members of the 2005 target.

Recommended reading

E. Bunn, 'Derivatives and hedging' *Corporate Finance*, No. 211, June 2002.

F.J. Fabozzi (ed.), *The Handbook of Financial Instruments*, Hoboken, N.J., Wiley, 2002.

S.G. Ryan, *Financial Instruments and Institutions – Accounting and Disclosure Rules*, Hoboken, N.J., Wiley, 2002.

Excellent up-to-date and detailed reading on the subject matter of this chapter and on much of the contents of this book is provided by the most recent edition of:

UK and International GAAP, A. Wilson, M. Davies, M. Curtis and G. Wilkinson-Riddle (eds), Ernst & Young, Butterworths Tolley, London. At the time of writing, the latest edition is the 7th, published 2001.

Questions

8.1 (a) Explain the main reasons for the introduction of FRS 4, Capital instruments. (7 marks)

(b) Explain how FRS 4, Capital instruments, deals with the accounting treatment of:

(i) convertible debt; and
(ii) redeemable preference shares,

making reference to any differences with International Accounting Standards. You should relate your comments to the underlying principles in the Statement of Principles, where appropriate. (9 marks)

(c) Errol plc borrowed £20 million on 1 January 2000 under an agreement with its bank to pay interest of 7% on 31 December 2000, 10% on 31 December 2001 and a final payment of interest and capital totalling £22 057 000 on 31 December 2002. The company prepares accounts to 31 December. Assume an overall effective annual rate of interest of 9%.

Requirement
Calculate and disclose the amounts that will appear on the face of the profit and loss accounts and balance sheets for each year affected by the loan. (6 marks)

ICAEW, Financial Reporting, December 2000 (**22 marks**)

8.2 You are the management accountant of Short plc. On 1 October 1993 Short plc issued 10 million £1 preference shares at par, incurring issue costs of £100 000. The dividend payable on the preference shares was a fixed 4% per annum, payable on 30 September each year in arrears. The preference shares were redeemed on 1 October 1998 at a price of £1.35 per share. The effective finance cost of the preference shares was 10%. The balance sheet of the company on 30 September 1998, the day before the redemption of the preference shares, was as follows:

	£ million
Ordinary share capital (non-redeemable)	100.0
Redeemable preference shares	13.5
Share premium account	25.8
Profit and loss account	59.7
	199.0
Net assets	199.0

Requirements
(a) Write a memorandum to your assistant which explains:

● how the total finance cost of the preference shares should be allocated to the profit and loss account over their period of issue;
● where in the profit and loss account the finance cost should be reported;
● where the preference shares should be disclosed in the balance sheet;
● the nature of any supporting information which is required to be disclosed in the notes to the financial statements regarding the preference shares.

Your memorandum should refer to the provisions of relevant Accounting Standards. (8 marks)

(b) Calculate the finance cost in respect of the preference shares for EACH of the five years ended 30 September 1998.   (7 marks)

(c) Assuming no changes other than those caused by the redemption of the preference shares, prepare the balance sheet of Short plc at the end of 1 October 1998. You should give an explanation for any changes to any of the headings or any new headings which are required.   (5 marks)

CIMA, Financial Reporting, November 1998   **(20 marks)**

8.3 Your managing director has recently read an article which referred to Financial Reporting Standard 4 (FRS 4) – Capital instruments. He has requested a report from you about FRS 4.

Requirement
Write a report to the managing director explaining the nature of capital instruments, giving *three* examples of capital instruments together with their required accounting treatment as specified in FRS 4.

CIMA, Financial Reporting, May 1995   **(20 marks)**

8.4 Tealing plc requires advice on the appropriate accounting treatment for the following transactions in capital instruments in the year ended 30 November 2002.

(1) The company issued convertible debt on 1 December 2001 for £500 000. This will be redeemed at the same amount or converted on 30 November 2006 when the holder of the debt has the option to convert to shares. Interest payable is 5.9% for the two years ended 30 November 2003 and 14.1 % for the remaining years.
Assume that the effective rate of interest is 10.33% per annum.

(2) 250 000 5% redeemable £1 preference shares were issued on 1 June 2002. Dividends are paid annually commencing on 30 November 2002 and the shares will be redeemed at a premium of £16 600 on 30 May 2006.
Assume that the effective rate of finance cost is 6.5% per annum.

(3) A loan from the company's bankers was obtained on 1 December 2001 for £400 000. No payments are required for the first four years and the repayment terms are four annual instalments of £168 400 starting on 30 November 2005.
Assume that the effective rate of finance cost is 10.06% per annum.

Requirements
(a) Calculate the amounts to be disclosed in the profit and loss account for the year ended 30 November 2002 and in the balance sheet of Tealing plc as at that date, preparing the appropriate extracts of these primary statements.   (10 marks)

(b) Explain the appropriate accounting treatment for each of the items in (a) with appropriate reference to the Statement of Principles, noting any differences in treatment to International Accounting Standards.   (7 marks)

ICAW, Financial Reporting, December 2002   **(17 marks)**

8.5 Standard setters have been struggling for several years with the practical issues of the disclosure, recognition and measurement of financial instruments. The ASB has issued a Discussion Paper on Derivatives and Other Financial Instruments and Financial Reporting Standard 13 on the disclosure of such instruments. The dynamic nature of international financial markets has resulted in the widespread use of a variety of financial instruments but present accounting rules in this area do not ensure that the financial statements portray effectively the impact and risks of the instruments currently being used.

Required

(a) (i) Discuss the concerns about the accounting practices used for financial instruments which led to demands for an accounting standard.   (7 marks)

    (ii) Explain why regulations dealing with disclosure alone cannot solve the problem of accounting for financial instruments.   (4 marks)

(b) (i) Discuss three ways in which gains and losses on financial instruments might be recorded in the financial statements, commenting on the relative merits of each method.   (8 marks)

    (ii) AX, a public limited company, issued a three-year £30 million 5% debenture at par on 1 December 1998 when the market rate of interest was 5%. Interest is paid annually on 30 November each year. Market rates of interest on debentures of equivalent term and risk are 6% and 4% at the end of the financial years to 30 November 1999 and 30 November 2000. (Assume that the changes in interest rates took place on 30 November each year.)

    Show the effect on 'profit' for the three years to 30 November 2001 if the debenture and the interest charge were valued on a fair value basis.   (6 marks)

ACCA, Financial Reporting Environment (UK Stream), December 1999   **(25 marks)**

8.6 One of the issues dealt with by the Accounting Standards Board in its *Statement of Principles for Financial Reporting* is the measurement of assets and liabilities in financial statements. The Statement notes that the historical cost system is the one most widely used in financial statements at present. However, the Statement suggests that financial reporting may well evolve towards a mixed measurement system, where some assets and liabilities are measured based on historical cost, while others are based on current values. The use of current values is already accepted practice for measuring certain categories of fixed asset, particularly properties. Recent developments appear to suggest that this practice may in future be applied to the measurement of financial instruments.

In September 1998, the ASB published FRS13 – *Derivatives and Other Financial Instruments: Disclosures*. Then, in December 2000, the ASB published a discussion paper that suggested measuring most financial instruments at current values, rather than merely providing information about current values in the notes to the financial statements. The discussion paper proposes that hedge accounting should be prohibited. Such a proposal, if implemented, would have a significant effect on current financial reporting practice in the UK. In particular, SSAP 20 – *Foreign Currency Translation* would need to be reviewed because this Accounting Standard currently permits hedge accounting in certain circumstances.

Required

(a) Identify the strengths and weaknesses of using a historical cost system of measurement for assets and liabilities.   (5 marks)

(b) Explain why a current value measurement system is more appropriate for financial instruments than a historical cost system.   (5 marks)

(c) Explain why the disclosure requirements of FRS 13 are insufficient on their own to satisfy the needs of users.   (4 marks)

(d) Discuss the effect of prohibiting hedge accounting on current UK accounting practice.   (6 marks)

CIMA, Financial Reporting – UK Accounting Standards, May 2002   **(Total = 20 marks)**

Substance over form and leases

There has long been a principle of financial reporting that, in deciding the appropriate method to record transactions, economic substance should take precedence over legal form. This is the basis of FRS 5 *Reporting the Substance of Transactions*, issued in 1994, to deal with the many complex transactions that had developed as a consequence of the ingenuity of the financial experts. We discuss FRS 5 in the first part of this chapter.

A very important example of the substance over form principle is to be found in the accounting treatment of leases. Indeed, so important is the example that the ASB produced a standard on the subject, SSAP 21 *Accounting for Leases and Hire Purchase Contracts* in 1984, some ten years before FRS 5 saw the light of day. SSAP 21 distinguishes between two different categories of lease – *finance*[1] and *operating* leases respectively, and requires very different accounting treatments of each. A lessee is required to capitalise a finance lease, that is to recognise both a fixed asset and a liability, charging depreciation of the asset and an interest or finance charge in respect of the liability in its profit and loss account. A lessee must not capitalise an operating lease, rather the rentals payable should be charged to the profit and loss account in accordance with the accruals concept. The accounting treatment of leases by the lessor mirrors the treatment by the lessee.

In the second part of this chapter, we explore the issues involved in the treatment of leases and explain the provisions of SSAP 21 in some detail. We illustrate the accounting treatment of finance and operating leases by both lessees and lessors. The provisions of the international standard IAS 17 are similar to those of SSAP 21 although there are differences, especially in the treatment of the income from finance leases by lessors.

In recent years, the view has emerged, both in the UK and overseas, that it is unrealistic to attempt to make a distinction between the two categories of leases and that in conceptual terms a strong case could be made for requiring the capitalisation of all non-cancellable leases. We explain this view, which is promulgated in two Discussion Papers issued by the G4+1 group, a view that now has strong support from both the ASB and the IASB, although it has yet to emerge in the form of an exposure draft.

In this chapter, we will discuss the following publications:

- FRS 5 *Reporting the Substance of Transactions* (1994, amended 1998)
- SSAP 21 *Accounting for Leases and Hire Purchase Contracts* (1984, amended 1997)
- IAS 17 *Leases* (revised 1997)
- G4+1 Discussion Paper *Accounting for Leases: A New Approach*, published by the FASB (1996)
- G4+1 Position Paper *Leases: Implementation of a New Approach*, also published as a Discussion Paper by the ASB (1999)

---

[1] This is the term used by the ASB and IASB. In the USA and Canada, finance leases are called capital leases or sales type leases.

Introduction

The vast majority of transactions of the vast majority of companies are simple and straight-forward. A fixed asset or an item of stock is purchased for cash or on credit and the impact on the company's assets and liabilities can be easily assessed. But occasionally a company will enter a complex set of transactions that involve a series of different events that, if viewed in isolation, might give a misleading picture.

Let us suppose X Limited 'sells' some land to Y Bank for £5m with an option to reacquire it for, say, £5.4m in six months' time.

Is it a genuine sale or is it a device to borrow money, 'off the balance sheet', for six months? And, if it is the latter, would the financial statements show a more realistic picture if the asset were not treated as a sale, but retained as an asset with the corresponding recognition of the obligation to 'repay' the bank?

The task is to determine the substance of the transaction. The doctrine of 'substance over form' is found in many attempts to construct a conceptual framework of accounting. Many interpretations have been made of the phrase but it is perhaps most readily understood as the belief that financial statements should, when there is conflict, be based on economic (or commercial) reality rather than legal form.[2]

Reflecting the substance of transactions

FRS 5 *Reporting the Substance of Transactions*

FRS 5 requires that the reporting entity's financial statements should report on the substance of the transaction into which it has entered (Para. 14).

FRS 5, as are many of the transactions to which it relates, is complex but there is a simple governing principle which is that, when determining the nature of a transaction, one needs to decide whether, as a result of the transaction, the reporting entity has created new assets or liabilities or whether it has changed any of its existing assets or liabilities (Para. 16). The standard hence adopts a strictly 'balance sheet' approach: identify the assets and liabilities and let the profit and loss account entry emerge.

In order to determine 'substance' FRS 5 emphasises the need to identify all aspects and implications of a complex transaction and points out that some aspects may be uncertain or contingent and that greater weight needs to be given to those aspects which are likely to have a commercial effect in practice. The standard suggests that the accountant needs to consider the expectations and motivation of all parties to the transaction and points out that, whatever is the substance of the transaction, it will normally have a commercial logic for all the parties and hence, if a transaction appears not to make sense, this might indicate 'that not all related parts of the transaction have been identified or that the commercial effect of some element of the transaction has been incorrectly assessed' (Para. 51). In other words it suggests that if the accountant digs deep enough the reality of the transaction will emerge.

---

[2] For a comprehensive discussion on the subject see B.S. Rutherford, *The Doctrine of Substance over Form*, Certified Accountants Publications, London, 1988.

The standard is relevant to those complex transactions whose substance is not readily apparent and whose commercial effect may not be fully reflected by their legal form. Common features of such transactions are:

1 the separation of legal title to an item from the ability to enjoy the principal benefits and exposure to the principal risks associated with it;
2 the linking of a transaction with one or more others in such a way that its commercial effect cannot be understood without reference to the series as a whole; and
3 the inclusion in a transaction of one or more options whose terms make it highly likely that the option or options will be exercised.

Scope of FRS 5

With certain exceptions, which are summarised in Table 9.1, the standard covers all transactions of all entities whose financial statements are intended to give a true and fair view of its financial position and profit or loss for a period. The standard is, for the most part, couched in pretty general terms and hence, when a transaction which would otherwise fall within the scope of the standard is also covered by another FRS, or a SSAP or specific statutory requirement, the standard or statute that contains the more specific provision or provisions should be applied (Para. 13).

Table 9.1 Transactions outside the scope of FRS 5 (unless part of a transaction that falls within its scope)

1 Forward contracts and futures
2 Foreign exchange and interest rate swaps
3 Contracts where a net amount will be paid or received based on the movement in a price or an index ('contracts for differences')
4 Expenditure commitments and orders placed, until the earlier of delivery or payment
5 Employment contracts.

The structure of FRS 5

The standard deals with the following main issues:

(a) the identification of assets and liabilities and tests for whether the asset or liability should be recognised in the balance sheet;
(b) transactions in previously recognised assets;
(c) the treatment of options;
(d) assets which are separately financed and, in particular, the circumstances where 'linked presentation' should be used (linked presentation means that, on the face of the balance sheet, the finance should be deducted from the gross amount of the asset which it finances);
(e) the, very limited, circumstances when it is permissible to offset assets and liabilities;
(f) the treatment of 'quasi-subsidiaries', when the relationship between the two entities is effectively, but not legally, one between a parent and its subsidiary.

We will examine the provisions of FRS 5 in the above order.

The identification of assets

An asset[3] is defined as:

> Rights or other access to future economic benefits controlled by an entity as a result of past transactions or events. (Para. 2)

While in the context of an asset, control is defined as:

> The ability to obtain the future economic benefits relating to an asset and to restrict the access of others to those benefits. (Para. 3)

Although the existence of future benefits is an essential criterion for the identification of an asset, it is not implied that the asset should be valued by reference to those benefits, although the present value of the asset's expected future benefits will provide an upper limit to its carrying value.

All assets carry some risk and the allocation of that risk between the various parties to a transaction will usually be a significant indication of whether the transaction has resulted in the acquisition or disposal of an asset. Risk is the potential variation between the actual and expected benefits associated with the asset and includes the potential for gain as well as exposure to loss. Normally the party that has access to the benefits also has to face the risks, and in practice the question of whether an asset should be identified is often dependent on an assessment of where the risk falls.

Control in this context is related to the means by which an entity ensures that the benefits accrue to itself and not to others and must be distinguished from the day-to-day management of the asset. Although control normally rests on the foundation of legal rights, the existence of such rights is not essential as commercial, or even moral, obligations may be significant factors.

The existence of an asset depends on a past and not a future event. Thus, in straightforward transactions it is easy to draw a distinction between a right to immediate control over future economic benefits and a right to acquire such control in the future. Both rights can be regarded as creating assets, but in the second case the asset is simply the option. The position in linked transactions may be different. An option may be simply a device to ensure that effective control of future benefits will be retained by the party who ceases, temporarily, to be the legal owner. Then the terms of the option may be such that the costs of exercising it are negligible compared to the benefits; in other words it would be commercial madness not to exercise the option. In such a case the accounting treatment (is there an asset and if so what is it?) will have to be decided by reference to the rights and obligations (including those taking effect in the future) that result from the transactions as a whole.

The identification of liabilities

A liability is defined as:

> An entity's obligations to transfer economic benefits as a result of past transactions or events. (Para. 4)

Little is said in FRS 5 on the general issue of liabilities but what is said is consistent and does not go beyond our discussion of the subject in Chapter 7.

---

[3] Although FRS 5 considerably predates the *Statement of Principles* there are no differences in substance between the key definitions of assets, liabilities, etc. provided in the two documents. We have examined the definitions of assets and liabilities in Chapters 1, 5 and 7.

Recognition of assets and liabilities

Assets and liabilities, although identified in terms of the above, should only be recognised in the balance sheet if:

(a) there is sufficient evidence of the existence of the item (including, where appropriate, evidence that a future inflow or outflow of benefit will occur); and

(b) the item can be measured as a monetary amount with sufficient reliability. (Para. 20)

An obvious example of an item which although identified may not be recognised in the balance sheet is a contingent liability.

The above general criteria for recognition are also to be found in Chapter 5 of the ASB's *Statement of Principles*, which we have discussed earlier in this book in Chapters 1, 5 and 7.

Transactions in previously recognised assets

The basic principle is straightforward. If, as a result of a transaction involving a previously recognised asset, there is no significant change in either the reporting entity's access to benefits or exposure to the risks inherent in those benefits, then the asset should continue to be recognised. The asset should cease to be recognised if both the access to benefits and the exposure to risks are transferred to others (Para. 22).

The range of possible outcomes can be well illustrated by the factoring of trading debts. If the terms of the deal are such that, although the legal title to the debts has been transferred, the finance charge that the 'seller' of the debts will have to pay will depend on the speed at which debtors pay or the seller retains responsibility for the whole or part of the bad debts, then the risk has not been transferred and the asset, debtors, should continue to be shown in the balance sheet as the total amount due from debtors. The amount received from the factors in respect of the debts that are still outstanding would be included in liabilities. (There is a possible exception that would arise if the transaction satisfies the condition for linked presentation, see p. 210). On the other hand, if the terms of the agreement are that the finance fee payable will be in no way affected by the future behaviour of the debtors then the whole of the risk has been transferred to the factors and the asset should cease to be recognised.

Special cases of transactions

Three special cases are mentioned in the standard:

(a) a transfer of only part of the asset;
(b) a transfer of all the item for only part of its life;
(c) a transfer of all the item for all its life but where the entity retains some significant rights to benefits or exposure to risks.

It may be helpful to provide some examples of the special cases:

1 The holder of a security might sell the right to receive the annual interest but retain the right to receive the principal.
2 The seller agrees to repurchase the asset it has sold after its use.
3 A company might sell its interest in a subsidiary in circumstances where the ultimate consideration depends in whole or in part on the future performance of the subsidiary.

The main point of the standard is pretty simple. In all cases an asset, albeit a different asset, continues to exist but its description and the amount at which it is included in the balance sheet will change, and it is, of course, possible that the 'new' asset will not pass the recognition tests to which we referred earlier.

Treatment of options

One of the characteristics of complex transactions may be the existence and use of options.[4] In deciding how to treat them, consideration needs to be given to all aspects of the series of transactions of which the option is part. If, after such consideration, it is decided that there is no genuine commercial possibility that the option will be exercised, the exercise of the option should be ignored whilst, if there is no genuine commercial possibility that the option will fail to be exercised, its future exercise should be assumed (Para. 61).

In assessing whether there is a genuine commercial possibility that an option will be exercised it should be assumed that the parties will act in accordance with their economic interests and that the parties will remain both liquid and solvent, unless it can reasonably be foreseen that either will not be the case. Thus, actions, which the party will take only in the event of a severe deterioration in liquidity or creditworthiness that is not currently foreseen, should not be taken into account.

There will be some circumstances that fall between the two certainties – the exercise or non-exercise of the option. In such a case the asset that would appear in the balance sheet of the entity with the right to acquire would not be the asset itself but the option to acquire the asset. Let us return to our simple example that involved X Limited 'selling' some land to a bank for £1m with an option to repurchase. If the price at which the option would be exercised is such that it is virtually certain to be less than the then market price, FRS 5 requires the transaction to be treated as a loan. If, conversely, the option price is virtually certain to be more than the prevailing market price then it would be presumed that the option would not be exercised and the transaction should be treated as a sale. But suppose there exists uncertainty, in that the option price lies within a range in which the market price of the land might reasonably be expected to fluctuate. In that case the asset that X Limited would show would be the option to reacquire the land, and the cost of that asset would be the extra finance costs that the borrower would incur in a transaction that involved an option as against a straightforward borrowing which did not include an option.

Linked presentation

A borrower can finance an item on such terms that the provider of finance has access only to the item financed and not to the entity's other assets. A well-known example of this is the factoring of debts. In some such arrangements, whilst the provider of finance has only recourse against the specified item, the 'borrowing' entity retains rights to the benefits generated by the asset, and can repay the finance from its general resources if it wishes to preserve those rights. In such situations the entity has both an asset and a liability and linked presentation would not be appropriate.

Linked presentation, which as we shall see involves setting off, on the face of the balance sheet, the liability against the asset, is only possible in situations where the finance has to be repaid from the benefits generated by the asset and the borrowing entity has no right to keep the item or to repay the finance from its general resources. The remaining conditions that have to be satisfied are set out in the standard at Para. 27; the essence of these conditions is that the borrower is under no legal, moral or commercial obligation to repay the loan other than from the benefits generated from the asset.

The question to be answered is, 'What is the nature of the asset which is retained by the borrowing entity and, in particular, what rights and benefits are associated with that asset?' The issue is best explained by introducing the example used in FRS 5.

---

[4] The disclosure requirements relating to options and other derivatives are discussed in Chapter 8.

Suppose that an entity transfers title to a portfolio of high quality debts of 100 in exchange for non-returnable proceeds of 90 plus rights to a further sum whose amount depends on whether the debts are paid. If we assume that the 90 is under no circumstances repayable then there are three ways of presenting the position in the balance sheet:

(a) Show the asset as 100 and a liability, distinct and separate, of 90. The problem with this form of presentation is that it would not reflect clearly the fact that the 90 liability has no relevance to the remaining assets of the entity and would, in particular, give a misleading view of the security of the entity.

(b) Set off the two amounts and show 10 as an asset. This may appear to be the most sensible procedure but it is argued that because the eventual return to the entity depends on the behaviour of the whole portfolio of debts which has been factored the risks remaining are the normal risks which could be related to that total portfolio of debt.

(c) Use what FRS 5 describes as the 'linked presentation' method: that is to show on the face of the balance sheet both the gross asset of 100 less possibly a small deduction for the normal provision against doubtful debts, and a deduction of 90. It is claimed that this presentation shows both that the entity retains significant benefits and risks relating to the whole portfolio of debts and that the claims of the provider of the finance are limited solely to the funds generated by the debts.

The art of financial statement preparation is not well served by over-elaboration and the drawing of fine distinctions based on immaterial differences. The 'linked presentation' provision smacks of over-elaboration and its application would provide only marginal assistance to the users of financial statements while adding the possibility of confusion. To take the ASB's own example, what is the asset, 100 or 10? Ignoring bad debts it is 10, the maximum that will be received in the future from the asset; 90 has been received but would in no circumstances have to be repaid, and so it is not a liability. Why suggest that it is? The obvious way of accounting for the transaction is to show the asset at 10 less an appropriate provision against doubtful debts. The fact that the provision is actually based on 100 rather than 10 can be explained in the notes if the fact is material.

However, the conditions that have to be satisfied if linked presentation is to be used are stringent and hence only apply to a small number of entities.

Offset

It is a general requirement of UK company law that assets and liabilities should not be netted off. The only exception is where the right of set-off exists between monetary assets and liabilities, such as, for example, in bank balances and overdrafts with the same party. The provisions of FRS 5 are more stringent and more precise than those found in company law and include the unambiguous statement that 'assets and liabilities should not be offset' (Para. 29). However, it goes on to state, in the same paragraph, that 'debit and credit balances should be aggregated into a single net item where, and only where, they do not constitute separate assets and liabilities'.

The offset should only be made when the balances are fundamentally linked such that the reporting entity would not have to transfer economic benefit arising from the credit balance without being sure that it would receive the benefits reflected by the debit balance.

The conditions under which offset should and must be applied are set out in para. 29 and may be summarised as follows:

(a) The items to be offset must be determinable monetary amounts denominated either in the same currency or in different but freely convertible currencies.

(b) The reporting entity has the ability to insist on a net settlement and this ability is assured beyond doubt. This means, for example, that the debit balance matures no later than the credit balance and that the arrangement is such that it would survive the insolvency of the other party.

Disclosure

In the world of complex transactions some assets may differ in some ways from most other assets, and some liabilities, such as limited recourse finance, may differ from the generality of liabilities. A common example of a different form of asset is one that, while it is available for use in the trading activities of the enterprise, may not be available as security for a loan.

The disclosure requirements of FRS 5 are less specific than admonitory, urging that:

> Disclosure of a transaction in the financial statements, whether or not it has resulted in assets or liabilities being recognized or ceasing to be recognized, should be sufficient to enable the user of the financial statements to understand its commercial effect. (Para. 30)

> Where a transaction has resulted in the recognition of assets or liabilities whose nature differs from that of items usually included under the relevant balance sheet headings, the differences should be explained. (Para. 31)

Quasi-subsidiaries

FRS 5 observes that there can be instances where, although the relationship between two companies may not constitute a parent/subsidiary relationship as defined by statute, the dominant company might have as much effective control over the assets of the other as would have been the case had the company been a subsidiary. A simple example is one where the dominant company holds less than 50 per cent of the equity of the other company but has an option to acquire additional shares which would take its holding over 50 per cent.

The standard refers to the controlled company as a quasi-subsidiary, which it defines as follows:

> A quasi-subsidiary of a reporting entity is a company, trust, partnership or other vehicle which, though not fulfilling the definition of a subsidiary, is directly or indirectly controlled by the reporting entity and gives rise to benefits for that entity that are in substance no different from those that would arise were the vehicle a subsidiary. (Para. 7)

The concept of substance over form requires that a company which is in effect a subsidiary should be treated as such and this is supported by s. 227(6) of the Companies Act 1985 as amended by the Companies Act 1989, which specifies that, if in special circumstances compliance with any provisions of the Act with respect to the matters to be included in a company's group accounts or in the notes thereto is inconsistent with the true and fair view requirement, the directors shall depart from that specific provision to the extent necessary to give a true and fair view. FRS 5 points out that the nature of quasi-subsidiaries is such that their existence will usually constitute such special circumstances. Thus, they should be included in the consolidated financial statements in the same way as legally defined subsidiary undertakings. If the dominant company does not have any subsidiaries it should provide, in its financial statements, consolidated financial statements of itself and the quasi-subsidiary (Para. 35). In addition, the notes to the financial statements should include summaries of the financial statements of the quasi-subsidiaries (Para. 38).

The conditions under which subsidiaries are required to be excluded are set out in FRS 2 *Accounting for Subsidiary Undertakings*, but the grounds for exclusion are not applicable to quasi-subsidiaries, which, by definition, need to be included in the consolidation if a true and fair view is to be provided. FRS 5 concludes that the only circumstances under which quasi-subsidiaries should be excluded are when they are held only with a view to subsequent sale and have not previously been included in the entity's consolidated financial statements (Para. 36). One set of circumstances is identified in the standard where the accounting treatment of a quasi-subsidiary would differ from that of a fully-fledged subsidiary. This occurs when the quasi-subsidiary holds either a single item or a single portfolio of similar items that are financed in such a way as to require the use of linked presentation. In the case of a quasi-subsidiary, linked presentation should be used in the consolidated balance sheet if the requirements that need to be met can be satisfied by the group (Para. 32). The difference in the case of a legal subsidiary is that linked presentation should only be used on the consolidated balance sheet if it is also applicable to the subsidiary's own balance sheet; in other words, all the conditions need to be met by the subsidiary itself. This particular refinement is required in order to comply with the Companies Act under which the subsidiary is part of the group as legally defined, and hence its assets and liabilities are assets and liabilities of the group and need to be treated in the consolidation in the normal way (Para. 102).

The section of FRS 5 on quasi-subsidiaries does not incorporate any major items of principle, unless the point about linked presentation discussed above is regarded as such, but mainly provides guidance and authority on the use of the override principle of the Companies Act.

Summary of FRS 5

The main elements of the standard have been dealt with in the text but we will summarise the main points in the following list:

1 The substance of transactions should be recorded; greater weight should be given to aspects that are likely to have a commercial effect.
2 Complex transactions should be analysed to see whether the entity's assets or liabilities have been affected.
3 If assets and liabilities are identified then general tests need to be applied to see whether they should be recognised. Reference may also need to be made to other FRSs, SSAPs or statute.
4 Essentially there are four possible outcomes to the analysis:
   (a) record the asset and liability separately;
   (b) apply linked presentation;
   (c) offset (very rare);
   (d) ignore the transaction.
5 Adequate disclosure is required, in particular (i) where the asset or liability recognised in the financial statements differs in some respects from the generality of assets and liabilities, and (ii) where, although identified, assets or liabilities are not recognised in the primary and financial statements.
6 Quasi-subsidiaries should be treated in much the same way as legal subsidiaries.

FRS 5 application notes

There are five application notes covering: consignment stock; sale and repurchase agreements; factoring of debts; securitised assets; and loan transfers. Each application note has three sections: features which describe the nature of the transaction; analyses of the transaction in terms of the framework of FRS 5; and required accounting which is the proposed standard covering recognition in the financial statements and disclosure in the notes. In addition each application note contains tables and illustrations that are intended for general guidance and which do not form part of the proposed standard.

Compliance with international accounting standards

There is no specific international accounting standard on this subject but a number of the provisions of FRS 5 can be related to certain international standards, of which the following are the more important:

- The provision in IAS 1 *Presentation of Financial Statements*, that departure from a specific requirement of IASs, is permitted, albeit only in exceptional circumstances.[5]
- The criteria for the recognition of assets and liabilities found in FRS 5 mirror those appearing in IAS 16.
- The offsetting provisions of FRS 5 differ from those of IAS 32 *Financial Instruments: Disclosure and Presentation*, in that the latter imposes somewhat less rigid criteria for offset to be applied. For example IAS 32 does not require the right of offset to be capable of surviving the insolvency of the other party.
- The conditions under which quasi-subsidiaries would be consolidated under the provisions of FRS 5 are similar to those laid down for the consolidation of special-purpose entities (SPEs) in SIC 12 *Consolidation – Special Purpose Entities*.[6]

Postscript to FRS 5

The provisions of FRS 5 are complex, as are the features of the transactions that it seeks to control. The provisions apply only to a small minority of financial statements but, where they do apply, their effect is often significant because complex transactions typically involve large amounts. The aim of the ASB in attempting to minimise off-balance-sheet financing is entirely laudable and the provisions of FRS 5 provide a set of principles that seem to be sufficiently comprehensive and robust to cope with the increasing ingenuity of the capital market.

Leases

Leasing and hire purchase agreements

To illustrate the issues involved in accounting for leases consider the affairs of Joel Jetway, the Managing Director of Creditor Airways. On Monday morning, because his car had broken down, his company rented a car for him for five days, in the afternoon the company signed a lease to 'rent' an aircraft for five years. The legal relationship between the two parties is the same in each case; the original owner, *the lessor*, retains title to the asset but allows, in exchange for suitable financial compensation, *the lessee* to have sole use of the asset[7] for the period stated in the agreement. Should the two contracts be accounted for in the same way?

---

[5] IAS 1, Paras 13 and 17. It is perhaps worth noting that US GAAP provides no similar override from the need to comply with the requirements of accounting standards.

[6] SIC 12 is an Interpretation of the Standing Interpretation Committee of, in this case, IAS 27 *Consolidated Financial Statements and Accounting for Investments in Subsidiaries*.

[7] The agreement might, however, allow the lessee to sublet the asset to others.

Prior to the issue of SSAP 21 in 1984 they would, in the UK, have probably been treated in the same way. Nothing would appear in the lessee's balance sheet as the rental payments would be shown as an expense in the profit and loss account. SSAP 21 changed all that and, as we shall describe later, prescribed that certain leases, known as *finance leases*[8] should be regarded not as a rental agreement but as if the asset had been purchased on credit. Thus on the signing of the lease the balance sheet of the lessee would include an asset and a liability and the payments made to the lessor would be split between finance costs and repayment of the liability. More recently the view has emerged, both in the UK and overseas, that it is unrealistic to attempt to make such a distinction and that all non-cancellable leases should be treated as finance leases, our motor car example escaping this treatment purely on the grounds of materiality. This approach has, however, not as yet, emerged in an exposure draft.

We start this section of the chapter by describing some of the main forms of leasing and hire purchase agreements. Under a hire purchase agreement the user has the option to acquire the legal title to the asset upon the fulfilment of the conditions laid down in the contract, usually that all the instalments are paid. By contrast, under a leasing agreement in the UK no legal title passes to the lessee at any time either during the currency of the lease or at its termination. The lessor rents the asset to the lessee for an agreed period and, although the lessee has the physical possession and use of the asset, the legal title remains with the lessor.

In some cases a lease will be for a relatively short period in the life of the particular asset and the lessor may lease the same asset for many short periods to different lessees and in such cases the lessor will usually be responsible for the repairs and maintenance of the asset. This type of lease is described as an operating lease. In other instances the lease may be for virtually the whole life of the asset with the lessor taking the whole of its profit from one transaction; such a lease is known as a finance lease. Typically, the lessee of a finance lease will in practical terms treat the leased asset in very much the same way as it would an owned asset; the lessee, for example, will often be responsible for the asset's repair and maintenance.

One of the major principles underlying SSAP 21 *Accounting for Leases and Hire Purchase Contracts*, is that a distinction can and should be drawn between finance and operating leases and that they should be subject to different accounting treatments. However, the view is emerging in the international accounting standards community that, for both conceptual and practical reasons, the distinction should not and cannot be made and that all non-cancellable leases should be treated as finance leases. We will discuss both the SSAP 21 approach and the more recent alternative view in the course of this chapter.

Basic accounting principles

Operating leases

For the accountant, operating leases pose few problems. Amounts are payable for the use of an asset. From the point of view of the lessee, the amounts payable are the costs of using an asset for particular periods and hence are charged to the profit and loss account using the accruals concept. So far as the lessor is concerned the amounts receivable represent revenue from leasing the asset and are credited to the profit and loss account. The leased asset is treated as a fixed asset by the lessor and depreciated in accordance with normal policy.

---

[8] This is the term used by the ASB and IASC; in the USA and Canada finance leases are called capital leases or sales type leases.

Finance leases

Lessees

Accounting for finance leases is a little more complicated. Prior to the introduction of SSAP 21, finance leases were usually treated by both lessee and lessor in the same way as operating leases. However, it was widely recognised that such treatment, while being justified on a strict legal interpretation of the agreement, failed to recognise the financial reality or substance of the transaction. The substance of the transaction was that the lessee acquired an asset for its exclusive use with finance provided by the lessor; which, in economic terms, has few (if any) differences from the case of an asset purchased on credit. If financial statements are to be 'realistic' it is necessary to find a way of accounting for finance leases which accords with the reality of the transaction rather than its legal form. As we saw earlier in this chapter the general issue is the subject of FRS 5 *Reporting the Substance of Transactions*, but, because of the growth of the leasing industry and the distorting effects of the then prevalent accounting treatment, the ASC issued SSAP 21 in advance of a comprehensive standard. Fortunately SSAP 21 is consistent with the provisions of FRS 5. The IASB also specifically requires that the substance and financial reality of a transaction, rather than its legal form, should determine the appropriate accounting treatment.[9]

The appropriate treatment of a finance lease, which accords with the substance of the transaction is, from the point of view of the lessee, to include in the lessee's balance sheet an asset representing the lease and a liability representing the obligation to make payments under the terms of the lease. At the inception of the lease the asset would be equal to the liability but this relationship does not hold thereafter. The asset would be depreciated over the shorter of its useful economic life and the length of the lease, while the liability would be eliminated by the payments. These payments are not, as in the case of an operating lease, charged entirely to the profit or loss account nor are they, in general, wholly set off against the liability. Instead the payments are split between that element which is regarded as representing the repayment of the liability and the remainder that is debited to the profit and loss account as the financing (or interest) charge. This approach is referred to as the capitalisation of the lease.

The lack of a faithful representation consequent upon the failure of a lessee to capitalise financial leases is highlighted by the problems that would be experienced when comparing two companies, one of which leases most of its assets, with the other purchasing fixed assets using loans of one sort or another. The latter company's balance sheet would show the assets which it used to generate its revenue thus allowing users of accounts to estimate the rate of return earned on those assets, whereas the former company's balance sheet would, if the leases were not capitalised, understate its assets. Similarly, the latter company's balance sheet would indicate the liabilities that would have to be discharged if it is to continue in business with its existing bundle of assets, whereas the former company's balance sheet would not.[10]

Lessors

We have so far considered only how the lessee should treat a finance lease. Let us now consider the matter from the point of view of the lessor. In the case of a finance lease the lessor's balance sheet would not include the physical asset but a debtor for the amounts receivable under the lease. Thenceforth the payments received under the terms of the lease should be

---

[9] IAS 1, Paras 9b and 17.

[10] It is for this reason that finance leases were described as providing an 'off balance sheet' source of finance.

split between that which goes to reducing the debt and the balance being credited to the profit and loss account. We shall see later in this section how the division can be made.

The principles illustrated

Lessees

We will start by examining the treatment of finance leases in the books of the lessee. This will not only enable us to show the basic principles involved but also introduce some terms which will make it easier to understand SSAP 21.

We will look at two examples. The first involves annual rental payments while the second involves more frequent rental payments, in our example six monthly payments, which brings an additional complication.

Example 9.1 An illustration of the basic principles of accounting for a finance lease in the accounting records of a lessee

Lombok Limited, a company whose year end is 31 December, leases a machine from Salat Limited on 1 January 20X1. Under the terms of the lease Lombok is to make four annual payments[11] of £35 000 payable at the start of each year. Lombok Limited is responsible for all the maintenance and insurance costs, so these are not covered by the payments under the lease.

The first step is to decide the amount at which the leased asset should be capitalised, i.e. shown as an asset and a liability in the first instance. SSAP 21 requires that:

> At the inception of the lease the sum to be recorded both as an asset and as a liability should be the present value of the minimum lease payments, derived by discounting them at the interest rate implicit in the lease. (Para. 32)

To do that we need to know what is meant by the minimum lease payments and the interest rate implicit in the lease. These terms are as defined in SSAP 21.

Minimum lease payments

> The minimum lease payments are the minimum payments over the remaining part of the lease term (excluding charges for services and taxes to be paid by the lessor) and:
>
> (a) in the case of the lessee, any residual amounts guaranteed by him or by a party related to him; or
> (b) in the case of the lessor, any residual amounts guaranteed by the lessee or by an independent third party. (Para. 20)

In the Lombok example we will assume that there are no residual amounts and thus the minimum lease payments at the inception of the lease are the four annual payments of £35 000.

---

[11] In practice lease payments are usually made at monthly, quarterly or six-monthly intervals, but, in order to illustrate more clearly the principles involved, in our example we will assume that the payments are made at annual intervals. Example 9.2 explains the treatment of six monthly rentals, and even more realistic examples of the type of calculations that have to be made in practice, including leases which do not, conveniently, start on the first day of the year, may be found in the guidance notes to SSAP 21.

▶

Interest rate implicit in a lease

The interest rate implicit in a lease is the discount rate that at the inception of a lease when applied to the amounts that the lessor expects to receive and retain produces an amount (the present value) equal to the fair value of the leased asset. The amounts which the lessor expects to receive and retain comprise (a) the minimum lease payments to the lessor (as defined above) plus (b) any unguaranteed residual value, less (c) any part of (a) and (b) for which the lessor will be accountable to the lessee. If the interest rate implicit in the lease is not determinable, it should be estimated by reference to the rate that a lessee would be expected to pay on a similar lease. (Para. 24)

A key element in the above definition is fair value and hence we need to know how this is found.

Fair value

Fair value is the price at which an asset could be exchanged in an arm's length transaction less, where applicable, any grants receivable towards the purchase or use of the asset. (Para. 25)

Note that while knowledge of the implied interest rate is required to determine the appropriate accounting treatment in the books of the lessee, it is found by reference to the cash flows of the lessor. In practice the lessee may not know or be able to estimate the various cash flows but we assume, at this stage, that the lessee can obtain all the necessary data.

If we let FV be the fair value, L_j the lease payment in year j (payable at the beginning of each year) and R_n the estimated residual values received at the end of year n, the last year of the lease, then using standard present value techniques the implied rate of interest r is found from the solution of the following equation:

$$FV = \sum_{j=0}^{n-1} \frac{L_j}{(1+r)^j} + \frac{R_n}{(1+r)^n}$$

If we assume in the case of the Lombok/Salat lease that the fair value is £108 720 and that there is no residual value (i.e. $R_n = 0$) then substituting in the above equation we get:

$$£108\,720 = \sum_{j=0}^{3} \frac{£35\,000}{(1+r)^j} \text{ or } \sum \frac{1}{(1+r)^j} = 3.1064$$

Inspection of tables showing the present value of an annuity shows that 3.1064 represents an interest rate of 20 per cent.[12] Thus the interest rate implicit in the lease is 20 per cent and hence the present value PV of the minimum lease payments can be found as follows:

$$PV = £35\,000(3.1064)$$
$$= £108\,720$$

This is of course equal to the fair value as, in the simple case, the only cash flows that the lessor will receive are the minimum lease payments. Later we will describe the circumstances where the two series of cash flows (i.e. the lessee's and the lessor's) might be different and the effect of these differences on the calculations.

We can now show how the lease should be treated in the books of Lombok (the lessee). The original entry recording the lease is:

---

[12] This and other necessary present value calculations can be made by use of standard computer packages. Care is needed if using a table or a program that assumes all cash flows take place at the end of a period. In this example the cash flows take place at the start of the period. This problem can be overcome by noting that the present value factor for an immediate payment is 1, and so deduct 1 from 3.1604 to give 2.1064 which when applied to the three remaining payments produces an interest rate of 20 per cent.

> *Dr* Leased asset   £108 720
>   *Cr* Liability under lease   £108 720

From this time onwards the two accounts are dealt with separately. The leased machine will be depreciated over the shorter of the length of the lease or the asset's expected life, using the company's normal depreciation policy for assets of its type, while the liability will be gradually extinguished as payments are made during the primary period of the lease. The only problem that remains is how to spread the total interest charge over the primary period of the lease. This same problem is, of course, encountered in accounting for hire purchase transactions.

The total interest charge may be calculated as follows:

	£
Payments under lease, 4 × 35 000	140 000
less 'Cost' as above	108 720
Interest	31 280

←Cal. 2 Charge.

Theoretically, the best approach is to use the actuarial or annuity method that produces a constant annual rate of interest (in this case 20 per cent) on the outstanding balance on the liability account. This is the method specified in SSAP 21, which does, however, allow the use of any alternative method that is a reasonable approximation to the annuity method.[13]

Assuming that all payments are made on the due dates, the liability account in the books of Lombok for the term of the lease can be summarised as follows:

	20X1	20X2	20X3	20X4
	£	£	£	£
1 Jan Opening balance (20X1 cost)	108 720	88 470	64 170	35 000
1 Jan Cash	35 000	35 000	35 000	35 000
	73 720	53 470	29 170	–
31 Dec Interest, 20% of above	14 750	10 700	5 830	–
31 Dec Closing balance	88 470	64 170	35 000	–

This account provides us with the interest charge to the profit and loss account for each year and the liability for inclusion in each balance sheet. The amount of interest charged to the profit and loss account declines over the life of the lease because the outstanding balance is reduced by the annual payments. It is, of course, necessary to distinguish between the current portion of the liability, that is the amount due to be paid in the coming twelve months, and the long-term liability for the purposes of balance sheet presentation. In this case, this is extremely easy as the only payment to be made in each of years 20X2 and 20X4 is £35000 per annum payable on the day following each balance sheet date. Hence the analysis of the liability into its current and long-term components is as follows:

	20X1	20X2	20X3	20X4
	£	£	£	£
Closing liability as shown above	88 470	64 170	35 000	–
Current portion of liability	35 000	35 000	35 000	–
Long term portion of liability – balance	53 470	29 170	–	–

---

[13] The method is the only one permitted under the provisions of FRS 4 *Capital Investments*.

Example 9.2 will explain the complication that arises in analysing this liability where rental payments are made more frequently than once a year.

One commonly used alternative to the annuity method is the 'sum of the year's digits' method or 'Rule of 78'.[14] If the sum of the digits method were used in the above illustration the results would be:

Total interest charge	£31 280
Sum of the year's digits, 1 + 2 + 3	6
Interest charged to profit and loss account	
20X1, $\frac{3}{6}$ of £31 280	15 640
20X2, $\frac{2}{6}$ of £31 280	10 430
20X3, $\frac{1}{6}$ of £31 280	5 210
	£31 280

Although the use of the annuity method is conceptually superior, a comparison of the annual interest charges under the two methods reveals similar patterns of interest charge and thus the 'sum of the year's digits' method is often used as a convenient approximation to the annuity method:

Year	Annuity method	Sum of the year's digits method
	(£)	(£)
20X1	14 750	15 640
20X2	10 700	10 430
20X3	5 830	5 210
	£31 280	£31 280

The impact of residual values

Let us now complicate matters by assuming that the asset that is the subject of the lease has a residual value. We will assume that the manufacturer who originally supplied the asset to Salat has agreed to reacquire the asset at the end of the lease. The sum is dependent on the condition of the machine and the market factors at the end of the lease, but the manufacturer has guaranteed to pay £10 000 whatever the circumstances. Let us assume that at the inception of the lease it is anticipated that the manufacturer will actually pay £20 000. Let us also assume that Lombok and Salat agree that they will divide any sums realised on the disposal of the asset in the ratio 35 : 65. Thus, at the inception of the lease it is estimated that Lombok will receive £7000 (of which £3500 is guaranteed) and Salat £13 000 (£6500 guaranteed).

For the purposes of calculating the implicit interest rate, the distinction between the guaranteed and unguaranteed elements of the residual value can be ignored as both have to be

---

[14] It is called the Rule of 78 because if the method is based on the monthly intervals and if the digit 1 is assigned to January, 2 to February and so on, the sum of the digits for the year is 78.

taken into the calculation, but the distinction may be important when deciding whether the lease is a finance or operating lease (see p. 225).

If we return to the equation on p. 218 and substitute the estimated value on realisation receivable by Salat, the equation becomes:

$$£108\,720 = \sum_{j=0}^{3} \frac{35\,000}{(1+r)^j} + \frac{13\,000}{(1+r)^4}$$

Use of tables or a programmable calculation on a computer shows that the above equation will be satisfied when r is approximately 25 per cent. This is a higher rate of interest than the 20 per cent that was previously calculated as Salat obviously earns a higher return due to the introduction of the residual value as an additional cash flow.

So far as Lombok is concerned the minimum lease payments are unchanged but they will now be discounted at the higher rate of 25 per cent that will produce an initial value of the leased asset of:

$$£35\,000(2.952) = £103\,320$$

The annual payments of £35 000 are the same as in the original example except that the liability that is to be paid off is lower (£103 320 not £108 720). Hence the finance charge in the profit and loss account will be higher in the second example. This reflects the fact that in the first example the lease payments can be regarded as acquiring the whole of the productive use of the asset, in that a zero residual value was assumed, whereas in the second case the same annual lease payments only acquired a proportion of the asset's productive capacity.

It will be noted that the estimated realisable value that Lombok expects to receive had no effect on the calculation of the amount by which the lease should be capitalised or on the way in which the annual lease payments should be split. This is because these depend on the minimum lease payments. The recognition of the estimated realisable value does have an effect on the amount that has to be depreciated which is the present value of the minimum lease payments less the estimated realisable value. Thus, the depreciation charges that would emerge from our two sets of assumptions are as follows (assuming the straight-line method is used):

$$\text{Assumption 1} \quad \frac{£108\,720}{4} = £27\,180$$

$$\text{Assumption 2} \quad \frac{£(103\,320 - 7000)}{4} = £24\,080$$

In the above examples we assumed that the lessee knows (or is able to find out from the lessor) the fair value of the asset and the estimated realisable value that the lessor expects to receive. In practice this may well not be the case and certain estimates will have to be made. Often the fair value will be known[15] and the interest rate estimated from a knowledge of other leases of a similar type.

[15] Unless the asset concerned is highly specific the prudent lessee will obviously wish to know how much it would cost to purchase the asset before signing a lease.

Example 9.2 Illustration of capitalisation of finance lease involving more frequent rental payments

In this example, we explain how to account for finance leases that involve rental payments occurring more frequently than once a year.

Java plc, whose year end is 31 December, entered into a non-cancellable agreement, on 1 July 20X1, to lease a machine for a period of five years. Payments under the lease are £55 200 payable six monthly commencing on 1 July 20X1. The interest rate implicit in the lease is 8 per cent per half year.

The fair value of the machine at 1 July 20X1 was £420 000.

Java plc uses straight-line depreciation applied on a strict time basis.

We need first to work out the present value of the minimum lease payments.

$$PV \text{ of the minimum lease payments} = £55\ 200\ (1 + PV \text{ of annuity of 1 per period for nine periods})$$
$$= £55\ 200\ (1 + a_{\overline{9}|} \text{ at } 8\%)$$
$$= £55\ 200\ (1 + 6.247)$$
$$= \underline{£400\ 000} \text{ approximately.}$$

The initial cost of the machine and the initial obligation should therefore be recorded at £400 000.

The lessee has the possession and use of the machine for five years so the annual depreciation using the company's method would be £80 000 (£400 000/5). In the year ended 31 December 20X1, Java has only had the use of the machine for six months and hence the depreciation should be £40 000. In summary, the machine will be depreciated over the term of the lease as follows:

		£
Depreciation	20X1	40 000
	20X2	80 000
	20X3	80 000
	20X4	80 000
	20X5	80 000
	20X6	40 000
		£400 000

A summary of the liability account for the first two years of the lease will appear as follows:

Period half-year	Opening balance	Payments on first day of period	Net amount on which interest is payable for each period	Interest at 8% per period	Closing balance
	£	£	£	£	£
1 July–31 Dec 20X1	400 000	55 200	344 800	27 584	372 384
1 Jan–30 June 20X2	372 384	55 200	317 184	25 375	342 559
1 July–31 Dec 20X2	342 559	55 200	287 359	22 989	310 348
1 July–31 Dec 20X3	310 348	55 200	255 148	20 142	275 560

The finance cost to be charged to the profit and loss account for the year ended 31 December 20X1 is £27 584 while that to be charged for the year to 31 December 20X2 will be £25 375 + £22 989 = £48 364.

The liability at 31 December 20X1 is £372 384 but we need to analyse this into its current and non-current portions for presentation in the balance sheet. One payment of £55 200 will be made on the following day, 1 January 20X2, so this will definitely reduce the liability at 31 December

20X1. There will another payment of £55 200 in the coming year, on 1 July 20X2, but not all of this will reduce the liability on 31 December 20X1. The payment on 1 July 20X2 will include interest for the period 1 January 20X2 until 30 June 20X2, which has not yet accrued and hence is not part of the liability on 31 December 20X1.

We may therefore calculate the current and long-term portions of the liability on 31 December 20X1 as follows:

	£
Current liability on 31.12.20X1	
Payments in next twelve months: 1.1.20X2	55 200
1.7.20X2	55 200
less Interest for period 1.1.20X2 to 30.6.20X2	
included in payment on 1.7.20X2	(25 374)
	85 026
Long-term liability on 31.12.20X1 – balance	287 358
Total liability on 31.12.20X1 – per ledger account	372 384

We may analyse the liability on 31 December 20X2 in a similar fashion:

	£
Current liability on 31.12.20X2	
Payments in next twelve months: 1.1.20X3	55 200
1.7.20X3	55 200
less Interest for the period 1.1.20X3 to 30.6.20X3	
included in payment on 1.7.20X3	(20 412)
	89 988
Long-term liability on 31.12.20X2 – balance	220 360
Total liability on 31.12.20X2 – per ledger account	310 348

We are now in a position to show how the lease would be reflected in the financial statements for the years ended 31 December 20X1 and 20X2 respectively.

Profit and loss accounts for the years ended 31 December	**20X1**	**20X2**
	£	£
Depreciation of leased machine	40 000	80 000
Finance charge	27 784	48 364

Balance sheets on 31 December		**20X1**	**20X2**
		£	£
Fixed asset			
	Leased machine		
	– at cost	400 000	400 000
	– *less* depreciation	40 000	120 000
	NBV	360 000	280 000
Creditors due in less than one year			
	Obligation under finance lease	85 026	89 988
Creditors due in one year or more			
	Obligation under finance lease	287 358	220 360

Barriers to the introduction of a standard

In order to understand part of the reason why leasing became popular, the reluctance on the part of most companies to capitalise leases and the provisions of SSAP 21, it is necessary to understand the way in which leases were in the past treated for the purposes of taxation. Unlike hire purchase contracts and credit sales agreements, where the user obtains grants and capital allowances, in a lease it is the legal owner, the lessor, who received grants and capital allowances on the asset. The lessee received no allowances but obtained tax relief on the amounts payable under the lease. Capital allowances are only of value to a company that has sufficient taxable profit. Hence, to their mutual advantage, one company with large taxable profits was able to lease assets to another company that did not have sufficient taxable profits to take full advantage of capital allowances. Thus the company with insufficient taxable profits could acquire fixed assets at a lower effective cost than would have been the case with alternative methods of financing.

The effect of what might well be described as the distortion of the tax system described above was undoubtedly one of the major causes of the growth of leasing. Hence, there was a good deal of opposition to the proposal that lessees should capitalise finance leases, as it was feared that a change in accounting practice might precipitate changes in taxation law whereby finance leases would be treated in the same way as hire purchase contracts.

Other factors which hindered the development of a standard requiring the capitalisation of finance leases included concerns about the possible extension of the principle to other types of non-cancellable contracts, for example those for the regular supply of raw materials or labour, and fears about the potential complexity of any standard. However, the ASC did issue SSAP 21 *Accounting for Leases and Hire Purchase Contracts* in August 1984 and, amongst other things, this required lessees to capitalise finance leases, and lessors to include in their balance sheets not the fixed asset but the debtor for the net investment in the lease.

It is perhaps somewhat ironic that, after studying the problem for some nine years, the ASC issued this standard just after the Finance Act 1984 had considerably reduced the tax advantages of leasing.

SSAP 21 *Accounting for Leases and Hire Purchase Contracts*

We are now in a position to discuss the specific requirements of SSAP 21. This is a detailed standard and we will not attempt to cover all its aspects but will instead concentrate on the important elements and those that might give rise to particular difficulties of understanding. The ASC published guidance notes on SSAP 21 and readers should refer to this booklet for a more detailed explanation of the provisions of the standard.

We will first deal with a number of general issues before concentrating on the impact of the standard on the accounts of lessees and hirers. A discussion of the more specialised topic of accounting for lessors will be deferred until later in the chapter.

Scope

The standard covers leases and hire purchases contracts and is applicable to accounts based on both the historical cost and current cost conventions. The standard does not apply to leases of the rights to exploit natural resources such as oil or gas, nor does it apply to licensing agreements for items such as motion pictures, videos, etc. Stress is also laid on the point that the standard does not apply to immaterial items, such as car rental, as discussed earlier.

Distinction between finance and operating leases

The apparent distinction between the two different types of leases has already been explained (see p. 215). The standard states that:

> **A finance lease is a lease that transfers substantially all the risks and rewards of ownership of an asset to the lessee. (Para. 15)**

It is presumed that a lease is a finance lease if at the start of the lease the present value of the minimum lease payments amounts to substantially all (normally 90 per cent or more) of the fair value of the leased asset. The present value should be calculated by using the interest rate implicit in the lease. However, the standard recognises that in exceptional circumstances this initial presumption may be rebutted if the lease in question does not transfer substantially all the risks and rewards of ownership to the lessee. Sometimes the lessor will receive part of its return by way of a guarantee from an independent third party, possibly the manufacturer of the asset, in which case the lease may be treated as a finance lease by the lessor but as an operating lease by the lessee.

There is nothing magic about using 90 per cent as a cut-off point, and the need to resort to the use of what is essentially an arbitrary criterion is one of the arguments used to support the view that there is no distinction to be made between the two different types of lease.

Hire purchase contracts

With the vast majority of hire purchase contracts the 'risks and rewards' pass to the hirer and hence may be regarded as being akin to finance leases. In such cases the standard specifies that they should be treated in a similar way to finance leases. However, in exceptional circumstances a hire purchase contract may be accounted for on the same principles as an operating lease.

Accounting by lessees

Finance leases

A finance lease should be capitalised; hence the lease should be recorded as an asset and an obligation to pay rentals. At the inception of the lease the asset will equal the liability (although this equality will not hold over the life of the lease) and will be the present value of the minimum lease payments, derived by discounting them at the interest rate implied in the lease.

The standard states that:

> the fair value of the asset will often be a sufficiently close approximation to the present value of the minimum lease payments and may in these circumstances be substituted for it. (Para. 33)

If the fair value cannot be determined, possibly because the asset concerned is unique, then the present value can be found by discounting the minimum lease payments by the interest rate implicit in the lease. If the latter cannot be determined the rate may be estimated from that which applied in similar leases.

Total payments less than fair value

In some circumstances the combined impact of any grants which may be available and taxation allowances received by the lessor may be such as to bring the total (i.e. not the present value of) lease payments below the fair value. The standard specifies (Para. 34) that if this occurs the amount to be capitalised and depreciated should be reduced to the minimum lease payments. A negative finance charge should not be shown.

In other words if, say, the total of the payments to be made under the lease is £10 000 and the fair value of the asset is £12 000, the asset and liability on the inception of the lease are both £10 000. The payments under the lease will all be applied to reducing the liability and no part of them will be charged to the profit and loss account as a finance charge. The only charge in the profit and loss account will be the annual depreciation charge.

Rentals

Rentals payable should be apportioned between the finance charge (if any) and a reduction of the outstanding obligation. The total finance charge should be allocated to accounting periods so as to produce a constant annual rate of charge (i.e. the annuity method), or a reasonable approximation thereto.

The guidance notes suggest that in most circumstances, especially where the lease is for seven years or less and interest rates are not high, the Rule of 78 (see p. 220) will be an acceptable approximation to the actuarial method. In the case of small (relative to the size of the companies) leases it is suggested that the straight-line method, whereby the total finance charge is recognised on a time basis, may be acceptable.

Note that FRS 4 *Capital Instruments* does not give any latitude as to use of the method of allocating finance charges (or finance costs as they are called in FRS 4); only the actuarial (or annuity) method is allowed. However, the concept of materiality could be cited to justify the use of a simpler method such as the Rule of 78 if the figures produced by the two methods are fairly close or the totals are not material in the context of the entity's total operation.

Depreciation

A leased asset should be depreciated over the shorter of the length of the lease or the asset's useful life. However, in the case of hire purchase contracts, because of the presumption that the asset concerned will be acquired by the hirer, the asset should be depreciated over its useful life.

Operating leases

The accounting treatment by the lessee in respect of operating leases is straightforward in that the whole of the payments are charged to the profit and loss account. The only slight complication is that the standard requires the rental to be charged on a straight-line basis over the lease term (unless another systematic and rational basis is more appropriate) even if the payments are not made on such a basis. Hence, if the term of the lease requires a heavy initial payment, a proportion of the payment can be treated as a prepaid expense.

More commonly, lessees are granted so-called 'rental holidays' in that they do not have to pay anything for an initial period. In such circumstances the standard requires a charge to be made to the profit and loss account for the period of the rental holiday that would be treated as an accrual in the balance sheet. Thereafter the charge to the profit and loss account would be less than the payments made in the year (as rental, like other holidays, has to be paid for), with the excess reducing the balance sheet accrual. Particularly significant examples of this type of arrangement are leases of buildings by government agencies to business in areas where the government wants to encourage the creation of jobs.

Disclosure requirements in the financial statements of lessees and hirers

Finance leases

For disclosure purposes information relating to hire purchase contracts with characteristics similar to finance leases should be included with the equivalent information regarding leases.

1 *Fixed assets and depreciation.* The lessee may either:
   (a) show separately the gross amounts, accumulated depreciation and depreciation expense for each major class of leased asset; or
   (b) group the above information with the equivalent information for owned assets[16] but show by way of a note how much of the net amount (i.e. net book value) and the depreciation expense relates to assets held under finance leases.
2 *Obligations.* The lessee must both:
   (a) disclose the obligations related to finance leases separately from other obligations and liabilities; and
   (b) analyse the net obligations under finance leases into three components (the figures may be combined with other obligations):
      – amounts payable in next year;
      – amounts payable in second to fifth years;
      – amounts payable thereafter.
3 *Finance charges.* The lessee must disclose the aggregate finance charge allocated to the period.
4 *Commitments.* The lessee must show by way of a note the amount of any commitment existing at the balance sheet date in respect of finance leases which have been entered into but whose inception occurs after the year end.
5 *Accounting policies.* Accounting policies adopted for finance leases must be stated.

Operating leases

1 *Current rentals.* The lessee must disclose the total rentals charged as an expense, analysed between amounts payable in respect of the hire of plant and machinery and those charged in respect of other operating leases. (The Companies Act, of course, requires disclosure of the charge for the hire of plant and machinery.)
2 *Future rentals.* The lessee must show the payments which it is committed to make during the next year, analysed between those in which the commitment expires:
   (a) within that year;
   (b) in the second to fifth years inclusive; and
   (c) over five years from the balance sheet date.
   Commitments in respect of leases of land and buildings and other operating leases must be shown separately.
3 *Accounting policies.* The accounting policies adopted for operating leases must be stated.

Accounting for finance leases by lessors – general principles

The provisions of SSAP 21 regarding the accounting treatment of finance leases by lessors are relatively difficult for two main reasons. First, the basic method is itself not simple since – as will be shown – it depends on complex calculations of what constitutes the lessor's

---

[16] Since it is the right to use the asset rather than the asset itself which is capitalised there is some doubt as to whether it should be called a tangible asset and included with the owned tangible assets. The ASC ignored such niceties and for the purposes of balance sheet presentation the leases are regarded as tangible assets.

investment in a particular lease and, second, the standard permits the use of alternative methods and simplifying assumptions so that a host of different methods can be justified under the terms of the standard.

We will first describe the basic principles underlying the provisions of SSAP 21 relating to the treatment of finance leases by lessors.

Balance sheet presentation – the measurement of net investment

Lessors should not include in their balance sheets the assets subject to the contracts which are finance leases but instead record as a debtor the *net investment* in the lease after making any necessary provisions for bad and doubtful debts. In order to explain this term and describe how profit is recognised, we will need to reproduce certain definitions included in SSAP 21.

Net investment

The net investment in a lease at a point in time comprises:

(a) the gross investment in a lease; less
(b) gross earnings allocated to future periods. (Para. 22)

Thus, we need to know what is meant by the gross investment and gross earnings.

Gross investment

The gross investment in a lease at a point in time is the total of the minimum lease payments [see p. 217] and any unguaranteed residual value accruing to the lessor. (Para. 21)

Gross earnings

Gross earnings comprise the lessor's gross finance income over the lease term, representing the difference between his gross investment in the lease [see above] and the cost of the leased asset less any grants receivable towards the purchase or use of the asset. (Para. 28)[17]

In order to illustrate the effect of the above definitions assume that the details relating to a particular lease are as follows:

Cost of asset	£12 000
Grant receivable by lessor	£2 000
Lease term	5 years
Annual rental	£3 000
Estimated residual value accruing to the lessor	£500

Let us see how one measures the net investment at the inception of the lease and at the end of the first year.

At inception:	£
Minimum lease payments, 5 × £3000	15 000
Estimated residual value	500
Gross investment	15 500
less Gross earnings (£15 500 – £10 000)	5 500
Net investment	£10 000

---

[17] The paragraph goes on to modify the definition to deal with the use of a possible option available in SSAP 21 relating to the treatment of tax-free grants.

Hence, at inception the net investment is equal to the cost of the asset less grants receivable by the lessor.

Assume that the gross earnings recognised in the profit and loss account in the first year are £2500 (we shall describe in the following section how this figure is calculated). Then the net investment at the end of the first year is:

	£
Minimum lease payments, 4 × £3000	12 000
Estimated residual value	500
	12 500
less Gross earnings allocated to future periods (£5500 − £2500)	3 000
Net investment	£9 500

The recognition of gross earnings

The total gross earnings on any lease are reasonably easy to calculate since the minimum lease payments will be known and, generally, the residual value, if any, can be estimated. The difficulty lies in allocating the gross earnings to the different accounting periods. The standard followed existing practice in the leasing industry by specifying that (other than in the case of hire purchase contracts) the interest should be allocated on the basis of the lessor's *net cash* investment in the lease and not on the basis of the net investment. Specifically, Para. 39 of SSAP 21 states:

> The total gross earnings under a finance lease should normally be allocated to accounting periods to give a constant periodic rate of return on the lessor's net cash investment in the lease in each period. In the case of a hire purchase contract which has characteristics similar to a finance lease, allocation of gross earnings so as to give a constant periodic rate of return on the finance company's net investment will in most cases be a suitable approximation to allocation based on the net cash investment. In arriving at the constant periodic rate of return, a reasonable approximation may be made.

To an extent the above is familiar in that it is the counterpart of the annuity method prescribed for use by lessees in that the annual finance charge should be such as to produce a constant rate based on the decreasing obligation. The difference is that although the reduction in the obligation is relatively easy to calculate, the determination of the net cash investment is somewhat more difficult.

The meaning of net cash investment

The meaning of the net cash investment can be more easily understood if one assumes that a separate company is established by the lessor for each lease and then measuring or estimating the cash flows in and out of that company. The net cash investment is then the balance of cash, which might be positive or negative, in the company at any point in time. The various cash flows may be summarised as in Table 9.2.

If one thinks in terms of a single lease company and the cash flows associated with it, it can be seen that the company will start with an 'overdraft' – the cost of the asset and of setting up the lease – but that this will be reduced if a grant is received and as capital allowances for the purchase of the asset are received. The overdraft will be reduced as lease payments are received but will be increased by virtue of the interest payments made on the overdraft. Profit may also be withdrawn (and for this purpose profit may be regarded as including the

Table 9.2 **Summary of cash flows**

Cash flows out	Cash flows in
1 Cost of the asset	(a) Grants received against purchase or use of asset
2 Cost of setting up the lease	(b) Rental income received
3 Tax payments on rental and interest received	(c) Tax reductions on capital allowances* and on interest paid
4 Interest payments on cash invested in the lease	(d) Interest earned when the net cash investment becomes a surplus
5 Profit withdrawn	(e) Residual value at the end of the lease

*Since in actuality the 'single-lease' company is not separate and distinct, the reductions in tax payments due to the receipt of capital allowance and the charging of expenses can be treated as cash receipts since they are covered by tax payment otherwise payable by the lessor (if this were not the case the lessor should not be in the leasing business in the first place).

contribution made by the 'single lease' company to the operating expenses of the enterprise of which it actually forms part) which will also increase the overdraft. At some stage the overdraft may be eliminated and replaced by a cash surplus on which interest may be deemed to be earned. The interest 'payments' and 'receipts' will also have taxation consequences that will respectively increase the cash surplus (or reduce the overdraft) or decrease the cash surplus. Finally, if the lessor receives a residual value this will increase the surplus.

It is on the basis of the above considerations that SSAP 21 defines net cash investment as follows:

> The *net cash investment* in a lease at a point in time is the amount of funds invested in a lease by a lessor, and comprises the cost of the asset plus or minus the following related payments and receipts:
>
> (a) government or other grants receivable towards the purchase or use of the asset;
> (b) rentals received;
> (c) taxation payments and receipts, including the effect of capital allowances;
> (d) residual values, if any, at the end of the lease term;
> (e) interest payments (where applicable);
> (f) interest received on cash surplus;
> (g) profit taken out of the lease. (Para. 23)

The actuarial method after tax

The guidance notes to SSAP 21 describe a number of ways of allocating the gross revenue to accounting periods based on the net cash investment. Of these the most accurate is the 'actuarial method after tax'. This method produces a constant rate of return on the net cash investment over that period of the lease in which the lessor has a positive investment (i.e. before any cash surplus is generated). The phrase 'after tax' does not imply that it is after-tax profit which is allocated but simply that the tax cash flows are included in the measurement of the net cash investment.

The actuarial method after tax is illustrated in Example 9.3.

Example 9.3 The actuarial method after tax

Gasp plc, the lessor, acquired an asset for £7735 that it leased out on the following terms:

Period	5 years
Rental	£2000 per year payable in advance on 1 January of each year
Residual value	Zero

Gasp's year end is 31 December and tax in respect of any year is payable on 1 January of the next year but one. The tax rate is 50 per cent and capital allowances of 100 per cent are receivable in the first year. (These rates are unrealistic but they have been chosen to simplify the figures and hence clarify the example.)

The annual rate of return earned over the period when there is a net cash investment is 12 per cent while it is estimated that surplus cash can be invested at 5 per cent (both rates are before tax).

The interest paid by Gasp on the funds invested in the lease will be ignored.

The cash flows and the profit recognised on the lease are set out in Table 9.3.

Table 9.3 Hypothetical cash flows – figures in brackets represent cash flows out

Date	Cost £	Rent £	Tax £	Profit taken on lease £	Interest on cash surplus £	Net cash investment £
1 Jan X0	(7735)	2000				(5735)
31 Dec X0				(688)		(6423)
1 Jan X1		2000				(4423)
31 Dec X1				(531)		(4954)
1 Jan X2		2000	2868			(86)
31 Dec X2				(11)		(97)
1 Jan X3		2000	(1000)			903
31 Dec X3					45	948
1 Jan X4		2000	(1000)			1948
31 Dec X4					98	2046
1 Jan X5			(1023)			1023
31 Dec X5					52	1075
1 Jan X6			(1049)			26
1 Jan X7			(26)			–

Notes:

(a) The profit taken on the lease has been calculated at 12 per cent of the net cash investment at the start of each year (e.g. £688 = 0.12 × £5735) while the interest on the cash surplus has been calculated at 5 per cent of the opening balance (e.g. £45 = 0.05 × £903). Interest on the cash surplus in 20X6 has been ignored (otherwise the calculation would never end).

(b) The tax computation for 20X0 (tax payable on 1 January 20X2) is as follows:

	£
Capital allowances (100%)	7735
less Rental income received	2000
Adjusted profit	5735
Tax thereon, 50% of £5735	£2868

In subsequent years the tax payment is 50 per cent of the sum of the rental income and the interest earned on the cash surplus.

Although the lease will generate an annual rental of £2000 for each of the five years after tax, profit recognised in respect of the lease is £688 in year 1, £531 in year 2 and £11 in year 3.[18]

It may be thought that this is a very imprudent way of recognising profit in that most of the profit is taken in the first two years of the lease. However, it must be recognised that the profit reported is that which is generated by the lessor's financing activities and is calculated by reference to the amount that the lessor has invested in the lease. As Table 9.3 shows, the investment falls to zero, to be replaced by a cash surplus by 1 January 20X3.

Arithmetically all the figures in Table 9.3 can be found if you know the cash flows, which will be specified in the agreement, and either the profit on the lease (12 per cent) or the re-investment rate (5 per cent). Thus, if one of the two rates is known the other can be calculated, with the aid of a computer or a lot of patient trial and error. In practice, of course, the lessor will have made the calculations of these rates when agreeing the terms of the rental with the lessee. Thus the lessor would start by deciding, on the basis of market conditions and competitive forces, the return required on the lease (taking into account the return on any surplus cash invested[19] and hence work out the rent that would need to be charged.

The next step is to calculate the proportion of the annual receipts of £2000, which is deemed to represent the reduction in the amount due from the lessee. The calculation is based on the figures in Table 9.4. This table also shows the necessary transfers to and from the deferred taxation account if it is judged necessary to establish such an account.

Table 9.4 To calculate capital repayment and deferred taxation transfers

	20X0 £	20X1 £	20X2 £	20X3 £	20X4 £	20X5 £	Total £
1 Rental	2000	2000	2000	2000	2000		10 000
2 Capital repayments	(624)	(938)	(1978)	(2045)	(2098)	(52)	(7 735)
3 Gross earnings	1376	1062	22	(45)	(98)	(52)	2 265
4 Interest				45	98	52	195
5 Profit before tax	1376	1062	22	–	–	–	2 460
6 Taxation	2868	(1000)	(1000)	(1023)	(1049)	(26)	(1 230)
7	4244	62	(978)	(1023)	(1049)	(26)	(1 230)
8 Deferred tax	(3556)	469	989	1023	1049	26	–
9 Net profit	£688	£531	£11	–	–	–	£1 230

Table 9.4 is constructed from the bottom up. The figures in line 9 are taken from Table 9.3. The net profit is then grossed up at the appropriate tax rate (50 per cent) to give line 5. Line 6, which shows the actual tax payments, is also taken from Table 9.3 which means that line 8 (deferred tax) can be derived. Line 4 is taken from Table 9.3 and hence the gross earnings (line 3) and capi-

---

[18] Observant readers will note that the sum of these is, at £1230, more than the 50 per cent of the difference between the minimum lease payments and the cost of the asset, i.e. 50 per cent of (£10 000 – £7735) = £1132. This is because the interest on the cash surplus is included in the total profit, i.e. £1230 = 50 per cent of £(10 000 – 7735 + 45 + 98 + 52).

[19] The surplus cash will probably be invested in another lease, thus the rate of return on the surplus cash will be the return from the new lease. The return on the new lease will depend *inter alia* on the return on any surplus cash it may generate which it may be presumed will be invested in yet another lease and so on *ad infinitum*. In practice, to avoid having to estimate returns on leases (or other investments) which will arise in the future, a prudent estimate of the return on surplus cash is used in the calculations.

tal repayments (line 2) can be deduced. If, taking into consideration the affairs of the company as a whole, it is decided that it is not necessary to account for deferred tax, one could start Table 9.4 at line 5 and work up from there.

It must be emphasised that Table 9.4 is used only to calculate the capital repayment and, if appropriate, the deferred taxation transfers. For the purposes of the balance sheet presentation SSAP 21 requires that the amount due from the lessee should be the net investment (not the net cash investment) in the lease. Thus in the instance of Gasp plc the asset would be recorded as follows:

Balance sheet date	Gross investment £	Gross earnings allocated to future periods £	Net investment £
31 Dec X0	8000	889	7111
31 Dec X1	6000	(173)	6173
31 Dec X2	4000	(195)	4195
31 Dec X3	2000	(150)	2150
31 Dec X4	–	(52)	52

The gross earnings allocated to future periods are found from line 3 of Table 9.4. Thus, for example, the figure at 31 December 20X0 is £(1062 + 22 − 45 − 98 − 52) = £889 and so on.

The method produces the apparently absurd result that the net investment at certain dates is greater than the remaining lease payments, the extreme case being that at 31 December 20X4 when a net investment of £52 is produced notwithstanding the fact that the lease has terminated. This odd result derives from the fact that a larger profit is taken in the early years of the lease in consequence of the anticipated return on the surplus cash invested; thus, for example, the net investment at 31 December 20X3 of £2150 can be regarded as representing the final lease payment of £2000 plus the anticipated interest receipts of £150 (£98 in 20X4 and £52 in 20X5).

Alternative approaches to accounting for finance leases and hire purchase contracts

As stated on p. 229, Para. 39 of SSAP 21 specifies that in the case of hire purchase contracts gross earnings can be allocated on the basis of the company's net investment. The reason for this is that in the case of hire purchase, capital allowances are granted to the hirer and hence the tax cash flows will not have the same significance to the hire purchase company as they have for a leasing company.

The same paragraph allows, for both hire purchase and leasing contracts, the use of alternative methods that would produce results that would be 'reasonable approximations' to the desired constant rate of return on the net cash investment. A number of alternatives are described in the guidance notes to SSAP 21, which include the investment period method, which is similar to the actuarial method after tax. Other methods described are the Rule of 78 and the actuarial method before tax. These two methods are primarily intended for use with hire purchase contracts but they can be used for finance leases where the amounts concerned are not judged to be material.

Lessors may, if they choose, write off the initial direct costs in arranging a lease over the period on a 'systematic and rational basis'.[20] This provision applies to both finance and operating leases.

[20] SSAP 21, Para. 44.

Accounting for operating leases by lessors – general principles

The basic principles are contained in Paras 42–44 of SSAP 21. These are:

> An asset held for use in operating leases by a lessor should be recorded as a fixed asset and depreciated over its useful life.
>
> Rental income from an operating lease, excluding charges for services such as insurance and maintenance, should be recognized on a straight-line basis over the period of the lease, even if the payments are not made on such a basis, unless another systematic and rational basis is more representative of the time pattern in which the benefit from the leased asset is receivable.
>
> Initial direct costs incurred by a lessor in arranging a lease may be apportioned over the period of the lease on a systematic and rational basis.

The accounting treatment of operating leases by the lessor is thus straightforward, subject only to the problems of dealing with cases where payment is not received on a straight-line basis and deciding on the circumstances where an alternative systematic and rational basis would be appropriate. These issues are similar to those faced by the lessee (see p. 226).

Disclosure requirements for the lessor in respect of finance and operating leases and hire purchase contracts

The requirements, contained in Paras 58–60 of SSAP 21, are as follows:

1 The net investment in (i) finance leases and (ii) hire purchase contracts should be disclosed. Note that separate totals need to be given for leases and hire purchase contracts. In the case of the remaining disclosure requirements, information regarding leases and hire purchase contracts can be combined.
2 The gross amount of assets held for use in operating leases and the related accumulated depreciation charge should be disclosed.
3 Disclosure should be made of:
    (a) the policy adopted for accounting for operating leases and finance leases and, in detail, the policy for accounting for finance lease income;
    (b) the aggregate rentals receivable in respect of an accounting period in relation to (i) finance leases and (ii) operating leases; and
    (c) the cost of assets acquired, whether by purchase or finance lease, for the purpose of letting under finance leases.

Sale and leaseback transactions

The standard makes specific reference to sale and leaseback transactions that arise when the vendor/lessee sells an asset but continues to have the use of it on the basis of a lease granted by the purchaser/lessor. No problems arise with regard to the treatment of a sale and lease-back transaction in the accounts of the lessor who will record the asset purchased at cost and then, depending on the nature of the lease, follow the provisions of SSAP 21 in the usual way. The position regarding the vendor/lessee is different in so far as there are circumstances where the sales and leaseback transactions will have to be accorded special treatment. The nature of the circumstances depends on the type of lease.

Finance leases

The key characteristic of a finance lease is that the 'risk and reward' associated with the asset rests with the lessee. Hence when a vendor engages in a sale and finance leaseback transaction, the 'risk and reward' is retained. It is therefore argued that in such circumstances it would be wrong to recognise a profit or loss on the sale of the asset concerned in the year in which the sale and leaseback is effected.

Thus SSAP 21 states:

> In a sale and leaseback transaction which results in a finance lease, any apparent profit or loss (that is, the difference between the sale price and the previous carrying value) should be deferred and amortized in the financial statements of the seller/lessee over the shorter of the lease term and the useful life of the asset. (Para. 46)

If the asset was sold for its fair value, the above provisions could be avoided by revaluing the asset prior to sale and hence removing any difference between the sale price and the carrying value. However, to the extent that the vendor retains the 'risk and reward' any profit on the sale should not be regarded as being realised, but it would be reasonable to recognise gradually the realisation of any profit over the shorter of the lease term and the useful life of the asset.

If the asset were not sold for its fair value it is likely that the consequence would be that the lease rental payments would be higher (if the asset were sold for more than its fair value) or lower than those which would be charged if the asset had been sold for its fair value. Hence it is reasonable to set the apparent profit or loss against the rental charges.

Operating leases

In the case of an operating lease the 'risks and rewards' are transferred along with the legal title to the asset. Hence any profit or loss on the sale of the asset should be recognised immediately as long as the asset was sold at its fair value.

If the asset is sold for an amount in excess of its fair value, the excess should be written back to the profit and loss account over the shorter of the remainder of the lease term or the period to the next rent review (if any).

Tax-free grants

SSAP 21 was amended in 1997 to cover tax-free grants that may be available to the lessor against the purchase price of assets acquired for leasing. These should be spread over the period of the lease and dealt with by treating the grant as non-taxable income (Para. 41)

Compliance with international standards

IAS 17 *Leases* (revised 1997), defines finance and operating leases in similar terms to SSAP 21 and requires the capitalisation of finance leases by lessees. However, there are differences. One example is that, whereas SSAP 21 makes reference to a figure of 90 per cent for the ratio of the present value of minimum lease payments to fair value in determining whether a finance lease exists, no such figure appears in IAS 17. The international accounting standard takes a more qualitative approach.

Both SSAP 21 and IAS 17 require that a lessor treats a finance lease as a debtor, rather than a fixed asset, in its balance sheet and takes credit for its finance income over the period of the lease. However whereas, as we have explained above, SSAP 21 requires a method based *on net cash investment* in the lease, IAS 17 requires the use of a method based upon the *net investment* in the lease. These different methods for spreading the finance income may give two very different answers.

The two standards also have somewhat different disclosure requirements.

Beyond SSAP 21

Accounting for Leases: A New Approach (1996)

A movement to treat all non-cancellable leases as finance leases has been under way for some time. The opening shot of the international campaign was the publication of a G4+1 Discussion Paper *Accounting for Leases: A New Approach* by the Financial Accounting Standards Board, in 1996. Although the author of the report is stated to be Warren McGregor, the paper is a report of a working party of the G4+1 group of standard setters, made up of representatives of the IASC and groups from five countries.[21] It confirms that leasing continues to be a major source of financing and suggests that it may become even more important in the future.

The authors of the paper, drawing largely on research carried out in Australia and the USA, conclude that there have been many examples of lease agreements for what are, in all material respects, finance leases that were drawn up in such a way to ensure that they qualified for treatment as operating leases and hence appear 'off the balance sheet'. The authors were sceptical of the ability of standard setters to produce criteria that would overcome this problem. They took a different approach and examined the issue from first principles, largely relying on the definitions of assets and liabilities contained in the IASC's Framework. These are very similar to the ASB definitions that we discussed at some length in Chapters 5 and 7:

> **An asset is a resource controlled by the enterprise as a result of past events and from which future economic benefits are expected to flow to the enterprise. (IASC Framework, Para. 49(a))**

> **A liability is a present obligation of the enterprise arising from past events, the settlement of which is expected to result in an outflow from the enterprise of resources embodying economic benefits. (IASC Framework, Para. 49(b))**

The report argues that, in respect of any non-cancellable lease, the lessee possesses both an asset and a liability and these should be reflected on its balance sheet. Hence, the report recommends that all non-cancellable leases should be capitalised. This recommendation is advanced on the grounds of both theory and pragmatism. This is normally a powerful combination but it appears to be working slowly in this particular case.

Leases: Implementation of a New Approach (1999)

While SSAP 21 remains in force, the battle continues. In 1999 the ASB published another discussion paper produced by the G4+1 group, *Leases: Implementation of a New Approach*. The 1999 report adopts the same position as its 1996 predecessor but advances the argument in a number of ways.

The cash flows on which the capitalisation is based

The 1999 paper addresses a range of practical issues concerned with the identification of the cash flows that should be capitalised to provide the measure of the initial asset and liability in

---

[21] The countries represented were Australia, Canada, New Zealand, the UK and the USA.

the books of the lessee, and covers such issues as possible variations in residual values, the question of contingent rentals and the treatment of long-term property leases.

One of the reasons why SSAP 21 is thought to be inadequate is the rich variety of types of leases that have been developed by the financial community. Many leases are far removed from the simple notion of a predetermined regular flow of resource from lessee to lessor over the life of the agreement. Much of the 1999 paper is concerned with examining the different types of leasing agreement that exist and discussing the basis on which they should be capitalised. We do not have the space to deal with the whole variety of leases discussed in the paper but it would be helpful to quote one as an example, both to provide a flavour of the document and to illustrate the thinking that underpins it.

The example we have selected is of a lease where the rent payable varies according to the revenue generated by the use of the asset. Specifically the example, example 4 in the paper,[22] is of an agreement where a lessee enters a three-year lease on a retail store. The annual rent comprises a minimum base rental of 10 000 plus $\frac{1}{2}$ per cent of the store's turnover during that year.

The question is whether the initial value of the lease should be based solely on the present value of the minimum payments, the three annual payments of 10 000, or whether account should be taken of the contingent rental based on turnover.

In this example, the authors came to the view that a fair value approach should be used and an estimate is made of what the rental payments would have been had there not been the turnover element. Suppose that this is 10 500 per annum, then the initial carrying value of the lease should be based on three payments of 10 500 and the differences between those amounts and the amounts actually paid should be credited or debited to the profit and loss account for the relevant year.

In general the approach taken in the paper is to capitalise on the basis of the minimum lease payments and to deal with variations on a year-by-year basis unless, as in the above example, the amount so derived would not provide a reasonable estimate of the fair value of the lease.

The discount rate to be used by the lessee

As we pointed out earlier, SSAP 21 requires the lessee to use the discount rate that it is implied in the leasing agreement and which is set by the lessor, which is not something that the lessee can always readily determine. The 1999 paper takes a much more sensible approach and argues that the discount rate to be applied by lessees should be an estimate of the lessee's incremental borrowing rate for a loan of a similar term and with the same security as is provided by the lease.[23] This proposal underscores the point that a lease is a form of finance and should be treated as far as possible in a comparable way to other sources of finance that the entity might employ.

The recognition of lease-related assets in the books of the lessor

The 1999 paper, unlike the 1996 version, deals with lessors as well as leases. The paper argues that, in the context of a lease agreement, a lessor possesses two distinct assets:

● the right to receive payments from the lessee; and
● the right to the return of the asset at the end of the agreement.

---

[22] *Leases: Implementation of a New Approach*, Para. 4.65.
[23] *Leases: Implementation of a New Approach*, p. 127.

The paper argues that these are distinct assets, one financial and one non-financial, and that they should be reported separately. The paper discusses a number of different ways by which the necessary measurements might be made.

The next step

The ASB asked for comments on the 1999 document with a deadline of 7 April 2000 and other members of the G4+1 group have acted in a similar way. One might by this time have expected some further progress, but it has not come speedily. The ASB position is that, due to the complexities involved and the time it will take to consider them, 'it is unlikely that a Financial Reporting Exposure Draft will be published in the near future'.[24] However, the ASB is presently taking the lead in an international project dealing with leases and IAS 17, *Leases*, is on the list of international standards due to be reviewed in 2003, so it now seems that the shelf-life of SSAP 21 is somewhat limited.

Summary

We have in this chapter concerned ourselves with the important topic of substance over form. We first examined the main provisions of FRS 5 and noted that it requires that an entity's financial statements should report on the substance of the transaction into which it has entered and that this essentially depends on whether the entity can recognise an asset or a liability.

We then examined a particularly important example of the concept, the accounting treatment of leases. The importance of the topic was such that the relevant accounting standard, SSAP 21, predated FRS 5 by some ten years. The need for haste in this area was because strict adherence to legal form meant that the balance sheets of many entities significantly understated assets and liabilities, the latter being more critical in entities in poor financial health. The resulting so-called 'off balance sheet financing' was a practice that had to be stopped.

We saw the way in which SSAP 21 sought to outlaw the practice by identifying a group of leases, finance leases, that had to be capitalised thus giving rise to both an asset and a liability in the books of the lessee. We also saw how SSAP 21 impacted on the financial statements of lessors.

We have discussed the criticisms that have been made of SSAP 21, in particular its view that certain types of leases, operating leases, should not be capitalised, and we have introduced two important discussion papers that appear to be taking us in a direction when all non-cancellable leases will be capitalised by the lessee. It now seems likely that the shelf-life of both SSAP 21 and the international standard IAS 17 will be rather short.

Recommended reading

The PricewaterhouseCoopers Leasing Team, *Leasing in the UK*, Tolley, Croydon, 2002.

B.A. Rutherford, *The Doctrine of Substance over Form*, Certified Accountants Publications Limited, London, 1988.

Excellent up-to-date and detailed reading on the subject matter of this chapter and on much of the contents of this book is provided by the most recent edition of:

---

[24] http://www.asb.org.uk/publications.

UK and International GAAP, A. Wilson, M. Davies, M. Curtis and G. Wilkinson-Riddle (eds), Ernst & Young, Butterworths Tolley, London. At the time of writing, the latest edition is the 7th, published 2001. See Chapters 18 and 19.

Questions

9.1 The objective of FRS 5 – *Reporting the substance of transactions*, is to ensure that a reporting entity's financial statements report the substance of the transactions into which it has entered.

You are the management accountant of BLFB plc. BLFB plc imports timber which it uses to manufacture and sell a large range of furniture products. BLFB plc makes up financial statements to 30 June each year.

On 1 June 1999, BLFB plc purchased for £40 million a large quantity of timber from an overseas supplier. The timber was intended to be used in the manufacture of a large quantity of high-quality furniture. Before manufacturing such furniture, it is necessary to keep the new timber in controlled conditions for at least five years from the date of purchase.

On 1 July 1999, BLFB plc sold the timber to Southland Bank plc for £45 million. The timber was physically retained by BLFB plc under the controlled conditions that were necessary to render the timber suitable for use. At the date of the sale on 1 July 1999, BLFB plc signed an agreement to re-purchase the timber from Southland Bank plc on 30 June 2004 for a price of £66.12 million. Responsibility for the security and condition of the timber remained with BLFB plc.

Your assistant, who is responsible for preparing the draft financial statements for the year ended 30 June 2000, has shown the transaction as a sale of £45 million and recorded a profit of £5 million.

Requirements

(a) **Write a memorandum to your assistant that:**
   (i) **describes what is meant by the 'substance' of a transaction and how to determine 'substance';** (5 marks)
   (ii) **explains why FRS 5 requires transactions to be accounted for according to their substance.** (5 marks)

(b) (i) **Prepare all the journal entries that should have been made in the financial statements of BLFB plc for the year ended 30 June 2000 in order to account correctly for the sale of timber to Southland Bank plc.** (4 marks)
   (ii) **Explain fully how the entries you have made comply with the relevant provisions of FRS 5. You should also explain why the treatment suggested by your assistant is incorrect.** (6 marks)

CIMA, Financial Reporting, November 2000 **(20 marks)**

9.2 You are the management accountant of Tree plc, a listed company that prepares consolidated financial statements. Your Managing Director, who is not an accountant, has recently attended a seminar at which key financial reporting issues were discussed. She remembers being told that:

● financial statements of an entity should reflect the substance of its transactions;

● the way to determine the substance of a transaction is to consider its effect on the assets and liabilities of the entity carrying out the transaction.

The year end of Tree plc is 31 August. In the year to 31 August 2001, the company entered into the following transactions:

Transaction 1

On 1 March 2001, Tree plc sold a property to a bank for £5 million. The market value of the property at the date of the sale was £10 million. Tree plc continues to occupy the property rentfree. Tree plc has the option to buy the property back from the bank at the end of every month from 31 March 2001 until 28 February 2006. Tree plc has not yet exercised this option. The repurchase price will be £5 million plus £50,000 for every complete month that has elapsed from the date of sale to the date of repurchase. The bank cannot require Tree plc to repurchase the property and the facility lapses after 28 February 2006. The directors of Tree plc expect property prices to rise at around 5% each year for the foreseeable future.

Transaction 2

On 1 September 2000, Tree plc sold one of its branches to Vehicle Ltd for £8 million. The net assets of the branch in the financial statements of Tree plc immediately before the sale were £7 million. Vehicle Ltd is a subsidiary of a bank and was specifically incorporated to carry out the purchase – it has no other business operations. Vehicle Ltd received the £8 million to finance this project from its parent in the form of a loan.

Tree plc continues to control the operations of the branch and receives an annual operating fee from Vehicle Ltd. The annual fee is the operating profit of the branch for the 12 months to the previous 31 August less the interest payable on the loan taken out by Vehicle Ltd for the 12 months to the previous 31 August. If this amount is negative, then Tree plc must pay the negative amount to Vehicle Ltd.

Any payments to or by Tree plc must be made by 30 September following the end of the relevant period. In the year to 31 August 2001, the branch made an operating profit of £2 000 000. Interest payable by Vehicle Ltd on the loan for this period was £800 000.

Required

(a) **Evaluate the extent to which the advice given to the Managing Director at the seminar is in accordance with generally accepted accounting principles.** (4 marks)

(b) **Explain how the transactions described above will be dealt with in the consolidated financial statements (balance sheet and profit and loss account) of Tree plc for the year ended 31 August 2001.**

(9 marks are allocated to transaction 1 and 7 marks to transaction 2)

(16 marks)

CIMA, Financial Reporting – UK Accounting Standards, November 2001 (**20 marks**)

9.3 Financial Reporting Standard 5 Reporting the Substance of Transactions requires an entity's financial statements to report the substance of transactions into which it has entered. The FRS sets out how to determine the substance of a transaction and whether any resulting assets and liabilities should be included in the balance sheet. The FRS came about partly as a result of concern over arrangements made by companies whereby assets and liabilities were omitted from the balance sheet.

Required

(a) **Explain the reasons why companies may wish to omit assets and liabilities from their balance sheets.** (5 marks)

(b) **Explain the reasons why the Accounting Standards Board felt it necessary to introduce FRS 5 Reporting the Substance of Transactions.** (5 marks)

(c) **Discuss the proposed treatment of the following items in the financial statements:**

   (i) **Beak plc sells land to a property investment company, Wings plc. The sale price is £20 million and the current market value is £30 million. Beak plc can buy the land back at any time in the next five years for the original selling price plus an annual commission of 1% above the current bank base rate. Wings plc cannot require Beak plc to buy the land back at any time.**

The accountant of Beak plc proposes to treat this transaction as a sale in the financial statements.   (7 marks)

(ii) A car manufacturer, Gocar plc, supplies cars to a car dealer, Sparks Ltd, on the following terms. Sparks Ltd has to pay a monthly fee of £100 per car for the privilege of displaying it in its showroom and also is responsible for insuring the cars. When a car is sold to a customer, Sparks Ltd has to pay Gocar plc the factory price of the car when it was first supplied. Sparks Ltd can only return the cars to Gocar plc on the payment of a fixed penalty charge of 10% of the cost of the car. Sparks Ltd has to pay the factory price for the cars if they remain unsold within a four month period. Gocar plc cannot demand the return of the cars from Sparks Ltd.

The accountant of Sparks Ltd proposes to treat the cars unsold for less than four months as the property of Gocar plc and not show them as stock in the financial statements.   (8 marks)

ACCA, Accounting and Audit Practice, December 1994   **(25 marks)**

9.4 FRS 5 – Reporting the Substance of Transactions – requires that a reporting entity's financial statements should report the substance of the transactions into which it has entered. FRS 5 states that in order to determine the substance of a transaction it is necessary to identify whether the transaction has given rise to new assets or liabilities for the reporting entity and whether it has changed the entity's existing assets or liabilities.

You are the management accountant of D Ltd which has three principal activities. These are the sale of motor vehicles (both new and second-hand), the provision of spare parts for motor vehicles and the servicing of motor vehicles.

During the financial year ended 31 August 1996, the company has entered into a type of business transaction not previously undertaken. With effect from 1 January 1996, D Ltd entered into an agreement whereby it received motor vehicles on a consignment basis from E plc, a large manufacturer. The terms of the arrangement were as follows:

(i) On delivery, the stock of vehicles remains the legal property of E plc.

(ii) Legal title to a vehicle passes to D Ltd either when D Ltd enters into a binding arrangement to sell the vehicle to a third party or six months after the date of delivery by E plc to D Ltd.

(iii) At the date legal title passes, E plc invoices D Ltd for the sale of the vehicles. The price payable by D Ltd is the normal selling price of E plc *at the date of delivery*, increased by 1% for every complete month the vehicles are held on consignment by D Ltd. Any change in E plc's normal selling price between the date of delivery and the date legal title to the goods passes to D Ltd does not change the amount payable by D Ltd to E plc.

(iv) At any time between the date of delivery and the date legal title passes to D Ltd, the company (D Ltd) has the right to return the vehicles to E plc *provided they are not damaged or obsolete*. D Ltd does not have the right to return damaged or obsolete vehicles. If D Ltd exercises this right of return then a return penalty is payable by D Ltd as follows:

Time since date of delivery	*Penalty as a percentage of invoiced price**
Three months or less	50%
Three to four months	75%
More than four months	100%

* i.e. the price that would otherwise be payable by D Ltd if legal title to the vehicles had passed at the date of return.

(v) E plc has *no right to demand* return of vehicles on consignment to D Ltd unless D Ltd becomes insolvent.

The managing director suggests that the vehicles should be shown as an asset of D Ltd only when title passes, and the purchase price becomes legally payable.

Requirement
Write a report to the managing director which:
(a) explains how (under the principles established in FRS 5) an asset or liability is identified, and when an asset or liability should be recognised and should cease to be recognised, in the financial statements of a business;   (12 marks)
(b) evaluates, in the light of the principles you have explained in (a), the correctness, or otherwise, of the managing director's suggested accounting treatment for the new transaction.   (8 marks)

CIMA, Financial Reporting, November 1996   **(20 marks)**

9.5 FRS 5 – *Reporting the Substance of Transactions* – requires that a reporting entity's financial statements should report the substance of the transactions into which it has entered.

You are the management accountant of S Ltd. During the most recent financial year (ended 31 August 1998), the company has entered into a debt factoring arrangement with F plc. The main terms of the agreement are as follows:

1   On the first day of every month S Ltd transfers (by assignment) all its trade debts to F plc, subject to credit approval by F plc for each debt transferred by S Ltd.
2   At the time of transfer of the debtors to F plc, S Ltd receives a payment from F plc of 70% of the gross amount of the transferred debts. The payment is debited by F plc to a factoring account which is maintained in the books of F plc.
3   Following transfer of the debts, F plc collects payments from debtors and performs any necessary follow-up work.
4   After collection by F plc, the cash received from the debtor is credited to the factoring account in the books of F plc.
5   F plc handles all aspects of the collection of the debts of S Ltd in return for a monthly charge of 1% of the total value of the debts transferred at the beginning of that month. The amount is debited to the factoring account in the books of F plc.
6   Any debts not collected by F plc within 90 days of transfer are regarded as bad debts by F plc and re-assigned to S Ltd. The cash previously advanced by F plc in respect of bad debts is recovered from S Ltd. The recovery is only possible out of the proceeds of other debtors which have been assigned to S Ltd. For example, if, in a particular month, S Ltd assigned trade debts having a value of £10 000 and a debt of £500 was identified as bad, then the amounts advanced by F plc to S Ltd would be £6650 [70% × £10 000 – 70% × £500].
7   On a monthly basis, F plc debits the factoring account with an interest charge which is calculated on a daily basis on the balance on the factoring account.
8   At the end of every quarter, F plc pays over to S Ltd a sum representing any credit balance on its factoring account with S Ltd at that time.

Requirement
Write a memorandum to the Board of Directors of S Ltd which outlines:
(a) how, under the principles set out in FRS 5, the substance of a transaction should be determined;   (10 marks)
(b) how the debt factoring arrangement will be reported in the financial statements of S Ltd.   (10 marks)

CIMA, Financial Reporting, November 1998   **(20 marks)**

9.6 You are the management accountant of Prompt plc, a UK company which prepares financial statements to 31 March each year. The financial statements for the year ended 31 March 1998 are due to be formally approved by the board of directors on 15 June 1998.

Your assistant has prepared a first draft of the financial statements. These show a turnover of £200 million and a profit before taxation of £18 million. Your assistant has identified a number of transactions [(a), (b) and (c) in Requirement, below] for which he is unsure of the correct accounting treatment. For each transaction, he has indicated the treatment followed in the draft financial statements. You have reviewed the transactions highlighted by your assistant.

Requirement
Draft a memorandum to your assistant which explains the correct accounting treatment for each transaction. Where the treatment adopted by your assistant in the draft financial statements is incorrect, your memorandum should indicate the reasons for this. For each transaction, your memorandum should refer to relevant provisions of company law and Accounting Standards.

Transaction (a)
During the year ended 31 March 1998, Prompt plc entered into an arrangement with a finance company to factor its debts. Each month 90% of the value of the debts arising from credit sales that month was sold to the factor, who assumed legal title and responsibility for collection of all debts. Upon receipt of the cash by the factor, the remaining 10% was paid to Prompt plc less a deduction for administration and finance costs. Any debtor who did not pay the factor within three months of the debt being factored was transferred back to Prompt plc and the amounts advanced by the factor recovered from Prompt plc. In preparing the draft financial statements, your assistant has removed the whole of the factored debts from trade debtors at the date the debts are factored. The net amount receivable from the factor has been shown as a sundry debtor.   (5 marks)

Transaction (b)
On 15 March 1998, Prompt plc decided to close one of its three factories. This decision was taken because the product (called product X) which was manufactured at the factory was considered obsolete. A gradual run down of the operation commenced on 15 April 1998 and was expected to be complete by 15 June 1998. The factory produced monthly operating statements detailing turnover, profits and assets, and the turnover for the year ended 31 March 1998 was £35 million. Closure costs (including redundancy) were estimated to be £2.5 million. Your assistant has made no entries in the draft financial statements in respect of the closure since it took place in the year ending 31 March 1999.   (12 marks)

Transaction (c)
On 30 June 1997, Prompt plc issued 100 million £1 debentures. The issue costs were £100 000. The debentures carry no interest entitlement but are redeemable on 30 June 2007 at a price of £259 million. Your assistant has included the nominal value of the debentures (£100 million) as part of shareholders' funds since they represent long-term finance for the company. The issue costs of £100 000 have been charged to the profit and loss account for the year, and your assistant suggests that the difference between the issue price and the redemption price should be dealt with in 2007 when the debentures are redeemed.   (8 marks)

CIMA, Financial Reporting, May 1998   (**25 marks**)

9.7 S plc is a large manufacturing company. The company needs to purchase a major piece of equipment which is vital to the production process. S plc does not have sufficient cash available to buy this equipment. It cannot raise the necessary finance by issuing shares because it would not be cost-effective to have a share issue for the amount involved. The directors are also unwilling to borrow because the company already has a very high level of debt in its balance sheet.

C Bank has offered to lease the equipment to S plc. The bank has proposed a finance package in which S plc would take the equipment on a two-year lease. The intention is that S plc will take out a second two-year lease at the conclusion of the initial period and a third at the conclusion of that one. By that time the equipment will have reached the end of its useful life.

C Bank will not require S plc to commit itself in writing to the two secondary lease periods. Instead, S plc will agree in writing to refurbish the equipment to a brand new condition before returning it to C Bank. This condition will, however, be waived if the lease is subsequently extended to a total of six years or more. Once the equipment is used, it would be prohibitively expensive to refurbish it.

S plc's directors are very interested in the arrangement proposed by C Bank. They believe that each of the two-year contracts could be accounted for as an operating lease because each covers only a fraction of the equipment's expected useful life.

Required

(a) Explain how the decision to treat the lease as an operating lease rather than a finance lease would affect S plc's profit and loss account, balance sheet and any accounting ratios based on these.   (6 marks)

(b) Explain whether S plc should account for the proposed lease as an operating lease or as a finance lease.   (4 marks)

(C) The relationship between debt and equity in a company's balance sheet is often referred to as the gearing ratio. Explain why companies are often keen to minimise the gearing ratio.   (5 marks)

(d) It has been suggested that the rules governing the preparation of financial statements leave some scope for the preparers of financial statements to influence the profit figure or balance sheet position. Explain whether you agree with this suggestion.   (5 marks)

CIMA, Financial Accounting – UK Accounting Standards, May 2001   (**20 marks**)

9.8 You are the financial director of Pilgrim plc, a listed company. Your new group managing director, appointed from one of Pilgrim plc's overseas subsidiaries, is reviewing the principal accounting policies and is having difficulty understanding the accounting treatment and disclosure of assets leased by Pilgrim plc as lessee, of which there are a substantial number (both finance and operating leases).

Requirement

Prepare a memorandum for your managing director explaining, in simple terms, the basics of accounting for leased assets in the accounts of listed companies (in full compliance with the relevant accounting standards and the Companies Acts). Your memorandum should be set out in sections as follows:

(a) Outline the factors which can influence the decision as to whether a particular lease is a finance lease or an operating lease.   (4 marks)

(b) As an example, taking the following non-cancellable lease details:
   – fair value (as defined in SSAP 21): £100 000
   – lease payments: five annual payments in advance of £20 000 each
   – estimated residual value at the end of the lease: £26 750 of which £15 000 is guaranteed by Pilgrim plc as lessee
   – interest rate implicit in the lease: 10%

   demonstrate whether the lease falls to be considered as a finance lease or an operating lease under the provisions of SSAP 21, explaining the steps in reaching a conclusion.

(4 marks)

(c) Explain briefly any circumstances in which a lessor and a lessee might classify a particular lease differently, i.e. the lessee might classify a lease as an operating lease whilst the lessor classifies the same lease as a finance lease or vice versa. (3 marks)

(d) Explain briefly any circumstances in which the requirements of SSAP 21 with regard to accounting for operating leases by lessees might result in charges to the profit and loss account different from the amounts payable for the period under the terms of a lease.

(3 marks)

(e) Draft a concise accounting policy in respect of 'Leasing' (as a lessee only) suitable for inclusion in the published accounts of Pilgrim plc and comment on the key aspects of your policy to aid your managing director's understanding. (4 marks)

(f) List the other disclosures Pilgrim plc is required to give in its published accounts in respect of its financial transactions as a lessee. (3 marks)

Note: Ignore taxation.

ICAEW, Financial Accounting 2, December 1992 (21 marks)

9.9 Flow Ltd prepares financial statements to 31 March each year. On 1 April 1998, Flow Ltd sold a freehold property to another company, River plc. Flow Ltd had purchased the property for £500 000 on 1 April 1988 and had charged total depreciation of £60 000 on the property for the period 1 April 1988 to 31 March 1998.

River plc paid £850 000 for the property on 1 April 1998, at which date its true market value was £550 000.

From 1 April 1998 the property was leased back by Flow Ltd on a ten-year operating lease for annual rentals (payable in arrears) of £100 000. A normal annual rental for such a property would have been £50 000.

River plc is a financial institution which, on 1 April 1998, charged interest of 10.56% per annum on ten-year fixed rate loans.

Requirements

(a) Explain what is meant by the terms 'finance lease' and 'operating lease' and how operating leases should be accounted for in the financial statements of lessee companies.

(7 marks)

(b) Show the journal entries which Flow Ltd will make to record:

● its sale of the property to River plc on 1 April 1998,

● the payment of the first rental to River plc on 31 March 1999.

Justify your answer with reference to appropriate Accounting Standards. (13 marks)

CIMA, Financial Reporting, May 1999 (20 marks)

9.10 Leese, a public limited company and a subsidiary of an American holding company operates its business in the services sector. It currently uses operating leases to partly finance its usage of land and buildings and motor vehicles. The following abbreviated financial information was produced as at 30 November 2000:

Profit and Loss Account for the year ending 30 November 2000

	£m
Turnover	580
Profit on ordinary activities before taxation	88
Taxation on profit on ordinary activities	(30)
Profit on ordinary activities after taxation	58

Balance Sheet as at 30 November 2000

Fixed assets	200
Net current assets	170
Creditors: amounts falling due after more than one year	
(interest free loan from holding company)	(50)
	320
Share Capital	200
Profit and Loss Account	120
	320

Notes

Operating lease rentals for the year – paid 30 November 2000:

	£m
Land and buildings	30
Motor vehicles	10

Future minimum operating lease payments for leases payable on 30 November each year were as follows:

Year	Land and Buildings	Motor Vehicles
	£m	£m
30 November 2001	28	9
30 November 2002	25	8
30 November 2003	20	7
Thereafter	500	–
Total future minimum operating lease payments (non-cancellable)	573	24

The company is concerned about the potential impact of bringing operating leases onto the balance sheet on its profitability and its key financial ratios. The directors have heard that the Accounting Standards Board (ASB) is moving towards this stance and wishes to seek advice on the implications for the company.

For the purpose of determining the impact of the ASB's proposal, the directors have decided to value current year and future operating lease rentals at their present value.

The appropriate interest rate for discounting cash flows to present value is 5% and the current average remaining lease life for operating lease rentals after 30 November 2003 is deemed to be 10 years.

Depreciation on land and buildings is 5% per annum and on motor vehicles is 25% per annum with a full year's charge in the year of acquisition. The rate of corporation tax is 30% and depreciation rates equate to those of capital allowances. Assume that the operating lease agreements commenced on 30 November 2000.

Required

(a) Discuss the reasons why accounting standard setters are proposing to bring operating leases onto the balance sheets of companies.   (7 marks)

(b) (i) Show the effect on the Profit and Loss Account for the year ending 30 November 2000 and the Balance Sheet as at 30 November 2000 of Leese capitalising its operating leases;   (10 marks)

   (ii) Discuss the specific impact on key performance ratios as well as the general business impact of Leese capitalising its operating leases.   (8 marks)

ACCA, Financial Reporting Environment (UK Stream), December 2000   **(25 marks)**

9.11 Accounting for leases has been a problematical issue for some years. In 1984, SSAP 21, – *Leases and hire purchase contracts* was issued. This Accounting Standard requires that lessee companies capitalise leased assets in certain circumstances. The Standard classifies leases as either finance leases or operating leases, depending on the terms of the lease. In December 1999, the Accounting Standards Board (ASB) published a Discussion Paper – *Leases: Implementation of a New Approach.*

Under the recommended approach, at the beginning of a lease the lessee would recognise an asset and a liability equivalent to the fair value of the rights and obligations that are conveyed by the lease (usually the present value of the minimum payments required by the lease); thereafter, the accounting for the leased asset and liability would follow the normal requirements for accounting for fixed assets and debt.

Expo plc prepares financial statements to 30 September each year. On 1 October 2001, Expo plc leased a fleet of cars for its sales force. There were 50 identical cars in the fleet. Relevant details for each car are as follows:

- Fair value on 1 October 2001 was £10 000.
- Lease term is 2 years.
- Estimated residual value of car on 30 September 2003 is £3000.
- Lease rentals are £9000 in total – a payment of £4000 on 1 October 2001 plus two payments of £2500 on 30 September 2002 and 30 September 2003.
- The payments of £2500 increase by £1 for every mile travelled in excess of an agreed annual maximum of 50 000 miles per car.
- The lessor is responsible for repair and maintenance of the fleet.

Required

(a) Explain the factors that led to the issue of the Discussion Paper in 1999.   (6 marks)

(b) Demonstrate the effect of the leasing arrangement on the profit and loss account of Expo plc for the year ended 30 September 2002 and its balance sheet at 30 September 2002,

- assuming Expo plc follows SSAP 21;   (7 marks)
- assuming Expo plc follows the proposals outlined in the Discussion Paper.

(7 marks)

Note: The discount rate to be used where relevant is 10%. In requirement (b), you should explain exactly where in the profit and loss account and balance sheet the relevant amounts will be reported.

CIMA, Financial Reporting – UK Accounting Standards, November 2002   (**20 marks**)

Pension costs

The provision of occupational pension schemes for employees is now common practice in the UK and in many other countries. Expenditure on pensions can be extremely significant, adding 20 per cent, or even more, to the costs of employees' remuneration.

Prior to the issue of SSAP 24 *Accounting for Pension Costs*, in 1988, the treatment of pension costs in financial statements was subject to very little regulation through either statute law or professional guidance. The result was that, in general, the financial statements failed to disclose a realistic figure for the costs of employing staff in that they did not indicate the actual costs of the pension and, accordingly, balance sheets often failed to disclose the liability that the company faced in discharging its obligations. SSAP 24 was a major step forward in bringing some degree of order to what had been a very disorganised field of accounting activity.

Despite, or possibly in part because of, the pioneering nature of SSAP 24, many commentators believed that it suffered from a number of conceptual weaknesses and allowed reporting entities too much scope. However it took a long time to bring forward an improved standard. It was only after many years' deliberation that the ASB published FRED 20 *Retirement Benefits*, in 1999, and it was not until November 2000 that the resulting standard, FRS 17 was published. That is not the end of the story because, for reasons we will explore in this chapter, FRS 17 has proved to be extremely controversial and the ASB has now decided that it will not be implemented in full until 2005. We will therefore need to deal in some detail with both standards in this chapter.

Thus in this chapter we will cover:

- SSAP 24 *Accounting for Pension Costs* (1988)
- FRS 17 *Retirement Benefits* (2000)
- IAS 19 (revised) *Employee Benefits* (revised 2000)
- FRED (unnumbered) *Amendment to FRS 17* (2002)

Introduction

We think it would be helpful if we started by describing the main types of pension schemes that are to be found and, at the same time, explaining some of the terms which have to be understood if the reader is to make sense of the rest of the chapter.

1 *Funded or unfunded*: In the case of the funded scheme, contributions are paid into a separate fund that is usually administered by trustees who invest the contributions and meet the pension commitments. The contributions are invested in a portfolio of property and/or securities either directly or indirectly by the purchase of insurance policies. In unfunded schemes, contributions are not placed in a separate fund but are reinvested in

the employer's business and pensions are subsequently paid on a 'pay-as-you-go' basis. An unfunded pension scheme is obviously the more risky from the point of view of the employees and the vast majority of pension schemes in the UK are funded.

2 *Defined benefits and defined contribution scheme*: In defined contribution schemes, the contributions are determined and the employees receive pensions on the basis of whatever amounts are available from those contributions and the returns earned from their investment. The risks in such a scheme fall entirely upon the shoulders of the employees. Such a scheme poses few problems for the accountant. The amount to be charged as the cost of providing pensions is clearly determinable as the amount payable to the scheme by the employer in respect of a particular year.

Under a defined benefit scheme the retirement benefits are determined, sometimes on the basis of average salary over the employee's period of service, but more often on the basis of salary in the final year or years before retirement. For such a scheme the cost of pensions in a particular year is, as we shall see, much more difficult to determine. It depends not only upon the contribution payable in respect of a year but also upon the pensions that will be paid in the future. The pensions payable depend on such factors as the future rate of increase in wages and salaries, the number of staff leaving the scheme before retirement and the life expectancy of pensioners and, where relevant, their dependants. In addition, the cost in the year of providing future pensions depends upon the rate of return to be earned on contributions and reinvested receipts. It is the need to take a very long-term view in the face of great uncertainties that makes accounting for defined benefit schemes such an interesting and difficult problem for the accountant.

Fortunately for many employees, but perhaps unfortunately for accountants, most UK pension schemes, certainly those of major employers, have been of the defined benefit variety. However, in recent years, a large number of major employers have closed down their defined benefits schemes to new employees and replaced them with defined contribution schemes.

3 *Contributory or non-contributory*: Some schemes are contributory, where the employees and the employer share the cost, while others are non-contributory, where the whole cost falls on the employer.

The issues

We will in this chapter concentrate on funded schemes where the assets are held by the trustees of the pension fund on whom falls the liability of paying the actual pension. Pension schemes are not normally subsidiaries, or quasi-subsidiaries, and it is not, therefore, appropriate to consolidate the scheme into the employer's financial statements. However, a pension scheme can give rise to assets and liabilities of the employer but only to the extent to which the employer is entitled to benefit from any surplus or has a legal or constructive obligation to make good any deficit.

The tasks that have to be performed are:

● determine the amount that must be paid into the pension fund each year in order to allow it to pay the promised pensions, this is sometimes called the regular contribution;
● measure the assets and liabilities of the fund;
● decide how any difference between the assets and liabilities should be reflected in the financial statements.

Pensions involve, by their nature, long-term issues including such things as life expectancy. Thus actuaries play a key part in assessing the regular contribution and in valuing the liabilities, although their role in valuing assets will be of less significance when the provisions of FRS 17 are applied in full.

We will illustrate the issues involved and the approach that might be taken by the actuary by describing a very simple scheme involving only one employee.

Let us suppose that at the inception of the scheme the sole employee, Mac, is aged 41 and is due to retire in 24 years' time at 65. It is currently estimated that his life expectancy on his date of retirement will be 15 years.

The actuarial calculations might proceed as follows:

> Present salary   £20 000
> Assume that Mac's salary will increase by 6% per year
> Hence, salary on retirement = £20 000 $(1.06)^{24} \approx$ £81 000.

If, on retirement, a pension of half final salary is payable, the fund will need to be sufficient to pay £40 500 per annum for 15 years. Assuming, for simplicity, that the retirement pension will be paid at the end of each year and that it is expected that the assets in the fund will earn 8 per cent per annum for the period following retirement, the capital value of the fund at retirement age will need to be £346 660.[1]

If we assume that, in the period until retirement, the annual return on investments is only 7 per cent, then 13 per cent of the staff member's salary will need to be paid into the fund.[2]

Actuarial gains and losses

Now let us see how things can go wrong, or to be more precise, how things might change. Few, if any, pension funds put all their investments in fixed-interest securities and so the return earned will probably not be 7 per cent. If the assets in, say, five years are worth more than the actuary had expected, how should that gain be treated? Should the surplus be credited to the profit and loss account immediately or over some future period? A different question is whether the difference between the expected and actual value of the assets should be returned to the employer immediately or used to reduce the future regular payments.

There may also be changes in the actuarial assumptions. Actuarial science is based on averages and people are, on average, living longer. Thus, suppose that five years into the scheme, the actuary revises his estimate of Mac's life expectancy and now expects that he will live for 18 years after retirement rather than 15. The fund will not be sufficient to pay the expected required pension, so what should be done? Should the extra cost be charged to the current profit and loss account immediately or spread over some future period? A different

---

[1] On the date of retirement the required balance on the fund x is given by:

$$x = £40\,500 \sum_{i=1}^{15} (1.08)^{-i} = £346\,660$$

or $x = £40\,500\ a_{\overline{15}|}$ at I = 0.08

[2] Let y be the required fraction of the annual salary which needs to be paid into the fund, then

$$£346\,660 = y\ £20\,000 \sum_{i=1}^{24} (1.06)^i\ (1.07)^{24-i}$$

from which $y = 0.13$.

question concerns whether the employer should immediately pay the extra required or simply increase the regular payments to reflect the new assumption.

The above are simple examples of what are termed actuarial gains and losses and as we shall see SSAP 24 and FRS 17 take very different lines as to how they should be treated.

Valuation of pension fund assets and liabilities

There are basically two ways of measuring pension fund assets: the *actuarial approach* (the basis underlying SSAP 24) and the *market approach* which is the one most commonly used in countries other than the United Kingdom and is the method specified in both FRS 17 and IAS 19 *Employee Benefits* (revised 1998).

The actuarial approach measures both the obligations of the fund and the assets of the fund by reference to the present values of the expected cash flows. In contrast, the market approach, as the name implies, values the assets by reference to their current market values while, in theory at least, the liabilities would be measured by the price that would have to be paid to purchase appropriate deferred annuities. These two methods are obviously not unconnected; for example, a change in the market's view as to long-term interest rates will affect the actuary's calculations of present values, the current value of investments and, in particular, the market value of deferred annuities. But in the short term, there may be considerable variations due to the short-term market fluctuations.

As we shall see, those who would advocate a market approach recognise that it is rarely possible to identify market values against which the obligations of the pension fund can be measured. Thus it is accepted that the fund's liability will have to be based on the present value of the expected pension payments but that still leaves open the choice of interest rate. Traditionally, the actuarial approach discounted the future pension payments at the same rate as that used to estimate the return on assets. An alternative approach, which is more in tune with the market approach, is to use a rate of interest that reflects the time value of money plus a risk premium relating not to the risks associated with the returns on the assets but to the risk that the employer will not be able to meet its obligations, see p. 262.

SSAP 24 and FRS 17– the differences in outline

We will look at the differences between SSAP 24 and FRS 17 in more depth after we have properly introduced the two standards but readers will find it helpful, before examining SSAP 24, to be aware of the major differences between the two approaches.

SSAP 24 focuses on the profit and loss account and is primarily concerned with matching revenue and expenses even if this results in some rather unsatisfactory estimates of assets and liabilities. Its stated objective is to require 'the employer to recognise the cost of providing pensions on a systematic and rational basis over the period during which he benefits from the employees' services'.[3] No mention here of the reporting of assets and liabilities.

In contrast, FRS 17 takes a much more 'balance sheet approach' and seeks to ensure that the fair values of the pension fund's assets and liabilities are the bases for determining whether the employer has an obligation to the fund or the fund has an obligation to the employer. Specifically the objectives of FRS 17 are to ensure that:

---

[3] SSAP 24, Para. 16.

a. financial statements reflect at fair value the assets and liabilities arising from an employer's retirement benefit obligations and any related funding;

b. the operating costs of providing retirement benefits to employees are recognised in the accounting period(s) in which the benefits are earned by the employees, and the related finance costs and any other changes in value of the assets and liabilities are recognised in the accounting periods in which they arise; and

c. the financial statements contain adequate disclosure of the cost of providing retirement benefits and the related gains, losses, assets and liabilities.[4]

The main consequences of the very different approaches taken by FRS 17 and SSAP 24 are:

- SSAP 24 allows certain types of differences, called experience differences, to be written off over the remaining service life of the current employees while FRS 17 calls for immediate recognition in the financial statements.
- SSAP 24 is based on the actuarial method of valuation, for both pension fund assets and liabilities, while FRS 17 is firmly rooted in the market approach.
- FRS 17 is much more prescriptive about the methods that should be used.

In addition, in line with the principle that users should be provided with more 'narrative' information that would enable them more easily to appreciate the information provided in the financial statements, the disclosure requirements of FRS 17 are more extensive than the not inconsiderable requirements of SSAP 24.

SSAP 24 *Accounting for Pension Costs*

The accounting principles underlying SSAP 24

Prior to the adoption of SSAP 24 many companies simply showed their contribution to the pension scheme as the pension cost for the period. The contribution may have been affected by factors other than those relating solely to the needs of the fund. Employers might, for example, increase the contribution for a year or for a limited period, with a view to reducing contributions in the future. Conversely, employers have in periods of financial stringency reduced their contributions. Such actions may have been effective in achieving the desired ability to manipulate the levels of reported profit, but they did little to help users of financial statements assess the total costs of employment for the period.

The accounting objective set by SSAP 24 was to require employing companies to recognise the cost of providing pensions on a systematic and rational basis over the period in which they benefit from the services of their employees and to recognise that, in many cases, this cost may well not be equal to the contribution made to the pension scheme in any period.[5]

Thus, in a very simple world, the actuary's task is to estimate what proportion of pensionable pay would have to be paid into the scheme each year to pay for the pensions, and the whole of this (in the case of a non-contributory scheme) or a part of this (in a contributory scheme) would represent the cost to the employer. This cost can be regarded as the regular pension cost.

---

[4] FRS 17, Para. 1.

[5] Since tax relief is based on the contributions paid to the scheme the difference has deferred tax implications. See Chapter 12.

But we do not live in such a state of simplicity and both the world and employers change their minds. The world changes its mind through altered interest rates, changes in the level of earnings and by allowing people to die other than when predicted by the actuary. Employers can also change their minds (or have their minds changed for them) and vary the conditions under which pensions are paid.

Thus, there will be variations to the regular cost and a large part of SSAP 24 is devoted to discussing how to account for these variations. Variations from the regular cost may be due to the following:

(a) the results of the world not being as the actuary expected it to be when he or she last worked out the regular cost – experience surpluses or deficiencies;
(b) changes in actuarial assumptions and methods and retroactive changes in benefits or conditions of membership;
(c) discretionary pensions increases.

Bases of the actuarial methods

In general SSAP 24 does not specify how the actuary should determine the actuarial value of pension fund assets and liabilities. Much is left for the actuary to decide:

> The selection of the actuarial method and assumptions to be used in assessing the pension cost of a defined benefit scheme is a matter of judgement for the actuary in consultation with his client, taking account of the circumstances of the specific company and its work force. (Para.18)

It would perhaps not be too great an exaggeration to say that, as far as SSAP 24 is concerned, it is a matter of 'anything actuarial goes'. FRS 17 is far more prescriptive and it will be convenient to defer our discussion of some of the main actuarial methods used to that section of the chapter in which we discuss FRS 17 in more detail.

Experience surpluses or deficiencies

In deciding whether the fund is in balance, that is whether it has sufficient assets to pay the required pensions given all the necessary assumptions about salary increases, rates of return and the like, the pension fund's assets are compared with its liabilities. Part of any difference may be due to changes in policy and assumptions about the future; these will be dealt with in the reassessment of the regular costs but, as noted above, part of the difference will, in all likelihood, be because some of the assumptions made at the last review proved to be incorrect, for example the rate of wage and salary increases might have been under- or overestimated. This part of the difference is known as experience surpluses or deficiencies, which are defined in SSAP 24 as follows:

> An experience surplus or deficiency is that part of the excess or deficiency of the actuarial value of the assets over the actuarial value of the liabilities, on the basis of the valuation method used, which arises because events have not coincided with the actuarial assumptions made for the last valuation. (Para. 63)

The definition refers, not to the market value of the assets, but to their 'actuarial value', which is a value based on assumptions about future cash flows and interest rates and which may well, from time to time, differ significantly from the current market value. As we explained earlier the use of actuarial rather than market values was a controversial issue and FRS 17 takes a very different approach.

But at this stage we will concentrate on the treatment of experience surpluses and deficiencies. Should they be credited (or charged) to the past, the current year or the future?

SSAP 24 specifies that, with certain exceptions to which we will refer later, material experience deficiencies, and surpluses, should be dealt with by adjusting current and future costs and not by immediately expensing (or crediting) the amount. In accordance with the main accounting objective of SSAP 24, the normal period over which the effect of the deficiency or surplus should be spread is the expected remaining service life of the current employees in the scheme after making suitable allowances for future withdrawals, or the average remaining service lives of the current membership.

There are three exceptions to the general rule:

(a) Where there is a significant reduction in the number of employees covered by the scheme (see below).

(b) Where prudence requires a material deficiency to be made up over a shorter period. This exception is strictly limited to cases where a significant additional payment has to be paid into the scheme arising from a major transaction or event outside the actuarial assumptions and normal running of the scheme; a possible example is the consequence of a major mismanagement of the assets of the pension scheme. The standard does not specify the period over which the additional charge should be spread; it merely allows a shorter period than would otherwise be required.

(c) Where a refund is made to employers subject to deduction of tax within the provisions of the Finance Act 1986, or similar legislation. In such cases the employer may (not must) depart from the normal spreading rule and recognise the refund in the period in which it occurs.

The exception arising from a significant reduction of employees merits further comment. There have been many instances in recent years where reorganisation schemes have resulted in significant redundancies. These have often led to large surpluses in the pension funds, with the result that future contributions are reduced or eliminated for a period (a 'contribution holiday'), or contributions are refunded.

In such instances, the benefit should not be spread over the lives of the remaining work force but instead recognised in the periods in which the benefits are received. They should, in general, not be anticipated in the sense of taking credit immediately the facts are known, but should be recognised on a year-by-year basis. But to this rule there is an exception, where the redundancies are related to a sale or termination of an operation, for in such a case FRS 3 *Reporting Financial Performance* must be followed. (SSAP 24, which of course predates FRS 3, refers to SSAP 6 in this context.) It may not be appropriate to defer recognition of a pension cost or credit, because FRS 3 requires that provisions relating to the sale or termination of an operation be made after taking into account future profits of the operation or on the disposal of the assets.

Changes in actuarial assumptions and methods and retroactive changes to the scheme

The effect of changes in the assumptions and methods used by the actuary should be treated in the same way as experience deficits and surpluses – they should be spread over the period of the expected remaining service lives of the current employees.

The same rule should be applied if there are retroactive changes in benefits and membership. Such changes, often called past service costs, may give improved benefits, e.g. increasing the proportion of final salary which will be paid as pension, or give employees credit for periods of service before they joined the scheme.

In some cases a surplus on a pension fund may be used to improve benefits and if, as a result, a provision that the company had made in its own accounts is no longer necessary, that provision should be released over the estimated remaining service life of the current employees.

Discretionary pension increases

A pension scheme might allow for pension increases within its rules, in which case they will be taken into account in the actuarial calculations, as should any increases required by legislation.

Other increases are discretionary on the part of the employer, whether paid direct or through the pension scheme. If such increases are granted on a regular basis, SSAP 24 states that the preferred treatment is to allow for them in the actuarial calculations. If this is not done, the full capital value of the increase should be provided in the year in which it is granted, not in the years in which it is paid, to the extent to which the increase is not covered by the surplus on the fund.

The same procedure should be followed in the case of an ex gratia pension granted to an employee on retirement, such as a long-serving member of staff who for some reason has not been a member of the scheme. Thus, for example, if it is estimated that the amount which would need to be invested to produce the desired pension at the estimated rates of interest is £400 000 then that amount should be charged to the profit and loss account in the year of retirement.

A non-recurring increase, which is granted for one period only with no expectation of repetition, should be charged to the period in which it is paid to the extent that it is not covered by a surplus.

The following example serves as a summary of the above and illustrates the variations between the contributions made to the scheme and the costs of pensions charged to the profit and loss account.

Example 10.1

Slick Limited is a small company that established a non-contributory defined benefit funded scheme in 20X1. Its year end is 31 December.

For arithmetical simplicity we will assume that the annual pensionable salary bill was £1 000 000 before the reorganisation referred to in paragraph C below and £600 000 thereafter.

(A) On the inception of the fund in 20X1 the actuary estimated that a contribution rate of 20 per cent on pensionable salaries would be required.

20X1–20X3
The charge to the profit and loss account will equal the contribution paid to the fund in each year, that is 20 per cent of £1 000 000 = £200 000.

(B) At the first triennial actuarial valuation in 20X4 the regular cost was estimated to be 21 per cent. There was at that stage an experience deficit of £75 000 which was paid into the fund by the employer in 20X4. The average remaining service life of the employees at that date was 15 years.

The position for each of the years 20X4–20X6 will be as follows:

20X4	£	£
Charge to profit and loss account		
Regular cost: 21% of 1 000 000		210 000
Experience deficit spread over 15 years		
75 000 ÷ 15		5 000
Amount paid to fund		
21% of 1 000 000	210 000	
Experience deficit	75 000	
	285 000	215 000
Prepayment at 31 December 20X4		70 000
	285 000	285 000

20X5	£	£
Prepayment at 1 January 20X5	70 000	
Charge to profit and loss account – as above		215 000
Amount paid to fund – regular cost – 21% of 1 000 000	210 000	
	280 000	215 000
Prepayment at 31 December 20X5		65 000
	280 000	280 000

20X6	£	£
Prepayment at 1 January 20X6	65 000	
Charge to profit and loss account – as above		215 000
Amount paid to fund – regular cost – as above	210 000	
	275 000	215 000
Prepayment at 31 December 20X6		60 000
	275 000	275 000

(C) The next valuation took place in 20X7, a year in which the company undertook a major reorganisation involving a substantial number of redundancies.

The surplus resulting from redundancies was estimated to be £200 000, which is to be recouped by a reduction of £50 000 in the contributions otherwise payable for each of the four years 20X7–20Y0. We shall assume that this event constitutes a 'sale or termination' of an operation as defined in FRS 3.

In addition there was an experience surplus of £56 000 arising from events other than the reorganisation. The remaining average service life of the employees was 14 years.

The regular cost is estimated to be 18 per cent of £600 000 and the experience surplus of £56 000 is to be deducted in arriving at the 20X8 (not 20X7) payment.

For each of the years 20X7–20X9 the accounting treatment will be as follows:

20X7	£	£	£
Prepayment at 1 January 20X7		60 000	
Charge to profit and loss account			
in respect of regular cost and			
experience deficit/surplus.			
Regular cost – 18% × 600 000	108 000		
add 20X4 experience deficit			
75 000 ÷ 15	5 000		
c/f	113 000	60 000	

20X7	£	£	£
b/f	113 000	60 000	
less 20X7 experience surplus			
56 000 ÷ 14	4 000		109 000
Credit to profit and loss account			
in respect of surplus on termination		200 000	
Amount paid to fund			
18% × 600 000	108 000		
Reduction in respect of surplus on termination	50 000	58 000	
		318 000	109 000
Prepayment at 31 December 20X7			209 000
		318 000	318 000

20X8	£	£	£
Prepayment at 1 January 20X8		209 000	
Charge to profit and loss account – as above			109 000
Amount paid to fund – as above	58 000		
less Experience surplus	56 000	2 000	
		211 000	109 000
Prepayment at 31 December 20X8			102 000
		211 000	211 000

20X9	£	£
Prepayment at 1 January 20X9	102 000	
Charge to profit and loss account – as above		109 000
Amount paid to fund – as 20X7	58 000	
	160 000	109 000
Prepayment at 31 December 20X9		51 000
	160 000	160 000

The above may be summarised as follows:

	Profit & loss account expense	Cash payment	Balance prepayment at year end
	£000	£000	£000
(A) 20X1–20X3			
20X1	200	200	–
20X2	200	200	–
20X3	200	200	–
(B) 20X4–20X6			
20X4	215	285	70
20X5	215	210	65
20X6	215	210	60
(C) 20X7–20X9			
20X7 Ordinary	109	58	209
Exceptional	(200)		
20X8	109	2	102
20X9	109	58	51

The prepayment at 31 December 20X9 may be analysed as follows:

	£
20X4 Experience deficit $\frac{9}{15} \times$ £75 000	45 000
20X7 Experience surplus $\frac{11}{14} \times$ £56 000	(44 000)
	1 000
20X7 Surplus on reorganisation £200 000 – £(3 × 50 000)	50 000
	51 000

Note: The deferred tax implications have been ignored.

We have now completed our main discussion of the accounting principles underlying SSAP 24, but we will deal with a number of related issues before turning to disclosure.

Related issues

The effect of discounting

SSAP 24 points out that financial statements normally show items at their face value without discounting, but by their very nature actuarial assumptions do make allowances for interest so that future cash flows are discounted to their present values. The statement points out that the question of whether items should be discounted in financial statements is a general one and on this general issue SSAP 24 should not be regarded as establishing standard practice.

In the special case of unfunded schemes the question of discounting cannot be avoided. The annual charge for pensions in any unfunded scheme is made up of two elements: the charge for the year (which is equivalent to the contribution to a funded scheme) plus interest on the unfunded liability. In an unfunded scheme the assets to support the pension are retained within the business and the latter element represents the return on those investments.

We will return to this topic when discussing FRS 17.

Group schemes

It is common for a number of companies in a group to use a single group scheme in which it is accepted that a common contribution rate can be used, even if when calculated company by company different rates would emerge. The standard allows this practice to continue and for lesser disclosure in the case of subsidiary companies, although full details have to be provided in the financial statements of the holding company.

Foreign schemes

In principle, all pension costs should be accounted for in accordance with the standard and hence consolidation adjustments may be required in the case of overseas subsidiaries. However, where countries overseas have very different pension laws or where the cost of making the necessary actuarial calculations is excessive, the contributions to the relevant overseas scheme may be treated as the costs for the period.

Scope

The standard is not restricted to instances where employers have a legal or contractual commitment to pay pensions; it also covers cases where the employers implicitly, through their actions, provide or contribute to employees' pensions.

Disclosure requirements

The main accounting principle is fairly straightforward. Estimate the regular cost and, subject to certain exceptions, spread the cost or benefit from variations over the remaining service lives of the current employees.

Given the uncertain nature of the estimates that are involved and the length of the time period over which they have to be made, it is not surprising that the standard requires extensive disclosure of surpluses or deficiencies in respect of defined benefit schemes, just stopping short of asking for the colour of the actuary's eyes.

It would not be helpful to repeat the requirements here but they can be summarised as follows:

(a) nature of the scheme;
(b) accounting and funding policies;
(c) date of last actuarial review and status of the actuary; i.e. whether or not an officer of the company;
(d) the pension cost for the period, together with an explanation of significant changes compared with the previous period, and any provisions or prepayments included in the balance sheet;
(e) the amount of any deficiency and action, if any, being taken in consequence;
(f) details of the last formal valuation or review of the scheme including:
   (i) actuarial method used and main actuarial assumptions;
   (ii) market value of the assets;
   (iii) level of funding expressed in percentage terms of the benefits accrued by members and comments on any material surpluses or deficiency so revealed;
(g) details of any commitments to make additional payments and the effect of any material changes in the company's pension arrangements.

An appendix to the standard provides some useful hypothetical examples of what might be disclosed by different types of companies but, a little surprisingly, does not provide an example of an unfunded scheme.

From SSAP 24 to FRS 17

The introduction of SSAP 24 in 1988 resulted in some reduction in the range of methods used for accounting for pension costs but, given the pioneering aspects of the standard, there was a need for a reasonably early review of the lessons learnt from its implementation. The review did not, however, come quickly, for the first of the two discussion papers relating to review, *Pension costs in the employer's financial statements*, was not published until 1995. The second paper, *Aspects of accounting for pension costs*, emerged in 1998 and this was followed by FRED 20 *Retirement Benefits*, issued in October 1999. The whole process culminated in the promulgation of FRS 17 *Retirement Benefits* in November 2000.

SSAP 24 had, even when it was issued, an old-fashioned air about it. While it was, in some ways, a radical document in that it attempted to bring some order to an important aspect of financial reporting that had previously been largely unregulated, it was also backward looking in that it did not seek to ensure that an entity's assets and liabilities were properly recorded. Examples of this include the provision that pension funds assets should be valued at the actuarial rather than their market value and that actuarial surpluses and deficits should be recognised over time rather than immediately.

There has over the period since 1988, and in particular since 1995, been a move towards the view that users of financial statements are generally better served if supplied with information about the fair values of assets and liabilities.

The 1995 discussion paper set out the two alternative methods of asset valuation but the response was overwhelmingly in favour of the actuarial method, the main reasons being the volatility of market values and the impossibility of estimating the market values of the pension liability. A majority of the members of the ASB agreed with this consensus but, at the same time, the Board recognised that there is no prospect of other countries adopting the actuarial approach and hence, as part of the move to international convergence, the 1998 paper proposed the acceptance of the market value approach. This proposal was accepted by the majority of the respondents to that paper.[6] While this seems to indicate a significant change of opinion over the three-year period, there are still considerable concerns about the greater volatility introduced by the use of the market approach.

FRS 17 *Retirement Benefits*

Actuarial methods

We will in this section concentrate on three key questions that faced the ASB when drafting FRS 17. They relate to the selection of actuarial methods.

- Should account be taken of the time value of money in determining the current service charge?
- Should account be taken of salary increases to which the employer is not yet committed?
- At what rate should the liabilities be discounted?

Should account be taken of the time value of money in determining the current service charge?

The annual cost of providing a pound of pension for an employee in her twenties is less than that of a counterpart in her fifties because a greater return will be earned on the assets transferred to the pension fund. Should this be recognised in determining the current service charge?

Two types of actuarial methods are mentioned in SSAP 24:

- accrued benefits methods;
- prospective benefits methods.

These differ in their treatment of the time value of money.

[6] FRS 17, Appendix IV, Para. 6.

Under an accrued benefits method, each period is allocated its share of the eventual undiscounted cost of the pension. The share of each period is then discounted and this produces a lower cost the further each period is away from the date of retirement. This results in a higher cost towards the end of an employee's service life than at the beginning because the effect of discounting the cost lessens as the employee approaches retirement.

Under a prospective benefits method, the total cost including all the interest that will accrue is spread evenly over the employee's service life.

The ASB believes the financial statements should reflect the fact that the cost of providing a defined benefit pension increases the closer the employee gets to retirement and therefore requires the use of an accrued benefits method.[7] We shall illustrate the application of an accrued benefit method in Example 10.2.

Should account be taken of salary increases to which the employer is not yet committed?

In terms of calculating the retirements benefits to which an employee is due, account should be taken of estimated salary increases to which the employer is not yet committed. In determining the percentage of salary that needs to be set aside to provide for these benefits, however, future salary increases should not be taken into account. Let us look at each in turn.

Likely benefits

The standard requires the defined benefit liability to be the best estimate of the present value of the amount that will actually be paid out.[8] Thus, for defined benefit schemes based on final salaries the liability should be based on the expected final salary, not the current salary. The Board accepts that there might be an argument, based on FRS 12 *Provisions, Contingent Liabilities and Contingent Assets*, that because the employer has some control over the future increases in salary it does not have a present obligation relating to those increases. This argument is rejected because the Board believes that there is a present commitment to pay a pension based on final salary, and that this liability should be reflected in the financial statements. It also points out that the use of expected final salaries is consistent with IAS 19 (revised) as well as with the US FAS 87.

Basis for the contributions

The approach adopted by FRS 17 is inconsistent, although, in determining the percentage of the salary that needs to be set aside to allow for the payment of the expected benefits, only the salaries expected to be paid in the following year are taken into account, as the method specified in FRS 17 *is the projected unit method*.[9] With this method the standard rate of contribution, the regular cost, is calculated by dividing the present value of the benefits expected to accrue in the year after the valuation (which will take into account the projected final earnings of employees) by the present value of the projected earnings of the employees in

---

[7] FRS 17, Appendix IV, Para. 11. In the case of a mature pension scheme where the average age of the employees is reasonably constant the two methods will yield pretty much the same result.

[8] FRS 17, Appendix IV, Para. 12.

[9] FRS 17, Para. 20.

that year.[10] There is an alternative actuarial approach known as the *attained age method* where the contribution rate is calculated by dividing the present value of the benefits which will accrue to the members of the scheme after the date of the valuation, as with the projected unit method, by the present value of the **total** projected earnings of the members of the scheme.

The attained age method would seem to provide a better basis of satisfying the FRS 17 objective of recognising the costs of providing retirement benefits in the accounting periods in which the benefits are earned. Unfortunately, the Board does not provide an adequate explanation of its preference for the projected unit method.

At what rate should the liabilities be discounted?

In the past, actuaries discounted liabilities in a defined pension scheme by using the estimated expected rate of return on the scheme's assets. While this approach does not seem unreasonable the Board take the view that a more realistic approach would be to use a discount rate that reflects the time value of money and the risk associated with the liability.[11] The point that employers could, if experiencing financial difficulties, mitigate their position by granting less than expected salary increases is made to support the view that the risk premium should be small. While the Board recognises that the risk premium will differ between schemes it requires, for the sake of both objectivity and international convergence, the use of a standard interest rate: the rate of return on a high quality corporate bond, i.e. one rated at AA or equivalent status.

Frequency of actuarial valuations

Full actuarial valuations should be undertaken by a professionally qualified actuary at least every three years but the actuary should review the most recent valuations at each balance sheet date and update them in the light of current conditions (Para. 35).

FRS 17 and the recognition of the costs of retirement benefits schemes

The nature of the costs

As we described earlier one of the major differences between SSAP 24 and FRS 17 is that the former requires certain differences to be written off over a period of time while the latter requires instant write-off, while believing that it is important to distinguish between those items that should appear in the profit and loss account and those whose place is in the statement of total recognised gains and losses. We will discuss the ASB's rationale for the approach taken by FRS 17 in a later section of the chapter dealing with the reaction to FRS 17 but we will first outline the relevant provisions of the standard.

---

[10] The reason why the calculation is based on the figures for the following year rather than the current year is that the method was developed by actuaries to determine the regular cost for the future period.
[11] FRS 17, Appendix IV, Para. 21.

First the standard, at Para. 50, analyses the costs as between periodic and non-periodic costs.

Periodic costs

- the current service cost;
- the interest cost;
- the expected return on assets;
- actuarial gains and losses.

Non-periodic costs

- past service costs;
- gains and losses on settlements and curtailments.

We have already introduced the current service, or regular, cost and actuarial gains and losses so we need to discuss the other terms

The interest cost

The interest cost measures the increase in the present value of a liability due to the passage of time, or, in the words of the standard, the interest cost is the 'expected increase during the period in the present value of the scheme liabilities because the benefits are one period closer to settlement' (Para. 2). This is sometimes known as the unwinding of the discount.

The expected return on assets

In designing any scheme estimates need to be made of the likely return on the assets. The expected rate of return is defined as:

> **The average rate of return, including both income and changes in fair value but net of scheme expenses, expected over the remaining life of the related obligation on the actual assets held by the scheme. (Para. 2)**

The standard makes it clear that the rate should be set by the directors, having taken advice from an actuary.[12] It does at first sight seem odd that the directors are able to select the figure that will appear in the profit and loss account although, as we will describe later, the choice is offset in the statement of total recognised gains and losses in which is found the difference between the expected and actual returns on assets. The choice of the expected rate will not therefore affect total owners' equity but is relevant to the issue of what appears in the profit and loss account and what in the statement of total recognised gains and losses.

Past service cost

This is the increase in the present value of the scheme liabilities related to employee service in prior periods arising in the current period as a result of the introduction of, or improvement to, retirement benefits.[13]

Under SSAP 24 such costs, in the case of current employees, are spread forward over their remaining working lives but the ASB, in FRS 17, is now of the view that these costs should be recognised immediately.

---

[12] FRS 17, Para. 54.
[13] FRS 17, Para. 2.

Gains and losses on settlements and curtailments

These are gains and losses that relate to changes in the scheme that are not allowed for in the actuarial assumptions. Such changes include the payment of a lump sum to a beneficiary or potential beneficiary in exchange for the payee giving up his or her rights to receive benefits or the transfer of scheme assets and liabilities relating to a group of employees leaving the scheme. The position under SSAP 24 is, as we discussed earlier, somewhat complicated. The FRS 17 approach is much more direct, immediate recognition in the profit and loss account.

Where should the costs be recognised?

Profit and loss account

The following amounts should be included within operating profit and be disclosed in the notes to the financial statements:[14]

- the current service cost;
- any past service cost;
- gains and losses on any settlements or curtailments.

The following should be included as part of other finance costs (or income) and should be disclosed separately in the notes to the financial statements:

- the interest cost;
- the expected return on assets.

Statement of total recognised gains and losses

The remaining items should be included within the statement of total recognised gains and losses and should also be included within the notes to the financial statements. These are:

- the difference between the actual and expected return on assets;
- experience gains and losses arising on the scheme liabilities.

It can be seen that the distinction as to what goes where does not relate to whether the item is periodic or non-periodic. Instead it depends on whether the amount can be regarded as relating to the normal operations of the business, in which case it should appear in the profit and loss account, or whether it is regarded as more akin to the revaluation of assets, and it is these 'revaluations' which are directed to the statement of total recognised gains and losses.

We will now illustrate the provisions relating to the treatments of the costs of providing a defined benefits retirement scheme in Example 10.2.

Example 10.2

A retirement benefits scheme which has only one beneficiary, Jane, was established on 1 January 20X1, four years before the date of her retirement. In order more clearly to illustrate the principles we will assume that the present value of the expected benefits payable to Jane at the date of retirement will be £120 000 and that her annual salary will be unchanged over the four years until retirement.

---

[14] As should any past service costs, any previously unrecognised surpluses deducted from past service costs and any previously unrecognised surplus deducted from the settlement or curtailment losses: FRS 17, Para. 82.

Assume:

(a) The appropriate discount rate for the scheme was 10% in 20X1 and 20X2 but fell to 8% for the rest of the period.

(b) That the contributions to the pension fund are made at the end of each year.

(c) The probability of Jane not completing four years of service is so low that it may be ignored.

(d) That the expected rate of return on assets is 12% for the whole of the period but the fair values of the scheme's assets were as follows:

Date	Fair value of assets £
31 December 20X1	21 353
31 December 20X2	45 412
31 December 20X3	78 693
31 December 20X4	121 302

On the basis of assumption (c), 25% of the £120 000 will be assigned to each of the years.

We will first calculate the current service and interest costs.

20X1

20X1 must 'contribute' £30 000 of the £120 000 but because the contribution will be made three years before the date of retirement the current service charge will be equal to £30 000/1.1^3 = £22 539.

The present value of the obligation at the year end is £22 539 and there is no interest cost in this, the first, year.

20X2

Current service charge

$$£30 000/1.1^2 = £24 793$$

Interest cost

Interest on the present value of the obligation at the start of the year, 10% of £22 529 = £2254.

The present value of the obligation at 31 December 20X2 is given by:

$$£60 000/1.1^2 = £49 586$$

which is made up of:

	£
Present value of liability as at 1 January 20X2	22 539
Current service charge 20X2	27 047
Present value 31 December 20X2	**49 586**

20X3

The discount rate fell from 10% to 8% as from 1 January 20X3.

Current service charge

$$£30 000/1.08 = £27 778$$

Interest cost

Interest on the present value of the obligation at the start of the year, 8% of £49 586 = £3967.

The fact that the discount on liabilities fell means that the opening present value of the liability is less than is now required so there will be an actuarial loss in 20X3.

	£	£
Required balance of the obligation		**83 333**
at 31 December 20X3, £90 000/1.08		
Less Present value of the liability at 1 January 20X3	49 586	
Interest cost on above, 8%	3 967	
20X3 contribution, £30 000/1.08	27 778	81 331
Actuarial loss		**2 002**

20X4

Current service charge
£30 000

Interest cost
Interest on the present value of the obligation at the start of the year, 8% of £83 333 = £6667.
We can see how the balance of £120 000 has been built up:

	Current service charge £	Interest cost £	Actuarial loss £	Total £
20X1	22 539			22 539
20X2	24 793	2 254		27 047
20X3	27 778	3 967	2002	33 747
20X4	30 000	6667		36 667
Total				**120 000**

The expected rate of return on assets and the differences between the expected and actual rates can be calculated as shown below. In doing so we will assume that all income from the assets has been reinvested and that the company makes its contributions to the scheme on the 31 December of each year based on the expected return of 12%.

Expected and actual returns on assets for the year	20X1 £	20X2 £	20X3 £	20X4 £
Opening balance	–	21 353	45 412	78 693
12% on opening balance	–	2 562	5 449	9 443
Contributions to scheme	21 353	23 916	26 786	30 000
Assets at year end based on expected return	21 353	47 831	77 647	118 136
Actual fair value at the year end	21 353	45 412	78 693	121 302
Difference between expected and actual return	–	–2 419	+1 046	+3 166

We are now in a position to show how the amounts relating to the retirements benefits scheme will appear in the financial statements.

Profit and loss account for the year	20X1 £	20X2 £	20X3 £	20X4 £
Included in operating profit				
– Current service cost	22 539	24 793	27 778	30 000
Included in other finance income				
– Expected return on pension scheme assets	–	2 562	5 449	9 443
– Interest on pension scheme liabilities	–	(2 254)	(3 967)	(6 667)
Net	**–**	**308**	**1 482**	**2 776**

Statement of total recognised gains and losses for the year	20X1 £	20X2 £	20X3 £	20X4 £
Actual return less expected return on pension scheme assets	–	(2 419)	1 046	3 166
Experience gains and losses arising on the scheme liabilities	–	–	(2 002)	–
Actuarial gain recognised in STRGL	–	**(2 419)**	**(956)**	**3 166**

Movement on the surplus or deficit for the year	20X1 £	20X2 £	20X3 £	20X4 £
Surplus in scheme at the beginning of the year		(1 186)	(4 174)	(4 640)
Movement in year				
Current service cost	(22 539)	(24 793)	(27 778)	(30 000)
Contributions	21 353	23 916	26 786	30 000
Other finance income		308	1 482	2 776
Actuarial gains		(2 419)	(956)	3 166
Surplus in scheme at the end of the year	**(1 186)**	**(4 174)**	**(4 640)**	**1 302**

In addition notes to the balance sheet would disclose the balances on the pension scheme that are given below.

Deferred taxation implications have been ignored.

Balance sheets on 31 December	20X1 £	20X2 £	20X3 £	20X4 £
Fair value of pension scheme assets	21 353	45 412	78 693	121 302
Present value of scheme liabilities	22 539	49 586	83 333	120 000
Net asset/(liability)	**(1 186)**	**(4 174)**	**(4 640)**	**1 302**

Disclosure requirements

The disclosure requirements of FRS 17 are extensive and it would be best if, at this stage, we summarised them rather than seeking to reproduce them in detail. The standard itself has an appendix that provides a helpful and comprehensive example of the disclosure provisions.

An initial comment is that FRS 17 seeks to ensure that the notes to the financial statements do more than analyse the amounts appearing in the statements but provide far more information about the basis underlying the key assumptions made in preparing the financial statements.

Defined benefits schemes

We have already discussed the disclosure requirements relating to the profit and loss account, statement of total recognised gains and losses and balance sheet so, at this stage, we will focus on those aspects that are to be included in the notes to the financial statements.

The information that has to be disclosed includes the following.

Details of the scheme

- the nature of the scheme, i.e. that it is a defined benefit scheme;
- the date of the most recent full actuarial valuation and, if it be the case, a statement that the actuary is an officer or employee of the entity;
- the contribution for the current period and any agreed future contributions;
- for closed schemes, and for those in which the age profile of the active membership is rising significantly, the fact that under the projected unit method the current service cost will increase as the members of the scheme approach retirement.

Assumptions

The major assumptions employed in the valuation of the pension scheme must be disclosed. These include assumptions about the rates:

- of inflation
- of salary increases
- of pension increases
- used to discount the scheme's liabilities

Assets

The fair value of the assets held by the scheme at the beginning and end of the period must be disclosed, together with the expected return for the current and following period. Separate amounts should be provided for equities, bonds and other investments.

History of amounts recognised in the statement of total recognised gains and losses

The following need to be disclosed for the current period and in respect of the previous four periods:

- the difference between the expected and actual return on assets expressed as an amount and as a percentage of the scheme assets at the balance sheet date;
- the experience gains and losses arising on the scheme liabilities expressed as an amount and as a percentage of the present value of the scheme liabilities at the balance sheet date;
- the total actuarial gain or loss expressed as an amount and as a percentage of the present value of the scheme liabilities at the balance sheet date.

Other notes

- the movement in the surplus or deficit during the year;
- an analysis of the reserves to show the amount relating to the defined benefit asset or liability, net of the related deferred tax.

The rationale underpinning FRS 17

The major differences between SSAP 24 and FRS 17 are in the valuation of assets and the treatment of actuarial differences. As we explain in many places in the book, the choice of the fair value basis of valuation is in line with the development of the Board's thinking in a number of areas of financial reporting so, at this stage, we will concentrate on the rationale underpinning the view that all differences should be recognised immediately and not written off over a period.

The main argument for 'recognising' rather than 'spreading' is that this ensures that the balance sheet shows either the surplus or deficit on the pension scheme based on the latest valuations and as such complies more closely with the Board's definitions of assets and liabilities. The Board also points out that the figures are 'transparent and easy to understand' and that the FRS 17 approach does not have to rely, as did SSAP 24, on complex and arbitrary rules for spreading gains and losses.[15]

Among the main concerns expressed in response to the Exposure Draft that preceded FRS17, was the effect of the far greater volatility in the pension costs that results from the combination of the use of market values and the ending of spreading. The Board's response was to affirm its belief that users of financial statements are sufficiently sophisticated to view figures in a proper context. Since we are here touching on matters that impact on the Board's overall approach it is perhaps useful to quote their arguments at some length.

> It is important to remember that the amounts reported in the statement of total recognised gains and losses *in any one period* have relatively little significance and should not necessarily cause concern. What matters is *the pattern that emerges over a number of years*. For example, if a substantial actuarial loss arises in one year, but then reverses over the next few years, there may well be no impact on future cash flows. If, on the other hand, the loss does not reverse and perhaps even is repeated, then it is more likely that additional contributions to the pension scheme will be required. Repeated gains or losses may also imply that pension costs in the future will be lower or higher as experience causes the actuary to change his assumptions. These trends will be highlighted by the disclosure of a five-year history of actuarial gains and losses.[16]

The Board also dealt with the concern that, as the standard does not allow for recycling, not all expenditure would flow through the profit and loss account. The hope here is that users will understand the significance of the distinction between the profit and loss account and the statement of total recognised gains and losses and will pay due attention to the messages provided by both statements.

The reaction to, and implementation of, FRS 17

It was perhaps unfortunate that FRS 17 came along at about the same time as a worldwide fall in share prices and fairly soon after changes in UK tax laws that removed benefits that had formerly been available to pension schemes. The combination of these factors was such that, even without FRS 17, many pension schemes reported a deficit, a position that would have been exacerbated by the removal of the 'helpful' spreading provisions in SSAP 24. As a consequence, a number of employers have, in recent years, closed their defined benefits retirement schemes to new employees and, sometimes, also to existing employees – replacing them with defined contribution schemes. While some of the blame for this was directed at FRS 17 it may be argued that this was criticism of the messenger which should more properly be directed at the underlying causes of the increasing cost of defined benefit schemes, namely the fall in the market values of shares and bonds, the withdrawal of tax benefits and increases in the life expectancy of pensioners.

---

[15] FRS 17, Appendix IV, 'The development of the FRS', Para. 40.
[16] FRS 17, Appendix IV, Para. 42.

Considerable pressure was put on the ASB not to implement FRS 17 or to do so over an extended period of time. The Board resisted these pressures but has, however, decided to defer the full implementation of FRS 17 for another reason. This was the decision by the IASB to review IAS 19 (revised) *Employee Benefits* and the associated risk that entities that had adopted the provisions of FRS 17 would very quickly have to change again in order to comply with a new international standard. Thus, in July 2002, the ASB issued an unnumbered exposure draft entitled *Amendment to FRS 17* setting out its proposals for dealing with the interim period while we await the issue of the international standard.

In this exposure draft, the Board reiterates its concerns about the weaknesses of SSAP 24 and, despite the problems that this would create for comparability, urges the voluntary adoption of all the provisions of FRS 17. It proposes, in any case, the full adoption of FRS 17 in respect of financial statements for accounting periods ending on or after 22 June 2005, and that the provisions of the standard relating to the disclosure of information in the notes to the financial statements should be implemented on the following timetable.[17]

Periods ending on or after	Provisions
22 June 2001	Details of the scheme
	Assumptions
	Fair values and expected returns on assets
	Movement of the surplus
22 June 2002	The information relating to the performance statements
	Information relating to the actuarial loss or gain for the current period only

Compliance with the international standard

The provisions of FRS 17 and IAS 19 (revised) are consistent in most respects but there is a major difference in the treatment of actuarial losses or gains. In contrast to FRS 17, IAS19 (revised):

- requires actuarial losses and gains to appear in the profit and loss account;
- allows gains or losses that do not exceed 10 per cent of the greater of the gross assets or gross liabilities of the scheme not to be recognised;
- allows gains or losses to be spread forward over any period up to the expected average remaining working lives of the employees participating in the scheme.

There is also a presentational difference in that under IAS 19 (revised) the items that FRS 17 would direct to the statement of total recognised gains and losses are recognised in the Income Statement.

The ASB is confident that its chosen approach is superior to that set out in IAS 19 (revised) but we must await the publication of an international exposure draft to learn whether the IASB is of the same mind.

---

[17] *Amendment to FRS 17*, Para. 1. The draft makes a number of more detailed proposals on the timetable for the publication of comparative figures that we have not included in the above.

Summary

We have, in this chapter, described the main forms of pension or retirement benefit schemes that are found in the UK and described the main issues relating to their treatment in financial statements. We traced the history of regulation in this area, which commenced with the issue of SSAP 24 in 1988. Although this standard is still in force the ASB is strongly of the view that it suffers from serious weaknesses, especially in the valuation of pension scheme assets and the treatment of actuarial gains and losses. We have explained that the Board favours the use of fair values to measure the assets and the immediate recognition of actuarial gains and losses. We have explained that this view is not shared by all, as there are serious concerns about the increased volatility in financial statements that the ASB's replacement standard, FRS 17, will undoubtedly introduce.

As with many other topics, accounting for retirement benefits is tied up with the international convergence programme and we have described how the provisions of FRS17 are being introduced gradually in the hope that a new international accounting standard, based on the same principles as the UK standard, will emerge before 2005, the target date for the full implementation of FRS 17.

Recommended reading

Excellent up-to-date and detailed reading on the subject matter of this chapter is provided by the most recent edition of:

UK and International GAAP, Butterworths Tolley, London. At the time of writing, the most recent edition is the 7th, 2001. A. Wilson, M. Davies, M. Curtis and G. Wilkinson-Riddle (eds), Ernst & Young. The relevant chapter is 23, 'Retirement benefits'.

More specialised reading includes the following:

P.G.C. Carne and P.P.E. Ogwuazor, 'Accounting for pension costs', *Accountants Digest*, No. 237, ICAEW, London, Winter 1989/90.

T. Sienkiewicz and D. Campbell, *Accounting for Pension Costs*, Tolleys, Croydon, 1990.

Staple Inn Actuarial Society, *A Users' Guide to FRS 17*, Staple Inn Actuarial Society, London, 2001.

Annual surveys of the ways in which companies treat retirement benefits in their financial statements are produced by Lane Clark and Peacock. The most recent edition was published by Tolleys, Croydon 2003.

Questions

10.1 (a) Identify and explain the main accounting issues in SSAP 24, Accounting for pension costs, for defined contribution schemes and defined benefit schemes.   (7 marks)

   (b) Provide a numerical illustration of accounting for a pension scheme surplus. You should explain the meaning of the resulting profit and loss account and balance sheet amounts, making appropriate reference to relevant accounting concepts and principles.

(8 marks)

ICAEW, Financial Reporting, December 2000   (**15 marks**)

10.2 Diverse plc has established a defined benefit pension scheme for all the company's full-time employees. The scheme receives contributions from the company and the participating employees. The scheme was originally established on 31 December 1991 and was actuarially valued at 31 December 1994. The scheme showed a deficit of £6 million. This deficit was caused by a reassessment of the original actuarial assumptions (an experience deficiency). No change to contribution levels was made as a result of the 1994 valuation. However, the deficit was funded by a one-off lump sum payment of £6 million into the scheme on 30 June 1995. The result of the 1994 valuation was not available when the 1994 financial statements of Diverse plc were approved by the Directors.

The scheme was actuarially valued for the second time at 31 December 1997. The results of this second valuation showed a surplus of £4 million. The actuaries advised that £3 million of this surplus was caused by a significant reduction in the number of scheme members because of a redundancy programme. The result of the 1997 valuation was not available when the 1997 financial statements of Diverse plc were approved by the Directors. No change was made to the normal contribution levels for 1998. Total contributions payable to the scheme for 1998 were £5 million. The average remaining service lives of participating employees in the scheme was estimated to be 20 years at the date of inception of the scheme. This estimate is reckoned to continue to be applicable in the medium term as older employees retire and younger employees join.

Requirements

(a) Explain the principles outlined in SSAP 24 – *Accounting for Pension Costs*, under which the profit and loss account charge for pension costs is determined in the financial statements of employing companies. You should indicate why the computation of the pension cost is more complicated in the case of defined benefit schemes than defined contribution schemes.   (7 marks)

(b) Compute the charge in the profit and loss account of Diverse plc in respect of the pension costs for the year to 31 December 1998.   (6 marks)

(c) Compute the pension asset or liability which would appear in the balance sheet of Diverse plc at 31 December 1998 and explain how it would be disclosed on the balance sheet.   (7 marks)

CIMA, Financial Reporting, November 1999   **(20 marks)**

10.3 You are the financial controller of C Ltd, a company which has recently established a pension scheme for its employees. It chose a defined benefit scheme rather than a defined contribution scheme.

C Ltd makes payments into the pension scheme on a monthly basis as follows:

● Employer's contribution of 12% of the gross salaries of the participating employees.
● Employees' contribution (via deduction from salary) of 6% of gross salary.
● Payments are made on the twentieth day of the month following payment of the salary.

C Ltd makes up financial statements to 31 December each year. On 30 June 1995 the scheme was subject to its first actuarial valuation. The valuation revealed a deficit of £2.4 million. The deficit was primarily caused by a change in the assumptions made by the actuary since the scheme was originally established. The deficit was extinguished by a one-off lump sum payment of £2.4 million into the scheme by C Ltd on 30 September 1995. The annual salaries of the scheme members for the year ended 31 December 1995 totalled £15 million, accruing evenly throughout the year.

Requirements
(a) Write a memorandum to your Board of Directors which explains:
- the difference between a defined contribution scheme and a defined benefit scheme,
- the accounting objective set out in SSAP 24 – *Accounting for Pension Costs* – concerning the determination of the charge for pension costs in the profit and loss account of the employing company,
- why the accounting objective is more difficult to satisfy for an employer with a defined benefit scheme.   (12 marks)
(b) Determine the total charge in the profit and loss account for pensions (EXCLUDING amounts deducted from employees' gross salaries) AND any balance sheet amounts in respect of pensions, explaining clearly where exactly on the balance sheet the amounts would be included.

Assume the provisions of SSAP 24 are followed by C Ltd.

You ascertain that at 30 June 1995 the average remaining service lives of the employees who were members of the pension scheme at that date was 24 years.   (8 marks)

Ignore deferred taxation.

CIMA, Financial Reporting, May 1996   (**20 marks**)

10.4 Court plc has a defined benefits pension scheme for all its employees. Based on actuarial advice the company has previously made contributions of £2 million per annum to the pension fund, being 10% of pensionable earnings. The average remaining service lives of the company's existing employees is ten years and pensionable earnings will continue at their present level.

An actuarial valuation of the fund as at 1 January 1991 has revealed a surplus of £3 million (i.e. the actuarial value of the pension fund's assets exceeds the actuarial value of the liabilities). The surplus has arisen solely because the investment performance of the pension fund has been better than anticipated. The actuary has suggested to the company the following funding options:

(a) Reduce contributions from 10% to 7.5% for the next ten years; or
(b) Have a one year pension holiday and reduce contributions to 9% in the following nine years; or
(c) Receive a refund of £3 million now and retain the 10% contribution.

All of these options can be assumed to comply with the requirements of the Taxes Acts (including Finance Act 1986) concerning pension fund surpluses.

In advance of a board meeting, the finance director of Court plc wishes to consider the impact of the various options on the accounts of the company and has asked you to prepare appropriate analyses building up to the average annual profit and loss account charge in accordance with SSAP 24 under each option for the next ten years. Also for each option the finance director wishes to know the balance sheet effect, if any.

Requirements
Note: In parts (i) and (ii), ignore taxation and the interest effect in respect of pension contributions advanced or deferred.
(i) Calculate the average annual charge to the profit and loss account of Court plc in respect of pension costs for the ten years commencing 1 January 1991 under each of the above options (a), (b) and (c).

For each option, (a), (b) and (c), detail the balance sheet effects of accounting for pension costs.   (6 marks)

(ii) Assume that Court plc follows option (b) above with effect from 1 January 1991 and that a further actuarial valuation as at 1 January 1996 leads the actuary to recommend reducing the pension contribution to 8% for 1996 only (with continuing contributions at 9%); under these assumptions calculate the profit and loss account charge for pension costs in each of the fifteen years commencing 1 January 1991, and the balance sheet provision at the end of each of those fifteen years. The average remaining service lives of existing employees can be assumed to remain at ten years.

(6 marks)

(iii) Set out, in note form, the practical accounting and presentational considerations, including taxation, which you would recommend the board of directors to take into account when deciding on an appropriate course of action in relation to the pension fund surplus as at 1 January 1991.

(6 marks)

ICAEW, Financial Accounting 2, December 1991   **(18 marks)**

10.5 (a) Accounting for retirement benefits remains one of the most challenging areas in financial reporting. The values being reported are significant, and the estimation of these values is complex and subjective. Standard setters and preparers of financial statements find it difficult to achieve a measure of consensus on the appropriate way to deal with the assets and costs involved. SSAP 24 'Accounting for Pension Costs' focused on the profit and loss account, viewing retirement benefits as an operating expense. However, FRS 17 'Retirement Benefits' concentrates on the balance sheet and the valuation of the pension fund. The philosophy and rationale of the two statements are fundamentally opposed.

Required

(i) Describe four key issues in the determination of the method of accounting for retirement benefits in respect of defined benefit plans; (6 marks)

(ii) Discuss how FRS 17 'Retirement Benefits' deals with these key issues and to what extent it provides solutions to the problems of accounting for retirement benefits.

(8 marks)

(b) A, a public limited company, operates a defined benefit pension scheme. A full actuarial valuation by an independent actuary revealed that the value of the pension liability at 31 May 2000 was £1500 million. This was updated to 31 May 2001 by the actuary and the value of the pension liability at that date was £2000 million. The pension scheme assets comprised mainly UK bonds and equities and the market value of these assets was as follows:

	31 May 2000	*31 May 2001*
	£m	£m
Fixed interest and index linked bonds (UK)	380	600
Equities (UK)	1300	1900
Other investments	290	450
	1970	2950

The pension scheme had been altered during the year with improved benefits arising for the employees and this alteration had been taken into account by the actuaries. The increase in the actuarial liability in respect of employee service in prior periods was £25 million (past service cost). The increase in the actuarial liability resulting from employee service in the current period was £70 million (current service cost).

The company had paid contributions of £60 million to the scheme during the period. The company expects its return on the pension scheme assets at 31 May 2001 to be £295 million and the interest on pension liabilities to be £230 million.

The company anticipates that a deferred tax liability will arise on the surplus in the scheme. Assume Corporation Tax is at a rate of 30 per cent.

Required

(i) Show the amount which will be shown as the net pension asset/pension reserve in the balance sheet of A plc as at 31 May 2001 under FRS 17, 'Retirement Benefits' (comparative figures are not required).   (4 marks)

(ii) Show a reconciliation of the movement in the pension surplus during the year stating those amounts which would be charged to operating profit and the amounts which would be recognised in the Statement of Total Recognised Gains and Losses (STRGL), utilising FRS 17, 'Retirement Benefits'.   (7 marks)

ACCA, Financial Reporting Environment (UK Stream), June 2001   **(25 marks)**

Reporting financial performance

We will in this chapter deal with a number of topics that might at first sight appear to be separate and discrete but which are in fact linked. The chapter falls into three parts.

The first part, A, is concerned with how the informational content of a set of financial statements can be improved by rearranging the ways in which the figures are presented. Hence we start with an examination of FRS 3 *Reporting Financial Performance*, a standard that deals with how the financial statements should distinguish between continuing and discontinued operations but which also introduced the distinction between those items that should appear in the profit and loss account and those that should appear in the statement of total recognised gains and losses (STRGL).

A related theme is that of segmental reporting, which is concerned with the extent to which figures in the financial statements should be disaggregated in terms of such factors as different types of products and different markets. We will look at the legal and stock market requirements as well as the content of SSAP 25 *Segmental Reporting*.

Part B of the chapter is concerned with the way in which information that is contained within the financial statements is modified or expanded for a number of reasons. The first relates to time, and here we discuss how happenings that have occurred after the year end may affect the financial statements. In other words we will discuss the treatment of post-balance-sheet events. The second concerns the relationship between the price of a share and earnings and the consequent need to calculate and report earnings per share on a consistent basis. The third matter that we discuss in this section, which impacts on the notes to the financial statements rather than the amounts included therein, is concerned with the transactions that the entity undertakes with so called related parties.

In the final part of the chapter we discuss the controversial subject of share-based payments and, in particular, the vexed question of employee share options. We describe the method of accounting for share-based payments that is being advocated by international standard setters and discuss the reactions, both positive and negative, that those proposals have evinced.

The various standards and exposure drafts covered in this chapter are:

- FRS 3 *Reporting Financial Performance* (1992)
- FRED 22 *Revision of FRS 3 'Reporting Financial Performance'* (2000)
- IAS 1 *Preparation of Financial Statements* (revised 1997)
- IAS 35 *Discontinuing Operations* (1998)
- SSAP 25 *Segmental Reporting* (1990)
- IAS 14 *Segment Reporting* (revised 1997)
- SSAP 17 *Accounting for Post Balance Sheet Events* (1980)
- IAS 10 *Events after the Balance Sheet Date* (revised 1999)
- FRED 27 *Events after the Balance Sheet Date* (2002)
- FRS 8 *Related Party Transactions* (1995)
- IAS 24 *Related Party Disclosures* (reformatted 1994)

- FRED 25 *Related Party Disclosures* (2002)
- FRS 14 *Earnings per Share* (1998)
- IAS 33 *Earnings per Share* (1997)
- FRED 26 *Earnings per Share* (2002)
- FRED 31 *Share-based Payments* (2002)

The number of exposure drafts in the list indicates the extent to which a number of the aspects covered in the chapter are, at the time of writing, part of the convergence programme.

Part A Reconfiguring the financial statements
Reporting financial performance

Financial statements report on past performance but they are also used as an aid in the prediction of future performance. Prediction is usually heavily dependent on an extrapolation of the past. Suppose, to take a simplistic example, one wants to predict future profits in order to place a value on a business. The obvious starting point is the current level of profit and recent rates of growth (or decline). Suppose the current profit is £3.0 million and growth has been on average 3 per cent per year over the recent past, the predictor would start by thinking whether the growth rate is likely to continue into the future or whether a different rate should be used. But in performing this simple extrapolation the predictor will need to consider the extent to which the future will differ from the past. In order to help achieve this there are two main ways in which the financial statements can be reconfigured.

One is to separate gains and losses between those that can be regarded as normal consequences of the course of business, and hence might reasonably be extrapolated, and those which are odd or unusual and which are not expected to recur on a regular basis. The second device is relevant only when an entity stops engaging in certain of its activities. If this occurs the financial statements should make a clear distinction between the results that derive from the part of the business that will be continued and that part that is being discontinued.

The desire to show separately what might be termed continuing or normal operating items and non-recurrent elements of the business resulted, in the past, in a loss of comparability in that different companies dealt with the issue in different ways. From time to time, abuses occurred because companies attempted to play down the effect of bad decisions by treating the resulting losses as a non-recurring item. New standards have been introduced that not merely seek to prevent such abuses but more positively attempt to ensure that the financial statements provide users with more relevant and helpful information. The approach that has now been adopted is well described in the *Statement of Principles*:

> The ability to use information in financial statements to make assessments is enhanced by the way in which it is presented. For example, the predictive value of information provided by the financial performance statement is enhanced if unusual or infrequent items of gains or losses are disclosed and if information is provided that helps users to assess the likely incidence of similarly unusual or infrequent gains or losses in the future. In the same way, presentations that help users to understand the recurring/non-recurring nature of the various gains and losses also improve the predictive value of the performance statement.[1]

---

[1] *Statement of Principles*, Para. 3.4.

The ASC first dealt with this topic in April 1974 through the issue of SSAP 6 *Extraordinary items and prior year adjustments*, which was reissued in a revised form in August 1986. SSAP 6 was replaced in 1992 by the more wide-ranging FRS 3 *Reporting financial performance*. The subject is now under review by the ASB and, as part of this work, the Board published a discussion paper *Reporting financial performance: Proposals for change* in 1999, followed by an exposure draft FRED 22 *Revision of FRS 3 'Reporting financial performance'* in December 2000.

SSAP 6 *Extraordinary Items and Prior Year Adjustments*

Since FRS 3 is in many respects a development of SSAP 6 it will be useful briefly to summarise SSAP 6 before dealing in more detail with the provisions of the FRS.

The problem that gave rise to the issue of SSAP 6 was the variety of practice concerning the treatment of income and expenditure that was regarded as being 'non-recurring'. Two extreme positions could be identified. At one extreme all items were passed through the profit and loss account, while at the other extreme any items which could be argued as not relating to the normal activities of the business (non-recurring items) were charged or credited direct to reserves or adjusted against the opening balance of retained profits. The latter method is known as 'reserve accounting'.[2] In practice, most companies adopted a position between the two extremes.

The argument in favour of reserve accounting was that a profit or loss based only on the 'normal activities' of the business gave a fairer indication of the business's maintainable profit. It was suggested that such a profit figure would provide the more useful basis for estimating future profits than the profit resulting from a profit and loss account that included all items irrespective of their nature.

The view of the ASC, as evidenced by the provisions of SSAP 6, was that all revenue items should pass through the profit and loss account. The reasons for this view were as follows:

(a) The inclusion and disclosure of the non-recurring items enables the profit and loss account for the year to give a better view of a company's profitability and progress.
(b) The exclusion of non-recurring items requires the exercise of subjective judgement and may lead to variation in the treatment of similar items and hence to a loss of comparability between the accounts of different companies.
(c) The exclusion of non-recurring items could result in their being overlooked in any review of results over a series of years. Thus, while the nature of the items will, by definition, change, many businesses, especially larger ones, will often have items that are 'non-recurrent' and continually to exclude them from the profit and loss account would result in a distorted view of profit being shown.

The wholly sensible view of the ASC was that the legitimate advantages of reserve accounting could be obtained, without the drawbacks listed above, if adequate disclosure is provided in accounts. In essence, SSAP 6 required that all profits and losses recognised in the year should be shown in the profit and loss account. There were, however, two exceptions – prior year adjustments and certain items that, either by law or under the provisions of an accounting standard, were specifically permitted or required to be taken directly to reserves.

While the standard did in general reject the use of reserve accounting, it did accept the notion that it is possible, and helpful to users, to distinguish between the results of ordinary

---

[2] The two approaches are also often described, particularly in the USA, as '*all inclusive income*' and '*current income*', respectively.

activities of the business and *extraordinary* (non-recurring) profits and losses. Thus the standard prescribed, if there were any extraordinary items, that the following elements should be included in the profit and loss account:

- post-tax profit before extraordinary items;
- extraordinary items (less taxation attributable thereto);
- post-tax profit after extraordinary items.

In addition, items of an abnormal size and incidence but which may be regarded as deriving from the ordinary activities of the business, *exceptional items*, should be disclosed but included in the derivation of the profit before extraordinary items.

The above provisions of SSAP 6 were incorporated into statute law by the Companies Act 1985 but the Act does not attempt to define the various terms, a task left to the standard setters.

FRS 3 *Reporting Financial Performance*

FRS 3 is based on the same principles as SSAP 6 but includes three important changes.

(a) It provides more precise and more useful definitions of the key terms and in particular limits drastically the circumstances under which an item can be classed as extraordinary.
(b) It puts greater emphasis on reporting the effects of discontinued operations. This has led to a change in the format of the profit and loss accounts of enterprises that have discontinued part of their operations during an accounting period.
(c) It requires the inclusion of three additional elements in the financial statements:
    (i) a statement of total recognised gains and losses, including the profit or loss for the period together with all other movements on reserves reflecting recognised gains and losses attributable to shareholders;
    (ii) a reconciliation of movements in shareholders' funds bringing together the performance of the period, as shown in the statement of recognised gains and losses, and all other changes in shareholders' funds in the period, including capital contributed by or repaid to shareholders;
    (iii) a note, which would be of relevance to companies which had revalued assets at some stage in their history, reconciling the profit or loss disclosed in the accounts with that figure which would have been disclosed had the company not revalued assets, i.e. the profit based on the strict application of the unmodified historical cost convention.

We will deal with each of these later in the chapter.

Exceptional and extraordinary items

The key definitions relating to ordinary activities and exceptional and extraordinary items provided in FRS 3 are:

Ordinary activities

Any activities which are undertaken by a reporting entity as part of its business and such related activities in which the reporting entity engages in furtherance of, incidental to, or arising from, these activities. Ordinary activities include the effects on the reporting entity of any event in the various environments in which it operates, including the political, regulatory, economic and geographical environments, irrespective of the frequency or unusual nature of the events. (Para. 2)

Exceptional items

Material items which derive from events or transactions that fall within the ordinary activities of the reporting entity and which individually or, if of a similar type, in aggregate, need to be disclosed by virtue of their size or incidence if the financial statements are to give a true and fair view. (Para. 5)

Extraordinary items

Material items possessing a high degree of abnormality which arise from events or transactions that fall outside the ordinary activities of the reporting entity and which are not expected to recur. They do not include exceptional items nor do they include prior period items merely because they relate to a prior period. (Para. 6)

The last sentence of the definition of 'Extraordinary items', which has to be read a few times to be understood, simply means that an item does not become extraordinary simply because it is recognised in the profit and loss account in a period following the one in which it occurred.

The definition of ordinary activities contained in FRS 3 is much wider than the corresponding definition in SSAP 6. As a consequence the definition of extraordinary items provided in FRS 3 is very much more restricted than the SSAP 6 version, with the result that, in the words of the ASB, extraordinary items are now likely to be '*extremely rare*' (Para. 48). Because of this, FRS 3, unlike SSAP 6, does not provide examples of extraordinary items. An illustration of the extent of the change is one of the examples provided in SSAP 6, the expropriation of assets, which is now regarded as part of the ordinary activities of the business because of the revised definition of that term. Another of the major examples of extraordinary items provided in SSAP 6 is the consequence of the discontinuity of a separate segment of the business that, as we will explain below, is now treated in an entirely different way.

The question of whether an item should be regarded as exceptional is essentially a matter of judgement related to whether knowledge of the item will provide the users of the financial statement with a clearer picture of the performance of the company. By definition, exceptional items must be material but thereafter the recognition of such items depends on size or incidence. The meaning of 'incidence' in this context is not clear, nor is it explained in FRS 3, but it presumably relates to items which lie somewhere between material and large but which will nonetheless have some significance in assessing the maintainable profits of the enterprise. Thus, for example, the profit or loss on the sale or termination of operations of a type which do not satisfy the rather tight conditions for recognition as discontinued operations (see p. 283) may not be large but may yet be significant in judging the future profitability of the business, perhaps because had the operation not been terminated large losses would have been sustained in the future.

Prior-period adjustments

These are defined as:

Material adjustments applicable to prior periods arising from changes in accounting policies or from the correction of fundamental errors. They do not include normal recurring adjustments or corrections of accounting estimates made in prior periods. (Para. 7)

In some ways it is unfortunate that the ASB did not use a different name for this type of adjustment because, as is pointed out in FRS 3 (Para. 60), the vast majority of items relating to prior periods arise from the corrections and adjustments which are the natural result of estimates inherent in periodic financial reporting and are therefore not covered by the definition of prior period adjustment; perhaps a title such as Fundamental Prior Period Adjustment would have been preferable.

The normal run of adjustments relating to prior periods are dealt with in the profit and loss account of the period in which they are identified. They are not exceptional or extraordinary merely because they relate to a prior period, but if their effect is material then they would be disclosed as an exceptional item or, in very rare cases, an extraordinary item.

The importance of consistency as a fundamental accounting concept is emphasised and it is stated that a change in accounting policy should therefore be made only when it can be justified that the new policy gives a fairer presentation of the financial position of the reporting company. An adaptation or modification of an accounting basis caused by transactions or events that are clearly different in substance from those which occurred in the past does not give rise to a change of accounting policy and hence does not result in a prior period adjustment (Para. 62).

The second element in the definition of prior period adjustments is the correction of fundamental errors. To be treated as prior period adjustments such errors would need to be of such significance that the financial statements that contained them could not show a true and fair view.

Prior-period adjustments and disclosure requirements

Prior period adjustments should be accounted for by adjusting the opening balance of reserves for the cumulative effect of the adjustments and by restating the comparative figures for the preceding period. In addition, the cumulative effect of the adjustment should be noted at the foot of the statement of total recognised gains and losses of the current period whilst the effect of the prior period adjustments on the results for the preceding period should be disclosed where practicable. (Para. 29)

Reflecting the results of discontinued operations

A company cannot maintain the profits of operations which it no longer carries out, and thus it seems reasonable to ensure that financial statements discriminate clearly between the results which have been achieved by that part of the enterprise which will continue, and the results achieved or losses sustained by those parts of the organisation which had been closed or sold during the course of the year.

In order to achieve this, FRS 3 calls for what is, in effect, two profit and loss accounts; one covering those operations that will continue in the future, which includes acquisitions made during the year, and one dealing with any part of the enterprise that was sold or terminated during the course of the year.

The way in which the information is disclosed, whether by way of note or on the face of the profit and loss account, is to a large measure left to the accountant, guided by two examples provided in the Appendix to FRS 3. The discretion is not unlimited, however, because as a minimum there should be shown on the face of the profit and loss account analyses of turnover and operating profit as between discontinued and continuing operations.

Adjustments are also required in the comparative figures because only the results of those operations which are regarded as continuing at the year end should be included in the preceding year's figures for continuing operations. This is an important measure that helps the users of the financial statements to gain a clearer picture of the progress of the company.

One of the two illustrations provided in the standard is reproduced in Table 11.1.

Table 11.1 **Illustration of profit and loss account format under FRS 3**

| | Continuing operations | | Discontinued operations | Total | Total |
| | 1993 | Acquisitions 1993 | 1993 | 1993 | 1992 as restated |
	£ million	£ million	£ million	£ million	£ million
Turnover	550	50	175	775	690
Cost of sales	(415)	(40)	(165)	(620)	(555)
Gross profit	135	10	10	155	135
Net operating expenses	(85)	(4)	(25)	(114)	(83)
Less 1992 provision			10	10	
Operating profit	50	6	(5)	51	52
Profit on sale of properties	9			9	6
Provision for loss on operations to be discontinued					(30)
Loss on disposal of discontinued operations			(17)	(17)	
Less 1992 provision			20	20	
Profit on ordinary activities before interest	59	6	(2)	63	28
Interest payable				(18)	(15)
Profit on ordinary activities before taxation				45	13
Tax on profit on ordinary activities				(14)	(4)
Profit on ordinary activities after taxation				31	9
Minority interests				(2)	(2)
[Profit before extraordinary items]				29	7
[Extraordinary items] (included only to show positioning)				–	–
Profit for the financial year				29	7
Dividends				(8)	(1)
Retained profit for the financial year				21	6
				1993	*1992*
Earnings per share				39p	10p
Adjustments				*xp*	*xp*
[to be itemised and an adequate description to be given]					
Adjusted earnings per share				*yp*	*yp*

[Reason for calculating the adjusted earnings per share to be given.]

Table 11.1 Continued

Required Note:	1993			1992 (as restated)		
	Continuing	Dis-continued	Total	Continuing	Dis-continued	Total
	£ million	£ million	£ million	£ million	£ million	£ million
Turnover				500	190	690
Cost of sales				385	170	555
Net operating expenses						
Distribution costs	56	13	69	46	5	51
Administrative expenses	41	12	53	34	3	37
Other operating income	(8)	0	(8)	(5)	0	(5)
	89	25	114	75	8	83
Operating profit				40	12	52

The total figure of net operating expenses for continuing operations in 1993 includes £4 million in respect of acquisitions (namely distribution costs, £3 million, administrative expenses, £3 million and other operating income, £2 million).

What constitutes discontinuity?

FRS 3 defines discontinued operations in the following way:

Operations of the reporting entity that are sold or terminated and that satisfy all of the following conditions:

(a) The sale or termination is completed either in the period or before the earlier of three months after the commencement of the subsequent period and the date on which the financial statements are approved.
(b) If a termination, the former activities have ceased permanently. ✓
(c) The sale or termination has a material effect on the nature and focus of the reporting entity's operations and represents a material reduction in its operating facilities resulting either from its withdrawal from a particular market (whether class of business or geographical) or from a material reduction in turnover in the reporting entity's continuing markets.
(d) The assets, liabilities, results of operations and activities are clearly distinguishable, physically, operationally and for financial reporting purposes.

Operations not satisfying all these conditions are classified as continuing. (Para. 4)

The objective of FRS 3 is clearly laudable in attempting to help users extrapolate past results into the future but the drawing of a distinction between continuing and discontinued operations is clearly open to abuse. Most businesses continually modify their range of operations; some product lines or activities will be dropped in the course of the year and these will usually be those that are less successful. Hence, if there were no limits on what could be designated as discontinued operations a business could make the 'continuing operations' part of the profit and loss account look very healthy by shunting the results of all abandoned product lines or activities into the discontinued operations section.

In order to prevent, or rather minimise, the opportunity for whitewashing the profit and loss account in this way, the ASB has laid down a rigorous definition of what constitutes discontinuity. As can be seen above there are four tests, all of which must be satisfied. The first two tests are fairly clear; the discontinuity must be completed either in the year or within three months of the balance sheet date, or even earlier if the date of approval of the financial statements is within that three-month period. Also, the termination must be permanent and not a temporary withdrawal from a particular market. Condition (d) is also reasonably straightforward. It requires that the 'operation' must have constituted a distinct chunk of the business in operational, physical and financial terms. Further elaboration of that point is provided in Para. 44 of the standard. To satisfy the condition, the operation must have been a revenue and cost centre to which all material items of revenue and costs were specifically assigned or, to put it another way, one where only a very small reliance had to be placed on the allocation of joint costs and revenues.

Condition (c) of the definition requires that the sale or termination must have had a material effect on the nature and focus of the enterprise but this does seem to beg the question of what is meant by the focus of the reporting entity's operations. The ASB goes some way to answering the question in that it states, 'including the aspects of both quality and location' (Para. 42). The nature and focus of the reporting entity's operations refers to the position of its products or services in their markets.

An example is given of a hotel company that sells its existing chains of hotels that operate at the cheaper end of the market and then buys a chain of luxury hotels. This, it is stated, can be regarded as 'changing its focus' and hence the sale could be treated as a discontinued operation even though the company stays in the hotel business. Similarly, a sale of all its hotels in one country might also be regarded as a discontinuity, even if, as a result, hotels are purchased in another country.

Two points need to be made about this example. The first relates to the use of the term 'chain' which implies that the hotels were operated as an identifiable group that was sold in its entirety. The sale of only the cheap hotels in a chain which were operated under the same name as the remaining luxury hotels and which shared common services would probably not satisfy the 'separateness' tests specified in condition (d).

The second point is that condition (c) requires that for the sale to be treated as a discontinuity it must represent 'a material reduction in its operating facilities resulting either from its withdrawal from a particular market (whether class of business or geographical) or from a material reduction in turnover in the reporting entity's continuing markets'(Para. 4c).

There is, perhaps, an ambiguity here. Can the sale be treated as a discontinuity if the material reduction in operating facilities in one market is replaced by an equivalent increase in another market? The example provided in Para. 42 suggests that it can but this is not clear from the wording of Condition (c) of the definition that places stress on the 'material reduction in operating facilities'. In reviewing the standard, the ASB might consider revising its definition to make it clear that a change in the style of operation that does not materially affect the totality of operating facilities can still be treated as a discontinuity for the purposes of the standard.

Acquisitions

In estimating future results it is necessary to take account of the effect of any acquisitions made during the year. Normally (the 'exception' being the use of the merger method of consolidation, see Chapter 13, only post-acquisition results will be included in the profit and loss account, but the user of the accounts will want to know the full year results of the company acquired. The Companies Act 1985 (Schedule 4A, Para. 13) requires that information relating to the profit or loss of any group or company acquired from the start of the financial year of the acquired undertaking to its date of acquisition should be shown in a note to the financial statement. The note must also state the date of the start of the financial year of the acquired undertaking and provide information relating to the previous accounting period.

The additional requirements of FRS 3 are that there should be shown:

(a) on the face of the profit and loss account: analyses between continuing operations, acquisitions (as a component of continuing operations) and discontinued operations of turnover and operating profit;

(b) on the face of the profit and loss account or in the notes: a similar threefold analysis of each of the statutory profit and loss format items between turnover and operating profit.

Acquisitions are shown as part of continuing operations except when an operation is both acquired and discontinued in the course of the year; then it should be treated as discontinued.

If it is not possible to determine the post-acquisition results of the new operation, then either an indication of the contribution of the acquired operation to turnover and operating profit should be disclosed or, if that is not possible, an explanation should be provided of the reasons for the company's inability to provide the information.

What should be included in the results of discontinued operations?

If an operation is sold or terminated in a year, two elements of profit or loss arise. One is the trading profit or loss to the date of termination, the other is the profit or loss on the disposal of the assets constituting the operation. FRS 3 provides that both should be included in the determination of the profit or loss on ordinary activities before taxation, albeit separately identified. This is in contrast to the provisions of SSAP 6, whereby profits or losses on the sale of a business segment were treated as extraordinary items and hence shown after the derivation of profit or loss on ordinary activities.

One of the members of the ASB, Robert Bradfield, did not vote for the adoption of the standard and one of his reasons for this, explained in his dissenting view (published alongside the standard), was the inclusion of profits or losses on the disposal of operations in the figure for pre-tax profit. Bradfield believed that the standard placed undue emphasis on the pre-tax profit figure which may be misleading if it includes the profits or losses on disposal, especially as the tax effects, as allowed by FRS 3, are only shown in the notes. The view of the majority of the members of the ASB, expressed in the section of the standard entitled 'A Development of the Standard', is that the FRS 3 approach does not place emphasis on a single number because the admittedly complex presentation is based on an 'information set' approach that highlights a range of important components of performance. However, if a single measure of performance is to be used – for example in calculating earnings per share – then it should be based on its 'all-inclusive' concept which avoids the inconsistencies which were experienced in the application of SSAP 6.

Provision for future losses

There is a great temptation to say that if the company has to take its medicine then it should drink deeply of it. Thus if the company decides that it should either eliminate entirely or reduce extensively its loss-making operations in, say, the United States, the announcement will have an adverse effect on share prices and there would be less confidence in the company's future; a confidence which the company will want to restore as quickly as possible. One way of helping to restore confidence quickly may be to lump as much of the loss into the 'bad news' year as possible and to relieve future years of the burdens of those losses.

To provide for everything in sight, and possibly just a wee bit more, may well be prudent but it is likely to be exceedingly misleading.

Consider the following two series of numbers:

Year			Results (£ million)			
	1	2	3	4	5	Total
A	L10	L2	–	P2	P4	L6
B	L16	P1	P2	P3	P4	L6

(L = Loss, P = Profit)

To oversimplify, let us suppose that series A represents the 'truth' but B represents the results of the company if an excess provision of £6 million is made in the 'bad news' year, year 1. The 'prudent' approach under B suggests that the company is immediately restored to profit in year 2 and then makes steady growth, whereas in fact the 'true' position is that profit is not restored until year 4 but that the real rate of improvement is then higher than is shown by the prudent approach.

Now let us see how this matter is dealt with in FRS 3, remembering that in accordance with normal practice any permanent diminution in asset values should be recorded. The essential point of FRS 3, Para. 18, is that provisions should be made for the direct cost of sale or termination and any operating losses of the operation up to the future date of sale or termination (after in each case taking account of related profits), if and only if there exists a binding sale agreement or the company is demonstrably committed to the sale or termination because, for example, the action is covered by detailed formal plans from which the company cannot realistically withdraw.

The provision would be included as part of discontinued operations only if the related event qualifies as a discontinuity. Note that the conditions for discontinuity and the condition precedent for making a provision are different and that provisions can be made for operations that are for the purposes of FRS 3 treated as continuing.

When in the subsequent period the operation is actually closed, its results for that period should not be lumped together but shown under the statutory format headings, but there also needs to be full disclosure on the face of the profit and loss account showing the way in which the provisions made in prior years have been utilised, indicating how much has been used to cover operating losses and how much to cover the loss on sale or termination of the discontinued operation.

The treatment of provisions for future losses specified in FRS 3 is consistent with the position adopted by the ASB in FRS 12 *Provisions, Contingent Liabilities and Assets*.

Taxation

In deciding how taxation should be disclosed, the ASB had before it two main options. One was to relate the tax charge on the face of the profit and loss account to its basic elements – for example, continuing and discontinuing operations, and extraordinary and exceptional items – and to show the total tax charge by way of a note. The alternative was to show the total tax charge on the face of the accounts and provide the analysis in the notes. By and large, with the exception of extraordinary items, the ASB adopted the latter approach.

The disclosure provisions at Para. 23 are of both a general and a specific nature. The general elements of the standard are:

(a) Any special circumstances that affect the overall tax charge or credit for the period, or that may affect those of the future periods, should be disclosed by way of a note to the profit and loss account and their individual effects quantified.
(b) The effects of a fundamental change in the basis of taxation should be included in the tax charge or credit for the period and separately disclosed on the face of the profit and loss account.

In addition there are specific disclosure provisions relating to:

(a) Profits or losses on the sale or termination of an operation.
(b) Costs of fundamental reorganisation or restructuring.
(c) Profits or losses on the disposal of fixed assets.

In each case relevant information should be provided in the notes showing their effect on the tax charge.

Taxation and extraordinary items

FRS 3 provides, in Para. 22, that the tax on extraordinary items should be shown separately as a part of the extraordinary profit or loss either on the face of the profit and loss account or in a note. Any subsequent adjustments to the tax on extraordinary profit or loss should also be shown as extraordinary items.

A dissenting view

We have already referred to the dissenting view of Robert Bradfield. One of the major elements of Bradfield's opposition to the provision of FRS 3 was his belief that users of accounts would not fully appreciate the taxation effect on the trading results attributable to shareholders (he made a similar point relating to minority interest). As an example, Bradfield quotes the case of an international group of companies where the pre-tax trading profits in a low-tax regime fell and those in a high-tax regime increased by an identical amount. Such a change would leave the shareholder materially worse off but this would be masked in FRS 3.

The point is a good one and needs further consideration. This needs to be conducted in the light of a broader consideration relating to the reaction of shareholders and other users of accounts to the far more complex structure of financial statements that have appeared as a result of FRS 3. A particular issue is the balance between the information disclosed in the primary financial statements and that in the notes to those statements.

Minority interests

In the case of consolidated financial statements the information disclosure requirements for minority interests are very similar to those for taxation. The effect of three specific items referred to above (the termination of an operation, the fundamental reorganisation of operations and the profit or loss on disposal of fixed assets) on minority interests should be noted. If there are any extraordinary items that affect minority interests then the extent of the extraordinary profit and loss attributable to minority shareholders should be shown separately as a part of the extraordinary item, either on the face of the profit and loss account or in a note.

The statement of total recognised gains and losses

We have already discussed the growing importance of this statement in a number of contexts including accounting for revaluations of tangible fixed assets in Chapter 5 and accounting for retirement benefits in Chapter 10.

One of the confusing aspects, especially so for the layperson, of pre-FRS 3 traditional accounting was the ambiguity surrounding the treatment of gains and losses which were thought sufficiently significant to be allowed to have an impact on the balance sheet but yet were not reflected in the profit and loss account, and were instead dealt with by direct transfer to and from reserves. A good example of this type of transaction was the unrealised surplus on the revaluation of assets.

The traditional profit and loss account was based on a 'narrow concept' of realisation that treats as profits only those gains that have resulted in the receipt of cash or the acquisition of assets that are reasonably certain to be turned into cash. Unrealised gains were shunted into reserves (because of the prudence convention, anticipated losses were generally taken to the profit and loss account) and were reported as part of the movement of reserves, a statement the significance of which was not readily appreciated by many users of financial statements.

FRS 3 did not fundamentally challenge the narrow concept of realisation but, in drafting the standard, the ASB emphasises that gains and losses may be excluded from the profit and loss account only if they are specifically permitted or required to be taken to reserves by an accounting standard or, in the absence of a relevant accounting standard, by law (Para. 37). However, even with this stipulation the ASB believes that an incomplete impression of the company's financial performance would be obtained if attention were directed exclusively to the profit and loss account.

Accordingly, FRS 3 requires that companies publish an additional primary statement, which should be presented with the same prominence as the other primary statements, the 'Statement of Total Recognised Gains and Losses', which shows the total of recognised gains and losses in so far as they are attributable to shareholders.

As we pointed out in Chapter 4, the ASB now takes a more relaxed attitude to realisation and in particular the extent to which unrealised gains and losses should be kept out of the profit and loss account. The important distinction, argues the ASB, is not between realised and unrealised gains and losses but between those which derive from operating activities and those which derive from changes in the value of those assets and liabilities that are held on a continuing basis for use in the entity's business and which provide its infrastructure. It is suggested that changes in value that do not directly affect current trading (including those resulting from the disposal of infrastructure assets) should be reported separately from the result of operating and financing.

Hence the ASB requires that 'gains and losses on those assets and liabilities that are held on a continuing basis primarily in order to enable the entity's operations to be carried out are reported in the statement of total recognised gains and losses, and not in the profit and loss account' while 'all other gains and losses are reported in the profit and loss account' (Paras 6.27 and 6.28).

The *Statement of Principles* goes further in this direction by not referring to realisation at all. In the context of the entity's operating cycle gains should be recognised at the incidence of the *critical event*[3] that normally occurs when the reporting entity has completed all its obligations while, in the case of revaluation, the critical consideration is reliability of measurement.[4]

---

[3] *Statement of Principles*, Para. 5.33.
[4] *Statement of Principles*, Para. 6.19.

The illustration in FRS 3 of the statement of total recognised gains is reproduced below.

Statement of total recognised gains and losses	1993	1992 as restated
	£ million	£ million
Profit for the financial year	29	7
Unrealised surplus on revaluation of properties	4	6
Unrealised (loss)/gain on trade investment	(3)	7
	30	20
Currency translation differences on foreign currency net investments	(2)	5
Total recognised gains and losses relating to the year	28	25
Prior year adjustment	(10)	
Total gains and losses recognised since last annual report	18	

It is, perhaps, worth making the obvious point that gains and losses should not be double counted.[5] Hence, a gain that was previously recorded as unrealised should not be recognised again in the period in which it is realised. For example, the realisation of a profit previously recognised when a fixed asset was revalued would be reflected in the statement of the movement of reserves, where it would appear as a transfer from the revaluation reserve to the profit and loss account reserve.

The prominence given to the statement of total recognised gains and losses is an example of the 'information set' approach which the ASB hopes will divert the focus of attention from the single 'bottom line' figure of profit for the period.

Two additional notes

Reconciliation of movements in shareholders' funds

The profit or loss for the period together with any recognised gains or losses not reflected in the profit and loss account measures the performance of the company during the period, but there are other changes in shareholders' funds that affect the company's financial position, notably the declaration of dividends and the injection and withdrawal of capital. FRS 3 hence requires the publication of an additional note reconciling the opening and closing balance of shareholders' funds.

Reconciliation of movements in shareholders' funds	1993	1992 as restated
	£ million	£ million
Profit for the financial year	29	7
Dividends	(8)	(1)
	21	6
Other recognised gains and losses relating to the year (net)	(1)	18
New share capital subscribed	20	1
Net addition to shareholders' funds	40	25
Opening shareholders' funds (originally £375 million before deducting prior-year adjustment of £10 million)	365	340
Closing shareholders' funds	405	365

[5] We shall return to the subject of recycling later in this chapter.

The note may be included as a primary statement but, if it is, it should be shown separately from the statement of total recognised gains and losses (Para. 59).

It is important to see how the profit and loss account, statement of total recognised gains and losses and the reconciliation of movements in shareholders' funds fit together. This can best be seen by studying the comprehensive note showing the movement of reserves required by company legislation. The example shown below is consistent with the previous illustrations.

Reserves	*Share premium account*	*Revaluation reserve*	*Profit and loss account*	*Total*
	£ million	£ million	£ million	£ million
At beginning of year as previously stated	44	200	120	364
Prior-year adjustment			(10)	(10)
At beginning of year as restated	44	200	110	354
Premium on issue of shares (nominal value £7 million)	13			13
Transfer from profit and loss account of the year			21	21
Transfer of realised profits		(14)	14	0
Decrease in value of trade investment		(3)		(3)
Currency translation differences on foreign currency net investments			(2)	(2)
Surplus on property revaluation		4		4
At end of year	57	187	143	387

Note: Nominal share capital at end of year £18 million (1992 £11 million).

Note of historical cost profits and losses

If there is a material difference between the results disclosed in the profit and loss account and that which would have been produced by an 'unmodified' (i.e. no asset revaluations) financial statement, a note of the historical cost profit or loss for the period should be presented. The note should include a reconciliation of the reported profit on ordinary activities before taxation to the equivalent historical cost figure and show the retained profit from the financial year as would have been reported on the historical cost basis.

The more common types of adjustments that will be found include:

(a) Gains recognised in prior periods in the statement of total recognised gains and losses but realised in the current period, as under the strict historical cost convention the whole of the gain would be reported in the current period.
(b) The difference between the depreciation charges based on historical cost and such charges based on the revalued amounts.

The standard, at Para. 55, allows two exceptions:

(a) adjustments made to cope with hyperinflation in foreign operations; and
(b) the practice of market makers and other dealers in investments of marking-to-market value where this is an established industry practice.

Where full historical cost information is unavailable or cannot be obtained without unreasonable expense or delay, the earliest available values should be used.

The note should be presented immediately following the profit and loss account or the statement of total recognised gains and losses. The FRS 3 example of the note is presented below:

Note of historical cost profits and losses	1993	1992 as restated
	£ million	£ million
Reported profit on ordinary activities before taxation	45	13
Realisation of property revaluation gains of previous years	9	10
Difference between a historical cost depreciation charge and the actual depreciation charge of the year calculated on the revalued amount	5	4
Historical cost profit on ordinary activities before taxation	59	27
Historical cost profit for the year retained after taxation, minority interests, extraordinary items and dividends	35	20

Two reasons are cited by the ASB to support the publication of this additional note:

● Undertakings are allowed to decide whether to revalue assets and, if so, when. The results of undertakings that have revalued assets at different times are thus not comparable but the strict historical cost profit figures can be compared.
● Some users of financial statements wish to assess the profit or loss on the sale of assets on the basis of their historical cost rather than, as required by the standard, on their revalued carrying amount.

Review of FRS 3

Accountants have struggled for a long time to find a way of separating out unusual items in order to help users make an informed judgement of the progress of the company and estimate its potential for the future. FRS 3 was an important milestone in that development.

Its provisions have resulted in the production of far more complex profit and loss accounts than had traditionally been produced, a development in tune with the view of the ASB that the desire for understandability should not mean that complex items should be excluded from financial statements if the information is relevant to decision making.[6]

A number of factors have led to the recognition that a review of the standard was appropriate, particularly the view that, although the ASB had made great strides with FRS, 3 there remained a number of areas, such as the treatment of gains and losses on assets, that would benefit from further work.

As part of the move towards international harmonisation of accounting standards the first stage of the review was carried out at an international level and this has resulted in a publication that comes in two parts. The first part is the discussion paper itself, issued by the ASB, while the second part consists of a 'position paper' produced by the 'G4+1' of standard setters.

---

[6] *Statement of Principles*, Para. 3.37.

Reporting financial performance: proposals for change

In the first part of the paper, the ASB sets out its thinking and poses questions that it would like answered in the consultative period; the detailed discussion is found in the second, international, part of the paper.

In its introduction, the ASB reiterates its view that the performance of a complex enterprise cannot be summarised by a single number and reaffirms its belief in the 'information set' approach, as introduced in FRS 3, which attempts to highlight a number of components of performance. However, this is not yet a view widely held by users, many of whom still give undue prominence to the profit and loss account at the expense of the STRGL.

The main points made in the paper which, as we will see, have been incorporated in FRED 22 *Revision of FRS 3 'Reporting financial performance'* (December 2000), are:

- the introduction of a single performance statement combining the profit and loss account and the STRGL;
- the final elimination of extraordinary items;
- that, in general, errors should be recognised in the year of discovery without separate identification;
- dividends should no longer be included in the statement of financial performance but instead be shown as part of changes in equity.

FRED 22 *Revision of FRS 3*

The exposure draft builds on the discussion paper and in particular proposes the use of a single performance statement. Some commentators have seen this as the elimination of the SRTGL but this is a mistaken view for the main thrust of the proposal is an endeavour to ensure that users of the financial statements give the same consideration to the items that presently appear in the STRGL as they give to the profit and loss items.

Proposed performance statement

The proposed performance statement would include all gains and losses recognised during the period and be divided into three sections:

- operating section;
- financing and treasury section;
- other gains and losses.

The Board believes that use of a consistent approach to the ordering of items in the statement would be of value to users and that, as a practical matter, it would be generally possible to distinguish between those items that relate to an entity's operations and those which relate to its financing and treasury activities. The 'other gains and losses' section would include holding gains and losses and arise from long-term items held for operating or financing purposes.

Recycling

The exposure draft proposes the elimination of recycling, whereby gains and losses are reported twice in the performance statements, when first recognised and subsequently when realised. Such an approach, which the Board has been championing vigorously for some time, adds to the greater clarity of financial statements and indicates the fact that far less emphasis is now being given to realisation in financial reporting.[7]

Discontinued operations

We introduced, on p. 283, the four conditions set out in FRS 3 that have to be satisfied if an operation is to be treated as being discontinued. These included the provisions that the discontinuation must be completed either in the period or close to the period end, that any sale must be irrevocable and every termination permanent. In contrast, the corresponding international standard, IAS 35, *Discontinuing Operations* (1998), requires that operations should be shown as discontinuing from the time a binding sales agreement has been signed or a decision to sell/terminate has been made and announced, but it allows for the possibility that the decision might be reversed.

Respondents to the discussion paper generally agreed with the proposition that a decision to sell or terminate should be irrevocable; however, some support was expressed for relaxing the requirement that the operations must be sold or termination completed in the reporting period or very shortly after the period end. The view was expressed that discontinuations representing a material reduction in operating facilities could take place over quite a long time and that a move towards the international approach would be appropriate.

In drafting FRED 22 the Board adopted most of the proposals of IAS 35 in the spirit of international co-operation, although with some reluctance, and proposed the removal of the requirement that the decision should be irreversible. However, the exposure draft still contains a far more rigorous test for the recognition of a discontinuity than IAS 35 and the ASB believes that, due to the existence of the test, the removal of the irreversibility condition would only very rarely have any practical effect. The test is found in the definition of an *initial disclosure event* that in respect to a discontinuing operation requires the occurrence of one of the following events:

> That the entity has entered into a binding sale agreement for substantially all of the assets attributable to the discontinuing operation; or the entity's board of directors or similar governing body has both:
>
> i. approved a detailed, formal plan for the discontinuance: and
> ii. made an announcement of the plan, and the actions of the entity are such that they have raised a valid expectation in those affected that it will carry out the planned termination. (Para. 2)

Extraordinary items

Extraordinary items, already rare, may now finally disappear for, while FRED 22 still provides for their continued existence by including a definition of the term that is, other than for minor drafting changes, identical to that included in FRS 3, the Board now cannot envisage any circumstance in which extraordinary items might be reported under the definitions in the proposed standard (Para. 68).

Dividends

In the UK and the Republic of Ireland, company law requires that dividends be shown on the face of the profit and loss account, a treatment that might suggest that dividends are

---

[7] See Chapter 4.

expenses rather than appropriations of profit. The ASB believes that it would be better, even given that changes in legislation would be required, to remove this confusion and show dividends as changes in equity. However, in order not to put too much distance between the operating results and the reporting of dividends, the draft proposes that dividends for the period should be shown as memorandum items at the foot of the performance statement, both in total and per share (Para. 96).

Notes to the financial statements

It is proposed that the note of historical cost profits and losses that is mandatory under the terms of FRS 3 (see p. 290) should now be optional (Para. 104). It is also proposed that, when exceptional items are reported in either the current year figures or those of a comparative period, a history of exceptional items reported should be shown in the notes to the statement. The note should show, for each of the last five years, a breakdown of the exceptional items reported with a description of each (Para. 63).

Compliance with international standards

The main differences between UK and international standards that would remain if the proposals of FRED 22 were implemented relate to the flexibility allowed in the presentation of the operating statements, the definition of discontinuity of operations and the treatment of losses and gains on the disposal of assets.

IAS 1 (revised 1997) *Preparation of Financial Statements*, requires the presentation of an income statement and a separate statement of changes in equity; the latter includes the net profit or loss for the period as reported in the income statement, but it is not described as a performance statement. In contrast, FRED 22 would require all gains and losses to be reported in a single primary performance statement. The exposure draft also divides the statement into sections and sets out requirements for the allocation of gains and losses to those sections. IAS 1 offers no particular order or groupings for gains and losses and no explanation as to why some gains and losses are reported in the income statement while some are reported in equity.

We have already pointed out (p. 293) that the FRED 22 test to decide whether a change in operational policy constitutes a discontinuity is more rigorous than the equivalent stipulation in IAS 35 *Discontinuing Operations*.

FRED 22 proposes that gains and losses on the disposal of fixed assets should be reported in the same way as revaluation gains and losses and impairment losses. The result is that gains on disposal (that are not reversals of previous impairments) and losses on disposal (that are not impairments), will be reported in other gains and losses (while impairments and their reversal will be reported in the operating section). This proposal would require a change to FRS 15. In contrast IAS 16 (revised 1998) *Property, Plant and Equipment*, requires gains or losses on disposal to be reported as income or expenses in the income statement for the period, while revaluation gains (that are not reversals of previous impairments) and revaluation losses (that are not impairments) are reported directly in changes in equity.

Post-FRED 22 developments

As at January 2003, the ASB was still engaged on a joint project with IASB in the area of reporting financial performance. The most recent publication providing details of the progress of the project is a Technical Note to be found on the ASB website.[8] The proposals and intentions set out in the note build upon those contained in FRED 22 and have the following overriding objective

> The objective of the format of the statement of comprehensive income is to categorise, order and display information so as to maximise predictive value with respect to forecasts of comprehensive income and its components.

In order to help achieve this objective the following principles were developed:

> Principle 1: A statement of comprehensive income should be able to distinguish the return on total capital employed from the return on equity.
>
> Principle 2: Components of gains and losses should be reported gross (that is they should not be set off) unless they give little information with respect to future income.
>
> Principle 3: Income and expenses resulting from the re-measurement of an asset or liability should be reported separately.
>
> Principle 4: A statement of comprehensive income should identify income and expenses where the change in economic value does not arise in the period in which it is reported.
>
> Principle 5: Within the prescribed format and without the use of proscribed subtotals, the statement of comprehensive income should allow reporting in the form of:
>
> ● information on the entity as a whole, analysed by nature or function;
> ● the activities disaggregated by business segments (geographic or product-based);
> ● additional distinctions according to managerial discretion.[9]

The ASB and IASB have tentatively agreed to develop a statement format that makes two main distinctions based on principles 1 and 3 above. The proposed format would allocate items into one of four categories in a 2×2 matrix format.

The two rows in this matrix would be based on a 'business/financing' distinction defined by principle 1 above. The financing section would report the return to providers of finance (i.e. interest and the unwinding of discounts on liabilities); hence, the business section would provide a measure of financial performance that is independent of the capital structure of the entity.

The proposed columnar distinction is driven by principle 3. Income and expenses that result from the re-measurement of assets and liabilities would be reported separately in the second column. This column would therefore include items such as fixed asset revaluations and actuarial gains and losses on defined benefit pension schemes.

The shape of the resulting performance statement is shown in Figure 11.1. This format will probably be adapted for specialised industries such as banking and insurance.

The exposure draft based on the above proposals is scheduled for publication in the first half of 2003.

---

[8] www.asb.org.uk.

[9] ABS, Reporting Financial Performance, Technical Activities, ASB website: **www.asb.org.uk/publications/ publication project.cfm?upid=66.**

	Income and expenditure arising from activities carried out in the current period	Income and expenditure resulting from the re-measurement of assets and liabilities
Operating items		
Finance items		

Figure 11.1 **Proposed structure for the performance standard**

Segmental reporting

The financial statements of a company and the consolidated financial statements of a group summarise the results and financial position for the reporting entity as a whole. Thus, subject to the possible exclusion of one or more subsidiaries from consolidation in accordance with the provisions of FRS 2, the financial statements summarise all of the activities of the reporting entity, no matter how diverse these activities may be. Many companies and groups of companies operate in a number of different industries and in a number of different geographical areas, perhaps manufacturing in certain countries and supplying customers in other countries. The industrial and geographical segments of the entity are very likely to enjoy different levels of profitability, may be subject to very different risks and may have very different growth potentials. If users are to be able to assess past performance and to predict likely future performance of the entity as a whole, it is argued that it is necessary for them to be provided with a detailed analysis in respect of the individual segments. The provision of such an analysis is known as segmental, analysed or disaggregated reporting.

Company law and the Stock Exchange have accepted the need for such segmental reporting for many years although, as we shall see, their requirements are limited. An international accounting standard was first issued on this subject in 1981 and subsequently reformatted in 1994. A revised version of IAS 14 *Segment Reporting*, was issued in 1997 and this draws heavily on the US standard.[10] In particular, the revised IAS 14 provides more guidance on the identification of segments and increases the disclosure requirements. As a consequence, SSAP 25 *Segmental Reporting*, which was issued in 1990, is now somewhat out of line with the revised IAS 14. Although the ASB considered possible changes to the standard in a Discussion Paper *Segmental reporting*, in 1996, it has concluded that, as there is general satisfaction with the present segmental reporting requirements, no further action will be taken at this time.[11]

The requirements of the Stock Exchange and company law

We shall look first at the requirements of company law and the Stock Exchange before turning to the provisions of SSAP 25.

---

[10] SFAS 131 *Disclosures about Segments of an Enterprise and Related Information*, June 1997.
[11] See 98 Financial Reporting Council, Annual Review, 1998, p. 47. Available on the FRC website, **www.frc.org.uk**.

So long as the disclosure of the information is not seriously prejudicial to the interests of the company, the Companies Act 1985 requires two analyses, the first where a company or group has carried on business of two or more classes that (in the opinion of the directors) differ substantially from one another, and the second where a company or group has supplied geographical markets that (in the opinion of the directors) differ substantially from each other.[12]

In the former case, the law requires a description of each class of business together with the turnover and the profit or loss before taxation attributable to each class whereas, for the geographical segments, the law requires only an analysis of turnover. For listed companies, the Stock Exchange increased the amount of disclosure by requiring 'a geographical analysis of both net turnover and contribution to trading results of those trading operations carried on . . . outside the United Kingdom and the Republic of Ireland', although the analysis of contribution is only required if the profit or loss from a specific area is out of line with the normal profit margin.[13]

The above requirements ensure the provision of a minimum amount of segmental information but leave a great many questions unanswered.

Although some would question the wisdom of leaving the selection of reportable segments to directors, this would seem to be inevitable given the variety and complexity of modern businesses.[14] Perhaps a more serious problem is that any segmental analysis provided may be highly misleading if there is substantial trading between segments, especially if this trading occurs at artificially determined prices, and yet the law and the Stock Exchange do not require the disclosure of any inter-segment turnover or the basis of inter-segment pricing. Where an analysis of profit or contribution is required, there is the problem of how to deal with common or joint costs that are not directly attributable to any one segment; examples would be interest cost and the cost of a head office. In addition, the segmental information would appear to be of limited use without some indication of the net assets employed in each segment but, immediately an attempt is made to provide such an indication of net assets, the accountant confronts the problem of how to deal with common or joint assets, that is assets used by more than one segment. We would expect to turn to the accounting standard for guidance on the above matters.

SSAP 25 *Segmental Reporting*

While the standard contains some provisions relating to the statutory segmental disclosure, which therefore apply to all companies, it also extends these requirements to any entity that:[15]

    (a) is a public limited company or that has a public limited company as a subsidiary; or

    (b) is a banking or insurance company or group . . . ; or

    (c) exceeds the criteria, multiplied in each case by 10, for defining a medium-sized company under section 247 of the Companies Act 1985, as amended from time to time by statutory instrument.

---

[12] Companies Act 1985, Schedule 4, Para. 55(1) to 55(5).

[13] See Stock Exchange, *Listing Rules.*

[14] SSAP 25, Para. 9 defines a reportable segment by reference to the relative size of the segment, namely 10 per cent or more of external turnover, results or net assets.

[15] SSAP 25, Para. 41.

Thus, segmental disclosure required by statute is increased for public companies and certain specialised companies as well as for large private companies, although such a large private company does not have to provide the additional information if its parent provides the required information.

The extent of the increase in disclosure may be seen in Para. 34 of the standard:

> If an entity has two or more classes of business, or operates in two or more geographical segments which differ substantially from each other, it should define its classes of business and geographical segments in its financial statements, and it should report with respect to each class of business and geographical segment the following financial information:
>
> (a) turnover, distinguishing between (i) turnover derived from external customers and (ii) turnover derived from other segments;
> (b) result, before accounting for taxation, minority interests and extraordinary items; and
> (c) net assets.

The geographical segmentation should be given by *turnover of origin*, that is the area from which products or services are supplied and for which results and net assets will be determined. However, it should also be given by *turnover of destination* where it is materially different.[16]

The division of turnover between external sales and inter-segment sales undoubtedly helps users to appreciate the interdependence of segments, although the effect of such interdependence on results will be impossible to ascertain without some knowledge of the way in which inter-segment prices are determined. While IAS 14 requires disclosure of the basis of inter-segment pricing, SSAP 25 does not require this.

The standard provides guidance on determining segmental results and increases the legal provisions by requiring the disclosure of net assets for each segment. As a consequence it should be possible to compute returns on capital employed for the different activities of the business.

Results are to be taken before taxation, minority interests and extraordinary items and normally before taking account of any interest receivable or payable. Net assets will normally be the non-interest-earning operating assets less the non-interest-bearing operating liabilities. Only if the interest income or expense is central to the business of the segment should it be included in arriving at the segmental result when, for consistency, the assets or liabilities to which it relates should be included in the segmental net assets. Interest not so apportioned and other common revenues and costs should be excluded from the segmental analysis but included in the total results. Similarly, common assets and liabilities should be excluded from the segmental net assets but included separately as part of the total net assets. This is essential if the segmental analysis is to agree with the related totals in the financial statements of the company or group and, where such agreement is not apparent, a reconciliation must be provided.[17]

The Appendix to SSAP 25 contains an illustrative segmental report covering both classes of business and geographical segment. Table 11.2 illustrates the sort of segmental report envisaged for classes of business only, although, for simplicity, we have excluded comparative figures.[18]

---

[16] SSAP 25, Para. 34.
[17] SSAP 25, Para. 37.
[18] Note that the table includes the aggregate share of the results and net assets of associated undertakings. This is required if such associated undertakings account for at least 20 per cent of its total results or 20 per cent of its total net assets (SSAP 25, Para. 36).

Table 11.2 Illustrative segmental report (excluding comparative figures)

Classes of business

	Industry A £000	Industry B £000	Group £000
Turnover			
External sales	700	250	950
Inter-segment sales	50	–	50
Total sales	750	250	1000
Profit before taxation			
Segment profit	150	100	250
less Common costs			60
			190
Share of profit before taxation of associated undertakings	40	–	40
Net assets			
Segment net assets	1 500	400	1900
Unallocated assets			100
			2000
Share of net assets of associated undertaking	300	–	300
			2300

From Table 11.2 it is possible to compare the profit margin on sales and the return on net assets for each segment. Thus, it can be seen that the smaller segment, that is industry B, has the higher profit margin and the higher return on capital employed:

> *Profit margin*
> Segment A $150 \div 750 = 20\%$
> Segment B $100 \div 250 = 40\%$
>
> *Return on net assets*
> Segment A $150 \div 1500 = 10\%$
> Segment B $100 \div 400 = 25\%$

In practice such results could be compared with those for previous years to build up a picture of past trends and hence likely future progress. For example, given the results disclosed, an investor would be much happier if the involvement of the company or group in industry B were growing as a proportion of its total activity than if the involvement in industry A were growing.

By requiring the disclosure of inter-segment sales and of segmental net assets, the standard has certainly improved the usefulness of the legally required segmental disclosure. However, it will be more difficult to draw conclusions from a segmental report the higher the level of inter-segment sales and the greater the proportion of common costs/revenues and common net assets.

Although, potentially, the segmental information should be of considerable benefit to users, the inevitable discretion permitted to directors may reduce that benefit substantially in practice.

Compliance with the international standard

There are a number of differences between SSAP 25 and IAS 14 *Segment Reporting* (revised 1997), in addition to the one relating to the disclosure of inter-segment pricing to which we have already referred. In general IAS 14 provides rather more guidance than SSAP 25 in such matters as definition of segments and of the elements to be disclosed.

IAS 14 adopts what has been termed a 'management approach' in that it places more stress on the organisational structure of the reporting entity in defining segments than does SSAP 25. It also adopts a primary and secondary reporting format whereby a decision is made as to whether the dominant source for different returns and risks is the different products of the entity or the different markets in which it operates. The dominant source provides the basis of the primary reporting segment, with the other being the basis for the secondary format. IAS 14 requires more information to be provided in respect of the primary source while SSAP 25 makes no such distinction. While these differences are on the surface quite significant, the flexibility allowed by SSAP 25 makes it possible to produce a statement that complies with both standards.[19]

Part B Extending the financial reporting envelope
Accounting for post balance sheet events

One of the desirable characteristics of accounting reports discussed in Chapter 1 was 'timeliness', i.e. the need to publish financial statements as quickly as possible. However, there will inevitably be some delay between the end of the accounting period and the date of publication (which is not to say that the duration of the delay could not often be reduced), and this leads one to the question of how the accountant should treat significant events which occur during this period.

SSAP 17 *Accounting for Post Balance Sheet Events*

The main principle underlying SSAP 17 *Accounting for Post Balance Sheet Events*, issued in 1980, is that users should be presented with information that is as up to date as possible and be informed of any significant events that have occurred since the end of the accounting period. The provisions are uncontroversial and straightforward and may therefore be briefly summarised.

A distinction is drawn between events that occur before and after the date on which the directors approve the financial statements, and the standard covers only those events that

---

[19] *International Accounting Standards: A Guide to Preparing Accounts* (2nd edn), ABG, London, 2000, Para. 16.13.

occurred prior to the date of approval. The point is made, however, that directors have a duty to ensure the publication of details of any events that occur after the date of approval if they have a material effect on the financial statements.

The date of approval is normally the date of the board meeting at which the financial statements are formally approved. In the case of consolidated financial statements, the date is that on which those statements are approved by the directors of the holding company.

Post balance sheet events are classified as either *adjusting* or *non-adjusting* events.

Adjusting events are those that provide additional evidence in respect of conditions existing at the balance sheet date and will therefore call for the revision of the amounts at which items are stated in the financial statements. A very obvious example of an adjusting event would be the receipt of cash from a debtor that could affect the provision against doubtful debts. Events such as the proposal of a dividend, a transfer to reserves and a change in the tax rate are also regarded as being adjusting events but the treatment of dividends would change if the provisions of FRED 27 *Events after the Balance Sheet Date* (May 2002), were implemented.

Non-adjusting events are those that do not relate to conditions existing at the balance sheet date and will not affect the figures included in the financial statements. Examples of non-adjusting events are the issue of shares, major changes in the composition of the company and the financial effect of the losses of fixed assets or stocks as a result of a disaster such as fire or flood. The last-mentioned instance is an example of a non-adjusting event because the fire or flood would not affect the condition of the asset concerned at the balance sheet date.

The standard also requires the disclosure, as a non-adjusting event, of the reversal after the balance sheet date of transactions undertaken before the year end with the prime intention of altering the appearance of the company's balance sheet. These alterations comprise those commonly referred to as 'window dressing'; for example, the borrowing of cash from an associated company to disguise an acute short-term liquidity problem.

It may be that some event occurs after the balance sheet date which, because of its effect on the company's operating results or financial position, puts into question the application of the going concern convention to the whole (or to a significant part) of the company's financial statements. The standard (Para. 22) requires that the financial statements should be amended as a consequence of any material post balance sheet event which casts doubt on the application of the going concern convention, even though Para. 21 specifies that the financial statements should be prepared on the basis of conditions existing at the balance sheet date. FRED 27 is more logical and does not include an equivalent provision to that set out in Para. 22.

The actual standard may be summarised as follows:

1 Financial statements should be prepared on the basis of conditions existing at the balance sheet date.

2 A material post balance sheet event requires changes in the amounts to be included in financial statements where:
   (a) it is an adjusting event; or
   (b) it indicates that the application of the going concern concept to the whole or a material part of the company is not appropriate. (Note that this seems to conflict with requirement 1.)

3 A material post balance sheet event should be disclosed where:
   (a) its non-disclosure would hinder the users' ability to obtain a proper understanding of the financial position; or
   (b) it is the reversal or maturity after the year end of a transaction, the substance of which was primarily to alter the appearance of the company's balance sheet (window dressing).

4 In respect of any material post balance sheet event which has to be disclosed under the provisions of (3) above, the following should be stated in the notes to the accounts:
   (a) the nature of the event; and
   (b) an estimate of its financial effect or a statement that it is not practicable to make such an estimate. The financial effect should be shown without any adjustment for taxation but the taxation implications should be explained if such is necessary to enable a proper understanding of the financial position to be obtained.

5 The date on which the financial statements were approved by the Board of Directors should be disclosed.

It should be noted that the Companies Act 1985 requires that all liabilities and losses in respect of the financial year (or earlier years) shall be taken into account, including those which only became apparent between the balance sheet date and the date of the approval of the financial statements.

FRED 27 *Events after the Balance Sheet Date*

This exposure draft was issued on May 2002 as part of the international harmonisation programme and differs from SSAP 17 in a number of ways.

Dividends no longer adjusting events

The SSAP 17 definition of an adjusting event includes the phrase 'events which because of statutory or conventional requirements are reflected in financial statements'.[20] The effect of this is that financial statements include dividends that are declared after the year end even though the subsequent declaration of a dividend does not affect the condition of the entity at the balance sheet date. The exposure draft proposes that this inconsistency, resulting from a reluctance to challenge existing legal practice that is inherent in SSAP 17, should not be carried forward to a new standard. The same change is being proposed in the corresponding international standard IAS 10 *Events after the Balance Sheet Date*. The convergence that would be achieved if the proposed changes to the UK and international standards were implemented would be accompanied by a divergence between UK company law and UK accounting standards in that Para. 3(7) of the Fourth Schedule to the Companies Act 1985 requires that paid and proposed dividends should be shown in the profit and loss account.[21] The necessary changes are being considered as part of the general review of company law.

Dividends from subsidiaries and associates declared after the balance sheet date

A change equivalent to the above is being proposed in respect of dividends from subsidiary and associate companies declared after the investing company's balance sheet date. SSAP 17 regards these as adjusting events, FRED 27 does not.

---

[20] SSAP 17, Para. 19.
[21] The equivalent provision in the Republic of Ireland is s. 4(15)(a) of the Companies Amendment Act 1986.

Adverse events and prudence

We pointed out earlier (p. 301) the inherent inconsistency contained in SSAP 17 in that, for reasons of prudence, Para. 22 of SSAP 17 requires that events that took place after the balance sheet date that cast doubt on the continuing application of the going concern concept, but did not affect the condition of the entity at the balance sheet date, might be regarded as an adjusting event. The prudence point is made in more general terms in the Appendix to the standard which states that, in exceptional circumstances, in order to accord with the prudence concept, an adverse event which would normally be classified as non-adjusting may need to be reclassified as adjusting. The more rigorous logical approach adopted by FRED 27 means that it does not contain similar provisions, although an event of the criticality that would put the future application of the going concern convention in doubt would need to be shown as a non-adjusting event with a note showing its likely financial effect.[22]

Compliance with the international standard

There would be no material differences between the UK and international standard if the proposed changes are implemented.

Earnings per share

One of the most widely used measures in finance is a share's price/earnings (P/E) ratio, that is the share's market value divided by the related earnings per share. Suppose:

- The ordinary shares of Wayne plc had a market value of £12 at 31 December 20X1.
- The most recent financial statements available for the company show a profit of £32m for the year to 30 September 20X1.
- The company has in issue 40 million ordinary shares but no preference or other shares.

The earnings per share (EPS) for the year ended 30 September 20X1 = £(32/40) = £0.8 and the best estimate of the P/E ratio as at 31 December 20X1 = 12/0.8 = 15. This is a best estimate because, like every price/earnings ratio, it relates the current market price with a historical figure for EPS.

The P/E ratio indicates the number of years it would take for investors to recoup their investment, in the above example 15 years. But things do indeed change and the current P/E ratio indicated the market expectation about how things will change; a high P/E ratio indicates that the market expects that the EPS will grow.

The market provides the price but the financial statements produce the EPS and so, given the wide use of the measure, it is not surprising to find that one of the first statements issued by the ASC covered this topic. The standard was SSAP 3, *Earnings per Share*, which was issued in 1972. While the calculation of earnings per share has had to change over the years, in particular because of changes in tax law and because of the gradual elimination of the special treatment of extraordinary items, the basic principles underlying SSAP 3 have

[22] FRED 27, Para. 20. It is rather odd that in the relevant section of the preface to FRED 27, dealing with the proposed changes to existing standards, reference is made to the removal of the phrase in the Appendix but not to the removal of the provision contained in Para. 22.

survived remarkably well. In fact in the section dealing with the development of its successor, FRS 14, also called *Earnings per Share* (1998), the ASB accepted that SSAP 3 was operating reasonably effectively and that the only reason for revising it was international developments in the area.[23]

FRS 14 *Earnings per Share*

Since the reason for the importance of reporting of EPS is its use in calculating a share's price earnings ratio, FRS 14 covers only those entities whose ordinary shares or potential ordinary shares are publicly traded and those entities that are in the process of issuing ordinary or potential ordinary shares in public security markets. Potential ordinary shares are financial instruments or rights that may entitle the owner to ordinary shares and these include convertible preference shares, options and rights granted under employee share plans.

The earnings to be used in the calculation are the net profit or loss for the period attributable to ordinary shareholders after deducting dividends and other appropriations in respect of non-equity shares. In the case of cumulative preference shares the amount to be deducted is the maximum dividend for the period irrespective of whether or not the full dividend was declared.

The definition of earnings is pretty straightforward, the complications arise with the denominator, the number of shares, and these relate to actual and possible changes in the capital structure that have changed, or may change, the number of equity shares in issue.

We will first discuss the treatment of actual changes in capital structure, which we shall do by considering a number of hypothetical examples.

Assume that MM plc's earnings attributable to equity shareholders for 20X5 is £2.0 million and that at 1 January, the start of its financial year, it had in issue 20 million ordinary shares of 25p each and that on 1 October it issued a further 4 million 25p ordinary shares. What is the EPS for 20X5? The answer depends on the nature of the issue, specifically whether it was a scrip (or bonus) issue or whether the issue was for cash (or other consideration) and, if for cash, etc., whether the issue was at, or below, the market price.

Scrip issue

A scrip issue does not raise extra cash and merely represents a rearrangement of the equity interest in a company in that a transfer is made from reserves to equity share capital. There are simply more shares in issue at the end of the year than there were at the beginning and, hence, to show the EPS appropriate to the new capital structure, all that is required is to apportion the earnings over the shares in issue at the year end, 24 million, and thus the EPS is (£2 000 000 ÷ 24 000 000) × 100 = 8.3p.

To assist comparability, the EPS for the corresponding period should be adjusted accordingly. Similar considerations apply if shares are split into shares of a smaller nominal value.

Issue at full market price

Let us now assume that the issue of shares was made at the full market price, while recognising that in practice such an issue is nowadays a rare event, as most issues for cash take the form of rights issues to existing shareholders at a price below that which prevails on the

---

[23] FRS 14, p. 48.

market. To calculate the EPS where there has been an issue at the full market price all that is necessary is to calculate the weighted average number of shares in issue in the course of the year and divide the result into the total earnings of the year. The average is weighted to take account of the timing of the share issue.

In this case the company had 20 million shares in issue for 9 months and 24 million for 3 months. The appropriate weightings to be applied are hence $\frac{3}{4}$ and $\frac{1}{4}$ and the weighted average is

$\frac{3}{4} \times 20\,000\,000 + \frac{1}{4} \times 24\,000\,000 = 21\,000\,000$, while the new EPS is ($£2\,000\,000/21\,000\,000$)

$\times 100 = 9.5$p.

It will be noted that this figure exceeds the 8.3p per share in the scrip issue example and it will be instructive to consider why this is so. A company which makes a scrip issue raises no extra resources and hence, all other things being equal, will not increase its earnings. Thus, the only effect of the scrip issue is to divide the earnings over a greater number of shares. In contrast, if shares are issued for cash, extra resources are obtained which, it is hoped, will increase earnings in the future. If the new investment generates the same rate of return as the existing assets of the business, then, all other things being equal, the EPS after an issue at the full market price will be the same as that which prevailed before the issue. However, in practice it will take some time to deploy the additional resources and in the first instance the additional cash will earn a small or even a negative return, hence the issue of shares for cash will normally reduce the EPS (from that which applied before the issue) until the new investment comes on stream.

Rights issue

A rights issue lies somewhere between the two extremes of a scrip issue and an issue at the full market price in that it combines elements of both, since while additional cash is raised the original shares lose some of their value.

In order to distinguish between the two elements of a rights issue it is necessary to find what is called the *theoretical ex-rights price*. This is the price per share following the issue which would make the stock market value of the company immediately after the rights issue equal to the sum of the market value before the announcement of the issue and the proceeds of the rights issue.[24] Once the theoretical ex-rights price is determined, the EPS calculation can be made on the assumption that there were two transactions: a scrip issue followed by an issue at the new market price.[25]

Let us assume that a company, RIG plc, has in issue 12 000 shares which had a market price of £2 and eight months after the start of the year RIG makes a rights issue of one for every three shares held (a 1 for 3 issue) at a discount of 25 per cent, i.e. 4000 shares were issued at a price of £1.50 each, so raising £6000. The theoretical ex-rights price, x, is given by:

$$16\,000x = 12\,000 \times £2 + 4000 \times £1.5$$
$$16\,000x = £24\,000 + £6000$$
$$x = £1.875$$

We need to find the size of a hypothetical scrip issue which would, all other things being equal, have reduced the market price per share from £2 to £1.875.

---

[24] The actual price per share following the issue is not likely to be equal to the theoretical ex-rights price as the actual price is likely to be affected by the market's expectations of future results and dividend policy. It might, for example, be thought that the total dividend per share would at least be held constant following the issue.

[25] Or the other way round.

Let X be the number of shares in issue following the scrip issue:

$$\text{then } X \times £1.875 = 12\,000 \times £2$$

$$\text{or } X = 12\,000 \times \frac{£2}{£1.875} = 12\,800$$

Thus the scrip issue would be such as to increase the number of shares in issue from 12 000 to $(12\,000 \times 2/1.875)$. We should note that the factor 2/1.875 is the:

$$\frac{\textbf{Actual market price (or fair value) before the issue}}{\textbf{Theoretical ex-rights price}}$$

We can now divide the rights issue into its two elements (a) the scrip issue and (b) the issue at the market price (or, in this case, at the theoretical ex-rights price).

Thus:

(i) The company started with 12 000 shares.
(ii) The hypothetical scrip issue increased the number of shares to $12\,000 \times 2/1.875$, i.e. an additional 800 shares.
(iii) The hypothetical issue of 3200 shares at £1.875 raised £6000.

Thus the company finished with 16 000 shares.

To calculate the EPS, it is necessary to remember that, in the case of a scrip issue, the earnings were simply divided by the number of shares ranking for dividend at the end of the year (irrespective of the date of the scrip issue), whereas in the case of an issue at market price the average number of shares was used (weighted on the basis of the time of the issue). To combine these two methods we draw a line after the hypothetical scrip issue and say that at the end of eight months there were 12 800 $(12\,000 \times 2/1.875)$ shares in issue but, as the increase was due to a scrip issue, we will calculate the EPS on the assumption that the company had 12 800 shares for the whole of the eight-month period. Thus, the weighted average number of shares will be calculated on the basis that the company had $12\,000 \times 2/1.875$ shares for eight months and 16 000 shares for four months. The weighted average number of shares is then:

$$12\,000 \times \frac{2}{1.875} \times \frac{2}{3} + 16\,000 \times \frac{1}{3} = 13\,867$$

and, if the earnings for the year were £1664, the EPS would be 12p.

The method described above is that set out in Para. 24 of FRS 14 which states that the factor that should be used to inflate the number of shares prior to the issue to adjust for the bonus element should be:

$$\frac{\textbf{Fair value per share immediately before the exercise of the rights}}{\textbf{Theoretical ex-rights value per share}}$$

In order to aid comparability, the EPS figure for the prior year needs to be adjusted to take account of the hypothetical scrip issue. If 12 000 shares were in issue for the whole of the preceding year then, for the purposes of restating the EPS, this figure needs to be increased to 12 800, i.e. to 12 000 × (fair value)/(theoretical ex-rights price). Actually, a short-cut can be taken as the same result can be obtained by multiplying the original EPS by the reciprocal of the above ratio, i.e. by (theoretical ex-rights price)/(fair value).[26]

Dilution

If, at the balance sheet date, the company has contracted to issue shares at some time in the future, the effect may be to dilute (reduce) the EPS in future. The same might happen if at the balance sheet date the company has already issued shares which have not yet ranked for dividend (and hence which have been excluded from the EPS calculation) but which may do so in the future. In such cases FRS 14 requires that the fully diluted EPS be shown on the face of the profit and loss account together with the basic EPS. In addition:

(a) equal prominence should be given to both the basic and the fully diluted EPS;
(b) the basis of calculation of the basic and the diluted EPS figure should be disclosed.

Examples of financial instruments that might be converted to ordinary shares include options, warrants and convertible preference shares.

Note the use of the word *diluted*: if the potential change in the capital structure will lead to an increase in the EPS there is no need to calculate and display a different EPS figure. The test of whether a potential ordinary share is dilutive can be illustrated by reference to the conversion of preference shares.

There are two impacts on the EPS figure of such a change. The profit available to equity shareholders will increase because of the elimination of the preference dividend and this will increase the EPS but, as a result of the operation, there are more equity shares in issue and this will reduce the EPS. It will all depend on where the balance falls as to whether the convertible preference shares need to be treated as *dilutive potential ordinary shares*. Consider the following example.

Suppose that a company has a net profit available to ordinary (equity) shareholders of £2 million and has 5 million shares outstanding. The EPS is 40 pence.

Further suppose that the company has in issue £3 million convertible 15% preference shares that are convertible:

Case 1, at one ordinary for one preference;
Case 2, at one ordinary for three preference.

In either case the conversion would increase the net profit attributable to ordinary shareholders by £0.45 to £2.45 but in case 1 the number of ordinary shares would increase to 8 million and the EPS would become 31 pence, while in case 2 the number of ordinary shares would only increase to 6 million which would produce an EPS of 41 pence.

Hence, only in case 1 do we have dilutive potential ordinary shares and would be required to disclose a full diluted EPS alongside the basic EPS.

In determining whether potential ordinary shares are, or are not, dilutive the yardstick to be used is the profit or loss from continuing operations. Since by definition discontinued operations have ceased they are not relevant to the question of whether or not the issue of the shares will of itself reduce EPS.

---

[26] Let P be the original EPS, P' the restated EPS, E the earnings, S the orginal number of shares in issue and F the ratio of the cum rights to the theoretical ex-rights price. Then:

$$P = \frac{E}{S} \text{ and } P' = \frac{E}{SF} = P \times \frac{1}{F}$$

If a company has more than class of potential ordinary in existence the order in which the exercise is done may affect the outcome. Therefore, in order to maximise the dilution of basic EPS, each issue or series of potential ordinary shares is considered in sequence from the most dilutive to the least dilutive.[27]

Contingently issuable shares

As the name suggests *contingently issuable shares* are those which will be issued depending on the outcome of a single event or a series of events. The standard makes it clear in a number of places that the EPS measure that emerges from the application of the rules of FRS 14 is a historical measure and not a prediction about the future. To give an example, suppose that a group of senior executives are offered shares if the average profit of a three-year period exceeds £40 million (assume for the sake of simplicity that a loss of any amount would be treated as zero for the purposes of the calculation) and that the profits for the first two years of the period amount to £115 million, that is £5 million short of the target. It does seem pretty certain that, short of an unexpected disaster, the goal will be achieved and the shares issued, but FRS 14 would not take these shares into account, as it treats the end of the reporting period as the end of the contingency period. The ASB accepts that there are arguments for adopting a different approach based on a projection of the future, but comes down against mainly, it seems, because it is not the method chosen by the IASB.

FRED 26 *Earnings per Share*

There are no differences in substance between FRS 14 and FRED 26; as we stated earlier the basic approach has stood the test of time. Perhaps the more significant changes relate to disclosure:

- FRED 26 proposes that basic and diluted EPS figures for both the net profit or loss for the period and also the profit and loss from continuing operations should be published on the face of the profit and loss account. FRS 14 does not require the publication of the figures for continuing operations.
- FRS 14 encouraged entities to provide additional EPS amounts which could be published in any part of the financial statements, the only stipulation being that they were not given greater prominence than the basic and diluted figures. Under the provisions of the FRED, all additional measures would need to appear in the notes, the only exception being EPS figures for discontinued operations.

Compliance with the international standard

The corresponding international standard is IAS 33 *Earnings per Share*, which is also under review. The text of FRED 26 is based closely on the text of the proposed revised IAS 33 and there are no material differences between the two sets of proposals.

[27] FRS 14, Para. 61.

Related party disclosures

Under traditional economic theory, a company is assumed to act in the interests of its owners, the equity shareholders, but, as we have seen in earlier chapters, many people have an interest in the affairs of a company and often the interests of different groups and individuals will conflict with one another. Companies must be managed and, in practice, directors and managers have to learn how to deal with these conflicting interests. Indeed, the directors and managers may well find themselves in a position where decisions which have to be taken on behalf of the company may be of considerable relevance, and possibly of benefit, to themselves in a private capacity. As has often been noted, it is a question of which hat is being worn, and the law and accounting standards try to ensure adequate disclosure of directors' interests and the benefits that they receive.

Another obvious example of a possible conflict of interest is where one company is controlled by an individual or another entity and enters into transactions with that 'related party' which are in the interest of the other party, rather than in the interest of the company itself.

The Department of Trade and Industry has investigated many cases involving related party transactions, including that of Pergamon Press Limited in 1969. The Chairman of Pergamon Press was Robert Maxwell and it is perhaps no coincidence that the impetus for related party disclosures stemmed from the scandal involving Robert Maxwell, Mirror Group Newspapers, Maxwell Communications Corporation and the Mirror Group Pension Funds that eventually surfaced in the early 1990s.

Various branches of the law, including company, trust and criminal elements, take more than a passing interest in the abuses which can flow from the existence of related party transactions, but our purpose here is confined to the disclosure issues involved.

There are two reasons why disclosure is required:

1 If transactions are not at arm's length, the users of financial statements may be misled; in particular, the financial statements may not provide a satisfactory basis for the prediction of future results. This would, of course, affect both parties to the transaction with the results of one party being overstated and those of the other party being understated. Disclosure might indicate the extent to which those with a legitimate interest in the company have gained or lost as a consequence.
2 Even in the absence of transactions, knowledge of the existence of a related party which controls the reporting entity will warn users that they may be subject to the effects of such transactions in future.

ED 46 *Disclosure of Related Party Transactions*, published by the ASC in 1989, proposed that companies should disclose abnormal transactions with related parties. By restricting the disclosure to abnormal transactions, it hoped to avoid lengthy disclosures. However, many commentators stressed the impossibility of distinguishing between normal and abnormal transactions and, when FRED 8 *Related Party Disclosures*, was issued in 1994, it followed international practice by requiring disclosure of all related party transactions. Both IAS 24 *Related Party Disclosures* (reformatted in July 1994), and FRS 8 *Related Party Disclosures* (November 1995), adopt this approach as has the exposure draft with the same name, FRED 25, issued in May 2002.

FRS 8 *Related Party Disclosures*

FRS 8 has as its objective:

> . . . to ensure that financial statements contain disclosures necessary to draw attention to the possibility that the reported financial position and results may have been affected by the existence of related parties and by material transactions with them. (Para. 1)

Thus it is a standard concerned with disclosure rather than measurement, although the existence of the standard may, of course, affect the amounts shown in the financial statements where the need for disclosure causes changes in the behaviour of the related parties.

The required disclosure may be summarised under two headings:

1 *Disclosure of existence and name of controlling party.* Where the reporting entity is controlled by another party, it is required to disclose the relationship and the name of the controlling party and, if different, that of the ultimate controlling party. This information is required whether or not any transactions have taken place between the controlling parties and the reporting entity in a particular year. Even if no transactions have occurred, the existence of a relationship which may give rise to such transactions in future is important information for those using the financial statements (Para. 5).

   For the purpose of FRS 8, control is defined as 'the ability to direct the financial and operating policies of an entity with a view to gaining economic benefits from its activities' (Para. 2.2).

2 *Disclosure of material transactions with related parties.* The reporting entity should disclose material transactions with a related party, irrespective of whether a price is charged, and this disclosure should include:
   (a) the names of the transacting related parties;
   (b) a description of the relationship between the parties;
   (c) a description of the transactions;
   (d) the amounts involved;
   (e) any other elements of the transaction necessary for an understanding of the financial statements;
   (f) the amounts due to or from related parties at the balance sheet date and provisions for doubtful debts due from such parties at that date;
   (g) amounts written off in the period in respect of debts due to or from related parties (Para. 6).

Related party transactions include purchases and sales of goods, purchases or sales of property, rendering or receiving of services, agency arrangements, licence agreements and management contracts. However, in order to avoid excessive detail, the standard normally permits transactions to be disclosed on an aggregated basis.

The definition of related parties

The purpose of the standard is clear; all that remains is to examine the definition of related parties. The key element in the definition is that the relationship between two or more parties is such that, through either influence or control, the interest of one of the parties may be subordinated to the interests of one of the other parties. In the words of FRS 8:

Two or more parties are related parties when at any time during the financial period:

(i)　one party has direct or indirect control of the other party; or
(ii)　the parties are subject to common control from the same source; or
(iii)　one party has influence over the financial and operating policies of the other party to an extent that that other party might be inhibited from pursuing at all times its own separate interests; or
(iv)　the parties, in entering a transaction, are subject to influence from the same source to such an extent that one of the parties to the transaction has subordinated its own separate interests. (Para. 2)

The standard provides two lists of related parties. One list consists of those which are automatically deemed to be related parties; the other of those who are presumed to be related parties unless there is evidence that neither party has influenced the financial and operating policies of the other in such a way as to inhibit the pursuit of its own separate interests. The first list therefore consists of those who are automatically guilty, whereas the second consists of those who are presumed guilty unless they can prove their innocence, a task which seems, philosophically, rather difficult. The lists are summarised in Table 11.3.

Table 11.3 **Lists of related parties**

Automatically related parties	*Presumed related parties unless there is evidence to the contrary*
Parent, subsidiaries and fellow subsidiaries	Key management of reporting entity or its parent
Associates and joint ventures	Person owning or able to control over 20 per cent of voting rights
Investors or venturers in respect of which the reporting entity is an associate or joint venture	Each person acting in concert in a way to exercise control or influence
Directors of the entity or its parent	An entity managing or managed by the reporting entity under a management contract
Pension fund for the benefit of employees in the reporting entity or a related party	
	Other presumed related parties
	Members of the close family of any individual deemed or presumed to be a related party. Partnerships, companies, trusts or other entities in which any individual or member of the close family deemed or presumed to be a related party has a controlling interest

Notes:

(a)　Where the parent is itself a subsidiary, the references to parent include the ultimate parent as well as any intermediate parent.

(b)　Close members of the family of an individual are those family members, or members of the same household, who may be expected to influence, or be influenced by, that person in their dealings with the reporting entity.

The lists are long but a number of exemptions are granted. So, for example, parties which can influence the behaviour of the reporting entity through their economic or commercial relationship with it are excluded. Thus, Para. 4 of the standard makes it clear that disclosure is not required of transactions with providers of finance, utility companies, government bodies, customers and suppliers, even where there is economic dependence. It recognises that such relationships may be extremely important but only requires disclosure if the entities mentioned fall within the definitions of related parties.

Fellow group members are obviously related parties but it would be extremely burdensome to report in detail on transactions between group members. Hence Para. 3 allows a number of exemptions which may be summarised as follows:

(a) It is not necessary to disclose in consolidated financial statements any inter-group transactions which have been eliminated on consolidation although it is, of course, necessary to disclose transactions with other related parties.
(b) It is not necessary to disclose related party transactions in a parent company's own financial statements where these are presented with consolidated financial statements.
(c) Where a subsidiary undertaking has 90 per cent or more of its voting controlled within a group, it is not necessary to disclose transactions with group entities provided that consolidated financial statements including the subsidiary undertaking are publicly available.

It also includes two other more specific exemptions:

(d) It is not necessary to disclose pension contributions paid to a pension fund.
(e) It is not necessary to disclose emoluments in respect of services as an employee of the reporting entity.

There are no exemptions for small companies and it is perhaps not surprising that no such exemptions are envisaged.

Materiality

The definition of related parties is widely drawn and the potential disclosure under FRS 8 is enormous. Are there ways of reducing the volume? The early approach of only reporting abnormal items was rejected but there still remains our old friend materiality, which might be relied on to reduce some of the noise. FRS 8, Para. 20, specifically refers to materiality by stating that 'transactions are material when their disclosure might reasonably be expected to influence the decisions made by the users of general purpose financial statements'. This could be used to avoid reporting many transactions with related parties but there is a sting in the tail. Paragraph 20 goes on to state that materiality must be judged, not only in terms of the reporting entity, but also in relation to the other related party where that party is a director, a key manager or other person who can influence the entity, a member of their close family or an entity controlled by the individual or close family member. Thus an amount that is quite small from the point of view of the reporting entity might still have to be reported if it is judged to be large from the point of view of the other party!

FRED 25 *Related Party Transactions*

While the basic principles are maintained there are a number of differences between FRED 25 and FRS 8, the most significant one being that the exposure draft does not require the publication of the names of the transacting related parties.

In general, FRED 25 gives less guidance, or perhaps is less directive, than the FRS in a number of areas including the determination of the nature of influence that would trigger related party status. The exposure draft states that such a relationship exists where a party has an interest that gives it a significant influence over an entity, where significant influence is defined as the power to participate in the financial and operating policy decisions of an entity. FRS 8 goes further by describing the necessary level of influence as being such that the interest of one of the parties may be subordinated to the interests of one of the other parties.

The exposure draft does not refer to materiality in the context of disclosure and hence the more general policies relating to materiality will apply. This means that materiality will be judged only in the context of the reporting entity and not in relation to the circumstances of the related party.

Other changes include:

- only wholly owned subsidiaries would be exempt from the requirement to disclose transactions with group entities; the cut-off point under FRS 8 is 90 per cent;
- the exemption from the requirement to disclose pension contributions is not included in FRED 25.[28]

Compliance with the international standard

FRED 25 is based on the text of the proposed revision of IAS 24, *Related Party Disclosures*; the only significant difference is that FRED 25, unlike the proposed amended IAS 24, includes a provision for the identification of the identity of the controlling party. IAS 24 only requires a statement that there is a controlling party. The ASB is of the view (which is not unreasonable) that the identity of the controlling party is relevant to the users. While the ASB has, with this exception, based FRED 25 on the IASB's proposals it continued to press its views that a number of the provisions of FRS 8 should be retained, including the clearer guidance on the degree of influence that constitutes control, the definition of materiality, the naming of the transacting related parties and the retention of the 90 per cent cut-off point for allowing exemptions for subsidiaries.[29]

Part C Share-based payments

The practice of acquiring goods and services through the issue of shares, or the promise of issuing shares, has greatly increased in recent years. While this method of payment is occasionally used to purchase goods and other services, it is most commonly used to reward employees, particularly the directors and other managers of large and listed companies. We will, in this section, concentrate on this use of share-based payments but readers should be aware that the basic principles also apply to the use of this device for other purposes.

In general, share-based payments are used to encourage executives and other employees to strive to ensure that shareholder wealth is maximised and to encourage staff to remain with the company. Hence payment is often only triggered if a target related to the value of shares is achieved and is only payable if staff members serve for a specified minimum period.

---

[28] This is of no great moment as the contributions have to be disclosed under the terms of FRS 17.

[29] Letter dated 4 October 2002 from Mary Keegan, chairman of the ASB, to Sir David Tweedie, Chairman of the IASB: **www.asb.org.uk**.

Different types of share-based payment

Schemes vary greatly in terms of both their complexity and their generosity. Some of the main variants are described below but it should be noted that in practice a scheme may comprise variations of or combinations of these plans.[30] In particular the schemes vary depending upon:

- whether the employees are promised a cash payment based on the excess of the market value of the shares at a specified future date over a stated price, often called share appreciation rights (SARs), or whether they are given an option to acquire shares in the employing company at a stated price;
- the extent to which stated performance criteria have to be achieved if the employee is to be entitled to benefit from the scheme. Performance criteria may include movements in share prices, return on equity or earnings per share growth. Share option schemes that do not require the attainment of targets are called 'plain vanilla' share options while those that do require target achievement are called performance-vesting schemes.

Existing practice

Prior to the publication of FRED 31, the only significant guidance offered in the UK was through UITF Abstract 17, *Employee share schemes*, revised in October 2000.[31] This required that, where share options are awarded to employees, a cost should be recognised in the financial statements. The minimum amount of this cost should be the difference between the fair value of the shares at the date of the grant and the amount of the exercise price, that is the consideration, if any, that the employees would be required to pay on exercise of the option. The Abstract takes the view that 'normally, the fair value of the shares will be estimated to be the market value of the shares at that time' (Para. 5) and this 'intrinsic value' is often very low or zero because, generally, the exercise price is equal to the market price at the date of the grant. The whole point of the scheme is, of course, to encourage executives to bring about a substantial increase in market value.

There is no guidance on share-based payments made to non-employees, other than the general requirements of FRS 4 that the issue of shares and warrants should be reported on the basis of the net proceeds received.

A major advance was the publication by the ASB of a Discussion Paper, *Share-based payments*, in July 2000, a document based on a discussion paper produced by a G4+1 working group. The main recommendation of these discussion papers was that where an entity obtains goods and services, including services from employees, and payment is in the form of shares or share options, the transaction should be measured at the fair value of the shares or options at the vesting date. The vesting date is the date upon which the other party (the employee) has performed all the services necessary to become unconditionally entitled to the shares or options.[32]

---

[30] A more detailed description can be found in the ASB Discussion Paper, *Share-based payments*, issued in July 2002.

[31] There was also UITF Abstract 13 *Accounting for ESOP Trusts*, which was concerned with the treatment of shares held on trust for employees in the period before they vested in the employees.

[32] ASB Discussion Paper, *Share-based payments*, Para. 8.1.

Since in many cases the fair value of an option at the vesting date is considerably higher than its intrinsic value at the grant date, the adoption of this proposal would have resulted in a considerable impact on the reported operating profits of companies issuing such options (see p. 318).

FRED 31 *Share-based Payments*

FRED 31 builds on some, but not all, of the recommendations of the discussion papers and is based upon an IASB exposure draft ED 2 *Share-based Payments*, issued at the same time in November 2002. Like the discussion papers, FRED 31 proposes that the expense should be based on the fair value of the shares or options but differs in that it proposes that the fair value should be measured at the grant date rather than the vesting date:

> The grant date being the date at which the entity and another party (including an employee) agree to a share-based payment arrangement, being when the entity and the counterparty have a shared understanding of the terms and conditions of the agreement.[33]

We shall discuss the implications of the different dates later in this section but we should start by describing the ways in which the fair value of an option can be measured. There are a number of models that are used to value options, of which the best known is the Black–Scholes model. While this Black–Scholes model is referred to in the commentary section of the exposure draft, entities are free to use other models. Both the IASB and the ASB make it clear that the proposed standard should focus on principles rather than on prescribing extensive application guidance which 'would be likely to become outdated'.[34] Any model would have to take into account variables such as the following:

- exercise price of the option;
- current market price of the share;
- volatility of the underlying shares;
- dividend yield;
- level of interest rates;
- time period during which the option can be exercised.

Equity-settled share-based payment transaction

Most employee share option schemes are based on share-based payments where 'the entity receives goods or services as consideration for equity instruments (including shares or share options)'. [35]

We will introduce the basic principles using one of the examples contained in Appendix B to FRED 31.

An entity grants 100 options to each of its 500 employees. Each grant is conditional on:

- the employee working for the entity for three years;
- the entity achieving an 18 per cent increase in its share price by the end of the three-year service period.

---

[33] FRED 31, p. 97.
[34] FRED 31, Para. BC 182.
[35] FRED 31, p. 96.

The entity estimates that the value of each option is Currency Units (CU) 15[36] before adjusting for the probability of staff leaving before the end of the period or for the probability that the target increase of 18 per cent will not be achieved.

Let us assume that the entity estimates that 20 per cent of its staff will not stay for the required three-year period and further that they will leave at a steady rate over the period; let us also assume that the entity estimates that the probability that the performance target will not be met is 0.85. On the basis of these, possibly heroic, assumptions the total fair value of the options at the grant date is given by the product of the estimated number of staff in post at the end of the period, the probability that the target will be achieved and the fair value of the options that are awarded to each individual:

$$500 \times 0.80 \times 0.85 \times CU15 \times 100 = CU510\,000$$

We also have to work out the expected number of years of service that will be supplied by the employees. Twenty per cent of the employees are expected to leave during the period and, as we are assuming that the departures will occur evenly over the period, we will expect that the 100 leavers will provide $100 \times 1.5 = 150$ years of service that together with the 1200 years of service from those who stay the course gives a total of 1350. Thus the estimated fair value of each unit (or year) of service is CU510 000/1350 = CU377.77.

Readers will note the nature of the assumptions that have to be made in order to arrive at this figure. First, it is necessary to determine the fair value of each option, here CU15, using an option-pricing model. This is a difficult task. Next it is necessary to estimate the rate of staff turnover, the rate of which is likely to be affected by changes in general economic conditions as well as by the introduction of the share option scheme itself. It is also necessary to estimate the probability of the agreed target not being achieved and it is difficult to see how a substantial element of objectivity can be introduced into this process. The nature and magnitude of the estimates that have to be made provides strong ammunition for those who are opposing the implementation of the proposals.

Let us suppose that the entity actually receives 430 units (years) of service in year 1, 400 in year 2 and 375 in year 3. Then the expense that will be recognised in each of the three years is as given below.

		CU
Year 1	430 × CU 377.77	162 441
Year 2	400 × CU 377.77	151 108
Year 3	375 × CU 377.77	141 664
Total		455 213

The actual expense recognised is less than the original estimate of CU510 000 because fewer units of service were provided than had been estimated; if more units of service had been provided the total would have been greater.

Each year the profit and loss account would be debited and equity credited with the appropriate amount. The element of equity that would be credited would in some countries be described as 'other equity' but in the UK would probably be described as ' potential share options'.

We now come to the end of the vesting period. Let us first assume that the financial target of 18 per cent growth in the share price has been achieved so that the share options can be

---

[36] In this more international world the ASB now expresses monetary amounts as Currency Units (CUs).

exercised. Then, in respect of those options that are exercised, cash would be debited with the consideration, if any, and share capital credited. Similarly a transfer would be made between other equity (share options), and share capital and share premium, where appropriate, of the amount previously credited in respect of the options that are taken up.

What if the options are not taken up, either because the performance target is not met or because some employees do not avail themselves of the right to acquire the shares? The answer which is perhaps surprising, is nothing. The argument is that the service has been rendered and that the consideration for the service was the fair value of the options granted. The lapsing of the option does not represent a gain to the entity because there is no change in the entity's net assets. The lapsing of the option merely represents the transfer of one type of equity, share options, to another part of the equity interest and hence the Board believes that the only accounting entry that would be required is a movement within equity to reflect the fact that the options are no longer outstanding.[37]

Had the Board adopted the discussion paper's proposal that the fair values should be calculated on their vesting day then it would have been necessary to make an estimate each year of the accrual based on the fair value of the shares or options at the year end. Consequently the charge for each year would be comprised of the charge for the services of the employees during the year together with a charge or credit reflecting changes in the previous accrual.[38] The Board rejected this approach, for the same reason as was advanced for not adjusting for cancelled options, that the changes to the accrual represent changes within equity and should not affect the profit and loss account.[39]

Cash-settled share-based payment transactions

With these schemes, the employees are paid in cash but the amount of the payment depends on the change in the price of the entity's shares or other equity interests. Here the accrual at any one time is the best estimate, using an option-pricing model, that will have to be paid to the employees still eligible under the scheme. As such schemes involve a potential reduction in resources through the payment of cash, adjustments to accruals are dealt with through the profit and loss account.[40] However, the Board believes that users will find it relevant to know the extent to which the charge for the year has been affected by changes in the estimates of fair values so Para. 52(b) requires the disclosure of the portion of the expense that is attributable to the transaction being measured as a cash-settled rather than an equity-settled transaction.

Other aspects of FRED 31

We have in this section concentrated on the basic principles underlying FRED 31 but it is a long document which has to deal with more complex arrangements including repricing, cancellation of schemes, reload features and share-based transactions which involve a choice between cash and equity settlements. Readers who wish to pursue this subject in more depth are referred to FRED 31 itself.

---

[37] FRED 31, Paras 16 and BC 205.
[38] ASB Discussion Paper *Share-based payments*, Para. 8.4.
[39] FRED 31, Para. BC 99.
[40] An example of a cash-settled scheme is provided in Appendix C to FRED 31.

The response to the Discussion Paper and FRED 31

FRED 31 is one of the more controversial exposure drafts to be issued, for the adoption of its principles will have a mighty impact on the reported profits of those companies that make extensive use of share-based incentive schemes, and has had a significant impact on those companies which have adopted it on a voluntary basis. For example, had Microsoft applied the principles in its financial statements for the year ended 30 June 2001, its net income would have fallen by 29 per cent from $7.7 billion to $5.5 billion.[41]

The proposals set out in the discussion paper that an expense should be recognised received strong support from the UK investment community but others, especially companies whose profits would be seriously eroded, expressed strong opposition. The Finance Director of Logica, for example, said that if the proposals were to be implemented, it would make 'many companies think very hard if they want to be in Britain'.[42] Similar differences in view are found in many other countries and, because of the vehemence of the opposition, it would be difficult for any country to issue a standard unilaterally. This is why the IASB sees this as a 'leadership project' which is designed to take political pressure off national standard setters. There are those who see the outcome of this particular battle as a major factor in establishing global accounting standards and believe that the credibility of the IASB will be severely dented if it is not able to impose this standard.[43]

The IASB proposes to introduce a new standard for periods beginning on or after 1 January 2004 so it remains to be seen whether or not it is successful in this extremely controversial area.

Summary

We have in this chapter introduced a number of stratagems that have been adopted by standard setters, negatively, to minimise the possibility of abuse through the manipulation of figures and, positively, to reconfigure the financial statements in order to provide users with more relevant information that will, in particular, help them predict future results.

We saw how FRS 3 built on its predecessor SSAP 6 in outlawing reserve accounting by ensuring that, in general, income and expenditure is reflected in a profit and loss account or statement of total recognised gains and losses, rather than being taken directly to reserves. In addition, FRS 3 clarified the way in which the results of discontinued operations should be reported. This standard also plays an important role in attempting to achieve a move away from a fixation on the 'bottom line', the post-tax profit, to what has been termed an 'information set' approach whereby users are encouraged to adopt a broader perspective when interpreting financial statements. Thus FRS 3 introduced the concept of the statement of total recognised gains and losses that standard setters believe should be treated on a par with the profit and loss account. We also discussed the work that has been done to build on the foundations laid down by FRS 3.

The issues surrounding four of the topics covered in the chapter, segmental reporting, accounting for post balance sheet events, earnings per share and related party disclosures are

---

[41] William A. Sahlom, 'Expensing Options Solves Nothing', *Harvard Business Review*, December 2002.

[42] *Independent on Sunday*, 3 June 2001, p. B1.

[43] Ron Paterson, 'Biting the Bullet', *Accountancy*, January 2003.

more pragmatic than theoretical. While the last three of these are currently the subject of review, it is unlikely that fundamental changes will be made to existing standards. The same might also be said of segmental reporting, which is the only topic covered in the chapter that is not yet being actively pursued as part of the convergence programme.

The most controversial subject covered in the chapter is share-based payments. This, as we saw, involves a number of interesting issues concerned with distinguishing between items that should appear in the operating statements and those that would only involve movements within equity. We also noted that, for many entities, the introduction of the accounting treatment proposed in FRED 31 would have a significant impact on reported earnings and, not surprisingly, this has generated considerable opposition. The use of share-based payment undoubtedly has a cost which should be recognised in the financial statements and the issue of a standard on this subject will be a true test of the ability of the IASB to set global accounting standards in controversial areas of accounting.

Recommended reading

J. Coulton, 'Accounting for executive stock options: a case study in avoiding tough decisions' *Australian Accounting Review*, Vol. 12, No. 1, March 2002.

IATA (in association with KPMG) *Segmental Reporting*, Montreal, IATA, 2000.

S. Lin, 'The association between analysts' forecasts revisions and earning components: the evidence of FRS 3' *British Accounting Review*, Vol. 34, No. 1, 2002.

Excellent up-to-date and detailed reading on the subject matter of this chapter and on much of the contents of this book is provided by the most recent edition of:

UK and International GAAP, A. Wilson, M. Davies, M. Curtis and G. Wilkinson-Riddle (eds), Ernst & Young, Butterworths Tolley, London. At the time of writing, the latest edition is the 7th, published in 2001.

Questions

11.1 The introduction of FRS 3, *Reporting Financial Performance*, has resulted in a considerably expanded profit and loss account with related disclosures and a new primary statement. The standard is intended to be based on the 'all-inclusive' concept of income.

Requirements
(a) **Discuss why FRS 3 was introduced and whether it has achieved its objectives.**

(7 marks)

(b) **Describe how the standard has implemented the 'all-inclusive' concept of income.**

(3 marks)

ICAEW, Financial Reporting, November 1994   (**10 marks**)

11.2 Discuss whether the range of information provided by the implementation of FRS 3, *Reporting financial performance*, is helpful to users of published financial statements.

ICAEW, Financial Reporting, May 1998   (**10 marks**)

11.3 FRS 3, *Reporting financial performance*, significantly supplements the financial information required under statutory formats.

Requirements

(a) Discuss the effect of the following disclosures on users' understanding of the financial performance of a limited company:

    (i) analysis of turnover down to operating profit between continuing operations, discontinued operations and acquisitions in the period;

    (ii) statement of total recognised gains and losses; and

    (iii) note of historical cost profits and losses.   (13 marks)

(b) Discuss how disaggregated data required by the disclosures in SSAP 25, *Segmental reporting*, assist users to analyse and interpret published financial information.

                                                 (7 marks)

ICAEW, Financial Reporting, June 2001   **(20 marks)**

11.4 A Ltd is a company which specialises in the processing of canned beans and canned spaghetti for sale to retail shops. The canned beans are processed from beans bought in directly from UK farmers. The canned spaghetti is processed from pasta which is purchased from suppliers in Italy. Processing and canning take place at one of two factories in the United Kingdom, one factory dealing with beans and one with spaghetti. Each factory maintains separate financial statements in order to produce a monthly operating report for Head Office.

Once canned, the products are transferred to one of four distribution centres (two centres per factory). The distribution centres (which also maintain their own individual financial statements) are used to transfer the products to shops and supermarkets following orders for sales. The accounting year end of the company is 31 December.

On 30 November 1995, a decision was made to rationalise the business. Due to adverse exchange rate movements it was decided to discontinue the processing and sale of canned spaghetti, and concentrate exclusively on canned beans. The consequence of this decision was that the factory which processed pasta into spaghetti and one of the associated distribution centres would be sold, and the majority of the personnel employed at these locations made redundant. It was decided to commence running down the processing operations and the distribution operations in the factory and the distribution centre to be closed on 15 January 1996, with an expectation to complete the closure by 31 March 1996. Apart from carrying out extensive negotiations with relevant Trades Unions regarding redundancy packages, no other closure activities were to be commenced before 15 January 1996.

On 30 November 1995, A Ltd also decided to rationalise its distribution operation. The rationalisation included closing one of the four centres (as noted above) and redefining the areas covered by the remaining centres (so that the three remaining centres took on the distribution formerly carried out by the four centres, with the work relating only to baked beans). The timetable for the rationalisation of the distribution operation in the three remaining centres was identical to that for the closure of the factory and the fourth centre (rundown of spaghetti distribution and reallocation of beans distribution commencing 15 January 1996, rationalisation complete by 31 March 1996).

You are the Chief Accountant of A Ltd, and one of the directors has recently visited you to discuss the accounting treatment of the rationalisation. The director is unsure as to whether the rationalisation will have any impact on the financial statements for the year ended 31 December 1995 given that the programme did not actually commence until 15 January 1996. The director is aware that there is an accounting standard which deals with the issue of discontinued operations but is unaware of any relevant details. The 1995 financial statements are currently in the course of preparation and are expected to be formally approved by the directors at the April 1996 board meeting. For the purposes of this question, you should assume that today's date is 29 February 1996.

Requirements

Write a memorandum for the Board of Directors which:

(a) explains how a discontinued operation is defined in FRS 3;   (6 marks)

(b) outlines the accounting treatment (if any) of the decision to close the factories and one of the distribution centres and to rationalise the operations of the remaining distribution centres, in the financial statements of A Ltd for the year ended 31 December 1995.

Your explanation should encompass the treatment in the balance sheet and profit and loss account and any additional information which is required in the notes to the financial statements.   (14 marks)

CIMA, Financial Reporting, May 1996   (**20 marks**)

11.5 Crail plc has the following matters outstanding before finalising its published financial statements for the year ended 30 April 2002.

(1) The company sold its European business operations, excluding the fixed assets, on 10 April 2002 at a profit of £500 000. The turnover and operating profit for the year ended 30 April 2002 relating to the European business amounted to £5 million and £100 000 respectively. The disposal of the fixed assets of the European business occurred on 10 May 2002 when a profit of £150 000 was realised. The European operations had been acquired in June 2001 as part of the acquisition of an unincorporated business.

(2) The company changed its accounting policy for research and development expenditure from capitalisation of development expenditure under SSAP 13, *Accounting for research and development*, to writing off all expenditure as incurred. As at 30 April 2002 the company had £400 000 of development expenditure capitalised with movements from 30 April 2001 being:

	£1000
As at 1 May 2001	250
Expenditure in year	200
Amortisation in year	(50)
As at 30 April 2002	400

The company has not yet implemented the new policy.

(3) The company revalued its land and buildings on 1 May 2001 to £5 million (land element – £1 million). The land and buildings were bought for £3 million (land element – £400 000) on 1 July 1997; the buildings had a total useful economic life of 50 years and there has been no change to this following the revaluation. It is company policy to:

– charge a full year's depreciation in the year of acquisition/revaluation;
– transfer the realised element of the revaluation reserve to realised profits annually.

The revaluation has not yet been accounted for but depreciation has been charged in the year ended 30 April 2002 based on historic cost.

(4) The company intends to pay an ordinary dividend of 10% of profits legally distributable.

(5) The company had a total turnover of £25 million and total operating profit of £1 million for the year ended 30 April 2002 before any adjustments for the above items. The company had opening balances of:

	£1000
Profit and loss account	6000
Revaluation reserve	–
Share capital	2000

(6) The taxation charge for the year ended 30 April 2002 is £350 000. No changes to this are required as a result of the above adjustments.

Requirement
Prepare the following disclosures for the financial statements of Crail plc for the year ended 30 April 2002:

> Profit and loss account (relevant extracts only)
> Statement of total recognised gains and losses
> Note of historical cost profits and losses
> Reconciliation of movement in shareholders' funds
> Movement on reserves disclosure note.

ICAEW, Financial Reporting, June 2002   **(20 marks)**

11.6 Glamis plc manufactures, distributes and retails glassware. The following matters relate to its financial statements for the year ended 31 July 1998:

(1) On 25 June 1998, one of the company's factories sustained damage from a freak storm. The cost of repairs in July 1998 was £500 000 and this has been provided for in the financial statements. The company's insurance does not cover this repair.

(2) The company disposed of a fixed asset for £1 million in June 1998. The asset cost £850 000 in August 1994 and had an expected life of five years. The asset was revalued to £900 000 in the financial statements on 1 August 1996; no change to its total useful economic life was recommended. The company does not charge depreciation in the year of disposal of an asset and has based the profit on disposal in the profit and loss account on the carrying value of the asset.

(3) The board of directors decided to close the company's retailing division on the basis of a formal plan submitted by the sales director. The company had accepted a firm offer of £3 million for the retail premises by 31 July 1998. The net book value of the premises was £2 million. Half of the staff involved in the retailing division were made redundant by 31 July 1998 at a cost of £500 000; the remaining staff were redeployed and retrained at a cost of £200 000. All these transactions have been included in the financial statements.

(4) The directors decided to change the accounting treatment of development costs to immediate write-off against profit as costs are incurred. This change has not yet been reflected in the draft financial statements. The balance on the development costs account at 31 July 1998 was £250 000 of which £200 000 was incurred by 31 July 1997.

The company's draft summarised profit and loss account shows:

	£000
Turnover	5500
Cost of sales	(3100)
Gross profit	2400
Distribution costs	(1100)
Administrative expenses	(500)
Profit before taxation	800
Taxation	(240)
Profit after taxation	560
Dividends	(100)
	460

Opening shareholders' funds as on 1 August 1997 were £1.2 million, as previously reported.

Requirements

(a) Advise the board of directors of Glamis plc on the most appropriate accounting treatment and disclosure for each of the above matters, preparing all necessary calculations. You should refer to relevant accounting standards and legislation as appropriate. (10 marks)

Note: You are not required to prepare extracts of the financial statements.

(b) Prepare the following extracts of the financial statements for Glamis plc:

   (i) Statement of total recognised gains and losses

   (ii) Note of historical cost profit and losses

   (iii) Reconciliation of movements on shareholders' funds. (9 marks)

Note: You should provide comparative figures as far as you can from the information available.

ICAEW, Financial Reporting, September 1998   **(19 marks)**

11.7 The Accounting Standards Board has published a Discussion Paper, *Reporting Financial Performance: Proposals for Change*. The proposals in the Discussion Paper build upon the strengths of, and are a progression from FRS 3, *Reporting Financial Performance*. It proposes that a single performance statement should replace the profit and loss account and the Statement of Total Recognised Gains and Losses, effectively combining them in one statement. The paper also takes the view that gains and losses should be reported only once and in the period when they arise, and should not be reported again in another component of the financial statements at a later date, a practice which is sometimes called 'recycling'.

Required:

(a) (i) Explain the reasons for presenting financial performance in one statement rather than two or more statements; (8 marks)

   (ii) Discuss the views for and against the recycling of gains and losses in the financial statements. (6 marks)

(b) Describe how the following items are dealt with under current Financial Reporting Standards, and how their treatment would change if the Discussion Paper were adopted:

   (i) Gains and losses on the disposal of fixed assets; (4 marks)

   (ii) Revaluation gains and losses on fixed assets; (4 marks)

   (ii) Foreign currency translation adjustments arising on the net investment in foreign operations. (3 marks)

ACCA, Financial Reporting Environment (UK Stream), December 2000   **(25 marks)**

11.8 Travis plc is a large grocery retailing and wholesaling organisation. It is presently drawing up its financial statements for the year ended 31 October 1993 and, mindful of the requirements of SSAP 25, has drafted the following segmental report:

Segment information

	Turnover		Profit before tax		Operating net assets	
	31.10.93	31.10.92	31.10.93	31.10.92	31.10.93	31.10.92
	£m	£m	£m	£m	£m	£m
By category						
Retailing						
Food	5 650	6 126	300	295	2 925	2 964
Drinks	1 951	2 047	219	136	987	917
Consumables	115	106	8	5	86	82
Wholesaling						
Warehousing	3 843	3 651	391	382	1 560	1 490
	11 559	11 930	918	818	5 558	5 453
By activity						
Retailing						
Hypermarkets	6 235	6 608	465	314	3 120	3 040
Large shops	545	534	43	40	560	538
Small shops	936	1 137	19	82	318	385
Wholesaling						
Warehousing	3 843	3 651	391	382	1 560	1 490
	11 559	11 930	918	818	5 558	5 453

Notes

Head office and service costs of £53 million (1992: £51 million) have been allocated according to the relative contribution of each segment to the total of continuing operations.

The group's borrowing requirements are centrally managed and so interest expense of £475 million (1992: £415 million) has been apportioned on the basis of average net assets for each segment.

Operating net assets represent the group's net assets adjusted to exclude interest bearing operating assets and liabilities.

Businesses discontinued during the year contributed £450 million (1992: £850 million) to turnover and £38 million (1992: £68 million) to profit before tax.

Requirements

(a) Discuss the objectives of segmental reporting in the context of each of the following user groups of financial statements:
  (i)   the shareholder group
  (ii) the investment analyst group
  (iii) the lender/creditor group
  (iv) Government.   (10 marks)
(b) Critically assess the presentation of Travis plc's draft 'Segment information' report, considering in particular its helpfulness to users of financial statements and its compliance with the requirements of SSAP 25. Outline any ways in which the information might be presented more effectively or in which the treatment of items might be improved.   (11 marks)

ICAEW, Financial Accounting 2, December 1993   **(21 marks)**

11.9 Spreader plc is a UK parent company with a number of wholly-owned subsidiaries in the USA and Europe. Extracts from the consolidated financial statements of the group for the year ended 30 April 1997 are given below.

Profit and loss account – year ended 30 April		1997	1996
		£000	£000
Turnover	*(Note 1)*	50 000	48 000
Cost of sales		(25 000)	(22 000)
Gross profit		25 000	26 000
Other operating expenditure		(15 000)	(14 200)
Operating profit		10 000	11 800
Interest payable		(1 000)	(900)
Profit before taxation	*(Note 2)*	9 000	10 900
Taxation		(2 800)	(3 600)
Profit after taxation		6 200	7 300
Dividend		(3 000)	(3 200)
Retained profit		3 200	4 100

Note 1 Analysis of turnover for the year by geographical segment

	UK		US		Rest of Europe		Total	
	1997	1996	1997	1996	1997	1996	1997	1996
	£000	£000	£000	£000	£000	£000	£000	£000
Total sales	15 000	20 000	10 000	8 000	30 000	25 000	55 000	53 000
Inter-segment sales	(2 000)	(2 500)	(1 000)	(500)	(2 000)	(2 000)	(5 000)	(5 000)
Sales to third parties	13 000	17 500	9 000	7 500	28 000	23 000	50 000	48 000

Note 2 Analysis of profit before tax for the year by geographical segment

	UK		US		Rest of Europe		Total	
	1997	1996	1997	1996	1997	1996	1997	1996
	£000	£000	£000	£000	£000	£000	£000	£000
Segment profit	3 000	6 000	1 500	1 200	6 000	5 000	10 500	12 200
Common costs							(500)	(400)
Operating profit							10 000	11 800
Interest payable							(1 000)	(900)
Profit before taxation							9 000	10 900

Note 3 Analysis of net assets at end of year by geographical segment

	UK		US		Rest of Europe		Total	
	1997	1996	1997	1996	1997	1996	1997	1996
	£000	£000	£000	£000	£000	£000	£000	£000
Segment net assets	15 000	13 500	6 000	5 000	20 000	20 000	41 000	38 500
Unallocated assets							2 000	1 800
Total net assets							43 000	40 300

Requirements

In your capacity as chief accountant of Spreader plc,

(a) prepare a report for the board of directors of the company which analyses the results of the group for the year ended 30 April 1997;　　　　　　　　　　　　　(21 marks)

(b) explain why the segmental data which has been included in the extracts may need to be interpreted with caution.　　　　　　　　　　　　　　　　　　　　(4 marks)

CIMA, Financial Reporting, May 1997　　　　　　　　　　　　　　　　　**(25 marks)**

11.10 (a) For enterprises that are engaged in different businesses with differing risks and opportunities, the usefulness of financial information concerning these enterprises is greatly enhanced if it is supplemented by information on individual business segments. It is recognised that there are two main approaches to segmental reporting. The risk and returns' approach where segments are identified on the basis of different 'risks and returns arising from different lines of business and geographical areas, and the 'managerial' approach whereby segments are identified corresponding to the enterprises' internal organisation structure.

Required
(i) **Explain why the information content of financial statements is improved by the inclusion of segmental data on individual business segments.** (5 marks)
(ii) **Discuss the advantages and disadvantages of analysing segmental data using the 'risk and returns' approach** (4 marks)
the 'managerial' approach. (3 marks)

(b) AZ, a public limited company, operates in the global marketplace.

   (i) The major revenue-earning asset is a fleet of aircraft which are registered in the UK and its other main source of revenue comes from the sale of holidays. The directors are unsure as to how business segments are identified. (3 marks)
   (ii) The company also owns a small aircraft manufacturing plant which supplies aircraft to its domestic airline and to third parties. The preferred method for determining transfer prices for these aircraft between the group companies is market price, but where the aircraft is of a specialised nature with no equivalent market price the companies fix the price by negotiation. (2 marks)
   (iii) The company has incurred an exceptional loss on the sale of several aircraft to a foreign government. This loss occurred due to a fixed price contract signed several years ago for the sale of secondhand aircraft and resulted through the fluctuation of the exchange rates between the two countries. (3 marks)
   (iv) During the year the company discontinued its holiday business due to competition in the sector. (2 marks)
   (v) The company owns 40% of the ordinary shares of Eurocat Ltd, a specialist aircraft engine producer with operations in China and Russia. The investment is accounted for by the equity method and it is proposed to exclude the company's results from segment assets and revenue. (3 marks)

Required
Discuss the implications of each of the above points for the determination of the segmental information required to be prepared and disclosed under SSAP 25 *Segmental Reporting* and FRS 3 *Reporting Financial Performance.*
Please note that the mark allocation is shown after each paragraph in part (b).

ACCA, Financial Reporting Environment (UK Stream), June 1999 **(25 marks)**

11.11 You are the Management Accountant of Global plc. Global plc has operations in a number of different areas of the world and presents segmental information on a geographical basis in accordance with SSAP 25 *Segmental reporting*. The segmental information for the year ended 30 June 2002 is given below:

	Europe		America		Africa		Group	
	2002	*2001*	*2002*	*2001*	*2002*	*2001*	*2002*	*2001*
	£m	£m	£m	£m	£m	£m	£m	£m
TURNOVER								
Turnover by destination:								
Sales to third parties	700	680	600	550	400	200	1700	1430
Turnover by origin:								
Total sales	720	685	610	560	440	205	1770	1450
Inter-segment sales	(20)	(5)	(10)	(10)	(40)	(5)	(70)	(20)
Sales to third parties	700	680	600	550	400	200	1700	1430
PROFIT BEFORE TAXATION								
Segment profit 1 (loss)	70	69	990	90	(20)	(40)	140	119
Common costs							(25)	(20)
Operating profit							115	99
Net interest							(18)	(15)
							97	84
Group share of associates' profit before taxation	10	9	12	5	–	–	22	14
Group profit before taxation							119	98
NET ASSETS								
Segment net assets	350	320	360	330	200	180	910	830
Unallocated assets							120	100
							1030	930
Group share of net assets of associates	55	52	36	30	–	–	91	82
Total net assets							1121	1012

Your Managing Director has reviewed the segmental information above and has expressed concerns about the performance of Global plc. He is particularly concerned about the fact that the Africa segment has been making losses ever since the initial investment in 2000. He wonders whether operations in Africa should be discontinued, given the consistently poor results.

Required
Prepare a report for the Managing Director of Global plc that analyses the performance of the three geographical segments of the business, based on the data that has been provided. The report can take any form you wish, but you should specifically refer to any reservations you may have regarding the use of the segmental data for analysis purposes.

CIMA, Financial Reporting – UK Accounting Standards, November 2002   (**20 marks**)

11.12 FRS 3, *Reporting Financial Performance*, requires that earnings per share should be calculated on the profit after tax, minority interest and extraordinary items. FRS 3 permits an additional measure of earnings per share to be disclosed provided it is presented on a consistent basis over time and reconciled to the amount required by the standard. There should also be an explanation of the reasons for calculating the additional version.

As a result, there is no longer a unique measure of performance. Is this a good thing and what problems might this give preparers and users of financial statements?

ICAEW, Financial Accounting 2, July 1994   (12 marks)

11.13 A plc is a company which is listed on the UK Stock Exchange. Your client, Mr B, currently owns 300 shares in A plc. Mr B has recently received the published financial statements of A plc for the year ended 30 September 1998. Extracts from these published financial statements, and other relevant information, are given below. Mr B is confused by the statements. He is unsure how the performance of the company during the year will affect the market value of his shares, but is aware that the published earnings per share (EPS) is a statistic which is often used by analysts in assessing the performance of listed companies.

Profit and loss accounts – year ended 30 September

	1998	1997
	£ million	£ million
Turnover	10 000	8 500
Cost of sales	(6 300)	(5 100)
Gross profit	3 700	3 400
Other operating expenses	(1 900)	(1 800)
Operating profit	1 800	1 600
Interest payable	(300)	(320)
Profit before taxation	1 500	1 280
Taxation	(470)	(400)
Profit after taxation	1 030	880
Equity dividend	(800)	(500)
Retained profit	230	380

Balance sheets at 30 September

	1998		1997	
	£ million	£ million	£ million	£ million
Fixed assets				
Intangible assets	3000		–	
Tangible assets	4000		3700	
		7000		3700
Current assets				
Stocks	1300		1000	
Debtors	1500		1200	
Cash in hand and at bank	100		90	
	2900		2290	

	1998		1997	
	£ million	£ million	£ million	£ million
Current liabilities				
Trade creditors	900		700	
Taxation	500		420	
Proposed dividend	800		500	
Bank overdraft	600		700	
	2 800		2 320	
Net current assets		100		(30)
Total assets less current liabilities		7 100		3 670
Creditors: amounts falling due after more than one year:				
Loan stock		(2 000)		(2 000)
		5 100		1 670
Capital and reserves				
Called-up share capital		1 500		500
Share premium account		2 700		500
Profit and loss account		900		670
		5 100		1 670

Information regarding share capital

The called-up share capital of the company comprises £1 equity shares only. On 1 April 1998, the company made a rights issue to existing shareholders of two new shares for every one share held, at a price of £3.30 per share, paying issue costs of £100 000. The market price of the shares immediately before the rights issue was £3.50 per share. No changes took place in the equity capital of A plc in the year ended 30 September 1997.

Requirements

(a) Compute the EPS figures (current year plus comparative) that will be included in the published financial statements of A plc for the year ended 30 September 1998.

(5 marks)

(b) Using the extracts with which you have been provided, write a short report to Mr B which identifies the key factors which have led to the change in the EPS of A plc since the year ended 30 September 1997. (10 marks)

(c) Comment on the relevance of the EPS statistic to a shareholder like Mr B who is concerned about the market value of his shares. (5 marks)

CIMA, Financial Reporting, November 1998 **(20 marks)**

11.14 Earnings per share is one of the most quoted statistics in financial analysis, coming into prominence because of the widespread use of the price earnings ratio as an investment decision making yardstick. In 1972 SSAP 3 *Earnings per share*, was issued and revised in 1974, and the standard as amended was operating reasonably effectively. In fact the Accounting Standards Board (ASB) has stated that a review of earnings per share would not normally have been given priority at this stage of the Board's programme. However, in June 1997 FRED 16 *Earnings per share*, was issued which proposed amendments to SSAP 3 and subsequently in October 1998 FRS 14 *Earnings per share* was published.

Required

(a) (i) Describe the main changes to SSAP 3 which have occurred as a result of FRS 14 and the main reasons for those changes.   (6 marks)

    (ii) Explain why there is a need to disclose diluted earnings per share in financial statements.   (5 marks)

(b) The following financial statement extracts for the year ending 31 May 1999 relate to Mayes, a public limited company.

	£000	£000
Operating profit		
Continuing operations	26 700	
Discontinued operations	(1 120)	
		25 580
Continuing operations		
Profit on disposal of tangible fixed assets		2 500
Discontinued operations		
(Loss) on sale of operations		(5 080)
		23 000
Interest payable		(2 100)
Profit on ordinary activities before taxation		20 900
Tax on profit on ordinary activities		(7 500)
Profit on ordinary activities after tax		13 400
Minority interest – equity		(540)
Profit attributable to members of parent company		12 860
Dividends:		
Preference dividend on non-equity shares	210	
Ordinary dividend on equity shares	300	
		(510)
Other appropriations – non-equity shares (note iii)		(80)
Retained profit for year		12 270

Capital as at 31 May 1999.	£000
Allotted, called up and fully paid ordinary shares of £1 each	12 500
7% convertible cumulative redeemable preference shares of £1	3 000
	15 500

Additional Information

(i) On 1 January 1999, 3.6 million ordinary shares were issued at £2.50 in consideration of the acquisition of June Ltd for £9 million. These shares do not rank for dividend in the current period. Additionally the company purchased and cancelled £24 million of its own £1 ordinary shares on 1 April 1999. On 1 July 1999, the company made a bonus issue of 1 for 5 ordinary shares before the financial statements were issued for the year ended 31 May 1999.

(ii) The company has a share option scheme under which certain directors can subscribe for the company's shares. The following details relate to the scheme.

Options outstanding 31 May 1998:
(i)   1.2 million ordinary shares at £2 each
(ii) 2 million ordinary shares at £3 each
both sets of options are exercisable before 31 May 2000.

Options granted during year 31 May 1999
(i)   One million ordinary shares at £4 each exercisable before 31 May 2002, granted
      1 June 1998.

During the year to 31 May 1999, the options relating to the 1.2 million ordinary
shares (at a price of £2) were exercised on 1 March 1999.

The average fair value of one ordinary share during the year was £5.

(iii) The 7% convertible cumulative redeemable preference shares are convertible at the
      option of the shareholder or the company on 1 July 2000, 2001, 2002 on the basis of
      two ordinary shares for every three preference shares. The preference share dividends
      are not in arrears. The shares are redeemable at the option of the shareholder on
      1 July 2000, 2001, 2002 at £1.50 per share. The 'other appropriations – non-equity
      shares' item charged against the profits relates to the amortisation of the redemption
      premium and issue costs on the preference shares.

(iv) Mayes issued £6 million of 6% convertible bonds on 1 June 1998 to finance the
     acquisition of Space Ltd. Each bond is convertible into 2 ordinary shares of £1.
     Assume a corporation tax rate of 35%.

(v) The interest payable relates entirely to continuing operations and the taxation charge
     relating to discontinued operations is assessed at £100 000 despite the accounting
     losses. The loss on discontinued operations relating to the minority interest
     is £600 000.

Requirement
**Calculate the basic and diluted earnings per share for the year ended 31 May 1999 for
Mayes plc utilising FRS 14 *Earnings per share*.**   (14 marks)

**(Candidates should show a calculation of whether potential ordinary shares are dilutive
or anti-dilutive.)**

ACCA, Financial Reporting Environment (UK Stream), June 1999   (25 marks)

11.15   Earnit plc is a listed company. The issued share capital of the company at 1 April 1999
was as follows:

●   500 million equity shares of 50p each.

●   100 million £1 non-equity shares, redeemable at a premium on 31 March 2004. The
    effective finance cost of these shares for Earnit plc is 10% per annum. The carrying
    value of the non-equity shares in the financial statements at 31 March 1999 was £110
    million.

Extracts from the consolidated profit and loss account of Earnit plc for the year ended
31 March 2000 showed:

	£ million
Turnover	250
Cost of sales	(130)
Gross profit	120
Other operating expenses	(40)
Operating profit	80
Exceptional gain	10
Interest payable	(25)
Profit before taxation	65
Taxation	(20)
Profit after taxation	45
Appropriations of profit (see note)	(26)
Retained profit	19

Note – appropriations of profit:

● to non-equity shareholders	11
● to equity shareholders	15
	26

The company has a share option scheme in operation. The terms of the option are that option holders are permitted to purchase 1 equity share for every option held at a price of £1.50 per share. At 1 April 1999, 100 million share options were in issue. On 1 October 1999, the holders of 50 million options exercised their option to purchase, and 70 million new options were issued on the same terms as the existing options. During the year ended 31 March 2000, the average market price of an equity share in Earnit plc was £2.00.

There were no changes to the number of shares or share options outstanding during the year ended 31 March 2000 other than as noted in the previous paragraph.

Requirements

(a) **Compute the basic and diluted earnings per share of Earnit plc for the year ended 31 March 2000. Comparative figures are NOT required.**   (10 marks)

(b) **Explain to a holder of equity shares in Earnit plc the usefulness of both of the figures you have calculated in part (a).**   (10 marks)

CIMA, Financial Reporting, May 2000   **(20 marks)**

11.16 (a) The Accounting Standards Board (ASB) believes that undue emphasis is placed on Earnings per share (EPS) and that this leads to simplistic interpretation of financial performance. Many chief executives believe that their share price does not reflect the value of their company and yet are pre-occupied with earnings based ratios. It appears that if chief executives shared the views of the ASB then they may disclose more meaningful information than EPS to the market, which may then reduce the reporting gap and lead to higher share valuations. The 'reporting gap' can be said to be the difference between the information required by the stock market in order to evaluate the performance of a company and the actual information disclosed.

Required

(i) **Discuss the potential problems of placing undue emphasis on the Earnings per share figure.**   (5 marks)

(ii) Discuss the nature of the 'reporting gap' and how the 'gap' might be eliminated.

(5 marks)

(b) Company X has a complex capital structure. The following information relates to the company for the year ending 31 May 2001:

(i) The net profit of the company for the period attributable to the preference and ordinary shareholders of the parent company was £14.6 million. Of this amount the net profit attributable to discontinued operations was £3.3 million.

The following details relate to the capital of the company:

	million
(ii) Ordinary shares of £1 in issue at 1 June 2000	6.0
Ordinary shares of £1 issued 1 September 2000	1.2
at full market price.	

The average market price of the shares for the year ending 31 May 2001 was £10 and the closing market price of the shares on 31 May 2001 was £11. On 1 January 2001, 300 000 partly paid ordinary shares of £1 were issued. They were issued at £8 per share with £4 payable on 1 January 2001 and £4 payable on 1 January 2002. Dividend participation was 50 per cent until fully paid.

(iii) Convertible loan stock of £20 million at an interest rate of 5% per annum was issued at par on 1 April 2000. Half a year's interest is payable on 30 September and 31 March each year. Each £1000 of loan stock is convertible at the holder's option into 30 ordinary shares at any time. £5 million of loan stock was converted on 1 April 2001 when the market price of the shares was £34 per share.

(iv) £1 million of convertible preference shares of £1 were issued in the year to 31 May 1998. Dividends are paid half yearly on 30 November and 31 May at a rate of 6% per annum. The preference shares are convertible into ordinary shares at the option of the preference shareholder on the basis of two preference shares for each ordinary share issued. Holders of 600 000 preference shares converted them into ordinary shares on 1 December 2000.

(v) Warrants to buy 600 000 ordinary shares at £6.60 per share were issued on 1 January 2001. The warrants expire in five years' time. All the warrants were exercised on 30 June 2001. The financial statements were approved on 1 August 2001.

(vi) The rate of taxation is to be taken as 30%.

Required
Calculate the basic and diluted Earnings per share for X for the year ended 31 May 2001 in accordance with FRS 14 *Earnings per share*.   (15 marks)

ACCA, Financial Reporting Environment (UK Stream), June 2001   (**25 marks**)

11.17 Related party relationships and transactions are a normal feature of business. Enterprises often carry on their business activities through subsidiaries and associates and it is inevitable that transactions will occur between group companies. Until relatively recently the disclosure of related party relationships and transactions has been regarded as an area which has a relatively low priority. However, recent financial scandals have emphasised the importance of an accounting standard in this area.

Required

(a) (i) Explain why the disclosure of related party relationships and transactions is an important issue.   (6 marks)

(ii) Discuss the view that small companies should be exempt from the disclosure of related party relationships and transactions on the grounds of their size.
(4 marks)

(b) Discuss whether the following events would require disclosure in the financial statements of the RP Group plc under FRS 8 Related Party Disclosures.

RP Group plc, merchant bankers, has a number of subsidiaries, associates and joint ventures in its group structure. During the financial year to 31 October 1999, the following events occurred:

(i) The company agreed to finance a management buyout of a group company, AB, a limited company. In addition to providing loan finance, the company has retained a twenty-five per cent equity holding in the company and has a main board director on the board of AB. RP received management fees, interest payments and dividends from AB.   (6 marks)

(ii) On 1 July 1999, RP sold a wholly owned subsidiary, X a limited company, to Z, a public limited company. During the year RP supplied X with second-hand office equipment and X leased its factory from RP. The transactions were all contracted for at market rates.   (4 marks)

(iii) The pension scheme of the group is managed by another merchant bank. An investment manager of the group pension scheme is also a non-executive director of the RP Group and received an annual fee for his services of £25 000 which is not material in the group context. The company pays £16m per annum into the scheme and occasionally transfers assets into the scheme. In 1999, fixed assets of £10m were transferred into the scheme and a recharge of administrative costs of £3m was made.   (5 marks)

ACCA, Financial Reporting Environment (UK Stream), December 1999   **(25 marks)**

11.18 (a) Explain the purpose of FRS 8, *Related party disclosures*, its relevance to users of published financial information and the main differences to international accounting standards.   (6 marks)

(b) The directors of Sidlaw Ltd have requested your advice on the appropriate accounting disclosures for the following:

(1) On 1 February 2001, Sidlaw Ltd purchased 75% of the ordinary share capital of Errol Ltd. Sidlaw Ltd sells £250 000 worth of goods to Errol Ltd every month and has done so for many years.

(2) Sidlaw Ltd has a self-managed pension fund for its employees and pays £4 million per annum into the fund. Sidlaw Ltd's directors also act as fund managers for which Sidlaw Ltd makes no charge to the pension fund.

(3) Mr Muir owns and controls Sidlaw Ltd and Kirric Ltd and has influence, but not control, over Glamis Ltd. All three companies buy and sell goods to each other but are not part of the same group.

Requirement

Advise the directors of Sidlaw Ltd on the appropriate accounting disclosures required under FRS 8, *Related party disclosures*, for all affected companies, providing brief reasons for your recommendations.   (7 marks)

ICAEW, Financial Reporting, June 2001   **(13 marks)**

11.19 Newcars plc is a vehicle dealership; it sells both new and good quality second-hand cars. The company is large and has a large number of shareholders. The only large block of shares is held by Arthur, who owns 25% of Newcars plc. Arthur is a member of Newcars plc's board of directors and he takes a keen interest in the day-to-day management of the company.

Arthur also owns 25% of Oldcars plc. Oldcars plc sells inexpensive second-hand cars which tend to be either relatively old or have a high mileage. Arthur is also a member of the board of directors of Oldcars plc.

Apart from Arthur, Newcars plc and Oldcars plc have no shareholders in common. The only thing that they have in common, apart from Arthur's interest in each, is that Newcars plc sells a large number of cars to Oldcars plc. This usually happens when a customer of Newcars plc has traded in a car that is too old to be sold from Newcars plc's showroom. Most of these cars are immediately resold to Oldcars plc and go into Oldcars plc's normal trading stock. These sales account for approximately 5% of Newcars plc's turnover. Oldcars plc acquires approximately 20% of its cars from Newcars plc.

Required

(a) Explain whether Newcars plc and Oldcars plc are related parties in terms of the requirements of FRS 8, *Related party disclosures*. List any additional information that you would require before making a final decision.   (7 marks)

(b) Assuming that Newcars plc and Oldcars plc are related parties, describe the related parties' disclosures that would have to be made in the companies' financial statements in respect of the sale and purchase of cars between the two companies.

                                                                                           (6 marks)

(c) Explain why it is necessary to disclose such information in respect of transactions involving related parties.   (7 marks)

CIMA, Financial Accounting – UK Accounting Standards, May 2001   **(20 marks)**

11.20 Engina, a foreign company, has approached a partner in your firm to assist in obtaining a Stock Exchange listing for the company. Engina is registered in a country where transactions between related parties are considered to be normal but where such transactions are not disclosed. The directors of Engina are reluctant to disclose the nature of their related party transactions as they feel that although they are a normal feature of business in their part of the world, it could cause significant problems politically and culturally to disclose such transactions.

The partner in your firm has requested a list of all transactions with parties connected with the company and the directors of Engina have produced the following summary:

(a) Every month, Engina sells £50 000 of goods per month to Mr Satay, the financial director. The financial director has set up a small retailing business for his son and the goods are purchased at cost price for him. The annual turnover of Engina is £300 million. Additionally Mr Satay has purchased his company car from the company for £45 000 (market value £80 000). The director, Mr Satay, owns directly 10% of the shares in the company and earns a salary of £500 000 a year, and has a personal fortune of many millions of pounds.

(b) A hotel property had been sold to a brother of Mr Soy, the Managing Director of Engina, for £4 million (net of selling cost of £0.2 million). The market value of the property was £4.3 million but in the overseas country, property prices were falling rapidly. The carrying value of the hotel was £5 million and its value in use was £3.6 million. There was an over supply of hotel accommodation due to government subsidies in an attempt to encourage hotel development and the tourist industry.

(c) Mr Satay owns several companies and the structure of the group is as follows:

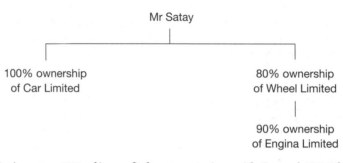

Engina earns 60% of its profit from transactions with Car and 40% of its profit from transactions with Wheel.

Required

Write a report to the directors of Engina setting out the reasons why it is important to disclose related party transactions and the nature of any disclosure required for the above transactions under the UK regulatory system before a Stock Exchange quotation can be obtained.   (25 marks)

The mark allocation will be as follows:

		Marks
Style/layout of report		4
Reasons		8
Transaction	(a)	4
	(b)	5
	(c)	4
		25

ACCA, Advanced Corporate Reporting, Pilot Paper (2002)

Taxation: current and deferred

In this chapter we look briefly at the treatment of current taxation and then, in more depth, at the subject of accounting for deferred taxation. While the former is concerned mainly with the presentation of corporation tax, income tax and overseas taxes in financial statements, the subject of deferred taxation poses a number of conceptual problems and is consequently both more difficult to understand and more controversial.

The main issues associated with current taxation concern the presentation of the current tax charge in the financial statements and the treatment of tax credits and withholding taxes. These are addressed in FRS16 *Current Taxes*, and, in a broadly similar way, in IAS 12 *Income Taxes*.

In the case of deferred taxation, the issues are whether to account for it at all and, if so, in what way. We look first at the perceived need to account for deferred taxation based on the view that taxation is an expense subject to the accruals or matching concept. The argument is that, if there are *timing* differences, that is differences between the periods in which revenues and expenses are recognised in the financial statements and the periods in which they are included when calculating the tax liability, then the tax expense shown in the financial statements should be the notional tax charge based on the revenues and expenses included in the financial statements rather than the tax payable in respect of the period.

We explain that, although SSAP 15 required partial provision for deferred taxation, FRS 19 *Deferred Taxation*, has now brought UK practice closer to the international standard IAS 12 *Income Taxes*, by requiring full provision for deferred tax using a liability method. However, we also examine the substantial differences between the UK and international standards, which will pose considerable difficulties in the attempt to achieve convergence, and cast serious doubt upon whether either method can really be called a full provision method at all.

In this chapter, we draw upon the following UK and international standards:

● SSAP 5 *Accounting for Value Added Tax* (1974)
● FRS 16 *Current Tax* (1999)
● FRS 19 *Deferred Tax* (2000)
● IAS 12 *Income Taxes* (revised 2000)

Introduction

The treatment of taxation in financial statements in the UK is regulated not only by the Companies Acts but also by three standards: SSAP 5 *Accounting for Value Added Tax* (April 1974), FRS 16 *Current Tax* (December 1999) and FRS 19 *Deferred Tax* (December 2000). The relevant international standard is IAS12 *Income Taxes* (revised October 2000).

SSAP 5 is probably the shortest and simplest standard one is likely to see. Its message is that Value Added Tax (VAT) should not be included in turnover nor included in expenses or as part of the cost of an asset except where the tax is irrecoverable. In other words, the VAT collected from customers on behalf of the government and the VAT paid on inputs do not appear in the financial statements, except to the extent that the balance due to or from the government is shown as a liability or asset respectively. While there are, from time to time, interesting legal disputes about which transactions are subject to VAT, these do not generally touch upon financial accounting concepts and we will not pursue the subject of Value Added Tax any further in this book.

In this chapter, we first deal with the treatment of current taxation, where the issues relate mainly to presentation. FRS 16 sets out standard accounting practice on how current tax should be reflected in financial statements and is especially concerned with the treatment of tax credits and withholding taxes. Its requirements are broadly consistent with the international standard IAS 12 *Income Taxes*, although, as we shall see later, there are some minor differences.

The main part of the chapter is devoted to deferred taxation, an area in which standard setters have found it extremely difficult to follow a consistent path. Deferred taxation becomes relevant when there are different rules for the treatment of income and expenses in financial statements and tax computations. Some differences may be *permanent*: a good example is business entertainment expenses where an expense properly charged in a profit and loss account has not been allowed as a tax expense in the UK for the past forty years or so. Permanent differences do not give rise to deferred taxation: the expense is not allowable for tax purposes, the taxable profit is higher than the accounting profit, and that is the end of the matter.

The perceived need to account for deferred taxation arises when there are *timing differences*, that is when the same revenue or expense is recognised in different periods in financial statements and tax computations. Where the timing difference reverses in the following period, there would be widespread agreement that it is necessary to account for deferred taxation. However, as we shall see, not all timing differences reverse so quickly. In some cases, the reversal of the timing difference may be remote, encouraging arguments that it should therefore be ignored. The previous accounting standard, SSAP 15 *Accounting for Deferred Tax*, went even further than this by taking the view that a provision for deferred tax was unnecessary where a timing difference expected to reverse in future would itself be replaced by a new originating timing difference in that same future period!

A deferred tax approach that takes account of all timing differences is known as *full provision* while one which takes into account only those timing differences which are expected to reverse in the foreseeable future is known as *partial provision*. As we shall see, even the so-called full provision methods required by current UK and international standards require important, although different, exclusions.

As with several other topics, relevant UK standards on this subject have not been consistent. The first standard, SSAP 11 *Accounting for Deferred Taxation*, published in 1975, required full provision for deferred taxation but the weight of opposition was such that this standard was withdrawn before its effective date. UK accountants had to wait until 1978 for SSAP 15, a standard that required the use of the partial provision approach. This partial provision method was very much a practical response to a set of circumstances existing in the late 1970s and early 1980s but, to cut a long story short, it had serious conceptual weaknesses, was open to manipulation by directors and is now completely out of line with international practice. Following earlier publications,[1] the ASB issued FRS 19 *Deferred Tax* in December 2000.

---

[1] The ASB issued a Discussion Paper *Accounting for Tax* (March 1995), which dealt with both current taxation and deferred taxation. It subsequently issued an exposure draft of a 'Proposed Amendment to SSAP 8: Presentation of Dividend Income' (October 1997). More recently it has dealt with current taxation and deferred taxation separately by the issue of FRED 18 *Current Taxation* (June 1999) and FRED 19 *Deferred Taxation* (August 1999).

FRS 19 requires full provision for deferred taxation on timing differences, using what is described as the *incremental liability* approach but, as we shall see, it exempts certain major timing differences and hence its requirements still fall rather short of full provision.

In the section of the chapter dealing with deferred taxation we explain timing differences and the perceived need for deferred taxation. We then examine the different approaches which could be adopted before we turn to the proposals of FRS 19 and IAS 12 respectively.

Current taxation

Readers are assumed to be aware of the law relating to the taxation of companies and we shall only refer to the system to the extent necessary to provide an understanding of the accounting implications of that system. For simplicity, we shall assume that a company makes up its financial statements for a year, rather than any other period, and that the rate of corporation tax is 30 per cent, the rate applicable to companies with chargeable profits in excess of £1 500 000.[2]

Corporation tax

The corporation tax of small companies is due in one amount payable nine months and one day after the end of its accounting period. However a large company, that is one which pays corporation tax at the standard rate, must pay corporation tax in instalments. These instalments are based on the company's own estimates of its corporation tax liability for the accounting year and, for a twelve-month accounting period, there are four equal annual instalments due on the 14th day of the seventh, tenth, thirteenth and sixteenth month after the start of the accounting year. So, for an accounting year ended 31 December 20X1, the corporation tax for the year would be due in four equal instalments payable on 14 July 20X1, 14 October 20X1, 14 January 20X2 and 14 April 20X2.

Although the system imposes upon companies the problem of estimating their taxable profits as the year proceeds in order to calculate the instalments payable, accounting for the resulting payments and liability for corporation tax is very straightforward. At the end of an accounting year, the liability will be the corporation tax payable for the full year less the two instalments which have been paid during the year.

Tax credits

When a UK company receives a dividend from a UK resident company or pays a dividend to its shareholders, that dividend carries a tax credit, presently at the rate of one-ninth of the amount received or paid. This reflects the fact that the dividend comes from income which has been subject to corporation tax, although there is no direct relationship between the rate of tax credit and the underlying corporation tax. To a company receiving a dividend with an associated tax credit, the tax credit has no value. However, individual shareholders receiving such a dividend would include the gross amount, that is dividend plus tax credit, as part of their income and then deduct the tax credit from the income tax payable for the year subject

---

[2] This is the rate for the financial year 2002, the year from 1 April 2002 to 31 March 2003. There is also a starting rate of 10% as well as a small companies rate of 20%.

to the proviso that an individual with a low taxable income cannot claim repayment of the tax credit. Thus an individual is able to obtain credit for the tax credit but not its repayment.

Withholding tax

Where a company receives interest from or pays interest to another company or individual, the position is somewhat different. Since the Finance Act 2001, UK companies have been able to pay interest and royalties gross to other UK companies.[3] However, in most other cases, the paying company must deduct income tax, presently at a rate of 20 per cent, from the gross interest and pay this tax over to the Inland Revenue on a quarterly basis. Such a tax is described as a withholding tax, a tax paid to the Inland Revenue by a company on behalf of the recipient, and is found in various forms around the world.

Overseas taxation

A company resident in the UK is liable to corporation tax on all its profits whether they arise in the UK or overseas. As profits which have arisen overseas are usually subject to taxation in the relevant overseas country, they may therefore be subject to double taxation. Similarly, where a UK company receives dividends from the taxed profits of an overseas subsidiary, such dividends are subject to UK corporation tax.

It is usually possible to obtain relief for such double taxation, although the precise nature of the relief depends upon the terms of any double taxation convention between the UK government and the relevant overseas government. Where there is no double tax convention, it is still possible to obtain unilateral relief for double taxation.

In some cases it is possible to obtain relief against UK corporation tax for the whole of the overseas taxation payable but, in other cases, some of the overseas taxation may be unrelieved. One example of the latter is where the rate of overseas taxation on overseas profits exceeds the rate of UK corporation tax on those same profits. To illustrate, let us suppose that a UK company has taxable profits of £300 000 overseas and an additional £2 000 000 in the UK. The rate of overseas corporation tax is 50 per cent while the rate of UK corporation tax is 30 per cent.

The corporation tax payable overseas is 50 per cent of £300 000, that is £150 000, while the corporation tax payable in the UK is 30 per cent of £(2 000 000 + 300 000), that is £690 000. As the UK corporation tax payable on overseas income is only £90 000 (30 per cent of £300 000), this is the maximum relief which may be given against the overseas taxation of £150 000.

The taxation charge in the profit and loss account would therefore include the following:

	£000
Corporation tax on income – 30% of £2 300 000	690
less Relief for overseas taxation	90
	600
Overseas taxation	150
	750

With this background, let us now turn to the provisions of FRS 16.

---

[3] Finance Act 2001, s. 85.

FRS 16 *Current Tax*

FRS 16 *Current Tax*, issued in December 1999, is a very short document which is concerned mainly with the way in which dividends and interest received and paid should be treated in the profit and loss account of a company when tax credits and withholding taxes are involved. Paragraph 2 of the standard provides a number of definitions including the following:

Tax credit

The tax credit given under UK tax legislation to the recipient of a dividend from a UK company.The credit is given to acknowledge that the income out of which the dividend has been paid has already been charged to tax, rather than because any withholding tax has been deducted at source. The tax credit may discharge or reduce the recipient's liability to tax on the dividend. Non-taxpayers may or may not be able to recover the tax credit.

Withholding tax

Tax on dividends or other income that is deducted by the payer of the income and paid to the tax authorities wholly on behalf of the recipient.

As we have seen above, an example of the former is the tax credit attributable to a dividend received from a UK company. Examples of the latter are income tax deducted at source from patent royalties or interest received from a UK company or foreign tax deducted at source from interest or dividends received from an overseas company.

The main purpose of FRS 16 was to lay down standard practice for the treatment of tax credits and withholding taxes; to be more specific, to rule on whether a relevant income or expense should be shown at the net amount or at a gross amount including the relevant tax. In the latter case, the relevant tax would have to appear as part of the tax charge in the financial statements. This is essentially a pragmatic question and the outcome favoured by a majority of the Board, as reflected in FRS 16, is to require the grossing up of actual receipts and payments for any withholding tax but to use the net approach for tax credits.[4]

The standard also stresses the need for consistency in where the taxation consequences of any gain or loss is reported. Thus, where a gain or loss is recognised in the profit and loss account, then the taxation charge or credit should be reported there as well. Where, however, a gain or loss is recognised in the statement of total recognised gains and losses, then the taxation charge or credit should be recognised in that statement too. An example of the latter would be the taxation consequences of an exchange gain or loss on foreign currency borrowing which hedge an equity investment in an overseas company.

It requires that the current tax expense in the profit and loss account and in the statement of total recognised gains and losses should be analysed into UK tax and foreign tax respectively and that each should be analysed to show tax estimated for the current period and any adjustments related to prior periods. Appendix I to the standard provides a possible, but non-mandatory, layout of a note to support the current tax charge shown in a profit and loss account and an example of this is provided in Table 12.1.

Finally FRS 16 provides guidance on what rate of tax should be used to calculate the corporation tax liability for a period:

Current tax should be measured at the amounts expected to be paid (or recovered) using the tax rates and laws that have been enacted or substantively enacted by the balance sheet date. (Para. 14)

---

[4] For the arguments considered in reaching this conclusion, see FRS 16, Appendix V, 'The development of the FRS', Paras 9 to 20.

A UK tax rate can be regarded as having been substantively enacted if it is included in either:

(a) a Bill that has been passed by the House of Commons and is awaiting only passage through the House of Lords and Royal Assent; or
(b) a resolution having statutory effect that has been passed under the Provisional Collection of Taxes Act 1968. (Para. 15).

FRS 16 is an extremely short standard which provides sensible and uncontroversial solutions to the question of accounting for current tax.

Table 12.1 Example of possible note disclosure relating to the current tax charge shown in a profit and loss account

	£000	£000
UK corporation tax		
Current tax on income for the period	1200	
Adjustments in respect of prior periods	150	
	1350	
Double taxation relief	220	
		1130
Foreign tax		
Current tax on income for the period	300	
Adjustments in respect of prior periods	(10)	
		290
Tax on profit on ordinary activities		1420

IAS 12 *Income Taxes*

IAS 12 *Income Taxes*, revised in 2000, covers both current tax and deferred tax. With regard to current tax, there are only relatively minor differences between the requirements of FRS 16 and those of IAS 12. For example, unlike FRS 16, IAS 12 has nothing to say on the tax treatment of dividends receivable and payable. Nor does it mention the recognition of current tax in a statement of total recognised gains and losses, which is not surprising given that most countries do not have a requirement for companies to publish such a statement. Instead, it requires current tax to be charged or credited directly to reserves if it relates to gains or losses, which have been credited or charged directly to equity. The international standard requires the separate disclosure of the current tax liability on the face of the balance sheet, while disclosure of this may be relegated to a note under UK law, and also requires the disclosure of any current tax expense relating to discontinued operations, on which FRS 16 is silent.

While the differences between FRS 16 and IAS 12 appear to be relatively minor, they could lead to considerable differences in reported profit in particular cases, especially where a company has a large amount of dividend income. As we shall see in a moment, when it comes to accounting for deferred taxation, the differences between FRS 19 and IAS 12 are much more important.

Deferred taxation

Timing differences

Although accounting profits form the basis for the computation of taxable profits in the UK, for most companies there are substantial differences between the two. Such differences may be divided into two categories: permanent differences and timing differences.

In the case of permanent differences, certain items of revenue or expense properly taken into account in arriving at accounting profit are not included when arriving at taxable profit. Examples are regional development grants received, amounts spent on entertainment and depreciation of non-industrial buildings.

In the case of timing differences, the same total amount is added or subtracted in arriving at both accounting profits and taxable profits over a period of years, but it is added or subtracted in different periods. It is the existence of such timing differences which gives rise to the perceived need to account for deferred taxation.

Although there are fewer differences than formerly, because revenue law has now accepted standard accounting practice for the purposes of taxation in a number of areas,[5] there are still a number of differences between accounting practice and taxation law which give rise to timing differences. The more important are:

(a) differences which result from the use of the receipts and payments basis in taxation computations and the accruals basis in financial statements; these differences often reverse in the subsequent accounting period although they may not always do so. An example of a timing difference which does not usually reverse in the next accounting period is pension contributions payable allowed for tax purposes that differ from the pension cost determined in accordance with the provisions of FRS 17 *Retirement Benefits*;

(b) availability of capital allowances in taxation computations which are different from the related depreciation charges in financial statements;

(c) interest or development costs capitalised in the financial statements but allowed as an expense for tax purposes when paid;

(d) unrealised revaluation surpluses on fixed assets, recognised in the statement of total recognised gains and losses, for which a taxation charge does not arise until the gain is realised on disposal of the asset;

(e) realised surpluses on the disposal of fixed assets, recognised in a profit and loss account, which are subject to rollover relief for taxation purposes;

(f) tax losses carried forward to be used against taxable profits which arise in the future;

(g) unrealised profits from inter-group trading which are removed in the consolidated financial statements;

(h) unremitted profits of subsidiaries, associates and joint ventures recognised in consolidated financial statements but not taxable until remitted.[6]

One of the four fundamental accounting concepts listed in company law is the 'accruals' concept, under which expenses are matched against the revenues recognised in a particular accounting year. While some accountants might argue that taxation is an appropriation of

---

[5] Interested readers are referred to Graeme Macdonald, *The taxation of business income: Aligning taxable income with accounting income*, The Tax Law Review Committee, The Institute for Fiscal Studies, London, April 2002.

[6] Fair value adjustments applied in a business combination treated as an acquisition are often treated as timing differences but we shall not deal with such complexities here. Interested readers are referred to the latest edition of *UK and International GAAP*, Ernst & Young, published by Butterworths Tolley, London.

profit, the vast majority would classify it as an expense. If it is so regarded, then it follows that taxation is subject to the accruals concept and that the taxation charge should be matched against the accounting profit to which it relates.

To illustrate, let us consider an example of a short-term timing difference.

Hongbo plc makes up its financial statements to 31 December each year and has a profit of £2 000 000 in both 20X1 and 20X2, before making any provision for reorganisation costs. During the year to 31 December 20X1 it made a provision for reorganisation costs amounting to £200 000 but these were not paid, and hence allowed for tax purposes, until the following year 20X2. If we assume a 30 per cent rate of corporation tax and make no provision for deferred taxation, the profit and loss accounts for the two years 20X1 and 20X2 would appear as follows:

Profit and loss accounts for the years ended 31 December

	20X1 £000	20X2 £000
Profit before provision	2000	2000
less Provision for reorganisation costs	200	–
Profit before taxation	1 800	2000
less Corporation tax:		
20X1: 30% × 2 000 000	600	
20X2: 30% × (2 000 000 – 200 000)		540
Profit after taxation	1200	1 460

The picture shown by these profit and loss accounts is, arguably, misleading: the payment of £200 000 for reorganisation costs in 20X2 brings with it a tax reduction of £60 000 (30 per cent of £200 000) but, while the provision is recognised in 20X1, the consequent tax reduction is recognised in 20X2.

If we follow the accruals concept, then the tax reduction should be recognised in the same accounting year as the expense and this is achieved by the use of a deferred taxation account as shown in the profit and loss accounts below:

Profit and loss accounts for the years ended 31 December

	20X1 £000	20X2 £000
Profit before provision	2000	2 000
less Provision for reorganisation costs	200	–
Profit before taxation	1800	2000
less Taxation:		
Corporation tax – as above		
30% of 2 000 000	600	
30% of (2 000 000 – 200 000)		540
Deferred taxation:		
On originating timing difference,		
30% of 200 000	(60)	
On reversing timing difference,		
30% of 200 000		60
	540	600
Profit after tax	1260	1400

In 20X1 the accounting profit is £200 000 less than the taxable profit while, in 20X2, the taxable profit is less than the accounting profit by that same amount. As may be seen above, the profit and loss account for 20X1 is credited with deferred tax on the originating timing difference so that the deferred tax account is debited while in 20X2 the deferred tax asset account is credited and the profit and loss account debited with tax on the reversing difference. The end result is that the profit and loss account for 20X1 reflects both the provision for reorganisation costs and the consequent reduction in taxation.

We have implicitly assumed that there are no permanent differences or other timing differences so that the total tax charge in each year reflects exactly 30 per cent of the reported accounting profit:

	20X1		20X2	
Total tax charge	540	= 30%	600	= 30%
Accounting profit	1800		2000	

Few would quarrel with the use of a deferred taxation account in such simple circumstances. However, things are not always so simple, so let us now explore the timing differences which arise where capital allowances exceed depreciation.

FRS 15 *Tangible Fixed Assets* requires that relevant assets should be depreciated as fairly as possible over the lives of those assets, estimated on a realistic basis. Subject to these parameters and, in particular, the opinions of its auditors, each company may select its own depreciation methods. A long-standing feature of the tax system is that the depreciation charge as shown in the financial statements is not an allowable charge in arriving at taxable profits. Instead, relief for tax purposes is given through capital allowances. The major reason for this has been the wish of governments to prevent companies from delaying the payment of tax by the adoption of unreasonably accelerated methods of depreciation. Conversely, at some times, the government has used the capital allowance system to encourage investment by granting generous capital allowances for expenditure on certain types of fixed asset.

In respect of expenditure on plant and machinery, there is currently a writing-down allowance of 25 per cent applied on a reducing balance basis. Even though this is much less generous than at many times in the past, substantial timing differences still arise and it is instructive to examine the case of an asset with a five-year life.

Let us assume that, as before, Hongbo plc makes up accounts annually to 31 December. On 1 January 20X1 it purchases a machine for £500 000. The machine has an expected life of five years at the end of which its residual value is expected to be £120 000.[7]

The company uses the straight-line method so that the annual depreciation charge is £76 000 ((500 000 − 120 000) ÷ 5).

The depreciation charge and writing-down allowance are therefore as given in columns (ii) and (iii) of Table 12.2. Amounts are rounded to the nearest £1000.

Table 12.2 shows how the deferred tax account is built up. In years 20X1 and 20X2 there are originating timing differences: capital allowances exceed depreciation so that taxable profits are lower than accounting profits. The tax charge in the profit and loss account must be increased and there is a resulting credit balance on the deferred taxation account. In years 20X3 to 20X5 there are reversing timing differences: capital allowances are less than depreciation so that taxable profits exceed accounting profits. The tax charge in the profit and loss account is reduced, thus *drawing down* and finally extinguishing the balance on the deferred taxation account.

---

[7] For illustrative purposes, the expected residual value has been assumed to approximate the tax written-down value at the end of five years, namely $£500\,000(1 - 0.25)^5 = £118\,652 \cong £120\,000$.

Table 12.2 Calculation of deferred tax account balance

(i) Year	(ii) Depreciation	(iii) Capital allowances	(iv) Difference (iii) – (ii)	(v) Tax on difference at 30%	(vi) Balance at year end on deferred tax a/c
	£000	£000	£000	£000	£000
20X1	76	125	49	15	15
20X2	76	94	18	5	20
20X3	76	70	–6	–2	18
20X4	76	53	–23	–7	11
20X5	76	38	–38	–11	–
	380	380	0		

If we assume that the company has a constant profit of £2m before depreciation and taxation and that there are no permanent differences or other timing differences, the consequences of accounting for deferred taxation may be seen in the profit and loss accounts:

Profit and loss account for the year to 31 December

	20X1 £000	20X2 £000	20X3 £000	20X4 £000	20X5 £000
Profit before depreciation	2000	2000	2000	2000	2 000
Depreciation	76	76	76	76	76
	1924	1924	1924	1924	1924
Taxation					
Corporation tax @ 30%[8]	562	572	579	584	589
Deferred tax – as per Table 12.2	15	5	(2)	(7)	(11)
	577	577	577	577	578
Profit after tax	1347	1347	1347	1347	1346

The use of a deferred taxation account in this situation results in a tax charge which is 30 per cent of the accounting profit of each period. It is therefore possible to argue that the use of the deferred taxation account is necessary to comply with the accruals concept and that comprehensive tax allocation, that is the making of a full provision for deferred taxation, provides useful information. However, it is important to bear in mind the simplifications which have been made.

First, we have assumed that the rate of corporation tax is the same in each of the five years. Were the rate of tax to change, then it would be necessary to make a choice on whether to apply the *deferral* method or the *liability* method of accounting for deferred taxation.

---

[8] Corporation tax payable for each year is calculated as follows (£000):
20X1 (2000 – 125) = 1875 × 30% = 562
20X2 (2000 – 94) = 1906 × 30% = 572
20X3 (2000 – 70) = 1930 × 30% = 579
20X4 (2000 – 53) = 1947 × 30% = 584
20X5 (2000 – 38) = 1962 × 30% = 589

Under the deferral method, all reversing timing differences in respect of an asset are, in principle, reversed at the same rate of tax as that applied to the originating timing difference on that asset. To apply this method to a multi-asset firm strictly involves extensive record keeping and hence, when it is used in practice, it is usual to apply an approximate 'net change' method. Thus, where there is a net originating difference for a group of assets in a particular year, it is dealt with at the current rate of tax. If, however, there is a net reversing difference in respect of those assets, it is reversed using some rule of thumb, such as FIFO or the average rate of tax on accumulated timing differences.

Under the liability method, whenever there is a change in the rate of tax, the balance on the deferred taxation account is adjusted to that current rate of tax on accumulated timing differences. The necessary adjustment is charged or credited to the profit and loss account and hence has an immediate impact on the shareholders' interest. Subsequent reversing differences are made at the new rate of tax. It follows that, to operate the liability method, it is not necessary to keep such detailed records as those required for the deferral method, as calculations may be made in total. To give one example: to calculate the balance on deferred taxation required because of the differences in capital allowances and depreciation on fixed assets, it is merely necessary to know the differences between the net book value and the tax written-down value of the relevant assets and the current rate of tax on the balance sheet date. The liability method is therefore much simpler to apply than the deferral method and has been the more popular of the two methods.

The second simplification we have made is to assume that Hongbo plc purchased one machine in 20X1 but made no further purchases in 20X2–X5. We shall now explore the position where a company makes regular purchases by assuming that Hongbo plc purchases one machine each year at a constant cost of £500 000. The depreciation charges and writing-down allowances for tax purposes are then as shown in columns (*ii*) and (*iii*) of Table 12.3.

Table 12.3 Calculation of deferred tax account balance

(i) Year	(ii) Depreciation	(iii) Capital allowances	(iv) Difference (iii) – (ii)	(v) Tax on difference at 30%	(vi) Balance at year end on deferred tax a/c
	£000	£000	£000	£000	£000
20X1 (1 machine)	76	125	49	15	15
20X2 (2 machines)	152	219	67	20	35
20X3 (3 machines)	228	289	61	18	53
20X4 (4 machines)	304	342	38	11	64
20X5 (5 machines)	380	380	–	–	64
20X6 (5 machines)	380	380	–	–	64

From Table 12.3 it can be seen that the balance on the deferred tax account gradually builds up and that, eventually, a steady state is reached in 20X5. From 20X5 capital allowances and depreciation are equal and originating timing differences offset reversing timing differences. Thus, if Hongbo plc continues to invest a constant amount each year, there will be no net reversal of timing differences and the balance on the deferred tax account will remain constant at £64 000.

We could develop this theme further by assuming that the cost of the machine increased year by year and, in such a case, we would find again that there would be no net reversing differences, with the consequence that the balance on the deferred tax account would become larger and larger. Such a deferred taxation balance was normally disclosed as a separate item in the balance sheet of a company and certainly not as part of the shareholders' equity. If the balance was not part of the shareholders' equity, then a knowledge of elementary accounting would suggest that it was a liability. However, this may be questioned. As we have seen, for many companies it may well not have been payable in the foreseeable future and, in such cases, its inclusion in the balance sheet may therefore have been regarded as inconsistent with the going concern concept.

The inclusion of a full provision for deferred taxation in the balance sheet of a company undoubtedly posed problems of interpretation. If the amount is not part of the shareholders' equity, then it must presumably be included as part of other long-term capital in measuring gearing. This resulted in many UK companies appearing to be very highly geared!

As we shall see, problems such as these persuaded the ASC to change from a requirement for companies to make a full provision for deferred taxation to a requirement that they should make a partial provision. We shall also see that, partly in response to subsequent changes in the taxation system but also in response to international developments, the ASB has now moved us back towards the use of a full provision, although it has stopped some way short of the terminus.

Attempts at standardisation: ED 11 to SSAP 15

The Accounting Standards Steering Committee made its first attempt at a standard method of accounting for deferred taxation when it issued ED 11, *Accounting for Deferred Taxation*, in May 1973. This proposed that companies should provide in full for deferred tax using the deferral method. The ensuing SSAP 11, which was published in August 1975, followed this approach, although it permitted companies to use either the deferral method or the liability method. SSAP 11 came under such heavy criticism from industry that its starting date was postponed indefinitely and it was eventually withdrawn.

ED 19, which was issued in May 1977, adopted a very different approach from SSAP11. Instead of requiring full provision for deferred tax, it permitted partial provision in certain circumstances. Thus, instead of requiring companies to perform a mechanical calculation to provide for deferred taxation on all timing differences, it recognised that not all timing differences would reverse in the foreseeable future and consequently permitted a more subjective approach which took into account the circumstances of the particular company. Even where a company took advantage of this permissive approach, it was still required to provide a note to the balance sheet showing the potential deferred taxation on all timing differences and this potential deferred taxation was to be calculated using the liability method.

The ensuing SSAP 15, originally issued in 1978 and reissued in a revised form in 1985, required companies to account for timing differences to the extent that it was probable that a liability or asset would crystallise but not to account for timing differences to the extent that it was probable that a liability or asset would not crystallise. The decision on whether deferred tax liabilities or assets would or would not crystallise involved looking into the future, taking into consideration the plans of the company's management. Under such a partial provision approach, only the liability method makes any sense and SSAP 15 required that this be used.

The partial provision approach may be seen as a pragmatic response to circumstances which existed in the UK in the 1970s and 1980s. High rates of price increase had led governments to introduce extremely generous capital allowances, in some cases 100 per cent in the year of purchase of a fixed asset, as well as allowances to compensate for the rising cost of stocks. These gave rise to enormous timing differences and frequently to ever-growing balances on deferred taxation accounts which, for the reasons we have discussed above, were difficult to interpret. By permitting companies to consider their future plans in estimating whether or not there would be net reversing differences in the foreseeable future, the ASC enabled companies to reduce provisions for deferred taxation and hence increase reported profits to what were considered to be more realistic amounts.

In the opinion of the authors, the partial provision approach lacks any sound conceptual foundation as it permits companies to ignore timing differences which will reverse in future if those reversing differences are expected to be exceeded by future originating differences. Where else in accounting do we ignore present creditors because they will be replaced by other creditors in future? The ASB found that such a pragmatic, but theoretically unsound, approach sat uncomfortably with its *Statement of Principles*. In addition, the generous tax incentives, which encourage the adoption of the partial provision approach, had long since disappeared and hence it could be argued that the approach had passed its 'sell-by date'.

The partial provision approach introduced considerable subjectivity into financial statements and resulted in companies in very similar positions often making very different provisions for deferred taxation. It had not found favour around the world and, as we shall see later in the chapter, partial provision is not now permitted by IAS 12.

Given all these factors, it is not surprising that FRED 19 *Deferred Tax*, published in August 1999, and the ensuing FRS 19, published with the same title in December 2000, rejected this partial provision approach in favour of full provision for deferred taxation. As we shall see in the next section, the approach of FRS 19 actually falls somewhat short of full provision!

FRS 19 *Deferred Tax*

FRS 19 requires that, for accounting periods ending on or after 23 January 2002, deferred taxation should be provided in full using what it calls an *incremental liability* approach. This approach requires the provision of deferred taxation on all timing differences subject to a number of important exceptions.

Thus, deferred taxation should be provided on all of the following timing differences:

- short-term timing differences;
- accruals for pension costs and other post-retirement benefits that will be deductible for tax purposes only when paid;
- accelerated capital allowances;
- elimination of unrealised inter-group profits on consolidation;
- unrelieved tax losses, provided it is more likely than not that there will be suitable taxable profits in future;
- gains or losses on assets which are continually revalued to fair value, with changes in fair value being taken to profit and loss account. An example would be the gains or losses on current asset investments marked-to-market;
- realised gains or losses on disposal of fixed assets where no rollover relief is available and tax becomes payable;
- unrealised gains or losses on fixed assets where there is a binding commitment to sell with no rollover relief becoming available.

However deferred taxation should **not** be provided on the following differences:

- realised gains or losses on disposal of a fixed asset where the gains are rolled over into replacement assets, or likely to be rolled over into replacement assets, such that no tax will become payable until disposal of the replacement asset at some time in the future in the absence of further rollover relief;
- unrealised gains or losses on the revaluation of fixed assets where there is is no binding commitment to sell the asset. In this case no tax will become payable until a sale at some time in the future and, even then, tax would only become payable if there were no rollover relief;
- unremitted earnings of subsidiaries, associates and joint ventures, that is the share of those earnings recognised in the consolidated profit and loss account, where there is no binding commitment to remit those earnings. Binding commitments to make such distributions would be extremely rare in practice.

Given the exemption of these timing differences, the FRS 19 approach falls somewhat short of requiring full provision for deferred tax. Its approach is driven by its *Statement of Principles* which, as we have explained in Chapter 1, only permits the recognition in financial statements of items which satisfy the definition of an asset or a liability. Thus the objective of the FRS is stated to be to ensure that:

(a) future tax consequences of past transactions and events are recognised as liabilities or assets in the financial statements; and

(b) the financial statements disclose any other special circumstances that may have an effect on future tax charges. (Para. 1)

Point (a) refers to liabilities or assets and, given that deferred taxation is usually a liability, rather than an asset, let us recall the definition of liability included in Chapter 4 of the *Statement of Principles* (see Chapters 1 and 7 above):

Liabilities are obligations of an entity to transfer economic benefits as a result of past transactions or events.

Many accountants, including the authors, would argue that the only obligation to transfer economic benefits existing at a balance sheet date is the remaining part of the current tax payable for the year. If this is the case, then it would follow that the only conceptually sound method of dealing with deferred tax is to use what is described as the 'flow through' approach to accounting for deferred taxation, jargon which means, quite simply, that deferred taxation should be ignored altogether.

The perceived need for deferred taxation rests upon the accruals or matching concept and this sits uneasily with the balance sheet oriented approach of the ASB *Statement of Principles* and, indeed, the IASB Framework. Hence it is possible to argue that the approach of FRS 19 rests on very shaky foundations, which is why many of the justifications that it uses for its proposed treatment seem somewhat contrived. The exemptions listed above identify situations where there is clearly a timing difference but where no payment or receipt of tax is likely to occur in the near future. The required approach, which requires companies to ignore such timing differences, would sit much more comfortably with the previous partial provision approach to deferred taxation than with the full provision approach that is stated to be the required approach of FRS 19!

For many companies, the change from partial provision to full provision would lead to substantial increases in provisions for deferred taxation but the effects of this would be mitigated if deferred taxation liabilities were to be discounted. Although not permitted by IAS 12, discounting is permitted, although not required, by FRS 19.

Discounting

For companies which choose to discount deferred taxation, the timing differences eligible for discounting would include those arising from accelerated capital allowances, revaluation gains and tax losses carried forward, to the extent that these have been recognised.

The full reversals of all relevant timing differences should be scheduled on a year-to-year basis. Tax on these reversing differences should then be calculated and discounted back to the balance sheet date using the post-tax yields to maturity on government bonds with maturity dates, and in currencies, similar to those of the deferred tax assets and liabilities.

Let us look at a very simple example of accelerated capital allowances for a company which makes up its financial statements to 31 December each year and which has just one machine. The machine cost £10 000 on 1 January 20X1 when it had an expected life of eight years and an expected residual value of £1000. The company uses the straight-line method of depreciation and the machine is eligible for capital allowances at 25 per cent on a reducing-balance basis.

If all goes according to plan, the annual depreciation will be $(10\,000 - 1000) \div 8 = 1125$ p.a. and this is shown in the third column (*iii*) of Table 12.4. The capital allowances are as shown in the second column (*ii*).

Table 12.4 Capital allowances, depreciation and timing differences

(i) Year to 31.12	(ii) Capital allowances	(iii) Depreciation	(iv) Timing difference
	£	£	£
20X1	2500	1125	1375
20X2	1875	1125	750
20X3	1406	1125	281
20X4	1055	1125	(70)
20X5	791	1125	(334)
20X6	593	1125	(532)
20X7	445	1125	(680)
20X8	335	1125	(790)
	9000	9000	0

As will be seen from Table 12.4, there are originating timing differences in the first three years which then reverse completely over the ensuing five years.

Let us suppose we are now at the end of the year 20X3 when the accumulated timing differences are £2406, that is 1375 + 750 + 281. If the corporation tax rate is 30 per cent, the credit balance on the deferred tax account at that time would be 30 per cent of £2406, which equals £722 to the nearest £1. We can easily schedule the reversals in years 20X4 to 20X8 in Table 12.5, using the relevant figures from Table 12.4.

The second column, (*ii*), of Table 12.5 shows the reversing timing differences in each future year and the third column, (*iii*), shows the undiscounted reversals of deferred tax. In order to arrive at the discounted amount, we need to determine the post-tax yield on government bonds for one year, two years, three years, four years and five years respectively. Gross yields for some of these years may be obtained from the yields for Treasury gilts published in the *Financial Times* and, where the particular number of years is not listed, the

Table 12.5 **Discounting of deferred taxation**

(i) Year to 31.12	(ii) Reversing difference	(iii) Tax @30%	(iv) Discount rate	(v) Deferred tax (discounted to 31.12.20X3)
	£	£	%	£
20X4	70	21	4.5	20
20X5	334	100	4.4	92
20X6	532	160	4.2	141
20X7	680	204	4.0	174
20X8	790	237	3.9	180
	2406	722		607

yields must be obtained by interpolation. In either case, tax must be deducted at 30 per cent, the rate which the company pays on its investment income.

If we assume that the relevant rates are as given in the fourth column, (*iv*) in Table 12.5, then it is easy to arrive at the discounted deferred tax by multiplying each reversal in column (*iii*) by the formula $1/(1+ i)$ to the power *n*, using the relevant discount rate. The discounted amounts are given in the final right-hand column and sum to a total of £607 compared with the undiscounted total of £722.

This is a very simple example to illustrate the principles involved and readers may wish to consult the more realistic example included in Appendix I to FRS 19. There is no doubt that, in practice, all sorts of approximations will have to be used to arrive at any discounted liability.

At the time of writing, it remains to be seen whether many companies will choose to discount deferred taxation. If some do but most do not, comparability between UK companies will be reduced. If many choose to discount, then comparability between UK companies and those in other countries, which are prohibited from discounting by the international standard, will be made even more difficult.

Presentation and disclosure

In addition to these fundamental changes in measuring deferred taxation, FRS 19 also requires extensive disclosure.

In the balance sheet, net deferred tax liabilities should be classified as provisions for liabilities and charges while net deferred tax assets should be classified as debtors, as a separate sub-category of debtors where material (Para. 55). Deferred tax liabilities and assets should be disclosed separately on the face of the balance sheet if the amounts are so material in the context of the total net current assets or net assets that, in the absence of such disclosure, readers may misinterpret the financial statements (Para. 58).

In the performance statements, deferred tax relating to a gain or loss which is recognised in the statement of total recognised gains and losses should be recognised in that statement (Para. 35). Deferred tax recognised in the profit and loss account should be included within the heading 'tax on profit or loss on ordinary activities' (Para. 59). Thus the tax expense for the year will comprise current tax, as explained earlier in the chapter, and deferred tax, including the effect of the unwinding of any discount in respect of any deferred tax which has been discounted.

The standard also requires appropriate analyses of the figures included in the financial statements and a considerable amount of narrative disclosure to enable readers of the financial statements to appreciate what has been done and why. These disclosures are specified in Paras 60 to 65 of FRS 19, to which interested readers are referred.

An important part of these required disclosures is the note reconciling the current tax charge in the profit and loss account with the tax charge which would be expected from applying the relevant standard rate of tax to the reported profit on ordinary activities before tax. Such a note will undoubtedly provide useful information and might take the form shown in Table 12.6.

Table 12.6 Reconciliation of tax charge

	20X2 £000	20X1 £000
Profit on ordinary activities before tax	2200	2000
Standard rate of tax of 30% applied to above profit	660	600
Effects of:		
Expenses not deductible for tax purposes, including unwinding of deferred tax liability	30	33
Capital allowances in excess of depreciation	(125)	(116)
Utilisation of tax losses	(19)	(17)
Changes in deferred tax discount rate	9	10
Current tax charge for period	555	510

We shall now turn to the international accounting standard.

The international accounting standard: IAS 12

Whereas the original IAS 12 *Accounting for Taxes on Income* (1979) permitted the use of either full or partial deferred tax accounting, the revised version, *Income Taxes* (2000),[9] now requires the use of full deferred tax accounting, using the liability method. It prohibits the discounting of deferred tax.

IAS 12 requires companies to account for deferred taxation not just on timing differences but on what it calls '*temporary differences*'. Like FRS 19, this approach adopts a balance sheet focus and requires deferred taxation to be provided in respect of differences between the carrying values of assets and liabilities in the balance sheet and their values for taxation purposes.

Temporary differences form a wider category of differences than timing differences but, because IAS 12 exempts a number of temporary differences from the need for deferred tax, its approach comes much closer to one based upon timing differences, like that of FRS 19.

[9] An earlier revised version of IAS 12 was issued in 1996.

However, this is not to say that there are no differences between the the two standards, for IAS 12 requires the provision of deferred taxation on a wider range of differences than FRS 19. We shall outline three major differences between the standards.

Realised gains on disposal of fixed assets

When a fixed asset is sold, FRS 19 does not require a provision for deferred tax if rollover relief is available or likely to become available. IAS 12 requires provision for deferred tax to be made whether or not rollover relief is available.

Unrealised gains on revaluation of fixed assets

When there are unrealised gains on revaluation of fixed assets, FRS 19 only requires a provision to be made for deferred tax if there is a binding agreement to sell the revalued asset in circumstances where no rollover relief is available. IAS 12 requires a provision for deferred tax to be made whether or not the asset will be sold and whether or not rollover relief is available.

Unremitted earnings

FRS 19 only requires a provision for deferred tax on unremitted earnings of subsidiaries, associates and joint ventures in the unlikely event that there is a binding agreement to distribute those earnings. IAS 12 requires a provision for deferred taxation on unremitted earnings in all circumstances.

It can be seen from these three major differences that IAS 12 requires provision of deferred taxation on more differences than FRS 19 and hence has greater claim to the description 'full provision' approach to deferred taxation than the UK standard.

While IAS 12 specifically states that unrealised gains on the revaluation of fixed assets and unremitted earnings are temporary differences rather than timing differences, the authors find this terminology unduly arcane. It would seem to us that all three differences above are timing differences due to the fact that gains that are recognised in one accounting period will be taxed in a future period.

It is, of course, very difficult to reconcile the difference in the two approaches with what are very similar conceptual frameworks. Some accountants would argue that there is only one method of dealing with deferred taxation that is consistent with the conceptual frameworks, the flow through method, which ignores deferred taxation completely. As we have argued elsewhere in the book, the problems that have arisen in connection with deferred tax cast serious doubts on the extent to which existing conceptual frameworks provide suitable guidance to resolve accounting problems.

Given the differences that we have described in this chapter, it is hard to see how it will be possible to achieve convergence between the UK standard and the international accounting standard in the near future. It will perhaps become even more difficult if large numbers of UK companies start to discount their deferred tax liabilities while those in other countries are not permitted to do so. Much talking will have to occur and one or other set of standard setters will have to make some fundamental changes.

Summary

In this chapter, we have looked first at accounting for current tax and then at accounting for deferred taxation.

The treatment of current tax poses few conceptual problems and we have examined the treatment of corporation tax and overseas taxation, as well as tax credits and withholding taxes. FRS 16 requires that amounts receivable and payable should be grossed for withholding taxes but not for tax credits. We have seen that FRS 16 and IAS 12 are broadly similar, except that IAS 12 has nothing to say regarding the treatment of tax credits on dividends.

Deferred taxation is a much more difficult and controversial topic. We have explained how the perceived need to account for deferred taxation rests upon the application of the accruals or matching concept to timing differences and illustrated the full provision approach.

After a number of years in which a partial provision approach to deferred taxation has been applied in the UK, FRS 19 now requires full provision using what the ASB describes as the *incremental liability* approach. This approach means that deferred taxation should be provided on timing differences but with a number of important exceptions. We have explained how the exceptions result in the approach of FRS 19 falling somewhat short of what most reasonable people would describe as a 'full provision' approach to deferred taxation.

IAS 12 also requires a full provision approach to deferred taxation but uses a *temporary differences*, rather than an incremental liability, approach. Here too, the IASB makes a number of exceptions which effectively result in companies accounting for deferred tax on timing differences but on a wider range of timing differences than that required by FRS 19.

We have explained that FRS 19 permits the discounting of certain deferred tax liabilities while IAS 12 prohibits discounting altogether.

Given these differences, it is difficult to see how convergence will be achieved in the area of deferred taxation. Both FRS 19 and IAS 12 have gone to extraordinary lengths to try to justify how their respective approaches tie in with the relevant conceptual frameworks but, given the differences in the standards and the similarities between these frameworks, the authors are not convinced. If the objective of the standard setters is to ensure that only things which satisfy the framework definitions of assets and liabilities are to appear in balance sheets, then only the flow through approach, that is, to ignore deferred taxation altogether, can be claimed to be conceptually sound.

Recommended reading

A.J. Arnold and B.J. Webb, *The Financial Reporting and Policy Effects of Partial Deferred Tax Accounting*, ICAEW, London, 1989.

G. Macdonald, *The Taxation of Business Income: Aligning taxable income with accounting income*, Tax Law Review Committee Discussion Paper No. 2, Institute for Fiscal Studies, London, 2002.

I.P.A. Stitt, *Deferred Tax Accounting*, ICAEW, London, 1985.

P. Weetman (ed.), S*SAP 15 Accounting for Deferred Taxation*, ICAS, Edinburgh, 1992.

In addition to the above, readers are referred to the latest edition of *UK and International GAAP* by Ernst & Young, which provides much greater detailed coverage of this and other topics in this book. At the time of writing, the most recent edition is the 7th edition, edited by A. Wilson, M. Davies, M. Curtis and G. Wilkinson-Riddle, published by Butterworths Tolley in 2001. The relevant chapter is 24.

Questions

12.1 [*Authors' note*: This question has been included for students who wish to consider the partial provision method of accounting for deferred tax, which was required by SSAP 15 but is now outlawed by FRS 19.]

The Accounting Standards Board (ASB) currently faces a dilemma. IAS 12 (revised), *Income Taxes* published by the International Accounting Standards Committee (IASC), recommends measures which significantly differ from current UK practice set out in SSAP 15 *Accounting for Deferred Tax*. IAS 12 requires an enterprise to provide for deferred tax in full for all deferred tax liabilities with only limited exceptions whereas SSAP 15 utilises the partial provision approach. The dilemma facing the ASB is whether to adopt the principles of IAS 12 (revised) and face criticism from many UK companies who agree with the partial provision approach. The discussion paper 'Accounting for Tax' appears to indicate that the ASB wish to eliminate the partial provision method.

The different approaches are particularly significant when acquiring subsidiaries because of the fair value adjustments and also when dealing with revaluations of fixed assets as the IAS requires companies to provide for deferred tax on these amounts.

Required

(a) Explain the main reasons why SSAP 15 has been criticised.   (8 marks)

(b) Discuss the arguments in favour of and against providing for deferred tax on:
    (i)   fair value adjustments on the acquisition of a subsidiary
    (ii) revaluations of fixed assets.   (7 marks)

(c) XL plc has the following net assets at 30 November 1997.

	£000	Tax value (£000)
Fixed assets		
Buildings	33 500	7 500
Plant and equipment	52 000	13 000
Investments	66 000	66 000
	151 500	86 500
Current assets	15 000	15 000
Creditors: Amounts falling due within one year		
Creditors	(13 500)	(13 500)
Liability for health care benefits	(300)	–
	(13 800)	
Net current assets	1 200	
Provision for deferred tax	(9 010)	(9 010)
	143 690	78 990

XL plc has acquired 100% of the shares of BZ Ltd on 30 November 1997. The following statement of net assets relates to BZ Ltd on 30 November 1997.

	£000 Fair value	£000 Carrying value	£000 Tax value
Buildings	500	300	100
Plant and equipment	40	30	15
Stock	124	114	114
Debtors	110	110	110
Retirement benefit liability	(60)	(60)	–
Creditors	(105)	(105)	(105)
	609	389	234

There is currently no deferred tax provision in the accounts of BZ Ltd. In order to achieve a measure of consistency XL plc decided that it would revalue its land and buildings to £50 million and the plant and equipment to £60 million. The company did not feel it necessary to revalue the investments. The liabilities for retirement benefits and healthcare costs are anticipated to remain at their current amounts for the foreseeable future.

The land and buildings of XL plc had originally cost £45 million and the plant and equipment £70 million. The company has no intention of selling any of its fixed assets other than the land and buildings which it may sell and lease back. XL plc currently utilises the full provision method to account for deferred taxation. The projected depreciation charges and tax allowances of XL plc and BZ Ltd are as follows for the years ending 30 November:

	£000	£000	£000
	1998	*1999*	*2000*
Depreciation			
(Buildings, plant and equipment)			
XL plc	7 010	8 400	7 560
BZ Ltd	30	32	34
Tax allowances			
XL plc	8 000	4 500	3 000
BZ Ltd	40	36	30

The corporation tax rate had changed from 35% to 30% in the current year. Ignore any indexation allowance or rollover relief and assume that XL plc and BZ Ltd are in the same tax jurisdiction.

Required

Calculate the deferred tax expense for XL plc which would appear in the group financial statements at 30 November 1997 using:
  (i)   the full provision method incorporating the effects of the revaluation of assets in XL plc and the acquisition of BZ Ltd.
  (ii) the partial provision method.   (10 marks)

(Candidates should not answer in accordance with IAS 12 (Revised) *Income Taxes*.)

ACCA, Financial Reporting Environment, December 1997   **(25 marks)**

12.2 The problem of accounting for deferred taxation is one that has been on the agenda of the Accounting Standards Board for some time. In December 2000, the Accounting Standards Board published FRS 19 – *Deferred Tax*. The Standard basically requires that full provision is made for deferred tax on all timing differences and therefore rejects the two alternative bases of accounting for deferred tax, the nil provision (or 'flow-through') basis and the partial provision basis. However, FRS 19 does not normally require companies to provide for deferred tax on revaluation surpluses or fair value adjustments arising on consolidation of a subsidiary for the first time.

Required
  (a) Explain why the ASB rejected the nil provision and partial provision bases when developing FRS 19.   (6 marks)
  (b) Discuss the logic underlying the FRS 19 treatment of deferred tax on revaluation surpluses and fair value adjustments and indicate any exceptions to the general requirement not to provide for deferred tax on these amounts.   (5 marks)

You are the management accountant of Payit plc. Your assistant is preparing the consolidated financial statements for the year ended 31 March 2002. However, he is unsure how to account for the deferred tax effects of certain transactions as he has not studied FRS 19. These transactions are given below:

Transaction 1

During the year, Payit plc sold goods to a subsidiary for £10 million, making a profit of 20% on selling price. 25% of these goods were still in the stock of the subsidiary at 31 March 2002. The subsidiary and Payit plc are in the same tax jurisdiction and pay tax on profits at 30%.

Transaction 2

An overseas subsidiary made a loss adjusted for tax purposes of £8 million (£ equivalent). The only relief available for this tax loss is to carry it forward for offset against future taxable profits of the overseas subsidiary. Taxable profits of the overseas subsidiary suffer tax at a rate of 25%.

Required

(c) **Compute the effect of BOTH the above transactions on the deferred tax amounts in the consolidated BALANCE SHEET of Payit plc at 31 March 2002. You should provide a full explanation for your calculations and indicate any assumptions you make in formulating your answer.** (9 marks)

CIMA, Financial Reporting – UK Accounting Standards, May 2002 (**20 marks**)

12.3 H plc is a major manufacturing company. According to the company's records, timing differences of £2.00 million had arisen at 30 April 2002 because of differences between the carrying amount of tangible fixed assets and their tax base. These had arisen because H plc had exercised its right to claim accelerated tax relief in the earlier years of the asset lives.

At 30 April 2001, the timing differences attributable to tangible fixed assets were £2.30 million.

H plc has a defined benefit pension scheme for its employees. The company administers the scheme itself.

The corporation tax rate has been 30% in the past. On 30 April 2002, the directors of H plc were advised that the rate of taxation would decrease to 28% by the time that the timing differences on the tangible fixed assets reversed.

The estimated corporation tax charge for the year ended 30 April 2002 was £400 000. The estimated charge for the year ended 30 April 2001 was agreed with the Revenue and settled without adjustment.

Required

(a) **Prepare the notes in respect of current taxation and deferred tax as they would appear in the financial statements of H plc for the year ended 30 April 2002.** (*Your answer should be expressed in £ million and you should work to two decimal places.*)
(7 marks)

(b) **The directors of H plc are concerned that they might be required to report a deferred tax asset in respect of their company pension scheme.**
Explain why such an asset might arise. (6 marks)

(c) **FRS 19 – *Deferred Tax* requires companies to publish a reconciliation of the current tax charge reported in the profit and loss account to the charge that would result from applying the standard rate of tax to the profit on ordinary activities before tax. Explain why this reconciliation is helpful to the readers of financial statements.**
(7 marks)

CIMA, Financial Accounting – UK Accounting Standards, May 2002 (**20 marks**)

12.4 Explain how the requirements of FRS 18, Accounting policies, and FRS 19, Deferred tax, reflect the Statement of Principles.

ICAEW, Financial Reporting, June 2002 (**15 marks**)

Business combinations and goodwill

This chapter is divided into two parts covering the closely related topics of business combinations and goodwill. In the first part of the chapter, we start by discussing the economic and business context of business combinations and the ways in which such combinations may be effected. We then describe and evaluate the two methods of accounting for business combinations, the *acquisition* method and the *merger* method. The former is based on the premise that there is a purchase by a dominant partner whereas the latter assumes a coming together of more or less equal partners. We explain the provisions of the UK standard and outline those of the international accounting standard while drawing attention to proposed changes in this area. In this part of the chapter, we therefore refer to:

- FRS 6 *Acquisitions and Mergers* (1994)
- IAS 22 *Business Combinations* (revised 1998)

Although FRS 7 *Fair Values in Acquisition Accounting* (1994) is also relevant to this topic, we defer consideration of that standard until the following chapter.

In the second part of the chapter, we turn to the thorny issue of accounting for goodwill. We explain why goodwill arises and then describe the attempts of the standard setters to arrive at an appropriate accounting treatment for this, often very valuable, phenomenon. Standard accounting practice for goodwill now involves impairment reviews so we also revisit this topic which was introduced earlier, in Chapter 5. We examine the relevant UK and international accounting standards, which are:

- FRS10 *Goodwill and Intangible Assets* (1997)
- FRS 11 *Impairment of Fixed Assets and Goodwill* (1998)
- IAS 22 *Business Combinations* (revised 1998)
- IAS 36 *Impairment of Assets* (1998)
- IAS 38 *Intangible Assets* (1998)

Business combinations

Introduction

Words such as merger, amalgamation, absorption, takeover and acquisition are all used to describe the coming together of two or more businesses. Such words do not have precise legal meanings and, as they are often used interchangeably, the American description 'business combinations' best describes the subject matter of this chapter.

A company may expand either by 'internal' or 'external' growth. In the former case it expands by undertaking investment projects, such as the purchase of new premises and plant, while in the latter case it expands by purchasing a collection of assets in the form of an established business. In this second case we have a business combination in which one company is very much the dominant party, acquiring control of that other business either with or without the consent of the directors of that business.

Where such 'external' growth is contemplated, it will be necessary to value the collection of assets it is proposed to purchase. It will usually be necessary to determine at least two values: (a) the value of the business to its present owners (this will determine the minimum price which will be acceptable); (b) the value of the business when combined with the existing assets of the acquiring company (this will determine the maximum price which may be offered).

In other circumstances two or more companies may both see benefits from coming together. Thus, two companies may consider that their combined businesses are worth more than the sum of the values of the individual businesses. For such a combination, the individual businesses must be valued to help in the determination of the proportionate shares in the combined business, although, of course, the ultimate shares will, to a considerable extent, depend upon the bargaining ability of the two parties.

Table 13.1 gives some indication of the importance of business combinations in the years 1991–2000. It shows acquisitions and mergers of industrial and commercial companies in the UK by UK companies.[1]

Table 13.1 **Acquisitions and mergers in the UK by UK companies: 1991–2000**

Year	Number of companies acquired	Consideration (£million)			
		Total	Cash	Ordinary shares	Fixed interest securities
1991	506	10 434	7 278	3 034	121
1992	432	5 941	3 772	2 122	47
1993	526	7 063	5 690	1 162	211
1994	674	8 269	5 302	2 823	144
1995	505	32 600	25 524	6 617	459
1996	584	30 742	19 551	10 926	265
1997	506	26 829	10 923	15 583	323
1998	635	29 525	15 769	13 160	595
1999	493	26 163	16 220	9 592	351
2000	587	106 916	40 074	65 570	1 272

Some reasons for combining

Purchase of undervalued assets

It is well recognised that the same collection of assets may have different values to different people. As a result, it is often possible for one business to purchase another business, that is a collection of assets, at a price below the sum of the values of the underlying assets. If we take limited companies, for example, the shares of a company may be standing at a relatively low

[1] This information has been taken from Table 6.1B of *Financial Statistics*, published monthly by the Office for National Statistics.

price because the current management is making poor use of the assets or has not communicated good future prospects to the shareholders. Even though the acquiring company purchases the shares at a price higher than the existing market price, it may be able to acquire underlying assets which have a much higher value than the price paid. Indeed, as many asset strippers have shown, even the sale of assets on a piecemeal basis may generate a sum considerably in excess of the price paid for those assets.

Economies of scale

The combination of two businesses may result in economies of scale, that is to say the cost of producing the combined output will be less than the sum of the costs of producing the separate outputs or, alternatively, the combined output will be greater for the same total cost. Such economies of scale may exist not only in production but also in administration, research and development and financing.

Concentrating first on production, economies of scale may arise for such reasons as the following: set-up costs and marketing costs may be spread over larger outputs; indivisible units of high-cost machinery may become feasible at higher levels of output; where capacity is dependent on volume and cost is dependent on surface area, as in the case of storage tanks, such area–volume relationships may result in less than proportionate rises in costs.

When we turn to administration, a large organisation may attract and make better use of scarce managerial talent and enable the firm to employ specialists. Large organisations may also be able to attract suitable people to administer research and development programmes and to use the results of those programmes more effectively. In addition, the larger organisation is often in a position to raise and service capital more cheaply than a smaller organisation.

Economics textbooks devote considerable space to discussions of the theoretical bases for economies of scale, and governments have often encouraged and supported combinations on the grounds that they would improve the efficiency of British industry, in particular its competitiveness in international markets. For reasons discussed below, there is now less confidence that benefits will be obtained from combinations.

Various techniques have been developed to examine whether and to what extent economies of scale exist in practice. Although there appears to be scope for economies of scale in many industries, these do not appear automatically after a business combination, but have to be planned. A number of studies have found that the performances of many combined businesses have been rather disappointing. In particular there are diseconomies of large organisations, due mainly to the problems of administering large units, which may often outweigh the benefits afforded by economies of scale.

Elimination or reduction of competition

By eliminating or reducing competition, it may be possible for a company to make larger profits; combining with another business may be one means of achieving this end. Although integration may occur for many reasons, one reason may be that it is possible to reduce competition both by vertical integration, that is by combining with a firm at an earlier or later stage of the production cycle, or by horizontal integration, that is by combining with a firm at the same stage in the production cycle.

To illustrate, a firm at one stage of production may combine with a firm at an earlier stage of production, that is a supplier, thus ensuring a ready source of supply and perhaps putting it in a position to charge a lower price than competitors at the second stage, and hence squeeze them out of business. The extent to which this is possible would depend upon the structure of the market, that is the extent to which there are monopolistic or competitive elements present.

Combination with a firm at the same stage of production would reduce the number of competitors by one and again may give rise to higher profits as a result of the increased industrial concentration, although much would depend upon the structure of the industry before and after the combination. The combination of two small firms in a very competitive industry might have little effect, whereas the combination of two giants might turn an oligopoly into a virtual monopoly.

There are obvious dangers to the public at large from mergers which reduce the level of competition and it is for this reason that we have legislation on monopolies and mergers.

Reduction of risk

By combining with a firm which makes different products, a business is often able to reduce risk. Thus one reason for a combination involving businesses in different industries may be a desire to generate an earnings stream which is less variable than the separate earnings streams of the two individual businesses. Such a reduction of risk is usually considered to be an advantage and will often lead to an increase in share values, although it may be argued that shareholders may be better able to reduce risk by the selection of their own portfolio of shares.

Use of price/earnings ratios

In many business combinations, one company has been able to increase the wealth of its own shareholders by combining with a company which has a lower price/earnings ratio. To illustrate let us take a simple example of two companies:

	Company A	*Company B*
Earnings	£10 000	£10 000
Number of ordinary shares	100 000	100 000
Earnings per share	10p	10p
Current market price	£1.50p	£1.20p
P/E ratio	15	12

Let us suppose that company A issues 80 000 shares valued at £120 000 (80 000 at £1.50) in exchange for 100 000 shares in company B valued at £120 000 (100 000 at £1.20). If there is no change in earnings after the combination, the earnings of the combined companies as reflected in the group accounts will be £20 000 and the earnings per share 11p, that is £20 000 divided by 180 000 shares in A. If the market continues to use the P/E ratio of company A, that is 15, the price of a share in company A after the combination will be £1.65. This is greater than £1.50, the price of a share in company A before the combination and hence advantageous to the original shareholders in the company. It is also advantageous to the original shareholders in company B who now hold 80 000 shares in company A valued at £132 000 compared with their former holdings of 100 000 shares in company B which were valued at £120 000.

It may be argued that the market is unlikely to apply the same P/E ratio to the combined earnings as it previously did to the earnings in company A as a separate company. An 'average' P/E ratio of 13.5, calculated as shown below, would perhaps be expected:

	Earnings	Values
Company A	£10 000	£150 000
Company B	£10 000	£120 000
Combined	£20 000	£270 000

The average P/E ratio is 270 000/20 000 = 13.5.

This does not appear to happen in practice, and the resulting P/E ratio is usually well above this 'average' P/E ratio because the market anticipates a better future.

Thus, even though benefits such as economies of scale and reduction of competition do not materialise, some companies have been able to increase the wealth of their shareholders by acquiring other companies with lower P/E ratios.

Managerial motives

Under traditional economic theory, the role of management is to respond in a rational, but more or less automatic, way to circumstances which present themselves. Thus if, for example, economies of scale are perceived to be likely if two businesses combine, such a combination will be pursued in order to maximise the wealth of shareholders.

A number of studies have suggested that the usual financial and economic reasons put forward for mergers were, in practice, not of prime importance. What seemed to be a more important determinant of mergers among large companies was the objectives of managers. In order to cope with increasing uncertainty, managers desired to increase their market power or to defend their market position. Although such activities could well further the interests of shareholders, they may have even greater benefits for the managers themselves. Thus, a less uncertain life, in particular less chance of the company itself being taken over, a larger empire and perhaps larger remuneration due to control of such an empire may be extremely important motivating forces.

Whatever the ultimate objective, managerial motives seemed to play a much larger role in merger activity than traditional economic theory allowed.

Methods of combining

In order to be able to account for combinations, we must first explore some of the methods which may be used to effect them. Such methods may best be classified as to whether or not a group structure results from the combination.

Let us take as an example two companies, L and M, and assume that the respective boards of directors and owners have agreed to combine their businesses.

Combinations which result in a group structure

Two such combinations may be considered.

In the first case, company L may purchase the shares of company M and thereby acquire a subsidiary company; alternatively company M may purchase the shares of company L.

The choice of consideration given in exchange for the shares acquired will determine whether or not the shareholders in what becomes the subsidiary company have any interest in the combined businesses. Thus, if company L issues shares in exchange for the shares of

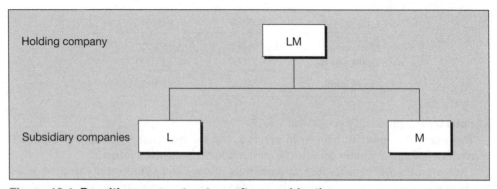

Figure 13.1 Resulting group structure after combination

company M, the old shareholders in company M have an interest in the resulting holding company and thereby in the group, whereas, if company L pays cash for the shares in company M, the old shareholders in M take their cash and cease to have any interest in the resulting group.

In the second case, a new company, LM, may be established to purchase the shares of both L and M. Thus, the shareholders in L and M may sell their shares to LM in exchange for shares in LM. The resulting group structure would then be as shown in Figure 13.1. The shareholders in LM would be the former shareholders in the two separate companies and their respective interests would depend, as in all the examples in this section, upon the valuations placed upon the two separate companies, which would in turn depend in part upon bargaining between the two boards of directors.

It is possible for company LM to issue not only shares but also loan stock in order to purchase the shares in L and M. It would be difficult for payment to be made in cash as LM is a newly formed company, although it could, of course, issue other shares or raise loans to obtain cash.

Combinations not resulting in a group structure

Again, two such combinations may be considered.

First, instead of purchasing the shares of company M, company L may obtain control of the net assets of M by making a direct purchase of those net assets. The net assets would thus be absorbed into company L and company M would itself receive the consideration. This would in due course be distributed to the shareholders of M by its liquidator.

As before, the choice of consideration determines whether or not the former shareholders in M have any interest in the enlarged company L.

Second, instead of one of the companies purchasing the net assets of the other, a new company may be formed to purchase the net assets of both existing companies. Thus, a new company, LM, may be formed to purchase the net assets of company L and company M. If payment is made by issuing shares in LM, these will be distributed by the respective liquidators so that the end result is one company, LM, which owns the net assets previously held by the separate companies and has as its shareholders the former shareholders in the two separate companies.

Preference for group structure

The above are methods of effecting a combination between two, or indeed more, companies although, in practice, virtually all large business combinations make use of a group structure, rather than a purchase of assets or net assets. Such a structure is advantageous in that separate companies enjoying limited liability are already in existence. It follows that names, and associated goodwill, of the original companies are not lost and there is no necessity to renegotiate contractual arrangements. All sorts of other factors will be important in practice; some examples are the desire to retain staff, the impact of taxation and whether or not there is a remaining minority interest. A group structure also permits easy disinvestment by sale of one or more subsidiaries.

Choice of consideration

As discussed above, the choice of consideration will determine who is interested in the single business created by the combination and will therefore be affected by the intentions of the parties to the combination. The choice of consideration will also be affected by the size of the companies and by conditions in the market for securities and the taxation system in force.

The main possible types of consideration are cash, loan stock, ordinary shares, some form of convertible security or any combination of these.

Let us look at the effect of each of these before turning to some factors which influence the choice between them.

Cash

Where one company purchases the shares or assets of another for cash the shareholders of the latter company cease to have any interest in the combined businesses.

From the point of view of the selling shareholders, they take a certain cash sum and will be liable to capital gains tax on the disposal of their shares.

From the point of view of the purchasing company, its cash holdings will decrease. It has sometimes been suggested that the use of cash will give a better chance of success if opposition is anticipated and, provided the earnings of the company which is purchased are greater than the earnings which would be made by using cash in other ways, there will be an increase in the earnings per share.

Loan stock

In this case the selling shareholders, either directly or indirectly, exchange shares in one company for loan stock in another company. Hence an equity investment is exchanged for a fixed-interest investment, which may or may not be an advantage, depending upon the relative values of the securities and the circumstances of the individual investor. Any liability to capital gains tax will be deferred until ultimate disposal of the loan stock.

From the point of view of the shareholders of the purchasing company, there may be an advantage in that the level of gearing will be increased. In addition, interest on the loan stock will be deductible for corporation tax purposes.

Ordinary shares

A share-for-share exchange is often the method used in combinations involving large companies. Here the shareholder simply exchanges shares in one company for shares in another company.

There are many potential benefits for the selling shareholders, although the extent to which they exist will depend upon the exact terms of the combination and the relative values of the shares. The selling shareholder continues to have an interest in the combined businesses, with the benefits mentioned in the second section of this chapter, and will not be subject to capital gains tax on the exchange. Against this the value of the security received is not certain but will depend upon market reaction to the combination.

From the point of view of the combined companies, a share exchange does not affect their liquidity. The extent to which it is beneficial for the existing shareholders of the company must depend upon the relative values of the shares.

Although shares were popular in the mid-1980s, cash has been the major part of the consideration in all but two of the ten years 1991 to 2000.[2]

Convertible loan stock

The issue of convertible loan stock has become more common and has sometimes been used in connection with business combinations. In such a case, the shareholders in one company exchange their shares for convertible loan stock in another company.

From the point of view of a selling shareholder, an equity investment is exchanged for a fixed-interest security, but one which is convertible into an equity investment at some time in the future. Thus, if in the future share prices move in the shareholder's favour, the shareholder will be able to take up the equity interest while, if they move against the shareholder, he or she will be able to retain the fixed interest investment. Again, any liability to capital gains tax is deferred until ultimate disposal of the convertible stock or equity shares issued in exchange.

From the point of view of the company issuing such securities, the interest on the loan stock is deductible for taxation purposes and the debt is self-liquidating if loan holders convert loan stock into ordinary shares. If loan holders do convert, the tax deductibility is, of course, lost and in addition there is a reduction in gearing and possible dilution of the existing shareholders' interest.

The choice in practice

As has been seen above, the various forms of consideration which may be used have advantages and disadvantages. The choice in any business combination will depend upon a large number of factors, some of which have been discussed in this section.

It is convenient to distinguish between an agreed combination where the two sets of shareholders in the individual companies are to be shareholders in the new or enlarged company and a situation where one party is dominant and is seeking to obtain control of the other company as cheaply as possible.

In the first of these cases the major part of the consideration must obviously be equity shares although, if a situation of surplus cash or low gearing is expected after the combination, an opportunity may be taken to pay part of the consideration in cash or some form of loan stock.

In the second case the choice of consideration will be affected considerably by the nature of the companies involved and the market situation. Where the biddee company is small or opposition is expected, a cash bid may be preferred. Loan stock may be attractive where rates of interest are low and especially if they are expected to rise. Where, however, it is felt that the shares of the dominant company are overpriced relative to those of the other company, then a share issue is likely to be most attractive.

---

[2] See the statistics on p. 360 for an analysis of the total expenditure for each of the years 1991–2000 between cash, ordinary shares and fixed-interest securities.

Accounting for business combinations

Accounting for business combinations is a topic which has been the cause of considerable controversy in many countries. The traditional method of accounting for combinations in the UK was the 'acquisition' or 'purchase' method but, in the 1960s, a new method began to find favour. This was the 'merger' or 'pooling of interests' method which had been extensively used in the USA. ED 3 *Accounting for Acquisitions and Mergers,* which was published in 1971, attempted to define situations in which each method should be used but was never converted into an SSAP. Changes introduced by the Companies Act 1981 made it possible to make progress and SSAP 23 *Accounting for Acquisitions and Mergers* was issued in April 1985. This standard was the subject of considerable criticism and, in 1990, the ASC issued a revised version ED 48. The ASB then issued its own exposure draft, FRED 6 *Acquisitions and Mergers,* in May 1993 and this was followed by FRS 6, with the same title, in September 1994. We shall explore these attempts at standardisation after we have distinguished between the 'acquisition' and 'merger' methods of accounting.

Acquisition and merger accounting

As stated above, the acquisition method has traditionally been used to account for business combinations in the UK and, where the consideration for shares or assets purchased is wholly cash or loan stock, this is agreed to be the correct method of accounting. However, where the consideration given is wholly or predominantly ordinary shares, many accountants would argue that the acquisition method is inappropriate. Here the shareholders in one company exchange their equity holding in that company for an equity interest in another company: a holding company if shares are purchased, or an enlarged company if net assets are purchased. In such circumstances, use of the acquisition method frequently produces inconsistencies in the treatment of the two combining companies. These inconsistencies are avoided by the use of the merger method but, as we shall see, consistency is obtained only at a price.

Under acquisition accounting, an investment in a subsidiary would normally be recorded at the fair value of the consideration given. Where the fair value of any shares issued exceeds their par value, a share premium account or merger reserve would normally be created in the parent company's financial statements.[3] In the consolidated financial statements, the investment would be replaced by the underlying separable assets and liabilities of the subsidiary at their fair values, representing their 'cost' to the group. Any difference between the cost of the investment and the sum of the values of the separable assets and liabilities is recorded as goodwill. Pre-acquisition profits of the subsidiary are no longer available for distribution and the results of the new subsidiary are only brought into the consolidated profit and loss account from the date of acquisition.[4]

Under the merger method of accounting, the investment in the subsidiary company would normally be recorded in the parent company's financial statements as the aggregate of the nominal value of any shares issued plus the fair value of any other consideration.[5] Thus,

---

[3] The conditions for the creation of a merger reserve, rather than a share premium account, will be discussed below.

[4] The acquisition method of accounting is considered in much greater depth in the next chapter. FRS 7 *Fair Values in Acquisition Accounting,* September 1994, provides guidance both on identifying assets and liabilities at the date of acquisition and on determining their fair values.

[5] As we shall see later in the chapter, any consideration other than equity shares must be a 'small' proportion of the total consideration for the use of merger accounting to be permissible.

the carrying value of the investment would not be equal to the fair value of the consideration given and no share premium account or merger reserve would be created.

In the consolidated financial statements, the investment would be replaced by the underlying separable assets and liabilities, not at fair value, but at their book values in the subsidiary's own accounts subject to adjustments necessary to achieve consistency of accounting policies for the group.[6] The pre-acquisition profits of the new subsidiary are not frozen but are aggregated with those of the parent company, and the results of the new subsidiary are brought into the consolidated profit and loss account for the whole period as if the companies had always been merged. No goodwill is recorded and any difference between the nominal value of shares issued plus the fair value of any other consideration given and the nominal value of shares purchased is treated as an adjustment to 'other reserves' in the consolidated financial statements. FRS 6 also makes it clear that any share premium account or capital redemption reserve in the subsidiary's balance sheet should also be treated as a movement in 'other reserves' (Para. 18).

The following illustration demonstrates the essential differences between the two methods when there is a share-for-share exchange.

Summarised balance sheets

	1	2	3
		After combination	
	Before combination	Acquisition method	Merger method
H Limited	£	£	£
Net assets (Fair values £1800)	1600	1600	1600
Shares in S Limited – at 'cost'		2400	800
	1600	4000	2400
£1 ordinary shares	1000	1800	1800
Share premium/merger reserve		1600	
Retained profits	600	600	600
	1600	4000	2400
S Limited			
Net assets (Fair values £1500)	1200	No change	
£1 ordinary shares	800	No change	
Retained profits	400		
	1200		

Column 1 shows the summarised balance sheets of H Limited and S Limited before a combination in which H buys the shares in S in a share-for-share exchange. In order to concentrate on the essential differences between the two methods, we will assume that the current value of a share in both H Limited and S Limited is agreed to be £3. Hence H issues 800 shares in exchange for the 800 shares in S. We shall also assume that the sum of the fair values of separable net assets in H and S are £1800 and £1500, respectively.

---

[6] It would, of course, be possible for these assets and liabilities to be revalued. Indeed it would be possible to revalue the assets and liabilities of both of the merging companies, and we discuss this possibility later in this section.

Columns 2 and 3 show the parent company's balance sheet using the principles of the acquisition method and merger method respectively.[7]

If the acquisition method is used, the shares issued by H will be valued at their fair value at the date of issue, that is at £3 per share. The investment in the subsidiary will be shown at a cost of £2400 while a share premium or merger reserve of £1600 will be recorded. Column 2 of the summarised balance sheets reflects these entries.

If the merger method is used, the shares issued by H will be valued at their par value and the investment in the subsidiary will be shown at a 'cost' of £800. This is shown in column 3 of the summarised balance sheet.

We may now prepare the consolidated balance sheet of H Limited and its subsidiary S Limited using the acquisition and merger methods respectively.

Consolidated balance sheet of H Limited and subsidiary S Limited

	1	2
	Acquisition method £	Merger method £
Net assets: H 1600 + S 1500	3100	
H 1600 + S 1200		2800
Goodwill on consolidation		
2400 – 1500	900	
	4000	2800
£1 ordinary shares	1800	1800
Share premium/Merger reserve	1600	
Retained profits: H only	600	
H + S		1000
	4000	2800

Column 1 shows the consolidated balance sheet immediately after the combination using the acquisition method. In preparing the consolidated balance sheet the excess of the cost of investment in the subsidiary (£2400) over the sum of the fair values of the separable assets and liabilities (£1500) is shown as goodwill on consolidation. The effect of using this method may be summarised as follows:

(a) *Retained profits.* Before the combination H had retained profits of £600 and S had retained profits of £400. However, the consolidated balance sheet only includes the retained profits of H and those of S have been frozen. Thus, if H receives a dividend from the pre-acquisition profits of S, this normally reduces the carrying value of the investment. The dividend received cannot be used as the basis for a dividend payment to the shareholders in H.

(b) *Net assets.* While the net assets of H are shown on the basis of their book values (£1600), those of S are included at their fair values (£1500).

---

[7] This is not strictly correct in that the treatment of the investment in the parent company's financial statements is legally independent of what method of accounting is used in the consolidated financial statements. Thus, if merger relief (see p. 371 later in section) is available, H does not have to create a share premium/merger reserve in its own financial statements even though such a merger reserve will be required to apply acquisition accounting in its consolidated financial statements. What we have done is logically consistent with the subsequent treatment of the combination in the consolidated financial statements.

(c) *Goodwill.* The goodwill in the consolidated balance sheet relates to S. None appears in relation to H.

Many would question whether this gives a true and fair view of the combination. After all, exactly the same people are interested in the net assets after the combination as before, although their proportionate interests will probably have changed as a result of the bargaining process. All that has happened is that the shareholders in S have exchanged their shares in S for shares in H, which now in turn owns S. Thus, two sets of shareholders have come together for their mutual benefit. Why then should the retained profits of one company be frozen while those of the other are not? Why should the net assets of one company be shown at fair values while those of the other are shown at their historical cost values? Why should we recognise goodwill for one company but not for the other?

A further criticism could be made of the method in that the consolidated balance sheet would look very different if, instead of the acquisition of shares in S by H, S had acquired the shares of H. This is a perfectly feasible alternative means of combination. The results produced will therefore vary depending upon what may in fact be an arbitrary choice of the holding company.

Consideration of questions like these has led to the development of merger accounting. Under the merger method, shares issued in exchange for other shares are valued not at their fair value, but at their par value. Thus, using our simple example, the 800 shares issued by H would be valued at £1 each, that is £800, rather than at £3 each. Correspondingly, the investment in S would be shown at a 'cost' of only £800. Column 3 of the summarised balance sheets (p. 368) reflects this entry.

Column 2 of the consolidated balance sheets provides the resulting consolidated balance sheet. From this it may be seen that the pre-combination retained profits of the two individual companies are still available for dividend while the net assets of both companies are shown at their historical-cost-based valuation. It is as if the companies had been combined since the cradle and it follows that, in preparing the consolidated profit and loss account, the results of both companies would be included for the whole year irrespective of the date on which the combination occurred.[8] In preparing the consolidated financial statements, necessary adjustments must, of course, be made to reflect uniform accounting policies throughout the group.

While the use of the merger method results in a consistent treatment of the profits and net assets of the two companies, it does, of course, have the result that all the assets are valued on the basis of old historical costs, which are arguably of little relevance to users of the financial statements. Under the acquisition method, the assets of at least one company are shown at their fair values at the date of the combination, and to move from such a position to one where all assets are shown on the basis of their historical costs to the separate companies is regarded by some accountants as a step in the wrong direction.

One way to avoid this consequence of merger accounting would be for both companies to restate the carrying values of the separable assets and liabilities at their fair values at the date of combination so that the assets and liabilities of both companies would be shown on a consistent basis at fair value rather than at out-of-date values. Such a method, known as the 'new entity', 'new basis' or 'fresh start' method, has not found favour with standard setters in the past, although the IASB has been exploring the possible use of this method of accounting in Phase II of its review of business combinations, discussed later in this chapter.

---

[8] This is to be contrasted with the position using the acquisition method of accounting where the consolidated profit and loss account will only include the results of a new subsidiary from the date of acquisition. This topic is considered in some detail in the following chapter.

In the above example the par value of the shares issued by H was the same as the par value of the shares purchased. In most combinations this will not be the case and, in addition, the consideration may include cash and loan stock. Any difference between the par value of the shares issued plus the fair value of any other consideration and the par value of the shares purchased and any share premium account in respect of these shares would be dealt with as a movement on the consolidated reserves.

We have now explored the differences between acquisition accounting and merger accounting. Provided shares are used to purchase shares or net assets in another company, so that two sets of shareholders have an interest in the resulting combined business, we have the theoretical possibility of applying the merger method of accounting. We shall now explore the way in which the use of such a method has been regulated by some of the official pronouncements.

Development of an accounting standard

The Companies Act 1981

Prior to the Companies Act 1981, there were severe doubts about the legality of the merger method of accounting. Although the ASC had issued ED 3 *Accounting for Acquisitions and Mergers* in 1971, it was unable to make progress in this area until the passage of the Companies Act 1981.

The Companies Act 1981 relieved companies from the need to create a share premium account in certain circumstances and these provisions are now contained in the Companies Act 1985, ss. 131–134. This so-called merger relief is available when one company issues equity shares to purchase equity shares in another company and ends up with an equity holding of 90 per cent or more. In such circumstances, the company does not have to create a share premium account in respect of either the equity shares issued or any non-equity shares issued in exchange for non-equity shares.[9]

Thus, if one company issues equity shares to acquire 95 per cent of the equity shares of another company, it is not necessary to create any share premium account in respect of that transaction. If, however, one company already holds 20 per cent of the equity shares in another company and then purchases an additional 75 per cent of those shares, the relief from the need to create a share premium account applies only to the equity shares issued to obtain the 75 per cent holding, that is the purchase which takes the total holding to 90 per cent or above.

The main consequence of the above provisions was that they permitted, although they did not require, the use of merger accounting.

Once the merger method had been legalised, the ASC was able to turn its attention to the circumstances in which this method should be used. Before we look at the provisions of SSAP 23 (April 1985) and its successor FRS 6 (September 1994), we shall examine some of the matters which had to be considered and resolved.

Criteria for use of the merger method

Use of merger accounting would seem to offer certain advantages where there is a uniting of interests, that is where the equity shareholders in two separate companies pool their interests to become equity shareholders in a combined entity.

---

[9] Relief from the requirement to create a share premium account is also provided in the case of certain group reconstructions which involve the transfer of ownership of a company within a group (Companies Act 1985, s. 132).

As described above, the Companies Act 1981 made changes that allowed, but did not require, the use of the merger method, provided at least 90 per cent of the equity shares of the acquired company were part of the pool or, to put it another way, even when up to 10 per cent of the equity shares did not become part of the pool. Within this legal framework, the ASC had to decide what conditions were necessary for the use of the merger method of accounting and whether, if those conditions were satisfied, use of the merger method should be obligatory or optional. In this section some of the factors that had to be considered are discussed briefly.

First, although there must be a uniting of interests, to what extent is it necessary to obtain the approval of the two sets of shareholders? Do all the shareholders in the two companies have to agree to the merger or only some minimum proportion? The law requires the holding in the offeree company to exceed 90 per cent but it says nothing about obtaining the agreement of the shareholders in the offeror company. Clearly it would be possible to impose much more stringent conditions here.

Second, there is the question of relative size. If one company is much smaller than the other then, even though all shareholders in both companies agree to a uniting of interests, the end result may well be a situation in which one set of shareholders is dominant in the combined entity, with the other set of shareholders having insignificant influence. Is this really a uniting of interests or merely an 'acquisition' using equity shares as the consideration?

Third, in order for there to be a uniting of interests, the consideration must be equity shares. If the consideration is wholly cash or loan stock, resources leave the combining businesses and one set of shareholders ceases to have any equity interest in the combination and there is definitely no uniting of interests. A difficulty arises where the consideration consists mainly of equity shares but also partly of cash or loan stock. Does this disqualify the combination for treatment as a merger? If it does not do so in principle, then what is the maximum percentage of the consideration that may be given in a form other than equity shares?

These were the main questions to be answered in specifying the circumstances in which merger accounting could be used, although, as we shall see, the Companies Act 1989 has subsequently restricted the proportion of non-equity consideration that may be included in the total consideration. Given the nature of the questions, answers can only involve arbitrary choice and hence it is not surprising that the selection of a suitable set of criteria has posed problems for standard-setting bodies in the UK and elsewhere.

The approach of SSAP 23

SSAP 23 permitted the use of merger accounting where a number of conditions were satisfied.[10] If we concentrate on a situation in which two companies are combining by forming a holding company/subsidiary company relationship and we assume that both companies have only voting equity shares in issue, these conditions may be summarised in the following way:

(i) Any initial holding of one company in the other could not exceed 20 per cent.
(ii) The offer had to be made to all remaining shareholders and had to result in a total holding of 90 per cent or more.
(iii) Not less than 90 per cent of the fair value of the total consideration given for shares, both in the present transaction and in past transactions, had to be in the form of voting equity shares. [11]

---

[10] SSAP 23, Para. 11.

[11] As we shall see below, this last condition has been tightened considerably by the Companies Act 1989, which requires that the fair value of any consideration other than equity shares must not exceed 10 per cent of the nominal value of equity shares issued.

Where the initial holding exceeded 20 per cent, there was a presumption, albeit rebuttable, of significant influence requiring the use of the equity method of accounting. The equity method, discussed in Chapter 15, is based on the principles of acquisition accounting and is therefore incompatible with the use of merger accounting.

The requirement that the total holding is 90 per cent or more was necessary to comply with the Companies Act condition for the use of merger relief, and the final condition that 90 per cent or more of the fair value of the total consideration was in the form of voting equity shares limited the non-share consideration to 10 per cent. Hence, a limit was imposed on the resources leaving the group.

The SSAP 23 conditions did not require the combination to be approved by the shareholders in the offeror company nor did it concern itself with the relative sizes of the two companies. Even when all the conditions were satisfied, the use of merger accounting was not compulsory: acquisition accounting could still be used.

The inclusion of these conditions in SSAP 23 led to a number of difficulties and they were superseded by new conditions for the use of merger accounting, inserted in the Companies Act 1985 by the Companies Act 1989.[12] We shall explore these difficulties and provisions before turning to the later thinking of the standard setters as embodied in FRS 6. They provide an excellent example of the difficulties which may arise when accounting standards contain detailed rules rather than principles.

Experience of SSAP 23

If we compare the consequences of using acquisition accounting and merger accounting in our simple example above, it is not hard to see why a company may prefer to use the merger method, if it is available, for a particular business combination. Under the merger method, the balance sheet figures for separable net assets are lower, and no amount emerges for goodwill. Subsequent reported profits will be higher, as depreciation will be based on lower asset values and there will be no goodwill to amortise. Thus, the merger method will result in the reporting of higher returns on capital employed in the company's subsequent financial statements than would be disclosed if the acquisition method were used.

Given the desire of companies to report their affairs in the best possible light, it is perhaps not surprising that numerous attempts were made to exploit the conditions included in SSAP 23 in order to be able to apply merger accounting. Let us look at a few examples.

Under SSAP 23 it was not possible to use merger accounting if the purchasing company held 20 per cent or more of the equity shares in the other company immediately prior to the offer. Where one company held more than 20 per cent in the other, it was easily able to reduce the holding below 20 per cent by 'warehousing' shares with a banker or other third party. Thus, by temporarily selling enough shares to take the holding below 20 per cent and buying them back in the general offer, it was able to satisfy this particular condition.

Other rather blatant exploitations of the specific conditions were the so-called 'vendor placing' and 'vendor rights' schemes. These were used where one company wished to buy shares in another for cash, or some other non-equity share consideration, but also wished to use merger accounting. A payment in cash would mean resources leaving the group and would require the use of acquisition accounting. In order to avoid this, some companies made a share-for-share exchange but gave the shareholders in the acquired company the power to convert the shares which they received into cash immediately, either by placing them with a third party or by selling them back to the shareholders in the acquiring company. The former was a vendor placing and the latter a vendor rights scheme. The end result

[12] Companies Act 1985, Schedule 4A, Para. 10.

was that shares had been purchased for cash but in such a way that merger accounting could be used. While no resources left the group, there was certainly no pooling or uniting of shareholders' interests of the two companies!

It is quite clear that some companies applied the letter rather than the spirit of the standard and the above perceived abuses of the standard brought much criticism from commentators.

FRS 6 Acquisitions and Mergers

Following the Companies Act 1989, which implemented the EC Seventh Directive on consolidated accounts, conditions for the use of merger accounting have been incorporated in the law, and these conditions differ somewhat from those included in SSAP 23. This change, together with the criticisms discussed above, necessitated a revision of SSAP 23.

The legal conditions for the use of merger accounting are contained in Schedule 4A to Companies Act 1985 and are listed in Table 13.2.[13]

Although the conditions in Table 13.2 do not fix a maximum shareholding immediately prior to the combination, condition 3, that the fair value of any non-equity consideration does not exceed 10 per cent of the nominal value of the shares issued, is much stricter than the SSAP 23 condition that it did not exceed 10 per cent of the fair value of the total consideration given. Whereas the purpose of the SSAP 23 condition was clear, the new legal condition appears to lack any economic validity whatsoever.

Table 13.2 Legal conditions for use of merger accounting

1	At least 90 per cent of the nominal value of the relevant shares in the undertaking acquired is held by or on behalf of the parent company and its subsidiary undertakings.
2	The proportion referred to in condition 1 was attained pursuant to an arrangement providing for the issue of equity shares by the parent company or one or more of its subsidiary undertakings.
3	The fair value of any consideration other than the issue of equity shares given pursuant to the arrangement by the parent company and its subsidiary undertakings did not exceed 10 per cent of the nominal value of the equity shares issued.
4	Adoption of the merger method of accounting accords with generally accepted accounting principles or practice.

Condition 4 leaves it to the standard setters to specify any further criteria for the use of merger accounting, and their thinking can now be found in FRS 6 *Acquisitions and Mergers*, issued in September 1994.

The approach taken in FRS 6 owes much to the Canadian standard setters[14] and restricts drastically the circumstances in which merger accounting may be used. The objective of the standard (Para. 1) makes this quite clear:

> to ensure that merger accounting is used only for those business combinations that are not, in substance, the acquisition of one entity by another but the formation of a new reporting entity as a substantially equal partnership where no party is dominant; to ensure the use of acquisition accounting for all other business combinations; and to ensure that in either case the financial statements provide relevant information concerning the effect of the combination.

[13] Schedule 4A, Para. 10. Schedule 4A was inserted into the Companies Act 1985 by Schedule 2 to the Companies Act 1989.

[14] See Canadian Institute of Chartered Accountants (CICA) Handbook, s. 1580, 'Business Combinations', 1973.

The relative sizes of the combining entities, considered unimportant in earlier definitions, now become extremely important in the FRS 6 definition of a merger:

> **A business combination that results in the creation of a new reporting entity formed from the combining parties, in which the shareholders of the combining entities come together in a partnership for the mutual sharing of the risks and benefits of the combined entity, and in which no party to the combination in substance obtains control over any other, or is seen to be dominant, whether by virtue of the proportion of its shareholders' rights in the combined entity, the influence of its directors or otherwise.**

The standard (Paras 6–12) then lists five criteria for determining whether this definition of a merger is met and these are summarised in Table 13.3. Where these criteria are met, merger accounting is compulsory. In all other circumstances, except certain group reconstructions, acquisition accounting must be used.

Table 13.3 **Criteria used to identify a merger**

1 No party is portrayed as acquirer or acquired by the board or management of either party.

2 All parties participate in selecting the management structure and personnel of the new entity by consensus rather than purely by the exercise of voting rights.

3 The relative sizes of the combining entities are not so disparate that one party dominates the combined entity.

4 Equity shareholders in the combining entities receive, as consideration, primarily equity shares in the combined entity. Any non-equity consideration must be an immaterial proportion of the fair value received. As we have seen, the law restricts the non-equity consideration to 10 per cent of the nominal value of the equity shares issued.

5 The equity shareholders in the combining entities must not retain a material interest in the future performance of only part of the combined entity. However, a combining entity may divest itself of a peripheral part of its business and still meet the definition of a merger.

Whether the combination is an acquisition or merger, the standard specifies minimum disclosure requirements to enable users to understand the effect of the combination. For all combinations, this disclosure must include the names of the combining entities, the date of the combination and whether merger accounting or acquisition accounting has been used.

When merger accounting has been used, the required disclosure includes an analysis of the principal components of the profit and loss account and statement of total recognised gains and losses into amounts related to the merged entity after the date of the merger and, for each party to the merger, amounts relating to that party for the period up to the date of the merger. Comparative amounts for the preceding financial year are also required. The standard also requires disclosure of the aggregate book values of the net assets of each party at the date of the merger and any adjustments made to these to achieve consistency of accounting policies between the parties as well as a statement of the adjustments made to consolidated reserves.

Few business combinations meet the criteria for the existence of a merger laid down in FRS 6 and hence the use of merger accounting is now extremely rare. As always, most business combinations will be acquisitions and the appropriate method of accounting will be acquisition accounting, as discussed in Chapter 14.

The international accounting standard

The relevant international accounting standard, IAS 22 *Business Combinations*, first issued in 1983 and subsequently revised in 1993 and 1998, is yet again under review. This standard distinguishes between two different types of combination, an acquisition and a uniting of interests, and specifies different methods of accounting for each of these. A uniting of interests only occurs when an acquirer cannot be identified[15] and is equivalent to what the ASB describes as a merger. All other business combinations are classified as acquisitions. Where there is an acquisition, the purchase method of accounting must be used. This is essentially the acquisition method as specified in FRS 6. However, when it comes to the detail of how the method is to be applied we find that there are numerous differences between the two standards. We shall examine some of these differences in the following chapter and provide just one example here.

In order to arrive at the initial values of assets and liabilities in an acquired entity, IAS 22 provides a choice between *a benchmark* treatment and an *allowed alternative* treatment. The difference between them is the way in which the share of any minority interest is valued.[16] Under the benchmark treatment, the proportion of the identifiable assets and liabilities in the acquired company which have been purchased are shown at their fair values while the proportion held by any minority interest are shown on the basis of their pre-acquisition carrying values. Under the allowed alternative treatment, the whole of the assets and liabilities of the acquired entity are shown at their fair values and the minority interest is shown at the appropriate proportion of those fair values. The benchmark treatment provides some rather odd numbers in a balance sheet and seems unlikely to survive the present review of IAS 22. However, until this happens, FRS 6 sensibly requires the use of the allowed alternative treatment, rather than the benchmark treatment, of IAS 22.

Where there is a uniting of interests, then the 'pooling of interests' method of accounting must be used. This is the same as the merger method of accounting specified in FRS 6.

While FRS 6 is consistent with, although somewhat more restrictive than, the provisions of IAS 22 on business combinations, there has recently been a movement towards the abolition of the merger/pooling of interests method of accounting. The group of international standard setters G4+1 issued a Position Paper in 1998 and this was subsequently published as a Discussion Paper by the ASB.[17] This paper considers whether there should be a single method of accounting for business combinations and, if so, what it should be. It comes to the conclusion that the purchase method, that is the acquisition method of accounting in British terminology, should be used for all business combinations.

The IASB is reviewing IAS 22 and has divided its review into two phases. The first phase is concerned with such matters as the definition of a business combination and appropriate methods of accounting, including the initial measurement of identifiable assets and liabilities and the treatment of provisions relating to the termination or reduction of the activities of the acquiree. This phase of the review is also concerned with accounting for goodwill, both positive and negative, and intangible assets, which reflects the wide coverage of the international accounting standard.

The second phase of the review is concerned with a number of matters including the way in which the acquisition method of accounting is to be applied and the possible use of the

---

[15] See IASC Standing Interpretations Committee, Interpretation SIC-9, *Business Combinations – Classification either as Acquisitions or Uniting of Interests*, 1998.

[16] See Chapter 14, p. 430.

[17] G4+1 Position Paper, 'Recommendations for Achieving Convergence on the Methods of Accounting for Business Combinations', FASB, 1998, and Discussion Paper, *Business Combinations*, ASB, London, December 1998.

new basis/fresh start method of accounting for business combinations under which the assets and liabilities of both parties are stated at their fair values, although probably only for those involving entities under common control. It is also looking at the treatment of contingent consideration and contingent assets and liabilities existing in the acquired entity at the date of the combination.

This two-phase review will, in due course, lead to the issue of exposure drafts and then to at least one International Financial Reporting Standard to replace IAS 22. At the time of writing, the IASB is very much in favour of abolishing the pooling of interests method of accounting, which would make life somewhat simpler for hard-pressed students of accounting. However there has been strong opposition to that stance by a number of countries, particularly Japan, and we must await the final outcome of the IASB deliberations.

The authors would welcome the abolition of the pooling of interests/merger method of accounting on both theoretical and practical grounds and await further developments in this area with interest.

Goodwill

Introduction

Goodwill is the term used by accountants to describe the difference between the value placed on a firm and the sum of the fair values of the assets and liabilities of the firm which are identified and recognised by the accounting system. There are two reasons why these values will not be equal. First, most firms possess not only the predominantly tangible assets listed in a balance sheet but also such intangible assets as 'managerial ability', 'efficient staff' and 'regional monopoly' which contribute to the value of the firm and yet are not included in a balance sheet. Second, there is the simple economic fact that assets operating together frequently have a much higher value than the sum of the values of those same assets operating separately.

Goodwill is usually only recorded in an accounting system when a company purchases an unincorporated business or acquires a subsidiary or associated undertaking and prepares consolidated accounts. In the former case the goodwill arises in the accounts of the purchasing company itself whereas, in the latter case, the goodwill arises only in the consolidated accounts. In both cases the goodwill is described as 'purchased goodwill' to distinguish it from internally generated goodwill.

In the past goodwill was sometimes calculated as the difference between the price paid and the sum of the book values of the individually identified assets less liabilities in the books of the acquired firm or company. Although this may simplify calculations, it makes little economic sense, as the values in the books of the acquired firm or company are irrelevant in determining the historical cost of assets to the acquiring company or group. In accounting for an acquisition it is necessary for the acquiring company or group to value the individual assets and liabilities at their fair values, which determine their historical cost to the acquiring company or group.[18] Thus, the total cost of the collection of net assets, tangible and intangible, must be apportioned between those assets and liabilities which are to be identified

---

[18] See Companies Act 1985, Schedule 4A, Para. 9, which requires the use of fair values when a subsidiary is acquired, and FRS 9, Para. 31(a), which requires a similar treatment in the case of an associate or joint venture. FRS 7 *Fair Values in Acquisition Accounting* (September 1994), specifies standard accounting practice in relation to both the identification of assets and liabilities at the date of acquisition and their valuation. We discuss this topic in Chapter 14.

separately in the accounting system and those which are not so identified. The latter group are recorded in the accounting system as a balancing figure which is described as goodwill. Such goodwill will normally be positive, but FRS 10 *Goodwill and Intangible Assets*, takes the view that it may be negative.[19] This may occur when the price paid for the collection of net assets is less than the sum of the fair values of the separable net assets, although the standard warns us that, where such negative goodwill emerges, the amounts allocated to the separable net assets should be reviewed to ensure that their fair values have not been overstated.

Internally created goodwill is not recorded, whereas goodwill which results from a market transaction is. It is therefore important to recognise that when a goodwill figure appears in a set of financial statements, it does not relate to the whole reporting entity but merely to one segment which has been acquired by purchase.[20] Once the purchase has been made, that segment may be merged with the other assets of the enlarged entity and will then no longer be separately identifiable.

With this background we may proceed to examine the problem of accounting for goodwill, assuming for the most part that the goodwill figure is positive.

Accounting for goodwill

Some possibilities

At the date of acquisition, goodwill represents the cost of acquiring certain intangible assets. In such a case, the accruals concept would seem to dictate that the cost should be carried forward and matched against revenues of the periods expected to benefit from the use of such intangible assets. However, the future benefits may be extremely uncertain and there may be no way of determining which benefits arise from the particular collection of intangible assets. Hence, the prudence convention would appear to be relevant and would mean that no asset should be recognised; rather that the amount paid for goodwill should be written off.

Given that there is a conflict between the accruals and prudence conventions, it is not surprising to find that various methods of accounting for goodwill have been proposed. If we ignore the impractical suggestion that goodwill for the whole entity be revalued on each balance sheet date, the various proposals may be summarised as follows:

(a) Retain goodwill at cost, unless there is a permanent fall in the value.
(b) Write off (amortise) the cost of goodwill over a period of years, which could be (i) its useful life, or (ii) a specific number of years, or (iii) its useful life subject to a maximum number of years.
(c) Write off goodwill immediately against reserves.

Some writers have argued that, in view of the unique nature of goodwill, the amount under (a) or (b) should appear, not as an asset, but as a 'dangling debit', that is as a deduction from share capital and reserves. This treatment can be regarded as a 'half-hearted' adoption of options (a) or (b) in that the information is provided but in such a way as to cast doubt upon its relevance.

---

[19] Many accountants would not admit this possibility, arguing that the price paid must place a ceiling on the sum of the 'costs' of the separable net assets. See the later section of this chapter on the IASB position.

[20] An exception to this general position occurs when the net assets of one firm are purchased by a newly formed entity. An example is the conversion of a sole tradership or partnership into a limited company. Provided the limited company acquires only the net assets of the firm and owns no other assets, the goodwill figure will relate to the whole business.

Let us look at each of the proposals in turn.

The retention of goodwill at cost would seem to be justified only if the asset has an indefinite life. It is expected that this would rarely be true in the case of the particular intangible assets purchased, although the purchased benefits may, of course, be replaced by subsequent activities. If the intangible assets acquired do not have an indefinite life, it is necessary to recognise the possibility of a fall in the value of goodwill, but the determination of whether or not such a permanent fall has occurred will be an extremely difficult, if not impossible, task. It will certainly be difficult where the segment of the business which gave rise to the goodwill is no longer separately identifiable.

The amortisation of goodwill over a period of years is also subject to difficulties. In the first case, it is usually very difficult, if not impossible, to determine the useful life of goodwill, a residual category of assets measured by a balancing figure. In the second case, the selection of a specific number of years such as 5 or 40 is merely arbitrary, although the selection of a long period has the advantage that the results of no one period are significantly affected. The third case merely combines the difficulty of the first with the arbitrariness of the second.

The third proposal recognises that, after the year of acquisition, the retention of a goodwill figure relating to part of the business is unlikely to provide information useful to those interested in the affairs of the entity. It therefore requires its removal from the balance sheet by an immediate write-off against reserves.

In view of the different proposals which have been made and their associated problems, it is not surprising that standard setters have experienced considerable difficulty in deciding upon an appropriate standard accounting practice.

The approach of SSAP 22

SSAP 22 *Accounting for Goodwill,* was issued in December 1994 and revised in July 1989. It was replaced by FRS 10 *Goodwill and Intangible Assets,* which we discuss below, in December 1997.

Unless it was prepared to use the true and fair override, the retention of goodwill at its cost was not an option available to the ASC in drafting the original SSAP 22. The Companies Act 1985 stated clearly that, where goodwill is treated as an asset, it must be amortised systematically over a period not exceeding its useful economic life.[21] However, this still left the possibility of amortisation or of immediate write-off of goodwill against reserves for, in the latter case, goodwill is not treated as an asset and hence the legal requirement for amortisation does not apply.

While SSAP 22 preferred companies to write off goodwill immediately against reserves, it also permitted them to capitalise goodwill and to amortise it in arriving at the profit or loss on ordinary activities.[22] Both methods could be used simultaneously in respect of different acquisitions.

The preferred method had two major advantages. First, it avoided the difficult task of estimating the useful life of goodwill. Second, it resulted in a consistent treatment of purchased goodwill and internally-generated goodwill. Given that the law does not permit companies to include internally-generated goodwill in their balance sheets, the write-off of purchased goodwill results in the consistent position that no company shows goodwill in its balance sheet.

A major bias with the above requirements was that, if goodwill was capitalised and amortised, future profits and earnings per share would be reduced, whereas, if goodwill was written off against reserves, there would be no impact on the profit and loss account at all!

[21] Companies Act 1985, Schedule 4, para. 21.
[22] SSAP 22, Paras 32–5.

Not surprisingly the vast majority of companies adopted the preferred method of accounting under SSAP 22, often taking some pretty extreme steps to be able to do so.

Experience of SSAP 22

Before we explore the ways in which companies responded to SSAP 22, it will, perhaps, be helpful if we illustrate how large goodwill may be in relation to the other net assets of a company at the date of acquisition. A good, but extreme, example was provided in the annual accounts of Saatchi and Saatchi Company plc, a consultancy firm, for the year to 30 September 1986. The prices paid for subsidiaries, the tangible net assets acquired, and the resulting goodwill in respect of that year were as follows:

	£m
Cost of acquisitions	443.2
Net tangible assets	41.2
Goodwill	402.0

Another example is provided in the annual financial statements of Thorn EMI plc for the year to 31 March 1993, a year in which Thorn EMI plc acquired the Virgin Music Group Limited from Richard Branson:

	Total	Virgin Music Group Ltd	Other
	£m	£m	£m
Cost of acquisitions	653.7	593.0	60.7
Fair value of net assets acquired	17.3	14.1	3.2
Goodwill	636.4	578.9	57.5

In both of these cases, goodwill dwarfed the identifiable net assets, as might be expected in any successful company or group where people are the most important assets.

Given that large amounts have been paid to acquire valuable goodwill, there was a considerable reluctance among many companies to write off that goodwill in accordance with SSAP 22. One response was to isolate an element of goodwill as 'brands' and to retain this in the balance sheet.[23] Such an approach raised considerable controversy and, in ED 52 *Accounting for Intangible Fixed Assets* (May 1990), the ASC attempted to outlaw separate accounting for brands. We shall examine the approach of the ASB later in this chapter.

Once faced with the need to account for goodwill in accordance with SSAP 22, it is perhaps not surprising to find that the vast majority of companies chose immediate write-off rather than amortisation through the profit and loss account with its consequent impact on earnings per share. The way in which many large companies did so makes interesting reading.

If a company wished to adopt the policy of immediate write-off, the first question which had to be answered, on which SSAP 22 was silent, was which reserves could be used for the purpose of writing off goodwill. There was widespread agreement that the balance on the profit and loss account and any merger reserve could be used for this purpose, but there was

---

[23] Some companies have gone further than this by including the values of internally generated brands as well as those which have been purchased. Good examples of companies which accounted for brands are Rank Hovis McDougall and Grand Metropolitan.

dispute over whether the law permitted the use of a revaluation reserve. Although there was a large body of opinion to the effect that a revaluation reserve could not be used for this purpose, many companies chose to ignore this opinion.[24]

The next problem arose when the 'available' reserves were too small to absorb a write-off of goodwill, and here we found two major responses.

Some companies effectively used share premium accounts to write off goodwill. They applied to the courts for a reduction of capital in order to be able to comply with the preferred method of accounting under SSAP 22. The share premium accounts were effectively relabelled, perhaps as a special reserve, thus becoming available to absorb the goodwill write-off.[25]

The second response was to create an appropriate reserve, a 'goodwill write-off' reserve, with a zero balance. The purchased goodwill could be written off against this goodwill write-off reserve resulting in a debit balance, a negative reserve, which was deducted from the share capital and reserves in the consolidated balance sheet.[26]

As well as provoking the above responses, the preference of SSAP 22 for immediate write-off appears to have had certain other consequences. By understating the fair values of the identifiable assets and liabilities, groups have been able to increase the amount labelled as goodwill and, given that this goodwill is written off to reserves, future reported profits benefited from reduced depreciation charges on the identified tangible and intangible assets purchased.

Particular variants of this have involved the creation, at the date of acquisition, of a provision for reorganisation costs and sometimes even a provision for future losses. Such provisions reduce the identified net assets and again increase the goodwill written off against reserves. They are then available to absorb costs which would otherwise have to be charged to the profit and loss account, and any unused amount could, in due course, be credited to the profit and loss account. Although it is possible to justify the setting up of such provisions, some groups have undoubtedly set up excessive provisions. As we have seen in Chapter 7, FRS 12 *Provisions, Contingent Liabilities and Contingent Assets,* now outlaws this approach as does FRS 7 *Fair Values in Acquisition Accounting,* to which we return in the following chapter.

It was developments such as those outlined above which caused the ASC to issue a revised version of SSAP 22 in July 1989. The purpose of this standard was not to change the practice of accounting for goodwill, but to provide additional disclosure to help the users of accounts to understand what had been done.[27] Thus companies were required to show how goodwill had been dealt with and to provide the table, subsequently required by law, showing the book values and fair values of each major category of assets and liabilities, together with an explanation of reasons for differences. In addition, it required disclosure of movements on provisions related to acquisitions and of information relating to the treatment of disposals of previously acquired businesses or business segments.

Even as the revised SSAP 22 was being issued, the accounting treatment of goodwill was under review and this led to the very different proposals in ED 47 *Accounting for Goodwill,* which was published in February 1990.

---

[24] Since the Companies Act 1989, the revalution reserve is definitely not available for the write-off of goodwill, Companies Act 1985, Schedule 4, Para. 34.

[25] Examples of companies which employed such an approach are Saatchi and Saatchi in 1985 and 1986 and Blue Arrow plc in 1987. A capital redemption reserve could presumably also be used in this way.

[26] Examples of groups which used this 'dangling debit disclosure' are Erskine House Group plc and TI Group plc.

[27] The additional disclosure requirements were contained in Paras 47–53 of the revised standard.

Towards a new standard

ED 47 took a very different view from SSAP 22. Whereas SSAP 22 favoured immediate write-off and permitted amortisation, ED 47 removed any choice and proposed that all goodwill should be amortised over its useful economic life. Whereas SSAP 22 attempted to achieve consistency between the treatment of purchased goodwill and that of non-purchased goodwill, ED 47 attempted to achieve consistency between the treatment of goodwill and that of other purchased intangible and tangible fixed assets. So, because buildings, machinery and trade marks are depreciated over their useful economic lives, it was argued that goodwill should be amortised.

ED 47 therefore proposed that positive goodwill should be amortised through the profit and loss account over its useful economic life using the straight-line basis or any other systematic basis which is more conservative and considered to give a more realistic allocation. However, it added the proviso that the useful economic life should not exceed 20 years, except in rare circumstances, and that the maximum life, even in those rare circumstances, should never exceed 40 years. These are provisions we do not find in standards dealing with tangible fixed assets! However, in common with similar provisions in respect of tangible fixed assets, ED 47 envisaged that there should be an annual review to ensure that the carrying value of goodwill was not excessive.

The exposure draft admitted the possibility of negative goodwill although, should such goodwill arise, it proposed a review of the fair values ascribed to the 'identifiable' assets and liabilities. Any negative goodwill remaining after such a review was to be credited to the profit and loss account over a suitable period.

The accounting treatment of goodwill proposed in ED 47 was very different from the preferred treatment of SSAP 22 adopted by the vast majority of UK companies. Given the potential impact of the proposed approach on reported profits, it is perhaps not surprising that there was considerable opposition to ED 47 and, partly due to the demise of the ASC, it was never converted into an accounting standard. As we shall see, the subsequent proposals of the ASB are rather more sophisicated, although we shall argue that the resulting standard, FRS 10 *Goodwill and Intangible Assets,* suffers from spurious sophistication.

ASB pronouncements

It was not until December 1993 that the ASB produced its first discussion paper on this subject entitled *Goodwill and Intangible Assets.*

In its proposed treatment of intangible assets the discussion paper was clear: purchased intangible assets, such as brands, should be subsumed within purchased goodwill and accounted for accordingly, although purchased legal rights, such as patents, attaching to internally created intangible benefits should be capitalised at their historical cost and amortised appropriately (Paras 1.7 and 3.1.3).

When it turned to the subject of accounting for purchased goodwill there was much less certainty. The paper identified the six methods of accounting for goodwill shown in Table 13.4. Three methods involved the recognition of goodwill as an asset while three methods involved the elimination of goodwill.

Although the discussion paper provided extensive discussion of the merits and demerits of the various methods, it failed to identify any single proposed approach. Indeed it identified two very different approaches which had support among Board members, namely methods A3 and B2 or B3. Method A3 is itself a combination of A1 and A2, while methods B2 and B3 both involve the creation of a separate goodwill write-off reserve, either with (B3)

Table 13.4 Methods of accounting for goodwill

A Asset-based methods

1   *Capitalisation and amortisation over a predetermined life* subject to a maximum number of years, possibly 20, and subject to the usual test of recoverability at the end of each year.

2   *Capitalisation and annual review.* Under this approach, the value of goodwill is assessed at each balance sheet date using certain 'ceiling' tests described at length in Appendix A to the Discussion Paper. These involve comparing the present value of the cash flows from the relevant segment of the business with the sum of the fair values of the separable assets and liabilities of that segment to determine the value of goodwill. Amortisation through the profit and loss account is only necessary if the value so determined is less than the existing carrying value of the goodwill.

3   *Combination of 1 and 2* with 1 being the norm and 2 being used when the goodwill has an indeterminate life expected to be more than 20 years.

B Elimination methods

1   *Immediate write-off against reserves*, the preferred method of SSAP 22.

2   *Creation of a separate goodwill write-off reserve* with disclosure as a 'dangling debit', a deduction from share capital and reserves. Under this approach no further adjustment would be made to the goodwill write-off reserve unless the acquired segment of the group to which it relates is disposed of or closed.

3   *Variant of 2* involving creation of a separate goodwill write-off reserve but with an annual assessment of recoverability to ensure that the goodwill write-off reserve is reduced if the value of the goodwill has fallen permanently.

or without (B2) a recoverability test. In other words, the Board envisaged possible ways forward which might have been described by a cynic as anything other than the preferred method of SSAP 22 – B1!

It came as no surprise that no consensus emerged in the responses to the discussion paper, although there was considerable opposition to the proposal that all intangible assets should be subsumed within purchased goodwill. To move matters forward, the ASB issued a working paper in June 1995 entitled 'Goodwill and Intangible Assets' for discussion at public hearings, the first such hearings to be held in the UK. This working paper and associated public hearings paved the way for the issue of FRED 12 *Goodwill and Intangible Assets,* in June 1996, and FRS 10, with the same title, in December 1997.

FRS 10 *Goodwill and Intangible Assets*

The ASB follows the provisions of company law by specifying that purchased goodwill should be capitalised and shown on the face of the balance sheet or consolidated balance sheet while internally generated goodwill should not be capitalised.

It requires that an intangible asset purchased separately should be capitalised at its cost while an intangible asset acquired as part of a purchase of a business should only be capitalised separately from goodwill if its fair value can be measured reliably; otherwise such an intangible should be subsumed within the amount shown for purchased goodwill.

On the purchase of a business, the amount of purchased goodwill will therefore be calculated as the difference between two values:

	£
Price paid to acquire business	X
less Sum of fair values of assets and liabilities identified and to be recorded separately in the accounting system, including intangible assets which can be measured reliably	X
Purchased goodwill, including intangible assets which cannot be measured reliably	X

We will deal first with the normal situation where purchased goodwill is positive and turn to negative goodwill later in the chapter.

FRS 10 is clear that, when purchased goodwill is positive, it must be recorded in the balance sheet as an intangible fixed asset. While most accountants would accept this position without question, it does pose considerable problems for an ASB which has issued a *Statement of Principles for Financial Reporting* specifying that a balance sheet should only include as assets, items which meet its definition of assets. (See Chapter 1, pp. 17–18.) The ASB is of the view that purchased goodwill does not meet its own definition of assets so has to wriggle somewhat to justify the inclusion of purchased goodwill in a balance sheet or consolidated balance sheet. Paragraph (b) of the Summary of FRS 10 says it all:

> The accounting requirements for goodwill reflect the view that goodwill arising on an acquisition is neither an asset like other assets nor an immediate loss in value. Rather, it forms the bridge between the cost of an investment shown as an asset in the acquirer's own financial statements and the values attributed to the acquired assets and liabilities in the consolidated financial statements. Although **purchased goodwill is not in itself an asset** [authors' emphasis], its inclusion among the assets of the reporting entity, rather than as a deduction from shareholders' equity, recognises that goodwill is part of a larger asset, the investment, for which management remains accountable.

The need for such a justification casts some doubt on the theoretical soundness of either the requirement for capitalisation of purchased goodwill or, more persuasively, the *Statement of Principles* itself.

Having required the capitalisation of purchased goodwill, the standard then attempts to ensure that 'capitalised goodwill and intangible assets are charged to the profit and loss account in the periods they are depleted' (Para. 1(a)). In the view of the ASB, such depletion only occurs 'to the extent that the carrying value of the goodwill is not supported by the current value of the goodwill within the acquired business' (Summary Para. (e)). We shall argue that this approach is fundamentally unsound.

In spite of these general principles, the ASB envisages that in practice goodwill and intangible assets will be amortised over their useful economic lives. Recognising the inevitable subjectivity, some would say impossibility, involved in estimating such lives and the potential desire of directors to overestimate them in order to minimise the amortisation expense in the profit and loss account, the standard contains a presumption that the useful economic life of purchased goodwill and intangibles does not exceed 20 years. The presumption is rebuttable so the standard accepts that the useful economic life may exceed 20 years and even that it may, in some cases, be indefinite so that no amortisation will be necessary. The grounds for adopting a life greater than 20 years must be clearly explained and, where an indefinite life is envisaged, the company must disclose the fact that it is invoking the true and fair override and explain why it is doing so.

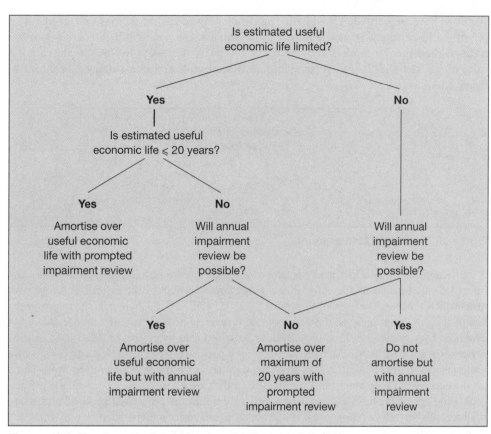

Figure 13.2 Treatment of positive goodwill and intangibles

In accordance with the provisions of FRS 11 *Impairment of Fixed Assets and Goodwill*, which we have explored in the context of tangible and intangible fixed assets in Chapter 5, it is necessary to ensure that the carrying values of goodwill and intangible assets do not exceed their recoverable amounts. This necessitates an impairment review but FRS 10 identifies two different triggers for an impairment review. One is when the estimated useful life is expected to exceed 20 years, in which case an impairment review must be conducted every year. When the estimated useful life is 20 years or less, an impairment review is required at the end of the first full financial year following the initial recognition and subsequently, if events or changes in circumstances indicate that its carrying value may not be recoverable in full. We shall describe the latter as a 'prompted' impairment review. Figure 13.2 summarises the requirements of FRS 10.

Impairment reviews

Company law requires that provision be made for the diminution in value of any fixed asset when the diminution in value is expected to be permanent. Such impairment occurs when the recoverable amount of an asset falls permanently below its carrying value and, as we have seen in Chapter 5, FRS 11, *Impairment of Fixed Assets and Goodwill*, attempts to standardise accounting practice in this area. As we shall demonstrate, it is usually more difficult to conduct an impairment review for goodwill than it is for other assets.

As we have explained, FRS 11 distinguishes between what we have described as a prompted impairment review and an annual impairment review but the conduct of the review is the same. To conduct an impairment review it is necessary to compare the carrying value of an asset with its recoverable amount. Recoverable amount is defined as shown in Figure 13.3.

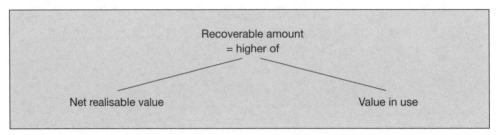

Figure 13.3 **Recoverable amount**

Net realisable value is the proceeds which would be received from selling an asset less any direct selling costs, while the value in use is the present value of the estimated future cash flows which the asset is expected to produce. As we have seen in Chapter 5, the major problem of applying such reviews in practice is that it is rarely possible to estimate the cash flows produced by a single asset because cash flows are produced by groups of assets used in conjunction with one another. FRS 11 therefore proposes that impairment reviews be undertaken for the smallest group of assets, defined as an income generating unit, which produce a largely independent income stream. In the case of purchased goodwill, the income generating unit is the business acquired which gave rise to the purchased goodwill and, as we shall see, this introduces conceptual and practical problems of a high order.

Let us assume first that the business acquired is not merged in any way with the business of the acquiring company but, rather, that it remains a separately identifiable business unit. According to FRS 11, an impairment review would require a comparison of the value of the acquired business on a subsequent balance sheet date with the sum of the carrying values of the assets and liabilities, including purchased goodwill, relating to that business unit on that same date. Provided the value of the business exceeds the sum of the carrying values there is no impairment whereas, if the reverse is the case, impairment must be recognised by writing down relevant assets.

If impairment on this basis has occurred then, if there is evidence that there is an impairment of any specific asset, that asset should be written down. Otherwise the impairment should be allocated as follows:

(a) first, to any goodwill in the unit;
(b) thereafter, to any capitalised intangible asset in the unit; and
(c) finally, to the tangible assets in the unit, on a pro rata or more appropriate basis.

(FRS 11, Para. 48)

Thus the more subjective values are written down first.

In our view, this approach is fundamentally flawed because the value of the business unit on any balance sheet date subsequent to the date of acquisition will reflect both goodwill created internally since the date of acquisition and any unrecognised gains and losses on the separable assets and liabilities shown in the balance sheet.

Let us explore this point in an example by supposing that a wholly owned subsidiary was acquired on 1 January 1993 and that it still exists as a separately identifiable unit 10 years later on 31 December 2002. Positive purchased goodwill of £90 000 was recognised on acquisition and this is being amortised on a straight-line basis over 30 years. To conduct an impairment review on 31 December 2002 it would be necessary to value the investment in the subsidiary, usually by discounting the expected future cash flows of the subsidiary, and to compare this value with the sum of the carrying values of assets and liabilities of the subsidiary plus the carrying value of the purchased goodwill:

	£000	£000
Value of investment in subsidiary – say		500
less Sum of carrying values:		
Separately identified assets and liabilities – say	400	
Purchased goodwill (90 000 – 10(3000))	60	
		460
Surplus		40

On the basis proposed by FRS 11, there is no impairment on the grounds that the carrying value of the purchased goodwill is supported by the current value of the goodwill within the acquired unit on 31 December 2002. However, the value of the investment on 31 December 2002 reflects goodwill generated internally since 1 January 1993 as well as any unrecognised gains and losses in respect of the tangible assets and liabilities. Let us suppose that we were to revalue the separately identified assets and liabilities to produce a sum of £420 000, rather than £400 000, and that we were able, in some magical way, to value the goodwill generated internally since acquisition at £50 000, the position would be as follows:

	£000	£000
Value of investment in subsidiary – as before		500
Sum of current values of separately identified assets and liabilities	420	
Carrying value of purchased goodwill	60	
Value of internally generated goodwill not recognised	50	
		530
Impairment		(30)

Given relevant information, there has clearly been an impairment and the carrying value of purchased goodwill should be written down by £30 000, from £60 000 to £30 000.
The FRS 11 approach fails completely to pick this up.

We are not suggesting for one moment that this alternative approach is feasible but, rather, illustrating why the ASB approach fails to identify whether or not impairment has occurred.

In addition to this fundamental flaw, there is a further problem. It will often be the case that an acquired business, for which purchased goodwill has been recognised, will be merged with other businesses of the acquirer. This would mean that the acquired business unit would no longer be identifiable at a subsequent balance sheet date. Although a sensible accountant might be tempted to recognise this as a clear example of a situation where an impairment review was impossible, the ASB attempts to provide a means of conducting a review in such circumstances and also provides us with a fall-back position.

Let us suppose that A plc acquired an unincorporated business B on 1 January 1993 and recognised purchased goodwill of £300 000, which is being amortised on a straight-line basis over its estimated useful life of 30 years. Let us also assume that the net assets of A plc and B have subsequently been merged to produce one income generating unit. How is it possible to conduct an impairment review after 10 years on 31 December 2002?

Using the approach promulgated in FRS 11, we would first have to estimate the internally generated goodwill in A plc at the date of acquisition, 1 January 1993; we will assume that this was £600 000. On 31 December 2002, we would then have to value the income generating unit, A plus B, and compare this value with the sum of the carrying values of the assets and liabilities in the balance sheet, which include purchased goodwill, together with the unrecognised internally generated goodwill which we have estimated, suitably amortised. If we assume that an appropriate amortisation method for the internally generated goodwill in A plc is straight line over, say, 20 years, then the calculation might run as follows:

Impairment review on 31 December 2002

	£000	£000
Value of income generating unit (A + B)		
– say		2000
Sum of carrying values of separately		
identified assets and liabilities	1900	
Purchased goodwill in B, less		
amortisation (£300 000 – [10 × £10 000])	200	
Unrecognised goodwill in A, less		
amortisation (£600 000 – [10 × £30 000])	300	
		2400
Impairment		(400)

FRS 11 requires that this impairment be allocated on a pro-rata basis to purchased and internally generated goodwill:

	£000
Impairment allocated to:	
Purchased goodwill 200/(200 + 300) × £400 000	160
Unrecognised goodwill 300/(200 + 300) × £400 000	240
	400

Only the amount allocated to purchased goodwill would be recognised in the financial statements. So the carrying value of purchased goodwill would be reduced by £160 000, from £200 000 to £40 000, and this amount would be charged to the profit and loss account.

While these calculations give the appearance of precision, the numbers produced are subjective and arbitrary and fundamentally flawed. Both the estimation of the internally generated goodwill in A plc on 1 January 1993 and the valuation of the income generating unit on 31 December 2002 are difficult tasks. But, even if reasonable estimates of these can be made, the approach suffers from the fundamental conceptual error that the valuation of the income generating unit on 31 December 2002 includes both unrecognised valuation changes in individual assets and liabilities as well as goodwill generated internally between 1 January 1993 and 31 December 2002.

While the ASB makes reference to extensive consultation and field testing of such impairment reviews, the conceptual and practical problems of conducting such reviews appear to be immense. We therefore take some consolation in the fall-back position that, where goodwill is not capable of continued measurement so that annual reviews are not feasible, the goodwill should be amortised over a maximum period of 20 years.

Even this suffers from conceptual problems. Where the expected useful economic life of goodwill does not exceed 20 years, what we have described as a prompted impairment review may become necessary. Such impairment reviews are necessary 'if events or changes in circumstances indicate that the carrying values may not be recoverable'. In an extreme situation where events or circumstances indicate that the value of the goodwill is zero, there will be no problem. However, in a less extreme situation, the FRS 11 approach puts us in an impossible position: an expected life not exceeding 20 years has been selected because it is impossible to conduct an impairment review but then an event or change of circumstances triggers the need for such a review! The logic of the ASB proposals here leaves much to be desired.

Purchased goodwill is the term used by accountants to describe a residual category of assets measured by a balancing figure. Given the difficulty of estimating the useful economic life of such a creature and the virtual impossibility of conducting sensible impairment reviews, we shall not be at all surprised to find that most companies amortise their positive purchased goodwill over a period of 20 years. Whatever they do, amounts attributed to goodwill in financial statements are likely to be rather short on economic meaning.

Negative goodwill

Let us turn next to the subject of negative goodwill, which occurs when the sum of the fair values of the individual assets and liabilities recognised on acquisition exceed the cost of the acquisition.

Given that accountants use fair values to determine the historical cost to the new owner of the individual assets and liabilities recognised at the date of acquisition, many accountants would argue that there can be no such phenomenon as negative goodwill. This is certainly the position taken by Accounting Principles Board (APB) Opinion 16 in the USA, which makes it absolutely clear that the sum of the 'costs' of the individually identified assets and liabilities cannot exceed the cost of the business or investment purchased. Where negative goodwill appears on an initial calculation, APB Opinion 16 requires that the recorded costs of the non-monetary assets be reduced to eliminate that goodwill. In our view, this is the only approach which is compatible with the use of historical cost accounting.

Neither FRS 10 nor the international accounting standard IAS 22 accepts this strict historical cost approach. The ASB envisages situations where negative goodwill may arise as, for example, when a bargain purchase has been made or where future reorganisation costs must be incurred consequential upon the acquisition but these costs do not satisfy the criteria for recognition as provisions at the date of acquisition. Where such negative goodwill emerges, the standard exhorts us to look more closely at the values attributed to the identified assets and liabilities to see whether these should be amended.

Once having permitted, indeed required, the recognition of negative goodwill, FRS 10 then has to confront the problem of how to account for it. The standard takes the view that negative goodwill should be shown next to positive goodwill among the assets in a balance sheet and that it should be recognised through the profit and loss account over the period when the non-monetary assets acquired are used or sold. Given that there will probably be a large collection of non-monetary assets with varying lives, the determination of this relevant period is beset with problems and is bound to be arbitrary. As with positive goodwill, any figure which appears in a profit and loss account or balance sheet in respect of negative goodwill is almost certain to lack any economic meaning whatsoever.

Disclosure requirements

FRS 10 requires substantial disclosures concerning positive goodwill, negative goodwill and intangible assets. We have not attempted to summarise this disclosure but rather direct readers to the relevant paragraphs of FRS 10, namely Paras 52 to 64.

The international accounting standards

There are a number of international standards relevant to the treatment of goodwill, namely:

- IAS 22 *Business Combinations* (revised 1998 and, at the time of writing, under review again);
- IAS 36 *Impairment of Assets* (1998); and
- IAS 38 *Intangible Assets* (1998).

IAS 38 prohibits the recognition of internally generated goodwill as an asset. IAS 22 requires that purchased goodwill should be recognised and accepts that it may be positive or negative.

Positive goodwill must be recognised as an asset and amortised, on a systematic basis, over its useful economic life. As under FRS 10, there is a rebuttable presumption that the useful economic life will not exceed 20 years. However, unlike FRS 10, IAS 22 takes the view that 'the useful life of goodwill is always finite' (Para. 51).

IAS 36 requires impairment reviews similar to those required by FRS 11, and IAS 22 requires that, as a minimum, there must be an annual impairment review when the estimated useful life of goodwill exceeds 20 years.

Like FRS 10, IAS 22 permits the recognition of negative goodwill and lays down rules on whether it should be credited to the income statement immediately or over a period of years equal to the average useful life of the identifiable acquired depreciable or amortisable assets acquired. As under FRS 10, IAS 22 requires the carrying value of negative goodwill to be shown as a deduction from assets under the same balance sheet classification as positive goodwill.

As we have explained in connection with business combinations earlier in the chapter, IAS 22 is under review and the accounting treatment of goodwill and intangibles is being examined in Phase I of that review. At the time of writing, it appears that the IASB will change the accounting treatment of negative goodwill to require it to be credited to the income statement immediately rather than over the average life of the collection of non-monetary assets which existed at the date of acquisition. If this change is made, at least one impossible task will be taken from the shoulders of accountants!

Conclusion

It is easy to be critical of the ways in which standard setters have dealt with goodwill but it is instructive to ponder why they have found the topic difficult and to suggest a different approach to the solution of the problem.

Under the conventional historical cost accounting system, purchased goodwill may be included in balance sheets but internally generated goodwill may not be included. As the ASB wisely points out, every method of accounting for this purchased goodwill is inconsistent with other aspects of financial accounting. If the purchased goodwill is recognised, this is inconsistent with the treatment of internally generated goodwill. If purchased goodwill is eliminated, this is inconsistent with the treatment of other fixed assets. While SSAP 22 preferred the elimination of purchased goodwill, FRS 10 has moved to the other end of the spectrum by requiring the recognition and amortisation of purchased goodwill.

As we have seen, FRS 10 even accepts that goodwill may have an indefinite life. The fundamental question here is whether after, say, 50 years of successful operations, the current goodwill is the original purchased goodwill or goodwill which has been created in the subsequent period. We have no doubts as to the answer to this question and are extremely sceptical of the view that goodwill can have an indefinite life. We therefore feel more comfortable with the view of IAS 22 that 'the useful life of goodwill is always finite'.

Even if we confine ourselves to a situation where the expected useful economic life of goodwill is finite, there must be severe doubts about any estimate of the useful economic life of this goodwill which is, after all, computed as a balancing figure representing a residual category of assets not recognised separately in the accounting system. Any estimate of the useful life of such a creature must be both subjective and arbitrary so that any figure for goodwill which appears in a balance sheet or profit and loss account is likely to be lacking in economic meaning.

The ASB seeks to ensure that the carrying value of goodwill does not exceed its recoverable amount but, as we have demonstrated, the FRS 11 approach to impairment reviews is conceptually unsound and may actually result in the inclusion of outlawed internally generated goodwill in the balance sheet in some circumstances.

In our view, the treatment of goodwill will remain an intractable problem while we continue to attempt to force all relevant financial information into an articulated set of financial statements. Even where individual assets and liabilities are shown at their current values, the financial statements of a business do not attempt to provide a valuation of the business. Goodwill usually derives from a past valuation of a part of the business. How can such different approaches possibly be reconciled?

Our preferred solution is quite simple. Given the impossibility of arriving at any meaningful figures for goodwill in the primary financial statements, all goodwill should be written off immediately. However, larger companies should then be required to present a separate statement which summarises and aggregates the current values of the individual assets and liabilities recognised in the financial statements on the balance sheet date and, in addition, provides an estimate of the valuation of the whole business, perhaps based on its market capitalisation. The difference between these two totals provides an indication of the value of goodwill of the company or group on the balance sheet date. Such a figure may be explained and discussed and would seem to sit comfortably with the ASB's attempt to deflect attention from any one number in the financial statements towards a larger set of relevant information.[28] It would also sit comfortably with the attempt to raise the profile of the *Operating and Financial Review*, discussed in Chapter 17.

The value for goodwill would, of course, be highly subjective but the subjectivity would be apparent and such an approach would be far from the spurious accuracy of the figures required by FRS 10.

We find it hard to imagine that FRS 10 will be the final word on accounting for goodwill and intangible assets.

Summary

The first part of the chapter deals with business combinations while the second part deals with the closely related topic of goodwill.

---

[28] As we explain in Chapter 21, a similar approach was proposed in the Discussion Document, 'Making Corporate Reports Valuable', Institute of Chartered Accountants of Scotland, Kogan Page, London, 1988. Readers are referred to the proposed 'Assets and Liabilities Statement' discussed in Chapter 7 of that report.

In the first part of the chapter, we provided some background on the reasons for business combinations and ways in which they may be effected, using different legal structures and different forms of consideration. We then explored the differences between the acquisition or purchase method of accounting and the merger or pooling of interests method of accounting for combinations. We examined the regulatory frameworks in the UK, as provided by company law and FRS 6, and by the IASB in IAS 22. We explained that the latter is at present under review and that the merger method of accounting, which is already rare, may disappear entirely when the review of IAS 22 is complete.

In the second part of the chapter, we examined the nature of goodwill and explored the possible ways of accounting for such a phenomenon. We then examined the regulatory framework in the UK, as provided formerly by SSAP 22 and now by FRS 10 and FRS 11, as well as the provisions of the relevant IASB standards, including IAS 22. Both the ASB and the IASB now require the amortisation of positive purchased goodwill over its useful economic life but, whereas FRS 10 envisages the possibility of an indefinite life, this is not envisaged by IAS 22. Both the ASB and the IASB accept the possibility of the existence of negative goodwill and lay down similar rules for its treatment.

We cast severe doubts on the rules contained in FRS 10 and FRS 11, particularly those relating to the impairment review, and expressed our concerns as to whether any figure in a set of financial statements purporting to represent goodwill has any economic meaning whatsoever. We have also suggested an alternative approach, one that appears to be in line with current developments concerned to increase and improve the extent of narrative reporting.

Recommended reading

J.A. Arnold, D. Egginton, L. Kirkham, R.H. Macve and K. Peasnell, *Goodwill and other intangibles*, ICAEW, London, October 1992.

P. Barwise, C. Higson, A. Likierman and P. Marsh, *Accounting for Brands*, London Business School and ICAEW, London, 1989.

T.E. Cooke, *Mergers and Acquisitions*, Blackwell, Oxford, 1986.

T.E. Cooke, *International Mergers and Acquisitions*, Blackwell, Oxford, 1998.

M.C. Miller, 'Goodwill – an aggregation issue', *The Accounting Review*, April 1973.

R. Perrier (ed.), *Brand Valuation*, 3rd edn, Interbrand, Premier Books, London, 1997.

H.R. Schwencke, *Accounting for Mergers and Acquisitions in Europe*, International Bureau of Fiscal Documentation Publications BV, Amsterdam, 2002.

M.A. Weinberg and M.V. Blank, *Takeovers and Mergers*, Vols 1 and 2, 5th edn by L. Rabinovitz, Sweet and Maxwell, London, 1989. This is published in loose-leaf form and updated regularly. At the time of writing the latest update was Release Bulletin number 25, January 2002.

Questions

13.1 'Accounting standards should narrow differences in reporting yet acquisition accounting and merger accounting result in significantly different results in the year of combination and thereafter.'

You are required to discuss the above statement stating, with reasons, whether there is a need for two different methods.

CIMA, Advanced Financial Accounting, May 1994 (15 marks)

13.2 The balance sheets of Left plc and Right plc at 31 December 1999, the accounting date for both companies, were as follows.

	Left plc	*Right plc*
	£000	£000
Tangible fixed assets	60000	40000
Stocks	10000	9000
Other current assets	12000	10000
Current liabilities	(9000)	(8000)
Quoted debentures	(15000)	(12000)
	58000	39000
Equity share capital (£1 shares)	30000	20000
Share premium account	10000	5000
Profit and loss account	18000	14000
	58000	39000

On 31 December 1999, Left plc purchased all the equity shares of Right plc. The purchase consideration was satisfied by the issue of 6 new equity shares in Left plc for every 5 equity shares purchased in Right plc. At 31 December 1999 the market value of a Left plc share was £2.25 and the market value of a Right plc share was £2.40. Relevant details concerning the values of the net assets of Right plc at 31 December 1999 were as follows:

● The fixed assets had a fair value of £43.5 million.

● The stocks had a fair value of £9.5 million.

● The debentures had a market value of £11 million.

● Other net assets had a fair value that was the same as their book value.

The effect of the purchase of shares in Right plc is NOT reflected in the balance sheet of Left plc that appears above.

Requirements
(a) **Prepare the consolidated balance sheet of the Left plc group at 31 December 1999 assuming the business combination is accounted for**
    ● **as an acquisition; and**
    ● **as a merger.** (14 marks)
(b) **Discuss the extent to which the business combination satisfies the requirements of FRS 6 – *Acquisitions and mergers* for classification as a merger. You should indicate the other information you would need to enable you to form a definite conclusion.**
(6 marks)

CIMA, Financial Reporting, May 2000 (20 marks)

13.3 AB, a public limited company manufactures goods for the aerospace industry. It acquired an electronics company CG, a public limited company on 1 December 1999 at an agreed value of £65 million. The purchase consideration was satisfied by the issue of 30 million shares of AB, in exchange for the whole of the share capital of CG. The directors of AB have decided to adopt merger accounting principles in accounting for the acquisition, but the auditors have not as yet concurred with the use of merger accounting in the financial statements.

The following summary financial statements relate to the above companies as at 31 May 2000.

Profit and Loss Accounts for the year ended 31 May 2000

	£000 AB	£000 CG
Turnover	45 000	34 000
Cost of sales	(31 450)	(25 280)
Gross profit	13 550	8 720
Distribution and administrative expenses	(9 450)	(3 820)
Operating profit	4 100	4 900
Interest payable	(200)	(400)
Profit before taxation	3 900	4 500
Taxation	(1 250)	(1 700)
Dividends (proposed)	(250)	
Retained profit for the year	2 400	2 800

Balance Sheets at 31 May 2000

	£000 AB	£000 CG
Tangible fixed assets	36 000	24 500
Cost of investment in CG	30 000	
Net current assets	29 000	17 500
Creditors: amounts due after more than one year	(2 000)	(4 000)
Total assets less liabilities	93 000	38 000
Capital and Reserves		
Ordinary shares of £1	55 000	20 000
Share premium account	3 000	6 000
Revaluation reserve	10 000	
Profit and loss account	25 000	12 000
	93 000	38 000

The following information should be taken into account when preparing the group accounts:

(i) The management of AB feel that the adjustments required to bring the following assets of CG to their fair values at 1 December 1999 are as follows:

Fixed Assets to be increased by £4 million;

Stock to be decreased by £3 million (this stock had been sold by the year end);

Provision for bad debts to be increased by £2 million in relation to specific accounts;

Depreciation is charged at 20% per annum on a straight line basis on tangible fixed assets;

The increase in the provision for bad debts was still required at 31 May 2000. No further provisions are required on 31 May 2000.

(ii) CG has a fixed rate bank loan of £4 million which was taken out when interest rates were 10% per annum. The loan is due for repayment on 30 November 2001. At the date of acquisition the company could have raised a loan at an interest rate of 7%. Interest is payable yearly in arrears on 30 November.

(iii) CG acquired a corporate brand name on 1 July 1999. The company did not capitalise the brand name but wrote the cost off against reserves in the Statement of Total Recognised Gains and Losses. The cost of the brand name was £18 million. AB has consulted an expert brand valuation firm who have stated that the brand is worth £20 million at the date of acquisition based on the present value of notional royalty savings arising from ownership of the brand. The auditors are satisfied with the reliability of the brand valuation. Brands are not amortised by AB but are reviewed annually for impairment, and as at 31 May 2000, there has been no impairment in value. Goodwill is amortised over a 10 year period with a full charge in the year of acquisition.

(iv) AB incurred £500 000 of expenses in connection with the acquisition of CG. This figure comprised £300 000 of professional fees and £200 000 of issue costs of the shares. The acquisition expenses have been included in administrative expenses.

Required
(a) **Prepare consolidated profit and loss accounts for the year ended 31 May 2000 and consolidated balance sheets as at 31 May 2000 for the AB group utilising:**
   (i) **Merger accounting;**
   (ii) **Acquisition accounting.** (19 marks)
(b) **Discuss the impact on the group financial statements of the AB group of utilising merger accounting as opposed to acquisition accounting. (Candidates should discuss at least three effects on the financial statements.)** (6 marks)

ACCA, Financial Reporting Environment (UK Stream), June 2000 **(25 marks)**

13.4 There are currently two possible methods of preparing consolidated financial statements when two or more separate legal entities combine to form a single economic entity in the form of a group. The most commonly used method is the acquisition method. However, another method is sometimes appropriate when two or more separate legal entities unite into one economic entity by means of an exchange of equity shares. This method is known as the merger method. Recent developments suggest that Standard setters are considering a change that would prevent the merger method ever being used and require that the acquisition method be used to prepare consolidated financial statements following a business combination.

Top plc and Bottom plc are two listed companies that operate in the same sector. The two sets of directors have been speculating for some time that it would be in the mutual interest of the two companies to combine together to form a single economic entity while maintaining the separate legal status of the two companies. Accordingly, on 30 April 2001 Top plc made an offer to all the equity shareholders of Bottom plc to acquire their shares. The terms of the offer were 4 equity shares in Top plc for every 3 equity shares in Bottom plc. The offer was accepted by all the equity shareholders in Bottom plc and the exchange of equity shares took place on 31 May 2001. The directors of Top plc wish to use merger accounting to prepare the consolidated financial statements for the year ended 31 January 2002. Any computational work in this question should assume that merger accounting principles will be adopted.

The relevant profit and loss accounts and balance sheets of Top plc and Bottom plc are given below:

Profit and loss accounts – year ended

31 January 2002	Top plc	Bottom plc
	£000	£000
Turnover	80 000	75 000
Cost of sales	(40 000)	(38 000)
Gross profit	40 000	37 000
Other operating expenses	(10 000)	(9 000)
Operating profit	30 000	28 000
Investment income	10 000	–
Interest payable	(5 500)	(4 000)
Profit before taxation	34 500	24 000
Taxation	(7 500)	(7 000)
Profit after taxation	27 000	17 000
Dividends paid 30 November 2001	(15 000)	(10 000)
Retained profit	12 000	7 000
Retained profit – 1 February 2001	20 000	18 000
Retained profit – 31 January 2002	32 000	25 000

Balance sheets at 31 January 2002	Top plc	Bottom plc
	£000	£000
Tangible fixed assets	89 000	65 000
Investments – see Note 1 [below]	40 800	–
Net current assets	27 200	25 000
Loans	(25 000)	(20 000)
	132 000	70 000
Called-up share capital – £1 equity shares	84 000	30 000
Share premium account	10 000	11 000
Revaluation reserve	6 000	4 000
Profit and loss account	32 000	25 000
	132 000	70 000

Note 1 – investment in Bottom plc
The investment in Bottom plc comprises:

	£000
40 million equity shares issued by Top plc	40 000
Merger expenses (including £500 000 issue costs of shares)	800
	40 800

Note 2 – accounting policies

Both companies have the same accounting policies in all respects other than valuation of stock. Bottom plc uses the LIFO method whereas Top plc uses the FIFO method. The directors of Top plc wish to use the FIFO method in preparing the consolidated financial statements. Details of the stocks of Bottom plc are as follows:

Date	Stock valuation under FIFO	Stock valuation under LIFO
	£000	£000
1 February 2001	9 500	9 000
31 May 2001	9 600	9 200
31 January 2002	10 200	9 300

Note 3

In preparing your answers to this question you should assume that the directors of Top plc wish to maximise the profit and loss reserve that is reported in the consolidated balance sheet.

Required

(a) Prepare the consolidated profit and loss account of the Top plc group for the year ended 31 January 2002, starting with turnover and ending with retained profit carried forward. Ignore deferred taxation.   (5 marks)

(b) Prepare the consolidated balance sheet of the Top plc group at 31 January 2002. Ignore deferred taxation.   (5 marks)

(c) Explain the concepts underpinning acquisition accounting and merger accounting and suggest why merger accounting might be considered invalid.   (10 marks)

CIMA, Financial Reporting – UK Accounting Standards, May 2002   **(20 marks)**

13.5 Growmoor plc has carried on business as a food retailer since 1900. It had traded profitably until the late 1980s when it suffered from fierce competition from larger retailers. Its turnover and margins were under severe pressure and its share price fell to an all time low. The directors formulated a strategic plan to grow by acquisition and merger. It has an agreement to be able to borrow funds to finance acquisition at an interest rate of 10% per annum. It is Growmoor plc's policy to amortise goodwill over ten years.

1. Investment in Smelt plc

On 15 June 1994 Growmoor plc had an issued share capital of 1 625 000 ordinary shares of £1 each. On that date it acquired 240 000 of the 1 500 000 issued £1 ordinary shares of Smelt plc for a cash payment of £164 000.

Growmoor plc makes up its accounts to 31 July. In early 1996 the directors of Growmoor plc and Smelt plc were having discussions with a view to a combination of the two companies.

The proposal was that:

(i) On 1 May 1996 Growmoor plc should acquire 1 200 000 of the issued ordinary shares of Smelt plc which had a market price of £1.30 per share, in exchange for 1 500 000 newly issued ordinary shares in Growmoor plc which had a market price of £1.20p per share. There has been no change in Growmoor plc's share capital since 15 June 1994. The market price of the Smelt plc shares had ranged from £1.20 to £1.50 during the year ended 30 April 1996.

(ii) It was agreed that the consideration would be increased by 200 000 shares if a contingent liability in Smelt plc in respect of a claim for wrongful dismissal by a former director did not crystallise.

(iii) After the exchange the new board would consist of 6 directors from Growmoor plc and 6 directors from Smelt plc with the Managing Director of Growmoor plc becoming Managing Director of Smelt plc.

(iv) The Growmoor plc head office should be closed and the staff made redundant and the Smelt plc head office should become the head office of the new combination.

(v) Senior managers of both companies were to re-apply for their posts and be interviewed by an interview panel comprising a director and the personnel managers from each company. The age profile of the two companies differed with the average age of the Growmoor plc managers being 40 and that of Smelt plc being 54 and there was an expectation among the directors of both boards that most of the posts would be filled by Growmoor plc managers.

2. Investment in Beaten Ltd

Growmoor plc is planning to acquire all of the 800 000 £1 ordinary shares in Beaten Ltd on 30 June 1996 for a deferred consideration of £500 000 and a contingent consideration payable on 30 June 2000 of 10% of the amount by which profits for the year ended 30 June 2000 exceeded £100 000. Beaten Ltd has suffered trading losses and its directors, who are the major shareholders, support a takeover by Growmoor plc. The fair value of net assets of Beaten Ltd was £685 000 and Growmoor plc expected that reorganisation costs would be £85 000 and future trading losses would be £100 000. Growmoor plc agreed to offer four year service contracts to the directors of Beaten Ltd.

The directors had expected to be able to create a provision for the reorganisation costs and future trading losses but were advised by their Finance Director that FRS 7 required these two items to be treated as post-acquisition items.

Required

(a) (i) Explain to the directors of Growmoor plc the extent to which the proposed terms of the combination with Smelt plc satisfied the requirements of the Companies Act 1985 and FRS 6 for the combination to be treated as a merger; and

    (ii) If the proposed terms fail to satisfy any of the requirements, advise the directors on any changes that could be made so that the combination could be treated as a merger as at 31 July 1996.   (8 marks)

(b) Explain briefly the reasons for the application of the principles of recognition and measurement on an acquisition set out in FRS 7 to provisions for future operating losses and for re-organisation costs.   (3 marks)

(c) (i) Explain the treatment in the profit and loss account for the year ended 31 July 1996 and the balance sheet as at that date of Growmoor plc on the assumption that the acquisition of Beaten Ltd took place on 30 June 1996 and the consideration for the acquisition was deferred so that £100 000 was payable after one year, £150 000 after two years and the balance after three years. Show your calculations.

    (ii) Calculate the goodwill to be dealt with in the consolidated accounts for the years ending 31 July 1996 and 1997, explaining clearly the effect of deferred and contingent consideration.

    (iii) Explain and critically discuss the existing regulations for the treatment of negative goodwill.   (9 marks)

ACCA, Financial Reporting Environment, December 1996   **(20 marks)**

13.6 FRS 10 – *Goodwill and Intangible Assets* – was issued in December 1997. At the same time, SSAP 22, the previous Accounting Standard which dealt with the subject of accounting for goodwill, was withdrawn. SSAP 22 allowed purchased goodwill to be written off directly to reserves as one amount in the accounting period of purchase. FRS 10 does not permit this treatment.

Invest plc has a number of subsidiaries. The accounting date of Invest plc and all its subsidiaries is 30 April. On 1 May 1998, Invest plc purchased 80% of the issued equity shares of Target Ltd. This purchase made Target Ltd a subsidiary of Invest plc from 1 May 1998. Invest plc made a cash payment of £31 million for the shares in Target Ltd. On 1 May 1998, the net assets which were included in the balance sheet of Target Ltd had a fair value to Invest plc of £30 million. Target Ltd sells a well-known branded product and has taken steps to protect itself legally against unauthorised use of the brand name. A reliable estimate of the value of this brand to the Invest group is £3 million. It is further considered that the value of the brand can be maintained or even increased for the foreseeable future. The value of the brand is *not* included in the balance sheet of Target Ltd.

For the purposes of preparing the consolidated financial statements, the Directors of Invest plc wish to ensure that the charge to the profit and loss account for the amortisation of intangible fixed assets is kept to a minimum. They estimate that the useful economic life of the purchased goodwill (or premium on acquisition) of Target Ltd is 40 years.

Requirements
(a) Outline the key factors which lay behind the decision of the Accounting Standards Board to prohibit the write-off of purchased goodwill to reserves.   (11 marks)
(b) Compute the charge to the consolidated profit and loss account in respect of the goodwill on acquisition of Target Ltd for its year ended 30 April 1999.   (5 marks)
(c) Explain the action which Invest plc must take in 1998/99 and in future years arising from the chosen accounting treatment of the goodwill on acquisition of Target Ltd.
                                                                                          (4 marks)

CIMA, Financial Reporting, November 1999   **(20 marks)**

13.7 Islay plc has acquired the following unincorporated businesses:

(1) 'Savalight', a business specialising in the production of low-cost, energy efficient light bulbs, acquired on 1 June 1996 for £580 000. The identifiable assets and liabilities of the business had a book value of £550 000 and were valued at £500 000 on 1 June 1996. The company estimated the useful economic life of the goodwill arising at five years and has been amortising this through the profit and loss account. It was anticipated that the goodwill would have a residual value of £20 000.

(2) 'Green Goods', a business specialising in the distribution of a range of environmentally friendly products, acquired on 1 June 1997 for £1.8 million. The identifiable assets and liabilities of the business had a book value of £1.1 million and were valued at £1.3 million on 1 June 1997, including goodwill of the business of £150 000. The company estimated the useful economic life of goodwill arising at 25 years and has been amortising this through the profit and loss account.

(3) 'Smart IT', a business specialising in the distribution of computers, acquired on 1 June 1998 for £900 000. The identifiable assets and liabilities of the business had a book value of £1 million and were valued at £1.2 million on 1 June 1998. Assume the major non-monetary assets in these amounts have a useful economic life of 15 years.

Islay plc revalued its tangible fixed assets during the year ended 31 May 1999 and created a revaluation reserve of £600 000. In addition, the company believes the goodwill arising on the purchase of 'Savalight' is now worth £350 000 and intends to reflect this in the financial statements for the year ended 31 May 1999.

The company's capital and reserves (**before reflecting any adjustments for the above acquisitions**) in the draft financial statements as at 31 May 1999 show:

Capital and reserves	£000
Called up share capital (5 000 000 ordinary shares of £1 each)	5000
Revaluation reserve	600
Profit and loss account (£200 000 for the year ended 31 May 1999)	700
	6300

Requirements

(a) Calculate and disclose the amounts for goodwill to be included in the financial statements for Islay plc for the year ended 31 May 1999, providing the following disclosures:

Balance sheet extracts

Disclosure note for goodwill

Disclosure note for movements on reserves.   (13 marks)

(b) Explain the accounting treatment you have adopted for any goodwill arising in acquisitions (1) to (3) above, referring to the provisions of FRS 10, 'Goodwill and Intangible Assets', and noting any current or future action Islay plc will have to take on goodwill recognised.   (4 marks)

ICAEW, Financial Reporting, June 1999   (**17 marks**)

13.8 Elie plc acquired 80% of the £1 million ordinary share capital of Monans Ltd on 1 July 2001 by issuing 200 000 £1 ordinary shares. Elie plc's ordinary shares were quoted at £17 on 1 July 2001. Expenses of the share issue amounted to £90 000.

A further amount of £94 500 is payable in cash on 1 July 2002. Elie plc's borrowing rate is 5%.

A further contingent consideration of shares with a value of £500 000 is dependent on Monans Ltd achieving a 10% increase in turnover in the year ended 31 October 2002. This would become due on 1 July 2003. Monans Ltd has achieved an increase in turnover over the past five years of 11%, 8%, 10%, 11% and 12% (from the earliest to the most recent year).

The net assets of Monans Ltd in its accounts as at 1 July 2001 were £3 million with fair value being £1 million higher than book value. Monans Ltd had the following reserves at 1 July 2001:

	£000
Revaluation reserve	400
General reserve	100
Profit and loss account	1500

A further acquisition of shares took place on 1 September 2001 when Elie plc purchased 60% of the £500 000 preference shares of Monans Ltd for £390 000.

Elie plc is intending to write off any goodwill arising over 9 years, charging a full year in the year of acquisition.

Elie plc has identified the following matters not reflected in the financial statements of Monans Ltd as at 1 July 2001:

(1) A contingent asset amounting to £200 000 existed at 1 July 2001; the company's lawyers consider it is probable this will be received in the near future.

(2) Operating losses of £300 000 are expected after acquisition.

(3) Reorganisation costs of £100 000 are to be incurred to bring Monans Ltd's systems into line with those of the group.

(4) A fall in stock value of £50 000 on 5 July 2001 due to a fire at a warehouse. The stock now has a net realisable value of £5000.

Requirements
(a) **Calculate the amount of goodwill arising on the acquisition of Monans Ltd that would be shown in the group accounts of Elie plc for the year ended 30 June 2002.**

(8 marks)
(b) **Explain your calculation of the goodwill arising in (a) including your treatment of items (1) to (4) above, referring to appropriate accounting standards.**   (12 marks)

ICAEW, Financial Reporting, June 2002   **(20 marks)**

13.9 FRS 11 – *Impairment of fixed assets and goodwill* requires that all fixed assets and goodwill should be reviewed for impairment where appropriate and any impairment loss dealt with in the financial statements.

The XY group prepares financial statements to 31 December each year. On 31 December 1998 the group purchased all the shares of MH Ltd for £2 million. The fair value of the identifiable net assets of MH Ltd at that date was £1.8 million. It is the policy of the XY group to amortise goodwill over 20 years. The amortisation of the goodwill of MH Ltd commenced in 1999. MH Ltd made a loss in 1999 and at 31 December 1999 the net assets of MH Ltd – based on fair values at 1 January 1999 – were as follows:

	£000
Capitalised development expenditure	200
Tangible fixed assets	1300
Net current assets	250
	1750

An impairment review at 31 December 1999 indicated that the value in use of MH Ltd at that date was £1.5 million. The capitalised development expenditure has no ascertainable external market value.

Requirements
(a) Describe what is meant by 'impairment' and briefly explain the procedures that must be followed when performing an impairment review.   (12 marks)
(b) Calculate the impairment loss that would arise in the consolidated financial statements of the XY group as a result of the impairment review of MH Ltd at 31 December 1999.

(4 marks)
(c) Show how the impairment loss you have calculated in (b) would affect the carrying values of the various net assets in the consolidated balance sheet of the XY group at 31 December 1999.   (4 marks)

CIMA, Financial Reporting, May 2000   **(20 marks)**

13.10 Acquirer plc is a company that regularly purchases new subsidiaries. On 30 June 2000, the company acquired all the equity shares of Prospects plc for a cash payment of £260 million. The net assets of Prospects plc on 30 June 2000 were £180 million and no fair value adjustments were necessary upon consolidation of Prospects plc for the first time. Acquirer plc assessed the useful economic life of the goodwill that arose on consolidation of Prospects plc as 40 years and charged six months' amortisation in its consolidated profit and loss account for the year ended 31 December 2000. Acquirer plc then charged a full year's amortisation of the goodwill in its consolidated profit and loss account for the year ended 31 December 2001.

On 31 December 2001, Acquirer plc carried out a review of the goodwill on consolidation of Prospects plc for evidence of impairment. The review was carried out despite the fact that there were no obvious indications of adverse trading conditions for Prospects plc. The review involved allocating the net assets of Prospects plc into three income-generating units and computing the value in use of each unit. The carrying values of the individual units before any impairment adjustments are given below:

	Unit A £ million	Unit B £ million	Unit C £ million
Patents	5	–	–
Tangible fixed assets	60	30	40
Net current assets	20	25	20
	85	55	60
Value in use of unit	72	60	65

It was not possible to meaningfully allocate the goodwill on consolidation to the individual income-generating units, but all the other net assets of Prospects plc are allocated in the table shown above. The patents of Prospects plc have no ascertainable market value but all the current assets have a market value that is above carrying value. The value in use of Prospects plc as a single income-generating unit at 31 December 2001 is £205 million.

Required
(a) Explain why it was necessary to review the goodwill on consolidation of Prospects plc for impairment at 31 December 2001.   (4 marks)
(b) Explain briefly the purpose of an impairment review and why the net assets of Prospects plc were allocated into income-generating units as part of the review of goodwill for impairment.   (5 marks)
(c) Demonstrate how the impairment loss in unit A will affect the carrying value of the net assets of unit A in the consolidated financial statements of Acquirer plc.
                                                                              (4 marks)
(d) Explain and calculate the effect of the impairment review on the carrying value of the goodwill on consolidation of Prospects plc at 31 December 2001.   (7 marks)

CIMA, Financial Reporting – UK Accounting Standards, May 2002   **(20 marks)**

Investments and groups

Investments by one entity in another take many different forms, ranging from simple or passive investments at one end of the spectrum to investments which command control of the investee's activities, assets and liabilities at the other end of the spectrum.

This chapter is divided into two sections. The first distinguishes different levels of investment and explains the treatment of investments in the financial statements of an investing company. The second examines accounting for groups using the acquisition method of accounting and pays particular attention to the treatment of acquisitions and disposals. We therefore draw upon the relevant provisions of the following UK and international accounting standards:

- FRS 2 *Accounting for Subsidiary Undertakings* (1992)
- FRS 6 *Acquisitions and Mergers* (1994)
- FRS 7 *Fair Values in Acquisition Accounting* (1994)
- IAS 22 *Business Combinations* (revised 1998)
- IAS 27 *Consolidated Financial Statements and Accounting for Investments in Subsidiaries* (revised 2000)

In the first section we also refer to the relevant parts of a number of other international accounting standards, namely:

- IAS 28 *Accounting for Investments in Associates* (revised 2000)
- IAS 31 *Financial Reporting of Interests in Joint Ventures* (revised 2000)
- IAS 39 *Financial Instruments: Recognition and Measurement* (revised 2000)

The international standards IAS 22, IAS 27, IAS 28 and IAS 39 are at present under review so we draw attention to likely changes where appropriate.

overview

Introduction

Many companies hold investments in other entities and it is therefore necessary to determine how these investments are to be treated in the financial statements of the reporting entity. As we shall see, the treatment of investments in the financial statements of an individual company is relatively straightforward but, as soon as an investment is sufficient to give influence or control over the affairs of the investee, things become more complicated.

Investments may range from simple or passive investments, held to obtain dividends and potential capital growth, to those which give the investing company control over the activities, assets and liabilities of the investee. The ASB *Statement of Principles for Financial Reporting* distinguishes four different categories of investment, as shown in Table 14.1.[1]

---

[1] *Statement of Principles for Financial Reporting*, ASB, London, December 1999: Chapter 8, 'Accounting for interests in other entities'. In drawing up this table, we have assumed that all four categories involve investment in entities. FRS 9 *Accounting for Associates and Joint Ventures* (November 1997) also identifies a Joint Arrangement which is Not an Entity, a 'JANE', which we discuss briefly in the following chapter.

Table 14.1 Four categories of investment

Degree of influence	Control	Joint control	Significant influence	Lesser or no influence
Resulting categorisation	Subsidiary	Joint venture	Associate	Simple or passive investment

We start by examining the accounting treatment of investments in the individual financial statements of the investing company. In the UK at present, this treatment is the same whatever the degree of control or influence the investor exercises over the investee. However, as we shall see, international accounting standards at present specify different possible accounting treatments for investments with different levels of influence.

We next move to the other end of the spectrum and, in the second section of the chapter, 'Accounting for groups', we focus on situations where the investment is large enough to give control. Where this occurs, the investee is a subsidiary undertaking and, subject to certain exceptions, the investing company must prepare group accounts that, since the enactment of the Companies Act 1989, must be consolidated accounts.[2] The relevant UK standard accounting practice is contained in FRS 2 *Accounting for Subsidiary Undertakings*. We examine the definition of a group and the possible exclusion of subsidiaries from the consolidated accounts before turning to some of the questions which must be answered in accounting for the purchase and sale of subsidiaries. As we have seen in Chapter 13, the use of merger accounting is extremely rare and likely to disappear completely in future so, in this chapter, we are concerned only with acquisition accounting.

In this section, we also examine the provisions of the relevant international accounting standards and draw attention to the main differences between UK and international pronouncements. As the relevant international standards are at present under review, we draw attention to changes which are likely to occur.

We will, in the following chapter, consider the intermediate categories of investment which give partial influence over the investee, that is investments in associates and joint ventures, as well as joint arrangements that are not entities.

Investments

Individual company financial statements

The key to determining the treatment of an investment in the shares of another company in the financial statements of the investing company is *intention*. If the investment is intended to be for the long term, it will be treated as a fixed asset; if for the short term, it will be treated as a current asset. In a traditional historical cost balance sheet, a fixed asset investment is shown at its historical cost unless its value has been impaired, in which case it is written down to its recoverable amount. A current asset investment is shown at the lower of cost and net realisable value. The carrying value used for an impaired fixed asset investment

[2] Companies Act 1985, s. 227, Para. 2.

will differ from that of a current asset investment when its value in use, or present value, exceeds its net realisable value and this sensibly reflects the management decision to retain, rather than to sell, the investment.

For both types of investment it is usual to take credit in the profit and loss account of the investing company for dividends received and receivable, although dividends receivable are only recognised to the extent that they are in respect of accounting periods ended on or before the accounting year end of the investing company and have been declared prior to approval of the investing company's own financial statements. Some companies are even more prudent and take credit only for dividends received in an accounting period.

The above accounting treatments provide limited information to users of the investing company's financial statements and, in order to remedy this, some companies have taken advantage of the alternative accounting rules to show investments at their current value.[3] In such cases, any revaluation surplus must be taken to a revaluation reserve and any revaluation deficit must be taken to the revaluation reserve to the extent that that reserve contains a revaluation surplus in respect of the same investment but otherwise must be charged to the profit and loss account. Amounts credited or debited to a revaluation reserve account must, of course, be reported in the Statement of Total Recognised Gains and Losses.

In its death throes in July 1990, the ASC issued Exposure Draft 55 *Accounting for Investments*, and this made proposals in respect of both fixed asset and current asset investments. It proposed that, where a company adopts the alternative accounting rules to show fixed asset investments at a valuation, that amount should be kept up to date by an annual revaluation. However, its major proposal for change was in accounting for certain current asset investments, namely those which are 'readily marketable'. It was the view of the ASC that such investments should be stated in a balance sheet at their quoted current value and that any difference between that current value and the previous carrying value should be reflected in the profit and loss account. Hence the profit and loss account would reflect not only the dividends receivable but also any changes in the value of such an investment during an accounting year. In the view of the ASC any such change would be a realised profit or loss on the grounds that it has been reliably measured by reference to a quoted price.[4]

While many accountants applauded the ASC for attempting to ensure that such changes in value are reflected in a profit and loss account, there were severe doubts about the legality of the proposed method of accounting for readily marketable current asset investments.[5] The method which was proposed did not comply with the historical cost accounting rules, which require such current asset investments to be shown at the lower of cost and net realisable value, nor with the alternative accounting rules which require any revaluation surplus to be taken, not to the profit and loss account, but to a revaluation reserve. The ASC was well aware that its proposals could only be introduced by relying on the true and fair override or if there were to be a change of law.[6] These were, of course, the days before FRS 3, the 'Statement of Total Recognised Gains and Losses' and the *Statement of Principles for Financial Reporting* but, even with this help, the ASB has not yet been able to resolve this

---

[3] The rules on what is an acceptable current value differ for fixed assets and current assets respectively. (See Companies Act 1985, Schedule 4, s. C, Paras 31(3) and 31(4).) Thus, a current asset investment may be shown at its current cost, while a fixed asset investment may be shown at its market value or any other value which the directors consider to be appropriate. In the latter case, the method of valuation adopted and the reasons for adopting it must be stated.

[4] ED 55 *Accounting for Investments*, July 1990, Para. 43. As we have seen in Chapter 4, there are different ways of defining realisation. ED 55 took the view that a profit or loss made due to a change in value of a readily marketable current asset investment is realised because the value of that investment can be reliably measured. In its view, the investment did not have to be converted into cash by sale before the profit could be treated as realised.

[5] R. Macve, 'Investments: conceptual clarity *v* legal muddle', *Accountancy*, March 1991, pp. 84–5.

[6] ED 55, Preface, Paras 1.17 and 1.18.

matter although it is seeking to move matters forward with the issue of FRED 30 *Financial instruments: Disclosure and presentation; recognition and measurement* in June 2002. However, as we have explained in Chapter 8, implementation of the proposals of FRED 30 would have to await changes in company law.

Considerable changes will be required if convergence is to be achieved because there are at present a number of significant differences between the UK and international standards, to which we now turn.

The international accounting standards

The position under international accounting standards is more complex as various standards lay down different rules for different levels of investment.

If we start with a simple passive investment, an investment which would be classified as an *available-for-sale financial asset* under IAS 39 *Financial Instruments: Recognition and Measurement*,[7] this should be stated at fair value provided such a value may be measured reliably. The company must then decide, as a matter of policy, whether gains or losses should be taken to the profit and loss account or direct to reserves and, as we have explained above, only the latter would appear to be possible at present under UK law. If the fair value cannot be measured reliably, then the investment should be shown at its cost.

IAS 27 *Consolidated Financial Statements and Accounting for Investments in Subsidiaries*, specifies the treatment of investments in subsidiaries in the investor's own financial statements. It gives a choice of three methods, requiring that investments in subsidiaries should be:

(a) carried at cost;
(b) accounted for using the equity method as described in IAS 28 *Accounting for Investments in Associates* and explained in the following chapter; or
(c) accounted for as an available-for-sale financial asset as described in IAS 39 *Financial Instruments: Recognition and Measurement* and discussed in Chapter 8 and summarised briefly above.

IAS 28 *Accounting for Investments in Associates* provides exactly the same choice of valuation bases in the financial statements of the investing company for investments in associates, thus permitting them to be valued at cost, by using the equity method or at fair values. The use of the equity method in the financial statements of an investing company is not permitted under present UK law.

The final type of investment, the joint venture, is at present covered by IAS 31 *Financial Reporting of Interests in Joint Ventures*, but this is silent on the treatment of investments carrying joint control in the financial statements of the investing company.

Clearly, the current international accounting standards are more flexible than UK practice but this looks likely to change as a consequence of the convergence programme. As we explained in Chapter 3, the IASB issued exposure drafts of its proposals to amend 12 international accounting standards in May 2002 and, in the same month, the UK ASB published six FREDs together with a Consultation Paper that deals with the remaining six of these IASB exposure drafts. One of the latter international exposure drafts addresses IAS 27, which it proposes to retitle '*Consolidated and Separate Financial Statements*' while another addresses IAS 28 *Accounting for Investments in Associates*.

The revised IAS 27 would prohibit the use of the equity method of accounting for the valuation of investments in the separate financial statements of the investing company.

---

[7] See Chapter 8

Investments in subsidiaries, associates and joint ventures would then have to be shown in the financial statements of the investing company either at cost or at fair value and the same method would have to be applied for each category of investments.

The IASB plans to introduce the changes for accounting periods commencing on or after 1 January 2003 and this would bring the international practice on accounting for investments closer to UK practice. However, the treatment of changes in the fair values of investments, that is whether they should be included in the profit and loss account or in the statement of total recognised gains and losses, is still likely to give rise to differences for some time to come for the reasons which we have discussed.

Accounting for groups

What is a group?

Subject to certain exceptions which we discuss below, any UK company which is a parent company at its year end must prepare group accounts in addition to its individual accounts. Since the Companies Act 1989, these group accounts must be a set of consolidated accounts for the parent company and its subsidiary undertakings.[8]

Prior to the Companies Act 1989, a subsidiary had to be a company, and a parent company/subsidiary relationship was defined as existing when the parent company was a shareholder and controlled the composition of the board of directors of the other company and/or when it held more than half of the equity share capital of that other company.[9]

This definition was thus based on both control and ownership and betrayed some confusion about why group accounts were required. While ownership and control usually go hand in hand, this is not always the case and, because the definition of 'equity share capital' was widely drawn, it was possible for a company to be simultaneously the subsidiary of more than one parent company. In response to the EC Seventh Directive, which we discussed in Chapter 3, the Companies Act 1989 introduced a much clearer concept of a group for accounting purposes.

First, it required that consolidated accounts include the parent and all *subsidiary undertakings*. The latter is a new term which is not restricted to companies but includes partnerships and 'unincorporated associations carrying on trade or business with or without view to profit'.[10]

Second, it introduced a new definition of a parent/subsidiary relationship based not upon ownership but upon control. Thus the relationship between a parent undertaking and a subsidiary undertaking is now defined as follows:[11]

> (2) An undertaking is a parent undertaking in relation to another undertaking, a subsidiary undertaking, if –
>
> (a) it holds a majority of the voting rights in the undertaking, or
> (b) it is a member of the undertaking and has the right to appoint or remove a majority of its board of directors, or

---

[8] Companies Act 1985 (as amended by the Companies Act 1989), s. 227. Before the Companies Act 1989, consolidated accounts were just one possible form which group accounts could take.

[9] Companies Act 1985, s. 736.

[10] Companies Act 1985 (as amended by the Companies Act 1989), s. 259.

[11] Companies Act 1985 (as amended by the Companies Act 1989), s. 258.

(c) it has the right to exercise a dominant influence over the undertaking –

    (i) by virtue of provisions contained in the undertaking's memorandum or articles, or

    (ii) by virtue of a control contract, or

(d) it is a member of the undertaking and controls alone, pursuant to an agreement with other shareholders or members, a majority of the voting rights in the undertaking.

...

(4) An undertaking is also a parent undertaking in relation to another undertaking, a subsidiary undertaking, if it has a participating interest in the undertaking and –

    (a) it actually exercises a dominant influence over it, or

    (b) it and the subsidiary undertaking are managed on a unified basis.

While subsection (2) is concerned with the existence of legal power of control, the rather wider subsection (4) reflects the very different definition of a group prevalent in Germany, namely a definition which rests on the existence of the *de facto* control rather than *de jure* control.

The more precise definition of a group introduced by the Companies Act 1989 helps us to keep clearly in our minds that the purpose of consolidated accounts is to show the assets and liabilities under common control and how these are being used. It also helps accountants to ensure that some of the many off-balance-sheet finance schemes which have exploited the previous definition of a subsidiary do now find their way on to the consolidated balance sheet. Indeed, as we have seen in Chapter 9, FRS 5 *Reporting the Substance of Transactions*, has attempted to go even further than this in requiring the inclusion of quasi-subsidiaries in the consolidated accounts.[12] Accountants in the UK are now much more aware of the need for such provisions following the collapse of the US corporation Enron in 2001. This spectacular collapse was undoubtedly delayed because of the company's use of numerous Special Purpose Entities which were not included in the consolidated financial statements.

The compass of group accounts

Group accounts must take the form of a set of consolidated accounts, the only exception now being where such a set of consolidated accounts would not give a true and fair view.[13] Thus a parent company must usually prepare a set of consolidated accounts showing the results and state of affairs of itself and all its subsidiary undertakings as a single economic entity.[14]

The law does, however, exempt the parent company from preparing group accounts in certain circumstances and permits the exclusion of subsidiary undertakings from the consolidated accounts in other circumstances. We shall deal with each in turn.

In view of the stated desire of successive governments to reduce the burdens on business, the law exempted a parent company from the need to prepare group accounts where the group qualifies as a small or medium-sized group, provided that it is not what is described as an ineligible group.[15] As with the definitions of small and medium-sized companies, the definitions for small and medium-sized groups are framed by reference to turnover, balance sheet total (assets) and number of employees.[16]

[12] See Chapter 9, pp. 212–13.
[13] Companies Act 1985, s. 227.
[14] Companies Act 1985, s. 228.
[15] Companies Act 1985, s. 248. A group is ineligible if any of its members is a public company, a banking company, an insurance company or an authorised person under the Financial Services Act 1986.
[16] Companies Act 1985, s. 249

In addition to these exemptions based on size, a parent company does not have to prepare group accounts where it is itself an intermediate holding company with an immediate parent company in the EU, provided consolidated financial statements are prepared at a higher level in the group. There are a number of conditions which must be satisfied if this exemption is to apply, in particular, the higher-level consolidated accounts must be prepared in accordance with law based on the EC Seventh Directive and must be filed with the UK parent's individual accounts together with certified translations, where appropriate.[17]

Where a parent company is not able to take advantage of the above exemptions, it must prepare consolidated accounts for all the companies in the group which are under the control of the parent company. However, the law *permits* the exclusion of subsidiary undertakings from the consolidated accounts in the following circumstances:[18]

(3) . . . a subsidiary undertaking may be excluded from consolidation where –

    (a) severe long-term restrictions substantially hinder the exercise of the rights of the parent company over the assets or management of that undertaking, or

    (b) the information necessary for the preparation of group accounts cannot be obtained without disproportionate expense or undue delay, or

    (c) the interest of the parent company is held exclusively with a view to subsequent resale and the undertaking has not previously been included in consolidated group accounts prepared by the parent company.

. . .

(4) Where the activities of one or more subsidiary undertakings are so different from those of other undertakings to be included in the consolidation that their inclusion would be incompatible with the obligation to give a true and fair view, those undertakings shall be excluded from consolidation.

This subsection does not apply merely because some of the undertakings are industrial, some commercial and some provide services, or because they carry on industrial or commercial activities involving different products or provide different services.

FRS 2 takes a more restricted view and specifically states that neither disproportionate expense nor undue delay can justify excluding material subsidiary undertakings from the consolidated accounts. However, whereas the law *permits* the exclusion of subsidiary undertakings from the consolidated accounts, FRS 2 *requires* their exclusion in certain circumstances and specifies the required accounting treatment for such excluded subsidiaries.[19] Thus, Para. 25 of FRS 2 states that a subsidiary *should* be excluded from consolidation in three circumstances:

(a) where severe long-term restrictions substantially hinder the exercise of the rights of the parent company over the assets or management of the subsidiary undertaking;

(b) where the interest in the subsidiary undertaking is held exclusively with a view to subsequent resale and the subsidiary undertaking has not previously been consolidated in group accounts prepared by the parent company;

(c) where the subsidiary undertaking's activities are so different from those of other undertakings to be included in the consolidation that its inclusion would be incompatible with the obligation to give a true and fair view.

---

[17] Companies Act 1985, s. 228.
[18] Companies Act 1985, s. 229.
[19] FRS 2 *Accounting for Subsidiary Undertakings*, Paras 25–30.

Table 14.2 Attitude to exclusion of subsidiary

	Companies Act 1985	FRS 2
Inability to exercise control	Permits	Requires
Disproportionate expense or undue delay	Permits	Forbids
Subsidiary acquired for resale	Permits	Requires
Different activities where inclusion would be incompatible with true and fair view	Permits	Requires*

*But extremely rare in practice.

All three of these required exclusions follow from the legal provisions quoted above, except that the circumstances envisaged under (c) are in practice, extremely rare. In particular, the explanation to the standard emphasises that any differences between banking and insurance companies/groups and other companies/groups, or between profit and not-for-profit undertakings, is not sufficient of itself to justify non-consolidation.[20]

Having specified the circumstances under which subsidiary undertakings should be excluded, FRS 2 specifies the accounting treatment to be applied to such subsidiaries and the information to be disclosed. The required accounting treatment may be summarised as follows:[21]

(a) *Severe long-term restrictions.* If the parent company is denied control but retains significant influence over the excluded subsidiary, use the equity method of accounting. The equity method of accounting, which is the required method of accounting for associates and joint ventures, is described in the following chapter.

If the parent does not even retain significant influence, treat the excluded subsidiary as a fixed asset investment showing it at the carrying value at which it would have appeared if the equity method had been in use when the restrictions came into force.[22] Subsequently take credit only for dividends actually received.

In either case, it is essential to write down the investment if there has been impairment.

(b) *Subsidiary held exclusively with a view to resale.* This should be treated as a current asset and shown at the lower of cost and net realisable value.

(c) *Different activities.* In the rare circumstances where a subsidiary undertaking is excluded for this reason, the investment should be recorded in the consolidated financial statements using the equity method of accounting, and a separate set of financial statements for the subsidiary should be included with the consolidated financial statements.[23]

Changes in the composition of a group

Consolidated accounts for a group are prepared to show the results of the group as a single economic entity. It follows that, subject to the cancellation of intercompany balances and the removal of unrealised intercompany profit, the consolidated profit and loss account should include the profits or losses of all companies in the group for the relevant periods during

---

[20] FRS 2, Para. 78e.

[21] FRS 2, Paras 27–32.

[22] This carrying value may be the cost of the investment if the restriction existed at the date of acquisition (FRS 2, Para. 27).

[23] Certain other disclosures are required in respect of subsidiaries, both included and excluded. Readers are referred to the Companies Act 1985, Schedule 5 and to FRS 2, Paras 31–34.

which they were members of the group. The consolidated balance sheet should show the combined assets and liabilities of companies which are members of the group at the accounting year end. This simple requirement gives rise to many accounting problems where there is an acquisition or disposal of a subsidiary during the course of a year.

The first problem is to decide exactly when an acquisition or disposal occurs. The negotiations which lead to such an event are often long and drawn out, involving preliminary discussions, agreement in principle, a drawing up of terms, an offer, an unconditional acceptance and then payment of the consideration. In the 1970s various of these possible events were selected as fixing the date of acquisition or disposal and often the selection of the date appeared to have been influenced by a desire to show the largest possible profit in the consolidated accounts. Thus, when a new profit-making subsidiary is acquired, the earlier the selected date of acquisition, the greater the profits which will be included in the consolidated profit and loss account. Similarly, when the shares in a loss-making subsidiary are sold, the earlier the date of disposal, the less the losses which serve to reduce the consolidated profits.

In order to remove discretion about the choice of possible date, FRS 2 defines the effective date of acquisition or disposal as the date on which control is obtained or relinquished.[24] Control usually passes when an offer becomes unconditional and, in the case of a public offer of shares, this will be the date when the necessary number of acceptances has been obtained.

The consolidated profit and loss account must include the profits of any new subsidiary from the date of acquisition, as defined above, to the end of the accounting year and the profits or losses of any subsidiary sold from the beginning of the accounting year to the date of disposal. As we have seen in Chapter 11, FRS 3 *Reporting Financial Performance,* specifically requires the disclosure of the aggregate results of continuing operations, acquisitions (as a component of continuing operations) and discontinued operations.[25]

Let us look first at the treatment of acquisitions and then consider some of the various types of disposal that may occur.

Treatment of an acquisition

Fair values and goodwill

When a company acquires a subsidiary undertaking, it pays a price to obtain control of the assets and liabilities of that subsidiary. In the balance sheet of the parent company it is necessary to record the investment at its cost while, in the consolidated balance sheet, it is necessary to recognise the individual assets and liabilities of that subsidiary.

When a subsidiary is acquired for cash, the determination of the cost of the investment is easy but, when shares in a subsidiary are acquired in exchange for an issue of shares or other securities in the parent company or where part of the consideration is deferred or contingent on some future event, the determination of the cost may not be so clear cut.

Where the consideration is an issue of shares, it is necessary to determine the fair value[26] of the shares and, if this exceeds the nominal value of the shares, to record a share premium or, where merger relief is available, a merger reserve.[27]

Similarly, where other securities are issued, these should be valued at their fair value. Fair value is the market price of the securities when control is obtained or, if the securities are unquoted, the best approximation to the market price.

---

[24] FRS 2, Para. 45.
[25] FRS 3 *Reporting Financial Performance,* ASB, October 1992, Para. 14.
[26] See Chapter 5, pp. 99–100.
[27] See Chapter 13, p. 371.

Where the consideration is deferred or contingent, a reasonable estimate of its fair value should be included.[28] This would be provided by the expected value of the amount payable, that is the present value of the amounts expected to be paid in future.

In preparing a consolidated balance sheet it is necessary to replace the investment in the subsidiary by the whole of the underlying assets and liabilities of the subsidiary showing any minority interest therein. Under the historical cost convention, these assets and liabilities must be included at their historical cost to the group and, for this purpose, the amounts at which they appear in the subsidiary's own balance sheet are, of course, irrelevant. Indeed the group may not recognise certain assets and liabilities which appear in the subsidiary's balance sheet and may recognise assets and liabilities which do not appear in the subsidiary's own balance sheet at all.

The difficulty which must be faced here is that the parent company has not bought the individual assets and liabilities of the subsidiary. It has paid a global price to obtain control over a collection of assets and liabilities and, in order to prepare a consolidated balance sheet, it is necessary to allocate the global price to the individual assets and liabilities using the concept of fair value.

The difference between the cost of the investment and the appropriate proportion of the sum of the fair values of the individual 'identifiable' assets and liabilities recorded will provide the amount of goodwill. The ASB follows the law in using the adjective 'identifiable' but, although we shall continue to use this adjective, it does seem to be rather inappropriate. Many assets such as a good management team, a considerable research potential or a regional monopoly may be identifiable but are not usually recognised in the consolidated accounts except as part of the goodwill figure.

FRS 7 *Fair Values in Acquisition Accounting* (September 1994), provides standard accounting practice for determining which assets and liabilities of the subsidiary should be recognised in the consolidated accounts and how they should be valued:

The identifiable assets and liabilities to be recognised should be those of the acquired entity that existed at the date of acquisition. (Para. 5)

The recognised assets and liabilities should be measured at fair values that reflect the conditions at the date of the acquisition. (Para. 6)

The standard makes it clear that certain assets and liabilities not recognised in the accounts of the subsidiary should be recognised at acquisition. Examples are pension surpluses and deficiencies, as well as contingent assets. However it also makes it quite clear that certain provisions which have sometimes been recognised in the past should not be made in future. This is in line with the thinking subsequently embodied in FRS 12 *Provisions, Contingent Liabilities and Contingent Assets,* which we have discussed in Chapter 7.[29] The banned provisions include those for reorganisation and integration costs expected to be incurred as a result of an acquisition, as well as provisions for expected future losses (FRS 7, Para. 7). The existence of such provisions results in post-acquisition costs bypassing the profit and loss account and, as we have seen in Chapter 7, such provisions have been difficult to police in practice. There is considerable agreement that, in the case of some groups, excessive provisions appear to have been made and now all such provisions have been banned.

Once the identifiable assets and liabilities have been listed, it is then necessary to obtain their fair values. Fair values are defined as follows:

---

[28] Further guidance is provided by FRS 7 *Fair Values in Acquisition Accounting,* ASB, September 1994.
[29] FRS 12 *Provisions, Contingent Liabilities and Contingent Assets,* ASB, London, September 1998.

The amount at which an asset or liability could be exchanged in an arm's length transaction between informed and willing parties, other than in a forced or liquidation sale. (FRS 7, Para. 2)

While this would imply the estimation of a value based upon a hypothetical transaction, the standard makes it clear that the fair value of tangible fixed assets and stocks and work-in-progress should not exceed their recoverable amounts. Recoverable amount is defined in turn as the greater of the net realisable value of an asset and, where appropriate, its value in use (Para. 2).

Although it does not use the term, FRS 7 sensibly requires us to include the assets acquired at their 'value to the business'. The value to the business of tangible fixed assets and stocks and work-in-progress, which has been discussed in Chapter 5, is given by the formula shown in Figure 14.1. However, as we have seen in Chapter 5, this is not the concept of fair value as understood at present by the IASB, so the move towards convergence may lead to a reduction in the use of the more relevant 'value to the business model' in future.

The replacement cost of the remaining service potential of a fixed asset should be based upon the market value, if assets similar in type and condition are bought and sold on an open market, or at depreciated replacement cost, reflecting the acquired business's normal buying process and the sources of supply and prices available to it.[30]

Whereas the fair values of short-term and certain long-term debtors and creditors will be equal to their face values, it will be necessary to discount any long-term debtors and creditors which do not carry interest at the current market rate.

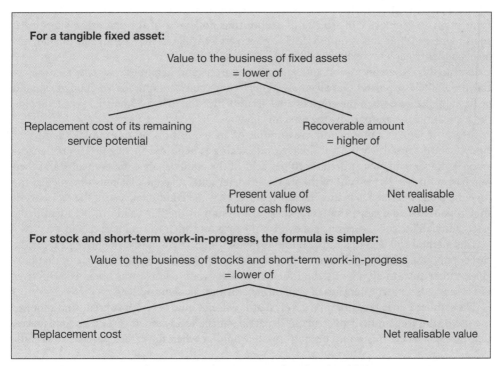

For a tangible fixed asset:

Value to the business of fixed assets
= lower of

Replacement cost of its remaining service potential

Recoverable amount
= higher of

Present value of future cash flows

Net realisable value

For stock and short-term work-in-progress, the formula is simpler:

Value to the business of stocks and short-term work-in-progress
= lower of

Replacement cost

Net realisable value

Figure 14.1 Determination of fair value as applied by the ASB

[30] FRS 7, Para. 9.

To help users of accounts to understand what has happened, company law requires companies to publish a table showing, for each class of assets and liabilities, the book values before an acquisition, the fair values at the date of acquisition and an explanation for any significant adjustment made together with the goodwill on acquisition.[31]

An example of the table required by law is given in Table 14.3.

Table 14.3 **Example of table required by company law**

	Book value at acquisition	Fair value adjustments	Fair value to the group
	£000	£000	£000
Tangible fixed assets	420	140	560
Current assets	340	50	390
Creditors due within one year	(190)	–	(190)
Creditors due in more than one year	(200)	(30)	(230)
Provisions for liabilities and charges	(50)	(10)	(60)
	320	150	470
Goodwill			130
Consideration paid			600

FRS 6 requires that the fair value adjustments are analysed between (a) revaluations, (b) adjustments to achieve consistency of accounting policies and (c) any other significant adjustments.[32] While this required disclosure is very sensible, it may be argued that adjustments under (b) are not really fair value adjustments at all.

In practice, the identification and valuation of assets and liabilities may take a considerable time. FRS 7 stipulates that all adjustments to fair values and purchased goodwill should be fixed by the date when the consolidated accounts for the first *full* financial year following the acquisition are approved by the directors.[33]

Before we look at a more complete example of an acquisition, let us examine the further complication caused when a subsidiary undertaking is acquired in stages. To take an example, one company may purchase 10 per cent of the equity shares of a company and then purchase a further 70 per cent of the shares at a later date. As control is only obtained at the time the latter purchase is made, the law requires that the combined cost of the 80 per cent should be matched against that percentage of the sum of the fair values of the identifiable assets and liabilities to determine goodwill at the date on which control is obtained.[34]

This method will lead to a rather dubious figure for goodwill in that the price paid for the earlier purchase related to the fair value of the net assets and goodwill at the date of that purchase rather than their value at the much later date when control was obtained. However FRS 2 sees it as a practical means of applying acquisition accounting.[35]

The standard does recognise, however, that it will not always be appropriate and requires the use of the true and fair override to depart from the legal rule in certain circumstances. One example where this would be appropriate would be when the earlier purchase was suffi-

[31] Companies Act 1985, Schedule 4A, Para. 12(5).
[32] FRS 6, Para. 25.
[33] FRS 7, Para. 25.
[34] Companies Act 1985, Schedule 4A, Para. 9.
[35] FRS 2, Para. 89.

cient to constitute the investee an associate for which equity accounting was appropriate. The application of the equity method of accounting requires the use of fair values at the initial purchase date and use of the legally specified approach, explained above, at a subsequent purchase which brings control would result in the post-acquisition profits and gains of the associate being reclassified as goodwill. In these circumstances, the standard requires that goodwill be calculated in stages, summing the differences between the cost of each purchase and the appropriate proportion of the fair value of the identifiable assets and liabilities at the date of each purchase. Such an approach would, of course, require the use of the true and fair override and the consequential disclosure that this had occurred.

The standard also deals with the situation where a company increases its stake in a subsidiary thus reducing or perhaps eliminating the minority interest.[36] In such a case it is essential to revalue the identifiable assets and liabilities in the subsidiary at the date of the increase in shareholding.

We have seen that the consolidated profit and loss account must include the results of a new subsidiary from the date of acquisition to the end of the accounting year and that the consolidated balance sheet must include the assets and liabilities of the new subsidiary which is a member of the group at the year end. This general statement is best explored in the context of an example.

Example 14.1

Let us take a company J Limited, which has many subsidiaries and makes up its financial statements to 31 December each year. J acquires a new wholly owned subsidiary, K Limited, during the year to 31 December 20X1. Control is obtained on 1 July 20X1. Summarised consolidated financial statements of the J group (excluding K) and financial statements for K Limited are given below:[37]

Summarised profit and loss accounts for the year ended 31 December 20X1

	J *Group*	*K* *Limited*
	£000	£000
Turnover	2000	500
less Expenses	1500	420
Profit from ordinary activities before tax	500	80
less Taxation	200	36
	300	44
less Minority interest	40	
	260	44
add Extraordinary profit (net of taxation and minority interest)	30	20
	290	64
less Dividends proposed	100	
	190	64

▶

---

[36] FRS 2, Para. 90.

[37] While the authors appreciate that FRS 3 has resulted in the virtual disappearance of the extraordinary item, we have included extraordinary profits in this and later examples for completeness.

Summarised balance sheets on 31 December 20X1

	J Group £000	K Limited £000
Fixed assets		
Goodwill – at cost less amortisation	100	–
Tangible fixed assets	500	156
Investment in K Ltd – 40 000 shares at cost	200	–
Net current assets	300	100
	1100	256
less Long-term loans	170	50
	930	206
Share capital (£1 shares)	250	40
Revaluation reserve (created 1 July 20X1)	–	20
Retained profits	500	146
	750	206
Minority interests	180	–
	930	206

As K Limited was acquired on 1 July 20X1, the date on which control passed, it is necessary to value the identifiable assets and liabilities at their fair values on that date. In practice it is extremely helpful if their fair values are incorporated in the individual financial statements of the subsidiary and this has been done in the balance sheet of K Limited to produce a revaluation reserve on 1 July 20X1 of £20 000.

We also need to calculate the cost of purchased goodwill and to estimate its useful economic life. In order to calculate this goodwill, we need to know the sum of the fair values of the identifiable assets and liabilities on 1 July 20X1. As these fair values have been incorporated in the financial statements of K, they are equal to the sum of the share capital and reserves of K at the date of acquisition, which may be calculated as follows:

K Limited

Net assets on 1 July 20X1	£000	£000
Share capital		40
Revaluation reserve		20
Retained profits		
On 1 January 20X1	82	
1 January to 30 June 20X1, $\frac{1}{2} \times$ £44 000	22	104
		164

J Limited has paid £200 000 to acquire net assets which have an aggregate fair value of £164 000 on 1 July 20X1. Hence it has paid £36 000 for goodwill. If we assume, for simplicity, that the estimated useful life of this purchased goodwill is six years, then the annual amortisation, using the straight-line method, will be £6000 and hence the amortisation for the six months 1 July to 31 December 20X1 will be £3000.

The consolidated profit and loss account must include the results of K Limited from 1 July 20X1 to 31 December 20X1 together with the amortisation of its goodwill. If we assume that the sales and operating profit of K Limited accrued evenly over the year and that the extraordinary profit did not arise until October 20X1, the consolidated profit and loss account must include the following post-acquisition profits of K from 1 July 20X1 to 31 December 20X1:

	Post-acquisition	
	£000	£000	£000
Turnover	$500 \times \frac{1}{2}$		250
less Expenses	$420 \times \frac{1}{2}$	210	
Amortisation of goodwill		3	213
			37
less Taxation	$36 \times \frac{1}{2}$		18
			19
add Extraordinary profit			20
			39

The consolidated profit and loss account with relevant workings, will appear as follows:[38]

Consolidated profit and loss account for the year ended 31 December 20X1

	£000	£000
Turnover		
J Group (excluding K)	2000	
K, $\frac{1}{2} \times £500\,000$	250	2250
Expenses		
J Group (excluding K)	1500	
K, $\frac{1}{2} \times £420\,000$	210	
Amortisation of goodwill in K	3	1713
Profit from ordinary activities before tax		537
less Taxation		
J Group (excluding K)	200	
K, $\frac{1}{2} \times £36\,000$	18	218
		319
less Minority interest (no change as new subsidiary is wholly owned)		40
		279
add Extraordinary profit (net of taxation and minority interest)		
J Group (excluding K)	30	
K (all post-acquisition)	20	50
		329
less Dividends proposed		100
Retained profit for the year		229

[38] We have assumed that the extraordinary profit of K Limited remains extraordinary within the context of the group.

**Movement on profit and loss account reserve for the
year ended 31 December 20X1**

	£000
Balance on 1 January 20X1 (old J Group only) (£500 000 – £190 000)	310
Retained profit for the year per consolidated profit and loss account	229
Balance on 31 December 20X1	539

Note that the retained profits brought forward do not include any profits in respect of K; after all, K did not become a member of the group until 1 July 20X1 so all retained profits before that date are pre-acquisition and represented by the net assets purchased on that date.

On the assumption that no major discontinuance is planned for K, the results of the new subsidiary will be included as part of the results of continuing operations and disclosed separately in accordance with the provisions of FRS 3.[39]

We next turn to the preparation of the consolidated balance sheet on 31 December 20X1. As K is a member of the group on that date, the balance sheet must include all of its assets and liabilities together with the purchased goodwill on acquisition shown at its cost less amortisation, that is at £36 000 less £3000.

The consolidated balance sheet on 31 December 20X1, together with appropriate workings, will appear as follows:

J Group
Summarised consolidated balance sheet on 31 December 20X1

			£000	£000
Fixed assets				
Intangible				
Goodwill	–	Old J group	100	
		K	33	133
Tangible	–	Old J group	500	
		K	156	656
Net current assets	–	Old J group	300	
		K	100	400
				1189
less Long-term loans	–	Old J Group	170	
		K	50	220
				969
Share capital, £1 shares				250
Retained profits, per consolidated profit and loss account				539
				789
Minority interest, as before				180
				969

---

[39] FRS 3, Para. 14.

Now that we have examined the basic principles for dealing with the acquisition of a new subsidiary, readers should be in a position to cope with various complications. Thus, the acquisition of a loss-making subsidiary or one in which profits do not arise evenly over the period should give few problems. Similarly, the acquisition of a partially owned subsidiary requires little modification to the approach we have adopted above.

Treatment of disposals

Just as companies acquire shares in subsidiaries, so too do they dispose of shares in subsidiaries. When we turn to disposals we may distinguish various categories of sales to outsiders[40] depending upon the shareholding, if any, which is retained:

(a) sale of total shareholding;
(b) sale of part of shareholding such that the investee company remains or becomes
   (i) a subsidiary;
   (ii) an associate;
   (iii) a simple investment.

In all cases it is necessary to recognise that different treatments are required in the individual accounts of the company making the sale and in the consolidated accounts.

We shall illustrate the principles involved in the context of a sale of the total shareholding and will then look briefly at partial disposals.

Sale of total shareholding

In the accounting records of the company which makes the sale, it is necessary to match the carrying value of the investment with the proceeds of sale to determine the profit or loss on disposal.

The disposal may, of course, have taxation consequences but, once the investing company has recognised the profit or loss and made any necessary provision for taxation, that is the end of the matter as far as that company is concerned.

When we turn to the consolidated accounts, matters are a little more complicated. In accordance with standard practice in the UK, as embodied in FRS 6, post-acquisition profits of a subsidiary are credited to the consolidated profit and loss account year by year, whether or not they are distributed as dividend to the investing company. Hence, year by year, we recognise profits which are retained by the subsidiary company and so increase the net assets shown in the consolidated balance sheet by these amounts.

In the consolidated financial statements, the profit or loss on disposal usually differs from that shown in the investing company's own profit and loss account. In the consolidated accounts, the profit or loss on disposal will be the difference between the sale proceeds and the appropriate share of the underlying net assets of the subsidiary at the date of sale plus any goodwill on acquisition which has not been written off in the consolidated profit and loss account. Thus the difference between the profit on disposal shown in the investing company's records and that in the consolidated financial statements will depend on the change in the net assets of the subsidiary since acquisition. To the extent that the net

---

[40] Intra-group sales may also occur. In addition, a parent company may lose control of a subsidiary even without a sale of shares where, for example, a rights offer by the investee is taken up by other shareholders but not by the existing parent. FRS 2 describes such a loss of control as a 'deemed disposal' and the principles involved in such a case are the same as those described in the text.

assets of the subsidiary have grown, due to the profits made and retained between acquisition and disposal, these have been recognised in the consolidated profit and loss account as part of the group's results.

Let us start with a very simple example. L Limited has two wholly owned subsidiaries, M Limited and N Limited. The respective summarised balance sheets on 31 December 20X1 are given below.

Summarised balance sheets on 31 December 20X1

	L	M	N
	£	£	£
Net assets	110 000	60 000	70 000
Investments in subsidiaries, at cost			
20 000 shares in M Limited	45 000		
30 000 shares in N Limited	70 000		
	225 000	60 000	70 000
Share capital, £1 shares	100 000	20 000	30 000
Retained profits	125 000		
at date of acquisition		10 000	20 000
post acquisition		30 000	20 000
	225 000	60 000	70 000

If we assume, for simplicity, that there are no fair value adjustments and that goodwill has not been amortised, the summarised consolidated balance sheet, with relevant workings, on 31 December 20X1, would appear as follows:

Summarised consolidated balance sheet on 31 December 20X1

	£	£
Goodwill		
M (£45 000 – £30 000)	15 000	
N (£70 000 – £50 000)	20 000	35 000
Other net assets		
(£110 000 + £60 000 + £70 000)		240 000
		275 000
Share capital, £1 shares		100 000
Retained profits		
L	125 000	
M post acquisition	30 000	
N post acquisition	20 000	175 000
		275 000

From this consolidated balance sheet we can see that the consolidated retained profits have been credited with £30 000 of post-acquisition profit retained by M and £20 000 post-acquisition profit retained by N. Thus, since acquisition, the net assets of these two companies have increased by £30 000 and £20 000, respectively, due to the making and retention of profits.

Let us now suppose that L sells its shareholding in M for £100 000 on 1 January 20X2. In the books of L it is necessary to compute the profit or loss on disposal by matching the carrying value of the investment, here its cost, against the sale proceeds. Sale proceeds are £100 000 and the cost was £45 000 so that the profit on disposal is £55 000.

In order to concentrate on principles, we shall postpone consideration of taxation until later in the chapter. The profit and loss account of L for the year ended 31 December 20X2 will therefore include the profit on disposal of shares in the subsidiary amounting to £55 000.

As the investment in M was sold on the very first day of 20X2, we shall prepare the consolidated profit and loss account for the year ended 31 December 20X2 by aggregating the profit and loss account items of L and N, the two companies in the group for this year. Concentrating only on the essential figures, we may produce a draft consolidated profit and loss account as follows:

Profit and loss accounts – year to 31 December 20X2

	L	N	Total
	£	£	£
Operating profit	80 000	60 000	140 000
less Taxation	40 000	20 000	60 000
			80 000
add Profit on disposal of shares in M	55 000		55 000
			135 000
add Retained profits brought forward			
L	125 000		
N (post acquisition)		20 000	145 000
Retained profits carried forward			280 000

Notice that the retained profits figure of £145 000 brought forward in this consolidated profit and loss account does not agree with the retained profits figure carried forward in the previous year's financial statements and shown in the consolidated balance sheet on 31 December 20X1 as £175 000. The difference is, of course, the £30 000 post-acquisition retained profits of M Limited, which ceased to be a member of the group on 1 January 20X2. We cannot now say that this £30 000 never existed. What has happened is that we have previously taken credit, in the consolidated financial statements but not in the parent company's financial statements, for profits of £30 000 which are represented in the net assets of company M. Any proceeds received for the shares are in respect of the underlying net assets at the date of disposal. What we must do is to return our profits brought forward to £175 000 by adding £30 000 and correspondingly to reduce the profit on disposal:

Workings for consolidated profit and loss account – year to 31 December 20X2

	Total	Adjustment	Draft consolidated P and L account
	£	£	£
Operating profit	140 000		140 000
less Taxation	60 000		60 000
	80 000		80 000
add Profit on disposal of shares	55 000	–30 000	25 000
	135 000		105 000
add Retained profits brought forward	145 000	+30 000	175 000
Retained profits carried forward	280 000		280 000

Notice that we have not changed the retained profits carried forward. These relate to L and its subsidiary N, the only two companies in the group at the year end. All we have done is to rearrange the items in the consolidated profit and loss account in order to give a true and fair view of what has happened:

	£	£
Sale proceeds		100 000
less Net assets of M at date of disposal	60 000	
Goodwill on acquisition	15 000	75 000
Profit on disposal		25 000

For ease of exposition, we have assumed that purchased goodwill has not been amortised. If goodwill had been amortised in the consolidated profit and loss account, only the unamortised amount applicable to M would be deducted in calculating the profit on disposal. To the extent that goodwill has been amortised in the past, it has already reduced consolidated retained profits.

The consolidated balance sheet on 31 December 20X2 poses no problems. At that date L has one subsidiary, N, and hence the consolidated balance sheet will be an aggregation for those two companies only.

Let us now complicate the example by assuming that the disposal occurs not on 1 January 20X2 but during the year to 31 December 20X2, for simplicity on 30 June 20X2. Let us assume that the proceeds on that date are £110 000 producing profit on disposal in the profit and loss account of L amounting to £65 000. Let us also assume that the profits of M arise evenly throughout the year.

M Limited
Summarised profit and loss account for the year to 31 December 20X2

	£
Operating profit	44 000
less Taxation	20 000
	24 000
add Retained profits brought forward	40 000
Retained profits carried forward	64 000

As explained above, we must make adjustments in the consolidated financial statements to show the results as far as the group is concerned. First, we must restore the retained profits brought forward to £175 000 and reduce the profit on disposal by £30 000, as we did before. However, we must, in addition, make a second adjustment. The operating profit and taxation figures included in the total column above relate only to L and N. However, the group consisted of L, N and M for the first six months of the year. The profits made and retained by M during those first six months should therefore be included in the group profits. Such profits are, of course, represented by net assets at the date of disposal and hence we must also reduce our profit on disposal. The appropriate adjustment will be as follows:

		£
Operating profits	$\frac{1}{2} \times$ £44 000	22 000
less Taxation	$\frac{1}{2} \times$ £20 000	10 000
		12 000

Our consolidated profit and loss account will therefore be arrived at as follows:

Draft consolidated profit and loss account of L Limited and its subsidiaries
M Limited and N Limited for the year ended 31 December 20X2

	Total (L and N) as above	Adjustments	Draft consolidated P and L account
	£	£	£
Operating profit	140 000	+22 000	162 000
less Taxation	60 000	+10 000	70 000
	80 000	+12 000	92 000
add Profit on disposal of shares in subsidiary	65 000	−12 000 ⎱ −30 000 ⎰	23 000
	145 000		115 000
add Retained profits brought forward	145 000	+30 000	175 000
Retained profits carried forward	290 000		290 000

Notice again that the retained profit carried forward relates only to L and N, the companies in the group on 31 December 20X2. The profit on disposal amounts to £23 000 and may be explained as follows:

	£	£
Sales proceeds		110 000
less Net assets at date of disposal:		
On 31 December 20X1	60 000	
Increase in 6 months to 30 June 20X2	12 000	
	72 000	
Goodwill on acquisition	15 000	87 000
Profit on disposal		23 000

We have now examined the basic approach to the accounting treatment of disposals. Before we explore partial disposals, let us consider first the treatment of taxation and, second, the disclosure of the disposal in the consolidated profit and loss account.

Taxation

Under the UK taxation system, a chargeable gain or loss will occur when an investing company sells shares. Assuming that there is a gain, the profit in the accounts of the selling company will be reduced by taxation.

When we turn to the consolidated profit and loss account the treatment is, as in the examples above, a little more complicated.

Let us take the last example in the previous section and assume that company L faces a liability to taxation at 25 per cent on the chargeable gain. Thus, on the gain of £65 000 in the accounts of L, the taxation would be £16 250 so that our profit on disposal in the profit and loss account of L would be as follows:

	£
Profit on disposal of shares in subsidiary	65 000
less Taxation	16 250
	48 750

When we turn to the consolidated profit and loss account, an analysis of the component parts of the profit on disposal would be as follows:

	£
Sales proceeds	110 000
less Cost of investment	45 000
	65 000
Recognised in consolidated accounts:	
Post-acquisition profits retained:	
to 31 December 20X1	30 000
6 months to 30 June 20X2	12 000
	42 000
Profit on disposal	23 000
	65 000

What is happening is that, although the post-acquisition profits have already borne corporation tax, they are being taxed again as a result of the disposal. It may therefore be argued that we should recognise this by apportioning the taxation charge to the three components:

	£		£
Post-acquisition profit			
to 31 December 20X1	30 000	× 25%	7 500
6 months to 30 June 20X2	12 000	× 25%	3 000
Profit on disposal	23 000	× 25%	5 750
	65 000		16 250

The second and third elements of this tax charge relate to the current year and should be included as part of the taxation expense in the consolidated profit and loss account. The first element relates to the retained profits brought forward and some accountants would argue that it should be treated as an adjustment to reserves. However, such a treatment appears to be inconsistent with FRS 3 and, in the view of the authors, all three elements should be included as part of the tax charge in the consolidated profit and loss account. All three elements have arisen because of the disposal during the current year and should be reflected in the consolidated profit and loss account, even though this may result in a relatively high tax expense in relation to the profits included.

This could, if desired, be isolated as taxation related to discontinued operations although, as we shall see below, this is not actually required by FRS 3.

Disclosure

In order to provide the results of the group, it is necessary to include as part of the consolidated profits those relating to the subsidiary M from the beginning of the year to the date of disposal. It is also necessary to include the profit on disposal of the subsidiary.

FRS 3 requires certain disclosures in the consolidated profit and loss account, namely that:

The aggregate results of each of continuing operations, acquisitions (as a component of continuing operations) and discontinued operations should be disclosed separately.[41]

The relevant analysis of turnover and operating profit must be included on the face of the consolidated profit and loss account but an analysis of other statutory format headings between turnover and operating profit must be included either on the face of the consolidated profit and loss account or in the notes to the financial statements.

If we assume that the sale of M falls within the FRS 3 definition of discontinued operations, an appropriate presentation for the relevant part of the consolidated profit and loss account for the L group would be as follows:

Consolidated profit and loss account – year to 31 December 20X2

	Continuing operations £	Discontinued operations £	Total £
Turnover			
Expenses – in accordance with statutory formats		Analysed appropriately	
Operating profit	140 000	22 000	162 000
Profit on disposal of discontinued operations	–	23 000	23 000
Profit on ordinary activities	140 000	45 000	185 000
Taxation	60 000		
(10 000 + 16 250)		26 250	86 250
Profit on ordinary activities after tax	80 000	18 750	98 750

FRS 3 does not require an analysis of the taxation charge between continuing operations and discontinued operations. We have included it for completeness.

Partial disposals

Where one company sells part of a holding in a subsidiary undertaking, the principles applied are the same as those illustrated above. However, the precise treatment depends upon the nature of the remaining investment. The investee may remain a subsidiary or the holding may be sufficient to make it an associate, otherwise it becomes a simple investment.

In all cases, it is essential to maintain a clear distinction between the entries in the accounting records of the selling company and those in the consolidation working papers.

In the records of the investing company it is necessary to match the appropriate proportion of the carrying value of the investment against the proceeds of disposal to produce a profit or loss on disposal. This may be subject to taxation but, now that we have explained the treatment of tax, we shall ignore it for the remainder of this chapter.

When we turn to the consolidated accounts, the position is somewhat different. We shall explore in detail the treatment where a subsidiary is retained and then look more briefly at the situation where an associate or a simple investment is retained.

[41] FRS 3 *Reporting Financial Performance*, ASB, October 1992, Para. 14.

Retention of subsidiary

At the beginning of the year the consolidated retained profit will include the post-acquisition profits of all subsidiaries based on the respective holdings of those subsidiaries at that particular date. In order to give a true and fair view of the operations of the year, the consolidated profit and loss account must include the appropriate portion of profits or losses of all companies which were members of the group during the year. The consolidated balance sheet at the end of the year will be an aggregation of the balance sheets of all companies in the group as at that date.

This is best illustrated with an example. P Limited acquired an 80 per cent interest in Q Limited many years ago when the reserves of Q were £20 000. The summarised balance sheets of the two companies, together with a summarised consolidated balance sheet on 31 December 20X1, were as follows:

Summarised balance sheets on 31 December 20X1

	P £	Q £	Consolidated £
Goodwill on consolidation			32 000
Investment in Q Limited: 32 000 shares			
at cost	80 000		
Other net assets	220 000	100 000	320 000
	300 000	100 000	352 000
Share capital, £1 shares	100 000	40 000	100 000
Retained profits	200 000		232 000
At date of acquisition		20 000	
Post acquisition		40 000	
Minority interest			20 000
	300 000	100 000	352 000

P sells 4000 shares in Q on 30 June 20X2 for £16 000. This produces a profit in the records of P amounting to £6000, as shown below, and leaves P with a 70 per cent shareholding in Q.

Sale of shares in subsidiaries

20X2		£	20X2		£
June 30	Investment account, cost of shares sold $\frac{1}{8} \times £80\,000$	10 000	June 30	Sale proceeds	16 000
	Profit on disposal	6 000			
		16 000			16 000

The consolidated profit and loss account must include the result of Q as an 80 per cent owned subsidiary for the first six months of the year and as a 70 per cent owned subsidiary for the second six months. Our consolidated balance sheet on 31 December 20X2 will, of course, be based upon the 70 per cent holding at that date.

A simple approach is to prepare initially a consolidated profit and loss account on the basis of the holdings at the end of the year. Assuming that there are no unrealised profits on intercompany trading and that we have the individual profit and loss accounts as shown in the first two columns, we may proceed as follows:

Workings for consolidated profit and loss account for the year ended 31 December 20X2

	P	*Q*	*Consolidated*
	£	£	£
Operating profit	50 000	20 000	70 000
less Taxation	20 000	8 000	28 000
	30 000	12 000	42 000
less Minority interest, 30% × £12 000			3 600
			38 400
add Profit on disposal of shares in Q Limited	6 000		6 000
			44 400
add Retained profit brought forward	200 000		
Post-acquisition group share (70% × £40 000)		28 000	228 000
Retained profit carried forward			272 400

As in the previous section, we may now make adjustments to show what has happened as far as the group is concerned. First, we must restore the retained profits brought forward to the figure shown in the consolidated balance sheet on 31 December 20X1 by adding £4000 and reduce the profit on disposal accordingly. Second, we must recognise that the minority interest was 20 per cent rather than 30 per cent for the first half of the year. Thus we must reduce the minority interest figure and also reduce the profit on disposal figure by 10 per cent of the profits of the first six months, which have of course increased the net assets underlying the shares sold. Assuming that the profits of Q arose evenly, we must therefore reduce the minority interest by £600 ($10\% \times \frac{1}{2} \times £12\,000$).

Workings for consolidated profit and loss account for the year ended 31 December 20X2

	Total based on 70% holding as above	*Adjustment*	*Draft consolidated P and L account*
	£	£	£
Operating profit	70 000		70 000
less Taxation	28 000		28 000
	42 000		42 000
less Minority interest	3 600	−600	3 000
	38 400		39 000
add Profit on disposal of shares in Q Limited	6 000	−600	
		−4 000	1 400
	44 400		40 400
add Retained profits brought forward	228 000	+4 000	232 000
Retained profits carried forward	272 400		272 400

Having made these adjustments, the operating profits of £39 000 after minority interest may be analysed as follows:

	£	£
Operating profit after taxation		
P (£50 000 – £20 000)		30 000
Q		
6 months to 30 June 20X2, 80% × ($\frac{1}{2}$ × £12 000)	4 800	
6 months to 31 December 20X2, 70% × ($\frac{1}{2}$ × £12 000)	4 200	9 000
Per consolidated profit and loss account		39 000

With some rearrangement and additional information on turnover and expenses, readers should be in a position to prepare a consolidated profit and loss account for the group.

As before, the closing consolidated balance sheet poses no problems. At 31 December 20X2 P has one subsidiary, Q, in which it has a 70 per cent interest.

Retention of an associate

Where a parent company sells shares in a subsidiary but retains a holding sufficient to give significant influence over the investee, it retains an associate. In the individual financial statements of the parent we match the relevant proportion of the cost of the investment against the proceeds of disposal to produce a profit or loss on disposal which may attract a taxation liability.

In the consolidated profit and loss account, we must recognise that the group has a subsidiary for part of the year but an associate for the remainder of the year. Thus for the first part of the year we must include all of the relevant profits of the subsidiary, subject to deducting any minority interests, together with the profit or loss on disposal. For the second part of the year we must include the appropriate proportion of the profits of the associate using the equity method of accounting.[42]

In the consolidated balance sheet at the year end, the investment in the associate will appear at its cost, less goodwill written off, plus the appropriate share of post-acquisition retained profits of that associate.

Retention of simple investment only

The treatment in the parent company's financial statements is exactly the same as for other disposals. However, the consolidated profit and loss account must include the whole of the profits of the subsidiary up to the date of disposal, subject to any minority interest, together with the relevant profit or loss on disposal. Subsequently there is only a simple investment so credit should be taken only for dividends received and receivable and the investment should be shown at the same value at which it appears in the parent company's own balance sheet.

While this sounds straightforward, it does give rise to the need to remove from the consolidated profit and loss account reserve the share of post-acquisition retained profit included in relation to the simple investment retained.

To give an example, let us suppose that a parent company disposes of 90 per cent of the equity shares in a wholly owned subsidiary, thus retaining a 10 per cent holding.

---

[42] The equity method of accounting is explained and discussed in the following chapter.

The consolidated profit and loss account reserve will have included 100 per cent of the retained profits of the subsidiary from the date of acquisition to the date of disposal and these will be reflected in the net assets of the subsidiary at the date of disposal. Whereas the post-acquisition retained profits relating to the 90 per cent holding sold will be taken into account in calculating the profit on disposal, those relating to the remaining 10 per cent holding must be removed if the investment is to be shown at its cost. Thus it would be necessary to have an adjustment to the consolidated profit and loss account reserve to remove the share of post-acquisition retained profits in respect of the remaining holding in a company which was previously a subsidiary.

In the consolidated balance sheet the investment would appear at its historical cost unless the directors had decided to revalue it at a higher amount or it had suffered impairment. As is the case with all disposals, preparation of the consolidated balance sheet poses few problems.

Having explored some of the major issues of accounting for groups in the UK, we now examine the international accounting standards on this subject.

The international accounting standards

There are two main international accounting standards which are relevant to the subject matter of this section of the chapter:

- IAS 27 *Consolidated Financial Statements and Accounting for Investments in Subsidiaries* (revised 2000)
- IAS 22 *Business Combinations* (revised 1998)

Both of these standards are under review so, as well as explaining the provisions of the current standards, we will draw attention to proposed changes.

IAS 27 defines the parent company subsidiary relationship in similar, although not identical, terms to UK company law and FRS 2, and requires the consolidation of subsidiaries. It exempts parent companies which are wholly owned or virtually wholly owned themselves from the need to publish consolidated financial statements and requires that subsidiaries be excluded from the consolidated financial statements when control is intended to be temporary or when the subsidiary operates under severe long-term restrictions which significantly impair its ability to transfer funds to the parent. Unlike FRS 2, it does not require the exclusion of subsidiaries from the consolidated financial statements when there is a fundamental difference between the activities of the parent company and those of the subsidiary although, as we have explained earlier in the chapter, exclusion for this reason is extremely rare in the UK.

As we explained earlier in the chapter, an exposure draft of a revised IAS 27 was issued by the IASB in May 2002 as part of its improvements project. This proposes that wholly owned or virtually wholly owned parent companies would only be exempted from the need to publish consolidated accounts if none of their securities was publicly traded and if the immediate parent company or ultimate parent company publishes consolidated financial statements prepared in accordance with international financial reporting standards. It would require exclusion of a subsidiary from consolidation only where control is intended to be temporary because the subsidiary is acquired and held exclusively with a view to its subsequent disposal *within 12 months from acquisition.* It takes the view that the existence of severe long-term restrictions casts doubt upon whether control exists and hence whether there is a subsidiary company at all.

IAS 27 makes no reference to the consolidation of quasi-subsidiaries which, as we have seen in Chapter 9, is required by FRS 5 *Reporting the Substance of Transactions*, in the UK. However Interpretation SIC 12,[43] *Consolidation – Special Purpose Entities* (June 1998), does require the consolidation of such entities under the control of the parent and the existence of this requirement undoubtedly boosted the standing of the IASB when the US corporation Enron collapsed in 2001 after failing to consolidate such Special Purpose Entities, a procedure which appeared not to be necessary under the voluminous US GAAP!

The mechanics of consolidation specified in international accounting standards are very similar to those in the UK. However IAS 22, *Business Combinations*, which we examined in the previous chapter, introduces a fundamental difference in the way in which assets, liabilities and minority interests are measured when using the acquisition method in consolidated financial statements which we will now explain and illustrate.

In this section of the chapter we have discussed the acquisition method of accounting and have, in particular, explained the need to use fair value, or more precisely in the UK context value to the business, in order to arrive at the historical cost of the separately identified assets and liabilities of a subsidiary to be included in the consolidated financial statements. Although IAS 22 and FRS 7 use the same term, 'fair value', IAS 22 actually requires the use of fair values while FRS 7 *Fair Values in Acquisition Accounting*, requires the use of the concept known as value to the business.[44]

Leaving this difference on one side, FRS 2 requires us to measure all of the assets and liabilities of a subsidiary at their fair values. Any minority interest in the subsidiary will then be measured as the relevant proportion of the aggregate of those fair values.

While this is the allowed alternative treatment under IAS 22, it is not the benchmark treatment. The benchmark treatment requires the use of fair values to the extent to which the subsidiary is owned by the group but requires that the minority interest be based upon the book values of assets and liabilities in the balance sheet of the subsidiary at the date of acquisition. This is best illustrated by means of an example.

Let us suppose that S plc acquires a 90 per cent interest in T plc. The aggregate book value of the net assets in the balance sheet of T at the date of acquisition is £400 000 and the sum of the fair values of those net assets is £600 000.

In accordance with UK practice and the allowed alternative treatment of the international accounting standard, the net assets would be shown at £600 000 and the minority interest would be shown at £60 000, that is 10 per cent of £600 000. However, under the benchmark treatment of IAS 22, the net assets and minority interest would be calculated as follows:

		£
Carrying value of net assets:		
S's interest	90% of £600 000	540 000
Minority interest	10% of £400 000	40 000
		580 000
Minority interest at date of acquisition		
10% of £400 000		40 000

---

[43] The Standing Interpretations Committee (SIC) was formed by the IASC in January 1997 and reconstituted in December 2001. Its role is to interpret international standards and provide timely guidance on financial reporting issues and it has issued some 33 Interpretations, which carry the prefix SIC. As we explained in Chapter 3, its name has now been changed to the International Financial Reporting Interpretations Committee.

[44] FRS 7, Para. 45.

This benchmark treatment results in strange carrying values for the individual assets and liabilities of the subsidiary in the consolidated financial statements and makes subsequent accounting for the group extremely complicated. However, it is the method which has long been part of US GAAP and became the benchmark treatment of IAS 22 in spite of considerable opposition from other countries. As we explained in Chapter 13, IAS 22 is at present under review and it is hoped that the benchmark treatment of that standard will disappear. There is no doubt in the minds of the authors that the allowed alternative treatment of IAS 22, that is the UK treatment, results in the provision of more sensible figures for users of consolidated financial statements.

Summary

In this chapter, we first examined the accounting treatment of investments in the financial statements of the investing company and then looked in much more detail at the subject of accounting for subsidiaries.

In the first section, we identified investments which give different levels of influence over the investee. These range from, at one end of the spectrum, a passive or simple investment through associates and joint ventures to investments which are sufficient to give control and hence create a parent/subsidiary relationship, We have seen that, in the UK, the rules for the treatment of all these investments in the investor's single-entity financial statements are the same while, under international accounting standards, the present treatment varies depending upon the level of influence which the investment carries. We have seen that changes in the international rules have been proposed which would prohibit the use of the equity method in the investor's single-entity financial statements.

In the second section, we explored the circumstances when consolidated financial statements must be prepared and when subsidiaries must be excluded from those consolidated financial statements. We then examined the mechanics of consolidation using the acquisition method of accounting. We concentrated heavily on the treatment of the acquisition of a new subsidiary, with the need to use fair values to arrive at the 'historical costs' of the assets and liabilities acquired, and on the disposal of shares in subsidiaries.

We saw that the ASB and the IASB interpret the term fair values in different ways and we have pointed out that UK practice adopts the allowed alternative treatment for the use of fair values, rather than the benchmark treatment of IAS 22. Both IAS 22 and IAS 27 are being revised and, while no change to the concept of fair value is expected, it seems likely that the benchmark treatment of fair values and minority interests will not survive the reviews.

Recommended reading

G.C. Baxter and J.C. Spinney, 'A closer look at consolidated financial statement theory', *CA Magazine*, January and February 1975.

R. Bryant, *Developments in group accounts*, 4th edn, Accountants Digest No. 425, ICAEW, London, 2000.

S.J. Gray (ed.), *International Group Accounting: Issues in European Harmonization*, 2nd edn, Routledge, London, 1993.

S.M. McKinnon, *Consolidated Accounts: The Seventh EEC Directive*, A.D.H. Newham (ed.), Arthur Young McClelland Moores, London, 1983.

C. Nobes, *Some Practical and Theoretical Problems of Group Accounting*, Deloitte Haskins & Sells, London, 1986.

A. Simmonds, A. Mackenzie and K. Wild, *Accounting for Subsidiary Undertakings*, Accountants Digest No. 288, ICAEW, London, Autumn 1992.

C. Swinson, *Group Accounting*, Butterworths, London, 1993.

P.A. Taylor, *Consolidated Financial Reporting*, Paul Chapman, London, 1996.

In addition to the above, readers are referred to the latest edition of *UK and International GAAP* by Ernst & Young, which provides much greater detailed coverage of this and other topics in this book. At the time of writing the most recent edition is the 7th, A. Wilson, M. Davies, M. Curtis and G. Wilkinson-Riddle (eds), Butterworths Tolley, London 2001. The relevant chapters are 5 and 14.

Questions

14.1 The accountancy profession has developed a range of techniques to measure and present the effects of one company owning shares in another company.

Briefly describe each of these techniques and how the resulting information might best be presented.
(The Companies Act 1985 disclosure requirements are not required.)

ACCA Level 2, The Regulatory Framework of Accounting, December 1986   **(20 marks)**

14.2 You are group financial accountant of a diverse group of companies. The board of directors has instructed you to exclude from the consolidated financial statements the results of some loss-making subsidiaries as they believe inclusion will distort the performance of other more profitable subsidiaries.

You are required to write a memorandum to the board of directors explaining the circumstances when a subsidiary can be excluded and the accounting treatment of such excluded subsidiaries.

CIMA, Advanced Financial Accounting, November 1993   **(15 marks)**

14.3 Fair value is a concept underlying external financial reporting.

You are required
(a) to explain why fair value accounting is required;   (4 marks)
(b) to explain how the fair value concept is applied;   (5 marks)
(c) to list three areas of application of fair value accounting.   (6 marks)

CIMA, Advanced Financial Accounting, November 1991   **(15 marks)**

14.4 Relevant balance sheets as at 31 March 1994 are set out opposite:

	£000 Jasmin (Holdings) plc	£000 Kasbah plc	£000 Fortran plc
Tangible fixed assets	289 400	91 800	7 600
Investments			
Shares in Kasbah (at cost)	97 600		
Shares in Fortran (at cost)	8 000		
	395 000		
Current assets			
Stock	285 600	151 400	2 600
Cash	319 000	500	6 800
	604 600	151 900	9 400
Creditors: amounts falling			
due within one year	289 600	238 500	2 200
Net current assets	315 000	(86 600)	7 200
Total assets less current liabilities	710 000	5 200	14 800
Capital and reserves			
Called up share capital			
Ordinary £1 shares	60 000	20 000	10 000
10% £1 Preference shares		4 000	
Revaluation reserve	40 000		1 200
Profit and loss reserve	610 000	(18 800)	3 600
	710 000	5 200	14 800

You have recently been appointed chief accountant of Jasmin (Holdings) plc and are about to prepare the group balance sheet at 31 March 1994.

The following points are relevant to the preparation of those accounts.

(a) Jasmin (Holdings) plc owns 90% of the ordinary £1 shares and 20% of the 10% £1 preference shares of Kasbah plc. On 1 April 1993 Jasmin (Holdings) plc paid £96 million for the ordinary £1 shares and £1.6 million for the 10% £1 preference shares when Kasbah's reserves were a credit balance of £45 million.

(b) Jasmin (Holdings) plc sells part of its output to Kasbah plc. The stock of Kasbah plc on 31 March 1994 includes £1.2 million of stock purchased from Jasmin (Holdings) plc at cost plus one-third.

(c) The policy of the group is to revalue its tangible fixed assets on a yearly basis. However the directors of Kasbah plc have always resisted this policy preferring to show tangible fixed assets at historical cost. The market value of the tangible fixed assets of Kasbah plc at 31 March 1994 is £90 million. The directors of Jasmin (Holdings) plc wish you to follow the requirements of FRS 2 'Accounting for Subsidiary Undertakings' in respect of the value of tangible fixed assets to be included in the group accounts.

(d) The ordinary £1 shares of Fortran plc are split into 6 million 'A' ordinary £1 shares and 4 million 'B' ordinary £1 shares. Holders of 'A' shares are assigned 1 vote and holders of 'B' ordinary shares are assigned 2 votes per share. On 1 April 1993 Jasmin (Holdings) plc acquired 80% of the 'A' ordinary shares and 10% of the 'B' ordinary shares when the profit and loss reserve of Fortran plc was £1.6 million and the revaluation reserve was £2 million. The 'A' ordinary shares and 'B' ordinary shares carry equal rights to share in the company's profit and losses.

(e) The fair values of Kasbah plc and Fortran plc were not materially different from their book values at the time of acquisition of their shares by Jasmin (Holdings) plc.

(f) Goodwill arising on acquisition is amortised over five years.

(g) Kasbah plc has paid its preference dividend for the current year but no other dividends are proposed by the group companies. The preference dividend was paid shortly after the interim results of Kasbah plc were announced and was deemed to be a legal dividend by the auditors.

(h) Because of its substantial losses during the period, the directors of Jasmin (Holdings) plc wish to exclude the financial statements of Kasbah plc from the group accounts on the grounds that Kasbah plc's output is not similar to that of Jasmin (Holdings) plc and that the resultant accounts therefore would be misleading. Jasmin (Holdings) plc produces synthetic yarn and Kasbah plc produces garments.

Required
(a) **List the conditions for exclusion of subsidiaries from consolidation for the directors of Jasmin (Holdings) plc and state whether Kasbah plc may be excluded on these grounds.** (4 marks)
(b) **Prepare a consolidated balance sheet for Jasmin (Holdings) Group plc for the year ending 31 March 1994. (All calculations should be made to the nearest thousand pounds.)** (18 marks)
(c) **Comment briefly on the possible implications of the size of Kasbah plc's losses for the year for the group accounts and the individual accounts of Jasmin (Holdings) plc.** (3 marks)

ACCA, Accounting and Audit Practice, June 1994   **(25 marks)**

14.5 Balmoral plc acquired 75% of the ordinary share capital and 30% of the preference share capital of Glenshee Ltd for £2 million on 1 November 1994. The draft profit and loss accounts for the companies for the year ended 31 October 1998 were:

	Balmoral plc £000	*Glenshee Ltd* £000
Turnover	2500	800
Changes in stocks of finished goods and work-in-progress	200	(100)
Own work capitalised	150	–
Raw materials and consumables	(1000)	(300)
Staff costs	(400)	(50)
Depreciation	(350)	(110)
Profit before taxation	1100	240
Taxation	(340)	(70)
Profit after taxation	760	170

Additional information

(1) The share capital and reserves of Glenshee Ltd at 1 November 1994 were:

	£000
Ordinary shares of £1 each	1500
10% preference shares of £1 each	500
Share premium account	100
Profit and loss account	400

There have been no subsequent changes to the share capital.

(2) The share capital of Balmoral plc comprises £2 million of 50p ordinary shares.

(3) The fair value of Glenshee Ltd's fixed assets was £200 000 higher than their net book value at 1 November 1994 and they have a useful economic life of 10 years.

(4) On 31 July 1998, Glenshee Ltd sold goods to Balmoral plc for £50 000 on the basis of cost plus a mark-up of one-third. By 31 October 1998, £40 000 of the goods remained in Balmoral plc's stock.

(5) Neither company has paid dividends in the year but both have proposed a final ordinary dividend of 5p per share and Glenshee Ltd proposes to pay the preference dividend in full. These proposed dividends are yet to be accounted for.

(6) Any goodwill arising is to be amortised over 10 years.

Requirements

(a) **Prepare the consolidated profit and loss account of Balmoral plc for the year ended 31 October 1998.**   (10 marks)

(b) **Discuss the benefits of consolidated accounts to the users of published financial statements.**   (5 marks)

ICAEW, Financial Reporting, December 1998   **(15 marks)**

14.6 Highland plc owns two subsidiaries acquired as follows:

1 July 1991   80% of Aviemore Ltd for £5 million when the book value of the net assets of Aviemore Ltd was £4 million.

30 November 1997 65% of Buchan Ltd for £2 million when the book value of the net assets of Buchan Ltd was £1.35 million.

The companies' profit and loss accounts for the year ended 31 March 1998 were:

	Highland plc £000	Aviemore Ltd £000	Buchan Ltd £000
Sales	5000	3000	2910
Cost of sales	(3000)	(2300)	(2820)
Gross profit	2000	700	90
Net operating expenses	(1000)	(500)	(150)
Other income	230	–	–
Interest payable and similar charges	–	(50)	(210)
Profit/(loss) before taxation	1230	150	(270)
Taxation	(300)	(50)	–
Profit/(loss) after taxation	930	100	(270)
Dividends proposed	(200)	(50)	–
	730	50	(270)

Additional information

(1) On 1 April 1997, Buchan Ltd issued £2.1 million 10% loan stock to Highland plc. Interest is payable twice yearly on 1 October and 1 April. Highland plc has accounted for the interest received on 1 October 1997 only.

(2) On 1 July 1997, Aviemore Ltd sold a freehold property to Highland plc for £800 000 (land element – £300 000). The property originally cost £900 000 (land element – £100 000) on 1 July 1987. The property's total useful economic life was 50 years on 1 July 1987 and there has been no change in the useful economic life since. Aviemore Ltd has credited the profit on disposal to 'Net operating expenses'.

(3) The fixed assets of Buchan Ltd on 30 November 1997 were valued at £500 000 (book value £350 000) and were acquired in April 1997. The fixed assets have a total useful economic life of ten years. Buchan Ltd has not adjusted its accounting records to reflect fair values.

(4) All companies use the straight-line method of depreciation and charge a full year's depreciation in the year of acquisition and none in the year of disposal.

(5) Highland plc charges Aviemore Ltd an annual fee of £85 000 for management services and this has been included in 'Other income'.

(6) Highland plc has accounted for its dividend receivable from Aviemore Ltd in 'Other income'.

(7) It is group policy to amortise goodwill arising on acquisitions over ten years.

Requirement
Prepare the consolidated profit and loss account for Highland plc for the year ended 31 March 1998.

ICAEW, Financial Reporting, May 1998   (13 marks)

14.7 You are the management accountant of Complex plc, a listed company with a number of subsidiaries located throughout the United Kingdom. Your assistant has prepared the first draft of the financial statements of the group for the year ended 31 August 1999. The draft statements show a group profit before taxation of £40 million. She has written you a memorandum concerning two complex transactions which have arisen during the year. The memorandum outlines the key elements of each transaction and suggests the appropriate treatment.

Transaction 1
On 1 March 1999, Complex plc purchased 75% of the equity share capital of Easy Ltd for a total cash price of £60 million. The Directors of Easy Ltd prepared a balance sheet of the company at 1 March 1999. The total of net assets as shown in this balance sheet was £66 million. However, the net assets of Easy Ltd were reckoned to have a fair value to the Complex group of £72 million in total. The Directors of Complex plc considered that a group reorganisation would be necessary because of the acquisition of Easy Ltd and that the cost would be £4 million. This reorganisation was completed by 31 August 1999. Your assistant has computed the goodwill on consolidation of Easy Ltd shown opposite.

	£ million	£ million
Fair value of investment		60
Fair value of net assets	72	
Less: reorganisation provision	(4)	
	68	
Group share		(51)
Goodwill relating to a 75% investment		9
Goodwill relating to a 25% investment ($\frac{25}{75}$)		3

Your assistant has recognised total goodwill of £12 million (£9 million + £3 million). The goodwill attributable to the minority shareholders (£3 million) has been credited to the minority interest account. The reorganisation costs of £4 million have been written off against the provision which was created as part of the fair value exercise.

Transaction 2

On 15 May 1999, Complex plc disposed of one of its subsidiaries – Redundant Ltd. Complex plc had owned 100% of the shares in Redundant Ltd prior to disposal. The goodwill arising on the original consolidation of Redundant Ltd had been written off to reserves in line with the Accounting Standard in force at that time. This goodwill amounted to £5 million.

The subsidiary acted as a retail outlet for one of the product lines of the group. Following the disposal, the group reorganised the retail distribution of its products and the overall output of the group was not significantly affected.

The loss on disposal of the subsidiary amounted to £10 million before taxation. Your assistant proposes to show this loss as an exceptional item under discontinued operations on the grounds that the subsidiary has been disposed of and its results are clearly identifiable. The loss on disposal has been computed as follows:

	£ million
Sales proceeds	15
Share of net assets at the date of disposal	(25)
Loss on disposal	(10)

Your assistant has noted that unless the goodwill had previously been written off, the loss on disposal would have been even greater.

Requirements

Draft a reply to your assistant which evaluates the suggested treatment and recommends changes where relevant. In each case, your reply should refer to the provisions of relevant Accounting Standards and explain the rationale behind such provisions.

The allocation of marks is as follows:

Transaction 1	(10 marks)
Transaction 2	(8 marks)

CIMA, Financial Reporting, November 1999 **(18 marks)**

14.8 Mull plc acquired shares in two companies as follows:

Skye Ltd
Ordinary shares – 8 million acquired on 1 June 1996 for £4.50 each.
Preference shares – £500 000 8% redeemable preference shares acquired, at par, on 1 June 1996.
At the date of acquisition the retained profits of Skye Ltd were £10 million.

Arran Ltd
Ordinary shares – 1 million acquired on 1 June 1998 for £6 each.
At the date of acquisition the retained profits of Arran Ltd were £5 million and the revaluation reserve was £11 million.
The draft balance sheets for the above companies at 31 May 1999 show:

	Mull plc £000	Skye Ltd £000	Arran Ltd £000
Fixed assets			
Freehold property	40 000	20 000	10 000
Plant and equipment	–	–	5 700
Fixtures and fittings	10 500	5 900	5 200
Investment in Skye Ltd	36 500	–	–
Investment in Arran Ltd	6 000	–	–
	93 000	25 900	20 900
Current assets			
Stock	19 000	13 000	11 000
Debtors	22 500	7 000	10 000
Cash in hand and at bank	1 000	570	780
	42 500	20 570	21 780
Creditors: amounts falling due within one year			
Bank overdraft	5 600	–	8 400
Creditors	18 400	9 600	7 500
Corporation tax payable	4 000	5 400	2 300
Proposed dividends	2 000	1 500	–
	30 000	16 500	18 200
Net current assets	12 500	4 070	3 580
Net assets	105 500	29 970	24 480
Capital and reserves			
Called up share capital			
Ordinary shares of £1 each	50 000	10 000	4 000
8% Redeemable preference shares	–	2 000	–
Revaluation reserve	10 600	–	11 000
Profit and loss account	44 900	17 970	9 480
	105 500	29 970	24 480

Additional information

(1) Skye Ltd has continued to account for its assets at their book value though their fair values on 1 June 1996 were:

Freehold land   – £2.5 million above book value

Fixtures and fittings   – £1.5 million below book value with an estimated remaining
              useful economic life of 5 years

The fair values of all other assets and liabilities for both Skye Ltd and Arran Ltd approximated to their book values.

(2) Skye Ltd's corporation tax payable at 31 May 1999 includes £1.4 million related to its year ended 31 May 1996. The company had originally provided £500 000 as the estimated liability as at 31 May 1996. Mull plc incorporated this estimate when establishing the fair values of Skye Ltd's net assets on acquisition. However, following a protracted Inland Revenue investigation, the final liability was agreed on 31 May 1999 at £1.4 million, £900 000 higher than the estimate.

(3) Skye Ltd paid its preference dividend during the year. All proposed dividends relate to ordinary shares. Mull plc has not yet accounted for any dividends receivable.

(4) Any goodwill arising is amortised over 10 years on the straight-line basis.

Requirements

(a) **Prepare the consolidated balance sheet of Mull plc as at 31 May 1999.**   (11 marks)
   Note: **You are not required to produce any disclosure notes.**

(b) **Briefly explain your accounting treatment of items (1) and (2) above, referring to the provisions of FRS 7, *Fair values in acquisition accounting*, where appropriate.**

(4 marks)

ICAEW, Financial Reporting, June 1999   **(15 marks)**

14.9 You are the management accountant of Faith plc. One of your responsibilities is the preparation of the consolidated financial statements of the company. Your assistant normally prepares the first draft of the statements for your review. The assistant is able to prepare the basic consolidated financial statements reasonably accurately. However, he has little idea of the principles underpinning consolidation and is unsure how to account for changes in the group structure. In these circumstances he asks you for guidance prior to beginning his work.

The profit and loss accounts of Faith plc, Hope Ltd and Charity Ltd for the year ended 30 September 2000 are given below:

	Faith plc £ million	*Hope Ltd* £ million	*Charity Ltd* £ million
Turnover	2000	1000	1200
Cost of sales	(1100)	(600)	(600)
Gross profit	900	400	600
Other operating expenses	(350)	(150)	(180)
Operating profit	550	250	420
Investment income	68		
Interest payable	(80)	(35)	(45)
Profit before taxation	538	215	375
Taxation	(160)	(65)	(114)
Profit after taxation	378	150	261
Proposed dividends	(160)	(70)	(100)
Retained profit for the year	218	80	161
Retained profit – 1 October 1999	780	330	526
Retained profit – 30 September 2000	998	410	687

Notes to the profit and loss accounts

Note 1 – Investments

Faith plc has made investments in the other two companies as follows:

- On 1 July 1993, Faith plc purchased 50% of the equity shares of Hope Ltd for a cash payment of £220 million. The net assets of Hope Ltd on 1 July 1993 had a fair value of £400 million. This value did not differ significantly from the carrying value in the balance sheet of Hope Ltd. The profit and loss account at that date showed a credit balance of £200 million. This investment gave Faith plc a reasonably significant influence over the operating and financial policies of Hope Ltd. However, on more than one occasion since 1 July 1993, the other shareholders have combined to prevent Hope Ltd embarking upon a course of action that was proposed by Faith plc.

- On 1 October 1999, Faith plc purchased a further 30% of the equity shares of Hope Ltd for a cash payment of £179 million. The net assets of Hope Ltd on 1 October 1999 had a fair value of £530 million. This value did not differ significantly from the carrying value in the balance sheet of Hope Ltd. This additional investment gave Faith plc control over the operating and financial policies of Hope Ltd.

- On 1 October 1999, Faith plc made a medium-term loan of £100 million to Hope Ltd. The rate of interest chargeable on that loan was 12% per annum. Both companies have correctly reflected that interest in their financial statements.

- On 1 January 1992, Faith plc purchased 70% of the equity shares of Charity Ltd for a cash payment of £460 million. The net assets of Charity Ltd on 1 January 1992 had a fair value of £600 million. This value did not differ significantly from the carrying value in the balance sheet of Charity Ltd. The profit and loss account at that date showed a credit balance of £300 million. This investment gave Faith plc control over the operating and financial policies of Charity Ltd.

The accounting policy for goodwill adopted by Faith plc is to amortise it over a 20-year period. Faith plc charges a full year's amortisation in the year of investment but no amortisation in the year the investment is sold.

Note 2 – Disposal

The business of Charity Ltd is significantly different from that of Faith plc and Hope Ltd. Following Faith plc's additional investment in Hope Ltd, the directors of Faith plc took a strategic decision to concentrate on the core business of the group. Following this decision, Faith plc sold all its shares in Charity Ltd for £750 million on 31 May 2000. The proceeds of sale were credited to a suspense account in the books of Faith plc. No further entries have been made in connection with the sale. The tax department estimates that taxation of £30 million will be payable in connection with the sale. A balance sheet was drawn up for Charity Ltd immediately prior to the sale of its shares by Faith plc. This showed net assets of £1000 million. The profits of Charity Ltd accrued evenly throughout the year ended 30 September 2000.

Note 3 – Inter-company trading

Following its securing control over the operating and financial policies of Hope Ltd, Faith plc began to supply Hope Ltd with a component that Hope Ltd was formerly purchasing from an outside supplier. For the year ended 30 September 2000, sales of this product from Faith plc to Hope Ltd totalled £60 million. In setting the selling price, Faith plc added a mark-up of one-third to the cost price. On 30 September 2000, the stocks of Hope Ltd included £20 million in respect of supplies of the component purchased from Faith plc.

Requirements

(a) Write a memorandum to your assistant that explains the impact of the changes in the group structure during the year on the consolidated profit and loss account. Your memorandum should include instructions regarding:
- the change of treatment of Hope Ltd caused by the additional share purchase;
- the profits of Charity Ltd that need to be included in the consolidated profit and loss account for the year ended 30 September 2000;
- the treatment of the sales proceeds that are currently credited to a suspense account;
- any separate disclosures that are necessary on the face of the consolidated profit and loss account as a result of the sale of the shares.

Your memorandum should include references to appropriate Accounting Standards.

(12 marks)

(b) Prepare the consolidated profit and loss account of Faith plc for the year ended 30 September 2000. You should start with turnover and end with retained profit carried forward. Your consolidated profit and loss account should be in a form suitable for publication.

(30 marks)

CIMA, Financial Reporting, November 2000   **(42 marks)**

14.10 You are the management accountant of Pulp plc, a company incorporated in the United Kingdom. Pulp plc prepares consolidated financial statements in accordance with UK Accounting Standards. The company has a number of investments in other entities but its two major investments are in Fiction Ltd and Truth Ltd. The profit and loss accounts of all three companies for the year ended 31 December 2000 (the accounting reference date for all three companies) are given below.

	Pulp plc £000	*Fiction Ltd* £000	*Truth Ltd* £000
Turnover	30 000	32 000	28 000
Cost of sales	(15 000)	(16 000)	(14 000)
Gross profit	15 000	16 000	14 000
Other operating expenses	(8 000)	(8 500)	(6 000)
Operating profit	7 000	7 500	8 000
Investment income	2 850		
Interest payable	(1 000)	(1 200)	(1 000)
Profit before taxation	8 850	6 300	7 000
Taxation	(1 900)	(1 900)	(2 000)
Profit after taxation	6 950	4 400	5 000
Dividends paid 30 June 2000	(3 000)	(2 000)	(1 500)
Retained profit	3 950	2 400	3 500
Retained profit – 1 January 2000	9 500	8 900	9 000
Retained profit – 31 December 2000	13 450	11 300	12 500

Note 1 – Investment by Pulp plc in Fiction Ltd

On 1 January 1995, Pulp plc purchased, for £13 million, 4 million £1 equity shares in Fiction Ltd. The balance sheet of Fiction Ltd at the date of the share purchase by Pulp plc (based on the carrying values in the financial statements of Fiction Ltd) showed the following balances:

	£000
Tangible fixed assets	7 000
Other net assets	3 000
	10 000
Share capital (£1 equity shares)	4 000
Share premium account	3 000
Profit and loss account	3 000
	10 000

Pulp plc carried out a fair value exercise on 1 January 1995 and concluded that the tangible fixed assets of Fiction Ltd at 1 January 1995 had a fair value of £8 million. All of these fixed assets were sold or scrapped prior to 31 December 1999. The fair values of all the other net assets of Fiction Ltd on 1 January 1995 were very close to their carrying values in Fiction Ltd's balance sheet.

Note 2 – Investment by Pulp plc in Truth Ltd

On 1 January 1994, Pulp plc purchased, for £12 million, 6 million £1 equity shares in Truth Ltd. The balance sheet of Truth Ltd at the date of the share purchase by Pulp plc showed the following balances:

	£000
Share capital (£1 equity shares)	8 000
Share premium account	4 000
Profit and loss account	2 000
Net assets	14 000

Pulp plc carried out a fair value exercise on 1 January 1994 and concluded that the fair values of all the net assets of Truth Ltd were very close to their carrying values in Truth Ltd's balance sheet.

Note 3 – Accounting policy regarding purchased goodwill

Pulp plc amortises all purchased goodwill over its estimated useful economic life. For the acquisitions of Fiction Ltd and Truth Ltd, this estimate was 20 years.

Note 4 – Sale of shares in Truth Ltd

On 1 April 2000, Pulp plc sold 2.8 million shares in Truth Ltd for a total of £10 million. Taxation of £500 000 was estimated to be payable on the disposal. The profit and loss account of Pulp plc that is shown above does **NOT** include the effects of this disposal. The write-off by Pulp plc of goodwill on consolidation of Truth Ltd for the year ended 31 December 2000 should be based on the shareholding retained **after** this disposal. The profits of Truth Ltd accrued evenly throughout 2000.

Note 5 – Administration charge

Pulp plc charges Fiction Ltd an administration charge of £100 000 per quarter. This amount was also charged to Truth Ltd but only until 31 March 2000. The charges are included in the turnover of Pulp plc and the other operating expenses of Fiction Ltd and Truth Ltd. Apart from these transactions and the payments of dividends, there were no other transactions between the three companies.

Your assistant normally prepares a first draft of the consolidated financial statements of the group for your review. He is sure that the change in the shareholding in Truth Ltd must have some impact on the method of consolidation of that company but is unsure exactly how to reflect it. He is similarly unsure how the proceeds of sale should be included in the consolidated financial statements.

Required

(a) Write a memorandum to your assistant that explains the effect of the disposal of shares in Truth Ltd on the consolidated financial statements of Pulp plc for the year ended 31 December 2000. Do not explain the mechanics of the consolidation in detail. You should refer to the provisions of relevant Accounting Standards.

(10 marks)

(b) Prepare the working schedule for the consolidated profit and loss account of the Pulp group for the year ended 31 December 2000. Your schedule should start with turnover and end with retained profit carried forward. You should prepare all calculations to the nearest £000. Do NOT produce notes to the consolidated profit and loss account.

(30 marks)

CIMA, Financial Reporting – UK Accounting Standards, May 2001   **(40 marks)**

14.11 (a) On 1 October 1999 Hepburn plc acquired 80% of the ordinary share capital of Salter Ltd by way of a share exchange. Hepburn plc issued five of its own shares for every two shares it acquired in Salter Ltd. The market value of Hepburn plc's shares on 1 October 1999 was £3 each. The share issue has not yet been recorded in Hepburn plc's books. The summarised financial statements of both companies are:

Profit and loss accounts: Year to 31 March 2000

	Hepburn plc £000	Hepburn plc £000	Salter Ltd £000	Salter Ltd £000
Turnover		1200		1000
Cost of sales		(650)		(660)
Gross profit		550		340
Operating expenses		(120)		(88)
Debenture interest		nil		(12)
Operating profit		430		240
Taxation		(100)		(40)
Profit after tax		330		200
Dividends– interim	(40)			
– final	(40)	(80)		nil
Retained profit for the year		250		200

Balance sheets: as at 31 March 2000

	Hepburn plc	Hepburn plc	Salter Ltd	Salter Ltd
Fixed Assets				
Land and buildings		400		150
Plant and Machinery		220		510
Investments		20		10
		640		670
Current Assets				
Stock	240		280	
Debtors	170		210	
Bank	20		40	
c/f	430	640	530	670

Balance sheets: as at 31 March 2000 (continued)

	Hepburn plc		Salter Ltd	
	£000	£000	£000	£000
b/f	430	640	530	670
Creditors: amounts falling due within one year				
Trade creditors	170		155	
Taxation	50		45	
Dividends	40		nil	
	(260)		(200)	
Net Current Assets		170		330
		810		1000
Creditors: amounts falling due after more than one year				
8% Debentures		nil		(150)
Net Assets		810		850
Capital and Reserves				
Ordinary shares of £1 each		400		150
Profit and loss account		410		700
		810		850

The following information is relevant:

(i)   The fair values of Salter Ltd's assets were equal to their book values with the exception of its land, which had fair value of £125 000 in excess of its book value at the date of acquisition.

(ii) In the post-acquisition period Hepburn plc sold goods to Salter Ltd at a price of £100 000, this was calculated to give a mark-up on cost of 25% to Hepburn plc. Salter Ltd had half of these goods in stock at the year end.

(iii) Consolidated goodwill is to be written off as an operating expense over a five-year life. Time apportionment should be used in the year of acquisition.

(iv) The current accounts of the two companies disagreed due to a cash remittance of £20 000 to Hepburn plc on 26 March 2000 not being received until after the year end. Before adjusting for this, Salter Ltd's debtor balance in Hepburn plc's books was £56 000.

Required

Prepare a consolidated profit and loss account and balance sheet for Hepburn plc for the year to 31 March 2000.   (20 marks)

(b) At the same date as Hepburn plc made the share exchange for Salter Ltd's shares, it also acquired 6000 'A' shares in Woodbridge Ltd for a cash payment of £20 000. The share capital of Woodbridge Ltd is made up of:

Ordinary voting A shares	10 000
Ordinary non-voting B shares	14 000

All of Woodbridge Ltd's equity shares are entitled to the same dividend rights; however during the year to 31 March 2000 Woodbridge Ltd made substantial losses and did not pay any dividends.

Hepburn plc has treated its investment in Woodbridge Ltd as an ordinary fixed asset investment on the basis that:

- it is only entitled to 25% of any dividends that Woodbridge Ltd may pay;

- it does not any have directors on the Board of Woodbridge Ltd; and

- it does not exert any influence over the operating policies or management of Woodbridge Ltd.

Required

Comment on the accounting treatment of Woodbridge Ltd by Hepburn plc's directors and state how you believe the investment should be accounted for.   (5 marks)

Note: **you are not required to amend your answer to part (a) in respect of the information in part (b).**

ACCA, Financial Reporting (UK Stream), Pilot Paper   **(25 marks)**

14.12 The balance sheets of United plc, Blue Ltd and Green Ltd at 30 September 2002, the accounting date for all three companies, are given below:

	United plc £000	United plc £000	Blue Ltd £000	Blue Ltd £000	Green Ltd £000	Green Ltd £000
Fixed assets:						
Intangible assets (*Note 1*)					1 200	
Tangible assets	25 000		22 000		20 000	
Investments (*Note 2*)	23 900		–		–	
		48 900		22 000		21 200
Current assets:						
Stocks	8 000		7 000		7 500	
Debtors (*Note 3*)	8 500		7 200		7 400	
Cash	900		600		500	
	17 400		14 800		15 400	
Creditors: amounts falling due within one year (*Note 3*)	(9 200)		(7 900)		(7 300)	
Net current assets		8 200		6 900		8 100
Total assets less current liabilities		57 100		28 900		29 300
Creditors: amounts falling due after more than one year		(12 000)		(10 000)		(9 000)
		45 100		18 900		20 300
Capital and reserves:						
Called up share capital (£1 ordinary shares)		20 000		10 000		10 000
Share premium account		5 000		4 000		3 000
Profit and loss account		20 100		4 900		7 300
		45 100		18 900		20 300

Notes to the financial statements
Note 1
The intangible fixed asset of Green Ltd represents capitalised development expenditure. United plc writes off such expenditure as it is incurred. At the date of its acquisition by United plc, the balance sheet of Green Ltd contained capitalised development expenditure of £400 000.

Note 2
Details of the investments by United plc are as follows:

Company	Number of ordinary shares acquired	Date of acquisition	Price paid	Reserves balance of acquired company at date of acquisition
Blue Ltd	8 million	1 October 1994	£14.8 million	£2 million
Green Ltd	7.5 million	1 October 1995	£13.5 million	£3 million

The following additional information is relevant:

- All shares carry one vote at annual general meetings.

- No fair value adjustments were necessary as a result of the acquisition of either company.

- Goodwill on acquisition is written off over 10 years.

- On 30 September 2002, United plc disposed of 2 million shares in Blue Ltd for proceeds of £4.4 million. Upon receiving the cash, United plc credited the proceeds of disposal to its investments account. Apart from this, United plc has made no other entries in respect of the disposal. Taxation of £200 000 is expected to be payable on the disposal.

- Neither Blue Ltd or Green Ltd has issued shares since the dates of acquisition by United plc.

Note 3
United plc provides goods and services to Blue Ltd and Green Ltd and the debtors of United plc at 30 September 2002 contained the following balances:

- Receivable from Blue Ltd   £500 000.

- Receivable from Green Ltd   £400 000.

The above amounts agreed to the amounts recognised in the trade creditors of Blue Ltd and Green Ltd. There were no goods in the stock of Blue Ltd or Green Ltd at 30 September 2002 that had been purchased from United plc.

Required
Prepare the consolidated balance sheet of United plc at 30 September 2002. Marks will be given for workings and explanations that support your figures.

CIMA, Financial Reporting – UK Accounting Standards, November 2002   **(20 marks)**

Associates and joint ventures

As we explained in the previous chapter, investments by one entity in another take many different forms, ranging from simple or passive investments at one end of the spectrum to investments which command control of the investee's activities, assets and liabilities at the other end. In this chapter, we focus on investments between these two extremes, namely investments in associates and joint ventures. Both such investments give the investor significant influence over the investee. In the case of joint ventures, this influence amounts to control, albeit shared with other venturers. We also refer to joint arrangements that are not entities, known by the acronym 'JANE'.

While it would be possible to account for these investments using cost or fair values, accounting standard setters have focused, instead, on two methods of accounting which are generally considered appropriate for such investments, namely proportional (or proportionate) consolidation and the equity method of accounting. We start by explaining each of these methods and demonstrate the similarities and differences between them. We then turn to current practice by explaining the provisions of the rather unhelpful legal rules now contained in the UK Companies Act 1985 and then examine the provisions of the relevant UK and international accounting standards, which are:

- FRS 9 *Accounting for Associates and Joint Ventures* (1997)
- IAS 28 *Accounting for Investments in Associates* (revised 2000)
- IAS 31 *Financial Reporting of Interests in Joint Ventures* (revised 2000)

IAS 28 is at present under review, as part of the IASB improvements project, and this is one of the six topics included in the ASB Consultation Paper, issued in May 2002, as part of the convergence programme. We draw attention to proposed changes where appropriate.

Introduction

Associated companies were the subject of the very first SSAP, issued in 1971.[1] Prior to the publication of SSAP 1, a long-term investment in another company was treated in one of two ways. Either it was a simple investment, to be treated as a fixed asset investment or it was an investment in a subsidiary, in which case it was normal to prepare a set of consolidated financial statements. Both of these treatments have been discussed at some length in the previous chapter. The main change brought about by SSAP 1 was the recognition of an intermediate category of investment, an investment in an associated company, where a long-term investment was such as to give the investor company significant influence over the

---

[1] SSAP 1 *Accounting for the Results of Associated Companies*, ASC, London, January 1971. This was issued as a revised SSAP 1 *Accounting for Associate Companies*, by the ASC in April 1983 and has been replaced by FRS 9 *Accounting for Associates and Joint Ventures*, issued by the ASB in November 1997.

investee company. The term associated company included both a joint venture, where significant influence took the form of joint control, and a long-term investment which carried significant influence. Although it has proved difficult to develop a precise definition, the essence of the relationship is that the investing company or group participates in and has significant influence over the commercial and financial policy decisions of the associated company, including decisions on the level of distributions.

As we shall see later in this chapter, the Companies Act 1989 introduced a new term, an associated undertaking, which it defined in an extremely unhelpful way and this made it difficult to develop standard accounting practice in this area. However, FRS 9 *Associates and Joint Ventures,* which was issued by the ASB in November 1997, has surmounted the legal obstacles to provide that standard practice in the UK.

The main methods of accounting that have been developed for investments which give the investor significant influence over the investee are proportional consolidation and the equity method of accounting. We shall explore the similarities and differences between these two methods of accounting before returning to examine the current regulatory framework, both UK and international, later in the chapter.

Possible methods of accounting

Where one company exercises significant influence over another company, it seems unhelpful to account for the investment in that company as a simple or passive investment. To take credit in the profit and loss account merely for dividends received and receivable is not sufficient where the directors of the investing company are able to influence the level of those dividends. To show the investment in the balance sheet at its historical cost gives no guide to what is happening to the underlying net assets, the use of which is influenced by the investing company's directors. In order to evaluate the stewardship of their directors, shareholders in the investing company require further information. It is also desirable to minimise the opportunities available to directors to manipulate the trend of reported profits.

One possible alternative would be to show such an investment at its fair value and then to take movements in the fair value, together with any dividends receivable, to the profit and loss account each year. This would immediately bring us into conflict with company law, which states that only realised profits should be included in a profit and loss account, but there are other major deficiencies with such a treatment. Where the shares in the investee are unquoted, the estimation of fair value will usually be a difficult task, involving subjective judgement, frequently leading to a rather unreliable value. Even where it is possible to arrive at a reliable fair value as, for example, when the shares in the investee are quoted, it may be argued that this is an inappropriate way to account for investments which are held for the long term and carry significant influence over the investee. As we have seen in Chapter 14, it is certainly not the method we use to account for a subsidiary.

If treatment as a simple investment at cost or fair value is inadequate, there would appear to be two closely related possibilities. The first is *proportional (or proportionate) consolidation,* and the second is the *equity method* of accounting and its variant, the *gross equity method,* which differs only in the level of detailed disclosure required. We shall look at each of these possibilities. In so doing we shall assume that the investee is an associate which is a company rather than an unincorporated body.

Using the method of proportional consolidation we remove the investment in the associate from the investing company's balance sheet and replace it by the proportionate share of the assets and liabilities of that associate on a line-by-line basis together with any goodwill on acquisition. In the profit and loss account of the investing company we remove any dividends received or receivable already credited and take credit, instead, for the appropriate proportion of the revenues and expenses of the associate on a line-by-line basis. The consolidated profits would then include the appropriate proportion of the post-acquisition profits retained by the associate. It would, of course, be possible to disclose separately the amount of each revenue, expense, asset and liability included in respect of the associate although this would, inevitably, result in a rather cluttered set of financial statements.

Using the equity method of accounting we value the investment in the balance sheet at cost plus the share of post-acquisition profits retained by the associate. Thus, the carrying value of the investment in the balance sheet is increased by the appropriate proportion of the increase in net assets of the associate due to retained profits. The profit and loss account is credited, not with dividends received and receivable, but with the appropriate proportion of the profits of the associate. Conversely, it would be debited with the appropriate proportion of any losses.

The net effect on the profit and loss account under both proportional consolidation and the equity method is the same but the way in which information is disclosed is different. Under proportional consolidation, the share of revenue and expenses of the associated company are added to those of the investing entity on a line-by-line basis. Under the equity method of accounting, as currently applied, it is usual to leave the revenues and operating expenses of the investing company or group unchanged and then to take credit for the share of the associate's operating profit as a separate item, including each subsequent item of income or expense on a line-by-line basis.

Let us explore a balance sheet using each method of accounting.

The summarised balance sheets of A Limited and B Limited on 31 December 20X2 are as follows:

Summarised balance sheets on 31 December 20X2

	A Limited £	B Limited £
Fixed assets		
Tangible assets	90 000	40 000
Investment in B Limited		
5000 shares at cost	22 000	–
Net current assets	10 000	24 000
	122 000	64 000
Share capital, £1 shares	50 000	20 000
Retained profits	72 000	44 000
	122 000	64 000

Let us assume that A purchased its 25 per cent holding in B Limited some years ago when the retained profits of B were £28 000. Provided there have been no changes in share capital, this tells us that B's summarised balance sheet at the date of acquisition was:

	£
Net assets	48 000
Share capital	20 000
Retained profits	28 000
	48 000

As we explained in the previous chapter in the context of a subsidiary, the book values of the assets and liabilities of B at the date of acquisition should be replaced by their fair values, or more precisely their value to the business, at that date. However, for ease of exposition, we shall assume that the book values at the date of acquisition were equal to their fair values. On the basis of this simplifying assumption, A has purchased a 25% interest in these net assets for £22 000 and has paid £10 000 (i.e. £22 000 less 25% of £48 000) for goodwill. We shall also assume, for the present, that goodwill has not been amortised.

Between the date of acquisition and 31 December 20X2, B has increased its retained profits by £16 000 (i.e. £44 000 less £28 000). A's share of this retained post-acquisition profit is 25 per cent or £4000. We may therefore replace the asset 'Investment in B Limited' shown in the balance sheet of A at £22 000, by the following items:

	£
Fixed assets	
Tangible assets, 25% of 40 000	10 000
Goodwill	10 000
Net current assets 25% × 24 000	6 000
	26 000
less Retained profits (share of post-acquisition retained profits)	4 000
	22 000

Using proportional consolidation we would produce the following balance sheet, grouping like items for the investing company and associate together on a line-by-line basis.[2]

A Limited – Summarised balance sheet on 31 December 20X2
Using proportional consolidation (with workings)

		£
Fixed assets		
Intangible		
Goodwill		10 000
Tangible	(90 000 + 10 000)	100 000
		110 000
Net current assets	(10 000 + 6 000)	16 000
		126 000
Share capital (£1 shares)		50 000
Retained profits	(72 000 + 4 000)	76 000
		126 000

It would, of course, be possible to expand the balance sheet to provide an analysis of the assets and liabilities of the two companies along the following lines:

[2] As we will see later in the chapter, IAS 31 *Financial Reporting of Interests in Joint Ventures* (revised 2000), requires the use of what it calls proportionate consolidation for joint ventures, and permits the use of both of the formats, illustrated here.

A Limited – Summarised balance sheet on 31 December 20X2 using proportional consolidation (with disclosure of separate amounts for associate)

	£	£
Fixed assets		
Intangible		
Goodwill in associate		10 000
Tangible		
A Limited	90 000	
Associate	10 000	
		100 000
		110 000
Net current assets		
A Limited	10 000	
Associate	6 000	16 000
		126 000
Share capital (£1 shares)		50 000
Retained profits		
A Limited	72 000	
Associate	4 000	
		76 000
		126 000

Using the equity method of accounting, the investment is simply shown at cost plus the share of post-acquisition profits retained by the associate, that is at £26 000 (£22 000 plus £4000):

A Limited – Summarised balance sheet on 31 December 20X2 (using equity method of accounting)

	£	£
Fixed assets		
Tangible assets		90 000
Investment in associate (see below)		26 000
Net current assets		10 000
		126 000
Share capital, £1 shares		50 000
Retained profit		
A Limited	72 000	
Associate	4 000	76 000
		126 000

The carrying value of the investment may be calculated in two ways:

Cost of investment	22 000
add Share of post-acquisition profits	
retained by B Limited	4 000
	26 000

or

Share of net assets of B Limited

25% of £64 000	16 000
Unamortised goodwill	10 000
	26 000

Comparison of the way in which the investment is shown using the equity method with the balance sheet using proportional consolidation makes it clear why the equity method is often referred to as a 'one-line consolidation'. The carrying value of the investment is equal to the appropriate proportion of the net assets of the associate plus any unamortised positive goodwill or less the balance of any negative goodwill.

Associates and acquisition accounting

Both proportional consolidation and the equity method of accounting are subsets of acquisition accounting, which we discussed in the context of accounting for subsidiaries in Chapters 13 and 14. It follows that many of the principles that we have discussed in the context of preparing consolidated financial statements for a parent and its subsidiaries also apply in the case of accounting for associates and joint ventures. We shall outline a number of such matters here.

Date of acquisition

Under acquisition accounting, only post-acquisition profits are included in the profit and loss account. Hence, when an interest in an associate or joint venture is acquired during a year, it will be necessary to calculate or estimate which revenues and expenses were preacquisition and which post acquisition. Only the post-acquisition revenues and expenses should be included in the profit and loss account prepared using proportional consolidation or the equity method of accounting.

Consistent accounting periods and policies

In order to produce meaningful aggregated amounts for the investor and investee, results for the same accounting periods using consistent accounting policies should be used. In practice, this may not always be possible and accounting standards can only provide limited guidance on what should be done in such circumstances.[3]

Use of fair values

As we explained in the previous chapter, the book values of the associate or joint venture are of no relevance in determining the 'cost' of assets and liabilities to the investor. For this purpose it is necessary to use fair values or, more accurately in the UK context at present, value to the business of assets and liabilities. The use of such values at the date of acquisition will usually have consequences for the subsequent measurement of profits or losses of the investee, most obviously in the area of depreciation and amortisation.

---

[3] See, for example, FRS 9 *Associates and Joint Ventures*, Para. 31(d).

Purchased goodwill and amortisation

As we saw in Chapter 13, it is now standard practice to amortise purchased goodwill over its expected useful economic life although, under FRS 10 *Goodwill and Intangible Assets*, there are circumstances where this is not necessary provided annual impairment reviews are conducted. The same rules apply to the treatment of purchased goodwill in associates and joint ventures.

Unrealised intercompany profits

Given the existence of significant influence of the investor over the investee, it would be wrong to include unrealised profits from intercompany trading when using proportional consolidation or the equity method of accounting. The part of such unrealised profits relating to the investor's share in the investee should be removed.[4]

The regulatory framework in the United Kingdom

The legal background

While the subject matter of SSAP 1 was associated companies, the Companies Act 1989 subsequently provided the following definitions of 'associated undertakings' and 'joint ventures':[5]

> An 'associated undertaking' means an undertaking in which an undertaking included in the consolidation has a participating interest and over whose operating and financial position it exercises a significant influence and which is not:
>
> (a) a subsidiary undertaking of the parent company, or
> (b) a joint venture dealt with in accordance with paragraph 19.
>
> Where an undertaking holds 20 per cent or more of the voting rights in another undertaking, it shall be presumed to exercise such an influence over it unless the contrary is shown.
>
> (Paras 20(1) and 20(2))

The above definition refers to 'a joint venture dealt with in accordance with paragraph 19'. The relevant part of this paragraph is as follows:

> Where an undertaking . . . manages another undertaking jointly . . . that other undertaking ('the joint venture') may, if it is not –
>
> (a) a body corporate, or
> (b) a subsidiary undertaking of the parent company, be dealt with in the group accounts by the method of proportional consolidation.
>
> (Para. 19)

This is really rather bizarre drafting, and it posed considerable problems for the ASB as it attempted to prepare a sensible standard. While the legal definition of associated undertakings always includes an incorporated joint venture, it includes an unincorporated joint venture only if the venturer chooses to apply the equity method of accounting rather than proportional consolidation. Thus, under the provisions of the Act, if a venturer chooses to apply the equity method to an unincorporated joint venture, that joint venture is an associated undertaking while, if the venturer chooses to apply proportional consolidation to that

---

[4] See FRS 9, Para. 31(b). The IASC Interpretation SIC – 3 *Elimination of Unrealised Profits and Losses on Transactions with Associates*, issued in July 1997, explains this requirement in more detail.
[5] Companies Act 1985, Schedule 4A, Paras 19 and 20.

unincorporated joint venture, it is not an associated undertaking because it has fallen under the provisions of Para. 19. To define a joint venture by reference to the method used to account for it posed some difficulties in attempting to develop an appropriate accounting method for joint ventures!

FRS 9 *Accounting for Associates and Joint Ventures*

In developing standard accounting practice for associates and joint ventures, the ASB has developed an approach which distinguishes investments in entities from a joint arrangement that does not fall within its definition of an entity. The crucial definition here is the FRS 9 definition of an entity, which can only be described as arcane:

> A body corporate, partnership or unincorporated association carrying on a trade or business with or without a view to profit. The reference to carrying on a trade or business means a trade or business of its own and not just part of the trades or businesses of entities that have interests in it.   (Para. 4)

Under this definition, a limited company, certainly an entity using any sensible definition of the word, may or may not be an entity under FRS 9. If the company carries on its own trade or business, it is such an entity while, if it merely carries on part of the trades or businesses of the investors, it is not such an entity.

The distinction which the ASB makes can only lead to confusion and undoubtedly gives rise to problems in practice in deciding whether a body corporate, partnership or unincorporated association is carrying on its own trade or business or parts of the trades and businesses of the entities which have interests in it!

Nevertheless, on the basis of the above definition, FRS 9 distinguishes investments in entities, that is associates and joint ventures, from a 'joint arrangement that is not an entity'. Although the term is not used in the standard, the latter has, perhaps not surprisingly, attracted the acronym 'JANE'.

The standard provides definitions of the three categories of investment which it has identified and then clearly specifies the required accounting treatment for each category:[6]

> An *associate* is an entity (other than a subsidiary) in which another entity (the investor) has a participating interest and over whose operating and financial policies the investor exercises a significant influence.

> A *joint venture* is an entity in which the reporting entity holds an interest on a long-term basis and is jointly controlled by the reporting entity and one or more other venturers under a contractual arrangement.

> A *joint arrangement that is not an entity* is a contractual arrangement under which the participants engage in joint activities that do not create an entity because it would not be carrying on a trade or business of its own. A contractual arrangement where all significant matters of operating and financial policy are predetermined does not create an entity because the policies are those of its participants, not of a separate entity.

The required accounting treatment for each of these is shown in Table 15.1.

From Table 15.1, it may be seen that the ASB does not permit the use of proportional consolidation for associates and joint ventures. It considers that use of such a method is wrong because

---

[6] FRS 9 *Associates and Joint Ventures*, ASB, London, November 1997, was preceded by a Discussion Paper and an Exposure Draft FRED 11, both with the same title, in July 1994 and March 1996 respectively. For definitions see FRS 9, Para. 4, and for the required accounting treatment, FRS 9, Paras 18–29.

Table 15.1 Required accounting treatment of associates, joint ventures and JANEs

Entities	Required treatment
Associate	Equity method
Joint venture	Gross equity method
Joint arrangement that is not an entity (JANE)	Account for shares of individual assets, liabilities, results and cash flows

it combines assets and liabilities over which the investor only has significant influence, with assets and liabilities under the full control of the investor. As we shall see later in this chapter, this is not the view taken in the international accounting standard on joint ventures.

The difference between the gross equity method and the equity method is merely presentational in that the gross equity method provides more detailed disclosure of the share of the investee's turnover, gross assets and gross liabilities.

The method specified for a JANE is to require the investor to account directly for its share of the assets, liabilities, results and cash flows of the joint arrangement. This will frequently produce the same results as proportional consolidation in practice although this will not be the case where the venturer holds the individual assets and liabilities in the joint arrangement in different proportions.

To illustrate the approach of FRS 9, let us first take a situation where the investing company, C Limited, has subsidiaries and prepares consolidated financial statements. C Limited also has an associate, D Limited, in which it holds 30 per cent of the equity shares. Abbreviated consolidated financial statements for the group, excluding the incorporation of D as an associate, together with the financial statements of D Limited for the year ended 31 December 20X2 are given below.

Summarised profit and loss accounts for the year ended 31 December 20X2

	C Limited Consolidated P&L a/c £	D Limited Associate P&L a/c £
Turnover	1 040 000	710 000
Cost of sales	670 000	230 000
Gross profit	370 000	480 000
Operating expenses	134 000	170 000
Operating profit	236 000	310 000
Dividend received from D Limited	24 000	–
	260 000	310 000
Interest payable	50 000	40 000
Profit from ordinary activities before tax	210 000	270 000
Taxation	80 000	60 000
Profit after tax	130 000	210 000
Minority interest	10 000	–
	120 000	210 000
Dividends paid and proposed	40 000	80 000
Retained profit for the year	80 000	130 000

Movement on reserves for the year ended 31 December 20X2

	C Limited Consolidated accounts	D Limited Associate
	£	£
Retained profits at 1 January 20X2	400 000	240 000
Retained profit for the year	80 000	130 000
Retained profits on 31 December 20X2	480 000	370 000

The profit and loss account of C Limited, and hence the consolidated profit and loss account, includes the dividend of £24 000 receivable from D Limited and this amount has been disclosed at the net amount in accordance with standard practice.

Summarised balance sheets on 31 December 20X2

	C Limited Consolidated accounts	D Limited Associate
	£	£
Fixed assets – at net book values		
Goodwill (on consolidation)	70 000	–
Tangible assets	493 000	420 000
Investment in associate:		
45 000 shares (30%) at cost	97 000	–
Net current assets	280 000	360 000
	940 000	780 000
less Long-term loans	100 000	150 000
	840 000	630 000
less Deferred taxation	80 000	60 000
	760 000	570 000
Share capital £1 shares	200 000	150 000
Share premium	40 000	30 000
Retained profits	480 000	390 000
	720 000	570 000
Minority interests	40 000	–
	760 000	570 000

C Limited acquired its 30 per cent interest in D Limited on 1 January 20X1 when the reserves of D comprised a share premium account of £30 000 and retained profits of £60 000. On the basis of the simplifying assumption that book values were equal to fair values at the date of acquisition, goodwill of £25 000 would have been recognised:[7]

	£	£
Cost of investment		97 000
less Share of net assets:		
Share capital	150 000	
Share premium	30 000	
Retained profits	60 000	
30% of	240 000	72 000
Purchased goodwill		25 000

---

[7] In addition to this simplifying assumption, we are implicitly assuming that there have been no changes to share capital or share premium since acquisition.

We shall assume that this goodwill, relating to the associate, had an expected useful economic life of five years and that it is being amortised over that period using the straight-line method.[8]

Let us focus first on the consolidated profit and loss account which, at present, includes £24 000 in respect of the dividend received or receivable from D. Using the equity method, this must be removed and replaced by the share of the associate's profit, whether or not this has been distributed. Under the provisions of FRS 9, the share of profit must be included after the group operating profit and then on a line-by-line basis.

	D Limited	30% share
	£	£
Operating profit	310 000	93 000
Interest payable	40 000	12 000
Profit from ordinary activities before tax	270 000	81 000
Taxation	60 000	18 000
Profit after tax	210 000	63 000

Inclusion of the share of these figures in the consolidated profit and loss account, together with the amortisation of goodwill, produces the following results:

**Summarised consolidated profit and loss account for the year ended
31 December 20X2 (including results of associate)**

	£	£
Turnover		1 040 000
Cost of sales		670 000
Gross profit		370 000
Operating expenses		134 000
Group operating profit		236 000
Share of operating profit of associate	93 000	
less Amortisation of goodwill	5 000	88 000
		324 000
Interest payable:		
Group	50 000	
Associate	12 000	62 000
Profit from ordinary activities before taxation		262 000
Taxation:		
Group	80 000	
Associate	18 000	98 000
		164 000
Minority interest		10 000
		154 000
Dividends paid and proposed		40 000
Retained profit for the year		114 000

We have brought in the share of profits amounting to £63 000 to replace the dividend receivable of £24 000. Thus we have taken credit for an extra £39 000, which is the share of the profit retained by the associate in respect of the year. We have also recognised the amortisation of the goodwill of the associate.

---

[8] It is worth noting that the goodwill which arose in respect of the purchase of subsidiaries would have already been amortised, if appropriate, in preparing the consolidated financial statements shown in the first column above.

When we turn to the movement on reserves, we must include the share of the post-acquisition profits retained by the associate less the accumulated amortisation of goodwill. The following statement includes the relevant workings.

Movement on reserves for the year ended 31 December 20X2

	£	£
Retained profits on 1 January 20X2:		
Group		400 000
Share of post-acquisition profits		
in associate:		
30% × (240 000 – 60 000)	54 000	
less Accumulated amortisation		
of goodwill: 1 year × 5000	(5 000)	49 000
		449 000
Retained profit for the year		114 000
Retained profits on 31 December 20X2		
Group	480 000	
Share of post-acquisition profits		
in associate:		
30% × (370 000 – 60 000)	93 000	
less Accumulated amortisation		
of goodwill: 2 years × 5000	(10 000)	
	563 000	563 000

By the end of the year 20X2, we have therefore increased consolidated reserves by £83 000, the share of the post-acquisition profits retained by the associate less the accumulated amortisation of purchased goodwill, and must increase the carrying value of the investment in the consolidated balance sheet by this amount to keep it in balance. The carrying value therefore becomes £180 000, which is the cost of £97 000 plus £83 000.

Summarised consolidated balance sheet on 31 December 20X2

	£
Fixed assets	
Goodwill	70 000
Tangible assets	493 000
Investment in associate	180 000
	743 000
Net current assets	280 000
	1 023 000
Long-term loan	100 000
	923 000
Deferred taxation	80 000
	843 000
Share capital	200 000
Share premium	40 000
Reserves: per Movement on reserves	563 000
	803 000
Minority interest	40 000
	843 000

The carrying value of the investment in the associate may be analysed as follows:

		£
Share of net assets in balance sheet of D: 30% × 570000		171000
Unamortised goodwill		
Cost of goodwill	25000	
less Amortised – 2 years at 5000	10000	15000
		186000

As we outlined earlier in the chapter, in order for the inclusion of these amounts to be meaningful, it is necessary for the accounting periods and policies of the associate to coincide with those of the group. In addition, adjustment may be necessary to remove the effect of any unrealised profits made from trading between the group and the associate.

Joint ventures and the gross equity method

As we explained earlier in this section, FRS 9 requires the use of the 'gross equity method' for joint ventures. This method is defined as follows:[9]

> A form of equity method under which the investor's share of the aggregate gross assets and liabilities underlying the net amount included for the investment is shown on the face of the balance sheet and, in the profit and loss account, the investor's share of the turnover is noted.

Thus the method is exactly the same as the equity method except that a little more disclosure is required. The additional information required is illustrated in the following pro-forma consolidated profit and loss account and balance sheet incorporating both a joint venture and an associate. Headings relating to the joint venture are shown in italics.

Consolidated profit and loss account for the year ended 31 December 20X2

	£	£
Turnover: group and share of joint venture	X	
less Share of joint venture's turnover	X	
Group turnover		X
Cost of sales		X
Gross profit		X
Operating expenses		X
Group operating profit		X
Share of operating profit in: *Joint venture*	X	
Associate	X	X
		X
Interest payable		
Group	(X)	
Joint venture	(X)	
Associate	(X)	X
Profit on ordinary activities before tax		X
Tax on profit on ordinary activities:		
Group, *joint venture* and associate		X
Profit on ordinary activities after tax		X
Minority interests		X
Profit on ordinary activities after tax and minority interests		X
Dividends		X
Retained profit for group and its share of *joint venture* and associate		X

Consolidated balance sheet on 31 December 20X2

	£	£	£
Fixed assets			
Tangible assets		X	
Investments			
Investment in joint venture:			
Share of gross assets	X		
Share of gross liabilities	(X)	X	
Investment in associate		X	X
Current assets			
Stock		X	
Debtors		X	
Cash at bank and in hand		X	
		X	
Creditors: amounts due within one year		(X)	
Net current assets			X
Total assets less current liabilities			X
Creditors: amounts due after more than one year			(X)
Provisions for liabilities and charges			(X)
			X
Capital and reserves			
Called up share capital			X
Share premium account			X
Profit and loss account			X
Shareholders' funds			X
Minority interests			X
			X

Approach where no consolidated financial statements are prepared

In the above examples we have assumed that consolidated financial statements have been prepared so that it was possible to apply the equity method or gross equity method of accounting in those consolidated statements. It is, of course, possible for a company without a subsidiary to have an investment in an associate or joint venture. In such a case, it is not possible to apply the equity method or gross equity method in the investing company's financial statements and yet there are no consolidated financial statements available for that purpose.

In order to comply with FRS 9[10] the investing company:

> should present the relevant amounts for associates and joint ventures either by preparing a separate set of financial statements or by showing the relevant amounts, together with the effects of including them, as additional information to its own financial statements.

In the former case, the treatment will be as illustrated above. In the the latter case, one or more supplementary notes to the company's own financial statements will be necessary. Thus there must be a note to the balance sheet showing what the carrying value of the investment would be using the equity method and, in the case of a joint venture, the share of the

[10] FRS 9, Para. 48.

gross assets and gross liabilities making up that value. There must also be a note to the profit and loss account showing the effect of applying the equity method of accounting.

On the basis of the following summarised profit and loss accounts for the year ended 31 December 20X2 of E plc and F Limited, a possible note to the profit and loss account of E plc, which has 25 per cent of the shares in its associate, F Limited, is illustrated below.

Summarised profit and loss accounts for the year ended 31 December 20X2

	E plc	F Ltd
	£	£
Operating profit	240 000	140 000
Dividends received and receivable from F Limited	10 000	–
	250 000	140 000
Taxation	80 000	60 000
Profit on ordinary activities after tax	170 000	80 000
Dividends paid and payable	100 000	40 000
Retained profit for the year	70 000	40 000

A possible note to the profit and loss account might run as follows:

Note to the profit and loss account of E plc
The effect of applying the equity method of accounting to the investment in the associate F Limited is as follows:

	£	£
Share of profit of associate		
(25% of 140 000)		35 000
Share of taxation of associate		
(25% of 60 000)		15 000
		20 000
add Profit of E plc		
Per profit and loss account	170 000	
less Dividends from associate	10 000	160 000
Profit from ordinary activities after taxation		180 000
less Dividends paid and payable		100 000
Retained profit for the year		80 000
Retained in investing company	70 000	
Retained in associate (25% × 40 000)	10 000	
	80 000	

Such a note could be easily expanded to provide the relevant disclosure for an investment in a joint venture.

Large investments in associates and joint ventures

In order to ensure that users have adequate information to interpret a set of financial statements, FRS 9 requires the disclosure of the name of each principal associate and joint venture, together with details of the proportional shareholding, its accounting period and an indication of the nature of its business. The equity method is then applied to all investments in associates and the gross equity method to all investments in joint ventures, either in the consolidated financial statements, where these are prepared, or as supplemenary information in the investing company's own financial statements.

Both the equity method and the gross equity method provide only very summarised information about the results, assets and liabilities of the investee entity and, hence, when the investee is particularly large in relation to the investing group or company, FRS 9 requires additional disclosure. It lays down thresholds that attempt to capture the relative size of the investee in the context of the investing group or company and require comparison, between the investor's share of the investee and that of the investor, of the following:

- gross assets
- gross liabilities
- turnover
- operating results on a three-year average.

Additional disclosure is then required in three circumstances:

(i)   where the *aggregate* of the investor's share in its associates exceeds a 15 per cent threshold;
(ii) where the *aggregate* of the investor's share in its joint venture exceeds a 15 per cent threshold;
(iii) where the investor's share in any *individual* associate or joint venture exceeds a 25 per cent threshold.

Readers are referred to the standard itself for precise details of the disclosure required in each case.[11]

Summary of the UK position

Where an investment is large enough to give the investor significant influence or joint control over the affairs of the investee, it is clearly not adequate to show that investment at cost and to take credit only for the dividends receivable. Some alternative is necessary, and it is possible to identify three such alternative accounting treatments for associates and joint ventures:

(a) to show the investment at its fair value and to take changes in fair value, as well as dividends receivable, to the profit and loss account;
(b) to use proportional (proportionate) consolidation;
(c) to use the equity method of accounting.

While, as we have seen in Chapter 8, the ASB is in favour of the use of fair values for many financial instruments, it recognises that the determination of the fair value of unquoted investments may be extremely difficult and unreliable in practice. It also recognises that, even if the shares of the investee are quoted, accounting for the investee by the recognition of movements in the fair value of its shares is hardly the best way of measuring the performance of a long-term associate or joint venture over which the investor exercises significant influence or joint control.

The method of proportional consolidation is simple to understand but is rejected by the ASB on the grounds that it results in the aggregation of assets and liabilities of associates and joint ventures, which are not controlled, with the assets and liabilities of the parent company

---

[11] FRS 9, Para. 58.

and subsidiaries, which are controlled by the parent company. In accordance with the provisions of Chapter 2 of its *Statement of Principles for Financial Reporting,* the ASB takes the view that a consolidated balance sheet should only show the assets and liabilities under direct and indirect control, that is those of the parent and any subsidiary companies.[12] As we shall see in the final section of this chapter, the IASB does not feel itself constrained in this way.

Having rejected the use of fair values and proportional consolidation, the ASB is left with the equity method of accounting as its preferred candidate for associates and joint ventures. We have seen that, under this method, the level of detailed disclosure may be varied quite considerably and the ASB introduces its own variant of the equity method, the gross equity

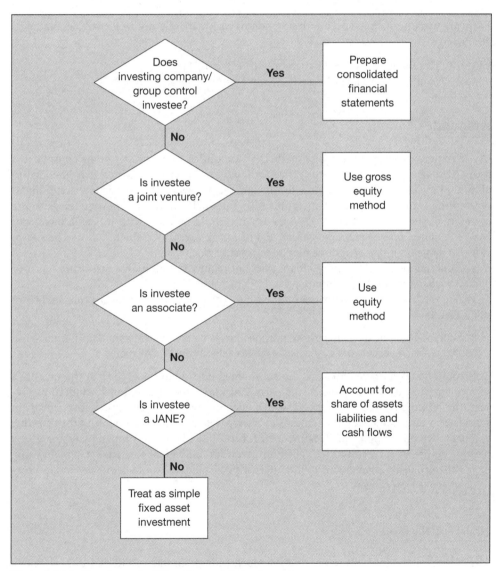

Figure 15.1 Treatment of fixed asset investments

---

[12] An exception is made for JANEs where the investor is required to account directly for its share of assets, liabilities, results and cash flows.

method, for joint ventures. It also increases the detailed disclosure requirements for both associates and joint ventures once certain thresholds are breached. The level of the thresholds and the extent of the detailed disclosure required are practical matters to which accounting theory has little to contribute at present.

Figure 15.1 provides a summary of the accounting treatment of fixed asset investments in the UK.

The international accounting standards

There are two international accounting standards which are relevant to the subject matter of this chapter:

● IAS 28 *Accounting for Investments in Associates* (revised 2000)
● IAS 31 *Financial Reporting of Interests in Joint Ventures* (revised 2000)

Associates

IAS 28 requires the use of the equity method of accounting for associates in the consolidated financial statements of the investor. There are two exceptions: first, when it is intended to dispose of the investment in the near future and, second, when the associate operates under severe long-term restrictions that significantly impair its ability to transfer funds to the investor. In such circumstances, the investment should be dealt with in accordance with IAS 39 *Financial Instruments: Recognition and Measurement,* under which it should be shown at its fair value or, if that cannot be measured reliably, at its cost.[13]

The international accounting standard does not require the additional disclosure specified by FRS 9 when certain thresholds are passed.

Where the investing company does not prepare consolidated financial statements, IAS 28 states that:

> It is appropriate that such an investor provides the same information about its investments in associates as those enterprises that issue consolidated financial statements.[14]

This could be taken to require that the equity method should be applied in the investor's own financial statements. While this is permitted under the international standard at present, the proposed revision of IAS 27, which encompasses the treatment of investments in subsidiaries, associates and joint ventures in the separate financial statements of the investing company, would prohibit this treatment in future.[15] Neither UK company law nor FRS 9 permit the use of the equity method in an investor's individual financial statements and, hence, the proposed amendment to the international standard would bring UK and international practice closer together.

Joint ventures

The definition of joint venture in IAS 31 is much wider than that of FRS 9. IAS 31 defines a joint venture in terms of contractual arrangements and distinguishes between jointly con-

---

[13] IAS 28 *Accounting for Investments in Associates* (revised 2000), Para. 8.
[14] *Ibid.*, Para. 15.
[15] See Chapter 14, pp. 406–7.

trolled operations, jointly controlled assets and jointly controlled entities. As we have seen, FRS 9 restricts the term joint venture to an entity and deals separately with joint arrangements that are not entities (JANEs).

The benchmark treatment of joint ventures under IAS 31 is proportionate, what we have called proportional, consolidation while the allowed alternative treatment is the equity method of accounting. However, the international standard makes it very clear that the IASB, or more precisely the IASC, considers the equity method to be very much second best:[16]

> This Standard does not recommend the use of the equity method because proportionate consolidation better reflects the substance and economic reality of a venturer's interest in a jointly controlled entity, that is control over the venturer's share of the future economic benefits.

This proportionate method may be applied using one of two possible formats along the lines of those that we have illustrated earlier in the chapter. Thus the venturer may either combine its share of each asset, liability, revenue and expense of the jointly controlled entity with similar items in its consolidated financial statements on a line-by-line basis or, alternatively, include its share of each class of assets, liabilities, revenue and expenses as separate lines in the consolidated financial statements.

As we saw, FRS 9 requires the use of the equity method, in its gross equity variant, for joint ventures so, here again, the UK standard requires application of the allowed alternative treatment, rather than the benchmark treatment, of the international accounting standard.

Given the aversion of the ASB to the use of proportional consolidation and the aversion of the IASB to the use of the equity method for joint ventures, it is not easy to see how convergence will be achieved in this area.

Proposed changes

The exposure draft, issued by the IASB as part of its improvements project in May 2002, proposes a number of changes to the above. We have already drawn attention to some of these proposed changes in both Chapter 14 and this chapter but will draw attention to two proposals here.

First, the exposure draft proposes to exclude from the scope of IAS 28 and IAS 31 investments, which would otherwise be classified as associates and joint ventures, when these are held by venture capital organisations, mutual funds, unit trusts and similar entities. It considers that, in the case of such investors, it is more appropriate to measure investments in associates and joint ventures at their fair values, in accordance with the provisions of IAS 39, *Financial Instruments: Recognition and Measurement*, where these are well established in the particular industry.

Second, it proposes to tighten up the situations where investments in associates and joint ventures should be excluded from treatment using the equity method of accounting or proportionate consolidation. At present, both IAS 28 and IAS 31 state that investments should not be accounted for using the equity method and proportionate consolidation in two situations:[17]

(a) when the investment is acquired and held exclusively with a view to its subsequent disposal in the near future; or

---

[16] IAS 31 *Financial Reporting of Interests in Joint Ventures* (revised 2000), Para. 33.
[17] See IAS 28, Para. 8, and IAS 31, Para. 35.

(b) where it operates under severe long-term restrictions that significantly impair its ability to transfer funds to the investor.

The IASB now proposes that such investments should only be excluded where the investment is acquired and held exclusively with a view to its subsequent disposal *within twelve months from acquisition*. It takes the view that, where an associate or joint venture operates under severe long-term restrictions, it is unlikely that significant influence over the investee actually exists. While the time horizon for the exclusion of temporary associates and joint ventures would be tightened to 12 months, there would be no change resulting from the proposals in respect of long-term restrictions: investments subject to severe long-term restrictions would still be excluded, albeit on the basis of a different criterion, and shown at fair values in accordance with the provisions of IAS 39.

Summary

In this chapter, we looked at accounting for investments which carry significant influence over or joint control over another entity, namely associates and joint ventures. For such investments, it is not sufficient to show them at cost or, except in special circumstances, at fair value. It is certainly not possible merely to take credit for dividends receivable when the level of those dividends may be influenced by the investor. We also looked at what FRS 9 calls Joint Arrangements which are Not Entities (JANEs) although these fall within the definition of a joint venture under IAS 31.

The two methods of accounting which standard setters consider to be appropriate for investments which carry significant influence or joint control are proportional (proportionate) consolidation or the equity method of accounting. We therefore explored each of these methods and demonstrated the similarities and differences between them.

We next examined the rather unhelpful provisions of UK company law in this area and saw how FRS 9 requires the use of the equity method to account for associates and the use of the gross equity method to account for joint ventures, while requiring something akin to proportional consolidation for JANEs. FRS 9 requires more detailed disclosure from joint ventures, i.e. it requires the gross equity method, and even more disclosure in respect of both associates and joint ventures, once certain size thresholds are crossed.

Finally, we examined the relevant international accounting standards, IAS 28 and IAS 31. These require the use of the equity method for associates and favour the use of proportionate consolidation for joint ventures. While IAS 31 does permit the use of the equity method for joint ventures as an allowed alternative treatment, the standard makes it very clear that the IASB (or, more precisely, its predecessor, the IASC) considers this method to be very much second best.

Thus we have seen that, although the required UK and international treatment of associates is similar, the preferred treatment of joint ventures is rather different.

Recommended reading

J.R. Edwards, *A history of financial accounting*, Routledge, London 1989.

T. Grundy, 'Acquisitions, joint ventures, alliances and divestment', *Business Digest*, issue 036, ICAEW, May 2000.

R. Ma, R.H. Parker and G. Whittred, *Consolidated accounting*, Longman, Cheshire, 1991.

C. Nobes, 'An Analysis of the International Development of the Equity Method', *Abacus*, Vol. 38, No.1, February 2002, pp. 16–45.

Readers are also referred to the latest edition of *UK and International GAAP* by Ernst & Young, which provides much greater detailed coverage of the subject matter of this chapter. At the time of writing the latest edition is the 7th, A. Wilson, M. Davies, M. Curtis and G. Wilkinson-Riddle (eds), Butterworths Tolley, London, 2001. The relevant chapter is 7, Associates, joint ventures and JANEs'.

Questions

15.1 Both the *Statement of Principles for Financial Reporting* and individual Accounting Standards make it clear that the treatment in consolidated financial statements of investments in other undertakings is dependent on the extent of the control or influence the investing entity is able to exercise over the other undertaking. Port plc has investments in three other undertakings:

- On 15 May 1990, Port plc purchased 40 million 50p equity shares in Harbour Ltd. The called-up equity share capital of Harbour Ltd on 15 May 1990 was 50 million 50p equity shares.

- On 15 June 1991, Port plc purchased 30 million £1 equity shares in Inlet Ltd. The called-up equity share capital of Inlet Ltd on 15 June 1991 was 75 million £1 equity shares. The remaining equity shares in Inlet Ltd are held by a large number of investors – none with more than 5 million equity shares.

- On 15 July 1992, Port plc purchased 25 million 50p equity shares in Bay Ltd. The called-up equity share capital of Bay Ltd on 15 July 1992 was 80 million 50p equity shares. Another investor owns 50 million equity shares in Bay Ltd. This investor takes an active interest in directing the operating and financial policies of Bay Ltd and on a number of occasions has required Bay Ltd to follow policies that do not meet with the approval of Port plc.

Equity shares in all of the companies carry one vote per share at general meetings. No party can control or influence the composition of the board of directors of any of the companies other than through its ownership of equity shares. There have been no instances where shareholders in any of the companies have acted together to increase their control or influence. None of the companies has issued any additional equity shares since Port plc purchased its interests.

Extracts from the profit and loss accounts of the four companies for their year ended 30 June 2001 are given below:

	Port plc £000	Harbour Ltd £000	Inlet Ltd £000	Bay Ltd £000
Turnover	65 000	45 000	48 000	40 000
Cost of sales	(35 000)	(25 000)	(26 000)	(19 000)
Gross profit	30 000	20 000	22 000	21 000

Note 1

Port plc manufactures a product that is used by Harbour Ltd and Inlet Ltd. During the year ended 30 June 2001, sales of the product to Harbour Ltd and Inlet Ltd were:

● to Harbour Ltd – £8 million;

● to Inlet Ltd – £7.5 million.

Opening and closing stocks of this product in the financial statements of Harbour Ltd and Inlet Ltd (all purchased from Port plc at cost plus 25% mark up, unchanged during the year) were as follows:

Company	Closing stock	Opening stock
	£000	£000
Harbour Ltd	3 000	2 400
Inlet Ltd	2 500	Nil

At 30 June 2001, there were no amounts payable by Harbour Ltd and Inlet Ltd in respect of stocks purchased from Port plc before 30 June 2001.

Note 2

There was no other trading between the companies other than the payment of dividends.

Required:

(a) State the alternative treatments of investments in consolidated financial statements that are set out in the *Statement of Principles for Financial Reporting* and UK Accounting Standards. Do NOT describe the mechanics of the methods.   (6 marks)

(b) Identify the correct treatment of the investments in Harbour Ltd, Inlet Ltd and Bay Ltd in the consolidated financial statements of Port plc.   (5 marks)

(c) Compute the consolidated turnover, cost of sales and gross profit of the Port group for the year ended 30 June 2001. You should ensure that your computations are fully supported by relevant workings.   (4 marks)

(d) Compute the adjustments that need to be made in respect of the transactions described in Note 1 above when preparing the consolidated balance sheet of Port plc at 30 June 2001. You should explain the rationale behind each adjustment you make.   (5 marks)

CIMA, Financial Reporting – UK Accounting Standards, November 2001   (**20 marks**)

15.2 (a) FRS 9, *Associates and Joint Ventures*, deals not only with the accounting treatment of associated companies and joint venture operations but covers certain types of joint business arrangements not carried on through a separate entity. The main changes made by FRS 9 are to restrict the circumstances in which equity accounting can be applied and to provide detailed rules for accounting for joint ventures.

Required:

(i) Explain the criteria which distinguish an associate from an ordinary fixed asset investment.   (6 marks)

(ii) Explain the principal difference between a joint venture and a 'joint arrangement' and the impact that this classification has upon the accounting for such relationships.   (4 marks)

(b) The following financial statements relate to Baden, a public limited company.

Profit and loss account for year ended 31 December 1998

	£m	£m
Turnover		212
Cost of sales		(170)
Gross profit		42
Distribution costs	17	
Administrative costs	8	(25)
		17
Other operating income		12
Operating profit		29
Exceptional item		(10)
Interest payable		(4)
Profit on ordinary activities before tax		15
Taxation on profit on ordinary activities		(3)
		12
Ordinary dividend – paid		(4)
Retained profit for year		8

Balance sheet as at 31 December 1998

	£m	£m
Fixed assets – tangible	30	
goodwill	7	37
Current assets	31	
Creditors: amounts falling due within one year	(12)	
Net current assets		19
Total assets less current liabilities		56
Creditors: amounts falling due after more than one year		(10)
		46
Capital and Reserves		
Called up share capital –		
Ordinary shares of £1		10
Share premium account		4
Profit and loss account		32
		46

(i) Cable, a public limited company, acquired 30% of the ordinary share capital of Baden at a cost of £14 million on 1 January 1997. The share capital of Baden has not changed since acquisition when the profit and loss reserve of Baden was £9 million.

(ii) At 1 January 1997 the following fair values were attributed to the net assets of Baden but not incorporated in its accounting records.

	£m	
Tangible fixed assets	30	(carrying value £20m)
Goodwill (estimate)	10	
Current assets	31	
Creditors: amounts falling due within one year	20	
Creditors: amounts falling after more than one year	8	

(iii) Guy, an associated company of Cable, also holds a 25% interest in the ordinary share capital of Baden. This was acquired on 1 January 1998.

(iv) During the year to 31 December 1998, Baden sold goods to Cable to the value of £35 million. The inventory of Cable at 31 December 1998 included goods purchased from Baden on which the company made a profit of £10 million.

(v) The policy of all companies in the Cable Group is to amortise goodwill over four years and to depreciate tangible fixed assets at 20% per annum on the straight line basis.

(vi) Baden does not represent a material part of the group and is significantly less than the 15% additional disclosure threshold required under FRS 9 Associates and Joint Ventures.

Required:

(i) Show how the investment in Baden would be stated in the consolidated balance sheet and profit and loss account of the Cable Group under FRS9 *Associates and Joint Ventures*, for the year ended 31 December 1998 on the assumption that Baden is an associate.   (9 marks)

(ii) Show how the treatment of Baden would change if Baden was classified as an investment in a joint venture.   (6 marks)

ACCA, Financial Reporting Environment (UK Stream), June 1999   **(25 marks)**

15.3 Wester Ross plc has acquired holdings in the following companies:

Ullapool Ltd – 75% of the ordinary share capital acquired on 1 February 2000 financed by the issue of 2 million £1 ordinary shares of Wester Ross plc at £7 per share and £6 million in cash.

Wester Ross plc also acquired 30% of the preference share capital at the same date for £1 million cash.

Glenelg Ltd – 30% of the ordinary share capital acquired on 10 March 1998 for £2 million cash.

The draft balance sheets of the companies at 31 October 2000 were:

	Wester Ross plc £000	Ullapool Ltd £000	Glenelg Ltd £000
Fixed assets			
Freehold property	15 000	8 000	2 000
Fixtures and fittings	27 000	10 000	1 000
Investments	9 000	–	–
Current assets			
Stocks	4 000	2 500	500
Debtors	8 500	1 700	400
Cash	–	700	–
Current liabilities	(5 000)	(1 300)	(200)
Long-term liabilities	(5 500)	(1 000)	(300)
	53 000	20 600	3 400

	Wester Ross plc £000	Ullapool Ltd £000	Glenelg Ltd £000
Capital and Reserves			
Ordinary shares of £1 each	35 000	12 000	1 500
Preference shares of £1 each	5 000	3 000	300
Revaluation reserve	10 000	2 000	–
Other reserves	–	1 000	–
Profit and loss account	3 000	2 600	1 600
	53 000	20 600	3 400

Additional information

(1) Wester Ross plc's investments were acquired when the reserves of the companies were:

	Ullapool Ltd £000	Glenelg Ltd £000
Revaluation reserve	1 500	–
Other reserves	500	–
Profit and loss account	2 000	600

There have been no changes to the share capital of the above companies since their acquisition.

(2) The fair value of the freehold property in Glenelg Ltd was £1.5 million above book value at the date of acquisition; all of this related to the land element of the property.

(3) Wester Ross plc has not yet accounted for the shares issued in acquiring Ullapool Ltd but has fully accounted for the cash element of the consideration for both Ullapool Ltd and Glenelg Ltd.

(4) Glenelg Ltd sold various items of fixtures and fittings to Wester Ross plc for £750 000 on 31 March 2000. The assets originally cost £1 million in the year ended 31 October 1995 and are being depreciated over 10 years on a straight-line basis. Wester Ross plc is depreciating the assets over their remaining useful economic life.

(5) It is group policy to:

– amortise goodwill over 10 years with a full year's charge in the year of acquisition
– charge a full year's depreciation on fixed assets in the year of acquisition and none in the year of disposal.

Requirements

(a) **From the above data, calculate the following amounts for the consolidated balance sheet of Wester Ross plc as at 31 October 2000:**
   (i) **Goodwill arising on the acquisitions of Ullapool Ltd and Glenelg Ltd;**
   (ii) **Investment in associate;**
   (iii) **Profit and loss account balance.**   (10 marks)
(b) **Explain the purpose of group accounts and the concepts underlying their preparation.**
                                                          (8 marks)

ICAEW, Financial Reporting, December 2000   (**18 marks**)

15.4 Ayr plc acquired holdings in two companies as follows:

Brodick Ltd – 80% of the ordinary share capital purchased on 1 December 1999 for £5 million.

– 20% of the preference share capital purchased on 1 June 2001 for £500 000.

Carluke Ltd – 30% of the ordinary share capital purchased on 1 April 2001 for £1.5 million.

The draft profit and loss accounts of the companies for the year ended 30 November 2001 were:

	Ayr plc £000	Brodick Ltd £000	Carluke Ltd £000
Turnover	4000	2000	1500
Cost of sales	(2800)	(1400)	(1050)
	1200	600	450
Distribution costs	(200)	(100)	(50)
Administrative expenses	(400)	(250)	(100)
	600	250	300
Taxation	(180)	(80)	(90)
Profit after taxation	420	170	210
Dividends – preference	(40)	(50)	–
– ordinary	(200)	(70)	(100)
	180	50	110

Additional information

(1) The reserves of Brodick Ltd and Carluke Ltd were:

	Date	Revaluation reserve £000	Profit and loss £000
Brodick Ltd	1 December 1999	400	300
	1 June 2001	500	200
Carluke Ltd	1 April 2001	–	70

The ordinary dividends of Carluke Ltd all relate to the post-acquisition period.

(2) There have been no changes in the companies' share capitals since acquisition. These are:

	Brodick Ltd £000	Carluke Ltd £000
Ordinary shares of £1 each	5000	3000
Preference shares of £1 each	2000	–

The preference dividends of Brodick Ltd were paid in two equal instalments on 31 May 2001, and 30 November 2001.

(3) On 1 December 1999, the value of the tangible fixed assets of Brodick Ltd was £200 000 higher than their net book value. This was due to the land element of freehold property.

(4) On 30 June 2001, Carluke Ltd sold £200 000 of goods to Ayr plc. Carluke Ltd operates a standard mark up of 25% on all sales. On 30 November 2001, Ayr Ltd still had 75% of these goods in stock.

(5) It is group policy to amortise goodwill over ten years with a full year's charge in the year of acquisition.

(6) Ayr plc has not yet accounted for any dividends receivable.

Requirements
(a) Calculate the following amounts as they would appear in the consolidated profit and loss account of Ayr plc for the year ended 30 November 2001:
   (i) Income from investment in associated undertakings
   (ii) Minority interests
   (iii) Profit after taxation. (13 marks)
   Note: Make all calculations to the nearest £000.
(b) Explain the rationale for the accounting treatment in (a) (i) and (ii) above.

(5 marks)

ICAEW, Financial Reporting, December 2001 (18 marks)

15.5 Ardrossan plc acquired holdings in two companies as follows:

Barmulloch Ltd – 75% of the ordinary share capital purchased on 1 August 2000 for £4 million.

Cumbernauld Ltd – 25% of the ordinary share capital purchased on 1 August 1999 for £1 million.

The draft balance sheets of the companies as at 31 July 2002 were:

	Ardrossan plc	Barmulloch Ltd	Cumbernauld Ltd
	£000	£000	£000
Fixed assets	4 500	2 500	1 500
Investments	5 000	–	–
Current assets			
Stock	1 400	900	600
Trade debtors	1 200	700	400
Dividends receivable	45	–	–
Cash at bank	450	–	200
	3 095	1 600	1 200
Current liabilities			
Bank overdraft	–	(400)	–
Trade creditors	(1 300)	(600)	(300)
Proposed dividends	(200)	(60)	–
Net current assets	1 595	540	900
Debentures 2006	(500)	–	–
	10 595	3 040	2 400
Ordinary shares of £1 each	8 000	3 000	2 000
Revaluation reserve	1 500	500	200
Profit and loss account	1 095	(460)	200
	10 595	3 040	2 400

Additional information

(1) The reserves of Barmulloch Ltd and Cumbernauld Ltd at the following dates were:

	Date	Revaluation Reserve £000	Profit and Loss Account £000
Barmulloch Ltd	1 August 2000	200	600
Cumbernauld Ltd	1 August 1999	200	100
Cumbernauld Ltd	1 August 2001	200	160

Assume profits accrued evenly in the year ended 31 July 2002.

(2) On 1 February 2002, Ardrossan plc sold its entire holding of shares in Cumbernauld Ltd for £1.3 million cash. This transaction has not yet been recorded in the accounts of Ardrossan plc. For any tax due on this transaction, assume a corporation tax rate of 30% and ignore indexation allowance.

(3) It is group policy to amortise any goodwill arising on consolidation over ten years with a full year's charge in the year of acquisition and none in the year of disposal.

(4) The trade creditors of Ardrossan plc include £25 000 payable to Barmulloch Ltd. The trade debtors of Barmulloch record the same amount as a debt receivable. None of these transactions. resulted in any stock at the year end.

Requirements

(a) **Calculate any profit or loss arising on the disposal of Cumbernauld Ltd to be included in the consolidated accounts of Ardrossan plc.**   (4 marks)

(b) **Prepare the consolidated balance sheet of Ardrossan plc as at 31 July 2002.**
                                                                                  (12 marks)

(c) **Explain the basis of your calculations in (a), making appropriate reference to accounting standards and concepts.**   (4 marks)

ICAEW, Financial Reporting, September 2002   **(20 marks)**

15.6 Aberdeen plc acquired shares in two other companies as follows:

Date of acquisition	Company	Percentage of equity shares acquired	Goodwill arising on acquisition	Company's profit and loss at acquisition
1 November 2000	Berwick Ltd	75%	£400 000	£1 200 000
1 May 2002	Coupar Ltd	30%	£150 000	£850 000

The summarised draft profit and loss accounts of the companies for the year ended 31 October 2002 were:

	Aberdeen plc £000	Berwick Ltd £000	Coupar Ltd £000
Turnover	10 500	7 500	4 400
Cost of sales	(7 350)	(5 000)	(3 200)
Gross profit	3 150	2 500	1 200
Other operating expenses	(1 700)	(1 100)	(450)
Profit before taxation	1 450	1 400	750
Taxation	(430)	(420)	(200)
Profit after taxation	1 020	980	550
Dividends proposed	(500)	(400)	(200)
Retained profit	520	580	350

Additional information

(1) It is group policy to amortise purchased goodwill over five years with a full year's charge in the year of acquisition.

(2) On 1 October 2002, Berwick Ltd sold goods to Aberdeen plc. These goods had a sales value of £200 000, Berwick Ltd having applied a mark up of 25%. As at 31 October 2002, Aberdeen plc still held £140 000 of these goods in stock.

(3) Aberdeen plc has not yet accounted for any dividends receivable from Berwick Ltd or Coupar Ltd. The dividends from Coupar Ltd all relate to the post-acquisition period.

(4) Aberdeen plc requires Coupar Ltd to bring its depreciation methods in line with group accounting policies. The directors have estimated that this would reduce the profit of Coupar Ltd for the year ended 31 October 2002 by £200 000. Ignore any effect on the taxation charge.

(5) The directors of Aberdeen plc propose a transfer of £100 000 to a general reserve and this should be accounted for.

(6) The retained profit brought forward at 1 November 2001 for the three companies was:

	£000
Aberdeen plc	2400
Berwick Ltd	1800
Coupar Ltd	600

Requirement
Prepare the consolidated profit and loss account, statement of reserves and disclosure note for Profit attributable to the members of Aberdeen plc, for the year ended 31 October 2002.

ICAEW, Financial Reporting, December 2002   (**15 marks**)

chapter 16

Overseas involvement

overview

International trade may be carried out by firms of all sizes and comes in many and various forms. A firm's involvement may be restricted to the purchase or sale of goods and services using a foreign currency but it could involve a foreign currency loan or an investment in a foreign subsidiary, associate or joint venture.

From an accounting point of view we need to identify two different situations:

1   Accounting for foreign currency transactions in the accounting records.
2   Translation of foreign currency financial statements as a preliminary to some form of consolidation.

We deal with each in turn.

We explore accounting for foreign currency transactions in the context of a number of examples. When we turn to the translation of foreign financial statements as a preliminary to full consolidation, proportional consolidation or use of the equity method of accounting, we concentrate on the translation of the financial statements of an overseas subsidiary and explore the two methods of accounting specified for this purpose in the UK standard, namely the closing rate/net investment method and the temporal method. Having first introduced the two methods, we discuss their strengths and weaknesses before exploring a more complex example of the closing rate/net investment method, the method used by the vast majority of companies in the UK.

We then turn to the provisions of the relevant international accounting standard.

In this chapter, we therefore draw upon:

● SSAP 20 *Foreign Currency Translation* (1983), and
● IAS 21 *The Effects of Changes in Foreign Exchange Rates* (revised 1993)

In May 2002, both the ASB and the IASB issued exposure drafts of proposed replacements for SSAP 20 and IAS 21 respectively. We draw attention to proposed changes at relevant points in the text and summarise them in a separate section towards the end of the chapter.

Introduction: the problems identified

Many firms based in the UK undertake transactions with firms in other countries and have branches and subsidiary and associated undertakings overseas.

Transactions undertaken between firms will often be expressed in foreign currencies and it will be necessary to translate these amounts into sterling in order to enter them in the accounting records of the UK firm. If the rate of exchange changes between the date of the transaction and the date of settlement it is necessary to decide how to deal with the resulting difference on exchange in the financial statements of the UK company. If there is an intervening balance sheet date, then it is necessary to decide which rate of exchange should be used at the balance sheet date and how the resulting difference on exchange should be treated.

Where there is an overseas branch, subsidiary or associated undertaking, it is usual for the accounting records of the overseas unit to be kept in the local currency: indeed, the local law may require the preparation and publication of financial statements in the local currency. In order to combine the results of the overseas unit with the sterling results of the investing company and those of any similar UK and other overseas units, the financial statements expressed in foreign currency must be translated into sterling.[1] When exchange rates between currencies fluctuate, this need for translation poses two problems. First, it is necessary to decide what rates of exchange are appropriate for the individual assets, liabilities, revenues and expenses in the financial statements of the overseas unit. No matter how this question is answered, the translation process invariably gives rise to differences on exchange. The second problem is therefore how to deal with these differences in the aggregated financial statements.

Until the ASC attempted to standardise the accounting treatment of exchange differences in 1975,[2] professional accountancy bodies in the UK had provided little guidance on how the above questions should be answered. Official pronouncements[3] tended to describe various methods and to emphasise that selection between them is a matter of professional judgement, without providing any guidance as to the principles on which that professional judgement should be based. As a result, many different methods were used in practice.

In this chapter, we look first at accounting for transactions denominated in foreign currencies and then turn our attention to the more complex subject of translating the financial statements of an overseas unit for the purposes of aggregation. The accounting treatment of both topics is presently regulated in the UK by SSAP 20, *Foreign Currency Translation*, issued in April 1983. The ASB is at present working on a replacement for this standard and, to this end, issued FRED 24 *The Effects of Changes in Foreign Exchange Rates* and *Financial reporting in hyperinflationary economies* in May 2002. FRED 24 has been drafted in an attempt to achieve convergence with a proposed revision of the international accounting standard on this topic, IAS 21 *The Effects of Changes in Foreign Exchange Rates*, as well as with IAS 29 *Financial Reporting in Hyperinflationary Economies*. IAS 21 was last revised in 1993 and the proposed revision of this standard was issued by the IASB as part of its proposed improvements project in May 2002.[4] The IASB has no plans to review IAS 29, which was reformatted in 1994. We shall draw attention to proposed changes at relevant points in the text and in a separate section towards the end of this chapter.

Accounting for foreign currency transactions

A UK company may purchase fixed assets, stocks or services from an overseas company and may, in addition, sell such items to an overseas company. It may also raise loans denominated in a foreign currency and make investments in the shares of an overseas company. When the amounts involved are expressed in a foreign currency, it will be necessary to translate those amounts into sterling in order to incorporate them into the accounting records of the UK company. The approach that should be adopted is best illustrated by means of a number of examples.

---

[1] Following the American terminology introduced by ED 21, the term 'conversion' is restricted to the exchange of one currency for another.
[2] ED 16 *Supplement to 'Extraordinary Items and Prior Year Adjustments'*, September 1975.
[3] See, for example, recommendation N 25 of the ICAEW, issued in February 1968.
[4] Exposure Draft of Proposed Improvements to International Accounting Standards, IASB, London, May 2002. This proposes revisions to 12 international accounting standards and was discussed in Chapter 3.

Example 16.1

Let us consider a UK company, Han Limited, which makes up its accounts to 31 December each year. On 15 September 20X1 it purchased a fixed asset, a machine, from a company in Druroland for 30 000 Druros when the rate of exchange was D3.00 to £1. It paid for this machine on 15 December 20X1 when the rate of exchange was D3.30 to £1.[5]

At the date of purchase, 15 September 20X1, it is necessary to translate the foreign currency amount to record the cost of the machine and the corresponding creditor in sterling. In the absence of an agreed rate of exchange for settlement, in which case the foreign company would bear the risk of any exchange rate movement, or a forward exchange contract, the rate ruling on the date of purchase, that is D3.00 to £1, should be used for this purpose.[6]

20X1			
Sept 15	*Dr* Machinery – at cost	£10 000	
	Cr Creditor company in Druroland		£10 000

Purchase of machine for D30 000 at exchange rate of D3.00 to £1

The sterling cost of the machine is £10 000 and it is this amount which will be depreciated over the expected useful life of the asset. No further adjustment to this cost is necessary, whatever subsequently happens to the rate of exchange. However, if the asset is subsequently revalued, it is necessary to translate the revalued amount at the rate of exchange ruling on the date that the new valuation is established.

In order to pay for the machine, Han Limited must arrange with its bankers to convert sterling into Druros. If bank charges are ignored, the payment of D30 000 on 15 December 20X1 will require an amount of £9091 in sterling given that the rate of exchange is D3.30 to £1.

20X1			
Dec 15	*Dr* Creditor company in Druroland	£9 091	
	Cr Cash		£9 091

Payment of D30 000 converted at D3.30 to £1

The debt is now settled but when we look at the account of the creditor in the records of Han Limited, it shows a credit balance of £909.

Creditor: Company in Druroland

20X1		£	20X1		£
Dec 15	Cash	9 091	Sept 15	Machine	10 000
	Difference: gain on exchange	909			
		10 000			10 000

---

[5] The currencies used in this and the following examples are fictitious currencies, and movements in the rates of exchange are exaggerated to illustrate the principles involved.

[6] FRED 24 proposes that the spot rate at the date of the transaction should always be used except where hedge accounting techniques are used in accordance with a proposed standard based upon FRED 23 *Financial Instruments: Hedge Accounting* (May 2002).

This is a difference on exchange, in this case a gain which arises because sterling has strengthened (that is become more valuable) against the Druro between the date of purchase and the date of settlement. The gain is, of course, realised and SSAP 20 requires that it be credited to the profit and loss account in arriving at the profit or loss from ordinary activities for the accounting year ended 31 December 20X1.

Example 16.2

In Example 16.1 we assumed that there was no contractually agreed rate of exchange for settlement or forward exchange contract in existence. SSAP 20, Para. 48 states that, where appropriate, contractually agreed rates of exchange *should* be used and *permits* the use of rates of exchange fixed in related or matching forward contracts.[7]

Let us assume that, as before, Han Limited purchased a machine from a company in Druroland for D30 000 on 15 September 20X1. However, let us also assume that, on that date, Han Limited entered into a forward exchange contract with its bank to purchase D30 000 for delivery on 15 December 20X1. Relevant rates of exchange are:

20X1		D to £1
Sept 15	Spot rate	3.00
	Forward rate – 3 months	3.10

Under SSAP 20, the company may record the cost of the machine at one of two amounts:

Cost of machine:	£
Using spot rate – as in Example 16.1	10 000
Using forward rate – 30 000/3.10	9 677

Given that the subsequent payment will be made at the agreed forward exchange rate of D3.10 to £1, the subsequent position will be as follows:

(i) Using spot rate

Creditor: Foreign company

20X1		£	20X1		£
Dec 15	Cash	9 677	Sept 15	Machine	10 000
	Gain on				
	exchange	323			
		10 000			10 000

(ii) Using forward rate

Creditor: Foreign company

20X1		£	20X1		£
Dec 15	Cash	9 677	Sept 15	Machine	9 677

---

[7] FRED 24 proposes that the spot rate should always be used in these circumstances.

Under the provisions of SSAP 20, Han Limited may choose to record the cost of the machine at either £10 000 or at £9677. Clearly this does little to standardise accounting practice in this area and reflects what may now be regarded as a rather naive approach by SSAP 20. The difference between the spot rate and the forward rate reflects differences between the interest rates in the two countries and it may be argued that the purchase of the machine and the forward exchange contract should be recognised as two different transactions. Under the more sophisticated approach adopted by the US Financial Accounting Standards Board (FASB) Statement No. 52 *Foreign Currency Translation*, the cost of the machine would be calculated using the rate of exchange at the date of purchase, the forward exchange contract would be recorded separately and 'marked to market' and the discount or premium under the forward exchange contract would be taken to the profit and loss account as part of the finance charge over the period of the contract. The difference between the US approach and the UK approach will, of course, be more marked where the contracts extend over two or more accounting periods.

SSAP 20 is now becoming rather long in the tooth and, in addition to a number of problems which we address in this chapter, it fails to deal satisfactorily with the various purposes for which forward exchange contracts, currency swaps and currency options are used. However, it has been difficult for the ASB to make progress in this area until the standard on financial instruments has been produced.[8] The proposed revision of SSAP 20, contained in FRED 24, would only permit the use of a forward exchange rate where hedge accounting techniques are used in accordance with the provisions of a standard to be based upon FRED 23 *Financial Instruments: Hedge Accounting.*

Example 16.3

The next complication which may arise is that the purchase and the payment occur in different accounting years. To illustrate this, let us assume that Han Limited purchased stock from a company in Sudarland for 200 000 sudars on 20 November 20X1 when the rate of exchange was 8 sudars to £1. It subsequently paid for the goods on 15 January 20X2 when the rate of exchange was 10 sudars to £1. The rate of exchange on 31 December 20X1, the intervening balance sheet date, was 9.5 sudars to £1. Following the principles explained in Example 16.1, the purchase would be recorded as follows:

20X1			
Nov 20	*Dr* Stock	£25 000	
	Cr Creditor – Foreign company		£25 000

Purchase of stock for 200 000 sudars at 8 sudars to £1.

The cost of stock is recorded at £25 000 and, as before, this figure is not affected by any subsequent changes in the exchange rate. If the stock is still held on 31 December 20X1 it is included in the balance sheet at the lower of cost and net realisable value. Cost will be determined in accordance with the company's normal accounting policy (e.g. FIFO, average cost, etc.).

When we turn to the creditor, a monetary amount, such an approach is not sensible and, in the absence of either contractually agreed exchange rates for settlement or forward exchange con-

---

[8] The ASB made precisely this point when, in May 1999, it withdrew the brief exposure draft 'Amendment to SSAP 20 "Foreign Currency Translation"' on the grounds that more substantial changes to SSAP 20 were necessary.

tracts, SSAP 20 requires that all monetary items are translated at the closing rate. The closing rate is defined more precisely as follows:

> **The closing rate is the exchange rate for spot transactions ruling at the balance sheet date and is the mean of the buying and selling rates at the close of business on the day for which the rate is to be ascertained.**[9]

On 31 December 20X1 the amount payable to extinguish the creditor is not £25 000 but a lower amount of £21 053, that is 200 000 sudars, translated at the closing rate of exchange on that day – 9.5 sudars to £1. When the liability is adjusted to this figure, the result is a gain on exchange:

Creditor – Foreign company

20X1		£	20X1		£
Dec 31	Balance c/d	21 053	Nov 20	Stock	25 000
	Profit and				
	loss account				
	– gain on exchange	3 947			
		25 000			25 000
			20X2		
			Jan 1	Balance b/d	21 053

The gain on exchange has occurred because the sterling value of the liability has fallen between 20 November 20X1 and 31 December 20X1 which is due to the strengthening of sterling against the sudar. SSAP 20 considers that, as there is objective evidence for the sterling value of the liability and, as such a gain on a short-term monetary item will shortly be reflected in cash flows, so the profit on exchange is a part of realised profit and hence should be included in the profit or loss from ordinary activities.

The gain recognised in 20X1 could, of course, be fully or partly offset by a loss in the subsequent year if sterling weakens against the sudar between 31 December 20X1 and the date of settlement, 15 January 20X2. The treatment adopted is, of course, consistent with the accruals concept: the gain occurred in 20X1 and is reported in 20X1, while the loss would occur in 20X2 and be reported in 20X2.

In this particular example there is, of course, no loss in 20X2 but a further gain on exchange when settlement is made on 15 January 20X2. Ignoring bank charges, the amount payable in sterling is £20 000 (200 000 sudars ÷ 10) so that the creditor's account appears as follows:

Creditor – Foreign company

20X2		£	20X2		£
Jan 15	Cash	20 000	Jan 1	Balance b/d	21 053
	Profit and loss				
	account – gain				
	on exchange	1 053			
		21 053			21 053

As in 20X1, the gain on exchange is credited to the profit and loss account, this time for the year ended 31 December 20X2.

SSAP 20 requires similar adherence to the accruals principle in the case of long-term monetary liabilities although, as we shall see, the standard adopts a different stance on the realisation of gains on exchange on such long-term liabilities.

---

[9] SSAP 20, Para. 41.

Example 16.4

Let us suppose that Han Limited raised a long-term loan of 400 000 sudars from a bank in Sudarland on 1 October 20X1 when the rate of exchange was 8 sudars to £1. The loan will be recorded in the accounting records of Han Limited at a figure of £50 000:

```
20X1
Oct 1   Dr Cash                    £50 000
           Cr Long-term loan                   £50 000
                                   ========    ========
        Being loan of 400 000 sudars
        translated at 8 sudars to £1
```

If, on 31 December 20X1, the rate of exchange is 9.5 sudars to £1 then, under the provisions of SSAP 20, the liability must be translated into sterling at that rate to produce a figure of £42 105 (400 000 ÷ 9.5):

Long-term loan
(denominated in sudars)

20X1		£	20X1		£
Dec 31	Balance c/d	42 105	Oct 1	Cash	50 000
	Profit and loss				
	account – gain				
	on exchange	7 895			
		50 000			50 000
		=====			=====
			20X2		
			Jan 1	Balance b/d	42 105

Restating the sterling liability at this figure produces a gain on exchange of £7895 and SSAP 20 requires that this be reported as part of the 'ordinary' profits of Han Limited.

Some accountants would argue that such a gain is realised on the grounds that there is objective evidence, in the form of an officially published exchange rate, that it actually occurred in 20X1. Others would argue that, because it relates to a long-term item which has not been repaid at the balance sheet date, the gain may be reversed by subsequent exchange rate movements before repayment and is therefore not realised at the balance sheet date. These two views reflect the lack of consensus on the precise meaning of realisation, which was discussed in Chapter 4.

Although SSAP 20 takes the view that exchange gains on unsettled short-term monetary items are realised, it takes the view that such gains on unsettled long-term monetary items are unrealised.[10] In the authors' view, this is an extremely uncomfortable position, for it may result in a situation where a gain on a short-term item will be treated as realised even though we may know, at the time of preparing the financial statements, that it has subsequently been reversed, whereas a gain on a long-term item, where we have no such certain knowledge of reversal, will be treated as unrealised. The ASC appears to have adopted different definitions of realisation for short-term and long-term items. In the former case, the existence of an objective exchange rate seems crucial, no matter what happens to the exchange rate subsequently. In the latter case, the existence of the objective exchange rate seems unimportant and uncertainty about the ultimate cash

---

[10] SSAP 20, Para 65.

payable appears to be dominant. Among such confusion, we should perhaps be thankful that, rightly or wrongly, there is little disagreement among accountants that the SSAP 20 view that all exchange losses on unsettled monetary items, whether short-term or long-term, are realised.

Given the ASC's conclusion that exchange gains on unsettled long-term monetary items are unrealised, many accountants argue that the prudence concept dictates that such gains should not be included in the profit and loss account. Indeed, they may quote statutory support for their argument in that the Companies Act 1985 specifically states that: 'only profits realised at the balance sheet date shall be included in the profit and loss account'.[11] However, the law permits directors to depart from this principle if there are special reasons, provided that the notes to the accounts give particulars of the departure, the reason for it and its effect.[12] SSAP 20 considers that such a departure from the realisation principle is essential if exchange gains and losses are to be treated symmetrically in accordance with the accruals principle. Thus, in contravention of SSAP 2, which was the relevant standard when SSAP 20 was issued, SSAP 20 requires that the accruals concept takes precedence over the prudence concept.[13] Hence, in the same way that exchange losses on long-term liabilities during the period are debited to the profit and loss account, so exchange gains for the period are credited to the profit and loss account.

Relevant disclosure must be made. It would also seem to be necessary to remove such unrealised profits, credited in profit and loss accounts, when calculating legally distributable profits. However, as we have seen in Chapter 4, the ASB has been attempting to change the concept of realisation to include such gains on exchange but whether this approach would be acceptable to the courts remains an open question.

Example 16.5

It is possible for a UK company to raise a foreign currency loan which it then invests in the shares of an overseas company. The loan and investment may be in the same currency or, alternatively, the loan may be raised in one currency while the investment is made in a country with a different currency. For ease of exposition we shall assume that only one currency is involved.

Let us assume that Han Limited raised a long-term loan of 300 000 Ruritanian dollars (R\$) on 1 October 20X1 when the rate of exchange was R\$1.5 to £1. It immediately invested the proceeds in the shares of a Ruritanian company so that, if we ignore the receipt and payment of cash, the summarised journal entry will appear as follows:

20X1			
Oct 1	*Dr* Investment in Ruritanian company	£200 000	
	Cr Long-term loan (Ruritanian)		£200 000

Being loan of R\$300 000 raised to finance investment in Ruritanian company translated at R\$1.5 to £1

---

[11] Companies Act 1985, Schedule 4, Para. 12(a).

[12] Companies Act 1985, Schedule 4, Para. 15.

[13] SSAP 2, Para. 14(b): 'provided that where the accruals concept is inconsistent with the "prudence" concept, the latter prevails'. SSAP 2 has subsequently been replaced by FRS 18 *Accounting Policies* (December 2000) and, as we have seen in Chapter 2, the ASB is playing down the role of realisation, as traditionally understood, in the recognition process.

The investment may constitute the Ruritanian company a subsidiary, an associate, a joint venture or merely a simple investment. Whichever is the case, the treatment in the accounting records of Han Limited will be exactly the same, although the treatment in any consolidated financial statements will differ.

Let us assume that the rate of exchange on 31 December 20X1 is R$1.4 to £1. If Han Limited follows the rules explained in previous examples, certain difficulties will arise. Unless there had been a permanent fall in the value of the investment, the investment would be shown in the balance sheet at its cost of £200 000 while the loan, a monetary amount, would have to be translated at the closing rate of exchange and shown as a liability of £214 286 (R$300 000 ÷ 1.4). Restating the loan at this amount produces a loss on exchange of £14 286 which would have to be charged to the profit and loss account.

Long-term loan
(denominated in Ruritanian dollars)

20X1			20X1		
Dec 31	Balance c/d	£214 286	Oct 1	Cash	£200 000
			Dec 31	Profit and loss account – loss on exchange	14 286
		214 286			214 286

It may be argued that to make such a one-sided adjustment is misleading. Because of the adherence to historical cost accounting, the investment is retained at its historical cost in sterling while the liability is shown at its current sterling equivalent. SSAP 20 recognises the logic of this argument and *permits*, although it does not *require*, Han Limited to translate the investment at the closing rate of exchange rather than at the historical rate of exchange, thus:

Investment in Ruritanian company

20X1			20X1		
Oct 1	Cost	£200 000	Dec 31	Balance c/d, 300 000 ÷ 1.4	£214 286
Dec 31	Gain on exchange	14 286			
		214 286			214 286

This produces an absurd sterling figure for the investment, a figure which is neither the historical cost in sterling nor a current value in sterling, but what has been achieved is the creation of a gain on exchange which may be used to offset the loss on exchange on the long-term loan. In this case the gain on the investment is exactly equal to the loss on the long-term loan and one may be offset against the other without any need to charge any gain or loss to the profit and loss account. If the loan and investment were for different currency amounts or in different foreign currencies, this equality of gain and loss is unlikely to exist. In such a case SSAP 20 requires that any exchange gain or loss on the investment should be taken direct to reserves. Any loss or gain on the loan should then be offset against the gain or loss on the investment but, if the exchange loss/gain on the loan exceeds the gain/loss on the investment, then the excess must be charged/credited to the profit and loss account.

The final problem addressed in this example is the extent to which such an offset should be permitted. Should it be necessary to identify a particular loan with a particular investment? Should the offset be restricted to situations where the loan and investment are in the same currency? Where a large company has many loans denominated in various foreign currencies and many investments in various foreign currencies, should a global approach be permitted whereby any gains are set off against any losses? What criteria should be laid down to govern the use of this offset arrangement?

After receiving many different recommendations from those who commented on the offset arrangements included in ED 27, SSAP 20 specified the following conditions:[14]

(a) in any accounting period, exchange gains or losses arising on the borrowings may be offset only to the extent of exchange differences arising on the equity investments;
(b) the foreign currency borrowings, whose exchange gains or losses are used in the offset process, should not exceed, in the aggregate, the total amount of cash that the investments are expected to be able to generate, whether from profits or otherwise; and
(c) the accounting treatment adopted should be applied consistently from period to period.

This must be recognised as a pragmatic solution to what is often a very difficult question to answer in practice: 'To what extent do foreign currency loans provide a hedge against foreign equity investments?'

Why the offset arrangement should apply to equity investments but not to other investments, such as a readily saleable property overseas, seems difficult to justify and displays the ad hoc nature of the UK approach to standard setting in the past. The topic of hedge accounting has now been addressed in a more systematic way in FRED 23 *Financial Instruments*: *Hedge Accounting*, issued in May 2002. As we saw in Chapter 8, this proposes that that there should be both a pre-designated hedge and an effective hedge for the use of hedge accounting to be permissible.

Summary

The accounting treatment of foreign currency transactions may be summarised as follows:

1 Non-monetary assets shown on basis of historical cost

Non-monetary assets shown at an amount based upon historical cost should be translated at the exchange rate at the date on which the historical cost was established. However, if there is a contractually agreed exchange rate for settlement, this *should* be used and, if there are related or matching forward exchange contracts in respect of trading transactions, the rates of exchange specified in those contracts *may* be used.[15] The cost of non-monetary assets purchased is not affected by subsequent changes in the exchange rate except where a company exercises the option to use the closing rate to translate the cost of foreign equity investments financed by foreign currency borrowings.

2 Non-monetary assets shown on basis of a revalued amount

Non-monetary assets which have been revalued, either upwards under the alternative accounting rules or downwards under the rules on impairment, should be translated at the rate ruling when the valuation was established.

---

[14] SSAP 20, Para. 51. FRED 24 does not contain any provisions permitting the use of such offset arrangements. Such offset arrangements would only be possible where hedge accounting is used in accordance with a standard based upon FRED 23 *Financial Instruments: Hedge Accounting* (May 2002).

[15] As we have explained above, FRED 24 proposes that, in future, the spot rate should be used, except where hedge accounting is used in accordance with a standard to be based upon the proposals of FRED 23.

3 Unsettled monetary items

Unsettled monetary items should be translated at the closing rate, unless there is a contractually agreed exchange rate for settlement, in which case the latter *should* be used. If there are related or matching forward contracts in respect of trading transactions, the rates of exchange specified in those contracts *may* be used.

4 Treatment of exchange gains and losses

All exchange gains and losses on settled and unsettled transactions should be credited or charged to the profit and loss account as part of the profit from ordinary activities (unless they relate to transactions which are treated as extraordinary items) but note that, according to SSAP 20, gains on unsettled long-term monetary items are not realised and hence it would seem necessary to make an adjustment when calculating the legally distributable profit of a company. Whether the legal definition of realised profits has progressed sufficiently to be consistent with the desire of of the ASB to define such gains as realised remains an open question.

Translation of the financial statements of an overseas subsidiary

Where a UK company has an overseas branch, subsidiary or associated undertaking which keeps its records in a foreign currency, it is necessary to translate financial statements in order to be able to combine the figures with those of the UK company or group. In this chapter we assume that the overseas unit is a subsidiary, although readers will appreciate that similar principles are appropriate for a foreign branch, associate or joint venture.

As explained in the first section of this chapter, when exchange rates are changing, the existence of an overseas subsidiary requires us to answer two questions. First, what rate of exchange should be used to translate the individual items in the accounts of the overseas subsidiary? Second, how should the resulting differences on exchange be treated in the accounts?

Turning first to the balance sheet of the overseas subsidiary, there are at least two rates of exchange which could be applied to each asset or liability. These are the historical rate or the closing rate. The historical rate is the rate of exchange ruling at the date the transaction occurred or, where appropriate, the rate of exchange ruling at the date of a subsequent revaluation. The closing rate is the rate of exchange ruling on the balance sheet date.

The major methods of translation which have been used employ a combination of these rates, and Table 16.1 illustrates how four methods deal with the major categories of asset and liability.

Under the current/non-current method, current assets and liabilities are translated at the closing rate while fixed assets and long-term liabilities are translated at the appropriate historical rates.

Under the monetary/non-monetary method, monetary assets and liabilities are translated at the closing rate while non-monetary assets are translated at the historical rate.

Under the temporal method, which is discussed in more detail later in this chapter, the rate of exchange depends upon the basis of valuation used in the balance sheet of the overseas subsidiary. If items are shown at current value, which is automatically the case with

Table 16.1 **Major methods of translation**

	Current/ non-current		Monetary/ non-monetary		Temporal		Closing rate	
	H	C	H	C	H	C	H	C
Assets								
Fixed assets								
At cost less depreciation	x		x		x			x
At current value	x		x			x		x
Current assets								
Stock								
At cost		x	x		x			x
At current value		x	x			x		x
Debtors		x		x		x		x
Cash		x		x		x		x
Liabilities								
Long-term loans	x			x		x		x
Current liabilities		x		x		x		x

H = historical rate; C = closing rate.

monetary assets and liabilities, the closing rate is used.[16] Where items are shown at a figure based upon historical cost, the historical rate is appropriate, and where items are shown at a figure based on a valuation, the rate of exchange at the date of the valuation is used.

From Table 16.1, it can be seen that there is very little difference between the temporal method and the monetary/non-monetary method within the context of historical cost accounts. The most frequent instance of a difference occurs where stock is shown at net realisable value.

Under the closing rate method all assets and liabilities are translated at the closing rate of exchange.

When we turn to the profit and loss account, three possible translation rates may be distinguished:

(a) historical rates, that is rates of exchange specific to each transaction;
(b) average rate ruling during the year;[17]
(c) closing rate on the balance sheet date.

Under the first of these, the appropriate rate of exchange is that ruling on the date of the transaction. So, if depreciation is based upon a historical cost, the rate of exchange at the date of acquisition of the asset is appropriate. If depreciation is based upon a revalued amount, the rate of exchange at the date of revaluation is appropriate. Where revenues and other expenses arise on a particular day, the rate of exchange on that day is appropriate. In

---

[16] This statement is only true within the confines of traditional financial statements. Arguably the current value of a monetary item should be its present value, which takes into account interest for the time period until maturity of the debt.

[17] This should, of course, be an appropriate weighted average, reflecting the way in which the currencies have moved during the year, and not merely a simple average of the opening and closing rates.

practice, for recurrent items such as wages, power, directors' remuneration, etc., an average rate is used as an approximation to the historical or specific rate of exchange.

Under the second option, an average rate of exchange is used in its own right, whereas with the third approach the closing rate of exchange is used for all items in the profit and loss account.

When we consider rates of exchange applied to balance sheet items and profit and loss account items, the following combinations have been found:

Balance sheet	Profit and loss account
Current/non-current	Historical or average
Monetary/non-monetary	Historical or average
Temporal	Historical or average
Closing rate	Average or closing rate

Thus there has been a wide choice in practice as to the appropriate combinations of rates of exchange.

Whichever combinations are used, there will inevitably be differences on exchange and there are various ways of dealing with them in the consolidated accounts:

(i)   Include as part of profit or loss from ordinary activities.
(ii) Treat as a movement on reserves.
(iii) Some combination of the above.

When the choice between relevant rates of exchange is coupled with the choice between the various ways of dealing with differences on exchange, there are a large number of possible combinations.

The SSAP 20 solution

ED 21, wrongly entitled, *Accounting for Foreign Currency Transactions*,[18] was issued in September 1972 as the first comprehensive attempt towards standardising the accounting treatment of foreign currencies in the UK. It permitted companies to use either the temporal method or the closing rate method and laid down rules on the rates of exchange to be used for translation and the treatment of the differences on exchange.

If ED 21 had become an SSAP, it would certainly have reduced the choice of methods available to companies by outlawing the use of the current/non-current and the monetary/non-monetary methods. However, when applied to historical cost accounts, the temporal method and the closing rate method usually produce very different results and, hence, the degree of standardisation proposed by ED 21 was limited and the exposure draft was heavily criticised.

The subsequent ED 27 *Accounting for Foreign Currency Translations*, issued in November 1980, and SSAP 20 *Foreign Currency Translation*, issued in April 1983, require the use of the closing rate/net investment method in the vast majority of cases although, as we shall see below, there are circumstances where the use of the temporal method is required.

---

[18] Wrongly entitled because it dealt almost exclusively with foreign currency translation and gave little attention to foreign currency transactions.

The words 'net investment' were added to the title of the method to indicate the view which the method implicitly takes of the investment in the overseas subsidiary. The majority of overseas subsidiaries are thought to have a large amount of autonomy and to operate primarily within the economic environment of an overseas country using the currency of that country. Using the terminology of the US FASB Statement No. 52, the 'functional currency' of the overseas subsidiary is usually that of the country in which it operates.[19] The holding company is therefore regarded as having an investment in the net assets of the subsidiary rather than in its individual assets and liabilities. It follows that only the net investment is at risk from movements in the exchange rate and, as we shall see, use of the closing rate/net investment method is consistent with this position.

In some cases, however, the overseas subsidiary may not have significant autonomy. Thus the affairs of the overseas company may be closely linked with those of the parent company, and its 'functional currency' may be sterling rather than the local currency. In such a case, SSAP 20 requires that the foreign financial statements be translated using the temporal method so that the results are included as if the transactions had been undertaken by the parent company itself.

SSAP 20 provides little guidance on how to recognise situations where the temporal method is appropriate and, given the variety of situations found in practice, it has to be recognised that it will sometimes be extremely difficult to decide which method of translation to apply.

To summarise, under the provisions of SSAP 20, it is expected that the vast majority of companies should use the closing rate/net investment method while a small number of companies will be required to use the temporal method. It is therefore essential for us to look at both methods.

In the following two sections of this chapter, we shall examine the principles of the closing rate/net investment and temporal methods using simple examples. We shall then compare and contrast the two methods before presenting a more complex example of the closing rate/net investment method.

Closing rate/net investment method

As we have seen, any method for translating the financial statements of an overseas subsidiary must specify which rates of exchange are to be used for the various items in the statements of that subsidiary and how the resulting differences on exchange are to be treated in the consolidated financial statements.

The SSAP 20 version of the closing rate/net investment method lays down the following rules:

(a) Assets and liabilities in the balance sheet of the overseas subsidiary are to be translated at the closing rate. This, of course, determines the amount of the shareholders' interest although, as we shall see, it may be sensible to translate the share capital and components of reserves at various rates of exchange.

(b) Profit and loss account items are to be translated at either the average rate or the closing rate.[20]

(c) Differences on exchange arising on translation are to be taken direct to reserves.

---

[19] See Appendix A to Statement of Financial Accounting Standard No. 52 for factors which should be taken into account in determining the functional currency of an overseas subsidiary.

[20] The forerunner to SSAP 20, ED 27, proposed the use of the average rate for profit and loss account items and, although this is standard international practice, the comments on ED 27 showed that there was considerable opposition to the exclusive use of an average rate in the UK. In spite of this opposition, FRED 24 (May 2002) follows the international standard by proposing that revenues and expenses should be translated at the exchange rates at the dates of transactions. In practice, this will usually require the use of average rates of exchange for many items.

When the rate of exchange between sterling and the overseas currency is fluctuating, a difference on exchange will arise in respect of the opening net assets of the subsidiary, which are translated at a different rate at the year end from that used at the beginning of the year. A second difference will arise if the average rate of exchange is used to translate profit and loss account items for, in such a case, the increase in net assets as shown by the retained profit or loss is translated at the average rate, whereas the resulting net assets are translated at the closing rate in the balance sheet. Both differences on translation are treated as movements on reserves.

Let us illustrate the method by means of a simple example.

Example 16.6

Widening Horizons Limited, a UK company which owns and rents out properties, established a wholly owned overseas subsidiary, Foreign Venture Limited, on 31 December 20X1. Widening Horizons Limited subscribed £100 000 in cash for one million shares of 1 groucho each. On 31 December 20X1, the rate of exchange between currencies was 10 grouchos to £1.

Foreign Venture Limited immediately raised a long-term loan of 500 000 grouchos and purchased freehold land and buildings, suitable for renting, at a cost of 1 200 000 grouchos.

After these transactions, the opening balance sheet of the new subsidiary, in both foreign currency and sterling, is therefore as given below:

Foreign Venture Limited
Opening balance sheet on 1 January 20X2

	Grouchos	Rate of exchange (grouchos to £1)	£
Freehold land and buildings			
At cost	1 200 000	10	120 000
Short-term monetary assets			
Cash	300 000	10	30 000
	1 500 000		150 000
less Long-term loan	500 000	10	50 000
	1 000 000		100 000
Share capital			
1 000 000 shares of 1 groucho	1 000 000	10	100 000

At this date only one rate of exchange is appropriate; it qualifies as both the historical rate and the closing rate. Once the balance sheet is translated into sterling, it is possible to match the cost of the investment shown in the records of Widening Horizons Limited at £100 000 against the share capital of Foreign Venture Limited to produce neither positive nor negative goodwill on consolidation.

During the following year to 31 December 20X2, Foreign Venture Limited collects rentals and incurs expenses with the result that its profit and loss account for the year and balance sheet on 31 December 20X2 are as follows:

Foreign Venture Limited
Profit and loss account for the year ended 31 December 20X2

	Grouchos	Grouchos
Rentals received		400 000
less Expenses		
Management expenses	115 000	
Depreciation of buildings	50 000	
Interest on long-term loan	75 000	240 000
Profit before taxation		160 000
less Taxation payable		60 000
Retained profit for year		100 000

Balance sheet on 31 December 20X2

	Grouchos
Freehold land and buildings	
At cost	1 200 000
less Depreciation	50 000
	1 150 000
Short-term net monetary assets	
(debtors plus cash less creditors)	450 000
	1 600 000
less Long-term loan	500 000
	1 100 000
Share capital	
1 000 000 shares of 1 groucho each	1 000 000
Retained profit	100 000
	1 100 000

Assuming that the relevant rates of exchange between grouchos and sterling are as given below, we may proceed to translate the financial statements in accordance with the closing rate/net investment method:

	Grouchos to £1
1 January 20X2	10
Average for year to 31 December 20X2	8
31 December 20X2	6

The average rate, rather than the closing rate, has been applied in the profit and loss account.

Foreign Venture Limited
Profit and loss account for the year ended 31 December 20X2

	Grouchos	Rate of exchange	£
Rentals received	400 000	8	50 000
less Expenses			
Management expenses	115 000	8	14 375
Depreciation of buildings	50 000	8	6 250
Interest on long-term loan	75 000	8	9 375
	240 000		30 000
Profit before taxation	160 000		20 000
less Taxation payable	60 000	8	7 500
Retained profit for year	100 000		12 500

Balance sheet on 31 December 20X2

	Grouchos	Rate of exchange	£
Freehold land and buildings			
At cost	1 200 000	6	200 000
less Depreciation	50 000	6	8 333
	1 150 000		191 667
Short-term net monetary assets	450 000	6	75 000
	1 600 000		266 667
less Long-term loan	500 000	6	83 333
	1 100 000		183 334
Shareholders' interest:			
Share capital	1 000 000	10(HR)	100 000
Retained profits	100 000	Per P and L a/c	12 500
	1 100 000		112 500
Difference on exchange	–	Balance	70 834
	1 100 000		183 334

Note: HR = historical rate.

The treatment of share capital merits special attention. It has been translated at the historical rate of exchange, that is the rate ruling at the date of acquisition.

If we assume for a moment that share capital had been translated at the closing rate of exchange of 6 grouchos to £1, this would have produced a sterling figure of £166 667 instead of the £100 000 shown. This would have reduced the difference on exchange, the balancing figure, by £66 667, but consideration must also be paid to the subsequent consolidation of the subsidiary's accounts with those of the parent company. In the consolidation workings the cost of the investment, £100 000, would be matched with the share capital of the subsidiary, £166 667, when translated at closing rate, to produce negative goodwill on consolidation of £66 667. This is clearly nonsensical since there was no goodwill on acquisition and the apparent negative goodwill would only have arisen because of the change in the exchange rate. In other words the £66 667 is a difference on exchange.

The wisdom of the method used in the example may now be seen. The application of the historical rate to share capital and, in a more general case, to pre-acquisition reserves as well, means, first, that the total difference emerges in the translation of the subsidiary's balance sheet and, second, that there is no risk that an erroneous adjustment will be made to the goodwill on consolidation. We shall return to this topic in the more comprehensive example of the closing rate/net investment method later in the chapter where positive goodwill on acquisition emerges. Once we recognise positive goodwill, it is necessary to consider where the goodwill is situated, for this determines whether it should or should not be retranslated at each subsequent balance sheet date.

The total difference on exchange, a gain of £70 834, must be credited to consolidated reserves. It has arisen for two reasons. First, the opening net assets were translated at one rate on 1 January 20X2 and at a different rate on 31 December 20X2. Second, the increase in net assets, the retained profit, has been translated at one rate in the profit and loss account and at a different rate in the closing balance sheet. We may analyse the difference as follows:

Analysis of difference on exchange

	Grouchos	Opening balance sheet (10 grouchos to £1) £	Closing balance sheet (6 grouchos to £1) £	Difference £
Opening net assets				
Freehold land and buildings	1 200 000	120 000	200 000	80 000 (gain)
Cash	300 000	30 000	50 000	20 000 (gain)
	1 500 000	150 000	250 000	100 000
less Long-term loan	500 000	50 000	83 333	33 333 (loss)
	1 000 000	100 000	166 667	66 667

Increase in net assets during year			
Retained profit for year			
Per profit and loss account, 100 000 grouchos at 8 grouchos to £1		12 500	
Per closing balance sheet (part of net monetary assets), 100 000 grouchos at 6 grouchos to £1		16 667	4 167 (gain)
Total gain on exchange			70 834

It is hoped that the above analysis helps to explain why the words 'net investment' have been added in the name 'closing rate/net investment' method. The loss on the opening long-term loan has effectively been offset against the gains on the opening assets so that it is only the gain on the opening *net* assets which is taken to reserves with the second part of the gain in respect of the retained profit for the year. If the closing rate had been used for profit and loss account items, this second part of the gain would not arise.

Let us assume that the financial statements of the parent company are as given in the left-hand column below. Provided there are no unrealised intercompany profits or similar consolidation adjustments, we may proceed to consolidate by adding the figures for the parent company with the translated figures for the overseas subsidiary, treating the difference on exchange of £70 834 as a movement on reserves and disclosing it in the Statement of Total Recognised Gains and Losses.

Widening Horizons Limited
Workings for consolidated profit and loss account
for the year ended 31 December 20X2

	Widening Horizons Limited £	Foreign Venture Limited £	Consolidated £
Rentals received	500 000	50 000	550 000
less Expenses			
Management expenses	120 000	14 375	134 375
Depreciation	60 000	6 250	66 250
Loan interest	100 000	9 375	109 375
	280 000	30 000	310 000
Profit before taxation	220 000	20 000	240 000
less Taxation	100 000	7 500	107 500
	120 000	12 500	132 500
less Dividends proposed	60 000	–	60 000
Retained profit for year	60 000	12 500	72 500

Workings for movement on reserves for year to 31 December 20X2

	Widening Horizons Limited £	Foreign Venture Limited £	Consolidated £
Reserves on 1 January 20X2	420 000	–	420 000
add Retained profit for year	60 000	12 500	72 500
Gain on exchange	–	70 834	70 834
Reserves on 31 December 20X2	480 000	83 334	563 334

Consolidated statement of total recognised gains and losses
for the year ended 31 December 20X2

	£
Profit for the financial year	132 500
Gain on exchange	70 834
Total recognised gains for the financial year	203 334

Workings for consolidated balance sheet on 31 December 20X2

	Widening Horizons Limited £	Foreign Venture Limited £	Consolidated £
Freehold land and buildings			
At cost	2 000 000	200 000	2 200 000
less Depreciation	350 000	8 333	358 333
	1 650 000	191 667	1 841 667
Investment in Foreign Venture Limited – at cost	100 000	–	–
Goodwill on consolidation – at cost	–	–	–
Short-term net monetary assets	330 000	75 000	405 000
	2 080 000	266 667	2 246 667
less Long-term loan	1 000 000	83 333	1 083 333
	1 080 000	183 334	1 163 334
Share capital	600 000	100 000	600 000
Reserves	480 000	83 334	563 334
	1 080 000	183 334	1 163 334

Once the translation has been undertaken, preparation of the consolidated financial statements poses only the normal problems faced when consolidating a UK subsidiary and preparing financial statements using the formats required by company law.

Temporal method

This method was first proposed by an American, Leonard Lorensen, in a study published by the American Institute of Certified Public Accountants.[21] It was the only method permitted by the US FASB in their standard on the subject, Financial Accounting Standard (FAS) 8, which was issued in October 1975. However, this standard attracted a great deal of criticism in the USA and has now been replaced by FAS 52, issued in December 1981, which, like SSAP 20 and IAS 21, favours the use of the closing rate method in most, but not all, circumstances.

Under the temporal method, the rates of exchange to be used for translation are determined by the basis of measurement used for the various items in the financial statements of the overseas subsidiary.

In the balance sheet, assets which are shown at a figure based on historical cost are translated at the relevant historical rate; assets shown on the basis of a revalued amount at some past date are translated at the rate of exchange ruling when the revalued amount was established; assets and liabilities shown at a current value, which includes all monetary assets and liabilities, are translated at the closing rate.

In the profit and loss account the rate of exchange used is similarly determined by the underlying basis of measurement: depreciation based on historical cost is translated at the

---

[21] L. Lorensen, *Reporting Foreign Operations of US Companies in US Dollars*, Accounting Research Study No. 12, AICPA, New York, 1972.

relevant historical rate; revenues and expenses which have accrued over the year are translated at an average rate; while revenues and expenses which relate to amounts established in previous years or to merely a part of the current year are translated at a specific rate or an appropriate average rate.

It follows that more extensive records are necessary than those required for use of the closing rate/net investment method.

Under the SSAP 20 version of the temporal method, all differences on exchange are credited or charged to the consolidated profit and loss account as a part of the ordinary profits for the year.[22]

Let us examine the temporal method by applying it to the same simple facts used in the previous example.

Example 16.7

The opening balance sheet of Foreign Venture Limited, the new subsidiary established by Widening Horizons Limited, in both grouchos and sterling is repeated below:

Foreign Venture Limited
Balance sheet on 1 January 20X2

	Grouchos	Rate of exchange	£
Freehold land and buildings			
At cost	1 200 000	10	120 000
Short-term monetary assets			
Cash	300 000	10	30 000
	1 500 000		150 000
less Long-term loan	500 000	10	50 000
	1 000 000		100 000
Share capital	1 000 000	10	100 000

Widening Horizons Limited paid £100 000 for the investment and hence at the date of acquisition there is no goodwill on consolidation.

The accounts of Foreign Venture Limited for the year ended 31 December 20X2 are given below. The left-hand column gives the financial statements in foreign currency while the right-hand column shows the results translated into sterling. For ease of reference, the relevant exchange rates are repeated:

	Grouchos to £1
1 January 20X2	10
Average for year to 31 December 20X2	8
31 December 20X2	6

In the profit and loss account the historical rate, that ruling when the land and buildings were purchased on 31 December 20X1, is applied to depreciation. For other items the average rate is an appropriate approximation to the historical rate. A simple average of the opening and closing

---

[22] Other variants of the temporal method exist. Thus some versions require the amortisation of unrealised gains or losses over the remaining life of the asset or liability.

rates would only be appropriate if the revenue and expenses arose reasonably evenly over the year and the rate of exchange moved reasonably evenly. Otherwise an appropriate weighted average would have to be used.

Foreign Venture Limited
Profit and loss account for the year ended 31 December 20X2

	Grouchos	Rate of exchange (see note)	£
Rentals received	400 000	8(AR)	50 000
less Expenses			
Management expenses	115 000	8(AR)	14 375
Depreciation of buildings	50 000	10(HR)	5 000
Interest on long-term loan	75 000	8(AR)	9 375
	240 000		28 750
Profit before taxation	160 000		21 250
less Taxation payable	60 000	8(AR)	7 500
Retained profit for year	100 000		13 750

Note: AR = average rate, HR = historical rate.

In the balance sheet, the freehold land and buildings, shown at depreciated historical cost, are translated at the historical rate of exchange on 1 January 20X2 while all monetary assets and liabilities are translated at the closing rate.

As explained in the previous example, it is sensible to translate the share capital and, in a more general case, any pre-acquisition reserves at the historical rate in order to maintain the goodwill on acquisition at its 'historical cost' of zero in the consolidated financial statements. It is also necessary to translate the retained profit for the year at the same sterling figure as shown for retained profit in the profit and loss account. When this has been done the difference on exchange emerges as the balancing figure.

Balance sheet on 31 December 20X2

	Grouchos	Rate of exchange (see note)	£
Freehold land and buildings			
At cost	1 200 000	10(HR)	120 000
less Depreciation	50 000	10(HR)	5 000
	1 150 000		115 000
Short-term net monetary assets	450 000	6(CR)	75 000
	1 600 000		190 000
less Long-term loan	500 000	6(CR)	83 333
	1 100 000		106 667
Shareholders' interest:			
Share capital			
1 000 000 shares of 1 groucho each	1 000 000	10(HR)	100 000
Retained profit			
Per profit and loss account	100 000	Actual	13 750
	1 100 000		113 750
Difference on exchange	–	Balance	(7 083)
	1 100 000		106 667

Note: HR = historical rate, CR = closing rate.

As explained above, SSAP 20 requires any difference on exchange arising under the temporal method to be included in the ordinary profits and losses of the group.

If we assume that the financial statements of the parent company are as given in the left-hand column below and that there are no consolidation adjustments for such matters as unrealised intercompany profits, we may proceed to consolidate. This requires adding the figures for the parent company with the sterling figures for the overseas subsidiary, treating the difference on exchange as part of the ordinary profits. We have not produced a Statement of Total Recognised Gains and Losses, as there are no gains/losses except for the profit for the financial year.

Widening Horizons Limited
Workings for consolidated profit and loss account for the year ended
31 December 20X2

	Widening Horizons Limited £	Foreign Venture Limited £	Consolidated £
Rentals received	500 000	50 000	550 000
less Expenses			
Management expenses	120 000	14 375	134 375
Depreciation	60 000	5 000	65 000
Loan interest	100 000	9 375	109 375
	280 000	28 750	308 750
Revenue less expenses	220 000	21 250	241 250
less Loss on exchange	–	7 083	7 083
Profit before taxation	220 000	14 167	234 167
less Taxation	100 000	7 500	107 500
	120 000	6 667	126 667
less Dividends proposed	60 000	–	60 000
Retained profit for the year	60 000	6 667	66 667

Workings for movement on reserves for year to 31 December 20X2

	Widening Horizons Limited £	Foreign Venture Limited £	Consolidated £
Retained profits on 1 January 20X2	420 000	–	420 000
add Retained profit for year	60 000	6 667	66 667
Retained profits on 31 December 20X2	480 000	6 667	486 667

Workings for consolidated balance sheet on 31 December 20X2

	Widening Horizons Limited £	Foreign Venture Limited £	Consolidated £
Freehold land and buildings			
At cost	2 000 000	120 000	2 120 000
less Depreciation	350 000	5 000	355 000
	1 650 000	115 000	1 765 000
Investment in Foreign Venture Limited			
At cost	100 000	–	–
Short-term net monetary assets	330 000	75 000	405 000
	2 080 000	190 000	2 170 000
less Long-term loan	1 000 000	83 333	1 083 333
	1 080 000	106 667	1 086 667
Share capital	600 000	100 000	600 000
Retained profits	480 000	6 667	486 667
	1 080 000	106 667	1 086 667

From workings similar to the above, it is quite straightforward to produce the consolidated financial statements for publication, although attention would have to be given to providing the more detailed information in accordance with the formats prescribed by company law.

As would be expected in this case, there is no goodwill on consolidation. The loss on exchange is charged in the profit and loss account and, under the rules of SSAP 20, would only be disclosed if it were an exceptional item.

There is no need to analyse the difference on exchange for the purposes of preparing the consolidated financial statements. However, it is instructive to do so.

No difference on exchange relates to the freehold land and buildings. In the opening balance sheet of Foreign Venture Limited the freehold land and buildings were shown at cost and translated at 10 grouchos to £1. In the profit and loss account, depreciation of 50 000 grouchos was provided and this was translated at 10 grouchos to £1. In the closing balance sheet the asset is shown at cost less depreciation, again translated at 10 grouchos to £1.

The difference arises, first, because monetary assets and liabilities are translated at different rates in the opening and closing balance sheet and, second, because, for certain items, different rates are used in the profit and loss account and closing balance sheet. It may be analysed as follows:

Analysis of difference on exchange   £

1 Opening balance of short-term net monetary assets	300 000	grouchos
In opening balance sheet, 10 grouchos to £1	£30 000	
In closing balance sheet, 6 grouchos to £1	£50 000	Gain 20 000
2 Opening balance on long-term loan	500 000	grouchos
In opening balance sheet, 10 grouchos to £1	£50 000	
In closing balance sheet, 6 grouchos to £1	£83 333	Loss 33 333
c/f		Loss 13 333

Analysis of difference on exchange (continued)   £

b/f   Loss 13 333

3 Increase in short-term net
   monetary assets during year
   Per profit and loss account

Retained profit	100 000	grouchos
add Depreciation	50 000	grouchos
	150 000	grouchos

At 8 grouchos to £1	£18 750
Per closing balance sheet as part of short-term net monetary assets, at 6 grouchos to £1	£25 000

Gain 6 250

Net loss   7 083

The differences on exchange may therefore be understood by thinking in terms of a flow of net monetary items:

Movement in net monetary assets/liabilities for the year ended 31 December 20X2

	Grouchos	*Grouchos*	*Rate*	*£*
Opening balance of net monetary liabilities:				
Long-term loan		500 000		
Short-term monetary assets		300 000		
		200 000	10	20 000
less Source of net monetary assets				
Retained profit plus depreciation		150 000	8	18 750
				1 250
Difference on exchange – balance (loss)				7 083
Closing balance of net monetary liabilities				
Long-term loan	500 000			
Short-term monetary assets	450 000			
	50 000			
		50 000	6	8 333

A critical look at the two methods

Some substantial differences

We have now demonstrated the mechanics of the two methods of translation, using the same example but rather large movements in the hypothetical exchange rates.

When exchange rates between currencies change over time, the methods produce very different results from the same set of foreign currency financial statements. Thus, if we compare the translated amount of the fixed assets of Foreign Venture Limited, in the simple examples in the two preceding sections, we find the following results:

Fixed assets of Foreign Venture Limited on 31 December 20X2

	Net book value
	£
Closing rate/net investment method	191 667
Temporal method	115 000

It is true that the rate of exchange moved from 10 grouchos to £1 at the beginning of the year to 6 grouchos at the end of the year, but there are substantial changes in practice in the exchange rates between currencies. Table 16.2 contains movements in the rate of exchange between sterling and a number of major currencies over a ten-year period.

Table 16.2 Movements in exchange rates over ten years

	Rates to £1 at end of December		Change as a percentage
	1991	2001	
US dollars	1.87	1.46	– 21.9
French francs*	9.70	10.72	+ 10.5
German Deutschmarks*	2.84	3.20	+ 12.7
Italian lire*	2150.30	3165.15	+ 47.2
Japanese yen	233.19	190.63	– 18.3
Swiss francs	2.54	2.42	– 4.7

Source: Bank of England Quarterly Bulletin.
* The currencies marked with an asterisk are now legacy currencies which have been replaced by the Euro from the beginning of 2002.

To illustrate the effect of the differences between the two methods, let us suppose that a German subsidiary bought land in December 1991 and that this was shown in the balance sheet on 31 December 2001 as:

Land, at cost   2 000 000 Deutschmarks

Under the closing rate/net investment method, this cost would be translated at the closing rate, while under the temporal method, it would be translated at the historical rate. Application of the two rates would produce very different sterling figures for the land:

Closing rate   2 000 000 ÷ 3.20 = £625 000
Historical rate   2 000 000 ÷ 2.84 = £704 225

When we turn to differences on exchange, we again find substantial differences between the methods. Under the closing rate/net investment method differences on exchange are treated as a movement on reserves, while under the temporal method they are considered to be part of the ordinary profit or loss for the year.

What then are the respective advantages and disadvantages of the two methods and why has SSAP 20 favoured the use of the closing rate/net investment method in most circumstances?

Advantages and disadvantages

How will the translated figures be used?

In order to evaluate the two methods of translation, we must bear in mind how the translated figures are going to be used. If we were studying the financial statements of an overseas company with a view to acquiring its shares, it might be useful to translate all items in the foreign currency statements into sterling at the closing rate of exchange in order to produce figures which are meaningful in the home currency. Use of a constant rate of exchange for all items would maintain the same relationships in the sterling financial statements as existed in the foreign currency statements. Thus, for example, long-term liabilities would be the same proportion of fixed assets and the current ratio would be the same in sterling as in the foreign currency accounts.

However, when considering the translation of the financial statements of a subsidiary company prior to consolidation, such a consideration would seem to be irrelevant. After all, we add the translated figures for the overseas subsidiary to those of the parent company and hence the relationship between items in the financial statements of the overseas subsidiary will be completely lost. What would seem to be more important for meaningful aggregation in the consolidated financial statements is that the bases of measurement used for the assets and liabilities are consistent.

The temporal method – the case for

If we accept the need to use consistent bases for consolidation then, in the context of historical cost accounting, it seems reasonable to aggregate the historical costs of the fixed assets and stocks of the subsidiary with the historical costs of the fixed assets and stocks of the parent company. Similarly, the amounts payable and receivable at the balance sheet date for both companies should be dealt with in a consistent manner.

Stated in this way, only the temporal method of translation is conceptually consistent with the historical cost basis of accounting and indeed any basis of accounting. The translation of a historical cost at a historical rate produces the historical cost in sterling, that is the amount which would have been incurred if a sum of money had been dispatched from the UK to purchase the asset. The translation of a historical cost at a closing rate must produce a conceptual nonsense.

It was arguments such as these which led the US FASB to require the exclusive use of the temporal method in FAS 8 issued back in 1975. However, the temporal method is not without its problems.

The temporal method – the case against

First, there is the practical problem of keeping records. In order to translate fixed assets and stocks at historical rates of exchange, a detailed analysis of these items together with the respective rates of exchange has to be kept. Such a record is not at present required by those companies which use the closing rate/net investment method.[23]

Second, the application of the method has caused large fluctuations in the reported profits of groups of companies from period to period, fluctuations which bear little relationship to

---

[23] IAS 21, Para. 30, requires that, in using the closing rate method, income and expenses of the foreign entity should be translated at exchange rates at the dates of the transactions, except when the foreign entity reports in the currency of a hyperinflationary economy, in which case the closing rate should be used. The proposed new international standard and UK standard both contain this provision and hence more extensive recordkeeping will be essential when using the closing rate/net investment method in future.

the underlying operating performance of the overseas subsidiaries. Such volatility of reported earnings arises because of the requirement to include exchange gains and losses on long-term monetary items in the ordinary profits of the group, and the problem could be solved by taking these particular exchange gains or losses direct to reserve or by spreading them over a period of years.

Third, the method produces misleading differences on exchange, which may in turn have adverse behavioural implications.

As an example of the third problem, let us take as an example a UK company which has an overseas subsidiary. In the balance sheet of the overseas subsidiary, fixed assets and stocks are shown on the basis of historical cost and these are usually financed by net monetary liabilities and an equity interest. During a particular year sterling is weakening against the overseas currency; that is, the other currency is becoming more valuable. In such a case the value of the overseas net assets to the UK company would be increasing and any potential dividends from the overseas subsidiary would be more valuable, as a given future dividend stream in the foreign currency would produce a greater amount of sterling. However, using the temporal method of translation, we would recognise no gains on the fixed assets but merely losses on the net monetary liabilities.

Thus, as a result of the movement in exchange rates, the overseas subsidiary is more valuable, but as a result of using the temporal method, the accounts show losses on exchange!

Under the provisions of both FAS 8 and SSAP 20, such losses on exchange reduced the profits from ordinary activities and hence the earnings per share. Given that boards of directors do not wish to undertake activities which reduce profits or produce losses in the financial statements, evidence was produced to indicate that 'profitable' overseas projects had been rejected because of the subsequent accounting losses which resulted from the use of the temporal method of translation.[24]

The closing rate/net investment method – its compensating virtues

The closing rate/net investment method does not produce these misleading differences. Because the closing rate is applied to non-monetary assets as well as monetary assets and liabilities, it is possible to set off exchange losses on foreign currency borrowings against exchange gains on real assets and therefore eliminate the need to charge such losses in the profit and loss account. The use of such a cover method is felt by many to reflect the reality of the situation where fixed assets and stocks are financed by money raised overseas. Indeed, under the offset arrangements included in SSAP 20, this cover method is extended to loans raised by the parent company or other companies in the group so that, where foreign currency borrowings have been used to finance, or provide a hedge against, group equity investments in foreign enterprises, exchange gains or losses on the borrowings may be set off against exchange differences arising on the retranslation of the net investment.[25]

Many would support the view that it is unhelpful to take into account exchange gains or losses on the monetary items without taking into account the exchange losses or gains on real assets. However, it is undoubtedly true that it would help users to understand what has happened and is likely to happen if companies provided a list of net investments in foreign

---

[24] See, for example, D.P. Walker, *An economic analysis of foreign exchange risk*, ICAEW Research Committee Occasional Paper No. 14, ICAEW, London, 1978.

[25] SSAP 20, Para. 57 specifies the conditions under which this offset arrangement may be applied. As we shall see in a later section of this chapter, the exchange difference on the retranslation of the net assets in the consolidated financial statements will usually differ from the exchange difference on the retranslation of the investment in the financial statements of the parent company.

entities and related borrowings, whose exchange gains or losses are offset as reserve movements, according to the principal foreign currencies involved.[26]

Summary

To summarise, the temporal method has the advantage of producing translated figures which are conceptually consistent with the underlying basis of measurement used, whereas the closing rate/net investment method has the advantage of simplicity and manages to avoid the reporting of fluctuating profits and misleading differences on exchange by the use of one rate of exchange for both assets and liabilities.

The ASC had to balance the respective advantages and disadvantages of the two methods in producing SSAP 20. As we have seen, it favoured the closing rate/net investment method for the majority of situations but required the use of the temporal method where the trade of the foreign enterprise is more dependent on the economic environment of the investing company's currency than that of its own reporting currency. It did, however, recognise the limitations of the closing rate/net investment method where the foreign country suffers from hyperinflation. In such a case it requires that the local currency financial statements be adjusted to reflect current price levels before the translation process is undertaken.[27]

In the view of the authors, the use of the closing rate/net investment method is inconsistent with the subsequent consolidation of the resulting sterling figures. In our view, the logic of the method should lead us to include the results of an overseas subsidiary in the consolidated financial statements by using the equity method of accounting.[28] In this way the consolidated profit and loss account would include the appropriate proportion of the profit or loss of the subsidiary while the consolidated balance sheet would show a net investment in the overseas subsidiary. This is surely what the title of the closing rate/net investment method implies!

One aspect of a larger problem

We have seen that both of the major methods of translation have advantages and disadvantages and that it has been difficult to choose between them.

The difficulties which we face here may be seen as part of the much larger problem discussed in the first part of this book. In Chapter 4 we have seen, for example, that the addition of historical costs which have been incurred at different points in time results in an unhelpful total when the value of the pound has been changing over time. The movement of exchange rates between currencies presents us with similar problems and, given that we have not yet solved the problems of accounting where only one currency is involved, it is not surprising that there is considerable confusion when we introduce two or more currencies.

It might be suggested that the major stumbling-block is the traditional reliance on historical cost accounts, which are known to have so many defects. We cannot expect the choice of

---

[26] It was to this end that the ASB published a brief exposure draft, *Amendment to SSAP 20 'Foreign Currency Translation': Disclosure*, in February 1999. This exposure draft was withdrawn shortly afterwards, in May 1999, on the grounds that more substantial changes to SSAP 20 are needed. The ASB has now issued FRED 24 (May 2002), which attempts to achieve convergence with the proposed new International Financial Reporting Standard (IFRS) on this topic.

[27] SSAP 20, Para. 26. This topic is addressed by IAS 29 *Financial Reporting in Hyper-inflationary Economies* (reformatted 1994) and UITF Abstract 9, 'Accounting for operations in hyper-inflationary economies' (June 1993). These specifically require adjustments prior to translation where the cumulative rate of inflation over a three-year period is approaching or exceeds 100 per cent.

[28] See Chapter 15 for a comprehensive discussion of the equity method of accounting.

exchange rate to remedy these defects. If we were to depart from historical costs and instead to show assets and liabilities of the overseas company at their current values, only one rate of exchange would be appropriate. The closing rate is required by both the temporal method and the closing rate method and the resulting sterling figures may quite properly be aggregated with the current values of assets and liabilities of the parent company. It would still be necessary to determine the treatment of resulting differences on exchange but a major problem would have disappeared.

There would still, of course, be other problems in connection with foreign currencies. In the examples above, we have assumed that our UK parent company prepares consolidated financial statements, so that sterling is the appropriate currency to use. Once we widen our horizons to look at a multinational company, which operates throughout the world and has shareholders in many countries, it is difficult to know even what the reporting currency should be, let alone what the resulting differences on exchange really mean.

To illustrate the sort of problem which we face, let us end this section with a very simple example.

Let us suppose that an individual habitually spends six months of every year in the UK and six months in the USA. On 1 January 20X2 he has wealth of $100 000 in the USA and £100 000 in the UK when the rate of exchange between the currencies is $2.0 to £1. During the year he lives on income arising in the respective countries and ends the year with exactly the same money wealth in each country when the exchange rate has moved to $1.5 to £1.

Let us compare his wealth at the beginning and end of the year in dollars and sterling, respectively:

	$	£
Opening wealth – 1 January 20X2		
(rate of exchange $2.0 to £1)		
UK, £100 000	200 000	100 000
USA, $100 000	100 000	50 000
	300 000	150 000
Closing wealth – 31 December 20X2		
(rate of exchange $1.5 to £1)		
UK, £100 000	150 000	100 000
USA, $100 000	100 000	66 667
	250 000	166 667
Gain during year	–	£16 667
Loss during year	$50 000	–

As can be seen, if we ignore changes in the purchasing power of the respective currencies, the translation process produces a loss of $50 000 or a gain of £16 667 during the year, even though our individual has the same money wealth at the end as he did at the beginning.

Problems such as those discussed above obviously bedevil the multinational company. Although such companies prepare their consolidated financial statements in the currency of the country where the parent company is situated, it must be admitted that the figures produced are of dubious significance to many shareholders.

A more complex example

Example 16.8 The closing rate/net investment method

(A) Some years ago, Home Country plc, a UK company, raised a long-term loan of $400 000 which it used to help purchase 80 per cent of the shares in Overseas Inc. at a total cost of $500 000.

(B) Relevant rates of exchange were as follows:

	Dollars to £1
At date of acquisition	5
On 31 December 20X1	4
On 31 December 20X2	3

(C) We shall first look at the treatment of the above transactions in the accounts of the parent company.

In accordance with the principles explained earlier in the chapter, the loan and investment would have originally been recorded at the following amounts:

Long-term loan ($400 000 ÷ 5)	£80 000
Investment in subsidiary ($500 000 ÷ 5)	£100 000

On 31 December 20X1 the loan would have been translated at the rate on that date and we shall assume that the company has also translated the investment at the closing rate at that date, as permitted by Para. 51 of SSAP 20. These items would have then appeared in the balance sheet as follows:

Home Country plc
Extract from balance sheet on 31 December 20X1

Long-term loan denominated in dollars	
$400 000 ÷ 4	£100 000
Investment in subsidiary	
$500 000 ÷ 4	£125 000

The difference on exchange between the date of acquisition and 31 December 20X1 would have been credited to reserves in past years, namely:

Exchange gain on equity investment	
£125 000 – £100 000	£25 000
less Exchange loss on dollar loan	
£100 000 – £80 000	£20 000
Net gain	£5 000

When the balance sheet on 31 December 20X2 is prepared, the foreign currency amounts will be translated at the closing rate of $3 to £1:

Home Country plc
Extract from balance sheet on 31 December 20X2

Long-term loan denominated in dollars
$400 000 ÷ 3 £133 333

Investment in subsidiary
$500 000 ÷ 3 £166 667

The difference on exchange to be treated as a movement on reserves in 20X2 in the financial statements of the parent company is therefore as follows:

Home Country plc
Part of movement on reserves for 20X2

Exchange gain on equity investment
£166 667 – £125 000 £41 667
less Exchange loss on dollar loan
£133 333 – £100 000 £33 333
Net gain £8 334

(D) The above figures for 20X2 are incorporated in the summarised financial statements of Home Country plc for the year ended 31 December 20X2 which appear below:

Home Country plc
Profit and loss account for the year ended 31 December 20X2

	£
Profit before taxation	117 000
Dividend receivable from Overseas Inc. (net)	
(80% of £20 000)	16 000
	133 000
less Taxation	60 000
	73 000
less Dividends payable	30 000
Retained profit for year	43 000

Home Country plc
Movement on reserves for the year ended 31 December 20X2

	£
Balance on 1 January 20X2	133 666
Retained profit for year	43 000
Difference on exchange	8 334
Balance on 31 December 20X2	185 000

Home Country plc
Balance sheet on 31 December 20X2

	£	£
Fixed assets		
Tangible assets		400 000
Investment in subsidiary (80% holding)		166 667
		566 667
Current assets		
Stocks	60 000	
Debtors	40 000	
Dividend receivable from Overseas Inc.	16 000	
Cash	5 666	
	121 666	
less Current liabilities	70 000	51 666
		618 333
less Long-term loans:		
Denominated in dollars	133 333	
Denominated in sterling	100 000	233 333
		385 000
Share capital		200 000
Reserves		185 000
		385 000

(E) We may now turn our attention to the financial statements of the overseas subsidiary.

The balance sheet of Overseas Inc. on 31 December 20X1 in dollars is given in the left-hand column below, while the relevant rates of exchange and resulting sterling amounts are given in the second and third columns, respectively. It has been assumed that the assets of Overseas Inc. were revalued at their fair values at the date of acquisition to produce a revaluation reserve of $150 000. Other reserves at the date of acquisition are assumed to have been $100 000.

Overseas Inc.
Balance sheet on 31 December 20X1

	$	*Rate of exchange*	£
Fixed assets			
At revalued amounts at date of acquisition and subsequent cost less depreciation	1 000 000	4(CR)	250 000
Current assets			
Stocks	300 000	4(CR)	75 000
Debtors	200 000	4(CR)	50 000
Cash	100 000	4(CR)	25 000
	600 000		150 000
less Current liabilities	400 000	4(CR)	100 000
Net current assets	200 000		50 000
	1 200 000		300 000
less Long-term loan	600 000	4(CR)	150 000
	600 000		150 000

Overseas Inc.
Balance sheet on 31 December 20X1 (continued)

	$	Rate of exchange	£
Share capital	100 000	5(HR)	20 000
Revaluation reserve – at date of acquisition by Home Country plc	150 000	5(HR)	30 000
Reserves			
Pre-acquisition	100 000	5(HR)	20 000
	350 000		70 000
Post-acquisition	250 000	Balance	80 000
	600 000		150 000

Notice that in translating the balance sheet, the share capital and pre-acquisition reserves have been translated at the historical rate at the date of acquisition with the intention of maintaining the goodwill on consolidation at its 'cost', which is:

	£
Cost of investment	100 000
less 80% of Net assets at their fair values 80% of £70 000	56 000
Purchased goodwill	44 000

This effectively treats the goodwill as a sterling asset, rather than a foreign asset, and appears to be the method envisaged by SSAP 20. While this articulated well with the regime of SSAP 22 under which goodwill was invariably written off immediately against reserves, it does not fit so comfortably with the FRS 10 approach under which goodwill continues to appear in consolidated balance sheets long after the acquisition of a subsidiary. If this goodwill is regarded as a foreign asset, rather than a sterling asset, then its cost would be $220 000, that is £44 000 translated at $5 to £1. If goodwill is regarded as a foreign asset, it should then be retranslated at the closing rate on each succeeding balance sheet date with any resulting difference on exchange being taken to reserves.

For ease of exposition, we shall continue to follow the former approach although we recognise that FRED 24 contains the proposal that purchased goodwill should be regarded as an asset of the foreign operation and hence translated at the closing rate on each balance sheet date.[29] For simplicity, we will also ignore any requirement to amortise goodwill over its expected useful economic life.

The balance of post-acquisition reserves, which is translated at £80 000, includes all exchange differences which have arisen since the date of acquisition. The size of these exchange differences depends upon when the post-acquisition reserves were earned and the rates of exchange prevailing at those dates. The less the fluctuation in exchange rates since acquisition, the lower will be the difference.

---

[29] FRED 24, Para. 45. This paragraph also requires that any fair value adjustments to the carrying values of assets and liabilities arising on the acquisition of a foreign operation should be treated as assets and liabilities of the foreign operation and hence translated at the closing rate on each balance sheet date. This has always been the case under UK GAAP and, unlike many US accountants, no UK accountant would consider doing anything different.

At first sight the use of historical rates for share capital and pre-acquisition reserves might be thought to be incorrect as far as the minority interest is concerned. However, the minority interest is 20 per cent of the net assets or total share capital and reserves, and the way in which the individual components of the share capital and reserves are translated has no effect on the total figure.

(F) The financial statements of Overseas Inc. for the year ended 31 December 20X2 are given below. The left-hand column is in dollars, the centre column gives the relevant rate of exchange and the right-hand column gives the resulting sterling figures.

The profit and loss account has been translated at the closing rate rather than the average rate and, as we have seen earlier in the chapter, this avoids one difference on exchange. A standard based upon FRED 24 would outlaw the use of both the closing rate and the average rate for it proposes that income and expenses shall be translated at exchange rates at the dates of the transactions, a much more complex process.[30]

Overseas Inc.
Profit and loss account for the year ended 31 December 20X2

	$	Rate of exchange (closing rate)	£
Operating profit	330 000	3	110 000
less Taxation	150 000	3	50 000
	180 000		60 000
less Dividends payable	60 000	3	20 000
Retained profit for year	120 000		40 000

Overseas Inc.
Balance sheet on 31 December 20X2

	$	Rate of exchange	£
Fixed assets			
At revalued amount or cost			
less depreciation	960 000	3	320 000
Current assets			
Stock	360 000	3	120 000
Debtors	240 000	3	80 000
Cash	160 000	3	53 333
	760 000		253 333
less Current liabilities			
(including dividend payable)	400 000	3	133 333
Net current assets	360 000		120 000
	1 320 000		440 000
less Long-term loan	600 000	3	200 000
	720 000		240 000

---

[30] FRED 24, Para. 37.

Overseas Inc.
Balance sheet on 31 December 20X2 (continued)

	$	Rate of exchange	£
Share capital	100 000	5(HR)	20 000
Revaluation reserve			
(created at date of acquisition)	150 000	5(HR)	30 000
Reserves			
Pre-acquisition	100 000	5(HR)	20 000
Post-acquisition			
		Per balance	
At 1 January 20X2	250 000	sheet 31.12.20X1	80 000
(Net assets on 1.1.20X2)	600 000	4	150 000
Post-acquisition			
		Per P and L	
Current year – 20X2	120 000	account	40 000
	720 000		190 000
Difference on exchange	–	Balance	50 000
	720 000		240 000

Note that the balance sheet contains a suitable analysis of reserves and, in particular, that it is necessary to translate the post-acquisition reserves so that they agree with the previous year's financial statements and with the profit and loss account balance for the year ended 31 December 20X2, respectively. An exchange gain of £50 000 emerges as the balancing figure. As the profit and loss account has been translated at the closing rate rather than the average rate, the whole of the difference on exchange relates to the opening net assets:

Difference on exchange

Opening net assets	$600 000	
Translation at beginning of year	$600 000 ÷ 4	£150 000
Translation at end of year	$600 000 ÷ 3	200 000
Gain on exchange		50 000

(G) In order to prepare consolidated financial statements, it is necessary to provide the usual analysis of the shareholders' interest in Overseas Inc. and to decide how to deal with the difference on exchange. In practice there will usually be many other adjustments in respect of such matters as unrealised intercompany profits, but these are problems faced on any consolidation and are therefore not dealt with here.

The shareholders' interest in Overseas Inc. may be analysed as follows:

Overseas Inc.
Analysis of shareholders' equity on 31 December 20X2

	Total £	Group 80% Pre-acquisition £	Post-acquisition £	Minority interest £
Share capital	20 000	16 000		4 000
Revaluation reserve	30 000	24 000		6 000
Other reserves				
Pre-acquisition	20 000	16 000		4 000
Post-acquisition				
At 1 January 20X2	80 000		64 000	16 000
Retained profit 20X2	40 000		32 000	8 000
Difference on exchange 20X2	50 000		40 000	10 000
	240 000	56 000	136 000	48 000
Cost of investment				
(original cost)		100 000		
Goodwill on consolidation		44 000		

(H) As shown in section (C) above, the financial statements of Home Country plc for 20X2 include an exchange gain on the equity investment of £41 667 and an exchange loss on the dollar loan of £33 333, together producing a net gain of £8334 which has been credited to reserves.

When we turn to the consolidated financial statements it is still possible to set the loss on the dollar loan, which appears in the parent company's financial statements, against the gain on the investment as permitted by SSAP 20, Para. 57. However, the appropriate exchange gain in the consolidated financial statements is the parent company's share of the exchange gain resulting from the translation of the subsidiary's financial statements, in this case 80 per cent of £50 000 = £40 000.

This treatment is in line with the general principle of consolidation whereby the cost of the investment in the parent company's balance sheet is replaced by the underlying net assets of the subsidiary.

As a consequence of this, the net difference on exchange, which is to be treated as a movement on reserves in the consolidated financial statements, will be:

	£
Gain on exchange in 20X2 in respect of Home Country's share of net assets in Overseas Inc., 80% of £50 000	40 000
less Loss on exchange in 20X2 in respect of dollar loan – per accounts of Home Country plc (see (C) above)	33 333
Net gain	6 667

(I) An adjustment similar to that discussed in (H) above is necessary to calculate the balance of consolidated reserves brought forward at 1 January 20X2.

It is insufficient just to add together the reserves of Home Country plc and 80 per cent of the post-acquisition reserves of Overseas Inc. As shown in section (C), the reserves of Home Country plc on 31 December 20X1 include the following net exchange gain made since acquisition:

	£
Exchange gain on equity investment	25 000
less Exchange loss on dollar loan	20 000
Net gain	5 000

While the exchange loss on the dollar loan may be properly charged against consolidated reserves, the relevant exchange gain in the consolidated financial statements is not that on the investment but the parent company's share of the gain on translating the subsidiary's financial statements. We do not know the amount of this exchange gain but we do know that it is included in the figure of £80 000 for post-acquisition reserves shown in (E) above.

The balance of consolidated reserves on 31 December 20X1, that is brought forward on 1 January 20X2, may therefore be calculated as follows:

	£
Home Country plc	
Per company's own balance sheet (see (D))	133 666
less Exchange gain on equity investment included in above figure (see this section above)	25 000
	108 666
Overseas Inc.	
Share of post-acquisition reserves at 1.1.20X2 including exchange differences on net assets since acquisition, 80% of £80 000 (see (E))	64 000
	172 666

(J)   We are now in a position to consolidate:

Home Country plc
Workings for consolidated profit and loss account for the year to 31 December 20X2

	£	£
Profit before taxation		
Home Country plc	117 000	
Overseas Inc.	110 000	227 000
less Taxation		
Home Country plc	60 000	
Overseas Inc.	50 000	110 000
		117 000
less Minority interest, 20% of (£110 000 – £50 000)		12 000
		105 000
less Dividends payable by parent company		30 000
Retained profit for the year		75 000

Workings for movement on reserves for year to 31 December 20X2

	£	£
Balance on 1 January 20X2 (per (I) above)		172 666
Retained profit for year – per consolidated profit and loss account above		75 000
Exchange gain (per (H) above)		
Gain on net assets	40 000	
less Loss on foreign currency borrowings	33 333	6 667
Balance on 31 December 20X2		254 333

Workings for consolidated balance sheet on 31 December 20X2

	£	£
Fixed assets		
Intangible assets		
Goodwill on consolidation – at cost per analysis of equity		
interest (see (G))		44 000
Tangible assets – at net book value		
Home Country plc	400 000	
Overseas Inc. (see note (a))	320 000	720 000
Net current assets (see note (b))		
Home Country plc	51 666	
Overseas Inc.	120 000	171 666
		935 666
less Long-term loans		
Home Country plc	233 333	
Overseas Inc.	200 000	433 333
		502 333
Share capital		200 000
Reserves – as above		254 333
		454 333
Minority interest, per analysis of equity interest		48 000
		502 333

Notes:

(a)   Note that the revalued amount of the fixed assets of Overseas Inc. at the date of acquisition represents 'cost' to the group.

(b)   An adjustment is necessary to cancel out the dividend receivable by Home Country plc. The amount is £16 000 but the effect on the total net current assets is, of course, nil.

It is now relatively straightforward to prepare the consolidated financial statements for publication in the normal manner, although a greater amount of detail would be necessary to satisfy the disclosure requirements of company law and accounting standards.

Note that, in order to simplify the example and concentrate on the translation process, we have assumed that purchased goodwill is a sterling asset, rather than a foreign asset, and that it has not been amortised. As explained above, FRED 24 proposes that purchased goodwill be treated as a foreign asset to be retranslated at each balance sheet date. FRS 10 *Goodwill and Intangible Assets* requires that positive purchased goodwill be amortised over its useful economic life.[31]

The international accounting standard

Although IAS 21 *Accounting for the Effects of Changes in Exchange Rates*, was first issued in 1983, it was reconsidered as part of the IASC comparability and improvements project and issued in a revised form as IAS 21 *The Effects of Changes in Foreign Exchange Rates* in

[31] See Chapter 13 for a comprehensive discussion of goodwill.

November 1993. This revised version was issued some 10 years after the issue of SSAP 20 and some 12 years after the issue of the US FAS 95 *Foreign Translation,* in December 1981. All three statements are based upon the same underlying principles although these are expressed rather differently. Inevitably, there are differences in detail.

In particular, IAS 21 makes it clear that it does not deal with hedge accounting except for items which hedge a net investment in a foreign entity; some guidance on hedge accounting has subsequently been provided in IAS 39 *Financial Instruments: Recognition and Measurement* (revised 2000).

Leaving this on one side, IAS 21 requires the same method of accounting for foreign currency transactions as SSAP 20. Thus transactions are initially recorded at the actual or spot rate of exchange. At subsequent balance sheet dates, non-monetary items must be translated at the historical rate, unless they are shown at a subsequent fair value, in which case the rate at the date on which the fair value was established must be used. Monetary assets and liabilities must normally be retranslated at the closing rate and any differences on exchange must be taken to the profit and loss account. The international standard does not have to concern itself with the thorny problem of whether exchange gains/losses are realised or unrealised, which bedevils discussion of this and many other topics in the UK. A cover method is required where a foreign currency liability is accounted for as a hedge of an enterprise's net investment in a foreign entity (see below) but the cumulative exchange differences relating to the investment should be recognised in the profit and loss account in the same period that the company recognises the gain or loss on disposal of the investment.

When we turn to the translation of foreign financial statements as a preliminary to some form of consolidation, IAS 21 distinguishes between a foreign entity, the activities of which are not an integral part of those of the reporting enterprise, and a foreign operation that is integral to the operations of the reporting enterprise. It requires the use of the closing rate/net investment method for the former and the temporal method for the latter. Thus it adopts the basic approach of SSAP 20 although it uses different terminology. However, in the context of the closing rate method to be used for foreign entities, it specifically requires that income and expense items should be translated at the exchange rates at the dates of transactions rather than the average rate for the period or closing rate as required by SSAP 20. Given the conceptual deficiencies of the closing rate method, discussed earlier in this chapter, this would seem to achieve spurious accuracy.

IAS 21 specifically refers to the treatment of goodwill and fair value adjustments within the context of the closing rate method. It allows these to be translated either at the historical rate or at the closing rate. Thus, as we explained in Example 16.8 in the context of a UK parent, they may be treated either as a sterling asset or as a foreign currency asset.

The disclosure requirements of IAS 21 are more stringent than SSAP 20. In particular, the requirements of the international accounting standard include disclosure of: [32]

(a) the amount of exchange differences included in the net profit or loss for the period;
(b) net exchange differences classified as equity as a separate component of equity, and a reconciliation of the amount of such exchange differences at the beginning and end of the period;
(c) the method selected . . . to translate goodwill and fair value adjustments arising on the acquisition of a foreign entity.

---

[32] See IAS 21, Paras 42–47 for full disclosure requirements.

The proposed new standards

As we have explained in Chapter 3, the IASB published an exposure draft of proposed Improvements to International Accounting Standards in May 2002. This exposure draft contained proposed replacements for 12 international accounting standards, one of which was IAS 21 *The Effects of Changes in Foreign Exchange Rates*. In the same month, the ASB issued FRED 24, which attempts to bring UK standard practice for foreign currency transactions and translations into line with the proposals of the IASB. Hence in this, as in many other areas of accounting, the ASB is shooting at a moving target!

While the IASB exposure draft makes no major changes in accounting for foreign currencies, it uses rather different terminology to the present IAS 21 and will have some considerable impact on UK practice if the proposals of FRED 24 are adopted. In keeping with the approach that we have adopted in this chapter, we will outline first the proposed changes in accounting for foreign currency transactions and second the changes in the translation of foreign currency financial statements.

The exposure draft requires the same approach to the translation of foreign currency transactions as that explained in this chapter, with the exception that contracted and forward exchange rates may only be used at the date of a transaction where hedge accounting techniques are used in accordance with a proposed replacement for IAS 39. As IAS 39 only applies to financial instruments, forward exchange contracts related to the purchase of goods and services will not be covered, although loans raised to hedge an investment in foreign equity shares will continue to be covered, provided some more stringent conditions are satisfied. Hence foreign currency transactions will usually be recorded initially using the spot rate of exchange at the date of the transaction and the choice between the spot rate and the forward rate, permitted by SSAP 20, will no longer be available.

With regard to the translation of foreign currency financial statements as a preliminary to consolidation, the exposure draft requires a similar approach to that of the current IAS 21 but uses rather different terminology. It distinguishes between a functional currency, the currency of the primary economic environment in which an entity operates, and a presentational currency, the currency in which the financial statements are presented. It proposes to permit companies to use any presentational currency they choose.

Where a foreign operation has the same functional currency as the parent, the foreign currency financial statements are to be translated as if the parent company had entered into the foreign currency transactions itself. In other words, the temporal method is to be used. Where the foreign operation has a different functional currency to the parent, the closing rate method should be used. It is in the application of the closing rate method that some important changes will be necessary in the UK.

The exposure draft proposes that, where the closing rate method is used, the income and expenses in the profit and loss account of the foreign entity shall be translated at exchange rates at the dates of transactions. This is, of course, far more complex than the use of the closing rate or average rate under SSAP 20 and, given the nonsense of the numbers produced by the closing rate method, appears to the authors to be aiming for spurious accuracy. The exposure draft also proposes that purchased goodwill and fair value adjustments arising on the acquisition of a foreign subsidiary should be regarded as foreign currency assets and hence retranslated at each balance sheet date. Under UK GAAP, fair value adjustments are always included as adjustments to the values of assets and liabilities of the subsidiary and hence would always have been retranslated at closing rates. However there has been no such consistency with the treatment of goodwill and the proposals, if taken forward, would lead to a more standard, although rather simplistic, treatment in this area.

The cover method, whereby exchange gains or losses on foreign currency borrowings may be offset against the losses or gains on the investment in a foreign operation will only be permitted if hedge accounting procedures are employed in accordance with the provisions of a revised IAS 39 *Financial Instruments: Recognition and Measurement*.

Finally, as we pointed out in Chapter 11, there is a fundamental difference of opinion between the ASB and the IASB on the issue of the recycling of gains and losses. Both IAS 21 and FRED 24 require gains or losses arising on a net investment in a foreign entity to be taken to reserves and, in the UK, these would be reported in the Statement of Total Recognised Gains and Losses (STRGL). Both the existing and proposed international accounting standards require accumulated exchange differences, which have been taken to reserves, to be recognised in the profit and loss account of the period in which the investment is sold. The ASB does not intend to permit such recycling of exchange gains and losses. As we have seen in Chapter 11, the ASB takes the view that once a gain or loss is reported in the STRGL, it cannot be reported a second time in the profit and loss account. Given that the vast majority of countries do not require the publication of a STRGL at all, let alone as a primary statement, it is hard to see how convergence will be achieved on this point!

Summary

In this chapter, we examined both the accounting treatment of foreign currency transactions undertaken by a UK company and the translation of the foreign currency financial statements of a subsidiary as a preliminary step to the preparation of consolidated financial statements.

We discussed the treatment of foreign currency transactions through a series of examples and have explained how SSAP 20 requires such transactions to be dealt with. We have explained some of the limitations of this SSAP 20 approach, including its approval of alternative approaches when forward exchange contracts are employed, the confusion surrounding what are and are not realised profits and the use of the cover method when foreign currency borrowings are invested in equity shares but not when they are invested in other equally saleable assets.

We then turned to the translation of foreign currency financial statements as a preliminary to the preparation of consolidated financial statements. While we have concentrated on a foreign subsidiary, we provided principles which are applicable to accounting for foreign associates and joint ventures as well. We identified two main methods of translation, namely the closing rate/net investment method and the temporal method, illustrated both of these and explained when SSAP 20 requires each to be applied. We explained the severe weaknesses of both methods and demonstrated why the SSAP 20 solution represents a compromise between two far from perfect alternatives. We then provided a more complex example of the closing rate/net investment method, which is the most common method in use in the UK.

Finally we examined the provisions of the international accounting standard IAS 21, and outlined the changes proposed by the exposure draft of Proposed Improvements to International Standards, issued by the IASB in May 2002, and reflected in the ASB FRED 24, published in that same month.

Recommended reading

Chartered Association of Certified Accountants, *The operation of SSAP 20 – a survey of opinion on the functioning of SSAP20 'Foreign currency translation'*, ACCA, London, 1992.

ICAEW, *The effects of changes in foreign exchange rates*, ICAEW Technical release TECH:12/02, London, 2002.

I.J. Martin, *Accounting and Control in the Foreign Exchange Market*, 2nd edn, Butterworths, London, 1993.

C. Nobes, 'A review of the translation debate', *Accounting and Business Research Number 40*, ICAEW, London, Autumn 1980.

C. Nobes and R. Parker, *Comparative International Accounting*, 7th edn, Financial Times Prentice Hall, Harlow, 2002: Chapter 17 ,'Foreign currency translation' by John Flower.

J. Pearcy, *How to Account for Foreign Currencies*, Macmillan, Basingstoke, 1984.

L. Revsine, 'The rationale underlying the functional currency choice', in *Accounting Theory and Policy*, R. Bloom and P.T. Elgers (eds), Harcourt Brace Jovanovich, Orlando, USA, 1987.

C.A. Westwick, *Accounting for Overseas Operations*, Gower, Aldershot, 1986.

Readers are also referred to the latest edition of *UK and International GAAP* by Ernst & Young, which provides much greater detailed coverage of this and other topics in this book. At the time of writing, the most recent edition is the 7th, A. Wilson, M. Davies, M. Curtis and G. Wilkinson-Riddle (eds), Butterworths Tolley, London, 2001. The relevant chapter is 8.

Questions

16.1 You are the Chief Accountant of JKL plc, a UK company that has three wholly-owned overseas subsidiaries.

- Company A is located in Spain. The company assembles computer terminals from materials provided by JKL plc. Once assembled, the computer terminals are shipped to the UK where JKL plc sells them.

- Company B is located in Singapore and produces computers using materials supplied by local companies. Company B sells the computers to customers throughout southeast Asia.

- Company C, operated on the same basis as Company A, is located in a country where recent legislation forbids the ownership of companies by foreign nationals and where strict currency and import/export controls have been introduced. These currency controls mean that JKL plc is unable to sell its interest in Company C.

You are required to explain how each of the three subsidiaries would be dealt with in the consolidated financial statements of JKL plc.

CIMA, Advanced Financial Accounting, May 1994   (15 marks)

16.2 You are the consolidation accountant of Home plc. Home plc is incorporated in the United Kingdom and prepares its financial statements using UK Accounting Standards. Home plc has a subsidiary, Away Ltd. Away Ltd is incorporated in a country that has the Tot as its unit of currency. The accepted abbreviation for the Tot is 'T'. The financial statements of Home plc and Away Ltd for the year ended 30 June 2001 are given opposite:

Balance sheets at 30 June 2001

	Home plc		Away Ltd	
	£000	£000	T000	T000
Fixed assets:				
Tangible assets	30 000		50 000	
Investment in Away Ltd	14 000			
		44 000		50 000
Current assets:				
Stocks	10 000		16 000	
Debtors	12 000		18 000	
Cash in hand	60		80	
	22 060		34 080	
Creditors failing due within one year:				
Trade creditors	7 000		11 000	
Taxation	1 000		2 000	
Proposed dividends	1 000		2 000	
Bank overdraft	3 000		5 000	
	12 000		20 000	
Net current assets		10 060		14 080
Total assets less current liabilities		54 060		64 080
Capital and reserves:				
Called up share capital (£1/T1 shares)		25 000		40 000
Profit and loss account		29 060		24 080
		54 060		64 080

Profit and loss accounts for the year ended 30 June 2001

	Home plc	Away Ltd
	£000	T000
Turnover	12 000	20 000
Cost of sales	(6 000)	(10 000)
Gross profit	6 000	10 000
Other operating expenses	(3 000)	(5 000)
Operating profit	3 000	5 000
Interest payable	(100)	(200)
Profit before tax	2 900	4 800
Tax	(900)	(1 600)
Profit after tax	2 000	3 200
Proposed dividends	(1 000)	(2 000)
Retained profit	1 000	1 200
Retained profit – 1 July 2000	28 060	22 880
Retained profit – 30 June 2001	29 060	24 080

Notes to the financial statements

1 On 1 July 1995, Home plc purchased 30 million shares in Away Ltd for 42 million Tots. The balance on the profit and loss account of Away Ltd on 1 July 1995 was 8 million Tots. Away Ltd has not issued any additional shares since 1 July 1995. Goodwill on consolidation is amortised over 10 years.

2 Home plc has not made any entries in its financial statements regarding the dividend receivable from Away Ltd.

3 On 30 June 2001, Home plc invoiced Away Ltd for a management charge of £250000 for the year ended 30 June 2001. This amount was included in the turnover and debtors of Home plc. Away Ltd received the invoice before closing its books for the year ended 30 June 2001 and entered it using the closing rate of exchange to translate the sum into Tots. The relevant amount was included in the other operating expenses and trade creditors of Away Ltd. There was no other trading between the two companies.

4 Relevant rates of exchange are as follows:

Date	Exchange rate (Tots to £l)
1 July 1995	3
30 June 2000	3.75
30 June 2001	4
Average for the year ended 30 June 2001	3.85

5 In previous years, the financial statements of Away Ltd have been translated into sterling for consolidation purposes using the closing rate method. The average rate of exchange for the year has been used to translate the profit and loss account. Exchange differences have been recognised in the consolidated statement of total recognised gains and losses. A junior accountant is puzzled by this treatment and has approached you for clarification. He cannot understand how the consolidated financial statements show a true and fair view if possibly significant exchange differences by-pass the consolidated profit and loss account.

Required

(a) Translate the balance sheet of Away Ltd into sterling (£) using the closing rate method.

(6 marks)

(b) Prepare the consolidated balance sheet of the Home group at 30 June 2001.

(12 marks)

(c) Prepare the consolidated profit and loss account of the Home group for the year ended 30 June 2001. You should start with turnover and end with retained profit for the year.

(6 marks)

(d) Prepare a statement that reconciles the opening and closing reserves of the Home group. [*Marks will be awarded for deriving each figure in the reconciliation, including exchange differences arising on consolidation.*]

(11 marks)

(e) Prepare a memorandum to the junior accountant that justifies the fact that exchange differences by-pass the consolidated profit and loss account and summarises recent developments regarding the destination of gains and losses in the performance statements.

(5 marks)

CIMA, Financial Reporting – UK Accounting Standards, November 2001   **(40 marks)**

16.3 Shott, a public limited company, set up a wholly owned foreign subsidiary company, Hammer, on 1 June 1999 with a share capital of 400000 ordinary shares of 1 dinar. Shott transacts on a limited basis with Hammer. It maintains a current account with the company but very few transactions are processed through this account. Shott is a multinational company with net assets of £1500 million and 'normal' profits are approximately £160 million. The management of Hammer are all based locally although Shott does have a representative on the management board. The prices of the products of Hammer are determined locally and 90% of sales are to local companies. Most of the finance required by Hammer is raised locally, although occasionally short term finance is raised through borrowing monies from Shott. Hammer has made profits of 80 000 dinars and 120 000 dinars after dividend payments respectively for the two years to 31 May 2001. During the financial year to 31 May 2001, the following transactions took place:

(i)   On 30 September 2000, a dividend from Hammer of 0.15 dinars per share was declared. The dividend was received on 1 January 2001 by Shott.

(ii) Hammer sold goods of 24 000 dinars to Shott during the year. Hammer made 25% profit on the cost of the goods. The goods were ordered by Shott on 30 September 2000, were shipped free on board (fob) on 1 January 2001, and were received by Shott on 31 January 2001. Shott paid the dinar amount on 31 May 2001 and had not hedged the transaction. All the goods remain unsold as at 31 May 2001.

(iii) Hammer has borrowed 150 000 dinars on 31 January 2001 from Shott in order to alleviate its working capital problems. At 31 May 2001 Hammer's financial statements showed the amount as owing to Shott. The loan is to be treated as permanent and is designated in pounds sterling.

The directors of Shott wish to use the closing rate to translate the balance sheet of Hammer and the average rate to translate the profit and loss account of Hammer but are unsure as to whether this is possible under accounting standards. On 1 June 2001 Hammer was sold for 825 000 dinars, and the proceeds were received on that day.

		Dinars to £1
Exchange rates:	1 June 1999	1.0
	31 May 2000	1.3
	30 September 2000	1.1
	1 January 2001	1.2
	31 January 2001	1.5
	31 May 2001	1.6
	1 June 2001	1.65
Average rate for year to 31 May 2001		1.44

Required

(a) (i)   **Advise Shott as to whether the temporal or closing rate/net investment method should be used to translate the financial statements of Hammer;**   (6 marks)

     (ii) **Discuss the claim by SSAP 20** *Foreign Currency Translation,* **that the usage of the temporal or net investment/closing rate method is based upon the economic relationship between the holding company and its foreign subsidiary.**   (5 marks)

(b) **Discuss how the above transactions should be dealt with in the consolidated financial statements of Shott, calculating the gain or loss on the disposal of Hammer on 1 June 2001 and stating how the cumulative exchange differences would be dealt with on the disposal.**   (14 marks)

ACCA, Financial Reporting Environment (UK Stream), June 2001   **(25 marks)**

16.4 Howard plc acquired 2 100 000 ordinary shares of Kroner 1 in Pau Ltd on 1 January 1985 when the reserves of Pau Ltd were Kr1 500 000 and the exchange rate was Kr10 to £1. Goodwill was eliminated against the consolidated reserves on 31 December 1985.

The profit and loss accounts of Howard plc and Pau Ltd for the year ended 31 December 1992 were as follows:

	Howard	Pau
	£000	Kr000
Turnover	9 225	94 500
Cost of sales	6 027	63 000
Gross profit	3 198	31 500
Distribution cost	1 290	7 550
Administrative expenses	1 469	2 520
Depreciation	191	2 100
	248	19 330
Dividends from subsidiary	315	
	563	19 330
Tax	195	7 570
Profit on ordinary activities after tax	368	11 760
Dividends paid 30.6.92	183	4 200
Retained profit for the year	185	7 560

The balance sheets of Howard plc and Pau Ltd as at 31 December 1992 were as follows:

	Howard	Pau
	£000	Kr000
Fixed assets		
Tangible assets	1 765	38 500
Investment in Pau Ltd	305	
Current assets		
Stock	2 245	3 675
Debtors	615	1 750
Cash	156	9 450
	3 016	14 875
Current liabilities		
Trade creditors	(2 245)	(4 375)
Creditors falling due after more than 1 year		
Loan	(1 230)	(8 680)
	1 611	40 320
Capital and reserves		
Share capital in £1 ordinary shares	600	
Share capital in Kr 1 ordinary shares		3 500
Profit and loss account	1 011	36 820
	1 611	40 320

The tangible assets of Pau Ltd were acquired 1 January 1985 and are stated at cost less depreciation.

Stocks represent six months' purchases and at 31 December 1991 the stock held by Pau Ltd amounted to Kr4 760 000.

Exchange rates have been as follows:

	Kroner to £1
1 January 1985	10
30 June 1991	10.5
30 September 1991	10
31 December 1991	9.5
Average for 1992	8
30 June 1992	8
30 September 1992	7.5
31 December 1992	7

In determining the appropriate method of currency translation, it is established that the trade of Pau Ltd is more dependent on the economic environment of the investing company's currency than on that of its own reporting currency.

Required
(a) Explain briefly how it would be established that the trade of Pau Ltd is more dependent on the economic environment of the investing company's currency than on that of its own reporting currency. (4 marks)
(b) Prepare the consolidated profit and loss account for the year ended 31 December 1992 and a balance sheet as at that date, using the temporal method of translation. (22 marks)
(c) Calculate the amount to be included in the consolidated balance sheet of the Howard Group as at 31 December 1992 if Howard plc had sold goods to Pau Ltd on 30 September 1992 for £14 000 which had cost £10 000 and which remained unsold at 31 December 1992 using:
   (i) the closing rate method;
   (ii) the temporal method. (4 marks)

ACCA, Advanced Financial Accounting, June 1993   **(30 marks)**

16.5 The balance sheets of UK plc and its subsidiaries France SA and US Inc at 30 September 1998 (the accounting date for all three companies) are given below:

	UK plc £000	UK plc £000	France SA Fr000	France SA Fr000	US Inc $000	US Inc $000
Fixed assets						
Tangible assets	26 000		95 000		56 000	
Investments (Notes 1 & 2)	25 500		–		–	
		51 500		95 000		56 000
Current assets						
Stocks (Note 3)	15 000		44 000		25 000	
Debtors (Note 4)	10 000		30 000		16 000	
Cash in hand	2 000		6 000		3 000	
	27 000		80 000		44 000	
Current liabilities						
Trade creditors (Note 4)	6 000		12 000		8 000	
Taxation	3 000		6 000		4 000	
Proposed dividend	2 000		8 000		3 000	
Bank overdraft	8 000		10 000		9 000	
	19 000		36 000		24 000	
Net current assets		8 000		44 000		20 000
c/f		59 500		139 000		76 000

	UK plc		France SA		US Inc	
	£000	£000	Fr000	Fr000	$000	$000
b/f		59 500		139 000		76 000
Long-term loans		(20 000)		–		(25 000)
		39 500		139 000		51 000
Capital and reserves						
Share capital (Note 5)		20 000		80 000		32 000
Profit and loss account		19 500		59 000		19 000
		39 500		139 000		51 000

Notes to the financial statements

Note 1

UK plc has owned 100% of the ordinary share capital of France SA since incorporation, subscribing for it at par. The date of incorporation of France SA was 25 May 1990. France SA acts as a selling agent for products manufactured in the UK by UK plc and has no manufacturing capacity of its own. UK plc has negotiated an overdraft facility for France SA and has guaranteed the overdraft. Apart from this overdraft, France SA receives all its funding from UK plc.

Note 2

On 30 September 1992, when the reserves of US Inc stood at $8 million, UK plc purchased 24 million shares in US Inc for $35 million. US Inc has a product range which is similar to that of UK plc and France SA, but is targeted more specifically towards the needs of the US market. The stock is manufactured in the USA, and US Inc negotiates its own day-to-day financing needs with US financial institutions. The $25 million loan which was outstanding at 30 September 1998 was originally taken out on 30 June 1976 for a 30-year period. The accounting policy of UK plc is to amortise premiums on acquisition over a 20-year period. In the case of US Inc, the first write-off took place in the year ended 30 September 1993.

Note 3

The stocks of France SA were acquired from UK plc on 31 August 1998. They represent a consignment which cost UK plc £3.6 million to manufacture but were invoiced to France SA at a price of 44 million Francs. This price represented the sterling transfer price of £4 million translated at the spot rate of exchange in force at 31 August 1998. The stocks of US Inc were all manufactured locally. The stock in hand of US Inc at 30 September 1998 represents 6 months' production.

Note 4

- The debtors of UK plc include dividends receivable from France SA and US Inc. These debtors have been translated into sterling using the rate of exchange in force at 30 September 1998.
- The trade creditors of France SA comprise 12 million Francs payable to UK plc. UK plc's debtors include the equivalent asset translated into sterling using the rate of exchange in force at 30 September 1998.
- There was no other inter-company trading.

Note 5

- The shares of UK plc are £1 shares.
- The shares of France SA are 1 Franc shares.
- The shares of US Inc are $1 shares.

Note 6

The dates of acquisition of the tangible fixed assets of France SA and US Inc were as follows:

30 September 1998 – Net Book Value of Fixed Assets

	France SA	*US Inc*
Date	Fr million	$ million
25 May 1990	10 000	2 000
30 September 1993	45 000	20 000
30 September 1997	40 000	34 000
	95 000	56 000

Note 7

Exchange rates at relevant dates were as follows:

Date	*£/Fr rate*	*£/$ rate*
25 May 1990	10	2.4
30 September 1992	9.5	2.0
30 September 1993	9	1.7
30 September 1997	10	1.6
31 March 1998	10.5	1.7
31 August 1998	11	1.8
30 September 1998	12	1.8

Requirements

(a) Explain how the financial statements [profit and loss account and balance sheet] of France SA and US Inc will be translated into sterling for the purposes of the consolidated financial statements of UK plc. Your answer should refer to relevant Accounting Standards and should explain the treatment of the exchange difference on translation in each case. (10 marks)

(b) Prepare the working schedule for the consolidated balance sheet of the UK plc group at 30 September 1998. Your schedule needs to show only one figure for consolidated reserves, so a separate analysis of the exchange differences is not required. (30 marks)

CIMA, Financial Reporting, November 1998　　　　　　　　　　　　　**(40 marks)**

16.6 One of the frequent criticisms of SSAP 20, *Foreign currency translation*, is that exchange differences on net investments in foreign enterprises, and on borrowings which are a hedge, never pass through the profit and loss account.

Discuss the validity of this criticism and suggest a possible solution to the perceived problem.

ICAEW, Financial Accounting 2, July 1993　　　　　　　　　　　　　**(13 marks)**

Expansion of the annual report

overview

The size of the annual reports of companies, particularly those of listed companies, has grown substantially as directors have chosen to provide much more information than is required by law. While much of this increased disclosure has been required or encouraged by the Stock Exchange and the ASB, much is provided voluntarily. It seems likely, on the basis of the Government White Paper, *Modernising Company Law*, published in July 2002, that there will be a considerable increase in the amount of information required by law. In this chapter, we examine a number of statements with which accountants need to be familiar, namely:

- Cash Flow Statement
- Operating and Financial Review
- Historical Summary
- Reporting about and to employees
- Summary Financial Statement

We therefore draw upon the following official pronouncements:

- FRS 1 *Cash Flow Statements* (revised 1996)
- IAS 7 *Cash Flow Statements* (revised 1992)
- ASB Statement *Operating and Financial Review* (1993)
- ED *Revision of the Statement Operating and Financial Review* (2002)

The Accounting Standards Board has also attempted to regulate other parts of the annual reporting package of listed companies and we shall conclude with a brief look at two recent ASB Statements:

- *Interim Reports* (1997)
- *Preliminary Announcements* (1998)

We outline the changes proposed by the White Paper in relevant sections of the chapters.

Introduction

Traditionally a set of accounts, as financial statements used to be described, consisted of just two statements albeit supported by, often voluminous, notes. The balance sheet summarised the position at the end of an accounting year while the profit and loss account explained what had happened since the previous balance sheet. Neither document pretended to tell the whole story and, in particular, the profit and loss account was uncomfortable about reporting increases in value not caused by operations. We have seen, in earlier chapters, how accounting practice has developed to deal with some of the deficiencies of the traditional approach by the introduction of a new primary statement, the Statement of Total

Recognised Gains and Losses, and a requirement for a Reconciliation of Movements in Shareholders' Funds. We have also examined proposals to replace the profit and loss account and statement of total recognised gains and losses by a single performance statement.[1] Such statements serve to provide a more coherent description of how things have changed but remain firmly based on the traditional reporting model.

In this chapter, we will discuss some different approaches to reporting. The differences come in varying forms. Some of the statements which we will consider, such as the Cash Flow Statement, try to provide a different perspective on what has happened during the year. Others, such as the historical summary and operating and financial review, provide a context for the current year's report. Other statements, such as the simplified statements prepared for shareholders and employees, attempt to address the needs of particular user groups. Yet other reports, namely interim reports and preliminary announcements, seek to provide users with more timely information.

While the statements discussed in this chapter share the common feature that they are not at present required by company law, they are certainly not all produced on a consistent basis. Some are widespread because they are required by the Stock Exchange or the Accounting Standards Board (ASB); examples of these are Interim Reports and Cash Flow Statements. Others are produced by some companies but not by others; examples are historical summaries, operating and financial reviews and simplified reports. However, all of these statements provide an important and different perspective on the activities of a company and are therefore all worthy of examination.

In broad terms the objectives of most additional statements are the same – to assist the users of financial statements to obtain a more comprehensive view of the progress and future prospects of the company. This broad objective can be served in a number of ways and it is helpful to have a framework within which the statements can be analysed. Essentially the statements can be seen as constituting two groups, depending on whether a statement:

(a) provides more data than are required by company law, or
(b) does not provide additional data but makes it easier to assimilate the data either by rearrangement of the figures or through the provision of simplified statements.

We might usefully refer to the first group as 'extended' statements and the second as 'rearranged and simplified' statements.

Extended statements include such documents as the Cash Flow Statement and Employment Report as well as the Operating and Financial Review.

Rearranged and simplified statements can be derived from the published financial statements of the company, except in the case of smaller companies, and include such documents as the simplified report to employees and the Summary Financial Statement which may be sent to the shareholders of listed companies.

It is interesting to question why companies should be required or should choose to publish such rearranged and simplified statements. In part, the reason may be behavioural in the sense that the publication of the document is intended to create better relations with employees and the community in general. Such an objective is clearly present in the case of simplified financial statements prepared especially for employees. Another possible reason is the wish to remove the 'competitive advantage' possessed by investors and potential investors who have technical knowledge themselves or have ready access to professional advice.[2]

---

[1] See Chapter 11, pp. 292–6.
[2] Supporters of the 'efficient market hypothesis' which, in its semistrong form, states that all available data relevant to the price of a share are immediately reflected in the market price, would presumably take the view that there is nothing to be gained from any requirement for companies to publish otherwise available data in a different form.

The first major developments in the drive towards the expansion of the annual report came in 1975 when the Accounting Standards Steering Committee issued both SSAP 10 *Statements of Source and Application of Funds*, and *The Corporate Report*.[3] SSAP 10 required all but very small enterprises to prepare a statement of source and application of funds as part of their audited financial accounts. It has since been superseded by FRS 1 *Cash Flow Statements*, first issued in September 1991 but subsequently revised in October 1996. *The Corporate Report* argued that the then current reporting practices did not fully meet the needs of the various users of accounts and recommended that all significant economic entities should publish the following additional statements:

(a) a statement of value added;
(b) an employment report;
(c) a statement of money exchanges with government;
(d) a statement of transactions in foreign currency;
(e) a statement of future prospects;
(f) a statement of corporate objectives.

The adoption of these recommendations would have resulted in the provision of substantially more information than that provided by the statutory financial accounts. While *The Corporate Report* remains an important document worthy of study, none of these recommendations has in fact been adopted by the ASC or ASB except to the the extent that some companies are encouraged to prepare an Operating and Financial Review, which is concerned in part with future prospects.

Even without legislative requirements, it is clear that the accountant must develop competence in producing and interpreting statements other than the traditional balance sheet and profit and loss account. In this chapter, we concentrate on the Cash Flow Statement and then examine, more briefly, the Operating and Financial Review, the Historical Summary, the subject of reporting about and to employees and the Summary Financial Statement which listed companies may send to their shareholders instead of the full financial statements. Finally, we examine the recent attempts of the ASB to regulate Interim Reports and Preliminary Announcements.

The Government White Paper, *Modernising Company Law*, published in July 2002,[4] makes a number of proposals in this area, which we outline in the relevant sections.

Cash flow statements

Background

It has long been recognised that the information provided by a balance sheet and profit and loss account gives users limited help in understanding how the liquidity of a company or group has been affected by its activities during a particular year. To remedy this, accounting standard setters in many countries required companies to prepare 'funds statements', that is statements showing the sources and applications of funds. So, in the UK, SSAP 10 *Statement of Source and Application of Funds*, first issued in July 1975, required all but the smallest companies to prepare such a statement.

---

[3] Accounting Standards Steering Committee, *The Corporate Report*, London, 1975.
[4] Cm. 5553-I and II.

One of the first difficulties which companies encountered in complying with SSAP 10 was that, although the statement defined net liquid funds as one component of funds, it did not actually define the term funds. As with profit, there are many possible definitions of funds including cash, working capital and all financial resources. The choice of definition determines what the statement seeks to explain and hence what is shown as a source or application. To take a simple example, the receipt of cash from debtors is a source of funds if the cash concept is adopted, but merely a change in the constituent parts of funds if the working capital concept is used. As a second example, the issue of shares in exchange for the purchase of fixed assets is neither a source nor an application if either the cash or working capital concepts are used, but it certainly changes the financial resources of a company.

In the USA, the funds statement had long been the subject of criticism[5] and, in November 1987, the FASB replaced the requirement for US companies to produce a funds statement with a requirement for them to produce a statement of cash flows, Statement of Financial Accounting Standards number 95, *Statement of Cash Flows*, which requires relevant US companies to prepare a statement explaining the change in cash and cash equivalents by showing cash receipts and payments.

Both the UK accounting standard setters and the International Accounting Standards Committee drew on this US standard in preparing FRS 1, *Cash Flow Statements* (1991) and IAS 7 *Cash Flow Statements* (1992) respectively. However, FRS 1 was revised in October 1996 and, in the revised version, the ASB has moved some considerable way from both the US and the international approach, which we shall discuss later in the chapter.

FRS 1 requires all relevant UK entities to prepare a Cash Flow Statement as one of its primary financial statements. The revised standard applies to all financial statements intended to give a true and fair view of financial position and profit or loss. Exemptions are, however, given to a number of entities, including small companies, subsidiary undertakings where 90 per cent or more of the voting rights are controlled within the group (provided relevant consolidated accounts are publicly available), as well as more specialised institutions such as pension funds and certain open-ended investment funds.[6]

While there is no legal requirement for companies to prepare a Cash Flow Statement at present, the White Paper, *Modernising Company Law* (July 2002) proposes that such a requirement should be included in the next Companies Act.[7] However, in keeping with its proposals on the form and content of financial statements generally, which we discussed in Chapter 2, the White Paper envisages that the specification of the detailed rules on the form and content of the Cash Flow Statement should be delegated to a new Standards Board. Hence, there is likely to be little change to the Cash Flow Statement as a consequence of any new legislative requirement for such a statement.

We turn first to the preparation of a Cash Flow Statement for a single company.

FRS 1 and the individual company

The objective of FRS 1 is to ensure that the reporting entities falling within its scope:

(a) report their cash generation and cash absorption for a period by highlighting the significant components of cash flow in a way that facilitates comparison of the cash flow performance of different businesses; and

---

5 See, for example, Loyd C. Heath, 'Let's scrap the funds statement', *Journal of Accountancy*, October 1978.

6 FRS 1 *Cash Flow Statements* (revised 1996), ASB, London, October 1996, Para. 5.

7 *Modernising Company Law*, Cm. 5553-I, Para. 4.13.

(b) provide information that assists in the assessment of their liquidity, solvency and financial adaptability. (Para. 1)

To this end, it requires relevant entities to prepare a Cash Flow Statement explaining the change in cash balances during a period. In order to permit comparisons over time and with other businesses, receipts and payments are to be analysed under the nine headings shown below:[8]

Cash flow statement for the year ended 31 December 20X1

	£
Net cash inflow/outflow from operating activities	X
Dividends received from associates and joint ventures	X
Returns on investment and servicing of finance	X
Taxation	X
Capital expenditure and financial investment	X
Acquisitions and disposals	X
Equity dividends paid	X
Cash inflow/outflow before use of liquid resources and financing	X
Management of liquid resources	X
Financing	X
Increase/decrease in cash during year	X

FRS 1 adopts a very narrow definition of cash:

Cash in hand and deposits repayable on demand with any qualifying financial institution, less overdrafts from any qualifying institution repayable on demand. Deposits are repayable on demand if they can be withdrawn at any time without notice and without penalty or if a maturity or period of notice of not more than 24 hours or one working day has been agreed. Cash includes cash in hand and deposits denominated in foreign currencies. (Para. 2)

In requiring companies to explain the change in cash during a period, the revised FRS 1 introduced the first true 'cash' flow statement. The original FRS 1, like the US standard 94 and the international standard IAS 7, had required companies to prepare a statement explaining changes in 'cash and cash equivalents'. As we shall explain later, the definition of cash equivalents gave rise to considerable problems in practice and the ASB was unable to develop a satisfactory definition to replace it.

In order to emphasise how the Cash Flow Statement articulates with the profit and loss account and balance sheet, FRS 1 requires that the statement be accompanied by two notes. The first provides a reconciliation between an item in the cash flow statements and one in the profit and loss account while the second provides a reconciliation between the net cash inflow or outflow and items in the opening and closing balance sheet:

1 Reconciliation of net cash inflow/outflow from operating activities with operating profit/loss.
2 Reconciliation of cash flows with the movement in net debt/net funds during the period.

---

[8] FRS 1 (revised 1996) required the use of eight headings but this has itself been revised by FRS 9 *Accounting for Associates and Joint Ventures*, which was issued in November 1997. FRS 9 requires the insertion of a new heading, 'Dividends received from associates and joint ventures'.

Net debt is defined in Para. 2 of the Standard, as:

> The borrowings of the reporting entity (comprising debt as defined in FRS 4 'Capital Instruments' (paragraph 6), together with related derivatives, and obligations under finance leases) less cash and liquid resources. Where cash and liquid resources exceed the borrowings of the entity reference should be made to 'net funds' rather than to 'net debt'.

With this framework, we shall examine the cash flows to be included under each of the nine main headings.

Net cash flow from operating activities

The net cash flow from operating activities is the cash flow relating to all those activities which are included in arriving at the operating profits of an entity. It is calculated by reference to the cash effects of all transactions relating to operating or trading activities, normally included in the profit and loss account in arriving at operating profit. These include cash flows relating to provisions in respect of operating items, even where the provision was not included in the operating profit of a particular year. So, where a provision is made for the costs of a reorganisation or restructuring in one period but the cash payments take place in a later period, those cash flows must still be included as part of the operating cash flows in that later period (Para. 58).

The net cash flow from operating activities may be calculated either by the direct method (the gross method) or the indirect method (the net method). The direct method is easy to understand as it focuses on the cash received in respect of operating activities and the cash paid out in support of those activities:

Direct method	£000
Cash receipts from customers	5250
Cash payments to suppliers	(1685)
Cash payments to and on behalf of employees	(3132)
Net cash flow from operating activities	433

However, this method requires information that is not provided routinely by the accounting systems of most companies, so it is usually easier to derive the net cash flow from operating activities by using the indirect method:

Indirect method	£000
Operating profit	444
Adjustments for items not involving a flow of cash:	
Depreciation	85
Increase in stocks	(68)
Increase in debtors relating to operating activities	(55)
Increase in creditors relating to operating activities	27
Net cash flow from operating activities	433

This indirect method effectively reverses all the accruals adjustments, including that for depreciation, which have been made in arriving at operating profit.

As we have explained above, FRS 1 requires companies to publish a note to the Cash Flow Statement reconciling the net cash inflow/outflow from operating activities to the operating profit. This note is, in fact, the calculation using the indirect method. It is an extremely useful note for both accountants and non-accountants because it helps them to understand why a healthy profit may not lead to a positive cash inflow. While the original FRS 1 sensibly relegated this reconciliation to a note, the revised FRS 1 permits it to be given either adjoining the cash flow statement or as a note. However, it points out clearly that:

> The reconciliation is not part of the cash flow statement; if adjoining the cash flow statement, it should be clearly labelled and kept separate. (Para. 12)

In the view of the authors, this rather subtle point that the first part of a published Cash Flow Statement is a note, rather than a part of the Statement, is likely to be lost on the majority of users!

Dividends received from associates and joint ventures

Following the issue of FRS 9 *Associates and Joint Ventures* in 1997, it is now necessary to include dividends received from associates and joint ventures under this separate heading. Their proximity to the net cash flow from operating activities in the cash flow statement reflects the treatment of the share of the operating profit of such investees in consolidated profit and loss accounts or in the notes or supplementary profit and loss accounts prepared by individual companies.[9]

Returns on investments and servicing of finance

FRS 1 requires the separation of returns on investments and payments to service financing from the capital flows to which they relate. The cash flows under this heading should therefore include the following items:

- interest received, including any related tax recovered;
- interest paid, including any tax deducted and paid to the relevant tax authority (the standard specifically requires the inclusion of interest paid even if it is capitalised and, of course, requires the inclusion of the interest element of finance lease payments);
- dividends received, net of tax credits;[10]
- dividends paid on non-equity shares.

Dividends paid on equity share capital are to be included under a separate heading 'Equity dividends paid' discussed below.

Taxation

The only amounts to be included under this heading are payments and receipts relating to tax on the company's revenue and capital profits. Thus this heading typically comprises payments of corporation tax and similar foreign taxes.

Taxes for which the company acts as a collecting agent for the government, such as VAT, would normally be dealt with as part of the operating activities of the company. Cash flows would then be shown net of any VAT and an adjustment would be made to reflect the change in the amount payable to or recoverable from the government.

---

[9] See Chapter 15.

[10] Where foreign dividends are received after deduction of overseas withholding tax, which is recoverable, it would seem appropriate to include the gross amount.

Capital expenditure and financial investment

This heading comprises all payments and receipts in respect of the purchase or sale of fixed assets, whether tangible, intangible or investments in the loans or shares of other entities. It excludes payments and receipts in respect of acquisitions and disposals of trades, businesses and investments in subsidiary undertakings, associates and joint ventures, which must be included under the next heading. However, it includes payments and receipts relating to any current asset investment which is not included in the company's definition of liquid resources. We shall discuss such liquid resources under the heading 'Management of liquid resources' below.

Some commentators had argued that the ASB should require companies to distinguish between capital expenditure incurred to maintain the size of the business and capital expenditure involving expansion. Not surprisingly, the ASB took the view that such a distinction would be difficult both to make and to police.

Acquisitions and disposals

This heading comprises receipts and payments in respect of acquisitions and disposals of trades and businesses as well as purchases and sales of investments in subsidiary undertakings, associates and joint ventures. As we shall see in a later section of the chapter, in dealing with the purchase or sale of subsidiary undertakings in consolidated financial statements, it will be necessary to show separately any balances of cash and overdraft of the subsidiary at the date of acquisition or disposal.

Equity dividends paid

The cash flows to be included here are the dividends paid on the reporting entity's equity shares.

Under the original FRS 1, such dividends were to be shown under the earlier heading 'Returns on investments and servicing of finance', which resulted in a consistent treatment of dividends received and paid as well as of interest received and paid. However, the revised FRS 1 requires that equity dividends paid, typically the dividends paid on ordinary shares, should be shown under this separate heading. The justification for this is presumably the fact that directors have a large measure of discretion over this payment in practice.

Management of liquid resources

Each company must decide and explain which current asset investments are regarded as 'liquid resources'. Liquid resources are defined as follows:

> **Current asset investments held as readily disposable stores of value. A readily disposable investment is one that:**
>
> **(a) is disposable by the reporting entity without curtailing or disrupting its business; and is either**
>
> **(b) (i) readily convertible into known amounts of cash at or close to its carrying amount, or**
> **(ii) traded in an active market. (Para. 2)**

As we have described earlier, the original FRS 1 required that a cash flow statement explained changes in 'cash and cash equivalents', terms which were defined as follows:

> **Cash: Cash in hand and deposits repayable on demand with any bank or other financial institution. Cash includes cash in hand and deposits denominated in foreign currencies.**

> **Cash equivalents: Short-term, highly liquid investments which are readily convertible into known amounts of cash without notice and which were within three months of maturity when acquired; less advances from banks repayable within three months from the date of the advance. Cash equivalents include investments and advances denominated in foreign currencies provided that they fulfil the above criteria. (Original FRS 1, Paras 2 and 3)**

Such a definition of cash equivalents attempted to ensure that the amounts receivable were not subject to fluctuations in value as a consequence of interest rate changes. However, the definition attracted an enormous amount of criticism. Many companies argued that it was too restrictive and out of line with their treasury management policies so that cash flow statements prepared using the definition failed to reflect their liquidity and financial adaptability. Although the ASB attempted to develop a new definition of 'cash equivalents', it was unable to develop one which was universally acceptable. Instead it decided to require a real cash flow statement and left it to individual companies to decide which investments they regarded as liquid resources. The revised FRS 1 requires companies to decide and explain which investments are regarded as liquid resources and then to show receipts and payments in respect of such investments under the heading 'Management of liquid resources'.

While this may have been the best approach achievable, it inevitably reduces comparability between companies. In the view of the authors, it is particularly unfortunate that the ASB has provided a definition of 'liquid resources' which excludes cash, the most liquid of all resources. The use of the term 'liquid investments' would surely have been more appropriate for its intended use!

Financing

This heading comprises the capital receipts from and payments to external providers of finance. Typical examples would be receipts from issuing shares or debentures and payments to repay loans and purchase or redeem share capital. However, the heading would also include receipts and payments in respect of short-term borrowing, except overdrafts, as well as payments of issue expenses and the capital element of finance lease rental payments.

The revised standard specifically permits the section for Financing to be combined with that for the Management of liquid resources, provided that separate sub-totals for each are provided.

With this summary of the cash flows to be included under each heading, we are now in a position to look at an example. We shall illustrate the preparation of a Cash Flow Statement supported by the two notes required by the revised FRS 1.

Example 17.1

The summarised financial statements of a manufacturing company, Kamina plc, for the year ended 31 December 20X2, together with an opening balance sheet, are given below. The two right-hand columns by the balance sheet merely list differences between the opening and closing balances. The '+' column contains increases in assets and reductions in liabilities, while the '–'column contains reductions in assets and increases in both liabilities and the shareholders' interest.

Balance sheets on 31 December 20X1 and 20X2

	20X1	20X2	Change +	Change –
	£000	£000	£000	£000
Fixed assets				
Tangible – at net book value (note (i)):				
Freehold properties	800	1140	340	
Plant and machinery	1100	1400	300	
Investments at cost	100	110	10	
	2000	2650	650	
Current assets				
Stock	1100	1680	580	
Debtors (note (ii))	490	730	240	
Government securities – at cost	150	250	100	
Cash at bank	200	–		200
	1940	2660		
less Short-term creditors				
Bank overdraft	–	85		85
Creditors (note (iii))	735	970		235
Taxation payable (note (iv))	155	205		50
Proposed dividend	140	160		20
	1030	1420		
Net current assets	910	1240		
	2910	3890		
less Long-term loans (note (v))	600	1000		400
	2310	2890		
less Deferred taxation (note (vi))	380	479		99
	1930	2411		
			1570	1089
Share capital and reserves				
£1 ordinary shares (note (vii))	1000	1100		100
Share premium (note (vii))	200	300		100
Retained profits	730	1011		281
	1930	2411	1570	1570

Profit and loss account for the year ended 31 December 20X2

	£000	£000
Turnover		6250
Cost of sales		3750
Gross profit		2500
Distribution costs	615	
Administrative expenses	1064	1679
Operating profit		821
Profit on sale of freehold property		40
		861
Dividend received		5
Interest received		12
		878
Interest payable (note (viii))		98
Profit on ordinary activities before tax		780
Taxation		
Corporation tax	180	
Deferred tax	99	279
Profit on ordinary activities after tax		501
less Equity dividends		
Paid	60	
Proposed	160	220
Retained profit for the year		281

Notes

The following information is relevant:

(i)   Fixed asset movements

	Freehold properties	Plant and machinery
	£000	£000
Cost		
On 1 January 20X2	1000	2000
Additions	440	720
Disposal	(60)	–
On 31 December 20X2	1380	2720
Depreciation		
On 1 January 20X2	200	900
Disposal	(10)	–
Profit & loss account charge	50	420
On 31 December 20X2	240	1320
Net book value 31 December 20X2	1140	1400
31 December 20X1	800	1100

(ii) A freehold property was sold for £90 000 and, at 31 December 20X2, £75 000 of this amount is included in debtors.

(iii) Short-term creditors have been analysed as follows:

	31.12.20X1	31.12.20X2
	£000	£000
Interest payable – £600 000 11% loan	33	33
£400 000 10% loan	–	10
Creditor for purchase of machinery	40	60
Trade and expense creditors	662	867
	735	970

(iv) Taxation payable has been analysed as follows:

	31.12.20X1	31.12.20X2
	£000	£000
Corporation tax payable	80	95
Value added tax	75	110
	155	205

(v) Long-term loans

	31.12.20X1	31.12.20X2
	£000	£000
11% loan	600	600
10% loan raised 1 April 20X2	–	400
	600	1000

Interest on the 11 per cent loan is payable annually on 30 June while interest on the new 10 per cent loan is payable half yearly on 30 September and 31 March.

(vi) Deferred taxation

	31.12.20X1	31.12.20X2
	£000	£000
Deferred taxation on timing differences	380	479

(vii) Share issues

40 000 £1 ordinary shares were issued for cash of £80 000 on 5 December 20X2 while a further 60 000 £1 ordinary shares were issued on 12 December 20X2 to acquire a freehold property valued at £120 000.

(viii) Interest payable is made up as follows:

	£000
Interest on long-term loans	
11% loan	66
10% loan (from 1 April 20X2 to 31 December 20X2)	30
	96
Interest paid on bank overdraft	2
	98

We shall now examine the workings for this example in detail. We shall assume that Kamina plc considers the current asset investment in government securities to be a liquid resource.

(A)   Change in cash

	£000
Cash at bank on 1 January 20X2	200
Bank overdraft on 31 December 20X2	85
Decrease in cash	285

(B)   Net cash inflow from operating activities using indirect method

	£000	£000
Operating profit		821
Adjustments:		
Depreciation – freehold buildings (note (i))	50	
– plant & machinery (note (i))	420	470
Increase in stocks		(580)
Increase in debtors from operating activities:		
per balance sheet on 31 December 20X2	730	
less debtor for sale of property (note (ii))	75	
	655	
per balance sheet on 31 December 20X1	490	(165)
Increase in creditors from operating activities:		
Trade and expense creditors per note (iii) (867 – 662)	205	
VAT per note (iv) (110 – 75)	35	240
Net cash inflow		786

Note: It is not necessary to deduct the profit on sale of the freehold property as this has not been included in arriving at the operating profit shown in the profit and loss account.

(C)   Returns on investments and servicing of finance

	£000	£000
Interest paid (see notes (v) and (viii))		
On £600 000 11% loan		
Amount paid 30 June 20X2	(66)	
(Check 33 000 + 66 000 – 33 000)		
On £400 000 10% loan		
Amount paid 30 September 20X2		
$\frac{1}{2} \times 10\% \times 400\,000$	(20)	
(Check 0 + 30 000 – 10 000)		
	(86)	
On bank overdraft (interest paid)	(2)	
		(88)
Interest received		12
Dividends received		5
Net payments		(71)

(D) Taxation – corporation tax

	£000
Corporation tax paid during year	
Opening creditor per note (iv)	80
Profit and loss account charge	180
	260
less Closing creditor per note (iv)	95
	165

(E) Investing activities

	£000	£000
Purchases of fixed assets using cash		
Freehold properties – additions per note (i)	(440)	
less Purchased by means of share issue per note (vii)	(120)	
Cash purchases		(320)
Plant and machinery – additions per note (i)	(720)	
less Increase in creditors for plant and machinery		
purchases per note (iii) (60 000 – 40 000)	20	
Cash purchases		(700)
		(1020)
Sale of fixed assets – freehold property		
Net book value per note (i)		
(60 000 – 10 000)	50	
add Profit on disposal – per		
profit & loss account	40	
Proceeds as given in note (ii)	90	
less Debtor at 31 December 20X2	75	15
		(1005)

(F) Equity dividends paid

	£000	£000
Dividend proposed at 31 December 20X1		140
add Dividends per profit		
& loss account:		
Paid	60	
Proposed	160	220
		360
less Dividend proposed at 31 December 20X2		160
Equity dividends paid		200
Check: Final dividend for 20X1	140	
Interim dividend for 20X2	60	
	200	

(G) Management of liquid resources

	£000
Payment to acquire government securities (£250 000 – £150 000)	100

(H) Financing

	£000
Issue of ordinary shares for cash per note (vii)	80
New long-term loan – per note (v)	400
	480

(I) Change in net debt

The second note to the Cash Flow Statement must show why the net debt has changed, thus linking the cash flow statement to the opening and closing balance sheets. In our example, the note must therefore explain why the net debt has changed from £250 000 to £835 000, an increase of £585 000:

	31.12.20X1	*31.12.20X2*
	£000	£000
Long-term loans	600	1000
Bank overdraft	–	85
less Cash at bank	(200)	(–)
Liquid resources	(150)	(250)
Net debt	250	835

There are three reasons for this change:

	£000
Decrease in the cash balance per (A)	285
New long-term loan per (H)	400
	685
less Purchase of liquid resources per (G)	(100)
	585

We are now in a position to prepare the cash flow statement and accompanying notes.

Kamina plc
Cash flow statement for the year ended 31 December 20X2

	£000	£000
Net cash inflow from operating activities		786
Returns on investment and servicing of finance:		
Interest received	12	
Interest paid	(88)	
Dividends received	5	(71)
Taxation		
Corporation tax paid		(165)
Capital expenditure and financial investment:		
Payments to acquire tangible fixed assets	(1020)	
Receipts from sales of tangible fixed assets	15	
Payment to purchase fixed asset investment (110 000 – 100 000)	(10)	(1015)
Equity dividends paid		(200)
Cash outflow before use of liquid resources and financing		(665)
Management of liquid resources		
Purchase of government securities		(100)
Financing		
Proceeds from issue of ordinary shares	80	
Proceeds from new loan	400	480
Decrease in cash during the year		285

Notes to the cash flow statement

1 Reconciliation of operating profit to net cash flow from operating activities (see Working (B)):

	£000
Operating profit	821
Depreciation of tangible fixed assets	470
Increase in stocks	(580)
Increase in debtors from operating activities	(165)
Increase in creditors from operating activities	240
Net cash inflow from operating activities	786

2 Reconciliation of net cash flow movement to movement in net debt:

	£000
Decrease in cash during the year	285
New long-term loan raised	400
Purchase of government securities	(100)
Increase in net debt resulting from cash flows	585
Net debt at 31.12.20X1 (see below)	250
Net debt at 31.12.20X2 (see below)	835

Net debt at 31 December	20X1	20X2
	£000	£000
Loans	(600)	(1000)
Cash balances/overdrafts	200	(85)
Liquid resources	150	250
Net debt	(250)	(835)

The cash flow statement which we have prepared shows that, although there was a positive net cash inflow from operating activities of £786 000, there has been a net cash outflow before the use of liquid resources and financing amounting to £665 000. This is due to net interest paid, net dividends paid and corporation tax paid but, principally, to the fact that net payments to acquire fixed assets amounted to £1 015 000.

Kamina plc has raised £480 000 by issuing shares for cash and taking a new loan. However, it has invested £100 000 in liquid resources. The net effect is that cash balances have fallen by £285 000 during the year.

Now that we have explored the preparation of a cash flow statement for an individual company, we turn to the additional considerations posed by the existence of subsidiaries, associates, joint ventures and foreign currencies.

Groups, associates and joint ventures

Groups

Where a company has subsidiary undertakings and prepares consolidated financial statements, the cash flow statement will reflect the cash flows of the group.

Following the normal consolidation techniques of acquisition accounting, which we discussed in Chapters 13 and 14, a consolidated balance sheet includes the whole of the assets and liabilities of the parent undertaking and subsidiary undertakings even when those subsidiary undertakings are only partly owned. The cash flow statement will therefore explain changes in the cash of all the undertakings in the group as shown in the consolidated balance sheets. Intercompany cash flows, resulting from sales, management charges or dividend payments between group companies, are irrelevant although dividends paid to any minority interests will, of course, be shown as a payment under the heading 'Returns on investments and servicing of finance'.

Where the parent company uses the direct or gross method to determine the cash flows from operating activities of the group, it will be necessary to have in place a system to collect the relevant information from subsidiaries and to ensure that intergroup cash flows are eliminated. Where the indirect or net method is used, it will be possible to rely largely on the adjustments made during the consolidation process although, even in this case, certain additional information will be necessary. Examples of such additional information are analyses of group debtors and creditors, so that those relating to operating transactions can be identified and changes therein included in computing the net cash flow from operations, while those relating to non-operating transactions can be dealt with in computing receipts and payments included under other headings of the statement.

When a company acquires a new subsidiary undertaking, and acquisition accounting is used, the consolidated profit and loss account will include the profits or losses of that new

subsidiary from the date of acquisition to the end of the period, and the consolidated balance
sheet will include the whole of the assets and liabilities of the subsidiary, whether it is wholly
or partly owned.[11] It follows that when we try to determine the reasons for differences
between items in the opening and closing balance sheets, we find that part of the change will
be due to the assets, liabilities and any minority interest of the subsidiary undertaking at the
date of acquisition as well as to the payment made to acquire the subsidiary. So, for example,
if we focus on the change in cash between the beginning and end of the year, we find that part
of the change is due to a cash payment made by the parent company to acquire the new subsidiary, and a further part is due to the balance of cash held by the subsidiary at the date of
acquisition. The cash payment which must be shown in respect of the purchase of subsidiary
undertakings under the heading 'Investing activities' is therefore calculated as follows:

	£000
Cash consideration paid	x
less Cash of subsidiary undertakings	
at date of acquisition	x
Cash payment	x

Where a subsidiary is acquired for a consideration other than cash, all that will appear in
the cash flow statement will be the cash balances of the subsidiary at the date of acquisition.

To enable users to understand what has happened, it is necessary to provide a note to the
cash flow statement showing a breakdown of the assets and liabilities acquired, together with
the consideration paid. Such a note would take the following form:

Purchase of subsidiary undertakings

	£000
Net assets acquired:	
Tangible fixed assets	16 000
Investments	40
Stocks	13 000
Debtors	5 000
Cash at bank and in hand	2 500
Bank overdrafts	(1 000)
Other creditors	(5 500)
Loans	(3 000)
Minority interests	(40)
	27 000
Goodwill	3 000
	30 000
Satisfied by:	
Shares allotted	25 000
Cash	5 000
	30 000

---

[11] See Chapter 14.

The analysis of net outflow of cash in respect of the purchase of subsidiary undertakings would be:

	£000	£000
Cash consideration		5000
Cash acquired		
Cash at bank and in hand	2500	
Bank overdraft	(1000)	1500
Net payment		3500

When a group disposes of a subsidiary undertaking the converse is the case. Any cash proceeds from the sale of shares in the subsidiary, less any positive balance of cash of the subsidiary at the date of disposal, will be recorded as a cash receipt under the heading 'Investing activities'. A note to the statement should then provide a list of the assets and liabilities of the subsidiary at the date of disposal together with the proceeds received and any profit or loss on disposal:

	£000
Net assets disposed of:	
Tangible fixed assets	5000
Stocks	2000
Debtors	3000
Cash	1000
Creditors	(4000)
	7000
Profit on disposal	1000
	8000
Satisfied by:	
Loan stock	4000
Cash	4000
	8000

The net cash receipt from the disposal of the subsidiary would be:

	£000
Cash received	4000
less Cash balances of subsidiary sold	1000
	3000

Associates and joint ventures

When an investing company purchases or sells its interest in an associate or joint venture, any payment or receipt of cash will be included under the heading 'Investing activities'.

As we saw in Chapter 15, standard accounting practice requires the use of the equity method of accounting for associates and joint ventures. Under the equity method of accounting, an investing company takes credit in its consolidated profit and loss account for its full share of the profits or losses of the associate or joint venture. The consolidated balance sheet includes the investment but the individual assets and liabilities do not include relevant amounts in respect of the associated undertaking. Hence cash in the opening and closing consolidated balance sheets do not include the respective amounts for the associate or joint venture.

Apart from the purchase and sale of an investment and, perhaps, the making and repayment of a loan, the only recurrent receipt from an associate or joint venture will be the dividend received. This should be shown as a receipt under the separate heading, 'Dividends received from associates and joint ventures', a heading which has been inserted into the Cash Flow Statement by FRS 9 *Associates and Joint Ventures,* issued in November 1997.

Foreign currency differences

As we have seen in Chapter 16, exchange differences frequently arise both when a company engages in foreign transactions and when the accounts of an overseas entity are translated prior to the preparation of consolidated financial statements. We shall examine the treatment of such differences in the preparation of a cash flow statement. Where a company enters into a foreign currency transaction then, unless there is an agreed rate for settlement or a forward exchange contract, the foreign currency amount will be translated into sterling at the rate on the transaction date. Any difference arising on monetary items between the date of the transaction and the date of settlement will be taken to the profit and loss account as part of the operating profit. Where a debtor or creditor is outstanding at a balance sheet date, the foreign currency amount will be retranslated at the closing rate and again any resulting difference on exchange will be taken to the profit and loss account as part of operating profit.

As far as the cash flow statement is concerned, the cash flows to creditors or from debtors are the amounts actually paid and received in sterling and, if a company wishes to use the direct method to calculate the cash flow from operations, it must ensure that it has an adequate accounting system in place to collect this information. However, it is possible to use the indirect method although it will then be necessary to analyse the difference on exchange which has been included in arriving at operating profit. To the extent that the differences on exchange relate to operating activities, no adjustment is necessary. However, to the extent that differences relate to other activities, such as the purchase of fixed assets on credit or the retranslation of a foreign currency loan, this must be removed from the operating profit to arrive at the net cash flow from operating activities.

To illustrate, let us take examples of a settled transaction, that is one where payment has been made, and an unsettled transaction, respectively. A company makes a purchase from an overseas supplier which is recorded in the accounting records at a sterling amount of £15 000. During the same accounting period, settlement is made of £16 500 resulting in a loss on exchange of £1500, which is deducted in arriving at the operating profit shown in the profit and loss account. The cash payment is, of course, £16 500 and this is the amount which has been deducted in arriving at operating profit, albeit in two parts:

	£
Purchase	15 000
Loss on exchange	1 500
	16 500

Turning to an example of an unsettled transaction, let us assume that a company makes a sale, denominated in foreign currency, to an overseas customer and that the foreign currency amount invoiced is translated at £24 000. If the amount is still due at the ensuing balance sheet date, it will be translated at the closing rate of exchange to produce a different amount of, say, £26 000. The gain on exchange of £2000 will be credited to the profit and loss account in arriving at the operating profit.

As far as the cash flow statement is concerned, there has been no receipt. If we take the operating profit and make the usual adjustment for the change in debtors, this is exactly what will be included in the net cash flow from operating activities:

	£
Operating profit (including gain on exchange):	
Sale	24 000
Gain on exchange	2 000
	26 000
less Increase in debtors	26 000
Cash flow from this transaction	–

Whereas no adjustment is necessary in respect of exchange differences relating to operating activities such as purchases and sales, adjustments to the operating profit will be necessary in respect of other exchange differences. So, for example, an exchange difference relating to the purchase of a fixed asset on credit or the retranslation of a long-term loan must feature as an adjustment in moving from operating profit to net cash flow from operating activities. In the latter case the exchange difference will also have to be included in the note reconciling the opening balance sheet value of the loan with its closing balance sheet value.

Let us now turn to the translation of the accounts of a foreign subsidiary or associate. Here FRS 1 makes it clear what should be done.

> Where a portion of a reporting entity's business is undertaken by a foreign entity, the cash flows of that entity are to be included in the cash flow statement on the basis used for translating the results of those activities in the profit and loss account of the reporting entity.[12]

The vast majority of companies in the UK use the closing rate/net investment method under which profit and loss account items are translated at average or closing rate and assets and liabilities in the balance sheet are translated at the closing rate. Differences on exchange are taken to reserves and these will relate to opening assets and liabilities and, where an average rate is used in the profit and loss account, to the increase in net assets which has occurred during the year. Such differences thus explain changes in the balance sheet amounts, including the change in cash. The relevant parts of these differences on exchange must be included in the note reconciling opening and closing amounts for cash. Similarly, the relevant parts of the difference on exchange must be included in the note reconciling opening and closing net debt. The parts of the difference relating to such items as opening fixed assets, stocks, debtors and creditors will, of course, appear in relevant notes to the accounts but do not represent any receipt or payment of cash.

Where a company uses the temporal method of translation, exchange differences are taken to the consolidated profit and loss account and their treatment in preparing the cash flow statement will be exactly the same as that explained above for foreign currency transactions

---

[12] FRS 1, Para. 41.

entered into by the company itself. After all, the purpose of the temporal method is to translate the foreign currency financial statements in such a way that the result is the same as if the investing company had itself entered into the transactions undertaken by the foreign entity.

The international accounting standard

IAS 7 *Statement of Changes in Financial Position* was first issued in 1977 and, like the UK SSAP 10, required enterprises to prepare a statement explaining movements in 'funds'. It was subsequently revised in 1992 and, like FRS 1, now carries the title *Cash Flow Statements*.

IAS 7 requires all enterprises to prepare a Cash Flow Statement and, unlike the UK standard, provides no exemptions for small companies. However the Cash Flow Statement required by the international standard differs from that required by FRS 1 in two major respects.

- IAS 7 requires the Cash Flow Statement to explain the change in 'cash and cash equivalents' which has taken place during a period. Cash and cash equivalents are defined as follows:[13]

  Cash comprises cash on hand and demand deposits.

  Cash equivalents are short-term, highly liquid investments that are readily convertible to known amounts of cash and which are subject to an insignificant risk of changes in value.

  In this respect, IAS 7 is closer to the original FRS 1 (1991) than to the revised FRS 1 (1996), which, as we have explained earlier in the chapter, now has a clear focus on changes in 'cash'.

- IAS 7 requires that the cash flows should be reported under three headings: operating, investing and financing activities respectively. These are defined as follows:[14]

  Operating activities are the principal revenue-producing activities of the enterprise and other activities that are not investing or financing activities.

It is therefore the default category under which all cash flows that cannot be clearly classified as investing or financing activities should be included.

  Investing activities are the acquisition and disposal of long-term assets and other investments not included in cash equivalents.

  Financing activities are activities that result in changes in the size and composition of the equity capital and borrowings of the enterprise.

Clearly, this is a very different set of headings from the nine specified in FRS 1 and poses a number of difficulties for companies attempting to classify their cash receipts and payments. An example of this difficulty is the classification of interest and dividends received and paid. Under which heading should these be included? Are they concerned with operating activities, investing activities or financing activities? IAS 7 makes it clear that they must be classified in a consistent manner from period to period but permits them to be classified as operating, investing or financing activities.[15] In practice, different companies classify their interest and dividends in different ways so it is difficult to see how the provision of such flexibility in the international standard achieves much in the way of improved comparability between companies.

---

[13] IAS 7, Para. 6.
[14] *Ibid.*
[15] IAS 7, Para. 31.

There are substantial differences between IAS 7 and FRS 1 and, in the authors' view, the more recent FRS 1 is likely to lead to greater comparability between the Cash Flow Statements of different companies than IAS 7. At the time of writing, there appear to be no plans to revise either IAS 7 or FRS 1 so it is difficult to see how convergence will be achieved in this important area of financial reporting.

Usefulness and limitations of the cash flow statement

Now that we have explored the preparation of a cash flow statement and examined major differences between the UK and international standards, it is time to explore briefly the usefulness and limitations of the statement.

As we saw in Chapter 1, most users are concerned with the future performance of an entity and turn to the financial statements, as well as to other sources, for help in making a judgement about likely future performance. In assessing the cash flow statement, it is therefore necessary to ask how it helps users in this task.

The statement supplements the traditional accounts by focusing on changes in cash in a way which provides answers to many pertinent questions which a user might wish to ask. Examples of such questions are as follows: Has there been an increase or decrease in the cash balance? To what extent has cash been generated by the operations of the company? Are payments of interest, taxation and dividends covered by the net cash inflow from operations? Has cash been used to finance the purchase of fixed assets? To what extent has cash been raised to pay for an acquisition?

Answers to such questions as these undoubtedly help users to assess what has happened and what is likely to happen in future. However, like all the figures shown in financial statements, they cannot be used in isolation but must be interpreted as part of the whole collection of information. This may be illustrated by just one example. A user may look at a cash flow statement and find that there has been a substantial purchase of fixed assets out of cash balances. By itself, this may be a little worrying. However, the failure of long-term finance to cover the purchase of fixed assets in a particular year may merely reflect the fact that there were large cash balances at the opening balance sheet date, balances which have now been reduced to more appropriate levels!

The Cash Flow Statement is an enormous improvement on its predecessor, the Statement of Source and Application of Funds, and the Cash Flow Statement required by the revised FRS 1 (1996) improves still further that required by the original FRS 1 (1991). Its clear focus on changes in cash and its treatment of 'liquid resources' are to be applauded. However, it is not without some problems.

First, as we explained above, the focus of the revised FRS 1 on cash and its requirement to list cash flows under nine headings is even more out of line with the international accounting standard than the original FRS 1. There is thus a lack of comparability of Cash Flow Statements in the international arena and there appear to be no plans to achieve convergence, even in the European Union, in the near future.

Second, the need to include both receipts and payments under standard headings frequently results in a statement which is riddled with brackets and which may therefore be confusing to users.

Finally the authors have reservations about the introduction of a definition of 'liquid resources', which excludes cash, the most liquid of all resources! In our view, the term 'liquid investments' would better fit the bill.

The operating and financial review

As a consequence of changes in company law and of the work of the standard setters, the annual financial statements of companies have expanded out of all recognition over the past thirty years or so. While this has ensured that a large volume of mainly quantitative information is available to investors and other users of the statements, it has been argued that it would help users to understand this information better if the directors were to put the information into context by explaining what is happening and by interpreting the financial statements for their benefit. After all, the directors have far more knowledge about the company than any outsider is ever likely to possess.

It was to this end that the ASB published the Statement, *Operating and Financial Review*, in July 1993. This is not an accounting standard but a statement of best practice intended to encourage companies, particularly listed and large companies, to include an Operating and Financial Review as part of their annual report:

> **The Operating and Financial Review (OFR) is a framework for the directors to disclose and analyse the business's performance and the factors underlying its results and financial position, in order to assist users to assess for themselves the future potential of the business. (Para. 1)**

Such an Operating and Financial Review may be provided as a stand-alone document but may be included as part of another statement, such as the Chairman's or Chief Executive's Report. Experimentation is encouraged and many approaches have been seen in practice.[16] The Statement lists the essential features of the review and then provides more detailed guidance on its contents.

The essential features of the Operating and Financial Review are set out as follows (Para. 3):

- it should be written in a clear style and as succinctly as possible, to be readily understandable by the general reader of annual reports, and should include only matters that are likely to be significant to investors;
- it should be balanced and objective, dealing even-handedly with both good and bad aspects;
- it should refer to comments made in previous statements where these have not been borne out by events;
- it should contain analytical discussion rather than merely numerical analysis;
- it should follow a 'top-down' structure, discussing individual aspects of the business in the context of a discussion of the business as a whole;
- it should explain the reason for, and effect of, any changes in accounting policies;
- it should make it clear how any ratios or other numerical information given relate to the financial statements;
- it should include discussion of:
  - trends and factors underlying the business that have affected the results but are not expected to continue in the future; and
  - known events, trends and uncertainties that are expected to have an impact on the business in the future.

---

[16] See, for example, Pauline Weetman and Bill Collins, *Operating and Financial Review: Experiences and Exploration*, ICAS, Edinburgh, 1996.

The detailed guidance in the Statement is intended to help directors implement these general principles in writing their review. Not surprisingly, such matters of detail are classified under two headings, Operating Review and Financial Review respectively. The former includes discussion of the operating results, the profit for the year and other gains and losses reported in the Statement of Total Recognised Gains and Losses, a discussion of the dynamics of the business and of the investments which have been made for the future. Discussion of investment should deal with not just capital investment but also revenue investment, such as expenditure on advertising and marketing, training and both pure and applied research. Such revenue investment affects future periods as well as the current financial year.

The Financial Review should seek to explain the capital structure of the company, its treasury policy and the dynamics of its financial position. Thus it should discuss such matters as the types of capital instruments used and the maturity profiles of debt, the policies for managing interest rate risk and exchange rate risk, the pattern of borrowing requirements and resources of the business, such as brands and intangible assets, which are not reflected in the balance sheet.

The Statement recognises clearly that what is important to one company may not be important in the context of another company. It also recognises that, in deciding what should be disclosed, directors must weigh the benefits of disclosure against the possible danger of disclosing confidential or commercially sensitive information. Unfortunately, it is inevitable that some Boards of Directors will have difficulty in providing a review which is balanced and objective, dealing even-handedly with both good and bad aspects!

When it published its Statement in 1993, the ASB was of the view that the Operating and Financial Review was not a topic for regulation by an accounting standard but, rather, an area in which directors should be encouraged to follow the spirit of the Statement within the context of their own company. Given developments in narrative reporting since 1993, the ASB issued an exposure draft, *Revision of the the Statement 'Operating and Financial Review'* in June 2002. However the Operating and Financial Review has been given a much higher profile in the report of the Company Law Review Steering Group,[17] published in June 2001, and the subsequent White Paper, *Modernising Company Law*,[18] published in July 2002. We will deal with the proposals of the exposure draft and White Paper in turn.

Exposure draft

The exposure draft envisages that any Statement on the Operating and Financial Review will continue to be persuasive, rather than mandatory, and that it will continue to be addressed to directors of listed and large companies. While few changes to the information which should be disclosed and explained in the Review are proposed, the draft statement is structured somewhat differently from its predecessor. It is divided into two main sections. The first provides a list of the principles that directors should follow in preparing a Review and the second provides guidance on the structure and contents of the review.

The principles include such matters as the purpose of the statement, the intended audience, namely investors, the time-frame, the need for reliability and comparability and the need to explain any measures used in the Review. The guidance provides a framework for applying these principles under the headings shown in Table 17.1.

---

[17] *Modern Company Law for a Competitive Economy*, Final Report, June 2001.
[18] *Modernising Company Law*, Cm. 5553-I and 5553-II, HMSO, July 2002.

Table 17.1 The Exposure Draft Guidance on the OFR: Main headings

The business, its objectives and strategy

Operating Review

- Performance in the period
- Returns to shareholders
- Dynamics of the business
- Investment for the future

Financial Review

- Capital structure and treasury policy
- Cash flows
- Current liquidity
- Going concern

The exposure draft recognises that the list is not comprehensive and that not all headings will be appropriate to all companies. Like the present statement, the exposure draft encourages directors to focus on the matters which are relevant in the context of their own company. It also continues to accept that some of the information may be given in other parts of the annual report, such as the Chairman's Statement, rather than all being given in one standalone document. The adoption of such an approach may, of course, lead to difficulties in comparing the information provided by different companies in different parts of their annual reports.

The White Paper, *Modernising Company Law*

It is clear from the White Paper[19] that the Government now considers the Operating and Financial Review to be a major part of the annual reporting package providing users with an important narrative report on the company's business, performance and future plans. The Company Law Review, which preceded the White Paper, recommended that all Operating and Financial Reviews should include coverage of the following compulsory elements:

(i) the company's business and business objectives, strategy and principal drivers of performance;
(ii) a fair review of the development of the company's and/or group's business over the year and position at the end of it, including material post year-end events, operating performance and material changes; and
(iii) the dynamics of the business – i.e. known events, trends, uncertainties and other factors which may substantially affect future performance, including investment programmes.

However, it also proposed that the Review should include narrative discussion of other matters where the directors of the company consider them material and specifically provided examples of such matters as corporate governance, key relationships and environmental, community, social, ethical and reputational issues.

The Government now intends to introduce law requiring not just listed companies but some 1000 large companies and groups to prepare such a Review, although it intends to

---

[19] Cm. 5553-I and 5553-II, HMSO, July 2002.

devolve the making of detailed rules for the compilation of the Operating and Financial Review to the proposed new Standards Board.[20] Hence, for these companies, the publication of an Operating and Financial Review would, if the proposals are implemented, become mandatory, rather than just good practice.

It remains to be seen what form the proposed law will take and whether the ASB will issue a revised persuasive Statement or await the new legislation before issuing a new mandatory Statement or Standard.

The historical summary

It is usually difficult to draw conclusions about the performance and position of a company from a profit and loss account and balance sheet without some yardstick of comparison. Company law clearly recognises this in requiring the disclosure of corresponding amounts for the preceding financial year.[21] Thus the law ensures that, at a minimum, users are able to compare the performance and position in the current year with those of the previous year. Although such information is undoubtedly useful, comparative information for a longer period would be even more helpful in enabling users of financial statements to appreciate trends.

It was for this reason that, in the 1960s, the then Chairman of the Stock Exchange recommended that all listed companies should publish tables of relevant comparative figures for a ten-year period. Although this recommendation has never been incorporated into the Stock Exchange Regulations, nor into company law or accounting standards, it has become accepted practice for listed companies to provide a historical summary covering a five-year period. Five years has perhaps been chosen because this is the period specified for accountants' reports in prospectuses.

Given the lack of regulation, it is not surprising to find that the information included in a historical summary differs considerably from one company to another. While some companies only provide figures for turnover and profit for each of the five years, others provide summarised profit and loss accounts and balance sheets for the period. These are often supplemented by financial ratios, particularly earnings per share and dividend per share, and sometimes by a segmental analysis and/or non-financial information for the five-year period. Examples of the latter include the number of employees and the area of retail floor space available in each year. Readers familiar with the non-financial performance indicators published by utility companies will appreciate just how much detailed information of this type may be provided.

Given the lack of regulation and the fact that the historical summary is not subject to audit, it is, of course, possible for directors to choose to disclose those elements of a company's performance which show their company in the most favourable light. Thus, they may choose to disclose increasing amounts for turnover and operating profit while suppressing the fact that the profit before taxation and earnings per share may have been declining. It is for this reason that some accountants have called for regulation of the content of the historical summary.[22]

---

[20] The Government proposals on the OFR are contained in Paras 4.28 to 4.41 of the White Paper and, for interested readers, Appendix D to that White Paper provides comments on a set of draft clauses on the Operating and Financial Review contained in Cm. 5553-II.

[21] Companies Act 1985, Schedule 4, Para. 4(1).

[22] See, for example, R.M. Wilkins and A.C. Lennard, 'Historical summaries', in *Financial Reporting 1987–88*, L.C.L. Skerratt and D.J. Tonkin (eds), ICAEW, London, 1988. Wilkins and Lennard suggested that the Stock Exchange should consider introducing a requirement for historical summaries and that this should be supplemented by a SORP, giving practical guidance on the detailed information to be included and how problems areas should be handled. No such developments have occurred.

In our view, the historical summary should include as a minimum the main headings and totals in the profit and loss account and balance sheet. Thus the profit and loss account disclosures would include:

- Turnover
- Operating profit
- Exceptional items
- Profit before taxation
- Profit after taxation
- Dividends paid and payable

These should be supplemented by ratios for earnings per share, dividends per share and dividend cover.

The balance sheet disclosures should include:

- Fixed assets
- Net current assets
- Borrowings
- Shareholders' interest

These should be supplemented by ratios for net assets per equity share.

In order to ensure comparability, in so far as this is possible, previously published figures should be adjusted to reflect changes in accounting policies and to correct any fundamental errors which have come to light. In addition, amounts shown for earnings per share, dividends per share and net assets per share should be adjusted to reflect any subsequent changes in the share capital such as bonus issues and rights issues. In order not to obscure trends, it is essential that exceptional items and indeed, any of those, now rare, extraordinary items should be disclosed separately. A brief description of these and of any major changes in the composition of the group should also be provided.

The main criticism we would make of published historical summaries is that the vast majority are not adjusted for inflation. Although many users are able to make approximate adjustments for changes in the value of money by use of the published Retail Price Index (RPI), the trend shown by unadjusted information may be misleading for less sophisticated users.

To illustrate, let us assume that a company has reported its turnover for a five-year period as shown in the first line of Table 17.2. On the basis of the reported figures, turnover has been growing consistently over the five-year period. However, the second line of the table provides values for the average RPI each year and the third line provides the turnover for each year measured in average pounds for 2000.[23]

Whereas the unadjusted figures show a steadily increasing turnover, once we adjust for the fact that the value of the pound has been falling, the 'real' turnover has fallen consistently throughout the five-year period.

The ASC recommended that such simple adjustments be made.[24] In our view it is quite indefensible for companies to publish five-year historical summaries without incorporating changes in the value of the pound. The need for such adjustments is, of course, greater the higher the rate of inflation.

---

[23] To measure the turnover for each year in average pounds for 2000 – £(2000)s – it is merely necessary to multiply the turnover for each year by the average RPI for 2000 and to divide by the average RPI for the year to which the turnover relates. Hence the turnover for 1996 measured in £(2000)s, rounded to the nearest £1000, is calculated as £610 × 170.3/152.7 = £680. See Chapter 19 for a comprehensive coverage of the system of Current Purchasing Power (CPP) accounting, which attempts to adjust historical cost accounts for inflation, as measured by a general index such as the RPI.

[24] See the Discussion Paper, *Corresponding amounts and ten-year summaries in current cost accounting*, ASC, 1982, and the Handbook, *Accounting for the effects of changing prices*, ASC, 1986, Chapter 7.

Table 17.2 Company's turnover for five-year period

Year to 31 December	1996	1997	1998	1999	2000
Turnover (£000)	610	615	620	625	630
Average RPI for year	152.7	157.5	162.9	165.4	170.3
Turnover measured in £(2000) 000s	680	665	648	644	630

Reporting about and to employees

As we have seen in the introduction to this chapter, *The Corporate Report* favoured the expansion of the annual report to include an employment report.

Companies and other entities employ a large number of people who look to those entities for employment security and prospects while society at large expects employers to maintain certain standards of conduct in relation to their employees. *The Corporate Report* therefore took the view that significant economic entities should report employment information and recommended that the annual report should be expanded to include an employment report which should provide the following information:

(a) numbers employed, average for the financial year and actual on the first and last day;
(b) broad reasons for changes in the numbers employed;
(c) the age distribution and sex of employees;
(d) the functions of employees;
(e) the geographical location of major employment centres;
(f) major plant and site closures, disposals and acquisitions during the past year;
(g) the hours scheduled and worked by employees, giving as much detail as possible concerning differences between groups of employees;
(h) employment costs including fringe benefits;
(i) the costs and benefits associated with pension schemes and the ability of such schemes to meet future commitments;
(j) the cost and time spent on training;
(k) the names of unions recognised by the entity for the purpose of collective bargaining and membership figures where available or the fact that this information has not been made available by the unions concerned;
(l) information concerning safety and health including the frequency and severity of accidents and occupational diseases;
(m) selected ratios relating to employment.[25]

In the introduction to this chapter, we distinguished two types of statement.

The employment report envisaged by *The Corporate Report* is an example of what we called an 'extended' statement. It is a general-purpose statement to be included in the annual report of a company, which would provide much more information on employment than that required by company law. It should not be confused with another document, the employee report, which is an example of a 'rearranged and simplified' report, in this case a document separate from the annual report, intended for the use of employees.

---

[25] *The Corporate Report*, Para. 6.19. Appendix 3 to that document provides an example of the sort of employment report envisaged.

Employee reports usually contain a simplified set of accounts together with a narrative review of those accounts. The emphasis is on making the information as easy to understand as possible and such reports try to avoid technical language and frequently include charts and diagrams which might show, for example, the changes in sales or profits over a number of years or the distribution of value added between the team members.

In large companies the employees are primarily interested in a part, rather than the whole, of the entity and frequently employee reports are used to give more detailed segmental information about geographical areas, divisions or plants. They can thus be tailor-made for the particular company and can be improved in response to suggestions from the users, that is the employees, themselves.

Perhaps not surprisingly, companies have been reluctant to publish employment reports, especially given the fact that there has been little published work explaining which users find the particular pieces of information useful and for what purposes they may be useful. On the other hand, employee reports are more widely used and these are often also issued to shareholders as a matter of course.

Summary financial statements

As we were reminded in Chapter 2, company law has long required limited companies to send copies of their annual accounts, directors' reports and auditors' reports to every member and debenture holder of the company. However, the Companies Act 1989 introduced new provisions whereby a *listed* company may instead send members a summary financial statement.[26] Such a statement must explain that it is a summary of the full financial statements, inform members that they are entitled to those full financial statements and carry a warning that the summary financial statement does not contain sufficient information to permit a full understanding of the results or position of the company or group. It must contain a report by the auditor that the statement is consistent with the full financial statements and that it complies with the law. It must also include any qualified auditor's report together with details of certain types of qualification.

While the Companies Act 1989 introduced these general principles, the detailed regulations have been introduced by statutory instrument.[27] This specified the minimum content of the summary financial statement which comprises certain information from the directors' report and the main headings and associated amounts from the profit and loss account and balance sheet.

With regard to the information from the directors' report, it is necessary to disclose the names of all directors who served during the financial year and to present either the whole, or a summary, of the fair review of results and position. Information about post-balance sheet events and likely future developments must also be included. The minimum contents of the summary profit and loss account are set out in Table 17.3. Given that almost all listed companies prepare group accounts, the table is that which is applicable to consolidated financial statements.

As may be seen from Table 17.3, the summary financial statement is indeed a highly simplified statement and, as the required warning states, it is unlikely to contain sufficient information to allow for a full understanding of the group's performance and position.

---

[26] Companies Act 1985, s. 251.
[27] The Companies (Summary Financial Statement) Regulations 1990, SI 1990/515.

However, given the increasing complexity of the main financial statements, such summary financial statements certainly have a role to play and have the added advantage that they reduce substantially the cost to listed companies of sending full financial statements to all shareholders.

Table 17.3 Minimum content of summary profit and loss account and balance sheet

Summary consolidated profit and loss account

	£
Turnover	x
Income from shares in associated undertakings	x
Other interest receivable and similar income less interest payable and similar charges	x
Profit (or loss) on ordinary activities before taxation	x
Tax on profit (or loss) on ordinary activities	x
Profit (or loss) on ordinary activities after tax	x
Minority interests	x
	x
Extraordinary items (if any)	x
Profit (or loss) for the financial year	x
Dividends paid and proposed	x
	x
Directors' emoluments (total only)	x

Summary consolidated balance sheet

	£	£
Fixed assets		x
Current assets	x	
Creditors: amounts falling due within one year	x	
Net current assets		x
Total assets less current liabilities		x
Creditors: amounts falling due after more than one year		x
		x
Provisions for liabilities and charges		x
		x
Capital and reserves		x
Minority interests		x
		x

The Government is so persuaded of the merits of the summary financial statement that the White Paper, *Modernising Company Law*, contains a proposal that all companies should be able to provide their shareholders with a simplified summary statement, with wider coverage than just a summary financial statement, of the annual reporting documents. Thus all companies, not just listed companies, would be able to draw up and circulate such a statement to their shareholders although such shareholders would retain the right to receive the full documents if they so wish. The Government proposes to delegate the making of rules on the form and content of the summary statement to the proposed Standards Board.[28]

Interim reports and preliminary announcements

So far in this chapter, we have concentrated on the annual reports of companies and their growth in size over the years. However, no matter how much information and how many statements are provided in such reports, annual reporting is unlikely to provide sufficient information for investors to make satisfactory investment decisions. More timely information is needed and it is to this end that the London Stock Exchange requires listed companies to publish half-yearly, that is interim, reports as well as preliminary announcements of the full year's results as soon as this is possible.

The Stock Exchange rules on the contents of these documents are rather rudimentary and the ASB has issued two non-mandatory Statements to provide guidance on best practice in these areas: 'Interim Reports' was issued in September 1997 while 'Preliminary Announcements' was issued in July 1998.

Interim reports

In order to ensure that the information is timely, the Statement encourages companies to make their interim reports available within 60 days of the end of the period. In the UK the interim period is a half year while in other countries, such as the USA, the reporting period is a quarter.

The purpose of the interim report is to provide an update to the previous annual report and the Statement recommends that it include the following:

- **Management commentary**.
- **Summarised profit and loss account**, including the analysis of turnover and operating profit required by FRS 3, and accompanied by segmental information and one or more earnings per share figures.
- **Statement of total recognised gains and losses**, where material gains or losses, other than profit for the period, are recognised.
- **Summarised balance sheet**.
- **Summarised cash flow statement**, providing a summary of cash flows using the nine headings required by FRS 1 and supported by the two notes required by that standard.

The management commentary should be a less comprehensive version of the Operating and Financial Review, discussed earlier in this chapter. It should highlight and explain what has happened since the previous annual report and is intended to help users to understand what has happened and to make judgements on what is likely to happen in future. The interim report will therefore provide both confirmatory and predictive information.

The Statement provides a list of the information which should be included in the summarised financial statements and Table 17.4 provides this listing for a consolidated profit and loss account and balance sheet. Comparative amounts are required.

---

[28] *Modernising Company Law*, Cm. 5553-I, Para. 4.43.

Table 17.4 Interim Report: Contents of summarised consolidated profit and loss account and balance sheet

Summarised consolidated profit and loss account

- Turnover
- Operating profit or loss
- Interest payable less interest receivable (net)
- Profit or loss on ordinary activities before tax
- Tax on profit or loss on ordinary activities
- Profit or loss on ordinary activities after tax
- Minority interests
- Profit or loss for the period
- Dividends paid and proposed

Summarised consolidated balance sheet

- Fixed assets
- Current assets
  - Stocks
  - Debtors
  - Cash at bank and in hand
  - Other current assets
- Creditors: amounts falling due within one year
- Net current assets (liabilities)
- Total assets less current liabilities
- Creditors: amounts falling due after more than one year
- Provisions for liabilities and charges
- Capital and reserves
- Minority interests

Note: Turnover and operating profit should be analysed as required by FRS 3 and there should be a separate identification of amounts relating to associates and joint ventures.

The interim financial statements should normally be drawn up using the same accounting policies as those in the previous annual financial statements. The exception would be when it is intended to change these policies in the next annual financial statements, in which case the new policies should be implemented in the interim statements and an explanation of the change should be provided.

For the accountant involved with such an interim report, two different approaches could be adopted in preparing the financial statements. The first, the discrete method, regards the half-year as a distinct reporting period. The second, the integral method, regards the half-year as merely a part of the longer annual reporting period. The ASB Statement recommends the use of the discrete method. This has the conceptual advantage that the elements included in the interim financial statements may be defined in the same way as they are for the annual financial statements. However, it also recognises that this approach will not be appropriate for all items of revenue and expense and specifically draws attention to taxation as one such expense. The calculation of the corporation tax expense for a separate half-year period would often produce a meaningless figure. In such a case, it would be necessary to estimate the corporation tax payable for the full year and to apportion the relevant amount to the half-year period. In practice, the preparation of the half-yearly financial statements will inevitably involve a compromise between the use of both the discrete method and the integral method.

Preliminary announcements

In the UK, listed companies are required to notify the Stock Exchange of their preliminary statement of annual results and dividends as soon as possible after these are approved by the Board of Directors. At present these preliminary announcements are also distributed to financial analysts and institutional investors, rather than to shareholders at large. The ASB Statement, 'Preliminary Announcements', encourages companies to distribute them more widely and, in particular, encourages companies to experiment with the use of electronic communication to achieve this end.

As with interim reports, the Stock Exchange requirements are minimal and rather out of date, so the ASB Statement is intended to lay down best practice in this area.

Given that both interim reports and preliminary announcements are providing new information to the market about the company's performance and position, it is not surprising that there is considerable overlap between the contents of the two statements. Thus the Statement recommends that the preliminary announcement include the same documents as the interim report, namely:

- Management commentary
- Summarised profit and loss account
- Statement of total recognised gains and losses
- Summarised balance sheet
- Summarised cash flow statement

The management commentary should provide a balanced coverage of developments since the last annual report and interim report. The ASB encourages directors to refer specifically to developments in the second half of the year, which might otherwise not be commented upon.

The contents of the summary financial statements should be the same as those in the interim report as discussed in the previous section and partially listed in Table 17.4.

A preliminary announcement can only be made once the preparation and audit of the, as yet unpublished, financial statements for the year are well advanced; approval of the preliminary statement of results by the Board and agreement of the auditors are required before publication. It follows that the preparation of the preliminary announcement for the year avoids many of the conceptual problems of preparing an interim report.

The Government is determined to speed up the publication of results by companies, especially listed companies. We have seen, in Chapter 2, how the White Paper, *Modernising Company Law,* has proposed a shortening of the time limits in which companies must file their financial statements with the Registrar of Companies. That White Paper also proposes the introduction of legislation to require listed companies to publish any preliminary announcement, as well as their annual reporting documents, on the Internet. It envisages a requirement that the annual reporting documents should be available on the Internet within four months of the end of the company's year end.[29]

---

[29] *Modernising Company Law,* Cm. 5553-I, Paras 4.50–4.51.

Summary

In this chapter, we have examined a number of documents that are frequently included in a company's annual reporting package, even though they are not at present required by UK company law.

The first and largest part of the chapter is devoted to the Cash Flow Statement, a primary financial statement required by both FRS 1 (1996) and IAS 7 (1993) and, probably, soon to be required by company law. We explain how to prepare a Cash Flow Statement using the nine headings required by FRS 1 and illustrate this for an independent company. We then explore the preparation of such a statement for a group and look at the treatment of acquisitions and disposals of subsidiaries as well as the impact that associates, joint ventures and foreign currencies have on the statement. We explain the major differences between FRS 1 and IAS 7, differences that are likely to cause considerable problems for the convergence programme.

We then turn to the Operating and Financial Review (OFR), which the ASB (in its Statement issued in 1993) encouraged listed companies to prepare. We explore the purposes of such a narrative statement and illustrate its content before examining the changes proposed by the exposure draft for a Revised Statement and by the Government White Paper, *Modernising Company Law*. The latter proposes to raise the status of this OFR by the introduction of a legislative requirement for some 1000 large companies or groups to publish such a review.

We then look more briefly at three topics, the Historical summary, Reporting about and to employees and the Summary financial statement. We outline the reasons for the publication of historical summaries and discuss their content. We point out that, in our view, it is indefensible that companies consistently publish five-year historical summaries without making adjustments for inflation. We distinguish between relatively rare Employment reports, which we classify as 'extended statements', and the simplified reports for employees, which are sometimes sent to shareholders as well. We explain that, although the law at present allows listed companies to provide their shareholders with a summary financial statement, the White Paper proposes that all companies should be able to publish a simplified summary statement subject to the right of shareholders to receive the full annual reporting package if they so desire.

Finally we examine the ASB's attempts to encourage and improve the reporting of interim results and preliminary announcements. We end by drawing attention to the proposal in the White Paper that all listed companies should publish, not only their preliminary announcements, but also their complete annual reporting documents on the Internet within four months of their year ends.

Recommended reading

Accounting Standards Steering Committee, *The Corporate Report*, London, 1975.

L.C. Heath and P. Rosenfield, 'Solvency: the forgotten half of financial reporting', in R. Bloom and P.T. Elgers (eds), *Accounting Theory and Policy: A Reader*, 2nd edn, Harcourt Brace Jovanovich, Orlando, 1987.

P. Weetman and B. Collins, *Operating and Financial Review: Experience and Exploration*, ICAS, Edinburgh, 1996.

Readers are also referred to the latest edition of *UK & International GAAP*, Ernst & Young, which provides much greater detailed coverage of this and other topics in this book. At the time of writing, the most recent edition is the 7th, A. Wilson, M. Davies, M. Curtis and G. Wilkinson-Riddle (eds), Butterworths Tolley, London, 2001. The relevant chapters are 29, 'Cash flow statements', 4, 'Corporate governance' and 33, 'Interim reports and preliminary announcements'.

A useful website

www.dti.gov.uk/companiesbill

Questions

17.1 In November 1996 the Accounting Standards Board issued FRS 1 (Revised) – *Cash Flow Statements*. The appendix to FRS 1 contains a number of examples of cash flow statements drawn up in accordance with the new Standard. The examples given present the cash flows under a number of standard headings, as shown below.

		£000
(i)	Cash flow from operating activities	X
(ii)	Returns on investments and servicing of finance	X
(iii)	Taxation	X
(iv)	Capital expenditure and financial investment	X
(v)	Acquisitions and disposals	X
(vi)	Equity dividends paid	X
		X
(vii)	Management of liquid resources	X
(viii)	Financing	X
	Decrease in cash in the period	X

Requirements
(a) Describe the cash flows which are reported under each of the headings (i) to (viii), given above. (10 marks)
(b) Summarise the changes which FRS 1 (Revised) made to the old FRS 1, and explain why each change was considered necessary by the Accounting Standards Board. (10 marks)

CIMA, Financial Reporting, November 1997 **(20 marks)**

17.2 The following information has been extracted from the draft financial statements of T plc:

T plc
Profit and loss account for the year ended 30 September 2001

	£000
Sales	15 000
Cost of sales	(9 000)
	6 000
Other operating expenses	(2 400)
	3 600
Interest	(24)
Profit before taxation	3 576
Taxation	(1 040)
Dividends	(1 100)
	1 436
Balance brought forward	4 400
	5 836

T plc
Balance sheets at 30 September

	2001 £000	2001 £000	2000 £000	2000 £000
Fixed assets		18 160		14 500
Current assets:				
Stock	1 600		1 100	
Debtors	1 500		800	
Bank	150		1 200	
	3 250		3 100	
Current liabilities:				
Creditors	(700)		(800)	
Proposed dividend	(700)		(600)	
Taxation	(1 040)		(685)	
	(2 440)		(2 085)	
Net current assets		810		1 015
		18 970		15 515
Long-term loans		(1 700)		(2 900)
		17 270		12 615
Deferred tax		(600)		(400)
		16 670		12 215
Ordinary share capital		2 500		2 000
Share premium		8 334		5 815
Profit and loss		5 836		4 400
		16 670		12 215

Fixed assets

	Land and buildings	Plant and machinery	Total
	£000	£000	£000
Cost			
30 September 2000	8 400	10 800	19 200
Additions	2 800	5 200	8 000
Disposals	–	(2 600)	(2 600)
30 September 2001	11 200	13 400	24 600
Depreciation			
30 September 2000	1 300	3 400	4 700
Disposals	–	(900)	(900)
Charge for year	240	2 400	2 640
30 September 2001	1 540	4 900	6 440
Net book value			
30 September 2001	9 660	8 500	18 160
30 September 2000	7 100	7 400	14 500

The plant and machinery that was disposed of during the year was sold for £730 000.

Required

(a) **Prepare T plc's cash flow statement and associated notes for the year ended 30 September 2001. These should be in a form suitable for publication.**   (15 marks)

After the publication of the balance sheet at 30 September 2000, the directors of T plc were criticised for holding too much cash. The annual report for the year ended 30 September 2001 claims that the company has managed its cash more effectively.

Required

(b) **Explain whether T plc's cash management appears to have been any more effective this year.**   (5 marks)

CIMA, Financial Accounting – UK Accounting Standards, November 2001   **(20 marks)**

17.3 Inverness plc has prepared the following draft financial statements for the year ended 31 October 1997:

Balance sheet as on 31 October 1997

	1997		1996	
	£000	£000	£000	£000
Fixed assets				
Freehold property – at cost/valuation	31 000		28 000	
– accumulated depreciation	–		(7 200)	
		31 000		20 800
Plant and machinery – at cost	20 000		16 400	
– accumulated depreciation	(8 600)		(5 400)	
		11 400		11 000
c/f		42 400		31 800

Balance sheet as on 31 October 1997 (continued)

	1997		1996	
	£000	£000	£000	£000
b/f		42 400		31 800
Current assets				
Stock	7 200		5 600	
Trade debtors	4 800		5 200	
ACT recoverable	475		550	
Investments	2 000		1 600	
Cash at bank and in hand	3 000		1 400	
	17 475		14 350	
Creditors: amounts falling due within one year				
Trade creditors	(5 200)		(3 700)	
Corporation tax	(2 000)		(3 700)	
ACT payable	(475)		(550)	
Proposed dividends	(1 900)		(2 200)	
	(9 575)		(10 150)	
Net current assets		7 900		4 200
		50 300		36 000
Creditors: amounts falling due after more than one year				
Debentures		(7 000)		(2 000)
		43 300		34 000
Share capital		25 000		24 000
Share premium		4 600		3 900
Revalution reserve		9 000		–
Profit and loss account		4 700		6 100
		43 300		34 000

Profit and loss account for the year ended 31 October 1997

	£000	£000
Turnover		34 200
Change in stocks of finished goods and work in progress		(6 600)
Own work capitalised		500
Raw materials and consumables		(14 000)
Staff costs		(5 200)
Depreciation – freehold property	(800)	
– plant and machinery	(4 000)	
		(4 800)
Loss on sale of fixed assets		(600)
Interest receivable		500
Interest payable		(1 000)
Profit on ordinary activities before taxation		3 000
Taxation		(2 500)
Profit on ordinary activities after taxation		500
Dividends proposed		(1 900)
		(1 400)

Additional information

(1) During the year an item of plant and machinery with a cost of £1.9 million was sold.

(2) The freehold property was revalued on 31 October 1997.

(3) Interest of £400 000 was capitalised during the year as part of additions to freehold property.

Requirements

(a) **Prepare a cash flow statement and related notes for Inverness plc for the year ended 31 October 1997 in accordance with FRS 1 (Revised),** *Cash flow statements.*

(13 marks)

(b) **Briefly explain the main reasons for the recent changes to FRS 1.** (4 marks)

[*Authors' note*: ACT recoverable and ACT payable refer to Advance Corporation Tax, which has been abolished. The current asset is equal to the current liability so both may be ignored in working this question.]

ICAEW, Financial Reporting, November 1997 **(17 marks)**

17.4 You are the management accountant of Holmes plc and you are in the process of preparing the consolidated cash flow statement. Your Managing Director is aware that the statement is required by FRS 1 – *Cash flow statements,* and that a number of notes to the statement must also be included. She has a reasonable understanding of the rationale behind the cash flow statement but is not clear as to why so many notes to the statement are required.

Requirements

(a) **Prepare the consolidated cash flow statement of the Holmes group for the year ended 30 September 1999 in the form required by FRS 1 –** *Cash flow statements.*
Show your workings clearly.
Do not prepare notes to the cash flow statement. (30 marks)

(b) **Write a memorandum to your Managing Director which explains the need for the following notes to the cash flow statement:**
● **reconciliation of operating profit to operating cash flows;**
● **reconciliation of net cash flow to movement in net debt;**
● **summary of the effect of the acquisition of Watson plc.**
Do not prepare any of these three notes for Holmes plc. (8 marks)

(38 marks)

Extracts from the consolidated financial statements of Holmes plc are given overleaf:

Consolidated profit and loss accounts for the year ended

	30 September 1999 £ million	30 September 1999 £ million	30 September 1998 £ million	30 September 1998 £ million
Turnover		600		500
Cost of sales		(300)		(240)
Gross profit		300		260
Other operating expenses (*Note 1*)		(150)		(130)
Group operating profit		150		130
Share of operating profit of associates		40		35
Interest payable:				
– group	50		45	
– associates	15		10	
		(65)		(55)
Profit before exceptional item		125		110
Exceptional item (*Note 2*)		10		–
Profit before taxation		135		110
Taxation:				
– group	35		25	
– associates	8	(43)	8	(33)
Profit after taxation		92		77
Minority interests		(10)		(6)
Group profit		82		71
Equity dividends		(25)		(25)
Retained profit for year		57		46

Consolidated balance sheets at

	30 September 1999 £ million	30 September 1999 £ million	30 September 1998 £ million	30 September 1998 £ million
Fixed assets				
Intangible assets (*Note 3*)	25		19	
Tangible assets (*Note 4*)	240		280	
Investments in associates	80		70	
		345		369
Current assets				
Stocks	105		90	
Debtors	120		100	
Investments	20		70	
Cash in hand	10		5	
	255		265	
Creditors falling due within one year				
Trade creditors (*Note 5*)	40		30	
Taxation	10		8	
Proposed dividends	25		25	
Obligations under finance leases	25		20	
Other creditors (*Note 6*)	6		5	
Bank overdraft	20		80	
	126		168	
c/f	129	345	97	369

Consolidated balance sheets at	*30 September 1999*		*30 September 1998*	
	£ million	£ million	£ million	£ million
b/f	129	345	97	369
Net current assets		129		97
		474		466
Creditors falling due after more than one year				
Obligations under finance leases		(80)		(70)
12% loan stock		–		(90)
Provisions for liabilities and charges				
Deferred taxation		(30)		(24)
Minority interests		(65)		(40)
		299		242
Capital and reserves				
Called-up share capital		100		100
Revaluation reserve		–		20
Profit and loss account		199		122
		299		242

Notes to the financial statements:

Note 1 – other operating expenses

	1999	1998
	£ million	£ million
Distribution costs	81	75
Administrative expenses	75	70
Investment income	(6)	(15)
	150	130

From time to time, the group invests cash surpluses in listed securities which are shown as current asset investments in the consolidated balance sheet.

Note 2 – exceptional item

This represents the gain on sale of a large freehold property sold by Holmes plc on 1 October 1998 and leased back on an operating lease in line with the practice adopted by the rest of the group. The property was not depreciated in the current year. The property had been revalued in 1990 and the revaluation surplus credited to a revaluation reserve. No other entries had been made in the revaluation reserve prior to the sale of the property.

Note 3 – intangible fixed assets

This comprises the unamortised balance of goodwill on consolidation which is written off over its useful economic life. During the year ended 30 September 1999, Holmes plc purchased 80% of the issued equity share capital of Watson plc for £100 million payable in cash. The net assets of Watson plc at the date of acquisition were assessed as having fair values as follows:

	£ million
Plant and machinery – owned	50
Fixture and fittings – owned	10
Stocks	30
Debtors	25
Cash at bank and in hand	10
Trade creditors	(15)
Taxation	(5)
	105

The goodwill arising was assessed as having a useful economic life of 16 years and a full year's write-off was made in the year ended 30 September 1999. Apart from the acquisition of Watson plc, there were no other changes to the group structure in the year.

Note 4 – tangible fixed assets

	30 September 1999	30 September 1998
	£ million	£ million
Freehold land and buildings	–	90
Plant and machinery – owned	130	100
Plant and machinery – leased	90	70
Fixtures and fittings – owned	20	20
	240	280

During the year the group entered into new finance lease agreements in respect of some items of plant and machinery. The amounts debited to fixed assets in respect of such agreements during the year totalled £40 million. No disposals of plant and machinery (owned or leased) or fixtures and fittings took place during the year. Depreciation of tangible fixed assets for the year totalled £58 million.

Note 5 – trade creditors
Trade creditors at 30 September 1999 and 30 September 1998 do not include any accrued interest.

Note 6 – other creditors
These comprise dividends payable to minority shareholders.

CIMA, Financial Reporting, November 1999

17.5 The following draft financial statements relate to the Duke Group plc:

Draft Group Balance Sheet at 31 May 2000

	2000	1999
	£m	£m
Fixed Assets:		
Intangible assets – goodwill	90	83
Tangible assets	1239	1010
Investments	780	270
	2109	1363
Current Assets:		
Stocks	750	588
Debtors	660	530
Cash at bank and in hand	45	140
	1455	1258
Creditors: amounts falling due within one year	(1501)	(1213)
Net Current Assets	(46)	45
Total assets less current liabilities	2063	1408
Creditors: amounts falling due after more than one year	(1262)	(930)
Minority interests – equity	(250)	(150)
	551	328

Draft Group Balance Sheet at 31 May 2000

	2000	*1999*
	£m	£m
Capital and Reserves:		
Called up share capital:		
– ordinary shares of £1	100	70
– 7% redeemable preference shares of £1 each	136	130
Share premium account	85	15
Revaluation reserve	30	10
Profit and loss account	200	103
	551	328

Draft Group Profit and Loss Account for the year ended 31 May 2000

	£m	£m
Turnover– continuing operations	5795	
– acquisitions	1515	
		7310
Cost of sales		(5920)
Gross profit		1390
Distribution and administrative expenses		(772)
Share of operating profit in associate		98
Operating profit– continuing operations	598	
– acquisitions	118	716
Profit on sale of tangible fixed assets		15
Interest receivable	34	
Interest payable	(22)	
		12
Profit on ordinary activities before taxation		743
Tax on profit on ordinary activities		(213)
(including tax on income from associated undertakings £15 million)		
Profit on ordinary activities after taxation		530
Minority interests – equity		(97)
Profit attributable to members of the parent company		433
Dividends	135	
Other non-equity appropriations	6	(141)
Retained profit for the year		292

Group Statement of Total Recognised Gains and Losses for the year ended 31 May 2000

	£m
Profit attributable to members of the parent company	433
Surplus on revaluation of fixed assets	20
Exchange difference on retranslation of foreign equity investment	(205)
Exchange difference on loan to finance foreign equity investment	10
	258

Reconciliation of Shareholders' Funds for the year ended 31 May 2000

Total recognised gains and losses	258
Dividends	(135)
Other movements:	
New shares issued	100
Total movements during the year	223
Shareholders funds at 1 June 1999	328
Shareholders funds at 31 May 2000	551

The following information is relevant to the Duke Group plc:

(i)   Duke acquired an eighty per cent holding in Regent plc on 1 June 1999. The fair values of the assets of Regent on 1 June 1999 were as follows:

	£m
Tangible fixed assets	60
Stocks	30
Debtors	25
Cash at bank and in hand	35
Trade Creditors	(20)
Corporation Tax	(30)
	100

The purchase consideration was £97 million and comprised 20 million ordinary shares of £1 in Duke, valued at £4, and £17 million in cash. The group amortises goodwill over ten years.

(ii) The tangible fixed asset movement for the period comprised the following amounts at net book value:

	£m
Balance at 1 June 1999	1010
Additions (including Regent)	278
Revaluations of properties	20
Disposals	(30)
Depreciation	(39)
Balance at 31 May 2000	1239

(iii) There have been no sales of fixed asset investments in the year. The investments included under fixed assets comprised the following items:

	£m 2000	£m 1999
Investment in associated company	300	220
Trade investment (including purchase of foreign equity investment of £400m equivalent during year to 31 May 2000)	480	50
	780	270

(iv) Interest receivable included in debtors was £15m as at 31 May 1999 and £17m as at 31 May 2000.

(v)   Creditors: amounts falling due within one year comprised the following items:

	£m 2000	£m 1999
Trade creditors (including interest payable £9m (2000) Nil (1999))	1193	913
Corporation tax	203	200
Dividends	105	100
	1501	1213

(vi) Duke had allotted 10 million ordinary shares of £1 at a price of £2 upon the exercise of directors' options during the year.

(vii) Included in creditors: amounts payable after more than one year is a bill of exchange for £100 million (raised 30 June 1999) which was given to a supplier on the purchase of fixed assets and which is payable on 1 July 2001.

(viii) The exchange differences included in the Statement of Total Recognised Gains and Losses relate to a transaction involving a foreign equity investment. A loan of £300 million was taken out during the year to finance a foreign equity investment in Peer of £400 million. Both amounts are after retranslation at 31 May 2000.

(ix) The preference share dividends are always paid in full on 1 July each year and at 31 May 2000 the preference shares have a par value of £130 million.

Required

(a) **Prepare a group cash flow statement using the indirect method for the Duke Group plc for the year ended 31 May 2000 in accordance with the requirements of FRS 1 (Revised),** *Cash Flow Statements.*

   Your answer should include the following:
   (i)   **a reconciliation of operating profit to operating cash flows;**
   (ii) **an analysis of cash flows for any headings netted in the cash flow statement.**

   The notes regarding the acquisition of the subsidiary and a reconciliation of net cash flow to movement in net debt are not required.   (24 marks)

(b) **Discuss the nature of the additional information which is provided by the Group Cash Flow Statement of the Duke group in (a) above as compared to the Group Profit and Loss Account and Group Balance Sheet of Duke.**   (6 marks)

ACCA, Financial Reporting Environment (UK Stream), June 2000   (30 marks)

17.6 You are the Consolidation Accountant of Worldwide plc, a UK company with subsidiaries located throughout the world. You are currently involved in preparing the consolidated financial statements for the year ended 30 September 2002. Your assistant has prepared the consolidated profit and loss account, the consolidated statement of total recognised gains and losses, the consolidated balance sheet and some supporting schedules. The material your assistant has prepared is given overleaf.

Worldwide plc – consolidated profit and loss account for the year ended 30 September 2002

	£ million
Turnover	4000
Cost of sales	(2200)
Gross profit	1800
Other operating expenses	(800)
Operating profit	1000
Gain on sale of subsidiary (*Note 1*)	58
Interest payable (*Note 2*)	(200)
Profit before taxation	858
Taxation	(180)
Profit after taxation	678
Minority interests	(128)
Group profit	550
Dividends paid:	
– preference shares	(40)
– ordinary shares	(200)
Retained profit	310

Worldwide plc – consolidated statement of total recognised gains and losses for the year ended 30 September 2002

	£ million
Group profit for the period	550
Exchange differences (Note 3)	47
Total gains and losses for the period	597

Worldwide plc – consolidated balance sheets at 30 September

	2002 £ million	2002 £ million	2001 £ million	2001 £ million
Fixed assets:				
Goodwill on consolidation	42		65	
Tangible assets (*Note 4*)	5900		4100	
		5942		4165
Current assets:				
Stocks	950		800	
Trade debtors	1000		900	
Short-term investments	60		80	
Cash	20		18	
	2030		1798	
Creditors: amounts falling due within one year:				
Trade creditors	450		400	
Accrued interest	25		20	
Taxation	130		120	
Obligations under finance leases	45		25	
Bank overdrafts	65		40	
	715		605	
c/f	1315	5942	1193	4165

Worldwide plc – consolidated balance sheets at 30 September (continued)

	2002 £ million	2002 £ million	2001 £ million	2001 £ million
b/f	1315	5942	1193	4165
Net current assets		1315		1193
Total assets less current liabilities		7257		5358
Creditors: amounts falling due after more than one year:				
Obligations under finance leases	225		140	
Long-term loans	1554		1200	
		(1779)		(1340)
Provisions for liabilities and charges:				
Deferred taxation		(278)		(218)
		5200		3800
Capital and reserves:				
Ordinary share capital		2500		2000
8% preference share capital		500		500
Share premium account		500		–
Profit and loss account		1157		800
		4657		3300
Minority interests		543		500
		5200		3800

Note 1 – gain on sale of subsidiary

On 1 April 2002, Worldwide plc disposed of a 75%-owned subsidiary incorporated in the UK for £250 million in cash. The balance sheet of the subsidiary drawn up at the date of disposal showed the following:

	£ million
Tangible fixed assets	200
Stock	100
Trade debtors	110
Cash	10
Trade creditors	(80)
Taxation payable	(25)
Long-term loan	(75)
	240

This subsidiary had been acquired on 1 April 1994 for a cash payment of £110 million when its net assets had a fair value of £120 million. Goodwill on consolidation is amortised on a monthly basis over 20 years.

Note 2 – interest payable

During the year, the group constructed a factory in the UK. Construction commenced on 1 November 2001 and the factory was ready for use on 1 June 2002. However, production did not begin at the factory until 1 August 2002. The construction of the factory was financed by general borrowings denominated in £s. Your assistant has included the interest relating to the period from 1 November 2001 to 1 June 2002 in the cost of tangible fixed assets rather than taking it to the profit and loss account. The amount of interest that was treated in this way is £10 million. The figure was arrived at by applying a relevant capitalisation rate to expenditure on the factory in the period 1 November 2001 to 1 June 2002.

Note 3 – exchange differences

	Total £ million	*Group share* £ million
Arising on retranslation of opening net assets:		
Tangible fixed assets	25	20
Stock	20	15
Debtors	20	16
Trade creditors	(9)	(6)
	56	45
Arising on retranslation of profit for the period	16	12
Offset of exchange loss on Worldwide plc loans (see below)	(10)	(10)
	62	47

Worldwide plc has taken out a number of long-term loans denominated in foreign currencies to partly finance the equity investments in its foreign subsidiaries. Your assistant has offset the exchange differences arising on the retranslation of these loans against the exchange differences arising on the retranslation of the net investments in the relevant subsidiaries. The exchange gain on retranslation of the profit and loss account (from average rate for the year to the closing rate) relates to operating profit excluding depreciation.

Note 4 – tangible fixed assets

- During the period, the depreciation charged in the consolidated profit and loss account was £320 million.

- Apart from the disposal mentioned in note 1, the group disposed of tangible fixed assets having a net book value of £190 million for cash proceeds of £198 million.

- During the period, the group entered into a significant number of new finance leases. Additions to tangible fixed assets include £250 million capitalised under finance leases.

Required:

(a) Prepare the consolidated cash flow statement of the Worldwide plc group for the year ended 30 September 2002. *You should use the indirect method.* Notes to the cash flow statement are NOT required. (30 marks)

(b) Evaluate the extent to which the accounting treatment for capitalising interest described in *note 2* above is in accordance with existing Accounting Standards. (5 marks)

(c) Evaluate the extent to which the accounting treatment of exchange differences described in *note 3* above is in accordance with existing Accounting Standards. Your answer should refer to any relevant current developments that have the potential to affect your evaluation. (5 marks)

Note: Your evaluations for requirements (b) and (c) should not change your answer to requirement (a) of this question.

CIMA, Financial Reporting – UK Accounting Standards, November 2002   (**40 marks**)

17.7   Portal Group, a public limited company, has prepared the following group cash flow statement for the year ended 31 December 2000:

Portal Group plc

Group Statement of cash flows for the year ended 31 December 2000 (draft)

	£m	£m
Net cash inflow from operating activities		875
Returns on investments and servicing of finance		
Interest received	26	
Interest paid	(9)	
Minority interest	(40)	(23)
Taxation		31
Capital expenditure		
Purchase of tangible fixed assets	(380)	
Disposals and transfers of fixed assets at carrying value	1585	1205
Acquisitions and disposals		
Disposal of subsidiary	(25)	
Purchase of interest in joint venture	(225)	(250)
Net cash inflow before use of management of liquid resources and financing		1838
Management of liquid resources		
Decrease in short term deposits		(143)
Increase in cash in the period		1695

The accountant has asked your advice on certain technical matters relating to the preparation of the group cash flow statement. Additionally the accountant has asked you to prepare a presentation for the directors on the usefulness and meaning of cash flow statements generally and specifically on the group cash flow statement of Portal.

The accountant has informed you that the actual change in the cash balance for the period is £165 million, which does not reconcile with the figure in the draft group cash flow statement above of £1695 million.

The accountant feels that the reasons for the difference are the incorrect treatment of several elements of the cash flow statement of which he has little technical knowledge. The following information relates to these elements:

(a) Portal has disposed of a subsidiary company, Web plc, during the year. At the date of disposal (1 June 2000) the following balance sheet was prepared for Web plc:

	£m	£m
Tangible fixed assets – valuation		340
– depreciation		(30)
		310
Stocks	60	
Debtors	50	
Cash at bank and in hand	130	
	240	
Creditors: amounts falling due within one year (including taxation £25 million)	(130)	110
		420
Called up share capital		100
Profit and loss account		320
		420

The loss on the sale of the subsidiary in the group accounts comprised:

	£m
Sale proceeds – ordinary shares	300
– cash	75
	375
Net assets sold (80% of 420)	(336)
Goodwill	(64)
Loss on sale	(25)

The accountant was unsure as to how to deal with the above disposal and has simply included the above loss in the cash flow statement without any further adjustments.

(b) During the year, Portal has transferred several of its tangible assets to a newly created company, Site plc, which is owned jointly with another company.
   The following information relates to the accounting for the investment in Site plc:

	£m
Purchase cost – fixed assets transferred	200
– cash	25
	225
Dividend received	(10)
Profit for year on joint venture after tax	55
Revaluation of fixed assets	30
Closing balance per balance sheet – Site plc	300

The cash flow statement showed the cost of purchasing a stake in Site plc of £225 million.

(c) The taxation amount in the cash flow statement is the difference between the opening and closing balances on the taxation account. The charge for taxation in the profit and loss account is £191 million of which £20 million related to the taxation on the joint venture.

(d) Included in the cash flow figure for the disposal of tangible fixed assets is the sale and leaseback of certain land and buildings. The sale proceeds of the land and buildings were £1000 million in the form of an 8% loan note repayable in 2002 at a premium of 5%. The total profit on the sale of fixed assets, including the land and buildings, was £120 million.

(e) The minority interest figure in the statement comprised the difference between the opening and closing balance sheet totals. The profit attributable to the minority interest for the year was £75 million.

(f) The net cash inflow from operating activities is the profit on ordinary activities before taxation adjusted for the balance sheet movement in stocks, debtors and creditors and the depreciation charge for the year. The interest receivable credited to the profit and loss account was £27 million and the interest payable was £19 million.

Required

(a) **Prepare a revised Group cash flow statement for Portal plc, taking into account notes (a) to (f) above.** (18 marks)

(b) **Prepare a brief presentation on the usefulness and information content of group cash flow statements generally and specifically on the group cash flow statement of Portal plc.** (7 marks)

ACCA, Advanced Corporate Reporting (UK Stream), Pilot Paper (2002)   (**25 marks**)

17.8 Pitted Prunes plc merged with Rosy Plums plc and changed its name to Pitted Rosy Plums plc in June 1987. The figures included in the accounts for the year ended 31 December 1987 included the results of both companies from 1 January 1987.

The financial highlights printed in the annual report showed:

	1987 £000	1986 £000
Turnover		
Pitted Prunes plc	46 434	43 354
Rosy Plums plc	110 420	78 050
	156 854	121 404
Profit before taxation		
Pitted Prunes plc	4 336	4 171
Rosy Plums plc	2 019	1 144
	6 355	5 315
Shareholders' funds	38 061	35 772

	Pence per share	
Earnings per ordinary share	19.6	16.80
Dividends per ordinary share (net)	5.9	5.12

The five-year review showed:

Year ended 31 December	Pitted Rosy Plums		Pitted Prunes			
	1987 £000	1986 £000 restated	1986 £000	1985 £000	1984 £000	1983 £000
Turnover	156 854	121 404	43 354	40 959	34 832	25 209
Percentage exported	52%	49%	44%	45%	44%	38%
Operating profit	8 437	6 476	4 174	3 137	2 607	1 569
Profit on ordinary activities before taxation	6 355	5 315	4 171	2 667	2 208	1 205
Profit on ordinary activities after taxation	4 538	3 940	3 040	2 072	1 836	952
Dividends:						
Preference	287	289	285	124	77	77
Ordinary	1 288	1 601	625	454	403	330
Shareholders' funds	38 061	35 772	15 470	13 529	10 066	8 590
Earnings per ordinary share	19.6p	16.8p	22.6p	16.0p	14.4p	7.1p
Dividends per ordinary share	8.1p	7.2p	7.2p	5.3p	4.7p	3.8p

Required

(a) **Explain the current requirements for a company to produce a five year summary with its annual report and the circumstances in which it may be necessary to restate the actual figures.** (5 marks)

(b) Discuss how historical summaries may be of interest and use to an investor or potential investor. (5 marks)

(c) Discuss the adequacy of the five year historical summary produced for Pitted Rosy Plums plc and the minimum content that you consider desirable. (10 marks)

ACCA Level 3, Advanced Financial Accounting, December 1989 (**20 marks**)

Capital reorganisation, reduction and reconstruction

overview

While the law cannot prevent the reduction of permanent capital (share capital plus non-distributable reserves) which occurs when a company makes losses, it seeks to protect the creditors and shareholders of a limited company by restricting the reduction of permanent capital in other circumstances. We have already explored an example of this in Chapter 4 where we saw that dividends may only be paid out of distributable profits. In this chapter, we discuss the circumstances where a reduction of capital is permitted and explain the strict procedures which must be followed in order to do so.

The law permits limited companies to purchase and cancel their own shares. While it is intended that public companies must keep their capital intact and may only make a 'purchase not out of capital', private companies may purchase their shares in a way which leads to a reduction of capital, a 'purchase out of capital'. We start this chapter with an explanation of both of these purchases.

We then turn to the legal rules which govern the reduction of capital in other circumstances and illustrate such capital reduction schemes. The Government White Paper, *Modernising Company Law*, issued in July 2002, proposes the introduction of new procedures for the reduction of capital based upon a solvency statement by the directors and we outline these procedures.

Finally we discuss the regulatory framework for a wide range of reconstruction schemes and provide an illustration of the design and evaluation of such a scheme.

Introduction

There are many reasons for making changes to a company's capital structure and these range from those which are virtually cosmetic to those where the company's capital base has almost disappeared.

At one end of the spectrum is the share split, which increases the number of shares in issue but does not change the total share capital. For example, shares with a nominal value of, say, one pound may be divided into two shares of fifty pence each or four shares of twenty-five pence each. In the case of quoted companies, this may be done when the price of a share becomes 'too heavy', that is when the market value moves above the range with which investors feel comfortable. There are very few shares quoted on the London Stock Exchange with a market value that exceeds £10.

A company that has large reserves, which it does not intend to distribute, may wish to tidy up its balance sheet by making a bonus issue from these reserves. This involves a transfer between reserves and share capital, thus signalling clearly that the permanent capital of the company has increased and reducing the value of each of the expanded number of shares.

At the other end of the spectrum is the capital reconstruction scheme entered into as the only possible alternative to liquidation of the company. In such a case, the value of the company's assets may be less than the value of its liabilities and the probable result is that the company will be unable to meet its debts as they fall due. The company must then reach some agreement with its debenture holders and other creditors about how their liabilities are to be treated. To achieve economic viability, it will often be necessary to raise new capital from existing shareholders and if, as is likely, the company has accumulated losses, the new shares would probably be unattractive to investors. The writing-down, or reduction, of share capital removes such losses from the balance sheet and brings a greater likelihood of earlier future dividends, thus making the shares more attractive. A possible alternative is that the creditors may take over ownership of the company as was the case with Marconi.

While the term capital reorganisation is a very general one, the term capital reduction has a more precise meaning, that is, it involves the reduction of the permanent capital of the company. Thus a company may wish to reduce its share capital in line with a smaller level of operations or, perhaps, to permit a shareholder director in a family company to retire. The term capital reconstruction is usually applied to those situations where a company is in severe financial difficulties and has to reconstruct its balance sheet. Such a capital reconstruction scheme will frequently involve a capital reduction. A capital reorganisation may be used to effect a change in the relative rights of different classes of shareholders, perhaps when a company is involved in a business combination. Taxation considerations are important in leading a company to reorganise its capital so that its earnings may be distributed to members in a tax-efficient way.

We will, in this chapter, concentrate on various reorganisations of capital permitted under the provisions of the Companies Act 1985.

First, we look at the redemption or purchase of its own shares by a company under the provisions of the Companies Act 1985. We deal with both the purchase of shares other than out of capital, which may be made by any limited company with a share capital, and a purchase out of capital, which may only be made by a private limited company. In the following section we examine the more wide-ranging powers to reduce capital contained in the Companies Act 1985. We also outline proposals to simplify the reduction of capital, which are included in the Government White Paper, *Modernising Company Law*, issued in July 2002.[1] Next we provide the background to other capital reorganisations including those which involve the alteration of creditors' rights. In the final section, we consider the design and evaluation of a capital reconstruction scheme to be undertaken as an alternative to liquidation.

Redemption and purchase of shares

Purchase not out of capital[2]

Until the Companies Act 1981, the only class of share that a company was able to redeem was redeemable preference shares. The Companies Act 1985 now permits limited companies both to issue redeemable shares of any class, and to purchase its own shares, whether or not they were issued as redeemable shares. The difference between a redemption and a purchase is that in the former case the shares will be reacquired on terms specified when the security was

---

[1] *Modernising Company Law*, Cm 5553-I and Cm. 5553-II, HMSO, London, July 2002. The second volume contains some of the draft clauses for a Companies Bill.

[2] The relevant legal provisions are contained in the Companies Act 1985, ss. 159–70.

issued, whereas in the case of a purchase the amount payable will depend on conditions prevailing at the date of purchase. Apart from this, the rules governing redemption and purchase are the same and, in order to avoid repetition, we shall merely use the term purchase throughout this section. In both cases the purchased shares must be cancelled and cannot be reissued, although the government is considering whether companies should be permitted to retain uncancelled purchased shares as investments as part of their treasury management policies.[3]

The Act distinguishes two categories of purchase: a market purchase and an off-market purchase. The market purchase is a purchase of shares quoted on a recognised investment exchange that is not an overseas investment exchange. It follows that such a purchase may only be made by a public company which has shares quoted on the relevant market. The off-market purchase is any other purchase of shares under a contract and may be made by both public and private companies. In view of the possibility that one particular shareholder may be beneficially treated, the Act lays down more onerous conditions for an off-market purchase than for a market purchase. Thus, while the market purchase may be made in accordance with a general authority passed by an ordinary resolution in general meeting, the off-market purchase requires approval of a specific contract by a special resolution in general meeting.

Private companies are, in certain circumstances, allowed to reduce their permanent capital by the purchase of their own shares and we shall deal with these provisions later in the chapter. With this exception, the 1985 Act lays down very detailed rules to ensure that the permanent capital is maintained intact following the purchase. The general principle, which has applied for many years on the redemption of redeemable preference shares, is that the purchase must be made either out of distributable profits or out of the proceeds of a new issue of shares made for the purpose, or by a combination of the two methods.

In many instances the purchase will be made at a premium, i.e. the purchase price will exceed the share's nominal value. Any premium payable on purchase must be paid out of distributable profits unless the shares being purchased were originally issued at a premium, in which case some or all of the premium payable may come from the proceeds of any new issue, rather than from distributable profits.[4]

Where the purchase is made out of distributable profits, an amount must be transferred to a capital redemption reserve, which is treated as paid-up share capital of the company. Section 170(2) of the Companies Act 1985 requires that the amount of the transfer be found by deducting the total proceeds of the new issue from the nominal value of the shares purchased. It would appear that the intention of the Act is that the amount of the transfer should be such as to ensure that the permanent capital, following the purchase, is maintained at the original level. However, probably unintentionally, due to the particular wording used in the Act, circumstances can arise which result in either an increase or a reduction in permanent capital. The circumstances might occur where shares are purchased at a premium out of the proceeds of a fresh issue of shares itself made at a premium and these will be illustrated in the examples which follow.

First, let us assume that a company purchases shares without making a new issue of shares. In such a case, the amount payable, including any premium, must come from distributable profits and, in order to maintain the permanent capital of the company, it is necessary to transfer an amount equal to the nominal value of the shares purchased from distributable profits to a capital redemption reserve, which is treated as paid-up share capital of the company. This is illustrated in Example 18.1.

---

[3] See URN98/713, Department of Trade and Industry, May 1998. Retention of uncancelled purchased shares as treasury investments is permitted in many other countries including the USA.

[4] This means that where some of the shares in issue were issued at par with others having been issued at a premium it will be necessary to identify which particular shares are being purchased.

Example 18.1

Bratsk plc has the following summarised balance sheet:

	£
Net assets	1500
Share capital – £1 shares	1000
Share premium	200
(Permanent capital)	1200
Distributable profits	300
	1500

It purchases 100 £1 shares for £160 out of distributable profits.
   Summarised journal entries together with the resulting balance sheet are as follows:

	£	£
Dr Share capital	100	
Premium on purchase	60	
Cr Cash		160
	160	160
Dr Distributable profits	160	
Cr Premium on purchase		60
Capital redemption reserve		100
	160	160

Summarised balance sheet after purchase of shares

		£
Net assets	(1500 – 160)	1340
Share capital	(1000 – 100)	900
Share premium		200
Capital redemption reserve		100
(Permanent capital)		1200
Distributable profits	(300 – 160)	140
		1340

Notice that the permanent capital of the company remains unchanged at £1200.

Next let us assume that a company purchases shares out of the proceeds of a new issue. We will assume first that the shares are purchased at their nominal (or par) value. We will deal with the more common situation where the shares are purchased at a premium in later examples. In the absence of any premium payable on purchase, the nominal value of the shares purchased is replaced by the nominal value of, and any share premium received on, the new issue.

Example 18.2

Chita Limited has the following summarised balance sheet:

	£
Net assets	1500
Share capital – £1 shares	1000
Share premium	200
(Permanent capital)	1200
Distributable profits	300
	1500

Chita purchases 100 £1 shares at their nominal value out of the proceeds of an issue of 80 £1 shares at a premium of 25p per share.

Summarised journal entries and the resulting balance sheet are as follows:

	£	£
Dr Cash	100	
Cr Share capital		80
Share premium		20
	100	100
Dr Share capital	100	
Cr Cash		100

Summarised balance sheet after purchase of shares

	£
Net assets	1500
Share capital (1000 + 80 – 100)	980
Share premium (200 + 20)	220
(Permanent capital)	1200
Distributable profits	300
	1500

Once again, the permanent capital has been maintained at £1200.

Frequently, as in the case of Bratsk (Example 18.1), a premium is payable on the shares purchased. Such a premium must be paid out of distributable profits except that, where the shares which are being purchased were originally issued at a premium, all or part of the premium now payable may be paid out of the proceeds of the new issue and charged against the share premium account. The amount which may be charged against the share premium account is the lower of:

(i) the amount of the premium which the company originally received on the shares now being purchased, and

(ii) the current balance on the share premium account, including any premium on the new issue of shares.

Example 18.3

Dudinka Limited has the following summarised balance sheet:

	£
Net assets	1500
Share capital – £1 shares	1000
Share premium	200
(Permanent capital)	1200
Distributable profits	300
	1500

Dudinka Limited purchases 100 £1 shares that were originally issued at a premium of 20p per share. The price paid is £180 and this is financed by the issue of 90 £1 shares at a premium of £1 per share.

Part of the premium payable may be financed from the proceeds of the new issue; the amount is the lower of the original share premium on the shares now being purchased, £20 (100 at 20p) and the balance of the share premium account, including the premium on the new share issue, £290 (£200 + £90), and hence £20 may be debited to the share premium account. The balance must come from distributable profits.

Summarised journal entries and the resulting balance sheet are as follows:

	£	£
Dr Cash	180	
Cr Share capital		90
Share premium		90
	180	180
Dr Share capital	100	
Premium on purchase	80	
Cr Cash		180
	180	180
Dr Share premium	20	
Distributable profits	60	
Cr Premium on purchase		80
	80	80

Summarised balance sheet after purchase of shares

	£
Net assets (1500 + 180 – 180)	1500
Share capital (1000 + 90 – 100)	990
Share premium (200 + 90 – 20)	270
(Permanent capital)	1260
Distributable profits (300 – 60)	240
	1500

So, even where the proceeds of the new issue are exactly equal to the amount payable on purchase, the restriction on the amount of any premium payable which may be charged against the share premium account will often result in part of the premium payable being charged against distributable profits and a consequent increase in the permanent capital of the company. As stated earlier, this appears to be an unintended consequence of the legislation.

In the final example in this section, we look at a company which purchases shares but raises only part of the finance by making a new issue of shares. We shall assume that the shares are purchased at a premium and that the new shares are issued at a premium. As we shall see, it is in this situation that a reduction in the permanent capital of the company may occur.

Example 18.4

Ivdel plc has the following summarised balance sheet:

	£
Net assets	1500
Share capital – £1 shares	1000
Share premium	200
(Permanent capital)	1200
Distributable profits	300
	1500

It purchases 100 shares which were originally issued at a premium of 50p per share. The agreed price is £180 and the company issues 40 shares at a premium of £1 per share to help finance the purchase.

The premium payable on purchase is £80 and part of this may come from the proceeds of the new issue and be charged to the share premium account. As explained above, this amount is the lower of the original premium (£50) and the balance on the share premium account after the new issue (£240). Hence £50 may be debited to the share premium account and the balance must be debited to distributable profits.

As part of the purchase price is being met from distributable profits, it is necessary to make a transfer to capital redemption reserve. Section 170(2) of the Companies Act 1985 requires the amount to be calculated by deducting the aggregate amount of the proceeds of the new issue from the nominal value of the shares purchased. In this case the amount of the transfer is therefore:

	£
Nominal value of shares purchased	100
less Proceeds of new issue	
(40 × £2)	80
Necessary transfer	20

▶

Necessary journal entries and the resulting balance sheet are given below:

	£	£
Dr Cash	80	
Cr Share capital		40
Share premium		40
	80	80
Dr Share capital	100	
Premium on purchase	80	
Cr Cash		180
	180	180
Dr Share premium	50	
Distributable profits	30	
Cr Premium on purchase		80
	80	80
Dr Distributable profits	20	
Cr Capital redemption reserve		20

Summarised balance sheet after purchase of shares

	£
Net assets (1500 + 80 − 180)	1400
Share capital (1000 + 40 − 100)	940
Share premium (200 + 40 − 50)	190
Capital redemption reserve	20
(Permanent capital)	1150
Distributable profits (300 − 30 − 20)	250
	1400

In this case, the permanent capital has been reduced from £1200 to £1150, which does not accord with the intended aim of maintaining permanent capital. The reason for the reduction is that the proceeds of the new issue are treated as financing part of both the nominal value and the premium payable but this is not recognised by the legislation in specifying the computation of the transfer to capital redemption reserve.

Let us illustrate: the proceeds of the new issue are £80 and, of this, £50 is used to finance the premium on purchase. This leaves only £30 to replace the nominal value of the shares issued. To maintain the permanent capital of the company, the transfer to capital redemption reserve should be calculated as follows:

	£	£
Nominal value of shares purchased		100
less Net proceeds of new issue:		
Total proceeds	80	
less Utilised to finance part of premium payable	50	
		30
Necessary transfer to capital redemption reserve		70

Such a transfer would maintain permanent capital at £1200 but, for the reasons given earlier, it is not the transfer required by law. Section 170(2) makes no reference to 'net' proceeds of the new issue and hence the law seems to permit such a reduction in capital for both public and private companies. The law has been poorly drafted with the consequence that it fails to achieve the objective of maintaining the company's permanent capital.

Purchase out of capital[5]

The permissible capital payment

While failure to maintain capital in the circumstances discussed above may be an unintended effect of the legislation, the 1985 Act specifically permits a private, but not a public, company to purchase its shares out of capital. This provides such a company with a means for reducing its permanent capital without the formality and expense of undertaking a capital reduction scheme, which we discuss in the next section. Such an ability to purchase shares out of capital is of considerable benefit to, for example, a family-owned company where a member of the family wishes to realise his or her investment but no other member of the family wishes, or is able, to purchase it.

A purchase of shares out of capital results in a fall in the resources potentially available to creditors and, as we shall see, the 1985 Act therefore provides a number of safeguards to protect their interests. One of these safeguards is that the company must use all of its distributable profits before it may reduce its capital. Similarly, if a company issues shares to finance the purchase, either wholly or in part, then these proceeds must be used before any capital reduction may occur. Thus the act specifies, what it calls the 'permissible capital payment':

	£	£
Amount payable to purchase shares		X
Less Distributable profits	X	
Proceeds of new issue	X	X
Permissible capital payment		X

The term 'permissible capital payment' is misleading in that it is not a payment but the maximum amount by which the permananent capital may be reduced.

If the total of the permissible capital payment and the proceeds of a fresh issue of shares is less than the nominal value of the shares purchased, there would be a reduction in permanent capital in excess of the permissible capital payment. To prevent this, the law requires that the difference be transferred to a capital redemption reserve but, for the reasons stated earlier, where the shares purchased at a premium had originally been issued at a premium, the reduction in permanent capital might still exceed the permissible capital payment.

If the permissible capital payment together with the proceeds of any fresh issue of shares exceeds the nominal value of the shares purchased, the excess may be eliminated by writing it off against any one of a number of accounts, including accounts for capital redemption reserve, share premium, share capital or unrealised profits. This ability to write off the excess to any one of these named accounts or, indeed, to deal with it in some other way, provides a private company with considerable flexibility to design its own capital reduction scheme.

We shall illustrate the above rules with two examples of the purchase of shares by private companies.

---

[5] The relevant legal provisions are contained in the Companies Act 1985, ss. 171–177.

In Example 18.5 the purchase of shares is made partly out of capital and partly out of distributable profits, whereas in Example 18.6 the purchase is, in addition, made partly out of the proceeds of a new issue of shares.

Example 18.5

Kotlas Limited has the following summarised balance sheet:

	£
Net assets	1250
Share capital – £1 shares	1000
Distributable profits	250
	1250

It purchases 200 £1 shares at a cost of £300. In the absence of a share premium account or a new issue of shares at a premium, the amount of the premium payable must be provided from distributable profits.

The permissible capital payment is:

	£
Amount payable	300
less Distributable profits	250
Permissible capital payment	50

As the permissible capital payment (£50) is less than the nominal value of the shares purchased (£200) it is necessary to make a transfer from distributable profits to a capital redemption reserve.

	£
Nominal value of shares purchased	200
less Permissible capital payment	50
Necessary transfer	150

Necessary journal entries and the resulting summarised balance sheet are given below:

	£	£
Dr Share capital	200	
Premium on purchase	100	
Cr Cash		300
	300	300
Dr Distributable profits	250	
Cr Premium on purchase		100
Capital redemption reserve		150
	250	250

Summarised balance sheet after purchase of shares

	£
Net assets (1250 – 300)	950
Share capital (1000 – 200)	800
Capital redemption reserve	150
(Permanent capital)	950

The permanent capital of the company has been reduced from £1000 share capital to £950. It has fallen by the amount of the permissible capital payment.

Example 18.6

Nordvik Limited has the following summarised balance sheet:

	£
Net assets	1250
Share capital – £1 shares	1 000
Share premium	200
(Permanent capital)	1200
Distributable profits	50
	1 250

Of the £1 shares, 500 were issued at par when the company was formed and 500 were issued at a premium of 40p per share some years later.

Nordvik purchases 200 of the shares, which were originally issued at par for an agreed price of £300, and finances the purchase in part by an issue of 50 shares at a premium of 60p per share.

As the shares purchased were not originally issued at a premium, no part of the premium payable may come from the proceeds of the new issue. The whole of the premium payable, that is the whole of the increase in value of these particular shares since their issue, must be charged against distributable profits.

In this case, the permissible capital payment is:

	£	£
Amount payable		300
less Distributable profits	50	
Proceeds of new issue (50 × £1.60)	80	130
Permissible capital payment		170

In order to determine whether or not a transfer to capital redemption reserve is necessary, we must compare the proceeds of the new issue and the permissible capital payment with the nominal value of the shares purchased.

	£	£
Nominal value of shares purchased		200
less Permissible capital payment	170	
Proceeds of new issue	80	250
		(50)

▶

In this case no transfer to capital redemption reserve is required. Rather the excess £50 may be charged to one of the accounts discussed above and we have chosen to debit it to the share premium account.

Necessary journal entries and the resulting summarised balance sheet are given below:

	£	£
Dr Cash	80	
Cr Share capital		50
Share premium		30
	80	80
Dr Share capital	200	
Premium on purchase	100	
Cr Cash		300
	300	300
Dr Distributable profits	50	
Share premium	50	
Cr Premium on purchase		100
	100	100

Summarised balance sheet after purchase of shares

	£
Net assets (1250 + 80 – 300)	1030
Share capital (1000 + 50 – 200)	850
Share premium (200 + 30 – 50)	180
(Permanent capital)	1030
Distributable profits	–
	1030

The permanent capital of the company has been reduced from £1200 to £1030 by the amount of the permissible capital payment of £170.

Further safeguards

In view of the fact that there is a reduction in the permanent capital, that is a reduction in the net assets available to creditors and the remaining shareholders, the law provides a number of safeguards where a company wishes to make such a purchase of shares involving a payment out of capital. Thus, not only must the payment out of capital be permitted by the company's articles of association and authorised by a special resolution of the company, but the directors must also provide a statutory declaration of solvency to the effect that, having made a full enquiry into the affairs and prospects of the company, they have formed the opinion that the company will be able to pay its debts both immediately after the payment and during the following year. As the protection of creditors and shareholders rests on this continuing solvency of the company, the law requires that a report by the company's auditors on the reasonableness of the directors' opinion is attached to the statutory declaration.

After the payment out of capital has been authorised, the company must publicise it in an official gazette and either a national newspaper or by individual notice to each creditor. Any creditor, or any shareholder who did not vote for the special resolution, may then apply to the court for the cancellation of the resolution and the court may then cancel or confirm the resolution and may make an order to facilitate an arrangement whereby the interests of dissenting creditors or members are purchased.

If the directors' optimism subsequently proves not to have been well founded and the company commences to wind up within a year of the payment out of capital and is unable to pay all its liabilities and the costs of winding up, then directors and past shareholders may be liable to contribute. The directors who have signed the statutory declaration and/or past shareholders, whose shares were purchased, may have to pay an amount not exceeding in total the permitted capital payment.

Thus the Companies Act 1985 provides safeguards to protect creditors. The use of its provisions to make a purchase of shares partly out of capital is undoubtedly much cheaper and less burdensome than a reduction of capital under the provisions to which we turn next.

Capital reduction

There are other sections of the Companies Act 1985 that give companies much wider powers to reduce capital than that discussed above, but the Act imposes more onerous conditions if these powers are exercised, including the need to obtain the confirmation of the court.[6]

Provided it is authorised to do so by its articles of association, a limited company may reduce its share capital by passing a special resolution, which must be confirmed by the court. The Act gives a general power to reduce share capital but specifically lists three possible ways to reduce capital:[7]

(a) extinguish or reduce the liability on any of its shares in respect of share capital not paid up; or

(b) either with or without extinguishing or reducing liability on any of its shares, cancel any paid-up share capital which is lost or unrepresented by available assets; or

(c) either with or without extinguishing or reducing liability on any of its shares, pay off any paid-up share capital which is in excess of the company's wants.

Capital reductions for the first and third of the possible reasons listed are extremely rare. With regard to the first, few companies now have partly paid shares in existence and hence there is seldom any liability in respect of partly paid capital which could be reduced. With regard to the third, although it might make good economic sense for directors to return 'permanent' capital to shareholders where better investment opportunities exist outside the company than within it, most directors have been loath to relinquish their control over such resources and have usually found some way to employ them within the company.

Both of these capital reductions ((a) and (c)) do, of course, result in a reduction in the potential net assets or actual net assets available to creditors. Thus, in the first case, there is a reduction in the liability of members and hence in the potential pool of net assets available to creditors on a liquidation. In the third case, resources actually leave the company, so directly reducing the pool of net assets to which the creditors have recourse. For these reasons the court must give any creditor an opportunity to object to the capital reduction and will usually only confirm the scheme if the debt of such a dissenting creditor is paid or secured.

---

[6] As we shall see later in this chapter, the White Paper, *Modernising Company Law* (July 2002), proposes the introduction of an additional, simpler procedure based on the issue of a solvency statement by a company's directors.

[7] Companies Act 1985, s. 135.

The second of the three possible capital reduction schemes is the one most commonly found in practice. Thus, where a company has made losses in excess of previous profits, its net assets will be lower than its permanent capital. Given that such a position has been reached, it will often be sensible to recognise the fact by reducing the capital and writing off the losses so that a more realistic position is shown by the balance sheet and the company is allowed to make a fresh start. In particular, after such a scheme the company will be able to distribute realised profits without the need to first make good the accumulated realised losses and, in the case of a public company, net unrealised losses.[8]

The simplest way of carrying out such a capital reduction scheme is to reduce proportionately the nominal value of the ordinary shares outstanding. This has no effect whatsoever on the real value of the ordinary shareholders' interest since the same number of shares in the same company are held in the same proportions by the same people! Each shareholder has the same proportional interest in the net assets of the company after the scheme as before. This demonstrates the irrelevance of the par value and supports the argument that companies should be permitted to issue shares of no par value.[9]

To illustrate such a scheme, let us look at an example.

Example 18.7

Perm plc has the following summarised balance sheet:

		£
Net assets		1200
Share capital		
1000 £1 ordinary shares, fully paid		1000
500 £1 10% preference shares, fully paid		500
		1500
Share premium		200
		1700
less Accumulated losses		500
		1200

The preference shares rank for dividend and repayment of capital in priority to ordinary shares. The company wishes to reduce its capital by an amount sufficient to remove the accumulated losses and to write down the net assets to a more realistic book value of £900. Thus it wishes to reduce permanent capital by £800, that is £(500 + (1200 − 900)).

For illustrative purposes we shall consider two possible capital reduction schemes, the first involving a reduction of ordinary share capital only and the second involving the reduction of both ordinary share capital and preference share capital.

---

[8] See Chapter 4.

[9] A government committee under the chairmanship of Mr Montague Gedge reported in favour of the issue of shares of no par value as long ago as 1954, Cmnd. 9112/5, HMSO, London, 1954. Similar proposals in favour of no par value shares have been made in various consultation documents of the Company Law Review Steering Group, but the White Paper, *Modernising Company Law* (2002), recognises that, because the EU Second Directive (77/91/EEC [1977] OJ L26/1) requires public companies to have shares with a par value, the movement towards shares of no par value can only be a long-term aim!

Scheme 1

As explained above, the total amount of the capital reduction is £800. However, for the purpose of a reduction of capital, a share premium account is to be treated as paid-up share capital of the company[10] so that £200 may be written off against the share premium, leaving £600 to reduce the ordinary share capital from £1000 to £400, that is from £1 to 40p per share.

The balance sheet after the capital reduction would therefore appear as follows:

Summarised balance sheet after capital reduction

	£
Net assets	900
Share capital	
1000 40p ordinary shares	400
500 £1 10% preference shares	500
	900

The interest of preference shareholders and ordinary shareholders in the liquidation value of the company has not altered. Preference shareholders would receive the first £500 while ordinary shareholders would receive the remainder. If the company continues to trade, both sets of shareholders gain, in the sense that the company will be able to pay dividends as soon as profits are made without any need to make good the past losses.

Scheme 2

Given the fact that preference shareholders as well as ordinary shareholders benefit from the capital reduction scheme, ordinary shareholders might argue that preference share capital as well as ordinary share capital should be reduced. However, as we shall see, a reduction in the par value of a preference share has a much more serious effect than the reduction in the par value of ordinary shares. Indeed, a reduction in the par value of both preference shares and ordinary shares, with no other changes, will lead to a fall in the real value of the preference shares but a rise in the real value of the ordinary shares. This may be illustrated as follows.

As before, let us assume that the amount of the capital reduction is £800 and that, of this, £200 may be written off against the share premium account, leaving £600 to be written off against share capital. Given that the ordinary share capital is £1000 and that the preference share capital is £500, it might be thought that the amount of £600 should be written off in the ratio 2:1 which would produce a balance sheet as follows:

Summarised balance sheet after capital reduction

	£
Net assets	900
Share capital	
1000 60p ordinary shares	600
500 60p 10% preference shares	300
	900

Although this may initially appear to be fair, a little thought will make it clear that the preference shareholders have been unfairly treated.

Given that the par value of a preference share determines the amount of the preference dividend and the amount which the preference shareholders receive on a liquidation, preference

---

[10] Companies Act 1985, s. 130(3).

shareholders will have suffered a real loss. They are worse off after the scheme than before. Conversely, the ordinary shareholders are better off. Not only would they receive more on an immediate liquidation, as less would be paid to the preference shareholders, but also they are likely to receive higher future dividends, as a lesser dividend would be paid to the preference shareholders.

Careful attention must be paid to the likely effect of reducing the par values of different types of share capital. A capital reduction such as Scheme 2 is unlikely to be acceptable to the preference shareholders unless they are given some other benefit, such as a holding of ordinary shares, which will give them an opportunity to share in any future prosperity.

The proposed simplification of capital reduction

As we have explained, the procedures for capital reduction contained in the Companies Act 1985 are rather cumbersome and, in particular, require the confirmation of the court, with its associated costs. Following recommendations of the Company Law Review Steering Group,[11] the White Paper, *Modernising Company Law*, issued in July 2002, makes proposals for companies to be permitted to reduce their capital without the need for confirmation of the court, provided that the directors of the company make a solvency statement. Draft clauses of these proposals are contained in the second volume of the White Paper.[12]

Under the proposals, both private and public limited companies would be permitted to reduce their share capital in any way by passing a special resolution. However, public companies would have to comply with publicity requirements to ensure that, as far as is possible, creditors are informed of the proposed reduction of capital. Creditors of the company would have six weeks from the date of the resolution to apply to the court for the resolution to be cancelled and the court would then either make an order cancelling the resolution to reduce capital or dismiss the creditor's application.

The crucial requirement of this new process is the solvency statement required of directors, which we have already met earlier in the chapter in connection with the purchase of shares out of capital by a private company. The draft clauses define the envisaged solvency statement as follows:[13]

> In this Chapter 'solvency statement', in relation to a proposed reduction of share capital, means a statement that the directors –
>
> (a) have formed the opinion that, as regards the company's situation at the date of the statement, there is no ground on which the company could then be found to be unable to pay its debts; and
> (b) have also formed the opinion –
>   (i) if it is intended to commence winding up the company within the year immediately following that date, that the company will able to pay its debts in full within the year beginning with commencement of the winding-up; or
>   (ii) if it is not intended so to commence winding up, that the company will be able to pay its debts as they fall due during the year immediately following the date of the statement.

---

[11] The Group proposed the abolition of the requirement for confirmation by the court and its replacement by the requirement for a declaration of solvency in Chapter 5.4 of the Consultative Paper, *Modern Company Law for a Competitive Economy: The Strategic Framework*, Department of Trade and Industry, February 1999.

[12] Cm. 5553-II, Part 3, Chapter 3, *Reduction of Share Capital*, Clauses 50–67.

[13] Cm. 5553-II, Part 3, Chapter 3, Clause 63.

In forming their opinion, the directors must take into account all liabilities of the company, including contingent and prospective liabilities, and, where a statement is made without reasonable grounds, the directors are guilty of an offence for which a penalty will be specified.

Such an approach focuses on what is really important, namely the ability of the company to pay its debts in full. It would simplify the law and would remove the necessity to have the separate rules which enable a private company to purchase its shares out of capital, discussed earlier in this chapter.

The legal background to other reorganisations

We have looked in some detail at the ways in which a company may reduce its share capital under the provisions of the Companies Act 1985 and examined proposed changes to this approach. As we saw in the introduction to this chapter, there are many other ways in which a company may wish to reorganise its capital. For example, it may wish to alter the respective rights of different classes of shareholders, or, if it is in financial difficulties, it may need to reduce not only share capital but also the claims of creditors. In this section we look briefly at the legal background to such reorganisations.

First, it is necessary to clarify that although the term 'capital reduction' has a clear legal meaning, as discussed above, the terms 'capital reorganisation', 'capital reconstruction' and, indeed, 'scheme of arrangement' do not. These terms tend to be used interchangeably although there is, perhaps, a tendency to use the term 'capital reconstruction' for the more serious changes in capital structure; so in the final section of this chapter we look at a capital reconstruction scheme undertaken as an alternative to liquidation of the company. In the remainder of this section we will use the term reorganisation.

Any reorganisation which involves creditors will invariably be carried out in accordance with the procedures laid down in ss. 425–426 of the Companies Act 1985. These procedures are designed to protect the various parties involved by requiring court approval for the reorganisation. This sounds fine in theory but the courts have been reluctant to pass judgement on the economic merits and fairness of schemes and have tended to concern themselves with deciding whether the scheme satisfies the required legal formalities.[14]

Under ss. 425–426, the company applies to the court which will then direct meetings of the various parties affected to be held. The company must then send out details of the proposed scheme and, provided a majority agree – in number representing three-quarters in value of those attending the various meetings – and provided the scheme is sanctioned by the court, it will become binding on all parties once a copy is delivered to the Registrar of Companies.

Sometimes a reorganisation entered into in accordance with the above provisions will involve the transfer of the whole or part of an undertaking from one company to another. In such a case, s. 427 gives the court wide powers to make provision for the transfer of ownership of assets, liabilities, rights and duties to the transferee company.

The above provisions may be used to effect a reorganisation even where there is no change in creditors' rights. However, alternative procedures are available in such cases which do not involve the formality and expense of going to court. Thus, it may be possible to vary the rights of two or more classes of shareholders by merely holding separate class meetings

---

[14] See L.C.B. Gower, *Gower's Principles of Modern Company Law*, 6th edn, edited by Paul L. Davies, with a contribution by Dan Prentice, Sweet & Maxwell, London, 1997, Chapter 28.

and obtaining the necessary majority votes, although a dissenting minority is given a right to object to the variation in an application to the court.

Another possible means of reorganisation is provided by s. 110 of the Insolvency Act 1986. Under this section, once a voluntary liquidation of the company is proposed, the liquidator may be given authority to sell the whole or a part of the undertaking to another company in exchange for shares or other securities in that other company. Thus, where it is desired to change the rights of two or more classes of its shareholders, the company may be put into voluntary liquidation and a new company may be formed with the desired mix of various classes of shares. The business of the transferor company may then be sold to the new company in exchange for the new shares, which may then be distributed to the shareholders in the transferor company to achieve the desired change. This procedure is much simpler than the use of a scheme under ss. 425–427 of the Act.

Invariably taxation considerations will be extremely important in most capital reorganisations and, in view of the complexity of the tax legislation, specialist advice is almost always necessary.

Capital reconstruction

In this section we shall concentrate on the design and evaluation of a capital reconstruction scheme for a company which is in severe financial difficulties. It will be assumed that, in the absence of a capital reconstruction scheme, the liquidation of the company would be inevitable. This assumption will affect both the design of the scheme and the way in which it will be evaluated by the interested parties.

As the alternative source of benefits to interested parties is the amount receivable on liquidation, it is essential for us to recall the order in which the proceeds from the sale of assets must be distributed by a liquidator.

Distribution on liquidation

It is the duty of a liquidator to sell the assets of a company as advantageously as possible and to pay costs, creditors and shareholders in the following order:

1 Debts secured by a fixed charge. These must be paid out of the proceeds of sale of the particular assets. In practice a receiver will usually be appointed to sell the assets which are the subject of the charge, and to pay the secured creditors the amounts due to them.

   It will rarely be the case that the proceeds of sale are exactly equal to the costs of the receiver and the amount of the debt. Any excess will be paid over to the liquidator of the company while, to the extent of any deficiency, the creditors are treated in the same way as other unsecured creditors.

2 Costs of the liquidation, in the order specified by law.

3 Preferential creditors. These are listed in Schedule 6 to the Insolvency Act 1986 and include income tax deducted from employees' emoluments under PAYE, value added tax, car tax, social security contributions, contributions to pension schemes and remuneration of employees. There are limits to each of these categories so, for example, PAYE is preferential to the extent of one year's deductions, value added tax to six months, social security contributions up to one year and remuneration of employees up to four months. To the extent that only a part of a debt is preferential, the remainder will be treated as an unsecured creditor.

4 Creditors secured by a floating charge.

5 Unsecured creditors, including the amounts mentioned in 1 and 3 above.

6 Shareholders of the company in accordance with their rights as laid down in the company's articles of association. Preference shares will normally be paid before any amounts are paid to ordinary shareholders.

Where the amounts available are insufficient to pay any of the above groups in full, each member of the particular group receives the same proportion of the amount of his debt. This proportion is determined as the amount available for a particular group divided by the total amounts due to that group.

Design of a capital reconstruction scheme

Where a company is in financial difficulties, the objective in the design of a capital reconstruction scheme will be to produce an entity which is a profitable going concern. In some cases the financial difficulties may be so severe that this is impossible for, no matter how skilfully a capital reconstruction scheme is designed, it is not possible to turn the sow's ear into a silk purse. Where the financial difficulties are less severe and the company is capable of operating profitably, a capital reconstruction scheme may have a high probability of success. In order to achieve that success, it will usually be necessary to relieve the company of its burden of immediate debts and will often be necessary to raise new finance, probably by a new issue of shares.

Any capital reconstruction scheme which affects the rights of creditors and shareholders will require the necessary majorities of votes in favour of the scheme as required by s. 425 of the Companies Act 1985, together with the sanction of the court. Hence, to stand any chance of success, the scheme must give each interested party the same amount as or more than they would receive on liquidation of the company. In addition the scheme must be accepted as equitable by the various interested parties. It must ensure that no one class of creditor or shareholder is favoured at the expense of any other, so that all creditors and shareholders are treated – and feel that they are treated – fairly.

The design of a capital reconstruction scheme is illustrated in the following example, and the resulting scheme is evaluated in the final section of this chapter.

Example 18.8

A summarised balance sheet of Sakhalin plc on 31 December 20X1 is as follows:

Sakhalin plc
Balance sheet on 31 December 20X1

	£000	£000
Fixed assets at cost less depreciation		
Land and buildings	2500	
Plant and machinery	1000	3500
Current assets		
Stock and work-in-progress	1000	
Sundry debtors	1500	2500
		6000
less Current liabilities		
Bank overdraft	3000	
Trade creditors	1000	
Arrears of debenture interest	250	4250
		1750
Financed by		
10% secured debentures (note (a))		1250
1 million authorised and issued £1		
5% cumulative preference shares	1000	
2 million authorised and issued £1		
ordinary shares	2000	
	3000	
less Accumulated losses	2500	500
		1750

The following information is available:

(a) The debentures are secured on the office premises, the net realisable value of which is estimated to be £900 000.

(b) The other land and buildings are estimated to have a net realisable value of £1 900 000.

(c) The net realisable value of the plant and machinery is estimated to be £500 000, of the stock and work-in-progress £750 000, and the recoverable debts are now estimated to be £1 425 000.

(d) The preference dividend has not been paid for four years.

(e) The debenture interest is two years in arrears.

(f) The articles provide that, on liquidation, the preference shareholders rank for repayment at par prior to any distribution to the ordinary shareholders.

From preliminary meetings of the directors and soundings of the interested parties the following information has also been obtained:

(g) The debenture holders are prepared to agree to a reconstruction scheme, provided the rate of interest is increased from 10 to 15 per cent p.a., and they are given a fixed security on the total land and buildings, rather than just the office premises, of the company. They are also willing to accept ordinary shares in lieu of £125 000, that is one of the two years' interest in arrears.

(h) The bank is prepared to agree to a reconstruction scheme provided its debt is secured by a floating charge over the assets of the company, thus improving its position *vis-à-vis* any other creditors of the reconstructed company. They would be willing to provide the same amount of finance for the medium term.

(i) The trade creditors are unlikely to agree to any reduction in their claims but are thought to be willing to supply the reconstructed company and to continue to grant credit on normal terms.

(j) The preference shareholders would be willing to forgo their arrears of dividend and to accept ordinary shares instead of preference shares.

(k) The directors consider that, if the company is able to raise an additional £1 million in cash by a rights issue, it will be able to commence trading successfully. Expected annual earnings before debenture interest and dividends will then be at least £300 000 and, due to accumulated tax losses, no corporation tax will be payable in the foreseeable future.

(l) Debenture holders, preference shareholders and ordinary shareholders are willing to subscribe for new ordinary share capital in the company.

(m) Costs of the reconstruction scheme are expected to be £60 000.

(n) In the absence of a satisfactory scheme the company will have to be liquidated involving costs of £295 000.

From the above information it is possible to calculate the amount of the capital reduction required, namely:[15]

		£000
(a)	To correct the value of plant and machinery	500
(b)	To correct the value of stock and work-in-progress	250
(c)	To correct the value of debtors	75
(d)	To eliminate the adverse balance on the profit and loss account	2500
(e)	To provide for the costs of the scheme	60
		3385
(f)	Less surplus on revaluation of land and buildings	300
		3085

In order to begin to decide who must bear this loss in the reconstruction scheme, we must first examine what each class of creditor and shareholder would receive if the company were to be liquidated.

---

[15] In a balance sheet, assets should be shown at their 'going concern value' rather than their net realisable value. In order to avoid complicating the example by the introduction of another set of values, the realistic going concern values, assets have been written down to their net realisable values.

The realisable value of the assets and the way in which they would be distributed are as follows:

	£000	£000
Office premises	900	
less Payable to debenture holders		
secured on office premises	900	–
Other premises		1900
Plant and machinery		500
Stock and work-in-progress		750
Sundry debtors		1425
		4575
less Costs of liquidation		295
Available for unsecured creditors		4280
Unsecured creditors:		
Bank overdraft		3000
Debenture holders		
Capital	1250	
Interest	250	
	1500	
less Paid out of security as above	900	600
Trade creditors		1000
		4600

For simplicity it is assumed that there are no preferential creditors.

There would be £4280 available to meet unsecured creditors of £4600 with the result that each of these creditors, including the debenture holders to the extent that they are unsecured, would receive 93p in the £1. The various parties would therefore receive the following amounts on liquidation of the company:

	£000
Bank (0.93 × £3 000 000)	2790
Debenture holders (900 000 + 0.93 × 600 000)	1460
Trade creditors (0.93 × 1 000 000)	930
Preference shareholders	0
Ordinary shareholders	0
	5180

Thus all parties would lose on a liquidation and there is an incentive for them to agree to a suitable reconstruction scheme. It is clear that any losses under the scheme must fall most heavily on the shareholders.

One possible scheme of reconstruction would be as follows:

		Reduction
		£000
(a)	2 million £1 ordinary shares each to be reduced to 1p ordinary shares	1980
(b)	1 million £1 preference shares to be cancelled in exchange for 1 million 1p ordinary shares	990
(c)	The granting of an increased rate of interest of 15 per cent p.a. and a fixed charge on all premises to the debenture holders and the waiving of £125 000 of interest in arrears in exchange for 1 million 1p ordinary shares (£10 000)	115
(d)	The granting of a floating charge on the debt due to the bank	–
(e)	Consolidation of the 4 million 1p ordinary shares into 40 000 £1 ordinary shares	–
(f)	The making of a rights issue of 25 £1 ordinary shares for each £1 ordinary share held, thus raising cash of £1 000 000. Thus finance would come from old ordinary shareholders (£500 000), old preference shareholders (£250 000) and old debenture holders (£250 000)	–
	Total reduction achieved as required	3085

After such a reconstruction scheme is carried into effect, the balance sheet would appear as shown below:

Sakhalin plc
Balance sheet after scheme

	£000	£000
Tangible fixed assets – at valuation		
Land and buildings		2800
Plant and machinery		500
		3300
Current assets		
Stock and work-in-progress	750	
Debtors	1425	
Cash	1000	
	3175	
less Current liabilities		
Bank overdraft (secured)	3000	
Debenture interest (1 year)	125	
Trade creditors	1000	
Cost of reconstruction	60	
	4185	(1010)
		2290
less 15% Debentures (secured on land and buildings)		1250
		1040
Share capital		
1 040 000 £1 ordinary shares, fully paid		1040

Note: The apparently poor current ratio is due to the fact that the bank overdraft is included in current liabilities, in accordance with normal practice, whereas it is in fact medium-term capital.

Evaluation of a capital reconstruction scheme

In evaluating a capital reconstruction scheme, as in designing it, the aim must be to establish the relative fairness of the changes in rights as a result of the scheme. In most cases, professional advisers are called upon by each class of member and creditor to evaluate the scheme from their point of view and, in order to do this, it is necessary to evaluate the scheme as a whole since the changes of relative rights will be extremely important.

The rights of participants fall into two classes: the capital repayment rights and the income participation rights. In order to make an appropriate comparison of these, it is helpful to set out the interest of the various parties in the company both before and after the proposed reconstruction.

In Example 18.9 we shall do this in respect of the scheme which has been proposed for Sakhalin plc in Example 18.8.

Example 18.9

Table 18.1 summarises the interests of the relevant parties before and after the scheme.

Table 18.1 Evaluation of proposed scheme – comparison of interests

Original class	Interest prior to scheme	Interest after scheme
Bank	£3 000 000 unsecured overdraft	£3 000 000 secured overdraft
Debenture holders	£1 250 000 partly secured 10% debentures *plus* £250 000 arrears of interest	£1 250 000 fully secured 15% debentures *plus* £125 000 arrears of interest *plus* one-quarter of the ordinary shares
Trade creditors	£1 000 000 unsecured debt	£1 000 000 unsecured debt
Preference shareholders	£1 000 000 £1 5% preference shares	One-quarter of the ordinary shares
Ordinary shareholders	All ordinary shares	One-half of the ordinary shares

We have already considered the amounts each class would receive should the scheme be rejected and the company forced into an immediate liquidation. These amounts need to be compared with the position following the reconstruction and we shall do so by evaluating three alternative possible outcomes. First, we shall assume that, despite the scheme, the company goes into liquidation immediately following the end of the capital reconstruction. Second, we will assume that the earnings are as expected, about £300 000 per annum. Finally, we will assume that the earnings are more than anticipated; we will, for this purpose, assume a figure of £500 000 per annum.

If we assume that the costs of the reconstruction scheme are paid, the position on the subsequent liquidation would be as follows:

Position on liquidation after scheme

	£000	£000
Amount receivable from sale of premises		2800
less Debentures		
Capital	1250	
Interest	125	1375
		1425
Amount realised from other assets		
Plant and machinery	500	
Stock and work-in-progress	750	
Debtors	1425	2675
Cash (1 000 000 – 60 000)		940
		5040
less Costs of liquidation		295
		4745
less Bank secured by floating charge		3000
		1745
less Trade creditors		1000
Available for ordinary shareholders		745
Divisible:		
Old debenture holders $\left(\frac{1}{4}\right)$		186
Old preference shareholders $\left(\frac{1}{4}\right)$		186
Old ordinary shareholders $\left(\frac{1}{2}\right)$		373
		745

So, on a liquidation subsequent to the scheme the original parties would receive the following amounts:

	£000
Bank	3000
Debenture holders (1 375 000 + 186 000)	1561
Trade creditors	1000
Preference shareholders	186
Ordinary shareholders	373
	6120

Debenture holders and preference shareholders have, of course, subscribed £250 000 each for new ordinary share capital while ordinary shareholders have subscribed £500 000.

    Let us next examine the interests of the various parties in the expected earnings of the reconstructed company.

As we have seen in note (k) on p. 599, the annual earnings before debenture interest and dividends are expected to be at least £300 000 and no corporation tax is likely to be paid in the foreseeable future. It follows that these earnings may be divided as shown:

	£	£
Old debenture holders		
Interest 15% × £1 250 000	187 500	
Share of balance $\frac{1}{4}$ (300 000 – 187 500)	28 125	215 625
Old preference shareholders		
$\frac{1}{4}$ (300 000 – 187 500)		28 125
Old ordinary shareholders		
$\frac{1}{2}$ (300 000 – 187 500)		56 250
		300 000

It is helpful to examine the position if earnings turn out to be higher or lower than expected and, for illustrative purposes, we look at the position if earnings are £500 000:

	£	£
Old debenture holders		
Interest – as above	187 500	
Share of balance $\frac{1}{4}$ (500 000 – 187 500)	78 125	265 625
Old preference shareholders		
$\frac{1}{4}$ (500 000 – 187 500)		78 125
Old ordinary shareholders		
$\frac{1}{2}$ (500 000 – 187 500)		156 250
		500 000

We are now able to set out in Table 18.2 the position of each party before and after the proposed scheme in order to draw conclusions about its acceptability.

Table 18.2 Positions of parties before and after proposed scheme

			Position after scheme		
Original class	Amount receivable on liquidation before scheme	New capital introduced	Amount receivable on liquidation after scheme	Share of earnings £300 000	Share of earnings £500 000
	£000	£000	£000	£000	£000
Bank	2790	–	3000	n/a	n/a
Debenture holders	1460	250	1561	215.625	265.625
Trade creditors	930	–	1000	n/a	n/a
Preference shareholders	–	250	186	28.125	78.125
Ordinary shareholders	–	500	373	56.250	156.250

The scheme would appear to offer advantages to all parties:

The bank converts unsecured debt into secured debt and stands to receive more in a liquidation after the scheme than in one before it.

On an immediate liquidation the debenture holders would receive £1 460 000, whereas if they invest a further £250 000 they will obtain a higher rate of interest on their debentures, a higher level of security and one-quarter of the ordinary shares in the reconstructed company. Although they would only receive £1 561 000 on a liquidation after the scheme, their share in future earnings is attractive. If the level of future earnings is £300 000 their rate of return is approximately 12.6 per cent, that is £215 625 divided by the amount of £1 710 000 (1 460 000 + 250 000) effectively invested. If future earnings are £500 000, the rate of return rises to approximately 18.2 per cent.

Trade creditors would receive more in a liquidation after the scheme than in one before it.

Both preference shareholders and ordinary shareholders would appear to benefit considerably from the scheme. Although they would not receive back their new investment if a liquidation occurred immediately after the scheme, their potential earnings yield is high. If future earnings are £300 000, the yield is 11.25 per cent (28.125/250) while, if earnings are £500 000, the yield rises to 31.25 per cent (78.125/250).

If all the parties are happy with the scheme, they will vote in favour of it at their respective meetings. Provided it is then confirmed by the court, the scheme will become operative as soon as a copy of the court order is lodged with the Registrar. If any of the parties are unhappy with the scheme, it will be necessary to amend it. If, at the end of the day, agreement on a satisfactory scheme cannot be reached, the company will be liquidated.

Summary

In this chapter, we have looked at the rather complex topics of capital reorganisation, reduction and reconstruction.

We started by looking at the rules governing the purchase by a company of its own shares. While both private and public companies are permitted to purchase their own shares for cancellation, only a private company is permitted to purchase its own shares out of capital. We have illustrated the legal rules and seen that the application of these rules does not always achieve what appears to be the intended purpose of the law.

We have next looked at the wide-ranging power of companies to reduce their capital subject to the confirmation by the court and illustrated how this may be done. The involvement of the court brings with it substantial costs and we have outlined the proposals, made in the White Paper, *Modernising Company Law,* to simplify company law in this area. Under these proposals, both private and public companies would be able to reduce capital in any way by passing a special resolution, provided that the directors make a 'solvency statement'.

We have outlined the legal background to other reorganisations and finished the chapter with an examination of capital reconstruction schemes. Here we have illustrated the principles involved in both designing such a scheme and evaluating a scheme on behalf of the various parties who may be affected by it.

Recommended reading

J.H. Farrar, N.E. Furey, B.M. Hannigan and O.P. Wylie, *Farrar's Company Law*, 4th edn, Butterworths, London, 1998.

L.C.B. Gower, *Gower's Principles of Modern Company Law*, 6th edn, P. L. Davies (ed.) with a contribution from D. Prentice, Sweet & Maxwell, London, 1997.

T. Johnson, *A private company's purchase of own shares*, Butterworths, London, 1997.

M. Wyatt, *Company Acquisition of Own Shares*, 4th edn, Financial Times Pitman Publishing, London, 1995.

M. Wyatt, 'Purchase of own shares', *Accountants Digest*, No. 376, ICAEW, London, 1997.

A useful website

www.dti.gov.uk/companiesbill

18.1 In recent years several large listed companies have purchased their own ordinary shares.

You are required to summarise:
(a) **the accounting requirements for a public listed company when it purchases its own shares;**   (9 marks)
(b) **six advantages of a company purchasing its own shares.**   (6 marks)

CIMA, Advanced Financial Accounting, November 1991   **(15 marks)**

18.2 H plc was established in 1996 to develop advanced computer software. The company was established with the financial backing of B Bank. B Bank invested £2 million in H plc's share capital, buying 2 million £1 shares at par. The agreement was that B Bank would leave this investment in place for five years. At the end of that period, H plc would buy the shares back from B Bank at a price that reflected the company's success during that period.

An independent accountant advised that B Bank's 2 million shares in H plc were worth £4.5 million. The shares were repurchased on 30 April 2001 for that amount.

H plc's balance sheet immediately before the repurchase was as follows:

H plc

Balance sheet at 30 April 2001 (before share repurchase)

	£ million
Net assets	18.0
Share capital	7.0
Profit and loss	11.0
	18.0

The net assets figure includes £8.0 million cash.

Required:
(a) **Prepare H plc's balance sheet as it would appear immediately after the share repurchase.**   (5 marks)
(b) **When a company repurchases its shares, it must normally make a transfer from its profit and loss account to its capital redemption reserve (CRR). It has been suggested that this transfer is necessary to protect the company's lenders. Explain how the transfer to the CRR protects the interests of lenders when a company repurchases its shares.**   (10 marks)
(c) **Explain why companies are permitted to buy back their own shares.**   (5 marks)

CIMA, Financial Accounting – UK Acounting Standards, May 2001   **(20 marks)**

18.3 Capital plc carried on business in four product segments, namely aircraft design, hairdressing salons, import agencies and beauty products.

The directors are now considering the dividend policy and the future capital structure of the company.

The draft accounts of Capital plc as at 30 November 1995 showed the following share capital and reserves:

Share capital		£m
Ordinary shares of £1 each	*Note 1*	500
8% Redeemable preference shares of £1 each	*Note 2*	50
Reserves – all credit balances		
Share premium		63
Capital redemption reserve		10
Fixed asset revaluation reserve	*Note 3*	43
Profit and loss account	*Note 4*	775

Note 1
The market value of ordinary shares as at 30 November 1995 was £1.60.

Note 2
The redeemable preference shares were issued in 1985. They are redeemable at par.

Note 3
A revaluation reserve of £45 million was created on 1 December 1994 on the revaluation of some of the buildings. A debit of £2 million was made to the reserve in 1995 arising from a permanent fall in value on the revaluation of certain computer equipment.

Note 4
The profit and loss account of Capital plc for the year ended 30 November 1995 contained the following items:

(i)   Exchange gain on a long-term German mark loan taken out on 1 December 1994   £6m

(ii) Depreciation based on historic cost of fixed assets   £68m

      Additional depreciation based on revalued amount of fixed assets   £13m

(iii) Development costs for the year written off   £22m

(iv) Profit attributed to long-term contracts in beauty products   £9m

At their next meeting the directors will be considering proposals for:

(a) the purchase 'off market' at £1.50 per share of 30% of the issued ordinary shares of Capital plc which are currently held by Venture plc, a venture capital company. The directors consider that the shares are substantially undervalued and that the company should purchase the shares and hold them as an investment classified under 'own shares' in the balance sheet;

(b) the redemption of the preference shares;

(c) the distribution to the shareholders of Capital plc of shares in Kind plc, which have been held as an investment. The investment appears at cost, £15 million, in the balance sheet and the directors estimate that it has a market value of £24 million at 30 November 1995;

(d) a bonus issue of one ordinary share for every 20 ordinary shares held; and

(e) the amount of the final dividend to recommend for 1995.

The finance director has been requested to present a report in relation to these proposals.

Required
(a) (i)   Advise the board on its proposed procedure for purchasing the issued shares in Capital plc held by Venture plc and on its intention to hold these as an investment.
    (ii) Draft the journal entries to record the purchase transaction assuming that the board acts in accordance with the requirements of the Companies Act 1985.   (4 marks)

(b) (i) **Explain the definition of distributable profits in a public company (ignore the rules relating to investment companies).**

(ii) **Identify which of the proposals (a) to (e) above would be classified as a distribution.**

(iii) **Describe the accounting treatment of proposal (c), distribution of shares held as an investment in Kind plc.** (5 marks)

(c) **Calculate the distributable profits as at 30 November 1995 on the assumption that the company had redeemed the preference shares and made the bonus issue but delayed action on the purchase of own shares and the distribution of the shares in Kind plc until 1996. Explain clearly your treatment of each item mentioned in the reserves.** (11 marks)

ACCA, Financial Reporting Environment, December 1995 (**20 marks**)

18.4 Renewal plc was incorporated in 1985 to carry on business as manufacturers of designer jewellery. The company has incurred recent trading losses but has now returned to modest profitability. The directors estimate that raising new capital for additional investment in plant would produce an increase in profit from £1 000 000 to £1 750 000 per year but in order to be able to pay dividends it it necessary to eliminate the debit balance on the profit and loss account.

The balance sheet of Renewal plc as at 31 May 1996 showed:

	£000	£000	£000
Capital and reserves			
Ordinary shares of £1 each – 80p paid up			4080
8% cumulative preference			
shares of £1 each			5440
Profit and loss account balance			(5046)
Profit attributable to arrears of preference			
dividends			1306
			5780
Fixed assets			
Freehold premises			2890
Plant and machinery			2040
Patents			578
Development expenditure			408
Current assets			
Stock	2108		
Debtors	2720		
		4828	
		4828	5916
Current liabilities; amounts due in less than one year			
Trade creditors	2176		
Overdraft	1768		
Loans from directors	1020		
		4964	
Net current liabilities			(136)
			5780

The directors have formulated the following scheme:

(a) The unpaid capital on the £1 ordinary shares to be called up.

(b) The ordinary shareholders to agree to a reduction of 70p on each share held with new shares having a nominal value of 50p and treated as 30p paid up.

(c) The preference shareholders to agree to the cancellation of their three years' arrears of dividend.

(d) The preference shareholders to agree to a reduction of 20p on each share held with the new shares having a nominal value of 80p and treated as fully paid up.

(e) The dividend rate on preference shares to be increased from 8% to 11%.

(f) The debit balance on the profit and loss account to be eliminated.

(g) Freehold premises have been professionally valued at £3 800 000.

(h) Plant is to be written down by £850 000; patents are to be written down to £340 000; development expenditure is to be written off; stock is to be written down by £406 000; a provision for doubtful debts of 10% is to be created.

(i) New capital to be raised by a rights issue with existing ordinary shareholders subscribing for two shares for every one share held, 30p payable on application, and preference shareholders subscribing for one new 80p preference share for every four preference shares held.

(j) The directors to agree to £420 000 of their loans to be written off and to accept ordinary shares of 50p each, at a value of 30p (paid up), in settlement of the balance of their loans. These shares are not affected by the rights issue in (i) above.

Required
(a) (i) Explain the procedure that a company needs to follow to readjust the rights of members under ss. 425 and 426 of the Companies Act 1985.
   (ii) Advise the directors on an alternative course of action if the ordinary shareholders are not prepared to accept new obligations arising from the proposal to issue partly paid shares. (5 marks)
(b) Prepare the balance sheet for Renewal plc on the assumption that the directors' scheme has been put into effect. (7 marks)
(c) Advise the preference shareholders whether they should participate in the scheme. (8 marks)

ACCA, Financial Reporting Environment, June 1996 **(20 marks)**

18.5 The Collapsible Chair Company Limited was incorporated in 1972 and traded profitably until the 1990s. During the early 1990s the entry of new competitors into the market led to a fall in demand for its product. Consequently, the company started making losses and no dividend has been paid to its equity shareholders since 1992.

A significant failure to co-ordinate production and sales, and a breakdown in credit control following staff illness, has led to an increase in stock and debtors. This, in turn, has led to an increase in the bank overdraft beyond the current limit of £1.3 million. Discussions with the bank have revealed a reluctance to increase the overdraft limit beyond the current level. The debentures, all of which are held by the bank, are due for repayment on 31 December 1997. Both the debentures and the overdraft are secured by a fixed charge over the premises. The bank has threatened to put the company into receivership so as to recover the amounts owed to it. The costs of a receivership and likely subsequent liquidation are estimated at £150 000.

The directors of the company approached a venture capitalist with the idea of using a new design to produce an alternative type of chair. With an investment of £1.2 million, production could begin to yield an annual operating profit before debenture interest and taxation of £600 000 which would result in a cash inflow of a roughly equal amount. However, the venture capitalist was reluctant to invest in the company unless a scheme of capital reorganisation was agreed, and did not wish to gain a controlling interest in the company.

The balance sheet of the company at 31 March 1997, before the implementation of the capital reorganisation scheme, was as follows:

	£000	£000
Fixed assets:		
Premises	3000	
Plant	2000	
		5000
Current assets:		
Stocks	2000	
Debtors	1500	
	3500	
Current liabilities:		
Trade creditors	1800	
Bank overdraft	1500	
8% debentures	2500	
	5800	
Net current liabilities		(2300)
		2700
Capital and reserves:		
Equity share capital (£1 each)		6000
Profit and loss account		(3300)
		2700

The directors have obtained the following estimates for the value of the assets of the company as a going concern, and in a liquidation, at 31 March 1997.

Asset	Going concern value	Liquidation value
	£000	£000
Premises	3500	3500
Plant	1600	400
Stock	1500	500
Debtors	1300	900

A scheme of capital reorganisation has been agreed with all interested parties and implemented by the directors. Details of the scheme are as follows:

(1) The equity shares of £1 were redesignated as 30p shares.

(2) The assets of the company were stated at their going concern values.

(3) The repayment date for the debentures was deferred to 31 December 2007 with the interest rate increased to 10% per annum.

(4) The bank was issued with 1 million 30p equity shares in return for its willingness to accept a deferred repayment of the debentures.

(5) The venture capitalist subscribed for 4 million new 30p equity shares at par.

(6) The accumulated losses were written off.

Requirements
(a) **Prepare the balance sheet of the company at 31 March 1997 which incorporates the scheme which has been implemented.**   (13 marks)
(b) **Assess the effect of the scheme from the point of view of EACH of**
  - **the equity shareholders;**
  - **the bank;**
  - **the venture capitalist.**   (12 marks)

CIMA, Financial Reporting, May 1997   **(25 marks)**

18.6 Medical Equipment plc was incorporated in 1970 to assemble medical equipment used in hospitals. The directors of the company had a major shareholding and were all engaged full time in the operational management of the company. The company had experienced operating losses and the directors believed that profit improvement depended on reducing labour costs. They accordingly decided to automate the assembly process by investing in the development of an automatic machine known as 'Auto-Assembler'.

The 'Auto-Assembler' was tested and developed in 1990 and by 31 December 1990 development expenditure of £157 300 incurred in the development of the 'Auto-Assembler' has been capitalised. It was estimated that its operational use would result in cost savings of £130 000 per annum before tax and that it could be made operational in 1991 for a capital outlay of £75 000. The directors had been building up a short-term investment during 1989–1990 to cover this capital outlay.

The production engineer estimated that as a result of automation an additional £40 000 investment would be required for working capital to meet the additional cost of higher specification materials.

In December 1990 the manager of the bank informed the directors that he wanted the overdraft reduced to around £75 000 from its present level of £270 480.

The directors immediately approached Mr Jeremiah, a partner in the accounting firm of Hard Reality & Co. who were the company's auditors. They believed in the potential profitability of the new automated assembly process and advised Mr Jeremiah that they believed that they would be able to negotiate long-term loan finance to clear the overdraft. At the request of the accountants the company produced the following:

(i)   draft accounts as at 31 December 1990

(ii) additional information on assets and liabilities.

Draft profit and loss account for the year ended 31 December 1990

	£	£
Sales		2 008 000
Cost of sales		
Materials	1 398 800	
Labour	300 000	
		1 698 800
Gross profit		309 200
Distribution costs		(213 200)
Administration expenses		(129 000)
Profit before interest and tax		(33 000)
Interest		(51 600)
Profit before tax		(84 600)

Draft balance sheet as at 31 December 1990

	£
Fixed assets	
Freehold land and buildings	312 000
Plant and machinery	197 600
Development cost of 'Auto-Assembler'	157 300
	666 900
Current assets	
Stock	302 400
Investments	52 000
Debtors	169 000
Cash	2 600
	526 000
	1 192 900
Current liabilities	
Creditors	(303 240)
Overdraft	(270 480)
	(573 720)
Non-current liabilities	
10% debentures	(208 000)
Capital employed	411 180
Capital and reserves	
Ordinary shares of £1 each	425 000
Share premium account	42 500
7% non-cumulative preference shares of £1 each	260 000
Profit and loss account	(316 320)
	411 180

Additional information on individual assets and liabilities as at 31 December 1990:

	Going concern values assuming 'Auto-Assembler' does NOT become operational	Going concern values assuming 'Auto-Assembler' DOES become operational	Values realisable on liquidation
	£	£	£
Freehold land and buildings	385 000	385 000	385 000
Plant and machinery	123 500	88 400	44 200
Stock	292 400	254 800	200 100
Debtors	149 000	149 000	119 840
Investments	52 000	52 000	81 000
Development costs	–	157 300	–

	£
The creditors comprised:	
Preferential creditors	34 700
Loan interest accrued on debentures	10 400
Trade creditors	258 140
	303 240

Trade creditors allow 60 days' credit.

The debentures were secured on the freehold land and buildings and were redeemable at par in 1997.

Mr Jeremiah was not convinced that the directors would be able to arrange long-term loan finance to replace the overdraft and was of the opinion that a scheme of internal reconstruction would become necessary. He requested one of his staff to draft a brief report to explain to the directors feasible ways forward.

Required

(a) **Prepare a balance sheet as at 31 December 1990 on the basis that the company ceased trading on that date and explain its significance for the relevant parties.**   (5 marks)

(b) (i) **Explain briefly the purposes of a scheme for reconstruction as it would apply to equity and loan stockholders.**   (4 marks)

　(ii) **Propose a scheme for the capital reconstruction of Medical Equipment plc.**
　Show your calculation of the loss involved in the scheme; state what you would do with this loss; calculate the working capital requirements of the company; calculate the possible additional equity capital that might be required.
　Note: **The revised balance sheet after the implementation of the scheme is not required.**   (16 marks)

　(iii) **Explain briefly to the directors how the scheme will be fair to all relevant parties.**
　　(5 marks)

ACCA, Advanced Financial Accounting, June 1992   **(30 marks)**

18.7 Aztec plc was incorporated in 1968 as an importer of silver artefacts from South America which it customised for the UK market. The company had sold its products in the luxury market and traded profitably until 1989. Since that date it has suffered continuous losses which have resulted in a negative balance on the profit and loss account. The balance sheet as at 31 December 1993 showed the following:

	£
Share capital and reserves	
Ordinary shares of 1 each	675 000
7% Preference shares of 1 each	135 000
Profit and loss account	(573 000)
Net capital employed	237 000
Fixed assets	
Leasehold premises	397 000
Vehicles and equipment	105 000
Machinery	250 000
Current assets	
Stock	295 000
Debtor	120 000
Current liabilities	
Suppliers	(288 000)
Wages VAT and PAYE	(80 000)
Hire-purchase liability on vehicles/equipment	(20 000)
Bank overdraft (secured by a fixed charge over the machinery)	(112 000)
Non-current liabilities	
Hire-purchase liability on vehicles and equipment	(25 000)
11% Debentures (secured by a floating charge)	(405 000)
Net assets	237 000

Since 1989 the company has been developing an export market for its products in Europe and the directors forecast that the company will return to profit in 1994. They expect profits before tax and debenture interest to be in the range of £70 000 to £140 000 per annum over the next three years. As a result of developing the export market, they expect that the company will require warehouse premises on the Continent in 1996 at a forecast cost of £250 000.

However, the directors are concerned that even if the company achieves a profit of £70 000 per year it will be a number of years before a dividend could be distributed to the ordinary shareholders and it would be difficult to raise fresh funds from the shareholders in 1996 if there were to be little prospect of a dividend until the year 2000.

The directors have been considering various possible courses of action available under the Companies Act 1985 and the Insolvency Act 1986 and have had initial discussions with their auditors.

As a result of these discussions it was agreed that the finance director would produce a draft proposal for reorganisation; the auditors would let the finance director have their comments on the draft proposal: and the finance director would then submit a proposal to the board of directors for their consideration.

The following additional information was obtained by the finance director concerning the assets and liabilities at 31 December 1993 and estimated costs of liquidating or reorganising:

(a) Fair values and liquidation values of assets were:

	Fair values on a going concern basis	Liquidation values on a forced sale basis
	£	£
Leasehold premises	360 000	100 000
Vehicles and equipment	85 000	35 000
Machinery	225 000	122 000
Current assets		
Stock	285 000	150 000
Debtors	110 000	100 000

(b) Preference dividends are four years in arrears.

(c) Wages, VAT and PAYE would be preferential creditors in a liquidation.

(d) The costs of liquidating Aztec plc were estimated at £55 000.

(e) The costs of reorganisation were estimated at £40 000; these would be paid by Aztec (Europe) plc and treated as part of the purchase consideration.

The finance director prepared the following draft proposal:

(i) A new company was to be formed, Aztec (Europe) plc with a share capital of £270 000 in 10p shares to acquire the assets and liabilities of Aztec plc as at 31 December 1993.

(ii) The ordinary shareholders were to receive less than 25% of the ordinary shares in Aztec (Europe) plc so that the existing preference shareholders and debenture holders each had a significant interest and acting together had control of the new company.

(iii) The arrears of preference dividends were to be cancelled.

(iv) The new company was to issue:
  – 900 000 ordinary shares and £70 000 of 13% debentures to the existing preference shareholders;
  – 1 200 000 ordinary shares and £200 000 of 13% debentures to the existing 11% debenture holders;
  – 600 000 ordinary shares to the existing ordinary shareholders.

(v) The variation of the rights of the shareholders and creditors was to be effected under s. 425 of the Companies Act 1985 which requires that the scheme should be approved by a majority in number and 75% in value of each class of shareholders, by a majority in number and 75% in value of each class of creditor affected and by the court.

(vi) The transfer of the assets to Aztec (Europe) plc was to be effected under s. 427 of the Companies Act 1985 which would ensure that the court dealt with the transfer of the assets and liabilities and the dissolution of Aztec plc to avoid the costs of winding up that company.

Assume a corporation tax rate of 35% and an income tax rate of 25%. Ignore ACT.

Required

(a) Assuming that the necessary approvals have been obtained for assets and liabilities to be transferred on the proposed terms on 31 December 1993:

   (i) Prepare journal entries to close the books of Aztec plc; and

   (ii) Prepare the balance sheet of Aztec (Europe) plc after the transfer of assets and liabilities.   (10 marks)

(b) Draft a memo to the finance director commenting on his draft proposals for a scheme of capital reduction and reorganisation.   (16 marks)

(c) Advise the directors as to the course of action they should take in order to be able to proceed with their plans for reorganisation if they learn that a creditor has obtained a judgment against the company and is considering seeking a compulsory winding-up order.   (4 marks)

ACCA, Financial Reporting Environment, June 1994   **(30 marks)**

PART
3

Accounting and price changes

Accounting for price changes

The traditional historical cost system of accounting has serious shortcomings when prices are changing. While these shortcomings are extremely serious when the rate of inflation is high, they do not disappear when the inflation rate is low nor are they corrected in any systematic way by piecemeal revaluations. The cumulative effect of a low annual rate of inflation may be highly significant and, even with an inflation rate close to zero, the rate of change of specific prices may be high.

Accountants in the UK experimented with different methods of accounting for price change in the 1970s and 1980s. We outline these experiments in the first part of this chapter before examining, in some depth, the system of Current Purchasing Power (CPP) accounting.

CPP accounting requires the adjustment of historical cost accounts for changes in the value of money as measured by a general price index such as the Retail Price Index in the UK. The system has the advantages of measuring all assets, liabilities, revenues and expenses in the same currency, pounds on the balance sheet date, and of measuring and disclosing gains and losses from holding monetary liabilities and assets in an inflationary or, indeed, deflationary period.

The figures for non-monetary assets which emerge in a CPP balance sheet are usually far from the current values of those assets and this perceived defect led to experimentation with Current Cost Accounting (CCA), to which we turn in the ensuing chapters.

Introduction

The 1970s and 1980s was an exciting period for accountants who welcomed change. The extremely high rates of inflation that were a feature of the period posed a considerable challenge to the traditional historically based financial accounting model. Within a period of less than twenty years, the professional accountancy bodies turned from conservative advocates of the historical cost status quo to radical reformers urging the introduction of new systems and ideas. As the dragon of inflation was tamed, the urge for radical change dimmed but reform did not come to an end. The challenge to the conventional wisdom that historical cost accounts were all one needed did not go away. The theoretical debate about the nature and purposes of financial accounting that accompanied attempts to take account of changing prices and the discussions about the merits of different models of measurement continued, to a large measure, in the area of standard setting. While the attempt to introduce a new orthodoxy based on the adoption of a system of financial accounting that comprehensively and systematically takes account of changing prices, general, specific or both, was halted, its impact can be found in many places, including the alternative accounting rules included in the UK Companies Act and the increasing attention now being given to fair values by UK and international standard setters.

In this third part of the book, we trace the history of accounting for changing prices and introduce some of the models that were developed in that heady period. We do this not simply to tell tales about the past but in a belief that, even in low inflationary periods historical cost accounting, even in its modified form, is an inadequate model and that, while it is a mistake to focus on only one way of describing an entity's financial position, a set of financial statements that does not report on how an entity was affected by changes in general and relative prices tells an incomplete story. It is also our view that a full appreciation of historical cost accounting depends, in part, on a clear understanding of those things about which historical cost accounting does not report.

In Chapter 4 'What is profit?', we suggested that the traditional system of accounting, based on historical cost asset measurement and financial capital maintenance, suffers from numerous shortcomings when tested against the purposes which financial reporting might sensibly be regarded as serving. This observation is not a new one,[1] but the case for reforming accounts to reflect price changes was not widely accepted in the UK, especially by accountants, until the 1970s.

The high rate of inflation which was a feature of the UK economy of that period highlighted the limitations of the conventional accounting model and, when the annual rate of inflation rose to 25 per cent in 1974, it was no longer possible for accountants and governments to ignore the phenomenon.

A striking example of the consequences of inflation on historical cost accounts was provided by the ASC in its 1986 publication *Accounting for the Effects of Changing Prices: a Handbook*, which will henceforth be referred to as the ASC Handbook. The example compared dividend distributions expressed as a percentage of (a) historical cost profit and (b) a measure of profit based on current cost principles. The results were derived from large samples of companies and covered the period 1980 to 1984, a period in which the UK had significantly lower inflation than in the 1970s. The results are shown in Table 19.1.

Note that, in using a historical cost perception, it appeared that company directors had on average pursued prudent distribution policies, but the results based on current costs indicate that in some years the average dividend exceeded the amount required to be retained in the business to sustain its existing scale of operations.

Table 19.1 Dividend distribution expressed as percentages of profit derived on (a) historical cost and (b) current cost principles

	Historical cost (%)	Current cost (%)
1980	37	97
1981	40	111
1982	48	130
1983	50	94
1984	52	64

[1] See Sir R. Edwards, 'The nature and measurement of income', originally published as a series of articles in *The Accountant*, July–October 1938; reprinted in *Studies in Accounting*, W.T. Baxter and S. Davidson (ed), ICAEW, London, 1977, pp. 96–140. This is only one, and by no means the earliest, of many references that could have been selected. In this classic paper Sir Ronald Edwards, an accountant who was both a university professor and successful buinessman, clearly outlined many of the problems inherent in conventional accounting and discussed many important matters which are still controverial issues.

So it seems that in periods of high inflation business financial results based on historical cost asset valuations and money financial capital maintenance paint a misleading and distorted picture of the financial progress of companies. But does the case for accounting reform disappear in periods when inflation is low? It is certainly true that support for reform on the part of most businesspeople and professional accountants does depend on the rate of inflation. When inflation is high there is a strong pressure for change and exposure drafts and standards are issued, whereas when inflation falls the advocates of the status quo gain supremacy and the exposure drafts and standards are withdrawn. But the case for reform does not disappear.[2]

In its 1986 Handbook the ASC stated, 'The limitations of historical cost accounts exist not only in periods of relatively rapid price changes but also when prices are changing more slowly'.[3] Three reasons were advanced to support this view:

(a) Even with low annual rates of inflation, the cumulative effect of inflation over time is significant; for example, with 5 per cent inflation, prices double every 14 years.

(b) The accounting effects of previous high rates of inflation persist over a number of years.

(c) Rates of change of specific prices may be substantial even when the rate of inflation is relatively low.

The progress of accounting reform

The UK path towards accounting reform, which is as yet incomplete, is outlined in Figure 19.1, which can be used as a guide to this and subsequent chapters.

Two lines are shown in Figure 19.1. One represents the current purchasing power (CPP) method, which takes account of general price changes but which ignores specific price changes; in terms of the analysis presented in Chapter 4 it is a system of accounting based on the combination of the adjusted historical cost asset valuation basis and the maintenance of real financial capital. A detailed exposition of CPP accounting is provided later in this chapter. The other line represents an approach generally known as current cost accounting (CCA) which, in the United Kingdom, combines a variant of the replacement cost approach to valuation with either the operating or the real financial capital maintenance concepts. This approach will be discussed in more detail in Chapter 20.

CPP accounting retains most of the significant features of historical cost accounting, and the only real change is the replacement of the money unit of measurement by the purchasing power unit. It will be seen that when compared to a system which attempts to measure current values, the CPP model involves a far less radical departure from the conventional method and it is perhaps not surprising that the first tentative steps on the path to accounting reform taken by the British accountancy profession were on the CPP route; much the same occurred in the United States and Australia.[4]

---

[2] Michael Mumford, 'The end of a familiar inflation accounting cycle', *Accounting and Business Research*, Vol. 9, No. 34, Spring 1978, pp. 98–104.

[3] *Accounting for the Effects of Changing Prices: a Handbook*, ASC, London, 1986, p. 11.

[4] For example, in the United States the FASB produced an exposure draft in December 1974 which was similar in content to ED 8, but the Securities Exchange Commission in 1976 called for the disclosure by larger companies of additional information concerning the replacement costs of fixed assets and stock. The subsequent US standard, FAS No. 33 *Financial reporting and changing prices*, September 1979, required supplementary disclosure of both types of information, but this statement was superseded by FAS No. 89, with the same title, in December 1986. This encouraged, rather than required, such disclosure.

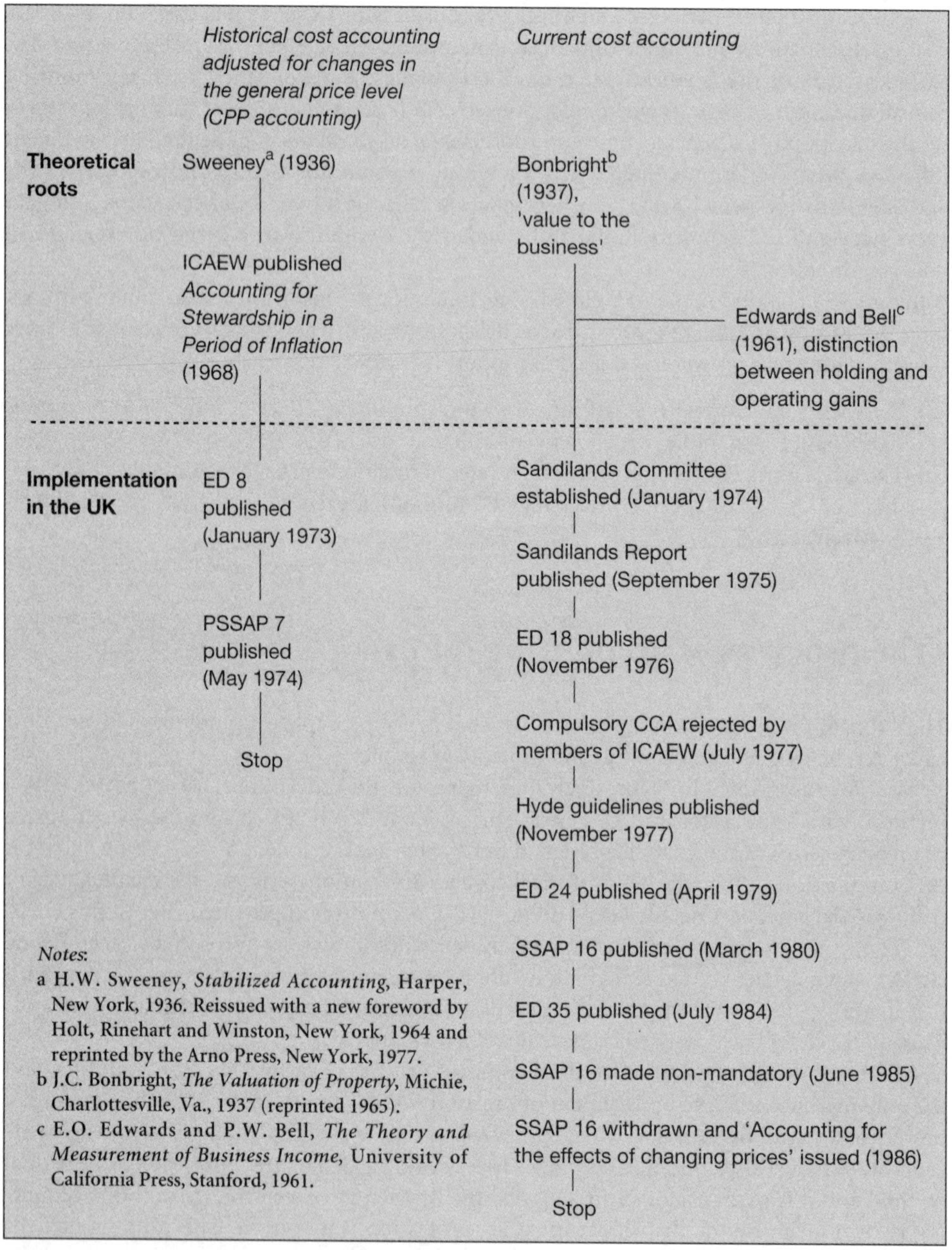

	Historical cost accounting adjusted for changes in the general price level (CPP accounting)	Current cost accounting
Theoretical roots	Sweeney[a] (1936)	Bonbright[b] (1937), 'value to the business'
	ICAEW published *Accounting for Stewardship in a Period of Inflation* (1968)	Edwards and Bell[c] (1961), distinction between holding and operating gains
Implementation in the UK	ED 8 published (January 1973)	Sandilands Committee established (January 1974)
		Sandilands Report published (September 1975)
	PSSAP 7 published (May 1974)	ED 18 published (November 1976)
		Compulsory CCA rejected by members of ICAEW (July 1977)
	Stop	Hyde guidelines published (November 1977)
		ED 24 published (April 1979)
		SSAP 16 published (March 1980)
		ED 35 published (July 1984)
		SSAP 16 made non-mandatory (June 1985)
		SSAP 16 withdrawn and 'Accounting for the effects of changing prices' issued (1986)
		Stop

Notes:
a H.W. Sweeney, *Stabilized Accounting*, Harper, New York, 1936. Reissued with a new foreword by Holt, Rinehart and Winston, New York, 1964 and reprinted by the Arno Press, New York, 1977.
b J.C. Bonbright, *The Valuation of Property*, Michie, Charlottesville, Va., 1937 (reprinted 1965).
c E.O. Edwards and P.W. Bell, *The Theory and Measurement of Business Income*, University of California Press, Stanford, 1961.

Figure 19.1 The path towards accounting reform

In 1968 the Research Foundation of the ICAEW published *Accounting for Stewardship in a Period of Inflation*. The title is instructive in that it suggests a far more restrictive view of the objectives of financial accounts than is accepted nowadays and does illustrate the extent of the changes that have since taken place. The methods outlined in that document were not original. They had been described in English by Sweeney in 1936[5] and his book was itself

5 H.W. Sweeney, *op. cit.*

based on work done in Germany during the period of hyperinflation which followed the First World War. The significance of the publication was that it was produced by a body associated with a leading professional accounting institute and indicated that that body was apparently prepared to initiate reform. The seeds took a long time to germinate, and the world had to wait until 1973 for the publication of ED 8 by the Accounting Standards Steering Committee (ASSC). ED 8 proposed that companies should be required to publish, along with their conventional accounts, supplementary statements which would, in effect, be their profit and loss accounts and balance sheets based on CPP principles. ED 8 was followed by the issue of Provisional Statement of Standard Accounting Practice (PSSAP) 7, in May 1974. The inclusion of the word 'provisional' in the title of this standard (the only occasion on which this was done by the ASSC) reflected the uncertainties in the mind of the accountancy profession on this matter, since it meant that companies were requested rather than required to comply with the standard.

Many users of accounting reports, including the Government, were dissatisfied with this approach. Consequently, the Government established its own committee of inquiry into inflation accounting in January 1974, i.e. after the issue of ED 8. The committee was chaired by Sir Francis Sandilands, and its report (usually referred to as the Sandilands Report) was issued in September 1975.[6] The committee recommended the adoption of a system of accounting known as 'current cost accounting' which is, as will be shown later, a very different creature from CPP accounting. As a result of the publication of the Sandilands Report, the ASC[7] abandoned its own proposals and set up a working party, the Inflation Accounting Steering Group (IASG) to prepare an initial Statement of Standard Accounting Practice (SSAP) based on Sandilands' proposals. The outcome of this group's labours was ED 18 *Current Cost Accounting*, which was published in November 1976. This publication came under a good deal of attack from many quarters, including those who supported the main principles of current cost accounting (CCA). The exposure draft was considered by many to be unnecessarily complicated and to deal with too many subsidiary issues. The draft was also attacked by many rank and file – some would say backwoods – members of the ICAEW, and their efforts resulted in the passing of a resolution in July 1977 by members of the Institute that rejected any compulsory introduction of CCA.

This did not halt the advance of CCA. The Government, in a discussion document issued in July 1977 (*The Future of Company Reports*), reiterated its support for the adoption of CCA, while in November 1977 the accountancy profession issued a set of interim recommendations to cover the period until a revised set of detailed proposals could be formulated. These recommendations were called the Hyde guidelines after the name of the chairman of the committee responsible for the recommendations. A second exposure draft, ED 24, was published in April 1979 and was followed by the issue of SSAP 16 *Current Cost Accounting* in March 1980. It was intended that SSAP 16 would prevail for three years while the effect of the introduction of CCA was evaluated.

With certain exceptions, SSAP 16 applied to all companies listed on the Stock Exchange and to large unlisted companies. Such companies were required to publish current cost accounts together with historical cost accounts or historical cost information. The intention was that primacy should be given to the current cost accounts although, as we shall see, things did not turn out in the way intended by the ASC.

Current cost accounts did not replace the historical cost accounts and they were often presented, and perhaps even more often regarded, as being supplementary to the main or, as

---

[6] *Report of the Inflation Accounting Committee*, Cmnd. 6225, HMSO, London, 1975.
[7] In 1976 the ASSC stopped steering and became the Accounting Standards Committee, see Chapter 2.

many no doubt believed, the 'real' accounts. Many companies simply failed to comply with the provisions of SSAP 16, and although auditors were obliged to refer to the absence of current cost accounts in the audit report, such references were not regarded as important qualifications and the companies concerned did not seem to suffer as a consequence of their non-compliance.

Following the evaluation of the impact of SSAP 16, ED 35 was published in July 1984. The basic principles of CCA were maintained, albeit with some modifications, but ED 35 proposed that companies should only be required to produce one set of accounts, based on historical costs with notes showing the effect of changing prices. The proposals of ED 35 were not implemented but instead SSAP 16 was made non-mandatory in June 1985. This was, however, not the end of the matter, for in 1986 SSAP 16 was withdrawn and the ASC published its Handbook, *Accounting for the Effects of Changing Prices*. At that time, the presidents of the five leading accountancy bodies in the UK issued a joint statement endorsing the view of the ASC that companies should appraise and, where material, report the effect of changing prices. In addition the presidents supported the view that accounting for the effect of changing prices is of great importance and agreed that a suitable accounting standard should be developed. Numerous reasons can be advanced to explain why it has not proved possible to introduce a generally acceptable system of current cost accounting. Prominent among them is the lack of agreement on the part of those advocating change as to how to account for changing prices, and the associated problem that very many businesspeople and accountants do not understand the basic principles underlying current cost accounting.

We shall continue this chapter with a discussion of the CPP method and will return to current cost accounting in Chapter 20.

Current purchasing power accounting

Introduction

The elements of aimed purchasing power (CPP) accounting were introduced in Chapter 4 – that is the adjusted historical cost basis of valuation coupled with profit measurement based on the maintenance of real financial capital. Before describing how these can be combined to produce a coherent accounting model it is necessary to consider how, and from whose point of view, the purchasing power of money should be measured.

The prices of different goods and services change by different amounts, and the problem faced by those responsible for measuring changes in the purchasing power of money is to find a suitable average value to reflect the different individual price changes which have taken place during the period under review. This could be done by considering all the different goods and services that are traded in the country during the period and to compare their prices with those prevailing in the comparison or base period. This is a massive task, but it is possible to arrive at the required answer by indirect methods, as is done in the United States in the calculation of the gross domestic product implicit price deflator.

An alternative approach is to select a sample of goods and services, measure the changes in their prices, and then average them. This method is used to construct the Index of Retail Prices (RPI), which is based on the price changes that affect 'middle income' households. In order to construct the index it is necessary to assign weights to the various price changes to take account of their relative importance. These weights are based on the spending patterns of a sample of householders that is drawn so as to exclude households with incomes that are significantly higher and significantly lower than the average.

One of the major provisions of PSSAP 7 was the stipulation that changes in the purchasing power of money should be measured by reference to the RPI. The consequence of this proposal was that changes in purchasing power were not to be measured from the point of view of the individual firm or even all firms but from the point of view of individual consumers. Thus it was the intention that CPP accounts should not be regarded as providing proxies to current value accounts, but rather as restatements of the conventional historical cost accounts in terms which attempted to adjust for the effect of inflation on shareholders and other individuals.

The basic principle underlying CPP accounts is that all monetary amounts should be converted to pounds of CPP in a manner which is analogous to the way in which sums expressed in different foreign currencies are translated to a common base. Assume that we are attempting to measure the CPP profit for a transaction that involved the purchase of goods for £2000 in January 1998 and their sale for £3000 in December 1998. The RPI was 159.5 at the date of purchase and 164.4 at the date of sale. If we wish to measure the profit in terms of purchasing power at December 1998 we would need to convert the £2000, which represented January 1998 purchasing power, in terms of December 1998 purchasing power. In order to carry out such calculations it will be helpful if we use symbols which indicate the purchasing power associated with the monetary amount; we will do this by specifying that £(Jan 98) means January 1998 pounds, and so on.

The calculation of CPP profit for the above transaction could then be shown as follows:

	£(Dec 98)
Sales	3000
Purchases, £(Jan 98) $2\,000 \times \dfrac{164.4}{159.5}$	2061
	939

The equation:

$$\pounds(\text{Jan } 98)\ 2000 \times \frac{164.4}{159.55} = \pounds(\text{Dec } 98)\ 2061$$

means that a consumer would require £2061 in December 1998 in order to be able to command the same purchasing power as was available from the possession of £2000 in January 1998.

The consequence of the extension of the basic CPP principle to the profit and loss account is that all items will be expressed in terms of current (i.e. year-end) purchasing power, and the same will be true in the balance sheet. Thus, all items in the balance sheet will have to be converted in terms of year-end purchasing power except the so-called monetary assets and liabilities which are automatically expressed in such terms. Example 19.1 illustrates the preparation of CPP accounts in the absence of monetary assets and liabilities. To provide clear illustrations in this and subsequent examples, we will assume rates of inflation higher than those that have been experienced in the very recent past.

Example 19.1

Bell Limited's historical cost and CPP balance sheets at 31 December 20X6 (on which date a hypothetical RPI was 120) are given below:

Bell Limited
Balance sheet as at 31 December 20X6

Historical cost		Note		CPP
		£		£(31 Dec X6)
Fixed assets				
Cost	10 000	(a)		12 000
Accumulated depreciation	4 000	(b)		4 800
	6 000			7 200
Stock	3 300	(c)		3 356
	£9 300		£(31 Dec 20X6)	10 556
Share capital	4 000	(d)		4 800
Retained earnings	5 300	(e)		5 756
	£9 300		£(31 Dec 20X6)	10 556

Notes:

(a) The fixed assets were purchased for £10 000 on 1 January 20X3 when the RPI = 100:

$$£(1 \text{ Jan X3}) \; 10\,000 \times \frac{120}{100} = £(31 \text{ Dec X6}) \; 12\,000$$

(b) Bell Limited depreciates its fixed assets on a straight-line basis over 10 years (assuming a zero scrap value). Thus, at the end of 19X6, four-tenths of the asset has been written off and the accumulated depreciation figure is thus:

$$4/10 \text{ of } £(31 \text{ Dec X6}) \; 12\,000 = £(31 \text{ Dec X6}) \; 4800$$

(c) The company's stock was purchased for £3300 on 30 September 20X6 when the RPI was 118:

$$£(30 \text{ Sep. X6}) \; 3300 \times \frac{120}{118} = £(31 \text{ Dec. X6}) \; 3356$$

(d) The share capital consists of 4000 £1 ordinary shares which were issued on 1 January 20X3 when the RPI was 100:

$$£(1 \text{ Jan. X3}) \; 4000 \times \frac{120}{110} = £(31 \text{ Dec. X6}) \; 4800$$

(e) Had CPP accounts been prepared in the past, the CPP retained earnings would have emerged in the same way that retained earnings emerge in the historical cost accounts. In this case the CPP retained earnings is found by treating it as the balancing figure in the CPP balance sheet. It is not possible to find the CPP retained earnings from its historical cost equivalent as the relationship between them depends on the aggregate of the differences between the CPP and historical cost figures of all the balance sheet items.

During 20X7 Bell Limited engaged in the following transactions:

(A) On 31 March 20X7 it sold half its stock for cash of £(31 Mar X7) 5500. £(31 Mar X7) 4400 of the proceeds were used to purchase additional stock while the balance was paid out as a dividend.
(B) On 1 July 20X7 one-quarter of the 1 January 20X7 stock was sold for £(1 July X7) 2750; the proceeds were used to pay for overhead expenses which may be assumed to accrue evenly over the year.

The RPI moved as follows:

Date	Index
1 January 20X7	120
31 March 20X7	121
1 July 20X7 (which may be assumed to be the average value for the year)	132
31 December 20X7	143

The CPP profit and loss account for the year ended 31 December 20X7 is given below:

Bell Limited
CPP Profit and loss account for the year ended 31 December 20X7

	£(31 Dec X7)	£(31 Dec X7)
Sales, £(31 Mar X7) 5500 $\times \frac{143}{121}$	6 500	
Sales, £(1 July X7) 2750 $\times \frac{143}{132}$	2 979	9 479
less Cost of sales		
Opening stock, £(30 Sep X6) 3300 $\times \frac{143}{118}$	3 999	
Purchases, £(31 Mar X7) 4400 $\times \frac{143}{121}$	5 200	
	9 199	
less Closing stock, £(30 Sep X6) 825 $\times \frac{143}{118}$		
$+$ £(31 Mar X7) 4400 $\times \frac{143}{121}$	6 200	2 999
Gross profit		6 480
less Overheads £(1 Jul X7) 2750 $\times \frac{143}{132}$	2 979	
Depreciation, £1(1 Jan X3) 10 000 $\times \frac{1}{10} \times \frac{143}{100}$	1 430	4 409
Net profit		2 071
less Dividends paid £(31 Mar X7) 1100 $\times \frac{143}{121}$		1 300
		771
Retained earnings, 1 Jan X7, £(1 Jan X7) 5756 $\times \frac{143}{120}$		6 859
Retained earnings, 31 Dec X7		7 630

Bell Limited
CPP balance sheet as at 31 December 20X7

	£(31 Dec X7)	£(31 Dec X7)
Fixed assets:		
Cost, £(1 Jan X3) 10 000 × $\frac{143}{100}$	14 300	
Accumulated depreciation,		
£(1 Jan X3) 5000 × $\frac{143}{100}$	7 150	7 150
Stock:		
£(30 Sep X6) 825 × $\frac{143}{118}$	1 000	
£(31 Mar X7) 4400 × $\frac{143}{121}$	5 200	6 200
		13 350
Share capital,		
£(1 Jan X3) 4000 × $\frac{143}{100}$		5 720
Retained earnings		
(from the profit and loss account)		7 630
		13 350

Example 19.1 illustrates the necessity of identifying the dates on which the different transactions took place in order to determine the denominator of the conversion factor (i.e. the RPI at the date of the transaction): the numerator is always the same – the RPI at the balance sheet date. In the example it was practicable to deal with each sale separately, but in practice it would usually be found necessary to make some simplifying assumption, e.g. that the sales accrued evenly over the year, which would mean that the average value of the RPI would be taken as the denominator in the conversion factor. A similar approach would usually be taken in respect to purchases and overhead expenses.

The treatment of depreciation merits special attention. Note that in Example 19.1 the conversion factor used in the calculation of the depreciation expense in the profit and loss account and the fixed asset items in the balance sheet is 143/100. The denominator, 100, is the RPI at the date on which the fixed asset was acquired. It is sometimes suggested that when calculating the depreciation expense, the denominator should be the average value of the RPI for the year on the grounds that 'depreciation is written off over the year'. This is indeed so, but the vital point that is missing in this argument is that the pound of depreciation that is being written off in 20X7 is a pound of 1 January 20X3, because it was pounds with a 1 January 20X3 purchasing power that were given up in exchange for the asset.

Monetary assets and liabilities

A common feature of inflation is that debtors gain in purchasing power while creditors lose.[8] And, because free lunches are not a common feature of our economy, it is – to use the

---

[8] It is possible for the contracts between lenders and borrowers to be drawn up in terms of purchasing power instead of monetary units. These are often called index-linked agreements.

terminology of game theory – a zero-sum game; the debtors' gains equal the creditors' losses. In other words, all other things being equal, one effect of inflation is to transfer purchasing power from creditors to debtors.

The reason for this is that a person who borrows money in a period of inflation, will repay it in pounds of lower purchasing power (value) than those that were obtained when the loan was granted. The longer the loan then, so long as the inflation continues, the greater will be the difference between the values of the pounds borrowed and of the pounds repaid.

It is, of course, possible for creditors to protect themselves in some cases by increasing the interest rate to take into account the expected rate of inflation. If this is done, the market rate of interest will be based upon the market's view of the likely future rates of inflation. Thus, a quoted rate of interest may be broken down into two parts: one, which we may term the 'real' interest rate, is that which would have been charged in the absence of inflationary expectations; the balance represents the inflation premium. This point has a good deal of relevance to some important questions about the treatment of gains and losses on monetary items. We will return to this point later.[9]

If the above analysis is extended to a company, it can be said that a company will lose purchasing power in a period of inflation if, taking the year as a whole, it holds net monetary assets (in simple terms if its cash plus debtors exceeds its creditors). Conversely, it will gain in purchasing power if, on average, it is in a net monetary liability position. The calculation depends on the meaning of monetary assets and liabilities.

In PSSAP 7 monetary items were defined as:

assets, liabilities, or capital, the amounts of which were fixed by contract or statute in terms of numbers of pounds regardless of changes in the purchasing power of the pound.[10]

Let us first consider the distinction between monetary and non-monetary liabilities. A non-monetary liability would be one in which the payment of interest, or the return on capital, or both, are not subject to a limit expressed in terms of a given number of pound coins. Such liabilities are rare in the private sector of the economy, but the British Government has issued a number of securities in which the returns are dependent on movements of the RPI. In contrast, the obligations on the part of the borrower of a monetary liability are fixed and are not affected by changes in purchasing power.

We will now turn to the distinction between monetary and non-monetary capital. Preference shares which do not entitle their owners to a share of any surplus on liquidation of the company are clearly monetary items in that the rights associated with them – the annual dividend and the repayment of principal – are subjected to upper limits which are expressed in monetary terms. Conversely, equity capital is a non-monetary item because no limits are placed on the amounts that can be paid to the owners of this type of capital. The effect of inflation on the relationship between equity and preference shareholders is similar to that on the relationship between debtors and creditors, i.e. equity shareholders will gain in purchasing power at the expense of preference shareholders because the latter's interests are fixed in money terms and will decline with a fall in the value of money. This point will be illustrated in Example 19.3.

Monetary assets are those assets the values of which are fixed in monetary terms, e.g. cash and debtors. Non-monetary assets, such as stock and fixed assets, are those assets the values of which may be expected to vary according to changes in the rate of inflation. Consider as examples debtors and stock, and suppose that a company has £100 invested in each of these

---

[9] See p. 630
[10] PSSAP 7 *Accounting for Changes in the Purchasing Power of Money*, Para. 28.

assets. Assume that as a result of some catastrophe the RPI increases by 100 per cent (or the purchasing power of money falls by 50 per cent) overnight. The violent change in the RPI will not affect the debtors' figure in that the asset will still only realise 100 £1 coins, but it is highly probable that it will have an effect on the stock figure as the cost of the stock will be likely to rise. In other words, it would take $(100 + x)$ £1 coins to buy the stock using the less valuable pounds.

The classification of investments into monetary and non-monetary categories often appears to be difficult, but this is not really so because we can employ the same analysis as was used in our discussion of capital. If the investment is in a fixed interest security where the dividend or interest and the repayment of principal are fixed in monetary terms, then it is a monetary item. An investment in equity shares where there is no limit on the amount that can be received is a non-monetary item.

The computation of gains and losses on a company's net monetary position

We showed earlier that one effect of inflation is to transfer purchasing power from creditors to debtors; we will now show how the amount of the creditors' loss and debtors' gains can be calculated. We will at this stage concentrate on interest-free credit and hence ignore the possibility of creditors reducing or eliminating their loss by incorporating an inflation premium in the rate of interest charged.

Suppose that A Limited borrowed £(1 Jan X4) 300 from B Limited on 1 January 20X4 which is repaid on 30 September 20X4. The year end for both companies is 31 December 20X4. Assume that the RPI moved as follows:

Date	1 January X4	30 September X4	31 December X4
Index no.	120	150	160

We will first consider the position from A Limited's point of view. The company borrowed 300 £1 coins when the index was 120 and repaid the same number of £1 coins when the index was 150. In order to calculate the gain on purchasing power involved we need to convert one or other of the pounds borrowed or repaid so that the comparison can be made in terms of common purchasing power. We will convert the pounds borrowed in terms of 30 September 20X4 purchasing power. The calculation could then be made as follows:

	£(30 Sep X4)
Purchasing power acquired,	
£(1 Jan X4) 300 × $\frac{150}{120}$	375
Purchasing power given up on repayment of the loan	300
Gain	75

The gain in purchasing power, expressed in 30 September 20X4 purchasing power, is thus £(30 Sep X4) 75. If the company's year end is 31 December, then for the purpose of the annual accounts the gain will have to be converted to 31 December 20X4 purchasing power:

$$\text{Gain} = \pounds(30 \text{ Sep X4}) \ 75 \times \frac{160}{150}$$
$$= \pounds(31 \text{ Dec X4}) \ 80$$

Note that the analysis has been confined to the borrowing made by A Limited. If A Limited has used all or part of the borrowing to invest in monetary assets (which would include keeping the cash in a bank) it would experience a loss in purchasing power due to the holding of a monetary asset in a period of inflation.

If we consider the creditor, B Limited, a similar analysis will show that its loss of purchasing power resulting from the loan is £(31 Dec X4) 80. In making the loan, B Limited gave up purchasing power amounting to £(1 Jan X4) 300 or £(30 Dec X4) 400. The repayment of the loan increased B Limited's purchasing power by £(30 Sep X4) 300 or £(31 Dec X4) 320. Thus its loss of purchasing power is £(31 Dec X4) 80.

The above analysis can be generalised as follows.

Suppose that a monetary asset of £(1)A was acquired at time 1 when the RPI was I_1, was sold at time 2 when the RPI was I_2 and that the year end is considered to be time 3 when the RPI was I_3. Then the purchasing power given up by virtue of the investment in the monetary asset is given by:

$$\pounds(1)A = \pounds(2)A \ \frac{I_2}{I_1}$$

The purchasing power regained from the disposal of the asset is given by £(2)A. The loss of purchasing power in time 2 purchasing power is:

$$\pounds(2)A \ \frac{I_2}{I_1} - \pounds(2)A = \pounds(2)A \left(\frac{I_1}{I_2} - 1 \right)$$

and the loss of purchasing power in time 3 (year end) purchasing power is:

$$\pounds(3)A \left(\frac{I_2}{I_1} - 1 \right) \frac{I_2}{I_1} = \pounds(3)AI_3 \left(\frac{1}{I_1} - \frac{1}{I_2} \right)$$

In the special case where the asset is still in existence at the year end, $I_2 = I_3$ and the loss can be stated as follows:

$$\text{Loss} = \pounds(3)AI_3 \left(\frac{1}{I_1} - \frac{1}{I_3} \right) = \pounds(3)A \left(\frac{I_3}{I_1} - 1 \right) \tag{19.1}$$

If £A is replaced by −£A the above approach can be used to calculate the gain in purchasing power resulting from holding a monetary liability in a period of rising prices.

In the above analysis we concentrated on a single monetary item, but in practice a company's net monetary position will fluctuate on a daily basis. The foregoing method can be adapted to deal with this problem in the following way.

Suppose that a company starts the year on 1 January with net monetary assets of £200, reduces its net monetary assets by £280 on 1 April and finally increases its net monetary assets by £100 on 1 October. If this were the case, the company would have held net monetary assets of £200 for three months (January–March), net monetary liabilities of £80 for the next six months (April–September) and been a net monetary creditor of £20 for the last three months of the year. An alternative way of viewing the position, which we will use to calculate the total loss or gain on the company's monetary position, is to say that it: (a) held a monetary asset of £200 for the whole of the year; (b) held a monetary liability of £280 for the nine-month period from April to December; (c) held a monetary asset of £100 for the three-month period from October to December.

Assume that the appropriate index numbers are:

Date	1 January	1 April	1 October	31 December
Index no.	100	140	150	180

The loss or gain on each of the three hypothetical items can then be calculated by substituting the appropriate values in equation (19.1) as follows:

$$\text{(a)} \quad \text{Loss} = £(31 \text{ Dec}) \, 200 \times \left(\frac{180}{100} - 1 \right)$$

$$\text{(b)} \quad \text{Loss} = -£(31 \text{ DEC}) \, 280 \times \left(\frac{180}{140} - 1 \right)$$

$$\text{(c)} \quad \text{Loss} = £(31 \text{ Dec}) \, 100 \times \left(\frac{180}{150} - 1 \right)$$

The total loss is given by:

$$£(31 \text{ Dec}) \left\{ 200 \left(\frac{180}{100} - 1 \right) - 280 \left(\frac{180}{140} - 1 \right) + 100 \left(\frac{180}{150} - 1 \right) \right\}$$

$$= £(31 \text{ Dec}) \left(-200 + 280 - 100 + 200 \times \frac{180}{100} - 280 \times \frac{180}{140} + 100 \times \frac{180}{150} \right)$$

$$= £(31 \text{ Dec}) \left(200 \times \frac{180}{100} - 280 \times \frac{180}{140} + 100 \times \frac{180}{150} \right) - £(31 \text{ Dec}) \, 20$$

Note that the second term in the right-hand side of the above expression, £(31 Dec) 20, is the balance of the company's net monetary assets at the year end. We can now see that it is possible to calculate a company's total gain or loss by first converting all changes to the company's net monetary assets to year-end purchasing power (this gives us the first term on the right-hand side of the expression) and then subtracting the actual balance of net monetary assets.

The loss in this case will be:

$$£(31 \text{ Dec}) \, 120 - £(31 \text{ Dec}) \, 20 = £(31 \text{ Dec}) \, 100$$

The above result may be interpreted as follows. If the company had been in a position to arrange its affairs so that cash, debtors and creditors had been in the form of non-monetary items of values that had changed exactly in step with inflation, it would have had 'net monetary assets' of £120 at the year end. It could have achieved this result had it been able to get its debtors to agree that they would repay the company with pounds which represented the same purchasing power as was represented by the amount of the debt at the date at which it was established, and had made a similar arrangement with its creditors. The company's bank balance is a special case of a creditor or debtor depending on whether or not the account is overdrawn.

The hypothetical £120 is then compared with the actual closing balance of £20 and it can be seen that the company's policy of holding net monetary assets over the year has resulted in a loss of purchasing power of £(31 Dec) 100.

The above argument can be generalised in the following fashion:

Let a_1 be the opening balance of net monetary assets plus the increases in net monetary assets for the first day of the year and let $aj, j = 2, \ldots, 365$, be the increases in net monetary assets for day j. Then the loss of the holding of net monetary assets expressed in terms of year-end purchasing power, £(day 365), using equation (19.1) on p. 631, is given by:

$$\text{Loss} = \pounds(\text{day } 365) \left[a_1 \left(\frac{I_{365}}{I_1} - 1 \right) + a_2 \left(\frac{I_{365}}{I_2} - 1 \right) + a_3 \left(\frac{I_{365}}{I_3} - 1 \right) + \ldots + a_{365} \left(\frac{I_{365}}{I_{365}} - 1 \right) \right]$$

$$= \pounds(\text{day } 365) \left(I_{365} \sum_{j=1}^{365} \frac{a_j}{I_j} - \sum_{j=1}^{365} a_j \right)$$

Note that $\sum_{j=1}^{365} a_j$ represents the actual closing balance of net monetary assets which we can call A. Therefore:

$$\text{Loss} = \pounds(\text{day } 365) \left(I_{365} \sum_{j=1}^{365} \frac{a_j}{I_j} - A \right)$$

The use of computing facilities makes the above approach feasible in practice but, in preparing CPP accounts, it was customary to take averages and assume that, depending on the circumstances, the increases in net monetary assets due to sales took place evenly either over the year as a whole or over each month or quarter, etc. If the annual assumption were made, the increase in net monetary assets would be assumed to have taken place at a date on which the general price index was at the average value for the year. If the calculation were done on a quarterly basis, the average values of the general price index for the quarters would be used.

Example 19.2 shows how one can calculate the loss or gain on a company's net monetary position.

Example 19.2

On 1 January 20X8 Match Limited's monetary items were as follows:

	£
Balance at bank	8000
Trade debtors	2000
Trade creditors	6000
Proposed dividend	1000

A summary of the company's cashbook for 20X8 revealed the following:

		£			£
1 Jan	Opening balance	8 000	1 Jan	Purchases of	
Jan–Jun	Cash sales	5 000		fixed assets	50 000
	Trade debtors	18 000	Jan–Jun	Trade creditors	16 000
1 July	Issue of ordinary shares	30 000	1 July	Payment of 19X7 dividend	1 000
July–Dec	Cash sales	8 000	July–Dec	Trade creditors	20 000
	Trade debtors	24 000	31 Dec	Closing balance	6 000
		£93 000			£93 000

Credit sales for the year were:

January–June	£21 000
July–December	£28 000

Credit purchases for the year were:

January–June	£14 000
July–December	£21 000

▶

The values of a suitable general price index at appropriate dates were

Date	1 January	Average Jan–Jun	1 July	Average July–Dec	31 December
Index	140	148	160	162	165

We must identify the changes in the company's net monetary balances. Note that the sale of goods results in an immediate increase in the company's net monetary assets regardless of whether the sale was made for cash or credit. If the sale was made on credit, the increase in debtors will increase the company's net monetary assets, but the consequence of this is that the payment of cash by debtors will not affect the total net monetary position of the company. Similarly, the payment of the proposed dividend does not affect the net monetary position of the company. It merely reduces cash and the liability of proposed dividends, both of which are monetary items.

The changes in the company's net monetary assets may be summarised as follows:

		Increase £	Decrease £	Net £	Balance £
1 Jan	Opening balance				
	Bank	8 000			
	Debtors	2 000			
	Creditors		6 000		
	Proposed dividend		1 000		
		£10 000	£7 000	£3 000	3 000
1 Jan	Reduction in cash				
	(purchase of fixed assets)		£50 000	£(50 000)	(47 000)
Jan–Jun	Increase in cash				
	(cash sales)	5 000			
	Increase in debtors				
	(credit sales)	21 000			
	Increase in creditors				
	(credit purchases)		14 000		
		£26 000	£14 000	£12 000	(35 000)
1 July	Increase in cash				
	(issue of shares)	£30 000		£30 000	(5 000)
July–Dec	Increase in cash				
	(cash sales)	8 000			
	Increase in debtors				
	(credit sales)	28 000			
	Increase in creditors				
	(credit purchases)		21 000		
		£36 000	£21 000	£15 000	£10 000[11]

[11] The closing balance of the net monetary assets is made up as follows:

	£
Bank	6 000
Debtors	9 000
	15 000
less Creditors	5 000
	10 000

The company's loss or gain on its monetary position can now be found by converting all changes in net monetary items to year-end purchasing power.

		Conversion factor	Increase £	Decrease £
1 Jan	Opening balance	165		
	£(1 Jan X8) 3000	140	3 536	
1 Jan	Decrease	165		
	£(1 Jan X8) 50 000	140		58 929
Jan–Jun	Increase	165		
	£(Jan–Jun) 12 000	148	13 378	
1 July	Increase	165		
	£(1 July X8) 30 000	160	30 938	
July–Dec	Increase	165		
	£(July–Dec) 15 000	162	15 278	
31 Dec	Balance			4 201
			63 130	63 130

	£(31 Dec X8)
Actual balance of net monetary assets	10 000
Balance from above	4 201
Gain £(31 Dec X8)	5 799

Note that the company gained in purchasing power even though it disclosed positive net monetary assets in both the opening and closing balance sheets because it was, over the year as a whole, a net monetary debtor.

Example 19.3 combines the features of Examples 19.1 and 19.2 in that it demonstrates how a set of CPP accounts can be produced in a case where a company holds net monetary items. It also shows how a set of historical cost accounts can be 'converted' into CPP accounts.

Example 19.3

(A) Parker Limited's historical cost and CPP balance sheets as at 1 January 20X5 (when the value of a hypothetical RPI was 150) are as follows:

Parker Limited
Balance sheets as at 1 January 20X5

	Historical cost £	Historical cost £	Notes, conversion factors	CPP £(1 Jan X5)	CPP £(1 Jan X5)
Fixed assets					
Net book value		8 000	(a) $\frac{150}{100}$		12 000
Current assets					
Stock	1 200		(b) $\frac{150}{140}$	1 286	
Debtors plus cash	600	1 800	(c)	600	1 886
		9 800		£(1 Jan X5)	13 886
Share capital					
£1 10% preference shares	2 000		(c)	2 000	
£1 ordinary shares	4 000	6 000	(d) $\frac{150}{80}$	7 500	9 500
Reserves		2 400	(e)		2 986
Owners' equity		8 400			12 486
15% debentures		1 000	(c)		1 000
Current liabilities		400	(c)		400
		£9 800		£(1 Jan X5)	13 886

Notes:
(a) The fixed assets were acquired when the RPI was 100.
(b) The stock was purchased over a period for which the average value of the RPI was 140.
(c) Monetary items.
(d) The ordinary shares were issued on a date at which the RPI was 80.
(e) The 'CPP reserve' is the balancing figure in the CPP balance sheet.

(B) During 20X5, Parker Limited issued 2000 £1 ordinary shares at a premium of 25 pence per share on 1 April when the RPI was 160 and purchased fixed assets of £(1 Sept X5) 3000; the RPI on 1 September 20X5 was 175.

Parker Limited's historical cost profit and loss account for 20X5 is given opposite.

Parker Limited
Profit and loss account

	£	£
Sales		12 000
less Opening stock	1 200	
Purchases	7 000	
	8 200	
less Closing stock	1 600	6 600
Gross profit		5 400
less Sundry expenses	1 450	
Debenture interest	150	
Depreciation (20% reducing balance)	2 200	3 800
		£1 600

No dividends were declared during the year.

A full year's depreciation has been provided on the fixed assets purchased on 1 September 20X5.

(C) In order to prepare the CPP accounts it is necessary to make certain assumptions about the dates on which the various transactions took place. It will be assumed that sales, purchases, expenses and debenture interest all accrued evenly over the year and that the average RPI for the year was 170. It will further be assumed that the average age of the closing stock was two months and that the RPI on 31 October 20X5 was 178. The RPI at the year end will be taken to be 180.

For convenience the RPI at appropriate dates are summarised below:

Date	Index
Issue of original ordinary shares	80
Purchase of original fixed assets	100
Purchase of opening stock	140
1 January 20X5	150
1 April 20X5 (issue of 2000 ordinary shares)	160
Average for 20X5	170
1 September 20X5 (purchase of fixed assets)	175
31 October 20X5 (purchase of closing stock)	178
31 December 20X5	180

(D) We will now calculate the losses or gains resulting from the company's monetary position. The loss or gain on short- and long-term items will be calculated separately. The calculations are usually done separately because of the different factors which give rise to a company's holding of short-term and long-term monetary items. The short-term items depend on the company's policy regarding its investment in working capital; in most cases the short-term items are equivalent to a company's net current assets excluding stock. The longer-term position is a consequence of the company's overall financing strategy and depends on the level of gearing at which the company operates.

The short-term position may be calculated as follows:

	Actual		Conversion	Year-end pounds	
	+	−	factor	+	−
1 Jan Opening balance	200		$\dfrac{180}{150}$	240	
1 Apr Issue of shares	2 500		$\dfrac{180}{160}$	2 812	
Average Sales less purchases, for year expenses + interest	3 400		$\dfrac{180}{170}$	3 600	
1 Sept Purchase of fixed assets		3 000	$\dfrac{180}{175}$		3 086
31 Dec Closing balance		3 100			3 566
	£6 100	£6 100		(31 Dec X5) £6 652	(31 Dec X5) £6 652

The company's actual balance of short-term monetary items is £3100, but had the company been able to maintain the purchasing power of these items it would have had £3566. Hence, the loss on holding short-term monetary items for the year is:

$$£(31 \text{ Dec X5}) [3566 - 3100] = £(31 \text{ Dec X5}) \ 466.$$

The company's long-term monetary liabilities consist of the preference shares and the debentures. The opening balances for these items are:

	£(1 Jan X5)
Preference shares	2 000
Debentures	1 000
£(1 Jan X5)	3 000

The above balance is equivalent in year-end pounds to:

$$£(31 \text{ Dec X5}) \left[3000 \times \frac{180}{150} \right] = (31 \text{ Dec X5}) \ 3600$$

However, since we are dealing with monetary items, these values are not affected by the changes in the price level and the value at the year end is £(31 Dec X5) 3000.

The company has therefore gained in purchasing power from holding monetary liabilities and the gain is given by:

$$£(31 \text{ Dec X5}) \left[3000 \times \frac{180}{150} - 3000 \right] = £(31 \text{ Dec X5}) \ 3000 \left[\frac{180}{150} - 1 \right]$$

$$= £(31 \text{ Dec X5}) \ 600$$

(E) We are now in a position to prepare the CPP profit and loss account and balance sheet.

Parker Limited
CPP profit and loss account for the year ended 31 December 20X5

	£(31 Dec X5)	£(31 Dec X5)
Sales, $12\,000 \times \dfrac{180}{170}$		12 706
less Opening stock, $1200 \times \dfrac{180}{140}$	1 543	
Purchases, $7000 \times \dfrac{180}{170}$	7 412	
	8 955	
less Closing stock, $1600 \times \dfrac{180}{178}$	1 618	7 337
Gross profit		5 369
less Sundry expenses, $1450 \times \dfrac{180}{170}$	1 535	
Debenture interest, $150 \times \dfrac{180}{170}$	159	
Depreciation,		
$0.20 \times 8000 \times \dfrac{180}{100}$	2 880	
$0.20 \times 3000 \times \dfrac{180}{175}$	617	5 191
Net trading profit		178
Gain on long-term monetary items	600	
less Loss on short-term monetary items	466	134
Profit for the year	£(31 Dec X5)	312

CPP balance sheet as at 31 December 20X5

	£(31 Dec X5)	£(31 Dec X5)
Fixed assets		
Net book value:		
$(8000 - 1600) \times \dfrac{180}{100}$	11 520	
$(3000 - 600) \times \dfrac{180}{175}$	2 469	13 989
Current assets		
Stock, $1600 \times \dfrac{180}{178}$	1 618	
Cash *plus* debtors less creditors	3 100	4 718
	£(31 Dec X5)	18 707
Share capital		
£1 10% preference shares	2 000	
£1 ordinary shares:		
$4000 \times \dfrac{180}{80}$	9 000	
$2000 \times \dfrac{180}{160}$	2 250	11 250
c/f		13 250

b/f		13 250
Reserves		
Share premium account,		
$500 \times \dfrac{180}{160}$	562	
Reserves, 1 January 20X5,		
$2986 \times \dfrac{180}{150}$	3 583	
Profit for 20X5	312	4 457
Owners' equity		17 707
15% Debentures		1 000
£(31 Dec X5)		18 707

The nature of the loss or gain on a company's net monetary position

One of the more important features of a set of CPP accounts is its disclosure of the loss or gain arising from the company's net monetary position. It attempts to show the results, from the point of view of the equity shareholders, of the financing policy adopted by the company in a period of changing prices.

The figures disclosed by CPP accounts have, however, been criticised on a number of grounds. One cause for criticism stems from the observation that the nominal interest normally includes some compensation for the fact that, in a period of rising prices, debtors will discharge their debts in pounds of a lesser value than that of the pounds, they borrowed. If, at the time the debt was issued, the market correctly assessed the future course of inflation, the 'gain' that apparently accrues to the borrower will be equal to the compensation for inflation that is included in the nominal rate of interest. If this were the case, it would seem sensible to set off the gain against the interest payable in the accounts of the borrower and to set off the corresponding loss against the interest receivable in the accounts of the lender. If this were done, the accounts would disclose the 'real' interest payable and receivable.

In practice the market will not be correct in its assessment of the future course of inflation and there will be a real loss or gain arising from the company's net monetary position. The loss or gain will depend on the difference between the anticipated and actual rates of inflation and thus, so far as interest-bearing loans are concerned, the debtor will not automatically gain nor the creditor automatically lose. The debtor will only gain if inflation turns out to be greater than that which was anticipated when the borrowing was made.

Suppose that £10 000 debentures were issued at a nominal rate of interest at 12 per cent and let us suppose that it is known that the market believed that prices would rise by 9 per cent each year for the period of the loan. It could thus be argued that the real rate of interest is 3 per cent.

Assume that the actual rate of inflation in 20X7 was 15 per cent. The items relating to the loan which would appear in the CPP profit and loss account for 20X7 would be:

Interest payable, 12% of £10 000	£1 200[12]
Gain on long-term borrowing, £10 000 $\left(\dfrac{115}{100}-1\right)$	£1 500

---

[12] For simplicity it has been assumed that interest is paid at the year end and the question of whether the interest should be deemed to have accrued evenly throughout the year, which would require the interest payment to be converted to pounds of year-end purchasing power, has been ignored.

It could, however, be argued that the following would provide a more realistic description of what in fact took place:

Interest payable, 3% of £10 000	£300
Gain on long-term borrowing, £10 000 $\left(\frac{115}{100} - 1\right)$ – 9% of £10 000	£600

In practice it is not possible to break down the nominal interest rate into the two elements – the real interest rate and the compensation for anticipated inflation – and hence it is not possible to present the CPP accounts in the above manner. However, it is clear that in the case of interest-bearing loans the loss and gain on the company's net monetary position will be overstated in the CPP accounts of the borrower and lender. There is thus a strong case for the suggestion that the loss or gain should be shown in the same section of the CPP profit and loss account as interest payable or receivable, and that the criticism referred to above is more concerned with the format of the CPP profit and loss account as proposed in PSSAP 7 than with the principles involved.

It must be emphasised that the above discussion refers only to interest bearing items. The CPP profit and loss account will not overstate the loss or gain on non-interest-bearing items such as cash at bank on current account or trade creditors.

It has also been argued that it is misleading to measure the loss or gain by reference to changes in the RPI, as this assumes that the alternative of putting, say, £10 000 into a bank account is the payment of a dividend of that amount. In reality only a very small proportion of the cash generated by a company is used to pay dividends; the greater proportion is recirculated in the business and is used to purchase stock and fixed assets and to pay wages and other overheads. It has been suggested that the loss in purchasing power experienced if a company deposited £10 000 in a bank account for one month should be measured by reference to the increase in prices of those items which will be purchased by the company.

The above argument can be countered by the assertion that the purpose of business activity is to increase future consumption and that physical assets are not acquired for their own sake. The objective of CPP accounts is to show the effect of changing prices on the consumption opportunities of the equity shareholders and not on the potential asset purchases of the firm.

Suppose that a slothful company starts the year with £100 000 in the bank and does nothing until the end of the year when it purchases assets the cost of which has increased by 10 per cent over the year. Let us also assume that the RPI has increased by 15 per cent over the same period. Is the loss on holding money £10 000 or £15 000? From the point of view of the equity shareholders it is £15 000. Had the £100 000 been distributed at the beginning of the year the shareholders could have consumed goods and services amounting to £100 000. As prices had on average gone up by 15 per cent over the year they would have required £115 000 at the year end to purchase an equivalent bundle of goods and services.

At the year end, the directors of the company must decide how best to maximise the total potential consumption over time of their shareholders. If the directors decide to invest the whole of the £100 000 in assets it must be on the basis of the belief that such action will be more beneficial to the shareholders than would the distribution of the cash. The shareholders would sacrifice immediate consumption in return for what are hoped will be greater consumption opportunities in the future.

It can be seen that there are two steps in the argument. First, the potential consumption opportunities of the shareholders have fallen by £15 000 (measured in year-end pounds) over the year. Second, a sacrifice of the consumption opportunity of £100 000 at the year end is required if the investment is to be made.

To show the loss on holding money as £10 000 would not reflect the fact that the potential consumption opportunity of the equity shareholders had fallen by £15 000 over the year.

Strengths and weaknesses of the CPP model

As we pointed out in Chapter 4, an accounting model can be appraised in terms of the selected capital maintenance test and asset valuation basis. We will now evaluate the CPP model in this way.

The real financial (money) capital maintenance test appears to be a sensible choice. Money is not of itself a valuable commodity – its utility depends on what can be done with it or, in other words, what it can buy either now or in the future. Thus, given that the purchasing power of money does vary over time, it seems reasonable to suggest that it is more helpful for many purposes to use a benchmark based on the maintenance of real money capital rather than on money capital. In particular, the use, in CPP accounting, of a price index based on changes in consumer prices does seem to be the appropriate basis for the preparation of financial statements which serve to show the impact of an entity's operations on the economic welfare of its owners. The case for the use of the real financial capital test in such circumstances can be highlighted by the presentation of a simple example.

Suppose that all the business of a sole trader is conducted on a cash basis such that the trader's only business asset is cash and that the business has no liabilities. Assume that the trader starts the year with £100 000 and has £120 000 at the end of the year, during which time no cash has been either introduced or withdrawn.

The profit which would be disclosed by the conventional accounting method that uses the money capital test is £20 000, but does this represent the owner's increase in 'well-offness' over the year? The question cannot be answered in the absence of any knowledge of the change in the purchasing power of money over the year. If the rate of inflation was less than 20 per cent, then it seems reasonable to suggest that the owner was better off at the end of the year than at the beginning of the year in the sense that more goods and services could be purchased. Similarly, if the rate of inflation was more than 20 per cent the owner would be worse off.

Let us now turn to the CPP basis of asset valuation. It is here that the CPP model is weak. As has already been stated, the CPP model does not purport to show the current economic value of assets since the basis of valuation is historical cost. With CPP accounting it is money and not the asset that is 'revalued'. Thus, the CPP model suffers from much the same limitations as historical cost accounting which were outlined in Chapter 4, and most authorities appear to agree that the CPP approach is not an adequate response to the criticisms of the conventional method.

Given the obvious usefulness of the real money capital test and the weakness of the CPP asset valuation basis, many people, including the authors, believe that it would be sensible to combine the profit measure based on real financial capital maintenance with a basis of asset valuation which does reflect current values. We will introduce such an approach in Chapter 21 but in Chapter 20 we will first introduce Current Cost Accounting.

Summary

In the first part of this chapter we have provided an account of the history of the attempts to introduce a new approach to financial accounting that would have systematically reflected the impact of changing general price levels or the changing values of specific asset and liabilities. We saw how, in periods of high inflation, strong support for the introduction of new methods of accounting emerged, even from those such as the professional bodies that had previously resisted reform.

In the second part of the chapter, we introduced CPP accounting and showed that while it has a number of useful features, such as disclosing the loss or gain arising from an entity's monetary position, it suffers from a number of important defects, not the least of which is its failure to recognise changes in relative prices.

Recommended reading

See end of Chapter 21.

Questions

See end of Chapter 21.

chapter 20

Current cost accounting

The rejection of Current Purchasing Power (CPP) accounting by the Sandilands Report in 1975 led to the development of a system of Current Cost Accounting (CCA). In this chapter, we look first at the theoretical roots of such a system, namely:

- The distinction between holding and operating gains – Edwards and Bell.
- The concept of deprival value – Bonbright and Baxter.

We then explore the basic elements of CCA, discussing the valuation of assets in a current cost balance sheet and the capital maintenance concept to be used in the measurement of current cost profit. There are two basic capital maintenance concepts to choose from:

- Operating capital maintenance.
- Financial capital maintenance.

We explain the following four adjustments that were developed to measure profit on the basis of operating capital maintenance:

- Cost of sales adjustment (COSA).
- Depreciation adjustment.
- Monetary working capital adjustment (MWCA).
- Gearing adjustment.

We also explain how the financial capital maintenance concept can be applied using money capital or real capital, that is inflation-adjusted capital, as the benchmark.

Introduction

With the rejection of Current Purchasing Power (CPP) accounting by the Sandilands Report in 1975, the ASC turned its attention to the development of the very different system of accounting, Current Cost Accounting (CCA), recommended in that report. The Sandilands Committee envisaged that current cost accounts would replace historical cost accounts but this proved politically unacceptable and SSAP 16 *Current Cost Accounting* (1980) required listed and large unlisted companies to prepare current cost accounts as well as historical cost accounts or historical cost information.

While SSAP 16 was withdrawn in 1986, the attempts to develop a system of current cost accounting, both in the UK and in several other English-speaking countries, remains one of the more interesting experiments in the attempts to reform accounting. We describe the basic elements of the system in this chapter but start by discussing the two theoretical roots of CCA identified in Figure 19.1, the contributions made by Edwards and Bell and by Bonbright.

We discuss first the ideas of Edwards and Bell, whose seminal work *The Theory and Measurement of Business Income*[1] was published in 1961. This book represented a major advance in the development of current value accounting and its particular contribution to the CCA model was the recognition of the distinction between holding gains and operating gains; we will concentrate on this aspect of their work.

Theoretical roots

The distinction between holding and operating gains

For the purposes of determining business profit[2] Edwards and Bell divided the activities of a company into holding intervals and sales moments – the latter being assumed to be instantaneous (see Figure 20.1). A sales moment is the instant in time when the company sells goods while a holding interval is the interval between successive sales moments.

Suppose that a company starts an accounting period with assets with a replacement cost of £40, and that at the end of the first holding period its assets have a replacement cost of £60. These are not necessarily the same assets, as the company might well have exchanged assets during the period. Thus a manufacturing company might have reduced its cash and increased its holding of raw materials, work-in-progress and finished goods. Since, by definition, the company has made no sales during the holding interval, the change in the value of the assets must be due to an increase in the replacement cost of assets owned by the company.

Immediately after the first sales moment, the replacement cost of the company's assets equals £90. These assets will consist of the receipts from sales plus those of the company's assets that were not sold. The total business profit so far (assuming that no capital has been introduced or withdrawn) is £50: the difference between the replacement cost of the assets immediately after the first sales moment and the equivalent value at the start of the accounting period.

The total business profit of £50 can be divided into two elements. Part of the profit, £20, is due to the increase in the replacement cost of the assets during the holding period. This, Edwards and Bell called the realisable cost saving, although other terms used to describe it are holding gain and revaluation surplus. We will use the term holding gain. The replacement cost of assets at the moment of the first sale was £60, but as they were acquired with assets which had a current cost of £40, the company has gained, or saved, £20 by virtue of acquiring or manufacturing the goods sold in advance of the date of sale.

The remainder of the business profit, £30, is termed the *current operating profit*. This is the difference between the replacement cost of the assets before and after the sales moment. Now many of the company's assets will remain unchanged during the sales moment (i.e. will not be sold) and the current operating profit can be stated in terms of the assets that do change. Thus the current operating profit can be said to be equal to the receipts from sales less the replacement cost of assets used up (or exchanged) in the sales moment.

---

[1] E.O. Edwards and P.W. Bell, *The Theory and Measurement of Business Income*, University of California Press, Stanford, Calif., 1961.

[2] Edwards and Bell, *op. cit.*, used the phrase 'business profit' to refer to the profit measurement related to assets valued at current cost. As defined by Edwards and Bell, an asset's current cost is usually (but not always) the same as its replacement cost. For simplicity at this stage, we will assume that current cost is the same as replacement cost.

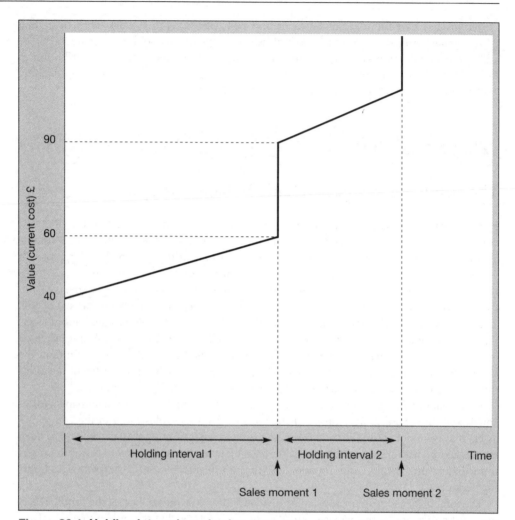

Figure 20.1 Holding intervals and sales moments of a company

The same approach can be used for each sales moment and, if we consider the accounting period as a whole, then, if it is assumed that no capital is introduced or withdrawn,

Business profit for period = Replacement cost of assets at end of period – Replacement cost of assets at beginning of period

= Sum of current operating profits for all sales moments + Sum of holding gains for all holding intervals.

The approach described above is illustrated in Example 20.1.

Example 20.1

Bow Limited started the year with the following assets:

	£
Stock, at replacement cost	600
Cash	400
	£1000

and finished the year with

	£
Stock, at replacement cost	900
Cash	500
	£1400

It will be assumed that the company has no operating expenses and that no capital was introduced or withdrawn. The total business profit is thus: £1400 – £1000 = £400.

The company's activities for the year were as follows:

				Stock £	Cash £
First	1 Jan	Opening balances		600	400
holding	17 Feb	Purchased stock for £200		200	(200)
interval		Stock had a RC of £900			
	31 Mar	at 31 March	HG	100	
				900	200
First	31 Mar	Stock with a RC of £300			
sales		sold for £450 (COP = £150)		(300)	450
moment				600	650
Second	1 Apr	Stock had a RC of £680			
holding		on 30 June	HG	80	
interval	30 Jun			680	650
Second	30 Jun	Stock with a RC of £280			
sales		sold for £300 (COP £20)		(280)	300
moment				400	950
Third	1 July				
holding	30 Sep	Purchased Stock for £450		450	(450)
interval		Stock had a RC of £900			
		at 31 Dec (the year end)	HG	50	
	31 Dec	Closing balances		£900	£500

where RC is the replacement cost, HG is the holding gain and COP is the current operating profit.

The total business profit of £400 can be analysed as follows:

Current operating profits	£	£
First sales moment £(450 – 300)	150	
Second sales moment £(300 – 280)	20	170
Holding gains		
First holding interval £(900 – 800)	100	
Second holding interval £(680 – 600)	80	
Third holding interval £(900 – 850)	50	230
Business profit		£400

We will discuss the problems involved in distinguishing between holding and operating gains later when we introduce the CCA model. However, it might be useful if we commented that a company's holding gains might be argued to give some indication of its success in the acquisition or manufacture of inputs, e.g. the extent to which it benefited by purchasing stock before a price increase. In contrast, the current operating profit might be said to provide information about the company's success as a seller of goods – the extent to which, because of its efficiency or position in the market, it can sell goods for a price that is greater than the current cost of replacing them.

The distinction between realised and unrealised holding gains

The total holding gain for a period may be split into two elements: the realised holding gain (RHG) and the unrealised holding gain (UHG). The RHG is that part of the total which is associated with the assets which have been used up or consumed in the period; that is, the RHG is the difference between the current value of the asset at the date at which it is consumed (e.g. the date of sale in the case of stock) and the historical cost of the asset. Conversely, the UHG arises from the increase in value of the assets which remain on hand at the end of the period and is equal to the difference between the current value of the assets at the end of the period and their historical cost or, in the case of assets owned at the beginning of the period, their value at that date.

The position is complicated slightly when we consider the consumption of assets that were owned at the beginning of the period because part of the RHG is effectively the realisation of part or the whole of the UHG of earlier periods.

Example 20.2 illustrates these points.

Example 20.2

Clive purchased 100 units of stock for £10 each on 1 December 20X7. No sales were made in December 20X7 and the RC of the units at 31 December 20X7 (Clive's year end) was £11 each.

Clive sold 60 units for £18 each on 30 June 20X8, at which date the RC of each unit was £13. No more sales were made in 19X8 but Clive purchased 20 units for £5 each on 10 October. The RC of stock on 31 December 20X8 was £16 per unit.

In 20X7 the only element of business profit is the UHG of £1 per unit or £100.

Now let us consider the year 20X8. Clive's assets at the start of the year, measured at RC, amounted to 100 units at £11 each or £1100. His assets at the end of the year were:

	£
Cash (60 × 18) − (20 × 15)	780
Stock 60 units at £16	960
	£1740

Clive's business profit for 20X8 was therefore £1740 − £1100 = £640. Clive's COP for the year is given by:

	£
Sales 60 × £18	1080
less RC of stock at the date of sale, 60 × £13	780
COP	£300

His RHG is given by:

	£
RC of stock at the date of sale	780
less Historical cost of stock, 60 × £10	600
RHG	£180

But of the above RHG of £180 a part represents the realisation of a portion of the 20X7 UHG, the amount involved being 60 × £1 = £60.

Clive's UHG in 20X8 is given by:

	£	£
RC at year end of closing stock of 60 units		960
less RC at 1 January of unsold closing stock held on 1 January, 40 × £11	440	
Historical cost of stock purchased in the year, 20 × £15	300	740
UHG		£220

The total business profit (BP) for the year is given by:

BP = COP + RHG + UHG − (that part of the RHG which was included in the UHG or previous years)

Substituting the monetary values, we have:

BP = £(300 + 180 + 220 − 60) = £640

The relationship between historical cost profit and business profit

The relationship can be easily seen if we resort to some simple algebra.

Let R be the revenue from sales, C be the current value of assets used up in generating sales, and H be the historical cost of those assets. Then the COP is given by $R - C$ while the RHG is equal to $C - H$.

The historical cost profit (HCP) is of course the difference between revenue and the historical cost of the assets consumed or, to use the above symbols:

$$HCP = R - H$$
$$= (R - C) + (C - H)$$
$$= COP + RHG.$$

In other words the historical cost profit is the sum of the current operating profit and the realised holding gains.

Let us now consider the implications of the above statement. The following discussion will serve as an introduction to the CCA model that will be developed later, as well as providing further evidence of the weaknesses of the historical cost accounting model.

It can be seen that historical cost profit has, when compared with business profit, two possible defects. First, historical cost profit combines two arguably distinct elements, COP and RHG, and the conventional accounting model makes no attempt to separate them. Second, the historical cost approach ignores UHG, i.e. it takes no account of the current value of the assets held at the end of the period.

The significance of these two observations depends on the view that is taken of the most suitable concept of capital for the purposes of profit determination. If the view is taken that the enterprise should be able to replace its assets as they are used up if it is to maintain its wealth or capital, i.e. the operating capital maintenance approach, then it might be argued that RHG should not be regarded as being part of the profit for the period.

Of course if one takes a different view of what constitutes 'well-offness' then it might be that RHG could be regarded as being part of profit. Such a view is implicit in the historical cost approach. However, it might still be argued that one of the defects of historical cost accounting is its failure to disentangle COP and RHG. This argument is based on the view that a company's COP and RHG are the result of different circumstances, and knowledge of the two elements might help the user of accounts to understand how the company obtained its historical cost profit. In particular, it might assist users to estimate future profits. For example, it might be that in a given year a company makes a very much greater profit than it had achieved in previous years because of the existence of RHGs. Those wishing to predict future profits would then no doubt consider the extent to which they believe that the opportunities to achieve RHGs will continue in the future.

To the extent that accounting practice in the UK and other countries allows companies to revalue assets for balance sheet purposes, UHGs are to be found in what are otherwise historical cost accounts. The recognition of UHGs in historical cost accounting has been partial, irregular (in the chronological and not moral sense) and has generally depended on the whim of the directors. Even after the issue of FRS 15 *Tangible Fixed Assets* (1998), directors will still enjoy considerable freedom as to which classes of assets are shown at current values.[3] Most adherents of current cost accounting would not wish to include UHGs as part of a company's profit. Even so, there is still a strong case for valuing assets at the current value, or in other words, systematically recognising UHGs. In CCA *all* UHGs on stocks and fixed assets are systematically recorded and reflected in the accounts.

The purpose of this section is to discuss the contribution of Edwards and Bell to the development of CCA. This can perhaps best be understood by noting that CCA makes a sharp distinction between current cost operating profit and holding gains.

---

[3] See Chapter 5.

It must, however, be noted that not all authorities agree that it is possible to make a clear and sharp distinction between operating profit and holding gains or that, even if it were possible, it would be desirable to do so. The distinction between operating and holding gains is clear in those cases when stock is replaced by more or less identical items. However, many traders do not act in this way but instead are prepared to switch from one line to another if they sense the opportunity of making greater profits. A trader might, for example, start the period with a warehouse full of carpets but use the cash flow generated from their sale to purchase refrigerators. In such a case it might be argued that it would not be realistic to include in the calculation of the trader's operating profit the replacement cost of carpets that the trader does not intend to replace. The designers of CCA systems have been forced to include special provisions to deal with such cases.

Some would go further and argue that even if stock is to be replaced, the distinction between holding and operating gains is artificial. Such advocates would say that the decision to carry on a business of necessity involves holding stock and hence most price changes in the stock holding period are just as much a part of the operations of the firm as the differences between current revenue and the current cost of goods sold.[4]

Which 'current value'?

In Chapter 4 we pointed out that there are several ways of valuing an asset, each of which is of relevance in the determination of periodic accounting profit. In other words there is not one unique measure of profit but a whole set, depending on the basis of asset valuation employed and the capital maintenance concept selected.

Let us for a moment ignore the problems associated with the choice of the capital maintenance concept and accept the argument that the present value approach to asset valuation should be rejected for the theoretical and practical reasons outlined in Chapter 4. We are then – if we are to use current values – left with the choice between the replacement cost and net realisable value approaches.

Clearly both are of relevance and a strong case can be made for requiring companies, or at least larger companies, to publish multi-columnar accounts which show both the replacement costs and the net realisable values of their assets and, possibly, their historical costs. Thus, companies would be required to report profit on more than one basis. Against this, the view has been expressed that the approach would be too costly for the producers of accounts and too complicated for the users of accounts.

The cost argument is not wholly convincing because if assets are to be employed properly businesspeople will need to be aware of both the replacement cost and the net realisable values of their assets. In addition, as will be seen, knowledge of both is required for the variant of current cost accounting that was favoured by the ASC. The second line of argument can – at least in the authors' view – be dealt with almost as easily. If it can be shown that there are a number of ways of measuring profit, then it surely is confusing and misleading to imply that there is only one. Considerations of practicability must limit the number of different profit figures that are reported, but it does seem reasonable to suppose that users of accounts should be able to cope with and benefit from the publication of two or three views of a company's results.[5]

---

[4] See D.F. Drake and N. Dopuch, 'On the case for dictomising income', *Journal of Accounting Research*, Autumn 1965, and P. Prakash and S. Sunder, 'The case against separation of current operation profit and holding gain', *The Accounting Review*, January 1979.

[5] This view would seem to be consistent with the ASB's support of the information set approach and their discouragement from focusing on one or two figures in the financial statements.

The foregoing argument was not accepted by those charged with the task of reforming accounting practice except in the period when it was advocated that both current cost and historical cost accounts should be published. Conventional wisdom decreed that one set of current value accounts was enough. The question of which asset valuation method should be adopted was therefore central to the current value accounting debate.

The net realisable value (NRV) approach possesses a number of virtues. The total of the net realisable values of a company's assets does provide some measure of the risks involved in lending to or investing in the company, in that the total indicates the amount that would be available for distribution to creditors and shareholders should the business be wound up. This point is, of course, dependent on the problems associated with the determination of net realisable values which were discussed in Chapter 4, and in particular the assumptions that are made about the circumstances surrounding the disposal of the assets. It has also been argued, notably by Professor R.J. Chambers, that the profit derived from a variant of the net realisable value asset valuation basis,[6] shows, after adjusting for changes in the general price level, the extent to which the potential purchasing power of the owners of an enterprise has increased over the period. However, the potential would only be realised if all the assets were sold, and it must be noted that in reality companies do not sell off all their assets at frequent intervals.

Advocates of net realisable value were, originally, mostly to be found in academia but, in the 1980s, support for this view emerged from a professional accountancy body in the form of a discussion document issued by the Research Committee of the Institute of Chartered Accountants of Scotland.[7] The model advocated by the committee and their arguments in favour of the net realisable value approach will be discussed in a little more detail in Chapter 21.

The general view of the supporters of CCA is that, in practice, companies continue in the same line or lines of business for a considerable time, making only marginal changes to the mix of their activities. It is therefore argued that if only one current value profit is to be published then it should be based on the replacement cost approach. For if it is assumed that a company is going to continue in the same line of business then it should only be regarded as maintaining its 'well-offness' if it has generated sufficient revenue to replace the assets used up. Thus, replacement cost was the preferred choice of those groups in the UK and most overseas countries that recommended the introduction of CCA. A strict adherence to the use of replacement cost, however, would not allow accounts to reflect the fact that companies do change their activities or the manner in which they conduct their present activities and that all the assets owned at any one time would not necessarily be replaced. Thus, some modification of the replacement cost approach is required.

Deprival value/Value to the business

A suitable basis of asset valuation, which would lead to the use of replacement cost in those circumstances where the owner would – if deprived of the asset – replace it and the use of a lower figure if the asset was not worth replacement, was suggested by Professor J.C. Bonbright in 1937. Professor Bonbright wrote, 'The value of a property to its owner is identical in amount with the adverse value of the entire loss, direct and indirect, that the owner might expect to suffer if he were deprived of the property'.[8] We have already introduced this approach in Chapter 5.

---

[6] A method known as Continuously Contemporary Accounting (CoCoA).
[7] *Making Corporate Reports Valuable*, Kogan Page, London, 1988.
[8] J.C. Bonbright, *The Valuation of Property*, Michie, Charlottesville, Va., 1937 (reprinted 1965).

Professor Bonbright's main concern was with the question of the legal damages which should be awarded for the loss of assets. He was not concerned with the impact of asset valuation on the determination of accounting profit. Others, notably Professor W.T. Baxter in the UK, recognised the relevance of this approach to accounting and developed the concept in the context of profit measurement. Professor Baxter coined the term 'deprival value', which neatly encapsulates the main point that the value of an asset is the sum of money that the owner would need to receive in order to be fully compensated if deprived of the asset. It must be emphasised that the exercise is of a hypothetical nature; the owner need not be physically dispossessed of the asset in order for its deprival value to be determined. This approach was proposed in the Sandilands Report and, renamed 'Value to the Business' or 'Current Cost', it became the asset valuation basis of CCA. Thus, in a current cost balance sheet, assets would be shown at their deprival value, while a current cost profit and loss account would show the current operating profit, determined as the difference between the revenue recognised in the period and the deprival values of the assets consumed in the generation of revenue.

As we have seen earlier the ASB had, for many years, accepted the view that the value-to-the-business model provides the most appropriate way of measuring the current value of an asset but that more recently, as a result of its desire to achieve greater international agreement, it has adopted a slightly different fair value approach (see, for example, Chapter 5).

Before turning to a discussion of CCA, it might be helpful if we explored the meaning of deprival value in a little more detail. Ignoring non-pecuniary factors, the deprival value of an asset cannot exceed its replacement cost, for the owner deprived of an asset could restore the original position through the replacement of the asset. The owner might of course incur additional costs (e.g. a loss of potential profit) if there was any delay in replacement – the indirect costs referred to in Professor Bonbright's original definition. There may be circumstances where these additional costs may be so substantial that they will need to be included in the determination of the replacement cost, but generally these additional factors are ignored.

The owner might not feel that the asset was worth replacing, in which case the use of the asset's replacement cost would overstate its deprival value. Suppose that a trader owns 60 widgets, the current replacement cost of which is £3 per unit. Let us also assume that the trader's position in the market has changed since acquiring the widgets, that it will only be possible to sell them for £2 each, and that this estimate can be made with certainty. The trader's other assets consist of cash of £100.

The trader's wealth before the hypothetical loss of the widgets is £220 (actual cash of £100 plus the certain receipt of £120). Let us now assume that the trader is deprived of the widgets. It is clear that the trader would only need to receive £120 in compensation, i.e. the net realisable value of the widgets, to restore the original position. The trader, if paid £180 (the replacement cost), would end up better off.

In order for an asset's deprival value to be given by its net realisable value, the net realisable value must be less than its replacement cost. Otherwise a rational owner (and in this analysis it is assumed that owners are rational) would consider it worthwhile replacing the asset.

We must now consider a different set of circumstances under which the owner would not replace the asset but has no intention of selling it. The asset may be a fixed asset that is obsolete in the sense that it would not be worth acquiring in the present circumstances of the business. The asset is still of some benefit to the business and it is thought that this benefit exceeds the amount that would be obtained from its immediate sale, i.e. its net realisable value. This benefit will, at this stage, be referred to as the asset's 'value in use'.

An example of this type of asset might be a machine that is used as a standby for when other machines break down. The probability of breakdowns may be such that it would not be worth purchasing a machine to provide cover because the replacement cost is greater than the benefit of owning a spare machine. It must be emphasised that the relevant replacement cost in this analysis is the cost of replacing the machine in its present condition and not the cost of a new machine. The machine may have a low net realisable value (which may be negative if there are costs associated with the removal of the machine) which is less than its value in use. In such circumstances an asset's deprival value will be given by its value in use, which would be less than its replacement cost but greater than its net realisable value.

As will be seen, the determination of an asset's value in use often proves to be a difficult task. In certain circumstances it may be possible to identify the cash flows that will accrue to the owner by virtue of ownership of the asset and thus, given that an appropriate discount rate can be selected, its present value can be found. In other instances the amount recoverable from further use may have to be estimated on a more subjective basis. However, this estimate will approximate to the asset's present value and hence we will, at this stage, use the term present value (PV) for simplicity.

The above discussion is summarised in Figure 20.2.

In the case of a fixed asset, the replacement cost is the lowest cost of replacing the services rendered by that asset rather than the cost of the physical asset itself. The replacement cost of stock will depend on the normal pattern of purchases by the business and thus it will be assumed that the usual discount for bulk purchases will be available.

The net realisable value of work-in-progress that would, in the normal course of business, require further processing before it is sold needs careful interpretation. The conventional definition of net realisable value in relation to stock is the 'actual or estimated selling price (net of trade but before settlement discounts) less (a) all further costs to completion and (b) all costs to be incurred in marketing, selling and distributing'.[9] There is an alternative definition that is the amount that would be realised if the asset were sold in its *existing* condition less the cost of disposal. For the purposes of determining the asset's deprival value, the higher of the two possible net realisable values will be taken.

Assume that a business holds an item of work-in-progress which could be sold for £200 in its existing condition, but which could, after further processing costing £30, be sold for £250.

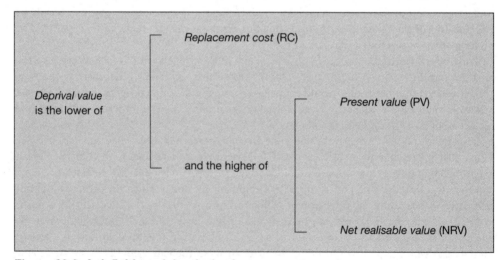

Figure 20.2 A definition of deprival value

---

[9] SSAP 9 *Stocks and Long-term Contracts*, revised September 1988.

Also assume that its replacement cost is £350 and thus its replacement cost does not yield its deprival value.

In this case the asset's deprival value is £220 so long as the period required to complete and market the stock is brief enough for us to be able to ignore the effect of discounting. It is clear that, before the hypothetical deprival of the asset, the business would expect to receive £220 from its sale after taking account of the additional processing costs. If, on the other hand, the increase in the sales proceeds that would be expected if the asset were processed was less than the additional manufacturing costs, a rational owner would sell the asset in its existing condition and the net sales proceeds under these circumstances would give its deprival value.

In the context of Figure 20.2, six different situations can be envisaged:

1 RC < NRV < PV; then the deprival value is given by the RC. In this case the asset's RC is less than both its NRV and PV. It is worth replacing and because its PV is greater than its NRV it is likely that the asset involved is a fixed asset that will be retained for use within the company.
2 RC < PV < NRV; then the deprival value is given by the RC. As (1) except that as the asset's NRV exceeds its PV the asset will be sold and is probably part of the trading stock of the business.
3 PV < RC < NRV; then the deprival value is given by the RC. The asset would be replaced and then sold. It is almost certain to be part of the trading stock.
4 NRV < RC < PV; then the deprival value is given by the RC. This is likely to be a fixed asset. It is worth replacing since its PV is greater than its RC.
5 NRV < PV < RC; then the deprival value is given by the PV. This asset is not worth replacing, but given that it is owned it will be retained since its PV is greater than its NRV. This is likely to be a fixed asset that would not now be worth purchasing but is worth retaining because of its comparatively low NRV.
6 PV < NRV < RC; then the deprival value is given by the NRV. This is the second case where the asset's value to the business is not its RC. The asset is not worth replacing nor is there any point in keeping it. It is obviously an asset that should be sold immediately. It might be an obsolete fixed asset whose scrap value is now greater than the benefit that would be obtained from its retention. Alternatively, the asset might be an item of trading stock in respect of which there has been a change in the business's place in the market, i.e. it can no longer acquire or manufacture the stock for an amount which is less than its selling price net of expenses.

It is clear that the deprival value of a fixed asset can only be given by its replacement cost or present value. The deprival value of an asset is based on its net realisable value only when it would be in the interest of the business to dispose of the asset. Thus, following the conventional definition of a current asset – an asset which will be used up within a year of the balance sheet date or within the operating cycle of the business, whichever is the longer – an asset whose deprival value is given by the net realisable value should be classified as a current asset.

The trading stock of a business is, by definition, an asset which is held for sale and hence its deprival value will either be its replacement cost or its net realisable value but not its present value (although in the case of stock which will not be sold for a considerable time its net realisable value may itself be based on the present value of future cash flows).

The deprival value of other current assets may be any of the three possible figures. Consider, as an example, the case of an unexpired insurance premium. Its deprival value is the loss that would be suffered if the insurance company could no longer honour its obligations. If the business felt that it was worth replacing the asset and would take out a new policy to cover the risk, the asset's deprival value would be given by its replacement cost. But suppose that it was believed that the cost of the new policy would outweigh the benefits that would be afforded by the policy. If the perceived benefits from the policy exceed the amount that could be obtained if the business surrendered the policy, the asset's deprival value would be its 'present value' (or value in use), which would be an amount which is less than the replacement cost but greater than its net realisable value (or the surrender value of the policy). It may be that the net realisable value exceeds the perceived benefit that would flow from the retention of the policy. In this instance, the deprival value of the asset is its net realisable value but, if this was indeed the case, the business should, in any event, surrender the policy.

The basic elements of current cost accounting

We are now in a position to introduce the basic elements of current cost accounting. In order to be able to concentrate on the principles involved we shall use very simple examples.

The current cost balance sheet

In a current cost balance sheet both assets and liabilities should in principle be shown at current cost, that is at deprival value or value to the business.

The current cost of short-term monetary assets will be the same as the amounts at which they appear in historical cost accounts. Hence, the assets that will appear at a different amount in a current cost balance sheet will be non-monetary assets, usually tangible fixed assets, investments and stocks.

In theory, liabilities should also be stated in terms of their 'current costs'. To do this we need to turn the definition of current cost around and ask how much the debtor would gain if he or she were released from the obligation to repay the debt. Clearly, all other things being equal, the longer the period before the debt is due, the less the gain from the extinction of the debt.

The 'current cost' or 'relief value' of a liability could be calculated by reference to its present value. Thus, if we ignore interest costs, the balance sheet figure for a debt of £100 000 repayable next month would be higher than a debt of the same nominal value repayable in ten years' time, the difference between the two figures depending on the discount rate.

In the early attempts to introduce CCA, liabilities continued to be recorded at their nominal values. However, there have been a number of developments in such areas as accounting for leases and retirement benefits, which are resulting in long-term liabilities being measured on the basis of their present values.

The total owners' equity in a current cost balance sheet is, as in a historical cost balance sheet, the difference between the assets and liabilities, but part of it will be treated as a reserve reflecting the amounts needed to be retained within the business to deal with the effect of changing prices. The size of the reserve, and its appropriate description, will depend on the selected capital maintenance concept (see Chapter 4).

The current cost profit and loss account

A current cost profit and loss account includes a number of items not found in one based on the historical cost convention. The actual number will depend on the chosen capital maintenance concept, which may be 'operating capital maintenance' or 'financial capital maintenance'. We shall look at each in turn.

Operating capital maintenance

We will first examine a current cost profit and loss account based on the maintenance of operating capital. Operating capital may be defined in a number of ways, but it is usual to think of it as the productive capacity of the company's assets in terms of the volume of goods and services capable of being produced. Thus, from this standpoint, a company will only be deemed to have made a profit if its productive capacity at the end of a period is greater than it was at the start of the period after adjusting for dividends and capital introduced and withdrawn.

The most convenient way of measuring a company's operating capital is by using, as a proxy, its *net operating assets*. So, a company will only be deemed to have made a profit if it has maintained the level of its net operating assets. As we shall see later, it is difficult to reach agreement as to what constitutes net operating assets. At this stage we will regard net operating assets as a company's fixed assets, stock and all monetary assets less current liabilities.

As explained in Chapter 4, if the company is partly financed by creditors, the profit attributable to the equity holders is different from, and in periods of rising prices greater than, the entity profit (current cost operating profit) on the assumption that part of the additional funds needed to maintain the operating capital is provided by creditors.

There are four 'current cost adjustments' which might appear in a current cost profit and loss account and which may be regarded as 'converting' a historical cost profit into a current cost profit. The first three are the 'current cost operating adjustments' and the fourth is the gearing adjustment:

1 *Cost of sales adjustment* (COSA): This is the difference between the current cost of goods sold and the historical cost.
2 *Depreciation adjustment*: This is the difference between the depreciation charge for the year based on the current cost of the fixed assets and the charge based on their historical cost.
3 *Monetary working capital adjustment* (MWCA): Monetary working capital may be defined as cash plus debtors less current liabilities. In order to operate, most companies need to invest in monetary working capital as well as in fixed assets, thus they might need to hold a certain level of cash and sell on credit but will also be able to buy on credit. All other things being equal, an increase in prices will mean that a company will have to increase its investment in monetary working capital, and the purpose of the MWCA is to show the additional investment required to cope with price increases. Of course, some companies can operate with negative working capital, for example a supermarket chain which buys on credit but sells for cash. In such instances an increase in prices will result in a reduction in monetary working capital and the MWCA would then be a negative figure reflecting that reduction.
4 *The gearing adjustment*: The gearing adjustment is the link between the current cost operating profit and the current cost profit attributable to the equity shareholders. It depends on the assumption that part of the additional funds required to be invested in the business as a result of increased prices will be provided by long-term creditors.

These adjustments are illustrated below.

Since X Limited started trading all prices have remained constant; hence the balance sheet as at 1 January 20X2, shown below, satisfies both the historical cost and current cost conventions.

Balance Sheet as at 1 January 20X2

	£		£
Share capital and		Fixed assets	
reserves	4500	purchased 31 Dec 20XI	3600
Loan (interest free)	4500	Stock (200 units)	2000
		Debtors	2400
		Cash	1000
	£9000		£9000

X Limited buys for cash and sells on one month's credit.

The company incurs no overhead expenses.

The fixed asset is to be written off over three years on a straight-line basis.

The mark-up is constant at 20 per cent on historical cost determined using the first-in first-out method of stock valuation.

Stock is held constant at 200 units: the monthly sales are 200 units. The cost of stock at the end of the previous month was £10 per unit; the cost of purchases increased by 10 per cent at the beginning of the month. The replacement cost of the fixed asset increased by 50 per cent on that date. Thereafter all prices are held constant.

All profits are paid out by way of dividend at the end of each month.

We will first present the historical cost accounts for January 20X2:

Historical cost profit and loss account for the month of January 20X2

	£	£
Sales, 200 × £10 × 1.2		2400
less Opening stock	2000	
Purchases, 200 × £10 × 1.1	2200	
	4200	
Less Closing stock	2200	2000
		400
Less Depreciation 1/36 of £3600		100
Profit for month		300
less Dividend		£300

Historical cost balance sheet as at 31 January 20X2

	£	£
Fixed assets		3500
Stock		2200
Debtors		2400
Cash £(1000 + 2400 – 2200 – 300)*		900
		£9000
Share capital and reserves		4500
Loan (interest free)		4500
		£9000

* Opening balance plus cash collected from debtors less purchases less dividends.

We will now look at the four adjustments on the assumption that the current cost of the assets is given by their replacement cost.

Cost of sales adjustment (COSA)

	£
Replacement cost of the 200 units sold	
$200 \times £10 \times 1.1$	2200
Historical cost of goods sold	2000
COSA	£200

Depreciation adjustment

	£
Depreciation charge for month based on the current cost of the fixed assets	
$1/36 \times £3600 \times 1.5$	150
Depreciation charge based on historical costs	100
Depreciation adjustment	£50

Note that in this simple introductory example we have assumed away the problem of the valuation of part-used assets, i.e. there is no prior or backlog depreciation.[10]

Monetary working capital adjustment (MWCA)

The company's opening monetary working capital consists of a cash balance of £1000, which represents half its monthly purchases (at the old prices) and debtors of £2400 (one month's sales). Hence, if it is assumed that for operational reasons the company will need to maintain the same relative position, an increase in the cost of purchases of 10 per cent will mean that the company's investment in working capital will also need to increase by 10 per cent.

Its opening monetary working capital was £3400;[11] hence the MWCA is 10 per cent of £3400 = £340.

The current cost operating profit and operating capability

Before turning to the gearing adjustment it is instructive to see what has happened so far. We started with a profit on the historical cost basis of £300 and have made three adjustments,

---

[10] Backlog depreciation represents the restatement of the depreciation charged in prior periods necessary to reflect the increase of the value of the asset that has occurred in the current period.

[11] Debtors include the profit on the sales. Strictly the profit element should be eliminated from the calculation of the MWCA as follows:

	£
Cost of stock with debtors	
$\frac{10}{12} \times £2400$	2000
Cash balance	1000
MWC	£3000
MWCA 10% of £3000	£300

We shall, however, ignore this complication.

the cumulative effect of which is:

	£	£
Historical cost profit		300
less COSA	200	
Depreciation adjustment	50	
MWCA	340	590
Current cost operating loss		£290

This example is based on the maintenance of operating capital, and the current cost operating loss of £290 can be related to the company's operating capacity as measured by its holding of net operating assets in the following way.

In order to be in the same position at the end of the month as it was at the beginning the company would need to:

(a) be able to replace that part of the fixed asset that has been consumed during the period (we will assume for the sake of the argument that the asset can be replaced in bits). At current prices it will need to set aside £150 to replace one-thirty-sixth of the asset (1/36 × £5400 = £150);
(b) hold stocks of £2200;
(c) carry debtors equal to one month's sales at the new price, £2640 (£2400 + 10% of £2400);
(d) hold a cash balance of £1100 (half the cost of one month's purchases).

We can now compare the required holding of assets with that which actually exists.

Required holding of assets

	£	£
Fixed assets		
remaining		3500
required for replacement		150
Stock		2200
Debtors		2640
Cash		1100
		9590
Assets available at the end of		
the month		
Fixed assets	3500	
Stock	2200	
Debtors	2400	
Cash	900	9000
Shortfall		590

The shortfall can be explained by two factors

	£
Dividend paid	300
Current cost operating loss	290
	590

Thus, it appears that, if it is the company's intention to maintain its operating capital, it should not have paid the dividend, but even if the dividend had not been paid, the company's operating capital would have been reduced by £290.

Many advocates of CCA would say that the above line of argument is unduly prudent because it ignores the fact that part of the company is financed by long-term creditors. They would include a gearing adjustment of some kind.

The gearing adjustment

The purpose of the gearing adjustment is to show how much of the additional investment required to counter the effects of increased prices would be provided by longer-term creditors[12] on the assumption that the existing debt-to-equity ratio, in this example 1:1, will be maintained.

Unfortunately, the gearing adjustment is another example of a failure to agree on the most appropriate method and there are at least two ways of calculating the gearing adjustment. The most commonly used, the so-called restricted or partial gearing adjustment, was based on the assumption that the current cost profit attributable to shareholders should bear the burden of only that part of the cost of sales, depreciation and monetary working capital adjustments financed by the shareholders, in this case 50 per cent. Thus, the restricted gearing adjustment is a credit to current cost operating profit of 50 per cent of the total of the three adjustments, i.e.:

	£
COSA	200
Depreciation adjustment	50
MWCA	340
	£590

The gearing adjustment, 50% of £590 = £295.

Putting all this together, the current cost profit attributable to shareholders can be determined as follows:

	£	£
Historical cost profit		300
less COSA	200	
Depreciation adjustment	50	
MWCA	340	590
Current cost operating loss		290
Add Gearing adjustment		295
Current cost profit attributable to shareholders		£5

Thus, the company could pay a dividend of £5 and still maintain its operating capital so long as the long-term creditors provide (or will provide if asked at some stage in the future) £295.

Some argue that this gearing adjustment is unduly restrictive because it fails to take into account unrealised holding gains (UHG) that will be reflected in a current cost balance sheet and which will reduce the debt-to-equity ratio thus affording the opportunity for further borrowings. In this case the unrealised holding gain on the fixed asset is 50 per cent of 35/36ths of £3600 = £1750.

The alternative, the natural or full gearing adjustment, is based on the sum of the UHG and the current cost adjustments – in this case 50 per cent of (£590 + £1750) = £1170, and thus the current cost profit attributable to shareholders becomes £880.

The use of the full gearing adjustment is based on the assumption that creditors would be prepared to lend the company an additional £1170 that would maintain the existing debt-to-equity ratio.

---

[12] Short-term creditors, such as trade creditors, have been ignored in this example. In practice, short-term creditors were included in monetary working capital.

The current cost accounts

The current cost profit and loss account for January, using the restricted gearing adjustment, can be presented as follows:

Current cost profit and loss account for the month of January 20X2

	£	£
Sales		2400
Cost of goods sold:		
Historical cost	2000	
COSA	200	2200
		200
Depreciation:		
Historical cost	100	
Depreciation adjustment	50	150
		50
MWCA		340
Current cost operating loss		290
Gearing adjustment (restricted)		295
Current cost profit attributable to shareholders		5
Dividend, assumed equal to Profit		£5

A distinction can be made between the three current cost operating adjustments. One, the depreciation adjustment, represents the restated value of the cost of an asset consumed during the period and will thus be credited to the provision for depreciation. The other adjustments relate to the additional investments required to maintain operating capability and will be credited to a *current cost reserve account*.

Another adjustment is required in the balance sheet in respect of the fixed asset. At the beginning of the month the fixed asset's current cost (equal in this instance to its historical cost) was £3600. This increased by 50 per cent to £5400 on the first day of the month. However, the decision to depreciate the asset on a straight-line basis assumes that one-thirty-sixth of the asset is used up in the month and hence 1/36 of the total gain of £1800, £50, is realised and the balance unrealised.

The total gain of £1800 is debited to the fixed asset account and credited to the current cost reserve account.

The gearing adjustment is debited to the current cost reserve account.

The current cost balance sheet as at 31 January 20X2 is therefore:

	£	£
Fixed assets at current cost	5400	
less Provision for depreciation	150	5250
Stock		2200
Debtors		2400
Cash (assuming a dividend of £5)*		1195
		£11045

	£	£
Share capital and reserves		4 500
Current cost reserve account (see below)		2 045
		6 545
Loan (interest free)		4 500
		£11 045
Current cost reserve		
Gain on fixed assets		1 800
COSA		200
MWCA		340
		2 340
less Gearing adjustment		295
		£2 045

*1000 + 2400 – 2200 – 5 = £1195

If we had used the full gearing adjustment, £1170, the current cost profit attributable to shareholders, and in this case the dividend, would be £880, thus reducing the assets to £10 170 and the current cost reserve to £1170. These figures illustrate the argument in favour of the full gearing adjustment because if the creditors did increase their loan by the amount of this gearing adjustment, £1170, the original debt-to-equity ratio of 1 : 1 would be maintained. The introduction of funds equal to the restricted gearing adjustment would not have the same effect because of the failure to recognise the unrealised holding gain.

The consequences of using the different approaches are illustrated in the following summary balance sheets that assume that additional borrowings, equal to the appropriate gearing adjustment, are obtained.

	Restricted gearing adjustment		Full gearing adjustment	
	£	£	£	£
Sundry assets		9 850		9 850
Cash		1 195		320
		11 045		10 170
Additional cash generated by fresh borrowings		295		1 170
		£11 340		£11 340
Share capital and reserves		4 500		4 500
Current cost reserve account		2 045		1 170
		6 545		5 670
Original loan	4 500		4 500	
Additional loan	295	4 795	1 170	5 670
		£11 340		£11 340
Debt-to-equity ratio		1 : 1.36		1 : 1

Financial capital maintenance

We will now consider current cost accounts in which profit is measured on the basis of financial capital maintenance. The focus here is on the shareholders and whether their interest in the company has increased or not. There are two versions of financial capital maintenance, one based on monetary units and the second based upon purchasing power units. While the former ignores inflation, the latter takes into account inflation, as measured, say, by the RPI, and hence attempts to show whether or not the interest of the shareholders in the company has increased in 'real' terms. For the remainder of this chapter, we shall confine ourselves to this real terms version of financial capital maintenance.

If it is assumed that no capital is introduced or withdrawn during the period, the 'real terms' profit can be found as follows:

(a) Measure the shareholders' funds at the beginning of the period based on the current cost of assets.
(b) Restate that amount in terms of pounds of purchasing power at the balance sheet date by use of a relevant index of general prices (such as the RPI).
(c) Compare the restated amount from (b) with the shareholders' funds at the end of the year, based on the current cost of assets. If shareholders' funds at the end of the period exceed the restated figure for the beginning of the period, a 'profit' has been made.

Using our earlier illustration and assuming that on average prices increased by 20 per cent over one month and that no dividends were paid, we can calculate the total real gain as follows:

(a) Shareholders' funds based on current costs as at 1 January 20X2, £4500.
(b) If prices increased on average by 20 per cent over the month, shareholders' funds would need to amount to £5400 (£4500 × 1.20) if real financial capital is to be maintained.
(c) **Calculation of total real gain**

	£
Shareholders' funds at 31 January 20X2	
at current cost	
Fixed assets	5 250
Stock	2 200
Debtors	2 400
Cash (before dividend)	1 200
	11 050
less Loan	4 500
Funds at 31 January 20X2	6 550
Funds at 1 January 20X2, restated in terms of	
31 January 20X2 purchasing power	5 400
Total real gains for January	£1 150

The above calculation gives no indication of how the gain was achieved. There are many ways of presenting a profit and loss account based on the maintenance of financial capital. One simple version based on our illustration is given below.

It starts in a similar fashion to the profit and loss account based on the maintenance of operating capital, in that it shows a current cost operating profit but without the inclusion of the monetary working capital adjustment which, along with the gearing adjustment, is inconsistent with the approach taken to monetary items in a system which does not seek to indicate the additional finance required to sustain a given level of net operating assets.

To the modified current cost operating profit are added the holding gains, distinguished between realised and unrealised. The cost of sales and depreciation adjustments are realised holding gains, which means that they are debited in the first part of the statement but are added back, or credited, in the second section.

The sum of the modified current cost operating profit and the total holding gains is described as the 'total gains'.

Finally, the 'inflation adjustment' is deducted from the total gains to give the total real gains.

Profit and loss account for January 20X2

'Real terms' (based on the maintenance of financial capital)

	£	£
Sales		2400
Cost of goods sold: historical cost	2000	
COSA	200	
Depreciation: historical cost	100	
depreciation adjustment	50	2350
Current cost operating profit		50
add Realised holding gains:		
Cost of sales adjustment	200	
Depreciation adjustment	50	
	250	
Unrealised holding gains: fixed asset	1750	2000
Total gains		2050
less Inflation adjustment (20% × £4 500)		900
Total real gains		£1150

Summary

We started the chapter by describing the theoretical roots of current cost accounting and paid tribute to the contributions made by Edwards and Bell, Bonbright and Baxter. We explained that Edwards and Bell developed the distinction between holding and operating gains while Bonbright and, subsequently, Baxter developed the ideas associated with the deprival value concept, which is also known as value to the business and current cost.

We then introduced the basic elements of Current Cost Accounting (CCA), using the deprival value concept of asset valuation and two different possible concepts of capital maintenance, operating capital maintenance and financial capital maintenance respectively. The first requires four current cost adjustments which we described and illustrated, namely the cost of sales, depreciation, monetary working capital and gearing adjustments. The second replaces the monetary working capital and gearing adjustments by an inflation adjustment based on a general index such as the Retail Price Index (RPI).

Recommended reading

See end of Chapter 21.

Questions

See end of Chapter 21.

Beyond current cost accounting

overview

In the previous two chapters we examined the attempts of the ASC to design a system of accounting to replace or supplement the traditional historical cost accounts. In Chapter 19, we explored the Current Purchasing Power (CPP) model while, in Chapter 20, we introduced the basic elements of the Current Cost Accounting (CCA) model.

In this chapter, we start by assessing the virtues of this CCA system for some of the main purposes for which periodic financial statements are used. We then explore an alternative system, real terms current cost accounting, which combines the most useful features of both CPP and CCA.

As long ago as 1988 the Institute of Chartered Accountants of Scotland publication, *Making Corporate Reports Valuable*,[1] took a much more revolutionary approach to the reform of accounting and we outline the major features of this report which include a call for further study of a system of accounting based upon the valuation of assets at their net realisable values rather than at their current cost.

Finally we explore the evolution of the ASB's approach to dealing with changing prices, an approach which undoubtedly reflects the reduced interest in such changes during the era of low inflation rates experienced in the last decade of the twentieth century and maintained in the early years of this century. The ASB approach has severe limitations, even in a period of low inflation, but nonetheless lays good foundations to cope with the situation when the merits of an approach to financial reporting based on a systematic use of current values becomes more widely accepted or, of course, when inflation rates begin to rise again.

The utility of current cost accounts

In Chapter 4 we identified some of the main purposes served by the publication of periodic financial statements and examined the extent to which traditional historical cost financial statements served those purposes. Here we assess the extent to which current cost accounts would satisfy those same purposes, namely control, taxation, consumption and valuation.

Control

Current cost accounts are likely to be more helpful than historical cost accounts or current purchasing power accounts in helping shareholders and others to assess how well or badly the directors have employed the resources which have been entrusted to them, especially

---

[1] P.N. McMonnies (ed.), *Making Corporate Reports Valuable*, Institute of Chartered Accountants of Scotland and Kogan Page, London, 1988.

through the use of such measures as return on capital employed. The current cost accounts attempt to show the current values of the assets of the company and whether or not the net assets have increased during a period after allowing for either specific or general price changes, depending upon which capital maintenance concept is applied. Thus, it may be argued that the current cost accounts would provide a better vehicle for the exercise of control by shareholders and others.

There were obvious weaknesses with the ASC's preferred current cost model, notably the complete absence of regard to changes in the general price level found in the operating capital maintenance variant, and the partial treatment provided by the financial capital maintenance approach.

Taxation

If one makes the not unreasonable assumption that a government would only wish to levy taxation on any surplus that is generated after the substance of the business has been maintained, then it can be seen that CCA is likely to provide a better basis for taxation than the historical cost or CPP methods.

It must be recognised that the amount of taxation payable by a company depends not only upon the way in which its taxable profit is calculated, but also upon the nominal tax rate applied to that taxable profit. Even if the government were to adopt current cost profits, rather than historical cost profits, as the basis for the computation of taxable profits, it might still wish to raise the same amount from the taxation of business profits. If such were the case, there would be a redistribution of the tax burden within the business sector, with no change in the total burden on that sector.

Current cost accounting does *prima facie* seem to provide a suitable basis for taxation, but since equity and clarity are desirable characteristics of any system of taxation much more will have to be done if taxes are to be based on current cost accounting. In particular, the degree of choice allowed to companies, especially with regard to the capital maintenance concept, would need to be reduced. It is unlikely that the Inland Revenue would accept the degree of subjectivity involved in any system of current cost accounting that has yet been developed.

The treatment of the gearing adjustment would also require careful consideration. It is reasonable to include the gearing adjustment in arriving at the profit subject to taxation, as it does offset the cost of interest which is charged to the accounts, so only the real cost of interest as opposed to the nominal charge would be allowed against tax. However, if this were done, there would be a strong case for not taxing the whole of the interest payments received by lenders, thus allowing them some relief from inflation. Such a change would have significant consequences for the whole of the tax system – both personal and corporate – and is unlikely to be made without a good deal of discussion.

Consumption

As is the case with taxation, the extent to which financial statements assist in the making and monitoring, by shareholders and others, of the consumption or dividend decision depends on the concept of capital that is to be 'maintained'. Although at its present state of development there is no general agreement as to the most suitable capital maintenance concept for CCA, it does not seem unreasonable to suggest that both the operating and financial capital bases provide more useful information than that provided by the historical cost model which, as we have argued at various places in this book, can be extremely dangerous in that dividends may be paid unwittingly out of capital.

In developing the CCA model, its advocates placed considerable emphasis on the dividend decision, but in some respects this aim resulted in a degree of complexity that hindered the acceptance of current cost accounting. The gearing adjustment was perhaps the most striking example. Such complexity may be inevitable in a system of accounting that does attempt to reflect reality – for reality is rarely simple. To take the dividend decision as an example, the desires of a short-term shareholder and a director/shareholder interested in security of employment will be very different. If CCA is complex because it tries to present information that will be of value to both groups, should such complexity be condemned?[2]

In developing CCA the emphasis was also placed on the needs of larger companies but it is often in the humbler parts of the business world that we find disasters caused by a level of consumption (through drawings or dividends) which is not supported by profits. If those responsible for the conduct of small and medium-sized enterprises are presented, as they are, with historical cost accounts which indicate they have generated a healthy profit, can one be surprised if some of them 'blow the lot', rather than intuitively estimating the cost of sales and other adjustments in order to see how much of that apparent profit needs to be retained to keep the business operating at its existing level?

If it is not yet possible to devise a suitable method for applying CCA principles in a way that would be appropriate to the circumstances of smaller enterprises, then, at the very least, the traditional historical cost accounts should carry a health warning.

Valuation

The sum of the values of the assets less liabilities of a business as shown in a current cost balance sheet will not, other than in the simplest of cases, be the same as the value of the businesses as a whole, but it is likely that the current cost total will give a better approximation to this value than the figures that are disclosed by the historical cost accounts.

It is not necessary at this stage to spell out the reasons why there is a difference between the total of the values of the individual assets less liabilities and the value of the business as a whole, as the subject of the valuation of a business was discussed earlier. The main reason for the difference is that which is covered by the concept of goodwill, which recognises that an existing business will usually possess substantial intangible assets such as reputation, established relationships with suppliers and customers, and managerial skills, which are not recorded in a balance sheet.

The above discussion of goodwill was based on the assumption that the value of the business was greater than the total of the values of the assets less liabilities. The reverse can also be true, and a potential weakness of the CCA model is that it can overstate the value of the assets in particular because of the existence of interdependent assets. This problem arises from the fact that assets will be valued at their replacement cost unless a permanent diminution in value has been recognised. If each asset is considered individually and the values aggregated, it may be seen that they are collectively not worth replacing and thus that a value less than the sum of their replacement values should be placed on them. A hypothetical example of this situation is that of a railway line which runs through two tunnels. Assume

---

[2] As is it is stated in the *Statement of Principles* (Para. 3.37), 'Information that is relevant and reliable should not be excluded from the financial statements simply because it is too difficult for some users to understand'.

that the present value of the railway line is £400 000 and the replacement cost of each tunnel is £250 000. If each tunnel is considered in isolation, it is clear that if either were destroyed it would be worth replacing, and thus would be valued for CCA purposes at £250 000. However, it is clear that if both tunnels were simultaneously destroyed they would not be replaced because the total replacement cost would exceed the benefit that would be derived from the action.

The appropriate action in the above example is to treat the railway line as an income-generating unit[3] and value the assets of the unit on the basis of their value in use. However, it will not always be possible to identify where such treatment is necessary and hence the risk of the overstatement of the assets still remains and is likely to be greater when applying current cost rather than historical cost accounting principles.

Thus, while it will generally be true that the current cost balance sheet totals will provide a closer approximation to the value of the business than historical cost information, there will still be substantial differences between the two values. This is not to be taken as a criticism of CCA in that the designers of the system did not set this as one of the objectives of CCA. However, it is likely that many laypeople will not fully appreciate this point, and there may well be some confusion on the part of the general public, who may believe that a system of current cost accounts should tell them how much a business is worth.

Interim summary

CCA is certainly not the perfect system of accounting in that there is more than one way of reflecting the activities of a business. Neither is it a perfect system of accounting in that, even within its own parameters, it is capable of improvement. The important practical question that had to be addressed was whether the benefits of current cost accounts exceeded the costs of developing the system and of preparing those accounts.

Attempts were made to try to answer this question, including studies commissioned by the ASC on the implementation of SSAP 16. The general conclusion was that there were some advantages to be gained from the publication of current cost information in that its availability provided a better basis for decision making than a complete reliance on historical cost accounts.

The fact that current cost accounts never really took hold suggests either that the benefits did not exceed the costs or that those parties on which the costs fell, the companies and auditors, have much more political clout with the standard setters than the users, who would be expected to benefit from the information.

CPP and CCA combined

The relationship between accounting for changes in specific prices and accounting for changes in general prices has always been uneasy. As described in Chapter 19, the early moves to reform in the UK tended to polarise the position – the reformed models were based on either CPP or CCA ignoring inflation. So why not combine the most helpful features of CCA and CPP? Such an approach has been advocated by a number of accountants,

---

[3] FRS 8 *Impairment of Fixed Assets and Goodwill*, see Chapter 5.

mostly of the academic variety.[4] The change in shareholders' equity derived from a set of fully stabilised[5] financial statements based on 'value to the business' asset valuation is the same as that derived from the ASC's approach, but there is an important difference because of the treatment of price changes during the year and because of the treatment of monetary items. A fully stabilised set of financial statements will, for example, show the loss or gain on holding monetary assets and liabilities.

The basic principles can be illustrated in the following example.

Example 21.1

Guy started a business on 1 January 20X3 with £1000 which he used to purchase 100 units of stock for £10 each. Trading was not overactive during the year and the only sales were 60 units for £18 each on 31 December 20X3.

For simplicity we will assume that he incurred no overheads during the year. Let us suppose that the general price level increased by 10 per cent over the year while the replacement cost of stock increased by 15 per cent. Then Guy's only sales transaction can be analysed as follows:

	£
Cost of sales	600
Inflation increase	60
Cost of sales restated in current pounds (at 31.12.19X3)	660
Price increase in excess of inflation	30
Replacement cost at date of sale	690
Sales	1080
Profit	£ 390

If we had prepared a standard CCA profit and loss account we would also have shown a profit of £390, as this is the difference between the sales proceeds and the current cost of the stock consumed. The major difference between the CCA approach and the above is that, in the latter, the CCA cost of sales adjustment of £90 has been broken down into two elements: (a) £60, which represents the amount by which the cost of the stock held needed to increase in order to keep step with inflation, and (b) £30, the amount by which the increase in the current cost of the stock exceeded inflation. The justification for disaggregating the CCA cost of sales adjustment in this way is that, if account is taken of the fall in the value of money, then the whole of £90 cannot be regarded as a realised holding gain, as £60 merely represents that which is required to keep step with inflation and is not a 'real gain'. In consequence, that element of the nominal gain which is required to keep step with inflation (£60 in this case) is sometimes known as the *fictitious holding gain*, whereas the *real realised holding gain* (or loss) is the difference between the current cost of the asset at the date at which it is consumed and the restated historical cost (i.e. the historical cost adjusted for the change in the general price level).

---

[4] See, for example, W.T. Baxter, *Accounting Values and Inflation*, McGraw-Hill, London, 1975.
[5] Fully stabilised means that all items are expressed in forms of a constant purchasing power, usually the unit of purchasing power on the balance sheet date.

If we now turn our attention to the closing stock the same approach can be used, i.e.:

	£	£
Current cost of closing stock £400 × 1.15		460
Historical cost of closing stock	400	
Inflation adjustment (fictitious unrealised holding gain) 10%	40	440
Real unrealised holding gain		£20

Opening financial capital was £1000 and, if real financial capital is to be maintained, this amount must be enhanced by 10 per cent to take account of the fall in the value of money.

On the basis of the above considerations, Guy's accounts for 20X3 would appear as follows:

Profit and loss account 20X3

	£
Sales	1080
Current cost of goods sold	690
Operating profit	£390

Statement of gains/losses 20X3

	£
Operating profit	390
Realised real holding gain	30
Unrealised real holding gain	20
	£440

Balance sheet as at 31 December 20X3

	£	£
Capital 1.1.X3	1000	
Inflation adjustment 10%	100	1100
Reserves		
Realised gains		
Operating	390	
Holding	30	420
Unrealised gains		20
		£1540
Stock at current cost (40 items @ £11.50)		460
Cash (60 @ £18)		1080
		£1540

The capital and reserves section of the balance sheet well illustrates the different views that may be taken with regard to distribution. If it is accepted that capital is maintained if assets less liabilities at the balance sheet date equal opening capital after adjusting for inflation, then the maximum that could be distributed without diminishing capital is £440. If it is argued that only realised profits should be distributed then the dividend should be restricted to £420. If it is argued that the business must retain sufficient funds to maintain the same level of activity (i.e. be able to replace the 60 units sold) the maximum dividend is equal to the realised operating gain of £390.

▶

This last line of argument brings us to the current cost account approach that it is the operating capability of the business that must be kept intact if capital is to be maintained. Thus, it can be seen that within the combined CCA/CPP approach it is possible to focus on a profit calculated on the basis of physical capital maintenance. The authors, along with most other writers on the subject, would not, however, advocate that this be done, as they believe that the concept of 'operating capability' is unclear and ambiguous. However, even if the maintenance of real financial capital is taken to be the benchmark used to measure profit, it may still be of value to show what proportion of the operating profit has been paid out by way of dividend so that users can see the extent to which the reserves of the business have increased or decreased after setting aside a sum to allow for increases in specific prices over the rate of inflation. The formulation used in the above simple example would allow this assessment to be made as well as showing the extent to which the total gains are realised.

Before turning to a slightly more complex example, we will discuss those issues, which we were able to sidestep in our very simple example – the monetary working capital and gearing adjustments.

The monetary working capital and gearing adjustments arise from the attempts to measure changes in operating capability. The first attempts to show the increased investment required in monetary working capital, and the second strives to show the extent to which the increased investment in stocks, fixed assets and monetary working capital would be provided by creditors. These adjustments are not required in a stabilised accounting system based on the maintenance of real financial capital. In such a system, the impact of inflation on monetary items is the loss or gain on both the business's short- and long-term monetary positions measured in the way described in Chapter 19.

Example 20.2 illustrates one way of combining current cost asset valuation with the maintenance of real financial capital.

Example 21.2

Suppose that Park Limited started business on 1 January 20X2. On that date the company issued 12 000 £1 shares and £4000 of debentures and purchased fixed assets for £12 000 and stock of £6000. The purchases were partly financed by an overdraft of £2000.

Park's balance sheet at 1 January 20X2 is then

	£		£
Share capital	£12 000	Fixed assets	£12 000
Debentures	4 000	Stock (100 units)	6 000
		Overdraft	(2 000)
	£16 000		£16 000

We will assume that all transactions took place on 1 July 20X2. On that date Park Limited purchased another 400 units for £75 (total £30 000) and sold 380 units for £36 000. Closing stock at FIFO cost is thus £9000.

Overhead expenses, including debenture interest, all paid for cash on 1 July 20X2, amounted to £5000. On 1 July the company paid its suppliers £27 000 and received £31 000 from its customers; thus trade creditors at 31 December 20X2 amounted to £3000 and trade debtors equalled £5000. The company's overdraft at the year end was:

	£
Overdraft at 1 January 20X2	2 000
add Paid to suppliers	27 000
Paid for overheads	5 000
	34 000
less Received from customers	31 000
Overdraft at 31 December 20X2	£3 000

Depreciation is to be provided at 20 per cent per annum on a straight-line basis.
Assume that the appropriate price indices moved as follows:

Date	1 January	1 July	31 December
General price index	90	100	110
Stock price index	80	100	120
Fixed asset price index	95	100	105

Note that the stock price index increased by more than the rate of inflation while the fixed asset price index rose by less (i.e. the price of the fixed assets fell in real terms).

In order to see clearly how certain elements of CCA can be combined with a set of CPP accounts, it is helpful to prepare first the CPP accounts. These will appear as follows:

CPP accounts

Profit and loss account for 20X2	£(31 Dec)	£(31 Dec)	*Workings*
Sales, 36 000 × 110/100		£39 600	
less Opening stock,			
£6000 × 110/90	7 333		
Purchases,			
£30 000 × 110/100	33 000		
	40 333		
less Closing stock,			
£90 000 × 110/100	9 900	30 433	
Gross profit		9 167	
less Overheads,			
£5000 × 110/100	5 500		
Depreciation,			
£2400 × 110/90	2 933	8 433	
		734	
Gain on short-term monetary items	344		(A1)
Gain on long-term monetary items	889	1 233	(A1)
CPP profit for the year		£1 967	

Balance sheet as at 31 December 20X2

	£(31 Dec)	£(31 Dec)
Fixed assets		
Cost		
£12 000 × 110/90	14 667	
less Accumulated		
depreciation,		
£2400 × 110/90	2 933	11 734
Current assets		
Stock, £900 × 110/100	9 900	
Debtors	5 000	
	14 900	
Current liabilities		
Creditors	(3 000)	
Overdraft	(3 000)	8 900
		20 634
Debentures		4 000
		£16 634
Share capital,		
£12 000 × 110/90		14 667
Retained profits		1 967
		£16 634

CPP workings

(A1)   Loss on short-term monetary items is given by:

		Actual £		Conversion factor	£(31 Dec)	
1 Jan	Opening balance		2 000	110/90		2 444
1 July	Sales	36 000		110/100	39 600	
	Purchases		30 000	110/100		33 000
	Overheads		5 000	110/100		5 500
31 Dec	Closing balance	1 000			1 344	
		£37 000	£37 000		£40 944	£40 944

Gain on short-term monetary items is £(31 Dec) (1344 − 1000) = £(31 Dec) 344.
Gain on long-term monetary liabilities is:

$$£(31 \text{ Dec}) \, 4000 \left(\frac{110}{90} - 1 \right) = £(31 \text{ Dec}) \, 889$$

Real holding gains

Four adjustments need to be calculated, the realised and unrealised real gains (or losses) on stock and fixed assets expressed in closing pounds.

(a) *Real realised gain on stock (the cost of sales adjustment)* Stock with a historical cost of £27 000 was sold on 1 July by which date the stock price index had moved to 100, i.e. the replacement cost at date of sale was:

Opening stock, £(1 Jan) 6000 × 100/80	£(1 July)	7 500
1 July purchases	£(1 July)	21 000
	£(1 July)	28 500

These are 1 July pounds and have to be converted to year-end pounds:

£(1 July) 28 500 × 110/100	£(31 Dec)	31 350
Cost of goods sold per CPP profit and loss account	£(31 Dec)	30 433
Cost of sales adjustment	£(31 Dec)	917

(b) *Real realised loss on fixed assets (depreciation adjustment)*

	£(31 Dec)
Depreciation charge based on movement in specific prices, £2400 × 105/95	2 653
Depreciation charge per CPP accounts	2 933
Depreciation adjustment (loss)	(280)

Note:
(i) Depreciation is based on year-end prices.
(ii) The loss means that the cost of the asset consumed (deemed to be 20% of the fixed assets) increased by less than the rate of inflation.

(c) *Real unrealised gain on stock*

	£(31 Dec)
Closing stock	
At replacement cost, £9000 × 120/100	10 800
At adjusted historical cost £900 × 110/100	9 900
Real unrealised gain	900

(d) *Real unrealised loss on fixed assets*

	£(31 Dec)
Net book value at 31 Dec	
At replacement cost 80% of £12 000 × 105/95	10 611
At adjusted historical cost (per CPP accounts), 80% of £12 000 × 110/90	11 734
Real unrealised loss[6]	(1 123)

We are now in a position to present the accounts, which we will do in summarised form:

Profit and loss account

	£(31 Dec)	£(31 Dec)
Sales		39 600
less: Current cost of goods sold	31 350	
Overheads	5 500	
Depreciation	2 653	39 503
Current cost operating profit		97

---

[6] Since this is the first year in the life of the assets and as depreciation is based on year-end values, there is no backlog depreciation.

Statement of gains and losses

	£(31 Dec)	£(31 Dec)
Current cost operating profit		97
Gains/losses on assets		
Realised		
Gain on stock	917	
Loss on fixed assets	(280)	637
Unrealised		
Gain on stock	900	
Loss on fixed assets	(1123)	(223)
Gains on monetary items (per CPP accounts)		
Short term	344	
Long term	889	1233
		1744

Balance sheet as at 31 December

	£(31 Dec)	£(31 Dec)
Fixed assets, net current replacement cost		10611
Current assets		
Stock at replacement cost	10800	
Debtors	5000	
	15800	
Current liabilities		
Creditors	(3000)	
Overdraft	(3000)	9800
		20411
Debentures		(4000)
		16411
Share capital		
Issued	12000	
Inflation adjustment[7]	2667	14667
Reserves		1744
		16411

A real alternative – *Making Corporate Reports Valuable*

Even a casual perusal of the earlier chapters of this book would lead the reader to conclude both that most accountants (both theoretical and practical) who have thought seriously about the issues agree that historical cost accounting is unhelpful and, in periods of rapid price changes, positively dangerous and that the current cost accounting path to reform has proved difficult to travel and may not bring us to the promised land. Perhaps we should approach the problem from another direction? Is there a real alternative? Some, but as yet very few, accountants believe that there is. In the 1960s and 1970s, a number of theoreticians, notably

---

[7] In years other than the first, the inflation adjustment would be applied to the opening balance of shareholders' equity. In this case the inflation adjustment is £12000 (110/90 − 1) = £2667.

Professors Chambers in Australia and Sterling in the United States,[8] advocated the use of the net realisable value basis for asset valuation. In 1988 their proposals received a powerful stimulus in the UK from the publication of the report of a major research project undertaken by the Research Committee of the Institute of Chartered Accountants of Scotland, entitled *Making Corporate Reports Valuable*.[9] The report is extremely stimulating and challenging and is an important contribution to the debate on accounting reform. It succeeds in its attempts to challenge preconceived ideas and is revolutionary rather than evolutionary. The revolutionary nature of its proposals is reflected in the committee's decision to reject traditional terms such as profit and loss account, balance sheet and auditor, which are replaced by phrases such as operations statement, assets and liabilities statement and independent assessor.

The report deals both with matters that could be addressed in the reasonably short term and with those that could only be implemented in the longer term. We will not attempt to summarise the whole of the 108-page document but focus on three aspects: the desirability of providing more contextual information; the incorporation in financial statements of the company's market capitalisation; and the longer-term proposals about a radically different form of financial reporting based on net realisable values.

More contextual information

In *Making Corporate Reports Valuable* (which will from now on be referred to as *MCRV*) four users groups are recognised: equity investors, loan creditors, employees and business contacts. It is suggested that the fundamental information needs of these external users are:

(a) information on an entity's objectives and its performance towards achieving them;
(b) a comparison of an entity's total wealth now as against that at the previous reporting date and the reasons for the change;
(c) the entity's likely future status, performance and resources;
(d) the present and projected environment of the entity; and
(e) information on the ownership and control of the entity and on the background of its management.[10]

In order to satisfy these needs, *MCRV* advocates the provision of a substantial amount of structured descriptive data to accompany the quantitative data. We have seen, in Chapters 2 and 17, how such an approach is now evident in the increasing emphasis being given to the Operating and Financial Review by both the ASB and the UK Government, in its White Paper on company law reform.[11]

Market capitalisation

Equity shareholders are very interested in the price at which they could sell their shares but the aggregate figure, i.e. the share price multiplied by the number of shares in issue, or market

---

[8] See R.J. Chambers, *Accounting, Evaluation and Economic Behaviour*, Prentice-Hall, Englewood Cliffs, N.J., 1966; R.J. Chambers, 'Second Thoughts on Continuously Contemporary Accounting', *Abacus*, September 1970; R.R. Sterling, *Theory of the Measurement of Enterprise Income*, University Press of Kansas, Topeka, Kans., 1970.

[9] P.N. McMonnies (ed.), *Making Corporate Reports Valuable*, Institute of Chartered Accountants of Scotland and Kogan Page, London, 1988.

[10] *Op. cit.*, Para. 9.9.

[11] *Modernising Company Law*, Cm. 5553-I and Cm. 5553-II, HMSO, July 2002.

capitalisation, is traditionally not thought to be of great relevance to statements about the financial success of the company. The conventional view is that the market price is a marginal price reflecting deals between the seller and purchaser of a small parcel of shares, and hence a poor guide to the value of the company as a whole, and that it is affected by changes in the market which do not relate specifically to the company concerned. In response to this traditional view, *MCRV* makes an important empirical observation when it suggests that it is believed that there is only one case on record in which the premium on a successful bid for a company quoted on the London Stock Exchange was negative.[12] Thus, it is suggested that the market capitalisation provides an estimate of the value of the entity that is consistently at or below the true value. The report goes on to suggest that the underestimation of the true value is likely to be in the region of 15–20 per cent on the grounds that this range covers the average amount of takeover premiums and that such an error is likely to be far less than that derived from a comparison of true value with the balance sheet net worth based on the historical cost convention. Thus *MCRV* suggests that the market capitalisation figure should have a prominent place in the financial statements and that directors should be required to explain the reasons for significant changes between the differences between market capitalisation and the reported figure for net identifiable assets.

A net realisable value accounting model

MCRV argues that the two main criteria for selecting a basis for asset and liability valuation should be additivity and reality.[13] By additivity is meant the quality that when all the numbers in a statement are added together, the sum should have the same meaning as each of the numbers taken on their own; *MCRV* reminds us of the old adage of the undesirability of adding apples and pears. The meaning placed on reality is that numbers in the accounts should reflect as closely as is practical one or more economic facts with which most skilled observers would agree, and not conjectures where there can justifiably be a considerable difference of opinion even amongst reasonable and skilled people.

In the view of *MCRV* both current replacement cost (the main element of current cost accounting) and net realisable value pass the additivity and reality tests, albeit with some difficulties.[14]

A number of reasons why NRV is preferred to current replacement cost are advanced, of which the following are perhaps the most important:

(a) NRV is a value that is readily understandable by investors and other users of accounts. *MCRV* points to evidence that some external users believe that this is the value that is actually disclosed by financial statements. Thus, it is suggested that the use of NRV would go some way to reducing the 'expectation gap' in financial reporting.[15]

(b) The use of current replacement cost still includes the making of 'arbitrary decisions' about such matters as depreciation. NRV is in this context far more elegant and simple for there is no need to allocate costs to different accounting periods. Assets are simply valued by reference to the market place, and their total value is the sum that would be obtained if all the assets were sold in an orderly fashion (i.e. not as a forced sale) – very additive and very realistic.

---

[12] *Op. cit.*, Para. 6.16.
[13] *Op. cit.*, Para. 6.4.
[14] *Op. cit.*, Para. 6.11.
[15] *Op. cit.*, Para. 6.20(b).

Of course the second of the two reasons given above can be turned round and used as a strong argument against NRV as a basis for valuation. An asset that is highly specific to the needs of a particular company may have a very low value in the market place, irrespective of its value to the company.

MCRV's answer is to question the definition or rather the delineation of the asset to be valued. A highly specific asset may, in the market place, be worthless in isolation but have a value when combined with other assets. To return to the railway example (see p. 668), the market value of a tunnel may be very low (depending primarily on its use for growing mushrooms or storing wine) but *MCRV* would argue that it is more meaningful to value the business unit of which the tunnel is a part.[16]

The question of whether the focus of asset valuation can be moved from the individual asset to the business unit is perhaps the key issue to be resolved if a practical and acceptable system of accounting based on NRVs is to be established. As we saw in Chapters 5 and 13, the ASB now certainly envisages, indeed requires, the use of such a focus on business units in the conduct of impairment reviews.

MCRV's structure for financial statements

As part of its longer-term proposals, *MCRV* suggests that there should be four main statements:

(a) Assets and liabilities statement
(b) Operations statement
(c) Statement of changes in financial wealth
(d) Distribution statement.

Assets and liabilities statement

This should show the entity's assets and liabilities at the end of the period, each stated at net realisable value. Trade creditors would normally be shown at their nominal value but, if the liabilities include securities that are traded, then that element could be included at market value.

For companies whose shares are traded, the statement would include its market capitalisation together with a statement from the directors explaining what they think are the main reasons for the difference, normally positive, between the market capitalisation and the total of the net identifiable assets.

A possible structure of an Assets and Liabilities Statement is:

Market value of assets (listed individually)		X
Debtors		X
Cash		X
		X
less Market value of long-term loans	X	
Creditors	X	
Deferred taxation	X	X
Net identifiable assets		X
Market capitalisation		X

---

[16] *Op. cit.,* Para. 6.8.

Operations statement

The operations statement shows the financial wealth created by trading. It differs from a profit and loss account in the following ways:

(a) there would be no depreciation charge;
(b) stock would be shown at NRV;
(c) only exceptional and extraordinary items of a revenue nature would be included; exceptional or extraordinary gains or losses relating to fixed assets would be included in the Statement of changes in financial wealth.[17]

An operations statement might be constructed as follows:

Sales		x
less Opening stock at market value	x	
Purchases	x	
	x	
Closing stock at market value	x	
	x	
Operating costs	x	x
		x
add Dividend income		x
Income from unusual events		x
		x
less Taxation		x
Financial wealth added by operations		£x

Statement of changes in financial wealth

This statement would show the change in the wealth of the business analysed into the main components; for example, change due to operations and changes due to movements in the market value of assets and liabilities.

It might appear as follows:

Financial wealth added by operations		x
Increase in value of quoted investments		x
Reduction in debenture liability		x
Increase in value of stock		x
		x
less Decrease in value of plant	x	
Decrease in value of vehicles	x	x
Distributable change in financial wealth		x
less Distributions		x
		x
New share capital		x
Change in financial wealth		£x
Movement in market capitalisation		£xx

---

[17] *MCRV* predates the issue of FRS 3 (1992) which has effectively abolished extraordinary items.

Perhaps one of the weaker aspects of the report is the *MCRV*'s treatment of changes in the general price level. It is not that the issue is ignored but more that its impact on the *MCRV* model is not explained clearly. The change in financial wealth shown by the statement is effectively measured on the basis of money capital maintenance but *MCRV* suggests that, in times of significant inflation, an adjustment should be made to reflect the effect of changes in the Retail Price Index.[18] Such an adjustment would be required in respect of the opening net identifiable assets and the proceeds of any share issue made during the year and would result in the disclosure of the change in financial wealth in real terms.

Distributions statement

This statement would articulate with the previous statement in that it starts with the distributable change in financial wealth for the year and then shows the undistributable surpluses brought forward, from which any distributions made or proposed would be deducted. The statement could also include an inflation adjustment derived from the application of the RPI to the value of shareholders' contributed capital at the start of the year; in addition an entity which wishes to maintain its operating capability in physical terms could make a further appropriation to maintain its asset portfolio.

The statement might be shown as follows:

Distributable change in financial wealth for the year		x
less Inflation adjustment	x	
Appropriation to maintain operating capability	x	x
		x
add Undistributed surpluses brought forward		x
less Dividends		x
Paid	x	
Proposed	x	x
Undistributed surpluses carried forward		£x

Additional statements

In addition to the above four main elements, *MCRV* advocates the publication of cash flow statements showing the inflow and outflow of cash analysed into its main components, both historical for the year past and projected for, say, the next three years. Segmental reporting is also regarded as being of importance. Where the amounts are significant it is suggested that the statements should be split:

(a) by type of product;
(b) by manufacturing location;
(c) geographically;
(d) by currency.

In the longer term, *MCRV* proposes the publication of much more descriptive information about such matters as innovation, the economic environment and staff resources.[19]

The longer-term proposals of *MCRV* are illustrated in Example 21.3.

---

[18] *Op. cit.*, Para. 7.25.
[19] *Op. cit.*, Para. 7.44.

Example 21.3

Egghead Limited is a management consultancy business that occupies its own premises. It has a small computer services division that has for the last 15 months been engaged in the production of a suite of software under contract for a company in the furnishing industry.

Egghead's summarised historical cost balance sheets as at 1.1.20X2 and 31.12.20X2 and its profit and loss account for the year ended 31.12.20X2 are shown below:

Balance sheets

	1.1.20X2		31.12.20X2	
	£000	£000	£000	£000
Fixed assets				
Freehold property				
Cost	1000		1000	
Acc. depr.	200	800	220	780
Vehicles and equipment				
Cost	400		440	
Acc. depr.	250	150	300	140
Investments, cost		200		200
		1150		1120
Current assets				
Work-in-progress	30		310	
Trade debtors	100		200	
Balance at bank	10		110	
	140		620	
Current liabilities				
Trade creditors	50		70	
Proposed dividends	30		80	
	80	60	150	470
		1210		1590
10% Debentures		500		500
		£710		£1090
Share capital		400		400
Unappropriated profits		310		690
		£710		£1090

Profit and loss account, year ended 31.12.20X2

	£000	£000
Fees		1200
Increase in work-in-progress		280
		1480
less		
Sundry expenses	900	
Depreciation		
Property	20	
Vehicles and equipment	50	
Debenture interest	50	1020
c/f		460

	£000
b/f	460
less Proposed dividend	80
Unappropriated profits for year	380
P and L account balance 1.1.20X2	310
P and L account balance 31.12.20X2	£690

(A) Additional information

1 The net realisable values of the fixed assets at 1.1.20X2 and 31.12.20X2 were as follows:

	1.1.20X2	*31.12.20X2*
	£000	£000
Freehold property	900	945
Vehicles and equipment	190	205
Investments	400	480

2 The only material work-in-progress relates to the computer services division's contract. The work done under the terms of the contract had a negligible value at 1.1 20X2 but it is estimated that the software developed under the terms of the contract could have been sold for £500 000 at 31.12.20X2.

3 The market values of the debentures were:

1.1.20X2	£400 000
31.12.20X2	£370 000

4 The shares of the company are traded on the Alternative Investment Market (AIM). The market capitalisation figures were:

1.1.20X2	£3 000 000
31.12.20X2	£2 900 000

5 Taxation and changes in the general price levels will be ignored.

We are now in a position to prepare the four main statements proposed by *MCRV*.

Assets and liabilities statement as at 31.12.20X2

	£000	£000
Market value of:		
Freehold property		945
Vehicles and equipment		205
Investments		480
Work completed by computer services division		500
Trade debtors		200
Balance at bank		110
		2440
Less		
Market value of debentures	370	
Trade creditors	70	
Proposed dividend	80	520
Net identifiable assets		£1920
Market capitalisation		£2900

Notes:

The directors would be required to comment on the possible reasons for the difference between the value of the net identifiable assets and the market capitalisation.

A case could be made for excluding proposed dividends from the above statement on the grounds that it is not a liability until approved by the shareholders.

Operations statement for the year ended 31.12.20X2

	£000	£000
Fees from services		1200
Increase in value of work done by computer services division		500
		1700
less		
Operating expenses	900	
Debenture interest	50	950
Wealth added by operations		£750

Note:

Because the increase in the value of the contracts undertaken by the computer services division is due primarily to the work undertaken by that group during the year, the increase in value has been included in the operations statement. If, in contrast, much of the work had been completed in 20X1 and the increase in value was due primarily to changes in the market value for such software, the increase of wealth would not be included in the operations statement but shown separately in the statement of changes in financial wealth.

Statement of changes in financial wealth for the year ended 31.12.20X2

	£000
Wealth added by operations	750
Increases in value of freehold property	45
Increase in value of investments	80
Decrease in value of debentures consequent upon an increase in interest rates	30
	905
less Decrease in value of vehicles and equipment (see Note (b))	25
Distributable change in wealth	880
less Distribution	80
Change in financial wealth	£800
Change in market capitalisation	£(100)

Notes:

(a) The directors would be required to comment on the reasons for the difference between the change in financial wealth and the change in market capitalisation.

(b) The fall in value of vehicles and equipment is found as follows:

	£000
NRV at 1.1.20X2	190
Cost of assets acquired during the year	40
	230
NRV at 31.12.20X2	205
	£25

Distribution statement for the year ended 31 December 20X2

	£000
Distributable change in financial wealth for the year	880
Undistributed surpluses brought forward (note (i))	720
Surplus available for distribution	1600
less Proposed dividend	80
Undistributed surpluses carried forward (note (ii))	£1520

Notes:

(i) The undistributed surpluses brought forward maybe derived thus:

	£000	£000
Assets, at NRV, at 1.1.20X2		
Freehold property		900
Vehicles and equipment		190
Investments		400
Trade debtors		100
Balance at bank		10
		1600
less MV of debentures	400	
Trade creditors	50	
Proposed dividend	30	480
		1120
less Share capital		400
Undistributed surplus at 1.1.20X2		£720

(ii) The articulation of the statements can be demonstrated by showing how this figure is derived:

Net identifiable assets at 31.12.20X2, per the assets and liabilities statement	1920
less Share capital	400
Undistributed surplus at 31.12.20X2	£1520

In the example we have ignored the effects of changes in the general price level, the treatment of which we have already identified as a weakness in the report. Further thought is needed on ways of accounting for changes in the general price level within the *MCRV* model. In other respects, the example does indicate the virtues of the approach. The statement of assets and liabilities is based on a clear and easily understandable principle. It indicates how much the assets would realise if sold in an orderly fashion. In contrast, a conventional balance sheet is, as we argued, vague in its concept and not readily understandable by users, especially laypeople.

The *MCRV* operations statement reflects not only its fees and expenses but what, for this company, has been an important event, the success of the programme of work for the design of software. A profit and loss account constructed on the historical cost basis, on the other hand, fails to recognise the event and hence gives only a partial picture of what actually occurred during the year.

The obvious concern about the *MCRV* approach is its subjectivity. The NRV of individual assets cannot always be ascertained with reasonable confidence but the estimation of NRV of 'business units', which are often unique, is even more difficult.

Two points can, however, be made in mitigation:

(a) The *MCRV* proposals that include the requirement for directors to provide systematic contextual information, including historical and projected cash flow statements, would enforce some discipline on those responsible for making the estimates. Wild guesses unsupported by reasoned arguments would be difficult to sustain in an MCRV system.

(b) The second point is related. The market would become suspicious of companies that habitually made wrong estimates. It may be that companies could for a year or two fool the market but, eventually, as chickens come home to roost, so estimates are converted into actual cash flows. If that suggests that the market should place less reliance on one year's figures, and in particular one year's 'bottom line', and take a longer view, then that would be no bad thing. The UK securities market does tend to take a short-term view and moves that would reduce the tendency would help the economy.

The *MCRV* approach remains fresh and imaginative and it seems to provide an excellent basis for further thought and experimentation. The ICAS published an annual report for a company, Melody Plc, based on the ideas in *MCRV* and expressed the hope that companies would be prepared to adopt and experiment with this approach. Unfortunately, there is little evidence that this happened.

The evolution of the ASB's thinking

Since its formation in 1990, the ASB has shown considerable enthusiasm for the greater use of current values in financial statements. However, in view of the earlier experience of the ASC with the introduction of current cost accounting and the desire to achieve an international convergence in accounting standards, it is not surprising that the ASB has chosen not to move too quickly towards the wholesale introduction of a comprehensive system based on CCA principles.

In its discussion paper, *The role of valuation in financial reporting*, issued in March 1993, the ASB clearly recognised the unsatisfactory nature of modified historical cost accounting. Nevertheless it proposed to retain the system but with more consistent revaluations of certain limited classes of assets for which supplementary information was already required by law and which were traded on a ready market. The assets to be shown at their current values were:

(a) properties;
(b) quoted investments; and
(c) stock of a commodity nature and long-term stock where a market of sufficient depth exists.

By the time it issued the first exposure draft of the *Statement of Principles for Financial Reporting* in November 1995, the ASB was considerably more enthusiastic about the use of current values. In Chapter 5 of that exposure draft, it compared the use of current values with the use of historical costs:

> Current values *sometimes* lack the attribute of reliability. Furthermore the costs of obtaining current values *may* outweigh the benefits of their use. On the other hand, the lack of relevance of the historical cost system is a *serious* deficiency. (Para. 5.10 emphasis added.)

It proceeded to outline its favoured system, which may be summarised as follows:

Assets: The appropriate current value is that given by the 'value to the business' rule. (Para. 5.35)

Liabilities: The use of the value to the business rule here is an unnecessary complication because the various values will converge to a single current value and thus market values may be used. (Para. 5.36)

Capital maintenance concept: The use of a real terms capital maintenance system with the disclosure of real holding gains and losses. (Para. 5.37)

Readers will observe that this is the real terms current cost accounting system that we have illustrated in Example 21.1, and the ASB provided a simple illustration in the appendix to Chapter 5 of the draft that is, in all fundamental respects, identical to that example.

By the end of Chapter 5, the ASB is quite clear in its preference for current values:

The Board therefore believes that practice should develop by evolving in the direction of greater use of current values to the extent that this is consistent with the constraints of reliability and cost. (Para. 5.37)

Such a clear statement was, perhaps not surprisingly, interpreted by many commentators as an attempt by the ASB to reintroduce a system of current cost accounting. As we have seen in Chapter 1, criticism of this and other matters led to the withdrawal of the exposure draft and its replacement by a revised exposure draft *Statement of Principles* in March 1999. The revised exposure draft proved to be less controversial and its contents quickly reappeared, with only minor changes, in the definitive *Statement of Principles* published in December 1999.

In the final version of the *Statement of Principles,* the ASB was much less willing to state its preference for current values than it was in the first draft. The statement advocates the continuation of the use of the 'mixed measurement' or 'modified historical cost' system, the system used by most quoted companies in Britain at the time of publication of the statement. Where current values are used, the ASB continued to favour the use of 'value to the business' to value assets[20] (Para. 6.7) although, as we have pointed out in Chapters 1 and 5, it is now moving towards an approach based upon market based fair values.

In measuring profit, it favours the use of the financial capital maintenance concept with no adjustment for general or specific price change even though it recognises that this approach is only satisfactory under conditions of stable prices. It accepts (Para. 6.42) that when the problems caused by changes in either general or specific prices become 'acute', something will have to be done. In the case of general price changes, there will be a need for an approach to be adopted that involves recognising profit only after adjustments have been made to maintain the purchasing power of the entity's financial capital (real financial capital maintenance) while, if the changes affect specific prices, the statement calls for a system that ensures that users are informed as to the significance of those specific price changes. The statement does not, however, comment on the level at which the problems become 'acute' but the use of a strong word such as this suggests that the Board is not readily disposed to encourage extensive use of the alternative methods of reporting at the present time.

It has nonetheless taken a number of steps that might assist the evolutionary introduction of a system of current cost accounting.

---

[20] The possibility of using 'relief value' to measure liabilities is mentioned (Para. 6.9) but its use is not advocated: see Chapter 7.

- One is the introduction of the Statement of Total Recognised Gains and Losses (see Chapter 11) that collects together the profit or loss for the year with other gains and losses recognised during the year. Such a statement already records unrealised holding gains and losses when assets are revalued and could readily be used to record holding gains or losses recognised under a full blown current value system of accounting.
- In Chapter 5 we explained how, in FRS 15, the ASB has introduced some order into the use of revaluations, as an alternative to historical costs, within the mixed measurement system. In particular, all assets within a particular class must be revalued and the measurement of assets at out-of-date current values has been outlawed. Where companies choose to show their assets at current values rather than at historical costs, they are required to use the fair value basis as their valuation concept. As a consequence, more and more accountants will become familiar with this powerful concept and it will not seem as strange in future as it did when CCA was first introduced in the 1970s.

A number of other current developments are providing further evidence of the inadequacies of the historical cost accounting approach; these include the work being done on such topics as financial instruments, retirement benefits, leases and share-based payments which we have discussed in earlier chapters. Once these developments have been completed, the introduction of an approach that systematically and comprehensively takes account of changing prices will not seem such a Herculean task.

Conclusion

Most married couples are only too aware that there is more than one way of perceiving and describing the facts. The same can be said of business: there is more than one way of telling what has happened.

At various stages in the debate on accounting reform, it has been suggested that financial statements should include two or more values for assets and liabilities and two or more profit figures based upon different capital maintenance concepts. This so-called multi-column approach has been rejected on the ground that it would confuse the users of financial statements. In our view, if more effort had been devoted to explaining that there is more than one way of explaining the results of complex businesses, we might be in a much better position than we are now. The ASB clearly recognises the limitations of any one bottom line figure and consistently encourages users to look at the whole package of information, both numerical and discursive, which is provided. However, it still advocates the one-column, rather than the multi-column, approach to the measurement of assets, liabilities and profit.

It may be that, in due course, the models presented in this chapter will provide the basis for more relevant financial reporting. Both the real terms CCA and the *MCRV* models of financial reporting provide information that is relevant to the needs of users and there seems no reason, other than the cost of producing the information, why they should not appear in a company's financial statements. As we have argued in the previous section, there is certainly now a framework in existence to facilitate a move towards a real terms CCA system.

In the meantime, despite the many weaknesses and limitations of the mixed measurement system, recognised by professional accountancy bodies as well as by academic accountants, these accounts continue to be regarded as the 'real' accounts. While this continues, it is difficult to argue with the old adage that an accountant is someone who prefers to be precisely wrong than approximately right!

Summary

We started the chapter by reviewing the utility of current cost accounts and then, in the second section, explained and illustrated how to prepare and present a fully stabilised set of current cost accounts that take account of changes in the general price level as well as changes in specific prices.

Next we examined an alternative approach based upon the use of net realisable value as the main basis of asset valuation and introduced the ICAS research publication, *Making Corporate Reports Valuable*, which, although published in 1988, remains a radical document full of fresh ideas.

The final section of the chapter is concerned with the way the ASB's thinking on the subject of current cost accounting has developed over the last ten or so years. We explain how it has put into place a system capable of coping with a much more widespread use of current values, which will undoubtedly occur over the coming decades.

Recommended reading

Accounting Standards Committee, *Accounting for the Effects of Changing Prices: a Handbook*, ASC, London, 1986.

W.T. Baxter, *Inflation Accounting*, Philip Allan, Deddington, 1984.

Institute of Chartered Accountants of Scotland, *Making Corporate Reports Valuable*, P.N. McMonnies (ed.), Kogan Page, London, 1988.

D.R. Myddleton, *On a Cloth Untrue*, Woodhead-Faulkner, Cambridge, 1984.

D. Tweedie and G. Whittington, *The Debate on Inflation Accounting*, Cambridge University Press, Cambridge, 1984.

G. Whittington, *Inflation Accounting: an Introduction to the Debate*, Cambridge University Press, Cambridge, 1983.

Questions

21.1

    (a) What do you consider to be the main weaknesses of historical cost accounting when prices are rising? (10 marks)

    (b) State two ways in which firms have adopted different accounting policies for specific items in historical cost accounts so that they partly reflect rising price levels.

        (4 marks)

    (c) The stewardship approach of traditional accounting has been said to have been replaced by a user-orientated approach. Briefly discuss this assertion in relation to historical cost accounts. (6 marks)

    ACCA Level 2, The Regulatory Framework of Accounting, June 1988   **(20 marks)**

21.2 In the ASC's handbook, *Accounting for the Effect of Changing Prices*, accountants are faced with a choice of systems of accounting when dealing with the effects of inflation.

Requirements

(a) Briefly describe the three factors which combine to make up these systems of accounting.
(3 marks)

(b) Explain the main advantages and disadvantages of two such systems.   (6 marks)

ICAEW, Financial Reporting II, May 1993   **(9 marks)**

21.3 (a) Explain the primary objective of current purchasing power accounting and outline the basic technique.
(8 marks)

(b) What do you consider are the advantages and disadvantages of current purchasing power accounting as a method of adjusting financial statements for price level changes?
(12 marks)

ACCA Level 2, The Regulatory Framework of Accounting, December 1988   **(20 marks)**

21.4 (a) Provide a definition of the deprival value of an asset.   (2 marks)

(b) For a particular asset, suppose the three bases of valuation relevant to the calculation of its deprival value are (in thousands of pounds): £12, £10 and £8.

Construct a matrix of columns and rows showing all the possible alternative situations and, in each case, indicate the appropriate deprival value.   (6 marks)

(c) Justify the use of deprival value as a method of asset valuation, using the matrix in (b) above to illustrate your answer.
(12 marks)

ACCA Level 2, The Regulatory Framework of Accounting, December 1988   **(20 marks)**

21.5 An assistant accountant of Changeling plc has been requested to prepare a profit and loss account using the CPP model for the year ended 31 March 1991. He has calculated the net operating profit for the year and the remaining entries are yet to be completed.

The profit and loss accounts for the year ended 31 March 1991 are set out below, comprising the historic cost profit and loss account and partially completed CPP profit and loss account.

	Historic cost £000	Index factor	CPP units as at 31.3.91 000
Sales	6500	2000/1875	6933
Opening stock	700	2000/1700	824
Purchases	4250	2000/1875	4533
	4950		5357
Closing stock	(900)	2000/1937	(929)
	4050		4428
Gross profit	2450		2505
Expenses	1150	2000/1875	1227
Depreciation:			
Original equipment	500	2000/1025	976
New equipment	50	2000/1813	55
Net operating profit	750		247
Tax	338		
c/f	412		

	Historic cost
	£000
Profit (loss) after tax	412
Gain (loss) on net monetary assets	–
Gain (loss) on long-term loans	–
Net profit (loss) for year	412
Dividends	187
Retained profit (loss) for year	225
Retained profit brought forward	750
Retained profit carried forward	975

Balance sheet as at 31 March 1990

	Historic cost	Index factor	CPP units as at 31.3.90	Index factor	CPP units as at 31.3.91
	£000		000		000
Capital	2500	1750	4605	2000	5263
Retained profit	750	950	1142	1750	1305
	3250		5747		6568
Fixed assets					
Equipment	5000	1750	8537	2000	9757
		1025		1750	
Depreciation	(1500)	1750	(2561)	2000	(2927)
		1025		1750	
Current assets					
Stock	700	1750	721	2000	824
		1700		1750	
Debtors	1050	–	1050	2000	1200
				1750	
Current liabilities					
Trade creditors	(875)	–	(875)	2000	(1000)
				1750	
Non-current liabilities					
Loan	(1125)	–	(1125)	2000	(1286)
	3250		5747	1750	6568

Balance sheet as at 31 March 1991

	Historic cost	Index factor	CPP units as at 31.3.91
	£000		000
Capital	2500	2000	5263
		950	
Retained profit	975	–	1142
	3475		6405
Fixed assets			
Equipment	5000	2000	9757
		1025	
Depreciation	(2000)	2000	(3903)
		1025	
New equipment	500	2000	552
		1813	
Depreciation	(50)	2000	(55)
		1813	
Current assets			
Stock	900	2000	929
		1938	
Debtors	1150	–	1150
	5500		8430
Current liabilities			
Trade creditors	(400)	–	(400)
Non-current liabilities			
Loan	(1625)	–	(1625)
	3475		6405

Assume that inflation index increased evenly throughout the year ended 31 March 1991.

Required

(a) Calculate the retained profit (loss) for the year using the CPP Model for the year ended 31 March 1991. (5 marks)

(b) Explain what the method of indexing is attempting to deal with and discuss the process from the viewpoint of both the entity and the proprietors. (5 marks)

(c) Write a brief report to the principal shareholder of Changeling Ltd who holds 20% of the issued share capital on the management of the company commenting on profitability, liquidity and financial structure. (10 marks)

ACCA, Advanced Financial Accounting, December 1991 (**20 marks**)

21.6 'The recognition and correct treatment of holding gains in company financial statements are vital for a proper understanding of the position and performance of the business entity.'

You are required

(a) to explain briefly the significance of the treatment of holding gains for the measurement of business profit; (5 marks)

(b) to set out the arguments for and against the recognition or holding gains. (10 marks)

CIMA, Advanced Financial Accounting, November 1994 (**15 marks**)

21.7 The accountant of Newsprint plc has produced three sets of accounts for the year ended 31 December 1988 using the historic cost, replacement cost with specific index adjustments and current purchasing power with general price index adjustments.

The historic and replacement cost accounts are set out below:

Profit and loss accounts for the year ended 31 December 1988

	Historic cost £	£	Specific index	Replacement cost £	£
Sales		357 500	–		357 500
Opening stock	41 250		240/200	49 500	
Purchases	178 750		–	178 750	
	220 000			228 250	
Closing stock	71 500			71 500	
Cost of sales		148 500			156 750
Gross profit		209 000			200 750
Wages	17 875			17 875	
Establishment and other charges	71 500			71 500	
Depreciation					
Fixtures	5 500		160/140	6 286	
Lease	5 500		220/160	7 563	
		100 375			103 224
Net profit		108 625	Operating profit		97 526

Balance sheets as at 31 December 1988

	Historic cost £	£	Specific index	Replacement cost £	£
Fixed assets					
Leasehold					
Premises	55 000		220/160	75 625	
Amortisation	5 500	49 500		7 563	68 062
Fixtures	55 000		160/140	62 857	
Depreciation	5 500	49 500		6 286	56 571
Current assets					
Stock		71 500	280/240		83 416
Cash		55 825	–		55 825
		226 325			263 874
Share capital					
Ordinary shares		90 200			90 200
Profit and loss account		108 625			97 526
					11 099[1]
					37 549[2]
Loan		27 500			27 500
		226 325			263 874

Note 1	£	
Stock	8 250	
Fixtures	786	
Lease	2 063	
		11 099

Note 2

Closing Stock

$$(71\,500 \times \frac{280}{240} - 71\,500) \qquad 11\,916$$

Fixtures

$$(49\,500 \times \frac{160}{140} - 49\,500) \qquad 7\,071$$

Lease

$$(49\,500 \times \frac{220}{160} - 49\,500) \qquad 18\,562$$

$$37\,549$$

The historic and current purchasing power accounts are set out below.

Profit and loss accounts for the year ended 31 December 1988

	Historic cost		General index	£CPP	£CPP
	£	£			
Sales		357 500	160/130		440 000
Opening stock	41 250		160/100	66 000	
Purchases	178 750		160/130	220 000	
	220 000			286 000	
Closing stock	71 500		160/130	88 000	
Cost of sales		148 500			198 000
Gross profit		209 000			242 000
Wages	17 875		160/130	22 000	
Establishment and other charges	71 500		160/130	88 000	
	89 375	209 000		110 000	242 000
Depreciation					
Fixtures	5 500		160/100	8 800	
Lease	5 500		160/100	8 800	
		100 375			127 600
Net profit		108 625	*Operating profit*		114 400

Balance sheets as at 31 December 1988

Fixed assets	Historic cost £	£	General index	£CPP	£CPP
Leasehold premises	55 000		160/100	88 000	
Amortisation	5 500	49 500	160/100	8 800	79 200
Fixtures	55 000		160/100	88 000	
Depreciation	5 500	49 500	160/100	8 800	79 200
Current assets					
Stock		71 500	160/130		88 000
Cash		55 825	–		55 825
		226 325			302 225
Share capital					
Ordinary shares		90 200	160/100		144 320
Profit and loss account		108 625			114 400
					16 005[3]
Loan		27 500			27 500
		226 325			302 225

Note 3
Loan
$(27 500 \times 160/100 - 27 500)$ 16 500
Purchases
$(178 750 \times 160/130 - 178 750)$ 41 250
Fixtures
$(55 000 \times 160/100 - 55 000)$ 33 000
Lease
$(55 000 \times 160/100 - 55 000)$ 33 000
Expenses
$(89 375 \times 160/130 - 89 375)$ 20 625
Cash
$(76 450 \times 160/100 - 76 450)$ (45 870)
Sales
$(357 500 \times 160/130 - 357 500)$ (82 500)

Required

(a) Explain briefly what the following amounts relate to and why they are in the balance sheets:

   (i) in the replacement cost model

     £11 099

     £37 549;

   (ii) in the current purchasing power model

     £16 005. (6 marks)

(b) Explain the case for and against the replacement cost model. (8 marks)

(c) Consider the implication of the replacement cost model figures for 1988 to the management of Newsprint plc. (8 marks)

(d) Explain to a shareholder why the historic cost net profit is different from the CPP operating profit using the data in the question to illustrate your answer and explain which figure is to be regarded as the base for calculating earnings per share under each model. (8 marks)

ACCA Level 3, Advanced Financial Accounting, June 1989 **(30 marks)**

21.8 The Paraffin Supply Company Limited acquired freehold land as a depot for its delivery vans and started business on 1 January 1986. It collected sufficient paraffin from a wholesaler each day to satisfy known orders. The wholesaler was paid in cash and the customers paid cash on delivery. The opening balance sheet at 1 January 1986 showed the following:

Balance sheet of Paraffin Supply Company Limited as at 1 January 1986

	£
Freehold land for use as garage premises	100 000
Delivery vehicles	96 000
	196 000
Financed by: Share capital	150 000
Long-term loan	46 000
	196 000

The company traded for 2 years until 31 December 1987. All profits had been retained in the business. There were no creditors, debtors or stocks. At 31 December 1987 the directors were considering whether to cease trading at 31 December 1988.

The accountant produced the following estimated accounts for the year ended 31 December 1988 with the 1986 and 1987 actual comparative figures:

Profit and loss accounts for the years ended 31 December

	1986 £	1987 £	1988 £
Sales	140 000	184 000	248 000
Less: Purchases	70 000	90 000	124 000
Administration expenses	21 400	22 000	27 500
Selling expenses	21 000	30 000	42 500
Depreciation	24 000	24 000	24 000
	3 600	18 000	30 000

	1986	1987	1988
Return on equity	$\dfrac{3\,600}{150\,000} \times 100$	$\dfrac{18\,000}{153\,600} \times 100$	$\dfrac{30\,000}{171\,600} \times 100$
	= 2.4%	= 11.7%	= 17.5%

In preparing the accounts the following conventions and policies had been followed:

(a) The capital maintenance concept is that capital will be maintained if the cost of assets representing the initial monetary investment is recovered against operations.

(b) The concept of profit is that profit for the year is regarded as any gains arising during the year which may be distributed while maintaining the amount of the shareholders' interest in the company at the beginning of the year.

(c) The measurement unit used is the medium of exchange.

(d) Depreciation of delivery vans is over 4 years using the straight-line method.

The directors had recently attended a seminar on the treatment of inflation in financial reports and they required the profits to be calculated using the general purchasing power income model and the replacement cost model.

The accountant obtained the following information to allow him to redraft the profit and loss account using these two models:

(a) The retail price index was as follows:

1 January 1986	100
31 December 1986	110
31 December 1987	120
31 December 1988 (Estimated)	130

(b) The replacement cost of the assets was:

	Garage premises £	Delivery vehicles £
31 December 1986	120 000	102 000
31 December 1987	130 000	115 000
31 December 1988 (Estimated)	141 000	128 000

Required

(a) (i) Prepare the profit and loss account for the year ended 31 December 1988 using the general purchasing power income model and explain the following:
The concept of capital maintenance used.
The concept of profit used.
The measurement unit used. (8 marks)

(ii) Mention four criteria for selecting an appropriate unit of measurement for financial reporting and briefly discuss whether the general purchasing power income model satisfies these criteria. (8 marks)

(b) (i) Prepare the profit and loss account for the year ended 31 December 1988 using the replacement cost model to show reported income on the assumption that backlog depreciation is not deducted in arriving at this reported income and explain the following:
The concept of capital maintenance used.
The concept of profit used.
The measurement unit used. (5 marks)

(ii) Discuss the arguments for and against excluding backlog depreciation when calculating the reported income. (4 marks)

ACCA Level 3, Advanced Financial Accounting, December 1988 **(25 marks)**

21.9 Air Fare plc is the subsidiary of an American parent company. It had been incorporated in the United Kingdom in 1985 to provide in flight packed meals for American airlines on return flights from the United Kingdom.

The fixed assets in the annual accounts have been carried at cost less depreciation but the directors have been considering the production of supplementary statements that are based on current values and show a profit after maintaining the operating capital and also a profit that encompassed gains on holding assets to the extent that these were real gains after allowing for general/average inflation.

The following information (i) to (vi) was available when preparing the supplementary statements for the year ended 31 December 1993.

(i) Draft profit and loss account for the year ended 31 December 1993 prepared under the historic cost convention.

	£000
Sales	11 441
Cost of sales	10 292
	1 149
Loan interest	625
	524
Tax	124
	400
Less: Proposed dividend	100
	300

(ii) The current cost values of the net assets representing shareholders' funds was £25 million at 1 January 1993.

(iii) Freehold premises had cost £8 million in 1985 and were being depreciated over 40 years which was the group policy specified by the American parent. The current gross replacement cost was £14 million at 31 December 1993 and £13.8 million at 1 January 1993.

Equipment had cost £12 million in 1991 and was being depreciated over 15 years. The gross replacement cost was £12.6 million at 31 December 1993 and £12.5 million at 1 January 1993.

(iv) The cost of sales had increased by £412 000 during the year due to price increases. The costs and price increases occurred evenly during the year.

(v) The retail price index had risen by 3% during the year.

(vi) Stock at the beginning of the year was £660 000 at cost and £670 000 at current replacement cost and stock at the end of the year was £750 000 at cost and £795 000 at current replacement cost.

The following information relates to a consideration not to provide for depreciation on the freehold property.

The freehold property consisted of the premises where the meals were prepared and packed. When the directors were reviewing the information prepared for the current value supplementary statements they noted that the current value of the freehold property exceeded the book value and decided that it was appropriate not to provide for depreciation.

The chief accountant advised them that it was probable that the auditor would qualify the accounts if depreciation were not provided in accordance with the provisions of SSAP 12 *Accounting for Depreciation*.

The directors had been discussing the problem over lunch at the local hotel and were surprised when the owner of the hotel informed them that the auditor of the company that owned the hotel had not required depreciation to be provided on the hotel premises. Further enquiry by the directors established that there were a number of companies that were not providing depreciation on freehold properties from a range of industries that included hotels, retail shops and banks. They even discovered that the Financial Reporting Review Panel had accepted one company's policy on non-depreciation of freehold buildings in respect of the accounts of Forte plc. They had therefore formed the view that non-depreciation was acceptable provided the auditors were offered and accepted the company's reasons.

They accordingly requested the chief accountant to prepare a brief report for the board of reasons to support a decision by the company to adopt an accounting policy of non-depreciation which they could subsequently discuss with the auditors.

Required

(a) (i) Prepare a profit and loss account that shows a result after maintaining the operating capital and also a result that encompasses the gains for the year on holding assets to the extent that these are real gains after allowing for inflation.

    (ii) Write a brief memo to the directors explaining the results disclosed in the profit and loss account prepared in (i). (10 marks)

(b) As chief accountant, prepare a brief report for the board giving reasons to support a decision by the company to adopt an accounting policy of non-depreciation of the freehold property. (10 marks)

ACCA, Financial Reporting Environment, June 1994 **(20 marks)**

21.10 It has been stated that: 'Current cost accounts allow for the impact of specific price changes on the net operating assets and thus the operating capability of the business. The same tools of analysis as those applied to historical cost accounts are generally appropriate. The ratios derived from current cost accounts... will often differ substantially from those revealed in historical cost accounts but should be more realistic indicators when assessing an entity or making comparisons between entities.'

Required

(a) Explain, with reasons, whether the value of the following ratios might differ if calculated using current cost accounts rather than the historical cost accounts.
    (i) Return on capital employed (ROCE)
    (ii) Stock turnover ratio (utilising the year end stock value)
    (iii) Debtors turnover ratio
    (iv) Gearing ratio (in the balance sheet) (8 marks)

(b) Explain the principal limitations of the specific historical cost ratios set out in part (a) when utilising them for the purpose of inter-firm comparison. (11 marks)

(c) Briefly discuss whether you feel that current cost based ratios are more realistic indicators of a company's performance than those ratios based upon historical cost accounts. (6 marks)

ACCA, Accounting and Audit Practice, June 1995 **(25 marks)**

21.11 You are a financial analyst specialising in the analysis of the profitability of organisations in the engineering sector. One such company is D Ltd. The directors of D Ltd have always been interested in the impact of price changes on the performance of their business and have adopted the practice of including current cost accounts (using the 'Real Terms' system) alongside the historical cost accounts in the published financial statements.

Extracts from the published financial statements for the year ended 31 March 1996 are given below:

Profit and loss accounts – year ended 31 March 1996

	Historical cost		*Current cost*
	£000	£000	£000
Sales	30 000		30 000
Operating costs (Note 1)	(16 000)		(19 000)
Operating profit	14 000		11 000
Interest payable	(2 000)		(2 000)
Profit before taxation	12 000		9 000
Taxation	(3 500)		(3 500)
Profit after taxation	8 500		5 500
Holding gains arising during the year	–	3 500	
Inflation adjustment to shareholders' funds	–	(2 000)	
Real gains	–		1 500
Profit for the year	8 500		7 000
Dividends	(7 000)		(7 000)
Retained profit	1 500		–

Balance sheet at 31 March 1996	*Historical cost*	*Current cost*
	£000	£000
Tangible fixed assets	20 000	24 000
Current assets (*Note 2*)	16 000	19 000
Current liabilities	(10 000)	(10 000)
Loans	(15 000)	(15 000)
	11 000	18 000
Shareholders' funds	11 000	18 000

Note 1		
Operating costs are as follows:	£000	£000
Cost of sales (excluding depreciation)	8 000	10 000
Depreciation	5 000	6 000
Other operating costs	3 000	3 000
	16 000	19 000

Note 2		
Current assets comprise:	£000	£000
Stocks	6 000	9 000
Debtors	9 000	9 000
Cash	1 000	1 000
	16 000	19 000

Requirements
(a) Compute (under both conventions) three accounting ratios for D Ltd which differ under the two conventions.   (6 marks)
(b) Explain, for each ratio you have computed, the reason why the current cost elements included in the ratio differ from the historical cost elements.   (9 marks)
(c) Explain the adjustments 'Holding gains arising during the year' and 'Inflation adjustment to shareholders' funds'.   (5 marks)

CIMA, Financial Reporting, May 1996   **(20 marks)**

Index